Second Edition

CompTIA Cloud+

T0354023

Guide to Cloud Computing

Jill West

Networking

Cengage

Australia • Brazil • Canada • Mexico • Singapore • United Kingdom • United States

CompTIA Cloud+Guide to Cloud Computing
2nd Edition
Jill West

SVP, Product: Erin Joyner

VP, Product: Thais Alencar

Product Director: Mark Santee

Product Manager: Natalie Onderdonk

Product Assistant: Ethan Wheel

Learning Designer: Carolyn Mako

Senior Content Manager: Brooke Greenhouse

Digital Delivery Quality Partner: Jim Vaughey

Technical Editor: Danielle Shaw

Developmental Editor: Lisa Ruffolo

VP, Product Marketing: Jason Sakos

Director, Product Marketing: Danaë April

Product Marketing Manager: Mackenzie Paine

IP Analyst: Ann Hoffman

IP Project Manager: Lumina Datamatics

Production Service: Straive

Senior Designer: Erin Griffin

Cover Image Source: Sanjatosic/Shutterstock.com

For product information and technology assistance, contact us at
**Cengage Customer & Sales Support, 1-800-354-9706
or support.cengage.com.**

For permission to use material from this text or product, submit all requests online at **www.copyright.com.**

Library of Congress Control Number: 2022910588

ISBN:978-0-357-88345-7

Cengage
200 Pier 4 Boulevard
Boston, MA 02210
USA

Cengage is a leading provider of customized learning solutions with employees residing in nearly 40 different countries and sales in more than 125 countries around the world. Find your local representative at **www.cengage.com.**

To learn more about Cengage platforms and services, register or access your online learning solution, or purchase materials for your course, visit **www.cengage.com.**

Notice to the Reader
Publisher does not warrant or guarantee any of the products described herein or perform any independent analysis in connection with any of the product information contained herein. Publisher does not assume, and expressly disclaims, any obligation to obtain and include information other than that provided to it by the manufacturer. The reader is expressly warned to consider and adopt all safety precautions that might be indicated by the activities described herein and to avoid all potential hazards. By following the instructions contained herein, the reader willingly assumes all risks in connection with such instructions. The publisher makes no representations or warranties of any kind, including but not limited to, the warranties of fitness for particular purpose or merchantability, nor are any such representations implied with respect to the material set forth herein, and the publisher takes no responsibility with respect to such material. The publisher shall not be liable for any special, consequential, or exemplary damages resulting, in whole or part, from the readers' use of, or reliance upon, this material.

Brief Contents

Table of Contents

Preface

CompTIA Cloud+ Guide to Cloud Computing, 2nd edition, is intended to serve the needs of students and professionals who are interested in mastering fundamental, vendor-independent cloud computing concepts. No previous cloud computing experience is necessary to begin learning from this course, although knowledge of basic computer, networking, and security principles is helpful. Those seeking to pass CompTIA's Cloud+ certification exam will find the course's content, approach, and numerous projects and study questions especially helpful. For more information on CompTIA Cloud+ certification, visit CompTIA's website at comptia.org.

Module Descriptions

The following list summarizes the topics covered in each module of this course:

Module 1, "Introduction to Cloud Computing," gives an initial overview of foundational cloud computing concepts, beginning with a survey of cloud certifications, a review of characteristics that define cloud computing, and a description of how an IT professional must adapt existing skills to succeed in a career focused on cloud technologies. The module then compares cloud deployment models (such as public cloud and hybrid cloud), cloud service models (such as PaaS and IaaS), and security concerns specific to each of these models. Finally, the module introduces popular cloud platforms, such as AWS (Amazon Web Services), Microsoft Azure, and GCP (Google Cloud Platform), and reviews sound troubleshooting methodology.

Module 2, "Virtual Hardware," begins with a description of virtualization technologies, including a thorough comparison of type 1 and type 2 hypervisors. The module then takes a deep dive into VM (virtual machine) configuration parameters, especially virtualized processing and virtual memory. It then applies these concepts specifically to the context of cloud computing, followed by a survey of VM allocation factors. The module concludes with coverage of VM alternative technologies such as serverless computing and containers.

Module 3, "Migration to the Cloud," focuses on how to get existing resources into the cloud. The module explores factors to be considered before, during, and after migration, including a comparison of migration strategies (such as lift-and-shift and lift-tinker-and-shift), and the timing of migration tasks that might affect user experience. Related migration topics include documentation, change management processes, and data transfer technologies. The module proceeds to discuss types of testing used to help the migration go smoothly. It also covers business processes that serve application development, such as project management and the application life cycle. The module concludes with a synopsis of common problems encountered during migration as well as planning for business continuity and disaster recovery.

Module 4, "Cloud Networking," initiates the discussion of cloud-based networking concepts with a comparison of the OSI Model and the cloud stack. The module includes a review of IP addressing and subnetting concepts followed by an exploration of networking services in AWS, Azure, and GCP. These sections include a thorough discussion of concepts such as regions, availability zones, VPCs (virtual private clouds), VNets (virtual networks), subnetting in the cloud, and the use of gateways and route tables to manage cloud traffic.

Module 5, "Cloud Connectivity and Troubleshooting," continues the cloud networking discussion with an exploration of technologies that connect the on-prem network with cloud-based resources. Network segmentation on-prem is contrasted with network segmentation in the cloud. The module explores technologies available to extend networking services across a hybrid or multi-cloud, such as DHCP, DNS, routing, and load balancing. It concludes with an overview of available CLI (command-line interface) commands used to troubleshoot cloud connectivity as well as situations where these tools might be useful.

Module 6, "Securing Cloud Resources," introduces security-related threats specific to cloud computing. While security is addressed throughout most of the modules, this module brings additional focus to cloud-based security strategies. The module highlights concerns and techniques specific to virtual network security, compute security, and data security, followed by an overview of common security weak spots in the cloud.

Module 7, "Identity and Access Management," furthers the security discussion with thorough coverage of IAM (identity and access management) techniques used to control access to cloud resources. The module covers account types that offer identity services to human users and application or cloud services, followed by a thorough discussion of authentication technologies and tools used in a cloud environment. Continuing with the theme of the three-tiered AAA (authentication, authorization, and accounting) approach to network access control, the module then explores options for managing authorization and permissions in AWS, Azure, and GCP. The module concludes with a brief discussion of how to extend IAM across a hybrid cloud as well as common IAM troubleshooting issues.

Module 8, "Cloud Storage," explains common storage technologies both on-prem and in the cloud, followed by storage optimization techniques. The module then highlights popular storage services in AWS, Azure, and GCP. It continues with an exploration of common backup types and techniques, including clones, snapshots, and redundancy levels. The module concludes with an emphasis on the security of cloud-hosted data storage.

Module 9, "Managing Cloud Performance," illustrates the need for effective monitoring techniques in the cloud along with an introduction to the benefits realized when automating cloud management tasks. Following a comparison of data collection tools—such as metrics, events, and logs—the module continues with coverage of analysis and response tools available in AWS, Azure, and GCP. Finally, the module explores common performance and capacity issues.

Module 10, "Cloud Automation," rounds out the foundations of cloud computing with further exploration into the possibilities and sheer necessity of using automation techniques in the cloud. Due to the fast-paced changes constantly occurring in cloud configurations and customer demand, automation through IaC (infrastructure as code) technologies provides adaptable and efficient modifications performed by tools covered in this module. The module then explores maintenance, security, and disaster recovery techniques that can be automated, including in-depth coverage of CLI and patch management tools available in AWS, Azure, and GCP. The module finishes with coverage of common obstacles to establishing successful automation workflows.

Features

To aid you in fully understanding cloud computing concepts, this course includes many features designed to enhance your learning experience.

- *Running scenario*—Each module begins with a running scenario giving real-world context for the technology and concepts presented. The ongoing story provides insight into a variety of cloud computing challenges from the perspective of an IT team preparing to migrate its data center to the cloud.
- *Module objectives*—Each module lists the concepts to be mastered within that module. This list serves as a quick reference to the module's contents and as a useful study aid.
- *Scenario-based practice questions*—Each module includes scenario-based questions similar to what you might encounter on the CompTIA Cloud+ exam. These questions put module content in real-world context and provide on-time application of covered concepts.
- *Colorful illustrations, screenshots, tables, and bulleted lists*—Numerous full-color diagrams illustrating abstract ideas and screenshots of various cloud platform consoles help you visualize common cloud computing tools, theories, and concepts. In addition, the many tables and bulleted lists provide details and comparisons of both practical and theoretical information that can be easily reviewed and referenced in the future.
- *Notes and CompTIA Cloud+ Exam Tips*—Each module's content is supplemented with Notes that provide additional insight and understanding, while CompTIA Cloud+ Exam Tips guide you in your preparations for taking the certification exam.
- *Cengage Unlimited cross-references*—If you have a Cengage Unlimited subscription, convenient cross-references to other publications with additional information on relevant concepts invite further study and exploration.
- *You're Ready prompts*—As you read through each module, you'll encounter prompts that indicate when you're ready for a specific project, inviting you to customize your learning path with what works best for your learning style.

- *Key Terms and Glossary*—Key terms emphasize the core concepts of cloud computing and are defined in the convenient Glossary.
- *Module summaries*—Each module concludes with a summary of the concepts introduced in that module. These summaries help you revisit the ideas covered in the module.
- *Acronyms table*—As in all things IT, cloud computing relies on extensive use of acronyms. The CompTIA Cloud+ objectives include a list of acronyms pertinent to the exam content, and a table at the end of each module indicates which of these acronyms are covered in that module.
- *Hands-On Projects*—Although it is important to understand the theory behind cloud computing technology, nothing beats real-world experience. To this end, each module provides several Hands-On Projects aimed at providing you with practical implementation experience as well as practice in applying critical thinking skills to the concepts learned in the module. Hands-On Projects use free trial or free student accounts in the three major cloud platforms: Amazon Web Services, Microsoft Azure, and Google Cloud Platform.
- *User-friendly organization*—Logical arrangement of content consolidates similar concepts for efficient coverage. This organization gives you the opportunity for deeper investigation of particularly rich concepts and skills that are emphasized in the latest CompTIA Cloud+ CVO-003 exam. Topics include a strong emphasis on security, troubleshooting, and business requirements, with expanded coverage of IoT (Internet of Things), containers, and cloud within a cloud concepts.

New to This Edition

Just as cloud technology continues to evolve, so does learning science and the insights available to course designers. In the interest of providing you with the most effective and durable learning experience, this latest edition is packed with improvements and enriched features:

- *Fully updated*—The content maps completely to CompTIA's Cloud+ CVO-003 exam for productive exam preparation.
- *Module outlines*—Each module begins with a brief outline of the content to help you organize the ideas in your mind as you read.
- *"Remember This" feature*—Section-specific learning objectives blend the Cloud+ exam objectives with the material covered in each section to help you focus on the most important points of that section.
- *Self-check questions*—Periodic multiple-choice questions sprinkled throughout the readings help you mentally complete the "learning cycle" as you practice recalling the information as you learn it. With answers and thorough explanations at the end of each module, you can check your own learning and assess your progress toward mastering each module's objectives.
- *Review questions*—A set of 10 review questions at the end of each module provides exam practice to help you assess the effectiveness of your learning and identify weak areas for further study.
- *Group activities*—One or more projects in each module offer optional group work activities to enhance the exploration of various concepts and skills.
- *Capstone projects*—Each module concludes with an in-depth project where you implement the skills and knowledge gained in the module through real design and deployment scenarios. In each Capstone project, you can use the cloud platform of your choice, whether that's AWS, Azure, GCP, or some other cloud platform. You can refer to guidance provided earlier in the module or course, and you can practice applying research skills to figure out how to complete new, related tasks.
- *Appendices*—New appendices provide exam-to-modules mapping, modules-to-exam mapping, a list of Cloud+ acronyms, and a grading rubric for projects and discussions.

Text and Graphic Conventions

Where appropriate, additional information and exercises have been added to this text to help you better understand the topic at hand. The following labels and icons are used throughout the text to alert you to additional materials.

Note ①

Prolific notes draw your attention to helpful material related to the subject being described and offer expanded insights to enrich your understanding.

Caution ①

Occasional Caution boxes alert you to potential issues.

Cloud+ Exam Tip ✔

The CompTIA Cloud+ Exam Tip icon provides helpful pointers when studying for the exam.

Grow with Cengage Unlimited!

Cengage Unlimited boxes provide cross-references to other Cengage materials if you need additional information about a topic.

   If you don't have a Cengage Unlimited subscription, you can find more information at cengage.com/unlimited.

Remember This

The Remember This feature highlights important points from each section as you finish reading that material. This invitation to pause and reflect helps you track your learning and ensure you're absorbing the most relevant concepts as you go.

Self-Check

To complete the learning cycle, these self-check questions help you practice recalling the information you've read. With answers and extensive explanations provided to readers at the end of each module, this low-stakes practice testing helps you assess how well you're learning and what material you might need to review before completing graded work.

You're Ready

These action pointers indicate when you've studied the concepts needed for each Hands-On Project at the end of the module. At each point, you can choose whether to take a break from reading to apply the concepts you've learned, or you can keep reading. These forks in the learning path encourage you to actively engage in choosing how you learn best.

Hands-On Projects

Each Hands-On Project in this course is preceded by a description of the project, required resources, and the relevant exam objective. Hands-On Projects help you understand the theory behind cloud with activities using some of the most popular cloud services.

Capstone Projects

Capstone Projects are more in-depth assignments that require a higher level of concept application. By providing less detailed guidance, these projects help you see the "big picture" of what you're learning. They challenge you to demonstrate a solid understanding and application of skills required for the CompTIA Cloud+ exam and a career in cloud computing.

Certification

Each main section of a module begins with a list of all relevant CompTIA Cloud+ objectives covered in that section. This unique feature highlights the important information at a glance and helps you better anticipate how deeply you need to understand the concepts covered.

Instructor's Materials

Instructors, please visit cengage.com and sign in to access instructor-specific resources, which includes the Instructor's Manual, Solutions Manual, PowerPoint Presentation, Syllabus, and Figure Files.

Instructor's Manual: The Instructor's Manual that accompanies this course includes additional instructional material to assist in class preparation, including suggestions for classroom activities, discussion topics, and additional projects.

Solutions Manual: Answers to Review Questions, Scenario-Based Questions, Hands-On Projects, Capstone Projects, Live Virtual Machine Labs, along with rubrics for Cloud for Life and Reflection activities, are provided.

PowerPoint Presentations: This course comes with Microsoft PowerPoint slides for each module. These are included as a teaching aid for classroom presentation, to make available to students on the network for module review, or to be printed for classroom distribution. Instructors, please feel at liberty to add your own slides for additional topics you introduce to the class.

MindTap for Cloud+ Guide to Cloud Computing

MindTap is an online learning solution designed to help you master the skills you need in today's workforce. Research shows employers need critical thinkers, troubleshooters, and creative problem-solvers to stay relevant in our fast-paced, technology-driven world. MindTap helps you achieve this with assignments and activities that provide hands-on practice, real-life relevance, and certification test prep. MindTap guides you through assignments that help you master basic knowledge and understanding before moving on to more challenging problems. MindTap activities and assignments are tied to CompTIA Cloud+ certification exam objectives. MindTap features include the following:

- *Integrated videos* are embedded in the module readings to show you concrete skills in four cloud platforms (Amazon Web Services, Microsoft Azure, and Google Cloud Platform). These author-led videos demonstrate skills, tools, and concepts covered in the modules, making abstract concepts and skills more concrete and preparing you to perform similar tasks in the Hands-On Projects. While videos assist in raising your comfort level with the platform(s) you're using in the projects, you'll benefit from watching videos for all the platforms to develop your expertise with those platforms and deepen your understanding of covered concepts.

- *Live Virtual Machine Labs* allow you to practice, explore, and try different solutions in a safe sandbox environment. Each module provides you with an opportunity to complete an in-depth project hosted in a live virtual machine environment. You implement the skills and knowledge gained in the module through real design and configuration scenarios.

- *Adaptive Test Prep (ATP)* app is designed to help you quickly review and assess your understanding of key IT concepts. Test yourself multiple times to track your progress and improvement by filtering results by correct answers, by all questions answered, or only by incorrect answers to show where additional study help is needed.

- *Pre- and Post-Assessments* emulate the CompTIA Cloud+ certification exam.

- *Cloud for Life* assignments encourage you to stay current with what's happening in the cloud industry.

- *Reflection* activities encourage classroom and online discussion of key issues covered in the modules.

Instructors: MindTap is designed around learning objectives and provides analytics and reporting so you can easily see where the class stands in terms of progress, engagement, and completion rates. Use the content and learning path as-is or pick and choose how your materials will integrate with the learning path. You control what the students see and when they see it. Learn more at cengage.com/mindtap/.

State of Cloud Computing in IT

Most organizations in nearly every industry rely on the cloud to some degree. The Flexera 2022 State of the Cloud Report (info.flexera.com/CM-REPORT-State-of-the-Cloud) polled 753 IT professionals from a wide range of industries in late 2021. All respondents currently use cloud services at their companies, with 96 percent in the public cloud and 84 percent using a private cloud. Organizations aren't limiting themselves to a single cloud platform, with 89 percent of respondents reporting their organizations employ a multi-cloud strategy. Furthermore, respondents reported that about half of their workloads run in a public cloud, and nearly half their data resides in a public cloud.

According to the same survey, the value of cloud computing shows in these organizations' budgets as well. More than half of the respondents, representing both small and large businesses, report their companies already spend more than $2.4 million annually for public cloud services. Over two-thirds of surveyed organizations report the operation of an existing cloud-specialist team, such as a CCOE (cloud center of excellence), with another fifth planning to create such a team in the near future.

Certifications

While unemployment rates for technology occupations are hitting record lows according to CompTIA (comptia.org/newsroom/2021/08/06/new-hiring-continuing-strong-employer-demand-drive-tech-unemployment-rate-to-its-lowest-level-in-two-years-comptia-analysis-reveals), rising salaries for jobs such as cloud architect, cloud infrastructure engineer, and cloud administrator reveal the soaring demand specifically for cloud computing expertise. According to the Global Knowledge 2021 IT Skills and Salary Report (globalknowledge.com/us-en/content/salary-report/it-skills-and-salary-report/), cloud computing pays more and is in higher demand than nearly any other IT sector, exceeded only by sales and marketing for pay and by cybersecurity for demand. Traditional degrees and diplomas do not identify the skills that a job applicant possesses, especially in relation to fast-changing cloud technologies. Companies are relying increasingly on technical certifications to adequately identify skilled job applicants, and these certifications can offer job seekers a competitive edge in the job market.

Certifications fall into one of two categories:

- Vendor-neutral certifications are those that test for the skills and knowledge required in specific industry job roles and do not subscribe to a vendor's specific technology solutions. Some examples of vendor-neutral certifications include all the CompTIA certifications (comptia.org) and certifications from CSA (Cloud Security Alliance) and (ISC)^2, which is the International Information System Security Certification Consortium.

- Vendor-specific certifications validate the skills and knowledge necessary to be successful while utilizing a specific vendor's technology. Some examples of vendor-specific certifications include those offered by Amazon Web Services (aws.amazon.com), Microsoft (microsoft.com), Google (cloud.google.com), Red Hat (redhat.com), Salesforce (salesforce.com), and Cisco (learningnetwork.cisco.com).

As employers struggle to fill open IT positions with qualified candidates, certifications are a means of validating the skill sets necessary to be successful within organizations. Furthermore, pursuing certifications helps ensure continued job satisfaction and relevance. According to the Global Knowledge report, most respondents reported pursuing training to improve their skill set, to earn a certification, and to seek a salary increase. In most careers, salary and advancement are determined by experience and education, but in the IT field, the number and type of certifications an employee earns also contribute to salary and wage increases.

Certification provides job applicants with more than just a competitive edge over their noncertified counterparts competing for the same IT positions. Some institutions of higher education grant college credit to students who successfully pass certification exams, moving them further along in their degree programs. For those already employed, achieving a new certification increases job effectiveness and satisfaction, which opens doors for advancement and job security. Certification also gives individuals who are interested in careers in the military the ability to move into higher positions more quickly.

What's New with the CompTIA Cloud+ Certification

Now in its third iteration, the CompTIA Cloud+ exam (CVO-003) reflects the maturation of the cloud industry with updated technologies and concepts framed in the larger context of business priorities and existing IT systems. With less emphasis on physical host configuration and much greater emphasis on cloud infrastructure, management, and security, the new exam requires proficiency with standard cloud services that demonstrates a student's understanding and knowledge in cloud networking, security, storage, and maintenance. These concepts are not directly transferrable from the on-premises data center to the cloud but, rather, require an abstraction of functions to a software-defined environment where everything is virtualized and underlying hardware is essentially invisible to the cloud consumer. Common compute, network, security, and storage standards must be reimagined to take full advantage of the cloud's potential. The new CompTIA Cloud+ exam invites candidates to contemplate these ideas more deeply and in ways more relevant to the cloud ecosystem.

The verbs in the exam's objectives indicate the increased depth of knowledge required for this new version of the exam. In the field of educational psychology, Bloom's taxonomy is an industry-standard classification system used to help identify the level of ability that learners need to demonstrate proficiency. It is often used to classify educational learning objectives into various levels of complexity. Bloom's taxonomy reflects the "cognitive process dimension" of learning and understanding that represents a continuum of increasing cognitive complexity, from remember (lowest level) to create (highest level).

There are six levels in Bloom's taxonomy, as shown in Figure A. The first CompTIA Cloud+ exam (CVO-001) was more heavily weighted toward level 2, Understand. Many of that exam's objectives began with the verb *explain* or *identify*. The next exam, CVO-002, contained only one objective at level 2 and was almost evenly distributed across level 3, Apply, and level 4, Analyze. The new exam, CVO-003, shifted again with a slight increase at level 2, Understand, and the heaviest emphasis on level 3, Apply. Many objectives use such verbs as *configure*, *apply*, *implement*, *perform*, or *troubleshoot*, all of which require practical, hands-on skills and greater understanding than what is needed to explain or identify related concepts.

Bloom's Taxonomy

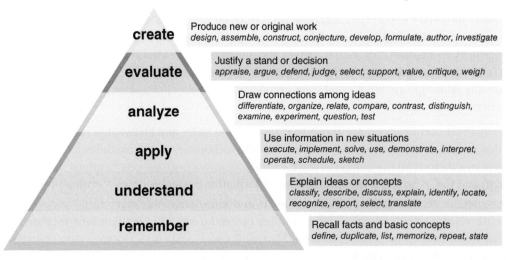

Figure A

In service of demonstrating these hands-on skills, this exam contains many performance-based questions. These questions present simulations with complex interactions designed to test a candidate's ability to apply concepts and analyze problems. Mastering, rather than simply memorizing, the material in this course will help you succeed on the exam and on the job.

Following are the domains covered on the new CompTIA Cloud+ exam:

CVO-003 domain	Percentage of examination
Domain 1.0 Cloud Architecture and Design	13%
Domain 2.0 Security	20%
Domain 3.0 Deployment	23%
Domain 4.0 Operations and Support	22%
Domain 5.0 Troubleshooting	22%

About the Author

Jill West authors Cengage courses for CompTIA Cloud+, CompTIA Network+, Data Communications, and the popular Technology for Success. She has taught kindergarten through college and currently teaches computer technology courses at Georgia Northwestern Technical College. Jill specializes in designing courses that teach to popular IT certifications, and she regularly presents at conferences and webinars on teaching cloud computing and computer networking, and on mentoring lifelong student learners in IT. She is a member of the 2019 inaugural cohort of Faculty Ambassadors for AWS Educate and is an AWS Academy Accredited Educator. Jill and her husband, Mike, live in north-west Georgia with two children at home and two off to college.

Acknowledgments

One of my greatest gifts in life is to get to work with the people who contributed to the development of this book. I've worked with many of these people through multiple projects, and I count them as friends. Lisa Ruffolo manages the numerous moving parts, keeping files flowing to their proper destinations. But more than that, she provides lively encouragement and constructive feedback—I always look forward to reading her comments on each module. Dani Shaw checks every module and project for technical accuracy, and I've come to rely on her eagle eyes to catch mistakes and contribute improvements. Carolyn Mako, though new to the team, jumped right in with insightful suggestions on learning design. I look forward to working with her again in the coming years. Our entire team was fortunate to have Brooke Greenhouse's warm and serene guidance to keep us on track and work her magic when challenges arose. And I'm personally grateful that Natalie Onderdonk continued on our team in her new role at the helm. She will always be one of my favorite geeks ever.

I would like to give a personal "thank you" to all our reviewers who contributed expertise, ideas, insights, and passion: Kim Green (Durham Technical Community College), Allan Pratt (Los Angeles City College), and Jeff Riley

Although my name goes on the cover, what you don't see is the myriad other people diligently contributing, brainstorming, checking, and rechecking to ensure you receive a cohesive and productive learning experience. It truly takes a village to develop an engaging, quality product such as this one.

Thank you to my kids—Winn, Sarah, Daniel, and Zack—for your patience as I work long hours. And thank you to my students for inspiring me to always do better.

A special thanks goes to my husband, Mike West, and all the ways he works tirelessly to keep our household running smoothly, covers the tasks I can't do when flooded with deadlines, and persistently encourages me through the struggles that come with intense schedules and high standards. Mike, I'm so grateful to be doing this life with you.

Read This Before You Begin

Getting into cloud computing is not as difficult as you might initially think. Many cloud providers offer generous free trials, especially for students. In this course, you'll have the opportunity to work in three public clouds: AWS (Amazon Web Services), Microsoft Azure, and GCP (Google Cloud Platform). You can choose any one, two, or all three of these platforms, depending on your needs, preferences, and available resources. They all offer some level of free trial credit and free tier services during the free trial, and some of these options don't even require a credit card if you have a school email account. Module 1 will walk you through the platform options. Regardless of which platform you decide to use, you can read through the material giving parallel information for the other platforms. You can also watch the videos for the other platforms so you can see those cloud services in action.

Finally, the Live Virtual Machine Labs in each module will give you practice with the AWS and Azure public cloud platforms. These labs are accessed through MindTap and let you work in fully functioning virtual machines to build your own cloud resources. With detailed steps and helpful screenshots, you'll find the support you need to perform complex provisioning tasks. Or you can explore and experiment beyond the parameters of the lab because these virtual machines are real systems and not simulations.

As for hardware and software, nearly all the projects in this course are completed through your browser. A decent computer with a good browser such as Chrome, Edge, Firefox, or Safari will work well. You will also need administrative access to your computer: In one project in Module 2, you will install and use VirtualBox, a free hypervisor. For this project, you will also need an ISO file for Windows or a Linux OS. You can instead use a different hypervisor for this project if you prefer. You will also use a drawing app, such as Visio, or you can use a free, online drawing app, such as app.diagrams.net.

These projects have been designed to make the cloud as accessible as possible for students and schools in all kinds of settings and circumstances. Nearly all the projects can be completed for free in their respective cloud platforms, especially if you're still within your free trial limits. Any steps that might accrue charges are identified, along with instructions on how to circumvent charges if you don't have free trial credits available.

Overall, the course offers many layers of options and resources that help you get into the cloud and build hands-on experience, making concepts concrete and memorable while helping you understand and apply the skills you're learning.

CompTIA.

Your Next Move Starts Here!

Get CompTIA certified to help achieve your career goals and gain a powerful, vendor-neutral credential that is trusted by employers.

Why get CompTIA certified?

Increase your confidence
91% of certification earners show increased confidence.*

Stand out to employers
64% of IT decision makers say certified employers add additional value.**

Earn more money
77% of IT pros got a raise within six months of earning their certification.*

Join a global community
92% of IT professionals hold at least one certification.**

Get ready for exam day.

• **Download the exam objectives:** Visit CompTIA.org to find the exam objectives for your IT certification and print them out. This is your roadmap!

• **Create your study plan:** Decide how many hours each week you are going to dedicate to studying, choose your preferred study tools and get to work. Studying is a unique experience. Download a study plan worksheet on CompTIA.org.

• **Get certified:** If you haven't already, use the coupon on this page when you purchase your exam voucher and schedule your exam. CompTIA offers flexible testing options to fit your busy life.

Choose your testing option.

Online testing
Earn a CompTIA certification online, from your home – or any quiet, distraction-free, secure location – at a time that's convenient for you.

In-person testing
Test at any of the Pearson VUE test centers around the world, where you can use their equipment under the supervision of a proctor.

To purchase your exam voucher and learn how to prepare for exam day, visit CompTIA.org.

*Pearson VUE 2021 Value of IT Certifications
**2021 Global Knowledge IT Skills and Salary Report

Module 1

Introduction to Cloud Computing

Module 1 Objectives

After reading this module, you will be able to:

1 Explain the primary characteristics of cloud computing.

2 Compare cloud deployment models.

3 Compare cloud service models.

4 Identify popular cloud service providers.

5 Apply troubleshooting methodology.

Module 1 Outline

Study this module's outline to help you organize the content in your mind as you read.

Module 1 Scenario

The clock says 8:56 a.m. as you slide in through the basement door of your building, shaking the rain off your umbrella and wiping your feet on the doormat. You're right on time for once! You notice the empty boxes still sitting by the doorway after yesterday's delivery of new cabling supplies. When you glance up at the security camera in the lobby area, you wonder yet again who might be sitting on the other side of that camera watching you move through the office space toward your desk. You make a mental note to ask Henry, the security guard at the front gate, where the camera feed goes and how often someone sits staring at the feeds ... just out of curiosity, of course.

As you hang your jacket on the back of your chair and prop your umbrella in the corner near your desk, Kendra, your boss, calls out from her office, "Come on, everyone—we've got a meeting!"

Oh, that's right. Your IT team is discussing the upcoming cloud migration today. At the meeting, the CIO of the private school you work for summarizes an Amazon Web Services (AWS) conference he recently attended touting the benefits of cloud computing. He's seeing dollar signs as he excitedly describes all the ways your school can save money by migrating to the cloud. "We won't have to pay so much for IT hardware anymore, our expenses will flex with our changing IT needs throughout the year, and even our electric bill will go down. Plus, the cloud apps we can use in the classroom are good for our students. We'll be able to attract more students from tech-savvy families moving to the area because of the tech start-ups and other IT companies migrating here."

Sounds like a good plan. Now it's up to your team to figure out how to do it. Your cloud conversion team will be led by your boss, Kendra, the network administrator. You've been recruited to help, along with a recently hired co-worker, Nigel, who passed his A+ certification exam last spring while taking night classes and then asked to be transferred to IT from his former position as a security guard. None of you have much experience with the cloud yet, other than binge-watching movies on the weekends and using your personal Gmail and social media accounts. The technology seems a little futuristic and "out there" when you think about it. But you're also secretly excited about learning some new stuff. Supposedly, "the cloud" is the next big revolution in the IT industry, and you'd rather be ahead of the curve than behind it on something so significant.

As the meeting rolls along, the entire team discusses what kinds of information you all need to know to have an intelligent conversation about the cloud. As you wrap up your action list in preparation for your next meeting, the questions you want to answer for yourself are the following:

- What is cloud computing?
- What new skills do I need to learn?
- Who owns the cloud?
- How does the cloud affect the security of my organization's data?

Section 1-1: Characteristics of Cloud Computing

 Certification

1.4 Given a scenario, analyze the solution design in support of the business requirements.

CompTIA (Computing Technology Industry Association and pronounced "comp-TEE-uh") released its first cloud computing certification, Cloud Essentials (CLO-001), in 2011 and updated to the current Cloud Essentials+ exam (CLO-002) in 2019. Cloud Essentials+ is intended for non-IT professionals or for IT professionals needing to bridge the gap between technical concepts and business concerns. The more technical Cloud+ certification (CVO-001) was first released in 2015, and the newest version of the Cloud+ certification, CVO-003, launched in mid-2021. While there are no prerequisites for taking the exam, Cloud+ builds on the knowledge required for other technical certifications (see Figure 1-1), including the following:

- **CompTIA A+**—Covers skills required for IT technical support specialists
- **CompTIA Network+**—Covers foundational networking concepts and skills
- **CompTIA Security+**—Surveys IT security technologies and strategies at a level necessary for any IT professional

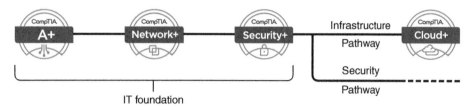

Figure 1-1   CompTIA Cloud+ is an infrastructure-specialty certification

Source: CompTIA, Inc.

While these certifications ("certs" for short) are not required for the Cloud+ exam, the knowledge covered by their objectives is directly relevant to the skills required of a Cloud+ certified technician. Cloud+ takes the foundational concepts covered in these earlier exams and applies that information to a cloud environment. This course assumes you are already at least somewhat familiar with A+, Network+, and possibly Security+ skills and concepts.

CompTIA Cloud+ Certification

One aspect that sets Cloud+ apart from most other cloud computing certs is that Cloud+ is vendor neutral. This means that, throughout this course, you will learn cloud computing concepts that span the full range of cloud computing services rather than targeting specific skills for working with any one cloud provider's platform. You might pursue a Cloud+ certification for the following reasons:

- To prepare for a new job or a promotion that likely will include responsibility for interacting with an organization's existing cloud services.
- To build a foundational understanding of cloud computing in preparation for vendor-specific cloud certifications.
- To complement certifications in other specialty areas (such as infrastructure, security, database management, or programming).
- To develop a big-picture perspective of cloud computing technologies, major players, and industry expectations in preparation for choosing vendors and migrating on-premises ("on-prem" for short) services to the cloud.

Other Cloud Certifications

Another vendor-neutral cloud certification is the more advanced CCSP (Certified Cloud Security Professional) certification from (ISC)[2], which is the International Information System Security Certification Consortium. The CCSP focuses on the security side of cloud computing at an expert level and requires a minimum five years of paid, full-time IT work experience, three years of which must be in information security and one year in work specific to one or more of the six exam domains. Alternatively, you must already have (ISC)[2]'s CISSP (Certified Information Systems Security Professional) certification.

Several highly respected, vendor-specific cloud certifications prove increasing levels of proficiency with specific cloud platforms and products. **CSPs (cloud service providers)**—such as Amazon, Microsoft, and Google—invest significant resources into providing training and certification programs for industry professionals. Some of the major vendor cloud certifications include the following:

- **AWS (Amazon Web Services)** holds the lion's share of the cloud platform market. AWS role-based certifications follow one of several certification tracks or learning paths, such as Architect, Developer, or Operations. Within each path, roles progress from Foundational and Associate to Professional and, in some cases, Specialty levels. Popular AWS certs include the three following certifications:
  - ○ *Cloud Practitioner*—This nontechnical, entry-level AWS certification is appropriate for professionals in technical, managerial, sales, purchasing, or financial roles.
  - ○ *AWS Certified Solutions Architect – Associate*—This intermediate AWS cert focuses on designing applications and systems in AWS. The related, advanced cert is AWS Certified Solutions Architect – Professional.
  - ○ *AWS Certified SysOps Administrator – Associate*—This intermediate AWS cert focuses on creating automated deployments of applications, networks, and systems in AWS. The related advanced cert is AWS Certified DevOps Engineer – Professional.
- Microsoft supports the Azure cloud platform and offers the following exam pathways to earn its Azure certifications:
  - ○ *Microsoft Certified: Azure Fundamentals*—This entry-level Azure certification is appropriate for candidates with nontechnical backgrounds or for technical professionals validating foundational knowledge of cloud services.
  - ○ *Microsoft Certified: Azure Administrator Associate*—This intermediate Microsoft cert focuses on implementing, monitoring, and maintaining Azure-based cloud solutions.
- **GCP (Google Cloud Platform)** is another major contender in the global cloud market and is quickly growing. While GCP offers fewer certifications, they are highly relevant if you will be working in a GCP ecosystem. Popular GCP certs include the following:
  - ○ *Cloud Digital Leader*—This nontechnical GCP certification requires knowledge of Google Cloud products and services in addition to basic cloud concepts.
  - ○ *Associate Cloud Engineer*—This entry-level GCP certification covers setting up, deploying, and securely operating a cloud solution. Google recommends at least six months related work experience before taking the exam.
  - ○ *Professional Cloud Architect*—This intermediate GCP cert focuses on designing, managing, optimizing, and securing a cloud solution architecture.
- **VMware**, a well-known provider of virtualization solutions, offers solutions that are highly integrated into some public cloud platforms. The following are two VMware cloud certs:
  - ○ *VMware Certified Technical Associate – Cloud Management and Automation*—This entry-level cert demonstrates a basic understanding of virtualization and cloud concepts.
  - ○ *VMware Certified Professional*—This intermediate exam requires skills to install, configure, and administer the VMware cloud environment.

Note 1

An entry-level cloud computing job might be called a junior cloud engineer, cloud implementation manager trainee, cloud technical architect, or junior cloud analyst, among many other possibilities. More advanced cloud computing positions might go by titles such as CSA (cloud systems administrator), senior cloud engineer, or cloud infrastructure engineer.

What Is Cloud Computing?

What makes cloud computing so attractive to companies looking to maximize their bottom line? According to NIST (National Institute of Standards and Technology), cloud computing has five essential characteristics, as shown in Figure 1-2:

- ***On-demand self-service***—In a traditional network or data center setting, network resources must be carefully planned, purchased, configured, and implemented. It can take months after deciding to institute a new

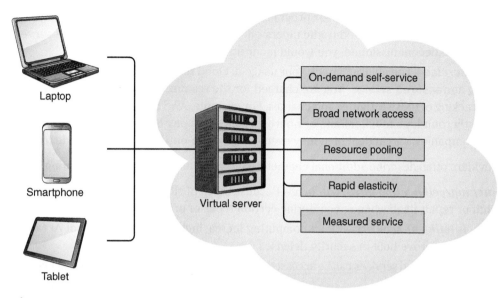

Figure 1-2   Characteristics of cloud computing

resource until that resource becomes available. Many people are typically involved in the decision-making and implementation processes. In contrast, cloud resources, such as VMs (virtual machines) or user accounts, can be created at any time by the service subscriber and other authorized users, which is called **on-demand self-service**. There's no built-in delay to order, install, and configure hardware because cloud resources are virtualized on top of existing hardware at the service provider's location. For example, suppose you need to add a web server to your network. Within a few minutes, you can spin up a VM in the cloud; optimize its virtual hardware resources (such as memory and processing power) and network settings to support web services; and then install the web server software, website files, and content to produce a live website. This process, once established, can even be automated.

- ***Broad network access***—Traditional network resources are mostly available only to users located within a specific geographic area. To access and configure these resources from outside the network, the user must "remote in" using a **VPN (virtual private network)** connection or similar remote access technology. Cloud services, however, can be accessed and configured from anywhere on the Internet and using any of a number of device types, such as a laptop, smartphone, or tablet. This type of access is called **broad network access**, and it gives cloud computing the flexibility of access to a larger user population in a wider variety of circumstances.

- ***Resource pooling***—In traditional networks, physical and virtual resources reside at the organization's own location, and all those resources are dedicated to the organization's own use. If a server is functioning at 10 percent capacity to meet the organization's needs, the remaining capacity is simply unused. Cloud providers use **resource pooling** to maximize the potential capacity of physical and virtual resources, which simultaneously serve multiple customers—called **tenants**—at any given time. The cost benefits of this efficiency are passed along to customers. A single server might be performing compute operations for three or four different cloud subscribers, and a single subscriber might be running a database whose data is held by multiple servers at multiple locations owned and operated by the cloud provider. In most cases, cloud customers don't know where their resources are hosted geographically; they only know how to access them through the Internet. Resource pooling is made possible by **multitenancy**, which means to support multiple customers' processes running on the same hardware. Multitenancy maximizes the potential capacity of physical and virtual resources by simultaneously serving multiple customers.

- ***Rapid elasticity***—**Rapid elasticity** refers to a cloud resource's ability to be added, released, increased, or decreased quickly—even automatically—according to demand. For example, suppose your company is preparing to run a Super Bowl ad and anticipates a tremendous increase in traffic to their website. On a traditional network, you would need to order additional servers to help support the increased traffic. This could take weeks of preparation and would be very expensive. After the ad traffic subsided, you would be left with several servers whose purpose had waned. If your web server is hosted in the cloud, however, you could provision additional web servers in minutes—or program them to auto-provision as needed—and then decommission those servers as the ad-generated traffic tapers off. You would only pay for the cloud servers while you used them, and once decommissioned, you would incur no additional costs.

- *Measured service*—The ability to track your usage of cloud resources at a granular level is what makes cloud computing a measured service. You are charged for the resources you use. Many cloud providers allow for detailed tracking of these activities and charges. For example, AWS bills for VM instances by the second, which avoids costly roundups to full-minute or hourly pricing. This pay-as-you-go approach, if configured properly, can save companies a great deal of money even before other optimizations are made for cloud technology.

Cloud providers often describe additional characteristics and benefits to cloud computing, including the following:

- *Self-patching/self-healing infrastructure*—Because much of cloud computing is automated, a cloud network can patch or repair itself when encountering certain types of problems.
- *Adaptive, intelligent security*—Cloud computing increasingly takes advantage of AI (artificial intelligence) technology to improve built-in security defenses.
- *Cross-platform*—Cloud services can be accessed and used from devices running different OSs (operating systems).

Organizations consider many reasons for transitioning to a cloud environment. They might be facing the expiration of a lease at their data center location; they might be looking for ways to optimize their services and become more competitive; or they might expect that cloud services will improve their bottom line. The cloud transition is not an overnight shift—organizations adopt cloud services in phases, and many will never become fully cloud-centric. Even after they've begun to make the transition to the cloud, business and user needs continue to change, and so do their cloud service requirements. Whether the changes are external, such as changes to regulations or laws, or internal, such as business mergers (two businesses blending into one), acquisitions (one business buying another), or divestitures (one business splitting off part of itself), the cloud services that support the business will need to be adapted, migrated, or replaced. All these changes require specialized skills from IT technicians to configure, deploy, secure, maintain, manage, and troubleshoot cloud computing services and resources.

What Do I Need to Know?

Cloud computing is a fairly recent—and rapidly changing—development in IT that is simultaneously revolutionizing the industry. Skills and knowledge from even five years ago are insufficient to meet the demands of managing today's cloud-hosted resources. IT professionals throughout the industry are asking what new skills will help them stay relevant as cloud computing technologies emerge and mature. The following list shows areas of professional growth most needed for cloud computing professionals—or any IT professional interacting significantly with the cloud:

- *Security skills*—Traditionally, IT security focuses on maintaining a protective perimeter around the on-prem data center, managing all traffic into and out of that secure perimeter (see Figure 1-3). As data, applications, and other resources move to the cloud, security must be built into the resources themselves so it travels with each resource. Administrators must also carefully consider what data can be outsourced to the cloud, as some types of regulated data are restricted to on-prem storage only. At the same time, cloud service providers offer options with built-in security compliance measures, which can relieve customers of needing to configure these requirements themselves. While the cloud customer is still responsible for enabling cloud security measures and configuring them in ways that best fit their needs, most cloud providers offer many tools—some that are free—to help with this effort. A cloud IT professional must become familiar with these tools and best practices in using them.
- *Cross-discipline expertise*—The broad possibilities inherent in cloud computing require that cloud technicians understand the business and organizational context of the services provided through the cloud. The more you understand, the more valuable you'll make yourself to potential employers. Important areas include the following:
  - The organization's business goals and the business processes and workflows that affect every department within an organization
  - Software development processes, including automation, configuration management, virtualization, monitoring, and CI/CD (continuous integration/continuous delivery)

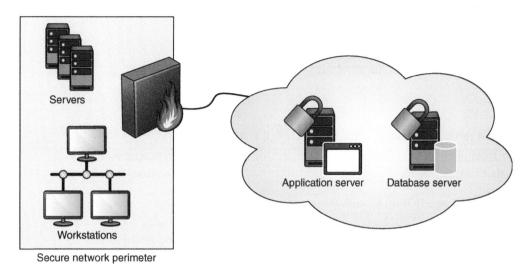

Figure 1-3   Cloud security can't rely on a secure perimeter

- ○ Infrastructure concepts, skills, and tools—networking in the cloud transitions the concrete configurations of a local network into a more abstract layer, which will only make sense to you if you thoroughly understand local networking
- ○ Security vulnerabilities, technologies, and best practices that are specific to cloud-hosted resources
- *Automation scripting skills*—One of the biggest advantages of moving to the cloud is gaining a greater degree of automation. The underlying virtualization layer and the encompassing monitoring techniques allow for granular and responsive automation. Developing the skills required to script extensive automation processes (called orchestration) in a way that is both efficient and reliable, and then continuing to refine them, is where cloud network admins often are most challenged.
- *Lifelong learning*—Cloud technologies are in constant flux, even more so than on-prem technologies. CSPs are innovating at an astonishing rate. A service that adequately meets your needs when you first migrate to the cloud could be overshadowed by a much improved—and cheaper—service a few months later. Staying relevant requires monitoring your own learning by identifying your blind spots, finding the information resources you need, and following through on your learning process. The most important computer skill is the ability to teach yourself.

You're Ready

You're now ready to complete Project 1-1: Research Cloud Computing Certifications. You can complete the project now or wait until you've finished all the readings for this module.

Remember This

- The CompTIA Cloud+ certification is a vendor-neutral, entry-level cloud computing certification that requires demonstration of technical skills.
- Popular cloud vendor certifications are published by CSPs such as Amazon, Microsoft, and Google.
- Cloud computing consists of five essential characteristics: on-demand self-service, broad network access, resource pooling, rapid elasticity, and measured service.
- Skills most needed by cloud professionals include security skills, cross-discipline expertise, automation scripting skills, and lifelong learning.

Self-Check

1. Which cloud platform does the CompTIA Cloud+ certification target?

    a. AWS

    b. Azure

    c. GCP

    d. None

2. Which of these certifications requires the least technical skill?

    a. CompTIA Cloud+

    b. Associate Cloud Engineer

    c. AWS Cloud Practitioner

    d. VMware Certified Professional

3. Which of the following is NOT an essential characteristic of cloud computing?

    a. Adaptive security

    b. Broad network access

    c. Rapid elasticity

    d. On-demand self-service

○ Check your answers at the end of this module.

Section 1-2: Cloud Deployment Models

Certification

1.1 Compare and contrast the different types of cloud models.

1.3 Explain the importance of high availability and scaling in cloud environments.

1.4 Given a scenario, analyze the solution design in support of the business requirements.

2.4 Given a scenario, apply data security and compliance controls in cloud environments.

One advantage of cloud computing is that a business can use someone else's hardware to host its applications, data, and network infrastructure. One disadvantage of cloud computing is that a business must typically rely on someone else's hardware to host its applications, data, and network infrastructure. Those statements aren't redundant or contradictory—cloud computing adds convenience while also reducing an organization's control of the hardware supporting their IT resources. This creates specific security concerns that vary according to the type of cloud services an organization decides to use. Most organizations don't jump directly into a cloud-only deployment, so you should be aware of the various options for who owns what resources in the cloud and how various security responsibilities are distributed between the CSP and cloud customer.

Public Cloud

When people think of cloud computing, the public cloud is generally what they have in mind. As shown in Figure 1-4, public cloud services are hosted on hardware resources at the CSP's location, and those physical resources can be shared with any other customer. The CSP might be a business, an academic organization, or a government entity. It provides cloud services (paid or free)—such as storage space, applications, compute capacity, or network functions—that are available to the general public.

With a public cloud, the CSP manages the hardware, which can't be accessed directly by the cloud customer. In this case, the customer relies deeply on the CSP's security measures to protect the data and other resources hosted in the public cloud. However, this doesn't mean the customer has no responsibility for its data security or that all CSPs

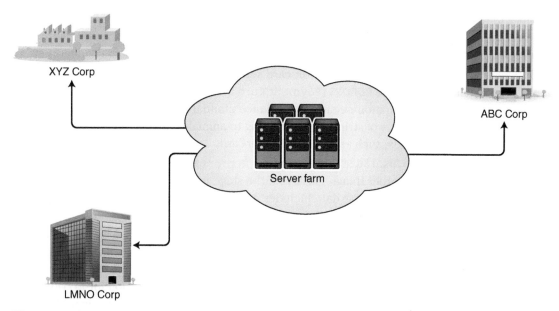

Figure 1-4   A public cloud is hosted on hardware shared by multiple customers

provide sufficient data center security. The following is a list of steps public cloud consumers can take to help ensure the security of their public cloud and its compliance with relevant industry standards:

- Research the CSP's industry certifications and audit compliance reports. Some of the most important to look for include the following:
  - *ISO/IEC 27001*—Developed by the ISO (International Organization for Standardization) and the IEC (International Electrotechnical Commission), the ISO/IEC 27001 standard provides an overarching model for organizations to use in keeping information secure. It addresses people, processes, and IT systems through a risk management process; all these components together are referred to as an ISMS (information security management system). An organization can become ISO/IEC 27001 certified by meeting these requirements, as determined by an audit conducted by an accredited certification body. Learn more about this certification at iso.org/isoiec-27001-information-security.html.

Note 2

The ISO (International Organization for Standardization) is an independent, nongovernmental international organization established in 1947 and is also responsible for having developed the seven-layer OSI (Open Systems Interconnection) model used in networking. Its shortened name, ISO, is derived from a Greek word meaning equal. The organization's founders chose this abbreviation to avoid confusion from having various acronyms for their name, depending on the language used.

  - *SSAE 18*—The SSAE (Statement on Standards for Attestation Engagements No. 18), developed by the AICPA (American Institute of Certified Public Accountants), is a standard used to determine audit compliance. The SSAE 18 replaced earlier standards such as SSAE 16, which replaced an even older standard, SAS 70 (Statement on Auditing Standards No. 70). Additional amendments continue to be made to the SSAE 18 where later releases, such as SSAE 19, replace certain portions of SSAE 18. Instead of resulting in a certification, an SSAE 18 audit results in various SOC (Service Organization Control) reports. Two types of SOC 1 (pronounced sock one) reports focus on internal financial controls. Most relevant to this discussion, however, are the SOC 2 and SOC 3 reports. Both reports address benchmarks as defined by the organization for information security, availability, processing integrity, confidentiality, and privacy. The SOC 2 report contains proprietary information and often requires a signed NDA (nondisclosure agreement) before release to a customer to restrict the customer from sharing proprietary information. The SOC 3 report is designed for public release. Learn more about this standard at aicpa.org/research/standards/auditattest/ssae.html *and* aicpa.org/interestareas/frc/assuranceadvisoryservices/serviceorganization-smanagement.html.

○ *PCI DSS*—For all companies that provide credit card services, including accepting, storing, processing, or transmitting credit card data, the PCI DSS (Payment Card Industry Data Security Standard) sets requirements for keeping that information secure. Compliance standards are determined by the PCI Security Standards Council in gradations of stringency according to annual transaction volume. The standards are enforced by credit card brands, such as Visa and MasterCard.

○ *HIPAA*—The HIPAA (Health Insurance Portability and Accountability Act) was enacted in 1996 to protect medical information. Among other things, HIPAA set the stage to establish and continually evolve specific guidelines for data security when that data includes any identifiable information about patients or their medical history. It also imposes stiff penalties and fines for data breaches, whether due to criminal intent or even simple negligence.

○ *GDPR*—A more recent development, the GDPR (General Data Protection Regulation) defines broad protections for any PII (personally identifiable information) and standards for how to handle breaches affecting that data. The regulations apply to any organization handling this type of information for EU (European Union) citizens, even if the organization is not based in Europe. The GDPR became effective in mid-2018 and, at the time of this writing, is still being tested with some recent breaches for how stringently the standards and penalties will be enforced.

○ *CCPA (California Consumer Privacy Act)*—Similar in purpose to the GDPR, the CCPA (California Consumer Privacy Act) applies only to medium and large businesses but enforces some standards that exceed those set by the GDPR. In some ways, this law more deeply impacts US business processes, especially due to its broader definition of what information qualifies as private data.

• Check security requirements as defined in the CSP's SLA (service level agreement). The SLA might include terms of agreement such as requiring encryption of all data in transit or in storage, geographic location of data storage (which might be regulated by law, depending on your organization and the type of data), consistency of service availability, and penalties for failure in any of these areas. Security failures can be quite costly for your organization, and the SLA should include some kind of compensation for damages resulting from problems on the CSP's end.

• Investigate the CSP's security measures. For example, ask about how the CSP protects against data leakage between tenants on their multitenant infrastructure. Ask whether the CSP relies on third-party vendors, what measures are in place to ensure those organizations' compliance with standards and compliance measures, and how those services are handled if there's an availability or other security concern with those vendors.

• Understand the CSP's recommendations and requirements for your own organization's security measures. This might include access monitoring, license management, self-service troubleshooting, trouble ticket reporting requirements, or encryption processes that you're responsible for.

Private Cloud

Private cloud services are hosted on hardware resources used exclusively by a single organization. This hardware might be located in a CSP's data center and dedicated to one customer, or the hardware might be located in the organization's own data center. What makes a cloud private is that no one else is allowed to use the hardware for their own cloud, regardless of where that hardware is located. This increases security and the organization's control over the exact configuration of the hardware used. In fact, the need to keep sensitive data on-site is often the motivating factor in deploying a private cloud on-prem.

You might wonder how a private cloud hosted on-prem is different from the traditional data center that most organizations already have. A traditional data center might use virtualization for network or data services. Virtualization is a time-tested technology designed to host many services on a single, physical server. While virtualization provides some flexibility in how the hardware interacts with virtual services, the configurations for these services are still closely tied to the underlying physical hardware. A cloud is more abstracted from the physical hardware in the data center, relying on a cloud API (application programming interface) layer of communication that is managed by comprehensive virtualization software. As shown in Figure 1-5, APIs provide the communication interface between various components of a deployment, such as a web server with serverless code or a database with an application. It's this sophisticated virtualization layer that more defines what "cloud" is, not necessarily access over the Internet. If you deploy cloud technology on your own hardware, you can have both at the same time: an on-prem data center that is running a private cloud. To qualify as cloud technology, all of NIST's five essential characteristics must apply, which is not true of older virtualization technologies.

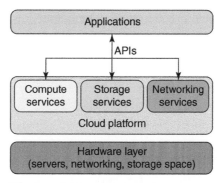

Figure 1-5 Cloud services and underlying hardware communicate with APIs

Grow with Cengage Unlimited!

If you'd like more information about virtualization and hypervisors, use your Cengage Unlimited subscription to go to *CompTIA Network+ Guide to Networks*, 9th edition, Module 7, and read the section titled "Virtual Architecture."

If you don't have a Cengage Unlimited subscription, you can find more information at cengage.com/unlimited.

Note 3

Private clouds aren't only for businesses. An individual might create a private cloud for their home network. For example, Nextcloud (nextcloud.com) is an open-source cloud storage and application service that can be installed on a home server and accessed through the Internet. It functions similarly to Dropbox (dropbox.com), except the cloud is owned and managed by the consumer rather than a third-party organization.

Private cloud security requires more of a traditional approach to securing a network perimeter. If the private cloud is hosted on-prem, security measures will cover everything from hardware to applications and data, where some of the security implementations will be virtualized within the private cloud. If the hardware resides at a CSP's location, you'll need to consider all the security concerns listed earlier for public cloud services. Some additional considerations include the following:

- Design for the future. Cloud security requires thinking outside the box or, in this case, outside the perimeter. Implement security measures that don't rely solely on having a secure boundary around network resources. These measures might include thorough and secure data encryption, host firewalls, internal network monitoring, and both internal and external access controls.
- Secure the virtual environment, hypervisor, VMs, and physical hosts.
- Ensure that security measures such as encryption and traffic monitoring are appropriately applied to traffic between virtual systems, even if it's never exposed to the Internet.
- Carefully investigate hypervisor vulnerabilities and apply all needed patches as they become available.
- Monitor VM security needs, applying patches and updates as needed, installing host firewalls, and using whatever other defenses you would normally use for a physical machine.

- Consider which virtual systems are placed on each physical host, isolating systems by security zone so low-security systems don't reside on the same physical machine as high-security systems.
- Segment virtual systems from host physical systems so that guest machines can't be used to inappropriately access the physical host's systems and configurations.

Hybrid Cloud

A **hybrid cloud** is a mix of both public and private cloud components, or a combination of some cloud and some traditional on-prem services, where those components and services interact with each other in a direct and seamless manner. See Figure 1-6. This scenario might occur as an interim phase during a company's transition to the cloud, or an organization might maintain a hybrid arrangement indefinitely.

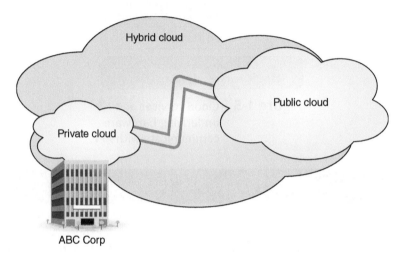

Figure 1-6   A hybrid cloud is a mix of public and private clouds
or a combination of cloud and on-prem services

Many organizations take a "cloud-first" or "cloud-centric" approach, where they migrate every application and service that reasonably can be moved to the cloud. Most of the time, the move must occur in phases. The organization might have begun its transition from its own hardware and software resources to cloud-based resources, but it is not yet a "cloud-only" network—some of its data and network resources are still hosted locally in its own, traditional data center.

Some organizations, however, find that not every application, data set, or service is suitable for the cloud. In these cases, organizations make a partial transition with the intent of maintaining some of their traditional data center. At the same time, the resources across the different hosting environments are integrated and directly interact with each other. Perhaps a database hosted on-prem communicates with a web server hosted in the cloud. Or compute resources hosted in a private cloud can rely on temporary, virtualized hardware resources in a public cloud to accommodate short spikes in demand, which is called cloud bursting.

In reality, a hybrid cloud model is the most common cloud deployment because relatively few organizations are ready or able to commit fully to the cloud. As might be expected, security measures for hybrid clouds include all relevant points listed for both a public cloud and a private cloud.

Multi-Cloud

A **multi-cloud** model involves using cloud services from multiple vendors at one time (see Figure 1-7). Some organizations commit to a single-cloud environment, such as AWS or Azure. All the cloud services they use are hosted by that one CSP. However, as cloud services mature and the demand for cross-environment functionality increases, many organizations choose the best-in-breed for any particular service. This means working with multiple CSPs to custom build a cloud best suited to the organization's needs.

On the simple side, a multi-cloud might look like a small business using two or more cloud applications from different vendors—such as email and office suite applications from Google (google.com), a file storage and sharing service from

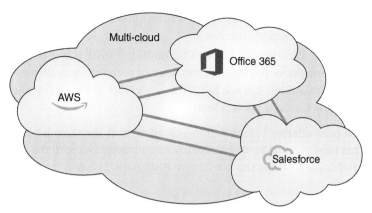

Figure 1-7   A multi-cloud intertwines cloud resources from multiple cloud providers

Dropbox (dropbox.com), and an online presentation platform like GoToMeeting (goto.com/meeting) from LogMeIn, Inc. On the more complex side, an organization might shift its payroll software to a cloud hosted by AWS (aws.amazon.com), and it might use a cloud-based **CRM (customer relationship management)** solution from Salesforce (salesforce.com) to help manage communications with customers, potential customers, vendors, and associates. What makes it a multi-cloud setup is that multiple CSPs are involved, even if the services themselves don't directly interact with each other.

> **Note 4**
>
> The rise in popularity of hybrid and multi-clouds necessitates an expansion of skills for IT professionals. No longer is it sufficient to develop expertise in only one cloud platform. Your skill set should cross several cloud platforms at many levels of available services.

Community Cloud

A **community cloud** is accessible to multiple organizations with similar concerns, but not to the general public. One example might be several regional hospitals that share access to patient records. The patient database in the cloud would be accessible to member hospitals but would not be available to other organizations or the general public. One of the member organizations might host and manage the community cloud resources either on- or off-premises, or it might be provided by a third party.

Cloud Within a Cloud

One cloud provider in particular has developed an innovative variation that is worth exploring here. As you read earlier, VMware offers widely popular virtualization products that many companies use to manage their virtualized resources on-prem. For example, if you want to create several VMs in your data center, you could use something like VMware's vCenter to manage all the VMs and their physical hosts.

As increasing numbers of customers flocked to the cloud, VMware looked for a way to hold onto their customer base. What they developed is sometimes referred to as a **cloud within a cloud**. Using this strategy, customers can migrate their vCenter virtualization environment onto a public cloud platform, such as AWS. They use all the same vCenter tools they're familiar with on-prem, and they can simultaneously benefit from hosting these resources in the public cloud.

This approach offers several advantages:

- *Cloud-native technologies*—Customers can take advantage of cloud-native technologies, such as containers, which you'll read about in a later module.
- *Unlimited scalability*—Running on a customer's own physical hardware limits expansion to the capabilities of the hardware itself. The cloud-within-a-cloud model benefits from the ability to scale almost without limit because the public cloud can offer expansion to as many physical resources as the customer is willing to pay for.

- *Familiarity*—Customers can continue using the virtualization and management tools they're used to rather than having to learn the cloud provider's interface.
- *Seamless migration*—Application workloads can be migrated from the private data center to the public cloud platform without interruption. Essentially, this kind of technology makes the virtualized environment cloud-agnostic, meaning the customer can run their VMware cloud on top of any hardware, whether their own (a private cloud) or someone else's (a public cloud).

VMware is not the only company offering a cloud-within-a-cloud service. For example, Snowflake provides cloud-based software for data analytics that runs in a public cloud network environment. As with the VMware example, this arrangement provides nearly unlimited scalability and the freedom to distribute the service across multiple cloud platforms.

Remember This

- Public cloud services are hosted on hardware resources at the CSP's location.
- Private cloud services are hosted on hardware resources used exclusively by a single organization.
- A hybrid cloud is a mix of both public and private cloud components, or a combination of some cloud and some traditional on-prem services, where those components and services interact with each other in a direct and seamless manner.
- A multi-cloud model involves using cloud services from multiple vendors at one time.
- A community cloud is accessible to multiple organizations with similar concerns, but not to the general public.
- When using a cloud-within-a-cloud solution, customers can migrate their vCenter virtualization environment onto a public cloud platform.

Self-Check

4. Which of these standards protects credit card information stored in a public cloud?
   a. PCI DSS
   b. HIPAA
   c. NDA
   d. ISO

5. What factor limits the capacity of a private cloud to provide resources to users?
   a. Operating system
   b. Security settings
   c. Hardware
   d. Geographic location

6. An AWS-hosted network using the G Suite productivity apps is an example of what kind of cloud?
   a. Community cloud
   b. Cloud-within-a-cloud
   c. Hybrid cloud
   d. Multi-cloud

○ Check your answers at the end of this module.

Section 1-3: Cloud Service Models

Certification

1.1 Compare and contrast the different types of cloud models.

1.4 Given a scenario, analyze the solution design in support of the business requirements.

2.5 Given a scenario, implement measures to meet security requirements.

Cloud computing takes functions and resources that would normally happen on a local network, abstracts those functions to a software-defined level, and then provides those services back to the local network from across the Internet or another network. For example, consider the traditional firewall appliance. These devices are installed in data center racks and positioned on the network to filter traffic between the internal network and the outside world. They can require a significant amount of upkeep to manage the firewall rules, logs, and updates. It is also expensive to upgrade these devices, which also have a limited life expectancy.

Cloud computing allows network administrators to export this firewall function to the cloud as a virtual firewall service, called FWaaS (Firewall as a Service). FWaaS can be expanded rapidly as needed, has no limits on life expectancy, and automates much of the maintenance and upkeep. Firewall coverage for remote office locations or work-from-home employees is more consistent. Firewall functions can be more granularly customized throughout the network. Cato Networks (catonetworks.com) and Palo Alto Networks (paloaltonetworks.com) both offer FWaaS product options.

While FWaaS is a specific type of cloud computing service, other service types are more encompassing. This section discusses the most common cloud service models, and it explores security concerns related to each model.

Common Cloud Service Models

The usual classifications of cloud service models, as defined by NIST and compared in Figure 1-8, are as follows:

- **SaaS (Software as a Service)**—Most cloud consumers are most familiar with SaaS (Software as a Service and pronounced sass), which is the provision of software through the cloud. Applications can be accessed from different types of devices without having to manage any of the underlying infrastructure such as the network, servers, operating systems, or storage. Google's office productivity suite (G Suite) is a great example of SaaS. Google Docs (docs.google.com), for example, is a document processing application that is accessed through a web browser and can be used on nearly any web-enabled computer or mobile device, regardless of the device's operating system or other installed apps. Dropbox (dropbox.com), an online file storage app, and GoToMeeting (goto.com), an online conference call app, are also popular examples of SaaS. The consumer might be able to manage user-specific configuration settings, such as sharing options, file storage location, view settings, contacts, permissions, or even default printer.

- **PaaS (Platform as a Service)**—PaaS (Platform as a Service and pronounced pass) is an intermediate level of cloud capability that allows consumers to deploy applications on various platforms without having to manage the lower-layer infrastructure such as the network, servers, or storage. The consumer can manage the applications and possibly some of the environment hosting those applications. For example, Google's App

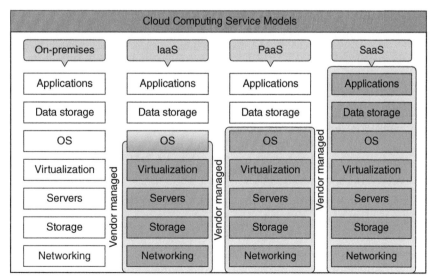

Figure 1-8   At each progressive level of these cloud computing service models, the vendor takes over more management and configuration responsibility for the organization

Engine can host a custom mobile app accessed by an organization's sales force, while another company uses App Engine to develop new games.

- *IaaS (Infrastructure as a Service)*—The more technically challenging IaaS (Infrastructure as a Service and pronounced i-as) allows consumers to deploy a cloud-based network with services such as storage, user desktops, network infrastructure devices (such as routers and load balancers), network security devices (such as firewalls and access control lists), and network services (such as DNS and authentication). The consumer doesn't control the underlying hardware but can manage operating systems, network configurations, and virtual devices. For example, a manufacturing plant might transition its entire server infrastructure to Google's Compute Engine, including web servers, Active Directory, and a SQL server.

Note 5

The "-aaS" acronym can be used to refer to nearly any service offered through the cloud. To refer to Anything as a Service, you might see the acronym XaaS, where "X" represents an unknown, just as it does in algebra. (And you thought you would never again use algebra.)

Some other -aaS examples include DBaaS (Database as a Service), DaaS (Desktop as a Service), DRaaS (Disaster Recovery as a Service), CaaS (Communication as a Service or Computing as a Service), BPaaS (Business Process as a Service), and even RaaS (Ransomware as a Service)—because hackers are getting on the cloud bandwagon, too!

Another way to think about these service models is according to how much a customer must know about configuring and managing cloud networks in order to use the service, and how much control that customer has over the exact configurations, features, and security measures. Consider the service models as they're shown in Figure 1-9. The smaller, upper end of the pyramid indicates how little a SaaS customer needs to understand and interact with a cloud provider's infrastructure to perform their work. In contrast, an IaaS customer interacts more heavily with the service provider's infrastructure for every aspect of their computing needs. The customer has more control and flexibility with configurations and security features, along with more responsibility for design and security.

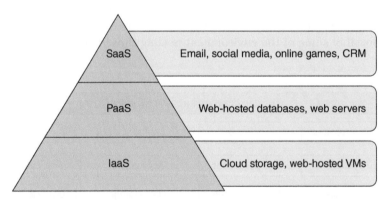

Figure 1-9   IaaS customers must understand more about configuring their cloud infrastructure—and they have more control—than do SaaS customers

At the same time, consider how accessible each type of cloud service is to users. In Figure 1-10, the triangle is upside down. Users, the largest group of cloud computing consumers, can easily access and use SaaS products without much setup, whereas IaaS products require extensive preparation by a much smaller group of more skilled network architects and administrators, who provide systems for their users. In the middle of this pyramid is PaaS, which is typically used by application developers—both professionals and laypersons—for testing their products. Customers at the lower layers of this pyramid build products that support customers at the higher layers, such as when a company subscribes to an IaaS product, on which it offers its own PaaS or SaaS products to its own unique market of customers.

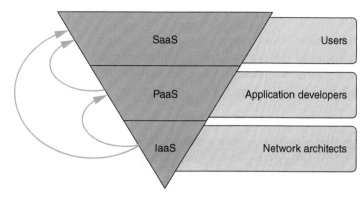

Figure 1-10   SaaS services are more immediately accessible to a wide market of users than other categories of cloud services

Service Model Security Concerns

As organizations transition to the cloud, security strategies must also evolve to protect new vulnerabilities and defend against new types of attacks. Sensitive data and other resources no longer reside within a secure perimeter. As data, applications, and the infrastructure move outside of a tightly controlled network perimeter, security must be associated with the data and applications themselves.

Each of the service models discussed here—IaaS, PaaS, and SaaS—present different types of security issues. The following discussion gives a general overview of security concerns and implementations for each service model. You'll dig much deeper into cloud security later in the course.

SaaS Security Concerns

Organizations using SaaS have two primary areas of security concerns:

- *Data security*—Data created, stored, and accessed through SaaS solutions must be encrypted both at rest (when stored) and in transit (as it travels between the CSP and the consumer). The SaaS provider bears some significant responsibility to offer and ensure data security measures. However, the SaaS customer must also ensure that private or regulated data is appropriately encrypted, protected, stored, and transmitted. In the end, some data is simply too sensitive to be stored in the cloud.

- *Application access*—Even when data is properly encrypted, it can still be compromised through social engineering attacks that result in unauthorized access to the SaaS products used to manage that data. Attack types such as phishing, Trojan horses, and keyloggers are major concerns for all organizations, whether they're in the cloud or not. However, with data stored in the cloud, user education becomes even more critical to the safety and security of that data.

PaaS Security Concerns

PaaS customers have the same concerns as SaaS users: data security and application access. In addition, PaaS presents additional concerns:

- *Application configurations*—Customers often subscribe to PaaS for the purpose of developing and hosting their own applications. The built-in security of these applications is a continuous concern for developers, with the need to ensure that applications can't be improperly reconfigured by hackers and won't release data to unauthorized users. Again, this is true for developers regardless of whether they're developing and deploying on a cloud platform or on-prem. However, because PaaS-hosted applications are easily accessed online, they have an increased vulnerability to hacking attempts.

- *Administrative/root access*—Public cloud services, by definition, have multiple tenants using shared hardware and network resources. PaaS providers must ensure that customers don't have administrative or root access to servers running PaaS instances. This will prevent tenants from accessing each other's services. These security measures also help prevent hackers from using unauthorized access to one tenant's resources to then access those of another tenant.

IaaS Security Concerns

IaaS customers must consider similar security concerns as when running their own, on-prem infrastructure. This includes compliance regulations, audit requirements, and identity management in addition to all the other concerns previously listed. Because IaaS customers have no control over the hardware underlying their cloud infrastructure, they must ensure that the CSP complies with standards common to the customer's industry.

Remember This

- The usual classifications of cloud service models, as defined by NIST, are SaaS, PaaS, and IaaS.
- Each of these common service models—SaaS, PaaS, and IaaS—present increasing layers of security issues, where SaaS requires data and access security, PaaS additionally requires configuration and root access security, and IaaS requires security measures similar to an on-prem network.

Self-Check

7. Which cloud service model requires the least skill to use?
   a. DRaaS
   b. IaaS
   c. PaaS
   d. SaaS

8. Which cloud service model requires the most skill to adequately secure?
   a. IaaS
   b. PaaS
   c. SaaS
   d. RaaS

○ Check your answers at the end of this module.

Section 1-4: Cloud Service Providers

 Certification

1.1 Compare and contrast the different types of cloud models.

CSPs offer a wide variety of cloud services, some specific to a particular market niche, and others more generalized to meet a wider base of consumer needs. For example, Salesforce (salesforce.com) hosts a popular SaaS-based CRM system that makes information regarding customer relationships readily available to employees in sales, customer service, marketing, and other organizational departments. Because the data is accessed through an online dashboard, employees throughout the company can use extensive and updated customer data to better perform their job duties.

Salesforce focuses on its SaaS CRM products. Although Salesforce also offers a few PaaS products, these are not the focus of their business. Other CSPs have emerged as leaders in the PaaS and IaaS markets, with AWS (Amazon Web Services), Microsoft Azure, and GCP (Google Cloud Platform) being three of the top contenders for market share as of 2022.

PaaS and IaaS Providers

As you learn about cloud technologies, it's important to follow changes in which providers offer what kinds of services and where they're positioned competitively. The following list explores some of these options:

- *AWS (aws.amazon.com)*—The market-leading cloud provider and the first major contender in the public cloud computing market, AWS is a subsidiary of Amazon and was founded in 2006. AWS offers a huge line of cloud computing products with more options added frequently. If anything, the plethora of options here can be overwhelming and is sometimes considered a weakness of AWS. The company offers extensive training tutorials through their website, along with many highly respected AWS-specific certifications.

- *Azure (azure.microsoft.com)*—Azure is the cloud computing arm of Microsoft's enterprise technologies. Designed for seamless compatibility with Microsoft's other tools, Azure also supports many other operating systems and cloud products. Azure first went live to the public in early 2010.

- *GCP (cloud.google.com)*—Hosted on the same infrastructure as other Google products, GCP brings IaaS and PaaS services to Google's extensive line of cloud products, such as the SaaS-based G Suite collection. App Engine, first released in 2008 and providing basic web application hosting, was Google's first entry into the public cloud market. Soon after, Google began adding other cloud services, which are now collectively referred to as Google Cloud Platform.

- *Alibaba Cloud (alibabacloud.com)*—Based in Hangzhou, China, Alibaba Cloud is a relative newcomer and yet offers a fast-growing public cloud platform primarily to Asian markets. Alibaba Cloud's parent company, Alibaba Group Holding Ltd., is the largest online commerce company in China and typically ranks in the top five global retailers by revenue.

- *IBM Cloud (ibm.com/cloud)*—IBM's cloud computing services suite, IBM Cloud, is a rebranding of earlier services from SoftLayer (which IBM acquired in 2013) and IBM's own Bluemix products. IBM Cloud was originally built on the open-source Cloud Foundry, which was originally developed by VMware. With IBM's purchase of Red Hat in 2018, IBM has taken a notable shift toward open-source technology that is intended to target markets across all public cloud platforms.

- *Oracle Cloud (oracle.com/cloud)*—Based in Redwood Shores, CA, Oracle is known primarily for its database software. In 2010, Oracle began rebranding its existing Oracle On Demand services, which allowed for running Oracle applications in an Internet browser, and adding new cloud computing services, all under the Oracle Cloud umbrella. The slower-growing Oracle Cloud platform takes advantage of Oracle's extensive success with databases and other software products to differentiate itself from other CSPs for Saas, PaaS, and IaaS services.

All these CSPs primarily provide public cloud platforms. You can also host your own private cloud—essentially DIY cloud computing—using cloud management software of some kind. A few examples include the following:

- *OpenStack (openstack.org)*—One of the most popular private cloud platforms. OpenStack is an open-source cloud computing platform designed by Rackspace and NASA to create do-it-yourself compute, storage, and networking cloud services. OpenStack can be deployed on the company's own data center, through an OpenStack-based public cloud, or in a hosted OpenStack private cloud.

- *VMware (vmware.com)*—A leading provider of data center virtualization solutions such as vSphere and ESXi, VMware is also a respectable force in the cloud market. VMware Cloud allows an organization to create a private cloud in its own data center. Alternatively, VMware solutions such as vSphere and vCenter can be installed over an existing public cloud infrastructure. Because so many organizations already use VMware virtualization products, VMware's partnerships with major public cloud providers such as AWS and IBM Cloud provide a natural extension to a customer's existing VMware infrastructure to create a seamless hybrid cloud or multi-cloud.

- *Eucalyptus (eucalyptus.cloud)*—Eucalyptus (Elastic Utility Computing Architecture for Linking Your Programs To Useful Systems—yes, it's an acronym) is a partially open-source platform that is designed specifically for building private or hybrid clouds to interact with AWS products. Originally developed by researchers at the University of California, Eucalyptus became a for-profit business in 2009, was purchased by Hewlett-Packard in 2014, and is now managed by AppScale Systems.

Exam Tip ✔

While the CompTIA Cloud+ exam is vendor neutral, you do need to be familiar with major CSP platforms and understand the basic ways they manage cloud services. This background knowledge will give you a more concrete understanding of the relatively abstract cloud computing concepts covered by the Cloud+ exam.

Common Cloud Services

While each CSP offers different cloud services and configures their user interfaces and product offerings in different ways, the major CSPs offer the same basic product types. These are the services you might use to configure your own cloud network, to host your resources on the cloud (such as applications, servers, or data), or to run the processes you need (such as authentication, machine learning, or batch processing). The following list describes some of these major categories of cloud services:

- *Compute*—Compute refers to cloud functions that process data in some way. The term primarily refers to running VMs or applications in the cloud and can also refer to developer tools used to create, test, and deploy applications. When working with compute services, you'll find many options for configuring the virtualized hardware on which these processes run—such as CPU cores, memory size, and I/O (input/output) compatibilities. You'll also find newer, cloud-native technologies for running code in the cloud, such as containers and serverless services. Grouped under the compute category, you might also find tools related to these processes, even though these tools might technically perform functions from other categories. For example, you might find a repository of OS images (a storage function) used to create VMs.

- *Storage*—The storage category covers cloud services that store or preserve data. This is a large category that is often subdivided into smaller categories, including databases (which is arguably a completely separate category from storage), block storage, object storage, file storage, data optimization services such as DFR (data footprint reduction), and data protection services such as backup and disaster recovery. You'll find virtualized hardware options, such as choosing storage volumes of various speeds and storage capacities, RAID options, data transfer speeds, and storage protocols (such as Ethernet, iSCSI, or InfiniBand, which bleeds over into networking concepts), as well as pricing options for accessing stored data. You might also find tools grouped under the storage category that enable mass migration of large amounts of data.

- *Networking*—Networking functions provide ways of moving data within the cloud or between networks and resources. Included in this category are options for configuring network functions such as connection configurations, subnets, IP addressing, VPNs, trunk lines, DHCP services, load balancing, and more. Other tools include migration resources and content delivery products, which might be grouped in their own categories.

- *Security*—As with a traditional data center, security functions in the cloud include perimeter security (firewalls, IPS/IDS, and proxies for the virtual network), identity management, certificate or key management, authentication services, access controls, and token or federation services. Cloud services, by definition, present a larger attack surface than do traditional networks, where access should be more tightly monitored and controlled. Therefore, the security tools you'll typically find at your disposal, especially when configuring a public cloud, will take the needs of this abstracted, remote environment into account.

- *Application components*—Tools from many of these categories can be used for building and hosting cloud-based applications. Cloud services optimized for app development might also be available, such as testing or hosting environments, microservices, templates, security auditing, e-commerce, machine learning, and mobile services.

- *Management tools*—Cloud platforms include a variety of management and monitoring tools, including dashboards (such as OpenStack's Horizon or Amazon's QuickSight), monitoring services (such as Google's Stackdriver or Amazon's CloudWatch), and data analytics services (such as Azure's Stream Analytics or Google's Cloud Machine Learning).

Table 1-1 shows some products in three of these categories from some of the major cloud platforms. You'll learn more about each of these products in later modules, and this table will help you begin to get familiar with the kinds of service names you'll encounter in this course.

Table 1-1   Popular cloud products and components from major cloud platforms

CSP	Compute	Network	Storage
AWS	EC2 (VMs) Fargate (containers) Elastic Beanstalk (web apps)	Virtual Private Cloud (networking) Direct Connect (dedicated cloud connection) Route 53 (DNS)	EBS (block storage) Glacier (archive storage) Snowball (petabyte-scale data transport)
Azure	Virtual Machines (VMs) Container Instances (containers) Azure Kubernetes Service (container orchestration)	Azure DNS (DNS) VPN Gateway (cross-premises connectivity) ExpressRoute (dedicated cloud connection) Traffic Manager (traffic routing)	Blob Storage (object storage) File Storage (file shares using SMB 3.0)
GCP	Compute Engine (VMs) App Engine (PaaS) Kubernetes Engine (containers)	Virtual Private Cloud (networking) Cloud Load Balancing (scalable load balancing) Cloud Interconnect (dedicated cloud connection) Cloud DNS (DNS)	Cloud Storage (object storage) Persistent Disk (block storage) Filestore (file storage)
OpenStack	Nova (VMs) Zun (containers)	Neutron (networking) Octavia (load balancing) Designate (DNS)	Glance (image storage) Swift (object storage) Cinder (block storage) Manila (file storage)

You'll encounter other categories in various cloud computing platforms, such as ML (machine learning), IoT (Internet of Things), media services, AR (augmented reality), and VR (virtual reality). Larger CSPs use more specific categories to make it easier for their customers to choose the products they need. These categories and the products in them change frequently as cloud technologies continue to mature.

Note 6

In this course, you'll need access to at least one major CSP's public cloud (for example, AWS, Azure, or GCP). You might want to sign up with more than one of these CSPs. The projects in this module show you the sign-up options for AWS, Azure, and GCP so you can choose the account type that best fits your needs and situation. Many students are concerned about having to provide a credit card number in order to create a cloud account. For this reason, some CSPs offer student-focused free trials that do not require a credit card.

Projects throughout the course that use these public clouds give instructions for AWS first. Additional projects provide instructions for performing the same or similar tasks in Azure and GCP. For any platform you're not using yourself, you can watch author-produced videos for projects in all three platforms. The idea is to give you lots of hands-on experience with at least one major CSP's public cloud and widespread exposure to all three platforms.

Internet of Things (IoT)

While this course doesn't directly address ML, AI, VR, or AR technologies, you will need to know some concepts related to IoT for the CompTIA Cloud+ exam. The **IoT (Internet of Things)** is a collection of all devices connected to the Internet. These aren't only your normal computing devices, like laptops and smartphones and printers; this is

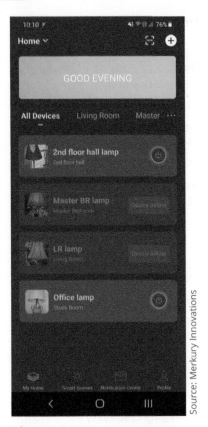

Source: Merkury Innovations

Figure 1-11   App-controlled IoT devices

anything that can communicate with the Internet. All sorts of things can be connected to a network, from toasters, refrigerators, bathroom scales, and garage doors to watches, lamps, cars, thermostats, doorbells, and even the kitchen sink.

One of the fastest-growing areas of IoT is personal monitoring devices, such as health monitors, exercise equipment, GPS locators, and smartwatches. Another exploding IoT market interconnects smart home devices. You might already be familiar with Amazon Echo, Apple HomePod, or Google Home. These voice-controlled smart speakers and their embedded personal assistant apps (such as Alexa, Siri, and Google Assistant) can interlink a plethora of devices, from locks and lights to security cameras and coffee pots. You can control these devices through voice commands while interacting with a smart speaker, or you can control IoT devices through an app on your smartphone (see Figure 1-11). All these connected devices within a home create a type of LAN called a HAN (home area network).

While IoT devices can function without cloud technology, most of these devices rely on cloud to optimize their functionality, as follows:

- **Communication**—IoT devices generally communicate over the Internet with a cloud service of some kind, like a SaaS, that allows the user to control their devices, especially when using a personal assistant app like Alexa.

- **Storage**—IoT generates massive amounts of data, which is often stored in the cloud. This is beneficial because you only pay for the storage space you use, and you can be confident the cloud's storage space can expand to accommodate whatever amount of storage you're willing to pay for.

You're Ready

You're now ready to complete the following projects:

- Project 1-2: Create an Account with AWS
- Project 1-3: Create an Account with Azure
- Project 1-4: Create an Account with GCP

You can complete these projects now or wait until you've finished all the readings for this module.

Remember This

- Market-leading IaaS and PaaS CSPs include AWS, Azure, and GCP. Other popular CSPs include Alibaba Cloud, IBM Cloud, Oracle Cloud, OpenStack, VMware, and Eucalyptus.
- Cloud services are grouped into categories, such as compute, storage, networking, security, application components, and management tools.
- The IoT (Internet of Things) is a collection of all devices connected to the Internet.

Self-Check

9. Which public cloud platform offers the most streamlined integration with Windows Active Directory?

   a. AWS
   b. Alibaba

   c. Azure
   d. Oracle

10. In which cloud category would you most likely find a service for configuring DNS records?

   a. Networking

   b. Security

   c. Compute

   d. Storage

11. Which IoT device provides access to a personal assistant app?

   a. GPS locator

   b. Smart speaker

   c. Security camera

   d. Smart toaster

○ Check your answers at the end of this module.

Section 1-5: Troubleshooting Methodology

Certification

5.1 Given a scenario, use the troubleshooting methodology to resolve cloud-related issues.

Throughout this course—and throughout your career—you'll be required to troubleshoot various problems. Taking a methodical approach to this process helps ensure efficiency and prevent costly delays and mistakes. As you become more familiar with the networks and other resources that you manage, you'll likely begin to rely more heavily on your experience and intuition. In the meantime, however, the troubleshooting method defined by CompTIA can help you organize your thoughts and your approach to solving problems. And when tackling an especially stubborn problem, you can fall back on this established method to help you work through the process one logical step at a time.

Exam Tip ✔

The Cloud+ exam might give you a troubleshooting scenario that requires you to identify the *next* step according to the troubleshooting method described in this section. To do this, you must use the information given to identify which steps of the troubleshooting process have been completed so far in the scenario, and then identify which step should come next and which of the task options would accomplish that step.

Common Cloud Computing Problems

At this point in your career, you've probably already developed a sense of how to troubleshoot a computer or network problem. In this course, you'll learn more about how troubleshooting processes apply specifically to cloud computing. You'll first explore a few common issues you might experience when working in cloud environments. When the troubleshooting steps are discussed later in this section, you'll see how those steps can be applied to common cloud issues. Consider some of these common issues:

- *Connectivity issues*—Obviously, using public cloud services relies heavily on access to the Internet. If your connection to your ISP (Internet service provider) goes down, you won't have access to your cloud services. Problems could also originate from your local network hardware or from endpoint configurations. Or you might have dedicated connections to a public exchange, and your connectivity is suffering from a routing misconfiguration.

- *Latency*—You might have connectivity, but it's really slow. This delay is called latency and is often caused by poor routing, insufficient bandwidth, or a bottleneck. Latency might be the ISP's responsibility, or you might need to upgrade your service with either your ISP or your CSP.

- *Capacity*—While you can certainly face capacity issues with a traditional data center, cloud services can be designed to auto-scale in order to avoid capacity-related problems. If this auto-scaling is not adjusting to current demands, you might need to adjust the related configurations or check for security issues that might be causing unexpected problems.
- *Security*—Cloud computing brings its own set of security vulnerabilities. When troubleshooting cloud services, you'll need to become familiar with the unique indicators of cloud-based security issues.

You'll learn more about each of these problems and how to solve them later in this course. In the meantime, take a look at the troubleshooting steps as defined by CompTIA.

Troubleshooting Steps

The following is a list of the steps in the CompTIA troubleshooting methodology, and they're also shown in Figure 1-12. As you read through the steps, think about how you've used these steps yourself in troubleshooting problems you've encountered:

1. *Identify the problem*—This includes questioning the user and identifying any changes the user has made recently to the computer or changes that have been made to the network or environment. Also, back up data on the computer or other system before making any changes to it yourself.
2. *Establish a theory of probable cause*—Beginning with the symptoms, look for internal and external clues for what might be causing the problem. Remember that the cause is not always complex—question the obvious!
3. *Test the theory to determine cause*—After you've confirmed your theory, decide what steps you should take next. If you can't confirm your theory, try again or escalate the problem to the next support tier.
4. *Establish a plan of action to resolve the problem and implement the solution*—However, don't make any changes without first considering corporate policies and procedures and the impact the change might have on other systems. Keep in mind that some changes must first be approved at higher levels.
5. *Verify full system functionality, and, if applicable, implement preventive measures*—This might include educating the user.
6. *Document findings, actions, and outcomes*—Most organizations keep a knowledge base of some kind for systematic documentation. Be sure to use professional communication skills, such as good grammar and thorough explanations, so your documentation will be easy for others to use later.

Preventive Measures

You can take several measures to help minimize the likelihood of problems cropping up in your cloud environment. Consider the following tips:

- Maintain good monitoring and analysis techniques.
- Thoughtfully configure your dashboards to show the most helpful information.
- Follow good change management processes.
- Understand your cloud services and how to identify where problems are likely to occur, how to locate those problems, and how best to address them.

These best practices will be covered in more detail throughout this course.

You're Ready

You're now ready to complete Project 1-5: Apply Troubleshooting Methodology. You can complete the project now or wait until you've finished other projects for this module.

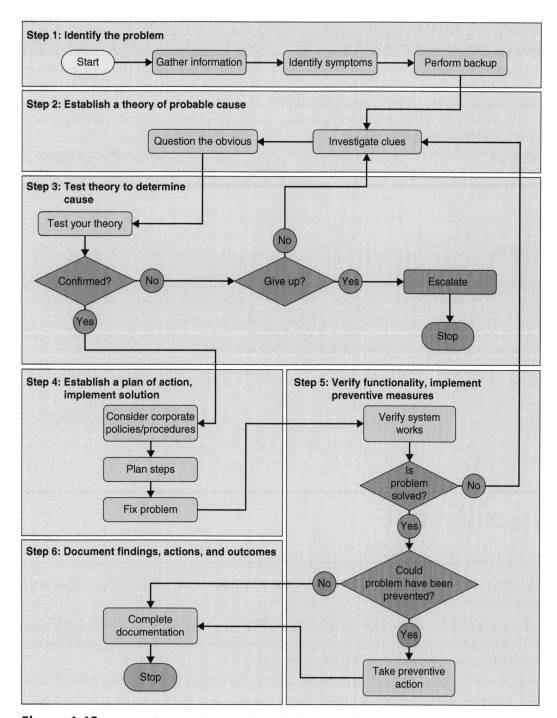

Figure 1-12   General approach to solving cloud computing problems

Remember This

- Common problems encountered with cloud technologies include connectivity issues, latency, capacity, and security.
- The steps for CompTIA's troubleshooting methodology are as follows: (1) Identify the problem; (2) establish a theory of probable cause; (3) test the theory to determine cause; (4) establish a plan of action to resolve the problem and implement the solution; (5) verify full system functionality, and, if applicable, implement preventive measures; and (6) document findings, actions, and outcomes.
- Preventive measures include good monitoring practices, thoughtful dashboard design, effective change management, and a clear understanding of a company's cloud infrastructure.

Self-Check

12. What cloud configuration technique can be used to compensate for capacity challenges?

   a. Latency

   b. Endpoint configurations

   c. Change management

   d. Auto-scaling

13. What is the last step of CompTIA's troubleshooting methodology?

   a. Documentation

   b. Verify functionality

   c. Test the theory

   d. Implement the solution

○ Check your answers at the end of this module.

Module Summary

Section 1-1: Characteristics of Cloud Computing

- The CompTIA Cloud+ certification is a vendor-neutral, entry-level cloud computing certification that requires demonstration of technical skills.
- Popular cloud vendor certifications are published by CSPs such as Amazon, Microsoft, and Google.
- Cloud computing consists of five essential characteristics: on-demand self-service, broad network access, resource pooling, rapid elasticity, and measured service.
- Skills most needed by cloud professionals include security skills, cross-discipline expertise, automation scripting skills, and lifelong learning.

Section 1-2: Cloud Deployment Models

- Public cloud services are hosted on hardware resources at the CSP's location.
- Private cloud services are hosted on hardware resources used exclusively by a single organization.
- A hybrid cloud is a mix of both public and private cloud components, or a combination of some cloud and some traditional on-prem services, where those components and services interact with each other in a direct and seamless manner.
- A multi-cloud model involves using cloud services from multiple vendors at one time.
- A community cloud is accessible to multiple organizations with similar concerns, but not to the general public.
- When using a cloud-within-a-cloud solution, customers can migrate their vCenter virtualization environment onto a public cloud platform.

Section 1-3: Cloud Service Models

- The usual classifications of cloud service models, as defined by NIST, are SaaS, PaaS, and IaaS.
- Each of these common service models—SaaS, PaaS, and IaaS—present increasing layers of security issues, where SaaS requires data and access security, PaaS additionally requires configuration and root access security, and IaaS requires security measures similar to an on-prem network.

Section 1-4: Cloud Service Providers

- Market-leading IaaS and PaaS CSPs include AWS, Azure, and GCP. Other popular CSPs include Alibaba Cloud, IBM Cloud, Oracle Cloud, OpenStack, VMware, and Eucalyptus.
- Cloud services are grouped into categories, such as compute, storage, networking, security, application components, and management tools.
- The IoT (Internet of Things) is a collection of all devices connected to the Internet.

Section 1-5: Troubleshooting Methodology

- Common problems encountered with cloud technologies include connectivity issues, latency, capacity, and security.
- The steps for CompTIA's troubleshooting methodology are as follows: (1) Identify the problem; (2) establish a theory of probable cause; (3) test the theory to determine cause; (4) establish a plan of action to resolve the problem and implement the solution; (5) verify full system functionality, and, if applicable, implement preventive measures; and (6) document findings, actions, and outcomes.
- Preventive measures include good monitoring practices, thoughtful dashboard design, effective change management, and a clear understanding of a company's cloud infrastructure.

Key Terms

For definitions of key terms, see the Glossary.

Alibaba Cloud
API (application programming interface)
automation
AWS (Amazon Web Services)
Azure
broad network access
CCPA (California Consumer Privacy Act)
cloud within a cloud
community cloud
CRM (customer relationship management)
CSP (cloud service provider)
Eucalyptus (Elastic Utility Computing Architecture for Linking Your Programs To Useful Systems)
GCP (Google Cloud Platform)
GDPR (General Data Protection Regulation)

HIPAA (Health Insurance Portability and Accountability Act)
hybrid cloud
IaaS (Infrastructure as a Service)
IBM Cloud
IoT (Internet of Things)
ISO/IEC 27001
knowledge base
latency
measured service
multi-cloud
multitenancy
NDA (nondisclosure agreement)
NIST (National Institute of Standards and Technology)
on-demand self-service
OpenStack
Oracle Cloud
orchestration

PaaS (Platform as a Service)
PCI DSS (Payment Card Industry Data Security Standard)
private cloud
public cloud
rapid elasticity
resource pooling
SaaS (Software as a Service)
SLA (service level agreement)
SOC (Service Organization Control) report
SSAE (Statement on Standards for Attestation Engagements No. 18)
tenant
virtualization
VMware
VPN (virtual private network)

Acronyms Checklist

The acronyms in Table 1-2 are listed in the Cloud+ objectives and could appear on the Cloud+ exam. This means that exam questions might use any of these acronyms in context so you must know the meaning of the acronym in order to answer the question correctly. Make sure you're familiar with what each acronym stands for and the general concept of the term itself. All these acronyms are used in context in this module.

Table 1-2   Module 1 acronyms

Acronym	Spelled out
AI	artificial intelligence
API	application programming interface
CRM	customer relationship management
CSP	cloud service provider or content service provider
DBaaS	Database as a Service
I/O	input/output
IaaS	Infrastructure as a Service
IoT	Internet of Things

Acronym	Spelled out
ISP	Internet service provider
ML	machine learning
PaaS	Platform as a Service
SaaS	Software as a Service
SLA	service level agreement
VM	virtual machine
VPN	virtual private network
XaaS	Anything as a Service

Review Questions

1. Your company transitions a dozen servers to the cloud instead of purchasing several new servers to replace aging equipment. The monthly cost of these cloud-hosted servers that can grow with the business is significantly lower than the anticipated cost of purchasing new hardware that would have, at first, greatly exceeded the current needs of the business. What feature of the cloud has your company taken advantage of?

   a. Broad network access
   b. Measured service
   c. Multitenancy
   d. Cross-platform compatibility

2. When you speak to Alexa, you initiate the processing of code that runs in the cloud without creating a new server to do so. Which cloud service model most likely provides the service that processes this code?

   a. SaaS
   b. PaaS
   c. IaaS
   d. DBaaS

3. Which of the following is NOT an advantage of a cloud-within-a-cloud deployment model?

   a. Unlimited scalability
   b. Minimal cost
   c. Platform familiarity
   d. Seamless migration

4. To deploy a series of test environments in the cloud, you want a script that will design and configure several servers, some network infrastructure, and firewall rules. What process will produce the script you need?

   a. Automation
   b. Self-healing infrastructure
   c. Multitenancy
   d. Orchestration

5. Which document can ensure you will receive compensation if your company's Internet service has an extended outage?

   a. GDPR
   b. NDA
   c. SLA
   d. HIPAA

6. Multitenancy enables what cloud characteristic?

   a. Rapid elasticity

   b. Broad network access

   c. On-demand self-service

   d. Resource pooling

7. Which document might require an NDA before you can read it?

   a. SSAE 18

   b. SOC 2

   c. ISO/IEC 27001

   d. SAS 70

8. As you're developing your hybrid cloud, you move a handful of servers and two applications to the cloud. Both applications need to communicate with a database that will remain on-prem. What technology will allow the applications to communicate with the database without human intervention?

   a. VPN

   b. CLI

   c. GUI

   d. API

9. For what purposes does the IoT often use cloud technologies? Choose TWO.

   a. Virtualization

   b. Storage

   c. Compute

   d. Communication

10. During which step of the troubleshooting process should you back up data?

   a. While testing your theory as to the probable cause

   b. While identifying the problem

   c. While verifying full system functionality

   d. While establishing a plan of action

Scenario-Based Questions

Question 1-1

Raul works for a small consulting firm that assists medical organizations, such as quick care facilities, and health professionals, such as doctors' offices or alternative care providers, to establish, update, and manage their IT systems. He regularly works with patient databases and must ensure that his clients' networks and other IT resources comply with strict government regulations. Raul's boss, Cheri, recently asked him to assist in upgrading their firm's data center. The CEO has decided they need to take a major step toward a more cloud-centric business model and asked Raul how the company can ensure that their cloud provider meets industry standard requirements for data security, service availability, and confidentiality. Which standard should Raul recommend they use to compare security ratings of various CSPs?

   a. PCI DSS

   b. HIPAA

   c. GDPR

   d. SSAE 18

Question 1-2

Raul's company has narrowed its options to a small handful of CSPs. All these CSPs offer a wide variety of cloud services and meet all of the company's security requirements. Cheri, Raul's boss, is now asking him to recommend what type of cloud services would best fit their needs. She explains they want to start with cloud-based email and an office productivity suite that enables easy file sharing among team members. Which cloud service model should Raul recommend they use to accomplish these goals?

   a. SaaS

   b. IaaS

   c. RaaS

   d. PaaS

Question 1-3

Anika has run into a problem with the VPN connection to her company's cloud-hosted database. She has a good Internet connection and can access her work email account, which uses the same sign-in credentials as the VPN. But she still can't pull reports from the database service. She calls Patrick, who works for the company's help desk. As Anika describes the problem to Patrick, he tells her to try again and make sure she's using the right password, then to restart her router, and if that still doesn't fix it, to restart her computer. Which troubleshooting step did Patrick fail to complete in the correct order?

a. Test the theory to determine cause

b. Document findings, actions, and outcomes

c. Establish a plan of action and implement the solution

d. Establish a theory of probable cause

Hands-On Projects

Note 7

Websites, applications, public cloud platforms, and related account options change often. While the instructions given in these projects were accurate at the time of writing, you might need to adjust the steps or options according to later changes.

Note to Instructors and Students: A rubric is provided for evaluating student performance on these projects. Please see Appendix D.

Project 1-1: Research Cloud Computing Certifications

Estimated time: 30 minutes

Objective 1.1: Compare and contrast the different types of cloud models.

Group work: This project includes enhancements when assigned as a group project.

Resources:

- Internet access

Context:

This course prepares you to take the CompTIA Cloud+ CVO-003 exam, which is a vendor-neutral exam covering a broad array of foundational and intermediate cloud computing concepts within the context of an organization's entire IT system. Other cloud certifications are offered mostly by cloud vendors, including Amazon, Google, VMware, OpenStack, Cisco, Microsoft, and IBM. Other vendor-neutral certifications are offered by Cloud Security Alliance (CSA) and Cloud Credential Council (CCC).

Passing the CompTIA Cloud+ exam will help prepare you to target more specialized and advanced cloud certifications later, such as those published by cloud vendors. Understanding what those certifications cover, how they're organized, and how they're related will help you make better choices about which certifications are the best fit for you and your career aspirations.

Use the web to research and answer the following questions:

1. What are the five domains of objectives for the CompTIA Cloud+ CVO-003 exam?
2. What kind of experience does CompTIA recommend you have before taking the Cloud+ exam?
3. What is the primary difference in purpose between the CompTIA Cloud+ exam and the CompTIA Cloud Essentials+ exam?
4. What are the domains of the AWS Cloud Practitioner certification?
5. What kind of experience does AWS recommend you have before taking the Cloud Practitioner exam?
6. What skills does the Microsoft Azure Fundamentals exam cover?

7. What are the four sections of the Cloud Digital Leader certification by Google?
8. **For group projects:** Each member of the group should research online for practice questions for a cloud certification, either one discussed in this project or a different certification. Group members should compare their sources to ensure no one uses the same source as someone else. Each group member quizzes the other group members with the practice questions and tallies their performance. Each group member then lists which exam objectives the group collectively demonstrates sufficient knowledge as required by each objective covered by that exam. Submit the name of the exam, the source of the practice questions, a brief summary of the group's performance on the practice questions, and the list of exam objectives currently mastered by the group collectively.

Project 1-2: Create an Account with AWS

Estimated time: 30 minutes
Objective 1.1: Compare and contrast the different types of cloud models.
Resources:

- Internet access
- If using a standard AWS account, a credit card
- If using an AWS Academy account, an invitation from the instructor to join a Learner Lab in AWS Academy

Context:

AWS offers multiple options for creating and accessing free resources for various purposes. The account itself is always free. While a typical AWS account requires a credit card (even if you don't accrue charges), you do have another option. Specifically, AWS Academy does not require a credit card and can be managed by your instructor. The following are the two different types of accounts you can use for this course:

- *AWS account*—This is a standard account type open to the public. It requires a credit card and allows full access to standard AWS services, including free-tier services. So long as you reliably shut down and delete the cloud resources you create for your projects, you should be able to complete all the AWS projects in this course without incurring any charges on your credit card.
- *AWS Academy account*—This account type is available to educators and students from accredited educational institutions, and it does not require a credit card. Instructors can customize the AWS environment students use, and instructors can enter each student's AWS console to help with troubleshooting or grading work. AWS Academy offers many appealing benefits, including free credits per account in addition to free credits allotted to each course a student takes in AWS Academy (this amount varies by course).

Note 8

NOTE TO INSTRUCTORS: At this time, the AWS Academy process begins with an application from your institution. There is no cost to join—it just requires filling out an application and waiting for approval. The application should be completed by an instructor or administrator who will oversee your school's participation in the program. This process should be completed before the course begins, as there might be a delay as your school's application is processed.

Once the institution is accepted, instructors are nominated for accreditation. Each instructor begins at the Foundation level with basic access to resources, which is sufficient for this Cloud+ course. An instructor can complete training and validation to achieve Associate level accreditation, but this is not necessary for the Cloud+ course.

The instructor sets up a course and invites students. Students get some credits they can use on their own to explore AWS, and they get additional credits they can use during the course for assigned activities. The best course type to choose for this Cloud+ course is the Foundational Services Learner Lab. Learner Labs provide a sandbox environment in the AWS cloud where students can experiment with certain AWS services using their credits.

Additionally, students can get discounts on AWS certification vouchers. Instructors also have access to their own training and voucher discounts for AWS certification exams. For more information, visit **aws.amazon.com/training/awsacademy/**. Note that this information changes often. For additional updates, please email the author at jillwestauthor@gmail.com.

(continues)

Hands-On Projects Continued

Check with your instructor to determine which type of account you should create. From the following steps, choose the set of steps that matches the type of account you will use, and then complete the steps to create your account.

If you're creating a **standard AWS account**:

1. Go to **aws.amazon.com** and click **Create an AWS Account**.
2. Complete the steps on the screen. You'll need a credit card number and an email address you check regularly.
3. Once your account creation process is complete, return to **aws.amazon.com** and sign in using your new account. Make sure you can get to the AWS Management Console. Spend a few minutes exploring the console.
4. Under AWS services, click **All services**. How many categories of services are listed?
5. Click a few services to see service-specific dashboards, such as the EC2 Dashboard. Do not create any new cloud resources.
6. In the upper-right corner of the window near your account name, notice that a region is listed. What region is currently selected in your account?
7. **Take a screenshot** showing your region and account name in the upper-right corner of your AWS Management Console; submit this visual with your answers to this project's questions.
8. When you're finished, sign out of your management console.

If you're creating an **AWS Academy account**:

1. Check your student email account for an invitation email from your instructor through AWS Academy.
2. Follow the instructions in the email to complete your account creation.
3. Once your account creation process is complete, use the portal address provided from your instructor or visit **awsacademy.instructure.com** to return to the AWS Academy portal and click **Student Login**. Sign in using your new account.

Note 9

Make sure to bookmark your AWS Academy portal address for future reference. You will use the page many times throughout this course.

4. On your Dashboard, click the tile for your Learner Lab course.
5. On your course's page, click **Modules**, and then click **Learner Lab – Foundational Services**.
6. The right pane contains instructions on how to use the lab environment. Take a few minutes to read through that information.
7. When you're ready, click **Start Lab**. It might take a minute or two for the lab environment to load. When the AWS dot turns from yellow to green and the information in the right pane updates, click **AWS**.
8. A new tab should open to your AWS Management Console. Spend a few minutes exploring the console.
9. Under AWS services, click **All services**. How many categories of services are listed?
10. Click a few services to see service-specific dashboards, such as the EC2 Dashboard. Do not create any new cloud resources.
11. In the upper-right corner of the window near your account name, notice that a region is listed. What region is currently selected in your account?
12. **Take a screenshot** showing your region and account name in the upper-right corner of your AWS Management Console; submit this visual with your answers to this project's questions.
13. When you're finished, close the AWS tab. On the Learner Lab tab, click **End Lab** and then click **Yes**. Completing cleanup steps at the end of each project will help preserve your course credits.

Project 1-3: Create an Account with Azure

Estimated time: 30 minutes

Objective 1.1: Compare and contrast the different types of cloud models.

Resources:

- Internet access
- Microsoft account
- If using a free trial or pay-as-you-go subscription, a credit card
- If using an Azure for Students subscription, a school-issued email address

Context:

Microsoft offers two options for a free Azure account that work for this course. To use Azure, you create a Microsoft account and then create one or more subscriptions within the account. If your school uses Office 365, you might already be able to authenticate to Azure using your existing Microsoft account. The two types of Azure subscriptions (there are others) most relevant to this course are as follows:

- *Free trial subscription*—This subscription is available to the public and requires a credit card. The $200 free credit expires after 30 days, whereas the free trial services last for 12 months. The subscription itself is free; any services you use beyond the free offers will be charged to your credit card. You will also be offered a technical support plan, starting at $29/month, which you can decline.

Note 10

Microsoft offers a generous amount of credit for the first 30 days of the free trial. A challenging disadvantage of the free trial is that, after 30 days, you must upgrade to a pay-as-you-go subscription without any remaining credits, and at that point, it can be difficult to identify which services are free and which are not. Azure doesn't mark the free services as clearly as AWS does. Those free services are only available for a year, at which point you're left with the "always free" services, which are fairly limited. Therefore, if you use Azure, carefully pay attention to resource configurations, run times, and potential charges.

- *Azure for Students subscription*—This subscription is available to full-time faculty and students (older than age 18) at an accredited, degree-granting educational institution. You must use a school-issued email account, but you do not need a credit card. You might also be able to generate an Azure for Students verification code through your school's Microsoft Azure Dev Tools for Teaching platform. Ask your instructor for additional information on this robust resource. You get $100 free credit that lasts 12 months, and you can renew your student subscription after a year for another disbursement of free credits.

Note 11

NOTE TO INSTRUCTORS: At this time, Microsoft's Azure for Students is managed by a team at Microsoft. Students apply directly through their program to confirm their status as a qualifying student.

Your school might already offer the Azure Dev Tools for Teaching program. If so, students might have an invitation from your program administrator, or they might be able to use their existing student email (if these emails are Microsoft accounts) to access their Azure resources. According to the Microsoft site, students must be at least 18 years old and must be a full-time student.

For more information, visit **https://azure.microsoft.com/en-us/offers/ms-azr-0170p/** or search for updated information to the Azure for Students program. Note that this information changes often. For additional updates, please email the author at jillwestauthor@gmail.com.

Check with your instructor to determine which type of account you should create. From the following steps, choose the set of steps that matches the type of account you will use, and then complete the steps to create your account.

(continues)

Hands-On Projects Continued ————————————————————————————

If you're creating a **standard Azure account using the free trial subscription**:

1. Go to **azure.microsoft.com**, activate the free trial, and create a Microsoft account or sign in with an existing Microsoft account. Complete the identity verification and agreement process. You can decline any technical support options. You're automatically taken to the Quickstart Center in your Azure portal. Click the **X** in the upper-right corner below your name to close the Quickstart Center and display the Home page.

If you are creating an **Azure account using the Azure for Students subscription**:

1. Go to **azure.microsoft.com/en-us/free/students/**, activate the Azure for Students offer, and create a Microsoft account or sign in with an existing account. Complete the identity verification and agreement process. You're automatically taken to the Quickstart Center in your Azure portal. Click the **X** in the upper-right corner below your name to close the Quickstart Center and display the Home page.

After you sign in, complete the following steps to explore the Azure portal:

2. Spend a few minutes exploring the portal. Under Azure services, on the right, click **All services**. How many categories of services are listed in the left pane?
3. Click a few services to see service-specific dashboards, such as the Virtual machines dashboard. Do not create any new cloud resources.
4. **Take a screenshot** showing your account name in the upper-right corner of your Azure portal; submit this visual with your answers to this project's questions.
5. When you're finished, sign out of your Azure portal.

Project 1-4: Create an Account with GCP

Estimated time: 30 minutes
Objective 1.1: Compare and contrast the different types of cloud models.
Resources:

- Internet access
- A Google account
- If not using an education option, a credit card
- If using an education option, information on how to sign up

Context:
Google Cloud offers an attractive free trial option available for all new accounts, which provides a generous amount of credit for a full year. Its biggest drawback is that it requires a credit card or bank account information in case you exceed the free credit amount. Projects in this course will not require that you use all your free credit so long as you remember to delete resources at the end of each project. GCP's education options must be organized through your school. Your instructor will give you this information if relevant for your specific course.

> ## Note 12
>
> NOTE TO INSTRUCTORS: At this time, Google offers the Google Cloud for Education program. The program offers free QwikLabs credits (not Google Cloud credits) to students and requires that work be completed within the QwikLabs environment, which does not grant free reign of GCP services. In QwikLabs, students can only complete the tasks assigned within each lab. While these QwikLabs activities can be informative, they do not provide much instructional support, and they are not sufficient for this course.
>
> For more information, visit **https://cloud.google.com/edu/students** or search for updated information to the Google Cloud for Students program. Note that this information changes often. For additional updates, please email the author at jillwestauthor@gmail.com.

Complete the following steps to create your account:

1. Go to **cloud.google.com** and sign up for the free trial.
2. Spend a few minutes exploring the Google console. An initial project has been created for you, which is listed at the top of the window just left of center. What is the name of your project?
3. Click the **Navigation menu** button to open the navigation pane. Under MORE PRODUCTS, notice that services are listed under each category name. How many categories are listed?
4. Click a few services to see service-specific dashboards, such as the Compute Engine dashboard. Do not create any new cloud resources.
5. In the upper-right corner, click to show your account name and email address. **Take a screenshot** showing your account name in the upper-right corner of your Google console; submit this visual with your answers to this project's questions.
6. When you're finished, sign out of your Google console.

Project 1-5: Apply Troubleshooting Methodology

Estimated time: 30 minutes
Objective 5.1: Given a scenario, use the troubleshooting methodology to resolve cloud-related issues.
Group work: This project includes enhancements when assigned as a group project.
Resources:
- A drawing app, such as Paint in Windows, or a web app such as jspaint.app, kleki.com, or app.diagrams.net

Context:
Most likely at this point in your IT career, you've already encountered some challenging troubleshooting scenarios with computers, mobile devices, and networks. Interestingly, you probably intuitively applied some sound trouble-shooting principles to the problem-solving process. To develop a deeper understanding of effective troubleshooting methodology, complete the following steps:

1. Think back to one of the more interesting scenarios you've faced, one where you were able to solve the problem. It could be something as simple as connecting two Bluetooth devices, solving a printer problem, or resolving an issue with an OS update. Take a few moments to write down the symptoms you encountered, the information you gathered, and the questions you asked. Try to remember the sense of confusion or concern that this lack of knowledge created.
2. Think through what theories you developed on the possible causes of the problem as well as the attempts you made to solve the problem. Write down as many details as you can remember about how you finally discovered the solution and how you arrived at that conclusion.
3. Look back at the troubleshooting flowchart in Figure 1-12. Using a drawing app such as Paint in Windows or a free web app such as jspaint.app, kleki.com, or app.diagrams.net, map your problem-solving experience to the steps shown in the flowchart, and include additional details as they come to you. **Save this image** as a .png file; submit this visual with your answers to this project's questions.

After developing your troubleshooting diagram, answer the following questions:

4. What theories did you test that turned out to be wrong? What information did you learn from those dead ends?
5. Did you involve anyone else in the problem-solving process? If so, who was that person, and how did they help?
6. What did you do to test your solution? What measures did you take to ensure the problem didn't happen again?
7. Considering what you've now learned about troubleshooting methodology, what could you have reasonably done differently to discover the solution more quickly?
8. **For group assignments:** Each member of the group should write a summary of the problem experienced in their scenario, steps taken, and outcome of the issue as if they were documenting this information in a knowledge base. Next, exchange this documentation with another member of the group. Each member then reads through the information written by their classmate and lists questions they still have about the events or information gaps that could cause problems in the future. Discuss your concerns with the author of the scenario. Submit this information and a summary of the group discussion.

(continues)

Hands-On Projects Continued

Capstone Project 1: Cloud Service Types

> **Note 13**
>
> Websites, applications, public cloud platforms, and related account options change often. While the instructions given in these projects were accurate at the time of writing, you might need to adjust the steps or options according to later changes.

Note to Instructors and Students: A rubric is provided for evaluating student performance on these projects. Please see Appendix D.

Estimated time: 30 minutes

Objective 1.1: Compare and contrast the different types of cloud models.

Resources:

- Internet access
- Cloud platform account

Context:

These Capstone Projects are intended to give you practice figuring out how to do tasks in the cloud without step-by-step guidance. While most of the popular cloud platforms offer extensive and well-written instructions, sometimes it's faster and easier to poke around and figure it out for yourself. Further, the tasks in these Capstones will help you practice recalling the steps you performed in the Hands-on Projects. The steps tell you what task to accomplish and ask questions along the way to help you think about what you're doing. However, the steps intentionally do not provide detailed information on how to perform the task.

Complete the following steps:

1. You can use AWS, Azure, or GCP for this Capstone project; alternatively, if allowed by your instructor, you can use another cloud platform such as Alibaba Cloud or IBM Cloud. Sign in to the cloud platform. Which platform are you using?
2. Study the service categories provided in this cloud platform, and complete Table 1-3.

Table 1-3 Cloud services

Service model	Name of a service that fits in each service model	Why do you think this service is included in this service model?
IaaS		
PaaS		
SaaS		

3. What is one category of services you think would be interesting to learn more about?
4. Choose one of the services listed in that category. What service did you choose?
5. Read about the service in the cloud platform or on the CSP's website. In your own words, what does this service do? Be sure to provide sufficient detail to show you understand the purpose of the service and the basics of its role in a cloud deployment.

Solutions to Self-Check Questions

Section 1-1: Characteristics of Cloud Computing

1. Which cloud platform does the CompTIA Cloud+ certification target?

   Answer: d. None

   Explanation: The CompTIA Cloud+ certification is vendor neutral and so does not target any specific cloud platform.

2. Which of these certifications requires the least technical skill?

   Answer: c. AWS Cloud Practitioner

   Explanation: The AWS Cloud Practitioner certification is a nontechnical, entry-level AWS certification appropriate for professionals in technical, managerial, sales, purchasing, or financial roles.

3. Which of the following is NOT an essential characteristic of cloud computing?

   Answer: a. Adaptive security

   Explanation: Cloud providers often describe additional characteristics and benefits to cloud computing, including adaptive, intelligent security that takes advantage of AI (artificial intelligence) technology to improve built-in security defenses. However, this is not an essential characteristic of cloud computing as defined by NIST.

Section 1-2: Cloud Deployment Models

4. Which of these standards protects credit card information stored in a public cloud?

   Answer: a. PCI DSS

   Explanation: For all companies that provide credit card services—including accepting, storing, processing, or transmitting credit card data—the PCI DSS (Payment Card Industry Data Security Standard) sets requirements for keeping that information secure.

5. What factor limits the capacity of a private cloud to provide resources to users?

   Answer: c. Hardware

   Explanation: Because a private cloud runs on hardware dedicated to only that cloud, its capacity is limited to the capabilities of the hardware on which it runs.

6. An AWS-hosted network using the G Suite productivity apps is an example of what kind of cloud?

   Answer: d. Multi-cloud

   Explanation: A multi-cloud model involves using cloud services from multiple vendors at one time, such as AWS and Google.

Section 1-3: Cloud Service Models

7. Which cloud service model requires the least skill to use?

   Answer: d. SaaS

   Explanation: With SaaS (software as a service), applications can be accessed from different types of devices without having to manage any of the underlying infrastructure such as the network, servers, operating systems, or storage.

8. Which cloud service model requires the most skill to adequately secure?

   Answer: a. IaaS

   Explanation: IaaS customers must consider similar security concerns as when running their own, on-prem infrastructure. This includes compliance regulations, audit requirements, and identity management in addition to all the other concerns for securing PaaS and SaaS solutions.

(continues)

Section 1-4: Cloud Service Providers

9. Which public cloud platform offers the most streamlined integration with Windows Active Directory?

   Answer: c. Azure

   Explanation: Azure is designed for seamless compatibility with Microsoft's other tools, such as Windows Active Directory.

10. In which cloud category would you most likely find a service for configuring DNS records?

    Answer: a. Networking

    Explanation: DNS is a networking function and will be found in the Networking category in most cloud platforms.

11. Which IoT device provides access to a personal assistant app?

    Answer: b. Smart speaker

    Explanation: Voice-controlled smart speakers offer access to embedded personal assistant apps such as Alexa, Siri, and Google Assistant.

Section 1-5: Troubleshooting Methodology

12. What cloud configuration technique can be used to compensate for capacity challenges?

    Answer: d. Auto-scaling

    Explanation: Cloud services can be designed to auto-scale in order to avoid capacity-related problems.

13. What is the last step of CompTIA's troubleshooting methodology?

    Answer: a. Documentation

    Explanation: Once a problem has been resolved, the symptoms, findings, actions, and outcomes should all be documented in a knowledge base for future reference.

Module 2

Virtual Hardware

Module 2 Objectives

After reading this module, you will be able to:

1 Explain compute virtualization technologies.

2 Optimize sizing of VM resources.

3 Deploy VMs in the cloud.

4 Describe serverless computing and container technologies.

Module 2 Outline

Study the module's outline to help you organize the content in your mind as you read.

Section 2-1: Virtualization Technologies
    Virtual Machines (VMs)
    Hypervisors
    Network Connection Types
    VM Configuration

Section 2-2: Virtualized Processing and Memory
    CPU Management
    Memory Management

Section 2-3: VMs in the Cloud
    VM Instance Types
    Instance Templates
    Affinity
    Allocation Factors

Section 2-4: VM Alternatives
    Serverless Computing
    Containers
    Supporting Containers
    Troubleshoot Applications in Containers

Module 2 Scenario

Three days after your first cloud-centric staff meeting, Kendra and Nigel shuffle into the conference room where you've been setting up a brief presentation on the projector. You've collected notes from the others and from your own research, and you've merged all the information into this overview so everyone will be up to date on what you've all learned. Part of the presentation covers services you can access in the cloud, and part of it gives a survey of popular cloud providers and the types of services they're best known for. It's a lot of good information, and you're actually kind of excited about it—but you dread doing any public speaking, even in front of your two co-workers. You feel your heart pounding in your chest, and imagining your boss as a purple unicorn isn't helping you relax.

As Kendra and Nigel chat about lunch plans, you knock over your coffee cup, squelch a few swear words, and quickly wipe up the mess. Thankfully, there wasn't much left in the cup, but you're annoyed to see your hands shaking. Deep breath. It's gonna be okay.

You start the presentation, and almost immediately Kendra and Nigel jump in with questions. Forty minutes later, you realize none of you paid much attention to the PowerPoint because you all had so much information you wanted to share and talk about and even more questions to explore. Kendra pauses and takes the metaphorical step back as she asks, "Okay, so what's next? We know we want to start moving to the cloud. How do we do this? Where do we begin?"

Nigel says, "Well, I know I'm the newbie here. But I wonder, what assets do we have in our network that could be moved to the cloud? I mean, how do we go from a server that's sitting in our rack to some kind of service in the cloud? I guess I don't really understand how that happens."

Kendra responds, "We don't actually ship the server computer to the cloud provider. We have to virtualize the services. That means, basically, we take the *idea* of the server—the work the server does—put it in its own virtual box, and then put a lot of those boxes all together in one place. Each box might think it's the only box there, but really, there are lots of boxes working side by side. Each server takes up less space, and each server takes turns using the hardware that is hosting all of them. It's almost like having several 'pretend' servers hosted by one real server."

You jump in as you get the idea of where she's going with this train of thought. "Right. And once we've created these 'pretend' servers—the virtual servers—it doesn't really matter where they live. They can all live on a physical server in our data center, or we can run them on someone else's hardware, like Google's or Amazon's."

Nigel looks a little confused. "How does all of that work? Does the host computer have an operating system? What about the pretend servers—er, I mean, virtual servers?"

"A hypervisor makes all the magic happen. It handles communications between the host and its guest systems," says Kendra. "We actually use a hypervisor already in our data center, and we have several virtual machines—that is, virtual computers—running services in our network." As she scrunches her face in thought, she adds, "I think we need to do some research into what virtualization is so the two of you have a thorough understanding of this concept before we move forward." She scratches out a list on her notepad and hands you a sheet of paper. Then she adds, "Here's what you'll need to research before our next meeting."

- How do hypervisors work?
- How are processor and memory resources shared between the host and its guests?
- How do you create a virtual computer in the cloud?

Section 2-1: Virtualization Technologies

Certification

1.2 Explain the factors that contribute to capacity planning.

1.3 Explain the importance of high availability and scaling in cloud environments.

3.1 Given a scenario, integrate components into a cloud solution.

3.3 Given a scenario, deploy cloud networking solutions.

3.4 Given a scenario, configure the appropriate compute sizing for a deployment.

4.3 Given a scenario, optimize cloud environments.

Virtualization is a virtual, or logical, version of something rather than the actual, or physical, version. Think about a house and the people who live there. A house's purpose is to provide a living space. Then take the logical *idea* of "living space for a family," and put a lot of those living spaces in one building, like an apartment complex. There's still only one building, but many families have their own living spaces within that building, each complete with a kitchen, living room, bedrooms, and so on. They share physical resources, such as electric and plumbing services, but they don't all have to furnish, decorate, or use their apartments the same way as everyone else in the building. Some apartments might have one bedroom, while others have two or three. Some apartments might be kept clean and decorated to a degree that's worthy of a magazine photo, while others are cluttered or have shag carpeting.

Virtualization works with much the same premise—the physical machine can be divided into pieces that support several virtual systems. You don't give one virtual system the CPU (central processing unit) and another virtual system the RAM (random access memory). Instead, you take the bandwidth each hardware component offers and divide that bandwidth among the virtual systems running on the physical host. These virtual systems are called virtual machines, as described next.

Virtual Machines (VMs)

VMs (virtual machines) are similar in concept to the apartments in an apartment building. Each VM can have its own OS (operating system), and all the VMs on a physical computer share the same hardware resources. For example, when you create an Ubuntu server VM on a Windows PC, the Windows machine is the physical computer, or host. The Ubuntu machine is the virtual, logical computer, or guest, that is hosted by the physical computer. This is made possible through the use of a hypervisor, also called a VMM (virtual machine manager), which creates and manages the VM and manages hardware resource allocation and sharing between a host and any of its guest VMs. Figure 2-1 shows a Windows 10 host machine with a hypervisor running an Ubuntu guest VM.

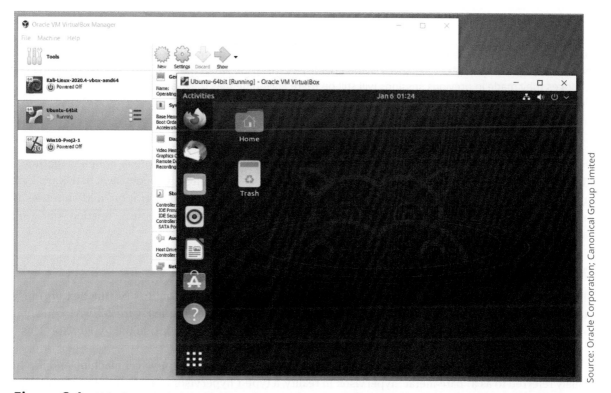

Source: Oracle Corporation; Canonical Group Limited

Figure 2-1   Windows 10 is installed on the physical machine while Ubuntu Desktop is installed in a VM running on the Oracle VM VirtualBox hypervisor

Together, all the virtual devices on a single computer share the same CPU, storage disks, DIMMs (dual in-line memory modules), and physical network interfaces. Yet each VM can be configured to use a different operating system, and it can contain its own applications. Figure 2-2 illustrates an example of some of the elements of virtualization when hosted on a user's computer as compared to the traditional, nonvirtual installation of a single OS and its applications.

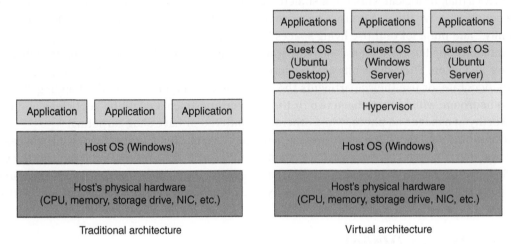

Figure 2-2   A hypervisor allows for installation of multiple guest VMs

A single physical machine with robust hardware that is hosting several VM servers can take the place of an entire rack of physical servers each hosting only a single OS. The hypervisor dashboard then provides central control of all the VMs and can thereby also eliminate the need for a KVM (keyboard, video, and mouse) switch on the rack.

Note 1

A server can also host a **VDI (virtual desktop infrastructure)** environment where users sign in remotely and are presented with a virtual desktop, such as Windows or a Linux distro. This eliminates the need for expensive workstations because with VDI, most of the processing is done on the server and not on the user's computer. VDI can also provide either persistent or nonpersistent instances. With a persistent instance, when the user remotes back into the desktop, any changes they made in previous sessions will still be there, including files they saved. With a nonpersistent instance, the desktop is reset each time someone signs in.

While virtualization is not required in order to host cloud services, it is by far the more common method of creating and providing cloud resources (as compared to hosting cloud services directly on physical hardware). Virtualization supports the cloud's elasticity and scalability features, allows for workload migration, and increases resource **resiliency**. A thorough understanding of virtualization will help you make better decisions in hosting your own private cloud and in configuring your resources in a public cloud.

Hypervisors

You might have already worked with common hypervisors such as Oracle VirtualBox (virtualbox.org) or VMware Workstation or Player (vmware.com). These hypervisors function as shown earlier in Figure 2-2, where the hypervisor is installed over an existing OS as an application, and then guest OSs are installed inside the hypervisor. This is called a **type 2 hypervisor**.

By contrast, a **type 1 hypervisor** is installed directly on the firmware of the physical machine and is sometimes erroneously referred to as a "bare-metal" hypervisor. In reality, a type 1 hypervisor is itself a minimal operating system, many of which are built on a Linux kernel. Like any OS, the hypervisor relies on firmware to enable communication with the underlying hardware. See Figure 2-3. Examples of a type 1 hypervisor include ESXi by VMware (vmware.com),

Hyper-V by Microsoft (microsoft.com), and Citrix XenServer (xenserver.org) powered by the open-source Xen Project hypervisor (xenproject.org).

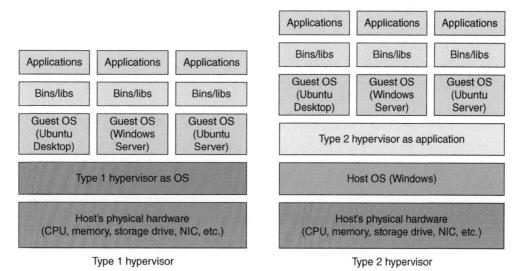

Type 1 hypervisor   Type 2 hypervisor

Figure 2-3   A type 1 hypervisor is installed directly on the host's firmware, while a type 2 hypervisor is installed as an application in an existing operating system

---

Note 2

Native to Linux OSs is a hypervisor called KVM (Kernel-based Virtual Machine). KVM (linux-kvm.org) has elements of both a type 1 and type 2 hypervisor. For example, KVM, when installed, effectively converts the existing Linux OS to a type 1 hypervisor. However, the original OS is still accessible and can still host other applications.

Hyper-V also has elements of both categories. Hyper-V is embedded in Windows Server 2008 and beyond, and in Windows 10 and beyond (sometimes called Client Hyper-V), where it appears to run more as an application and therefore looks more like a type 2 hypervisor. In reality, when Hyper-V is enabled in Windows, it creates a virtualization layer underneath the existing OS installation, thereby establishing its role as a type 1 hypervisor. This arrangement is unique, however, in that the host's Windows OS continues to be given privileged access through the virtualization layer to the underlying hardware, while guest OSs in VMs are not given this level of access.

Because there is no underlying host operating system using hardware resources or limiting the hypervisor's access to those resources, a type 1 hypervisor is more powerful than a type 2 hypervisor. It's also faster and more secure. However, compatibility with attached hardware can be more of an issue with type 1 hypervisors because guest VMs can't rely on drivers in the host OS to use the hardware.

It's also helpful to understand the core differences between type 1 and type 2 hypervisors by looking at what happens when the host computer is booted, as shown in Figure 2-4 and described here:

- With type 1 hypervisors, such as ESXi, the motherboard's BIOS or UEFI firmware hands the start-up process to the installed hypervisor, which then boots any VMs it's configured to start up automatically.

- With type 2 hypervisors, such as VirtualBox installed on a Windows computer, the motherboard's BIOS or UEFI firmware hands the start-up process to the host machine's OS. After boot, the user can start the hypervisor application and then boot up VMs inside the hypervisor.

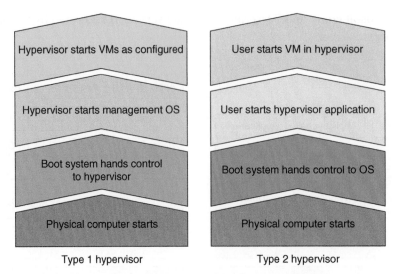

Type 1 hypervisor   Type 2 hypervisor

Figure 2-4   A type 1 hypervisor manages the physical machine's boot process, while a type 2 hypervisor runs as an application within the installed OS

For a CPU to support virtualization by a hypervisor, the CPU must have the HAV (hardware-assisted virtualization) feature turned on in the motherboard's UEFI/BIOS setup. On Intel chips, this feature is called **VT (Virtualization Technology)**, and on AMD chips, the feature is called **AMD-V (AMD virtualization)**. To turn on a chip's virtualization capability, enter UEFI/BIOS setup, find the relevant setting, and make sure it's enabled. Figure 2-5 shows where an Intel CPU's virtualization is enabled in an ASUS motherboard's UEFI setup utility.

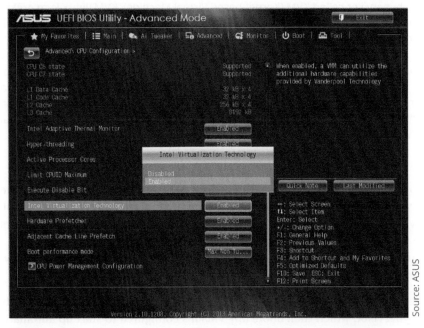

Source: ASUS

Figure 2-5   Enable virtualization in the motherboard's UEFI/BIOS setup utility to create VMs in a hypervisor

Note 3

Intel VT is sometimes referred to as Intel VT-x. Intel VT has several extensions that each provide different features. VT-x is the most recognized extension.

Network Connection Types

Each VM on a host can have one or multiple virtual NICs (network interface controllers), or **vNICs (virtual NICs)**, that can connect the VM to other machines, both virtual and physical. The maximum number of vNICs on a VM depends on the limits imposed by the hypervisor. For example, VirtualBox allows up to eight vNICs per VM. Upon creation, each vNIC is automatically assigned a MAC address.

A vSwitch (virtual switch) in the host's hypervisor connects the vNICs to a network. One host can support multiple virtual switches, which are controlled by the hypervisor. Each VM can be configured to network with other machines on the physical network or only to its host and other VMs on the same host. The most common of these networking modes, as shown in Figure 2-6, are as follows:

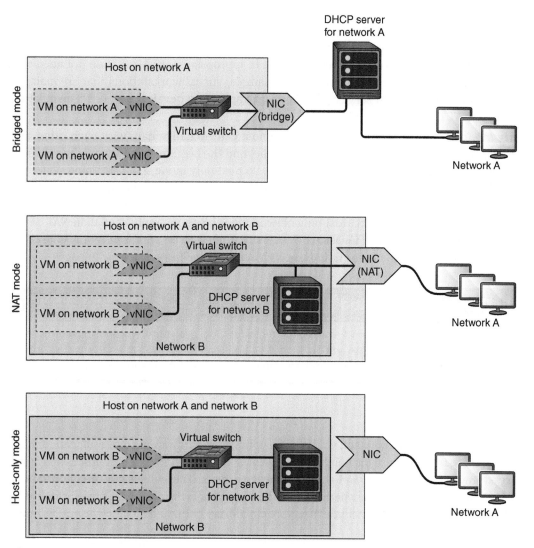

Figure 2-6   The network mode determines which network the VM is part of and which devices (physical or virtual) it can reach

- **Bridged mode**—In bridged mode, a vNIC accesses a physical network using the host machine's NIC. In other words, the virtual interface and physical interface are bridged. The vNIC obtains its own IP address, default gateway, and subnet mask information from the physical LAN's **DHCP (Dynamic Host Configuration Protocol)** server, which is a network service that assigns IP addresses to clients on the network. When connected using bridged mode, a VM appears to other nodes as just another client or server on the network. VMs that must be available at a specific IP address, such as mail servers or web servers, should be assigned bridged network connections. However, VMs that other nodes do not need to access directly can be configured to use the NAT networking mode, described next.

- *NAT mode*—In NAT (network address translation) mode, a vNIC relies on the host machine to act as a NAT device. In other words, the VM obtains IP addressing information from its host, rather than from a server or router on the physical network, and the NAT feature performs address translation on communications between the VM and the physical network. To do this, the hypervisor must act as a DHCP server. A vNIC operating in NAT mode can still communicate with other nodes on the network and vice versa. However, other nodes communicate with the host machine's IP address to reach the VM; the VM itself is invisible to nodes on the physical network. The NAT network connection type is appropriate for VMs that do not need to be accessed at a known address by other network nodes. For example, virtual workstations that are mainly used to run stand-alone applications, or that serve as test beds for application development or OS installations, are good candidates for NAT network connections.

- *Host-only mode*—In host-only mode, VMs on one host can exchange data with each other and with their host, but they cannot communicate with any nodes beyond the host. In other words, the vNICs never receive or transmit data via the host machine's physical NIC. In host-only mode, as in NAT mode, VMs use the DHCP service in the host's virtualization software to obtain IP address assignments. Host-only mode is appropriate for test networks or if you simply need to install a different OS on your workstation to use an application that is incompatible with your host's OS. Host-only networking is less commonly used than NAT or bridged mode networking because it won't work for virtual servers that need to be accessed by LAN-based clients or for virtual workstations that need access to LAN or WAN services such as email or web pages.

VM Configuration

When configuring VMs inside of a hypervisor, you're given options for hardware resource allocation. Important criteria for deciding among these resources are the number and size of CPUs and GPUs (graphics processing units), amount and type of memory, storage type and space, and access to device drivers. These decisions are important whether you're building the VM in your own hypervisor or whether you're building VMs in the cloud. Let's briefly look at how these decisions work with a local hypervisor, and later you'll explore cloud-based CPU and memory resources more extensively.

CPUs

It might seem that the more **vCPUs (virtual CPUs)** a VM has, the better, but this isn't necessarily true. Through a process called CPU scheduling, the hypervisor schedules a VM's access to the physical CPU cores available on the host machine. This scheduling gives each VM and the host the access they need to available processing power. Giving a VM more vCPUs than it really needs can cause unnecessary delays from the additional scheduling required to give all those vCPUs processing time. The situation is like having too many people in the kitchen when you're trying to prepare a large meal. Sometimes it's better to have a few people doing multiple tasks rather than having lots of people with each person doing a single task that accomplishes only a little bit of the work.

   Unless you already know a VM will need a high number of vCPUs, best practice when creating a VM is to start with one vCPU and then test the system when it's running its normal processes for all VMs on the server. If you do increase the number of vCPUs for any VM, be sure to carefully plan the ratio of physical CPU cores to vCPUs needed at any given time.

GPUs

When you're building a high-performance computer such as a gaming system, you'll typically include a graphics card to increase its graphics processing capability. The graphic card's onboard **GPU (graphics processing unit)** brings additional cores to the computer's hardware resources. While GPU cores tend to run a bit slower than CPU cores, they are designed to handle high volumes of parallel functions, and a GPU can typically offer higher overall numbers of cores than a CPU can within the same price point. A GPU's parallel processing is especially helpful for tasks such as machine learning and scientific computation of large data sets.

You can also allocate virtual GPUs to a VM on a hypervisor or in the cloud. When allocating GPU resources to guest VMs, you can take one of two approaches:

- *Pass-through*—In this scenario, the GPU can only be used by one VM at a time.
- *Virtual or shared*—In this scenario, the GPU's resources are artificially divided into portions that can be allocated at the same time to multiple VMs. Each partial allocation of GPU resources is sometimes referred to as a vGPU (virtual GPU).

The decision of which approach to use is typically decided by the physical GPU in your system (that is, whether it's capable of supporting shared GPUs) and the virtualization software (that is, which of these options it offers).

Memory

Whether virtual or physical, more memory is better in nearly all cases. The challenge when configuring VMs on a physical machine is to make sure that each system—including the host—gets the memory it needs. When a VM is running, it will typically reserve the amount of physical memory allocated to it whether or not it's using that memory (although some hypervisors allow for dynamic allocation of memory, which reserves only what it needs for currently running processes). This reserved memory is called **vRAM (virtual RAM)**. It's important that you leave enough physical memory for the host machine even when you have multiple VMs running.

Similarly, make sure each VM can reserve sufficient memory for the OS and applications installed in it. Because of these requirements, the memory allocated to VMs on your local machine will necessarily be limited by the amount of physical RAM you have available. This is why a workstation customized for hosting VMs should be given as much physical RAM as your budget will allow.

Storage

A VM needs storage space not only for saving files but also for running software such as an OS and applications. Most hypervisors allow for dynamic storage configuration for VMs. This means the VM will only use as much storage space as it actually needs for its existing data. You might provision 100 GB of a 1 TB hard disk for a VM, but if it only has 50 GB of data, the other 50 GB of space will remain available to the host or other VMs. This works fine until the VMs or the host start to use up most of their allotted storage space. You can overcommit the storage space and then add more physical disks to expand the available space only when you need it.

However, another complication arises from using dynamic storage space. Say you have a host with three VMs (see Figure 2-7). The host's hard disk has 500 GB available, and each VM is allocated 100 GB of dynamic storage space to be reserved only as needed. The host has already used the first 75 GB for its own purposes, and then each of the VMs uses another 20–25 GB as they're created and installed.

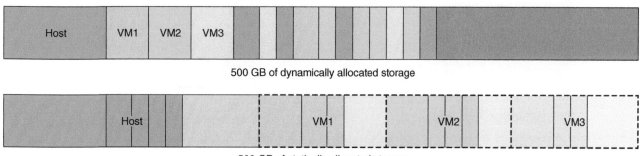

500 GB of dynamically allocated storage

500 GB of statically allocated storage

Figure 2-7   Statically allocated storage space is accessed more efficiently

Over time, the disk space is used a little here and there by the host and each VM. Accessing data spread randomly across the disk becomes increasingly time-consuming. Before too long, you start to notice performance issues in accessing stored data. This is because each machine's data is distributed throughout various storage areas on the disk. This problem could have been avoided by reserving a consolidated portion of the disk to each VM from the beginning so each VM stores its data in consecutive locations on the disk. Consider which of these options might be best for your situation.

You've seen here how the processing, memory, or storage resources a VM is using can be very different from the physical resources available on the host. Similarly, when you take these virtual machines into the cloud, you'll find even more built-in flexibility. Cloud computing services are known for their elasticity, meaning that a service can be expanded and contracted as needed. For example, a VM might be configured with up to 500 GB of storage space. As it approaches that maximum, its allocated storage space might be set to autoscale to a larger number to ensure the VM continues to operate with optimal efficiency. Some of the cost savings of cloud services is due to the difference between the initially proposed resources for a service versus the available services, which are autoscaled up or down as needed.

Device Drivers

CPUs, GPUs, RAM, and storage drives aren't the only hardware that can be passed through to a VM. The VM can also be given access to attached peripheral devices, such as security dongles and USB flash drives, or PCIe-connected devices, such as a network card. If you've ever worked with a VM in a hypervisor, such as VirtualBox, and interacted with the VM, you might have noticed that your mouse and keyboard work only for the host or one VM at a time. This is because these devices rely on pass-through technology in the hypervisor.

Whether you're passing through a GPU, a PCIe device, or a peripheral device, the VM will need its own copy of the device's driver, which is the firmware an OS uses to know how to interact with a device. Three types of drivers are available:

- *Generic*—Most OSs include some generic drivers that might be sufficient for a basic device such as a mouse or keyboard.

- *Vendor*—If the generic driver doesn't work, you might need to get a copy of the driver from the vendor's website. In some cases, the OS can do this for you automatically. Even simple devices, such as a mouse or keyboard, might incorporate configuration options that can only be accessed with the vendor's drivers and software. For example, Figure 2-8 shows configuration options for a Logitech keyboard. When troubleshooting device functionality in any system—whether physical or virtual—always check for updates to the vendor's drivers as part of the troubleshooting process.

Figure 2-8   Logitech driver provides detailed keyboard configuration options

- *Open source*—Some devices, such as graphics hardware, can use open-source drivers. Open-source drivers have often been designed specifically to provide additional functionality beyond that offered from the vendor's drivers. These drivers are typically available for download from common repositories, such as GitHub (github.com), and some vendor-sourced drivers are classed as open source when the source code is posted for public review.

Remember This

- Each VM (virtual machine) can have its own OS (operating system), and all the VMs on a physical computer share the same hardware resources.
- A type 1 hypervisor is installed directly on the firmware of a physical machine, whereas a type 2 hypervisor is installed as an application in an existing OS.
- Each VM can be configured to network with other machines on the physical network or only to its host and other VMs on the same host.
- When configuring VMs inside of a hypervisor, you're given options for the number and size of CPUs and GPUs, amount and type of memory, storage type and space, and access to device drivers.

Self-Check

1. When starting a VM in a type 1 hypervisor, which component starts first?
   - **a.** The guest VM's OS
   - **b.** The hypervisor
   - **c.** An application on the host machine
   - **d.** An application on the guest VM

2. Which network mode requires a VM to receive an IP address from the physical network's DHCP server?
   - **a.** NAT
   - **b.** Dynamic
   - **c.** Bridged
   - **d.** Host-only

3. Your hypervisor can allocate use of the host's GPU to only one VM at a time. Which deployment technique is the hypervisor using?
   - **a.** Generic
   - **b.** Pass-through
   - **c.** Shared
   - **d.** Virtual

○ Check your answers at the end of this module.

Section 2-2: Virtualized Processing and Memory

Certification

1.2 Explain the factors that contribute to capacity planning.

1.3 Explain the importance of high availability and scaling in cloud environments.

3.1 Given a scenario, integrate components into a cloud solution.

3.4 Given a scenario, configure the appropriate compute sizing for a deployment.

4.3 Given a scenario, optimize cloud environments.

Now that you have a basic understanding of how various hardware components support virtualization, let's dig deeper into a discussion of virtual processing and virtual memory. Either of these components might require extensive configuration to reach an optimal level of functioning for your VMs.

CPU Management

Whether you're building VMs in the cloud or on your own hypervisor, you'll need to decide how many vCPUs to give the VM. To understand the significance of your options, let's take a brief stroll through the history of CPU cores (see Figure 2-9):

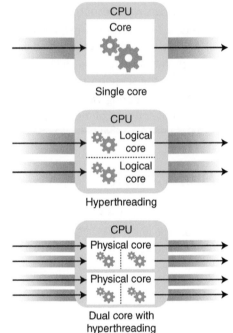

- **Single core**—In the "old days" (before 2002), each CPU socket on a motherboard could hold a single CPU chip that had a single core. The **core** is the processor in a CPU and can perform one task at a time. The series of tasks the core performs is called a **thread** (or thread of execution). For the computer to perform more than one task at a time, it needed multiple CPUs.

- **Logical core**—In 2002, Intel released its Xeon server processor and Pentium 4 desktop processor that could perform hyperthreading. **HT (hyperthreading)** allows the CPU to alter its processing logic so that a single physical core can schedule two tasks at a time and appear to the computer as two logical cores. In reality, the physical core is still processing only a single task at a time, but it switches between the two tasks so quickly that it appears to be performing both tasks at once. AMD eventually followed suit and offered its own version of this logical multitasking. The brand-agnostic term for this feature is **SMT (simultaneous multithreading)**.

- **Multicore**—In 2005, AMD released their first dual-core processor, which had two physical cores in the CPU. In 2006, Intel also released a dual-core processor and, by 2007, offered quad-core processors as well. When SMT is enabled on a CPU, each of those physical cores can function as two logical cores, doubling the number of available cores on a CPU. A server CPU with eight cores, for example, can support up to 16 threads. If the server has two of those CPUs, it can support up to 32 threads—that's 32 tasks being performed virtually at the same time. The count of threads can be calculated using the following formula:

# of threads = # of CPUs × # of physical cores × 2 if using SMT

Figure 2-9   Iterations of CPU core technology for multitasking

Note 4

Today's operating systems and hypervisors are smart enough to know that running simultaneous tasks on two threads offered by a single, hyperthreaded core is not as efficient as running those tasks on two different physical cores. When possible, the OS or hypervisor will use only one thread per physical core first. It will start using the additional logical thread per physical core only when needed. This is called CPU load balancing.

You can find out how many sockets, cores, and logical processors are on your computer by using reporting features in the OS. For example, Figure 2-10 shows a Windows 10 desktop computer's CPU information in Task Manager. This motherboard offers one CPU socket, which provides four cores and eight logical processors. Each thread's individual performance potential is partially determined by the CPU's clock speed and IPC (instructions per cycle). Notice in the figure that virtualization is enabled.

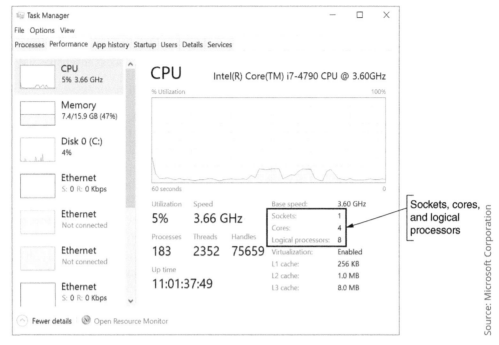

Figure 2-10   This one CPU provides four cores and eight logical processors

From this history lesson, you can see there are multiple ways to accomplish CPU multitasking across threads. This information about a CPU directly correlates to how many vCPUs a host machine can support in its guest OSs. Let's see how that works.

Oversubscription Ratio

A running VM with a single vCPU will use one thread from its host's physical CPU to function. If you allocate two vCPUs to the VM and it's running an application that can use multiple threads, it will at times claim two threads from the host CPU. When hosting VMs on a server or desktop computer, you can allocate as many vCPUs for a VM as you want *up to* the number of logical cores available on the physical host. However, if you are running multiple VMs on the host, you'll need to carefully consider how many vCPUs the host can offer. If multiple VMs are allowed to lay claim to all of the host's threads, you'll have performance issues while each VM has to wait for its turn with those threads.

On the other hand, most VMs don't use all their available threads at all times. The highest demand for processing power is usually at boot-up and during spurts of intense activity in multithreaded applications such as video editing programs. For this reason, you can overcommit (or oversubscribe) the number of vCPUs to available threads with the understanding that most VMs won't use all their vCPUs at any given time. This number of vCPUs to available threads is called the **overcommitment ratio**.

Note 5

Technically, "overcommitment" and "oversubscription" aren't exactly the same thing. While these terms are often used synonymously, "oversubscription" technically refers to the VM configurations on a host exceeding the host's physical resources, and "overcommitment" technically refers to running VMs that, collectively, require more physical resources at any given time. Oversubscription relies on the assumption that not all the VMs will require use of their allocated resources at the same time. Overcommitment requires some kind of technology to handle the excessive demand, such as multiplexing.

Similarly, some technicians make the distinction that "overcommitment" applies to memory while "oversubscription" applies to the CPU. In reality, you'll see these two terms used interchangeably both colloquially and in technical documentation.

In theory, you can overprovision as much as you want. For maximum performance, however, you'll find there's usually a "sweet spot" for the overcommitment ratio that depends on what kinds of tasks you're running in your VMs. A common overcommitment ratio for active VMs is three vCPUs per thread (logical core) on the host, and it's written 3:1. For VMs running simple apps, you might find higher ratios, such as 5:1. For process-intensive VM tasks, you'll find lower ratios, perhaps even as low as 1:1.

Optimizing CPU Allocation

While SMT can significantly increase the number of vCPUs a host can support, there are cases where disabling SMT results in performance improvements. If tasks running simultaneously on multiple logical cores tend to use many of the same resources, you might be creating a bottleneck somewhere else in the system. Think about the analogy of having too many cooks in the kitchen. If each cook is working on different dishes and needs different tools, it can be helpful to have several people in the kitchen at one time because the available resources rarely limit any individual's work. However, if multiple cooks frequently need the same tools, such as when only one oven is available for five cooks who each need to bake a casserole at different temperatures, then having all five cooks work on their dishes at the same time will cause conflicts. If only one casserole can bake at a time, there's no benefit in having more than one cook working on casseroles. Similarly, with CPU cores, if multiple cores are frequently trying to use the same resources (such as cache, RAM, files, or network interfaces) when performing parallel tasks, it might be better to have fewer cores that perform those tasks in a more serial manner. Disabling SMT can accomplish this goal.

Note 6

While you don't have access to a UEFI/BIOS setup utility when using cloud resources, you can still disable SMT for cloud instances in some platforms.

There are other reasons to minimize vCPU allocation to your VMs. For example, licensing could be an issue. Most people are familiar with obtaining software licenses per user or per device. The technical term for this arrangement is CAL (client access license). In many cases, however, costs for **volume-based licensing** (which is designed for many users under one license) are calculated not according to the number of users or the number of machines on which the software is installed but, instead, according to the number of CPU sockets in a system or (more recently) according to the number of logical CPU cores used to execute that software. In the case of cloud VM instances, this means the number of vCPUs. When using core-based licensing, cloud administrators might need to minimize the number of vCPUs for instances hosting certain applications so they can manage software license expenses more efficiently.

Memory Management

When activities on a computer demand more memory than the computer has available, the OS can resort to a variety of techniques collectively called memory management to handle the memory shortage. One of the most common techniques is called memory paging.

Most of the time, data stored in dynamic memory is quickly accessible from RAM cards installed on the motherboard. When the capacity of these cards is exceeded, this data is instead stored as fixed-size files called pages in a section of the hard disk called **virtual memory**. Virtual memory is significantly slower than physical memory. However, using virtual memory is a helpful fallback method to handle periods of intense demand on memory resources.

This technique comes in handy when allocating memory resources to VMs on a host. As with CPU threads, it's possible and even advisable at times to overcommit physical memory to guest OSs. Let's explore how that works.

Note 7

When a computer's virtual memory is also overused, it results in thrashing, which is poor performance caused by the computer relying too heavily on paging. Running processes stall while they wait for information to be swapped between virtual memory and physical memory.

Overcommitment Ratio

Most type 1 hypervisors allow you to configure various RAM settings for each VM:

- The minimum memory or memory reservation is the amount of the host's physical memory that must be available for the VM to claim for it to boot up. This amount of physical memory continues to be reserved for the VM as long as it's running.
- The maximum memory or memory limit is the highest amount of physical memory that can be allocated to a VM.
- The start-up memory is the amount of memory made available to a VM for a short time only when it first boots.

The variation between these settings is called dynamic memory, which allows for an overcommitment, or over-subscription, of the host's physical memory. Several VMs can use memory at the low end of their memory range and increase memory consumption up to the maximum limit when needed, which is sometimes called **memory bursting**. This arrangement maximizes the number of VMs a single host can support while minimizing the amount of unused physical RAM. However, problems start to occur when one or more VMs need more than their minimum allocated memory at the same time.

Memory Reclamation

In response to higher VM demand for memory, the hypervisor must find ways to manage memory more efficiently. Several techniques are employed by various hypervisors, with the most common technique being ballooning. To understand ballooning, consider that the hypervisor does not communicate directly with a guest VM's OS. Therefore, the hypervisor cannot directly manage whatever memory is allocated to a VM—only the VM's OS can do that. **Ballooning** is a way to trick the guest OS into releasing some of its RAM so the hypervisor can allocate it elsewhere.

A VM might report a higher usage of its allocated memory than what it really needs to function well. A VM with overallocated memory will typically use that excess memory for its file system caches. This memory is therefore not really going to waste, but you might decide it could be used more effectively in a different VM. Ballooning allows the hypervisor to reclaim some of that memory for other running VMs.

Ballooning seems counterintuitive until you understand that the idea is to trick the guest OS into releasing its claim on physical memory space. Recall that an OS will export some of its memory pages to its hard drive if it starts running out of memory. A VM's OS will do the same thing when it runs out of allocated memory. However, you typically can't change a VM's memory allocation while it's running—you have to shut the VM down, make the change, and then restart it. Instead, your goal with ballooning is to *temporarily* adjust how much physical memory the VM is using without having to restart the VM.

To do this, the hypervisor installs a small balloon driver inside each guest OS where ballooning is enabled. When a high-priority VM on the host needs more memory, the hypervisor identifies a lower-priority VM that is currently allocated more than its minimum RAM, and it begins a memory reclamation process. Because the hypervisor can't seize physical memory from a running VM, it instead siphons off some of the memory capacity by tricking the guest OS into resorting to its own memory management techniques.

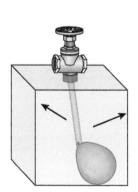 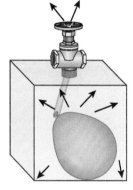

As shown in Figure 2-11, imagine a deflated balloon inside a closed cube. The pressure inside the cube is in equilibrium with the outside air. Using an air pump, you start to inflate the balloon. Gradually, the air pressure inside the cube increases until a pressure valve at the top is triggered and the excess air pressure escapes the cube.

A similar process occurs with the VM's allocated memory. The hypervisor instructs the balloon driver to "inflate" the balloon process, which appears to use up some of the VM's physical memory. This memory capacity is siphoned off to the hypervisor and made available to a higher-priority VM. In the meantime, the lower-priority VM behaves as if it has maximized its allocated physical memory, removes file system caches from its memory, and perhaps even resorts to

Figure 2-11 Increasing the balloon size reduces the space available for air inside the cube

sending memory pages to its own virtual memory (space on its virtual storage drive). The lower-priority VM experiences degraded performance, while the higher-priority VM receives a much-needed memory boost.

You're Ready

You're now ready to complete Project 2-1: Create a VM in a Hypervisor. You can complete the project now or wait until you've finished all the readings for this module.

Remember This

- Whether building VMs in the cloud or on a hypervisor, a technician will need to decide how many vCPUs to give the VM.
- Most type 1 hypervisors allow you to configure various RAM settings for each VM: minimum memory, maximum memory, and start-up memory.

Self-Check

4. How many threads does an SMT-enabled, 16-core CPU offer?
   - **a.** 16
   - **b.** 32
   - **c.** 64
   - **d.** 128

5. Which of the following license types do you use when you purchase and install Microsoft Office on your personal computer?
   - **a.** Core-based license
   - **b.** Volume-based license
   - **c.** Socket-based license
   - **d.** Client access license

6. Which memory management technique borrows memory from one VM for another VM?
   - **a.** Ballooning
   - **b.** Oversubscription
   - **c.** Bursting
   - **d.** Allocation

○ Check your answers at the end of this module.

Section 2-3: VMs in the Cloud

Certification

1.2 Explain the factors that contribute to capacity planning.

1.3 Explain the importance of high availability and scaling in cloud environments.

3.1 Given a scenario, integrate components into a cloud solution.

4.3 Given a scenario, optimize cloud environments.

4.6 Given a scenario, perform disaster recovery tasks.

5.3 Given a scenario, troubleshoot deployment issues.

Now that you've learned the basics of how virtualization works on-prem, let's take some of these concepts to the cloud. Many of the same principles still apply, and at the same time, some of the options and steps involved are different.

VM Instance Types

In the cloud, you can create VM instances using one or more cloud services. For example, in AWS, VM instances are provided through the EC2 (Elastic Compute Cloud) service. In Azure, you use the Virtual machines service, and in GCP, you use Compute Engine. As you create each instance, you'll have the opportunity to choose its features, such as number of vCPUs, amount of memory, disk storage type and size, connectivity options, network placement, and more.

When deploying VM instances in the cloud, CSPs (cloud service providers) such as AWS, Azure, and GCP offer preconfigured instance types in which CPU and memory capacity are automatically allocated in a fixed ratio. Table 2-1 shows various classes of instance types offered by AWS, Azure, and GCP. Notice that you can determine some information about the instance size by the name of the instance type. For example, AWS uses size names to identify relative instance sizes (micro, medium, large, etc.). Azure states the number of vCPUs in the instance name, as does GCP. Also, different optimizations are classed by family, such as the general purpose T2 family in AWS or the D2 series in Azure. Within each family are size combinations that generally keep the same ratio of vCPUs to memory but incrementally increase the actual sizes. Table 2-1 shows some examples for each CSP. You can find more information about instance options on their respective websites.

Table 2-1 Instance types for AWS, Azure, and GCP

Instance type	AWS samples	Azure samples	GCP samples
"General purpose" or "standard" for testing, small to medium databases, and low to medium traffic web servers	• t2.medium (2 vCPUs and 4 GiB memory) • t4g.xlarge (4 vCPUs and 16 GiB memory)	• Standard_D2d_v5 (2 vCPUs and 8 GiB memory) • Standard_D4d_v5 (4 vCPUs and 16 GiB memory)	• e2-standard-2 (2 vCPUs and 8 GB memory) • e2-standard-4 (4 vCPUs and 16 GB memory)
"Compute optimized" or "high-CPU"	• c6g.2xlarge (8 vCPUs and 16 GiB memory)	• Standard_F4s_v2 (4 vCPUs and 8 GiB memory)	• c2d-standard-4 (4 vCPUs and 16 GB memory)
"Memory optimized" or "high-memory"	• r6g.2xlarge (8 vCPUs and 64 GiB memory)	• Standard_E2_v5 (2 vCPUs and 16 GiB memory)	• m1-ultramem-40 (40 vCPUs and 961 GB memory)

Note 8

GiB stands for gibibyte, which is similar to GB (gigabyte) but uses powers of two instead of multiples of 10. For example, 1 GB is 1000 MB, whereas 1 GiB is 1024 MiB (mebibytes). GB and GiB are often used interchangeably. GCP, for example, uses the "GB" unit to identify memory usage but states in their pricing information that they calculate 1 GB as 2^{30} bytes, which is 1 GiB. In contrast, AWS and Azure both use the GiB unit of measurement throughout their websites. Ki (kibi-), Mi (mebi-), and Gi (gibi-) are called binary prefixes.

Instance Templates

When launching many instances of the same configuration, you can use a **template** to ensure every instance is configured the same way. In AWS, for example, an EC2 template determines the following parameters:

- *AMI (Amazon Machine Image) ID*—Choosing an AMI applies a standard template for the root volume that determines, among other things, the instance's OS. You can use a prebuilt image provided by AWS, choose a shared image available from the community, buy an image from a third party, or create your own custom image. To create your own image, you might first create an instance from a standard image, make configuration changes to the image, and then create a new image from the customized instance. This perfected image is sometimes called a golden image and should be kept updated, especially with security updates and configurations. Other cloud platforms offer similar options for using custom images.

- *Instance type*—The instance type determines the instance's virtual hardware resources, including vCPUs, RAM, and storage space.

- *Network and security settings*—Network and security settings can include the instance's network interfaces and IP configuration, subnet, key pair, and security group.

- *Storage volumes*—The AMI includes parameters to create a boot volume. You can also specify additional volumes and related settings, such as size, volume type, and whether it's encrypted.

Additional parameters are also available within the launch template. Figure 2-12 shows the configuration screen to create an EC2 template. Alternatively, you can create a launch template from an existing EC2 instance. When using templates, be aware that a template could cause problems if it is misconfigured. Especially when you pull a template from an outside source, check the configuration carefully.

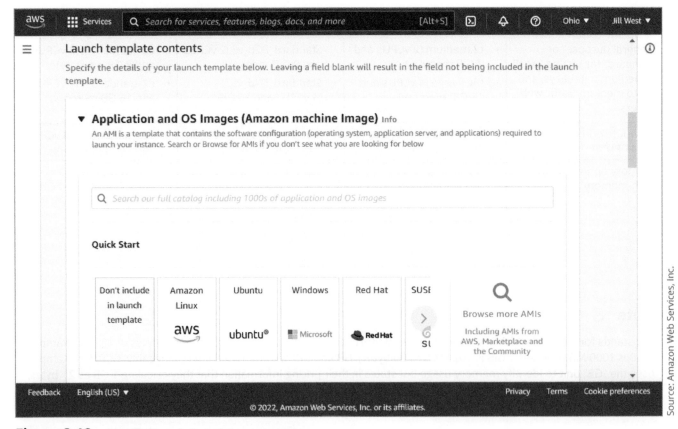

Figure 2-12   Specify launch template parameters

Note 9

Templates can be used in other platforms and services as well, especially for IaC (Infrastructure as Code) services. For example, Azure uses ARM (Azure Resource Manager) templates to deploy multiple services and resources at once. Later in this course, you'll learn about AWS CloudFormation templates.

Affinity

Most of the virtualization scenarios discussed earlier in the module consist of a single physical host supporting multiple VMs. What if you want to distribute several VMs across multiple physical hosts? This would offer several advantages, including the ability to scale up your deployment and the reliability of backup hosts taking over in the event of a host failure. When done on-prem in a LAN, this scenario is sometimes called a CAB (cluster across boxes). It relies on some key configurations between the physical hosts and shared storage provided by a SAN (storage area network). While cloud data centers use a more wide-scale version of this concept, the same idea applies—instances might reside on any of several physical hosts collaborating to provide the virtualized environment.

Whether you're responsible for configuring these clustered hosts or if you're creating VM instances in the cloud, you can choose whether certain VMs reside on the same host or different hosts. Guest VMs residing on the same host are part of an affinity group. You accomplish this restriction by setting an affinity rule on the VM instances. If, instead, you prefer these VMs *not* share the same physical host, such as for availability reasons, you can set an anti-affinity rule.

When the hypervisor starts these VMs, it will attempt to abide by the affinity or anti-affinity rule, which might be set as required or preferred:

- *Required*—If the affinity or anti-affinity rule is required and the rule cannot be observed (for example, if there are not enough physical hosts available to start the number of requested VMs on separate hosts), then the requested instances are not started.
- *Preferred*—If the affinity or anti-affinity rule is only preferred, the hypervisor will give its best effort at complying with the rule but will still start the VMs even if the rule cannot be observed.

Public cloud platforms offer multiple methods to control the affinity of cloud instances. One of the easiest methods is to set a desired geographical location of an instance. In AWS, for example, this is handled through regions and AZs (availability zones). As you'll learn in Module 4, an AZ (availability zone) represents one or more physical data centers, and a region is a collection of AZs. When you configure an EC2 instance, you can choose its region and its AZ. If you want another EC2 instance in a different data center to improve availability, you can configure the next instance in a different AZ.

Most CSPs, such as AWS, automatically attempt to spread your instances across physical hosts even when all these instances are hosted within the same data center. If you need to influence this distribution in AWS and other cloud platforms, you can use placement groups, which are logical groups of instances all hosted in the same AZ. AWS offers three types of placement groups:

- *Cluster*—A cluster is a group of devices or resources that appear as a single device or resource to the rest of the network. In AWS, instances in a cluster placement group are all hosted as closely together as possible within the AZ to support low-latency communications. See Figure 2-13. This placement scenario is commonly used in HPC (high-performance computing) clusters in support of applications that require high-speed, parallel operations.
- *Spread*—This arrangement distributes each instance within a small group (no more than seven) across diverse physical hosts. See Figure 2-14. This is commonly used when very high availability is required so that, if any one instance's host fails, the others will not be affected by the same host failure. Each instance's physical host relies on separate network connections and power sources within the same data center.

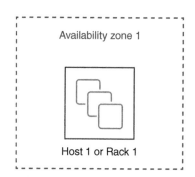

Figure 2-13 Cluster placement group

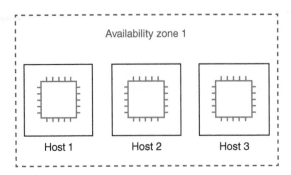

Figure 2-14 Spread placement group

- *Partition*—These instances are grouped into partitions (no more than seven partitions), and then the partitions are distributed across different physical host systems. See Figure 2-15. Each partition contains multiple instances, and each partition's instances reside on different hosts in different racks than the instances in another partition.

Figure 2-16 shows the option to add an EC2 instance to a placement group as the instance is being configured.

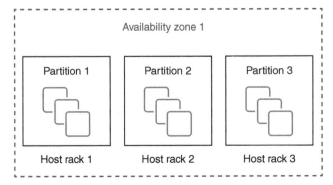

Figure 2-15 Partition placement group

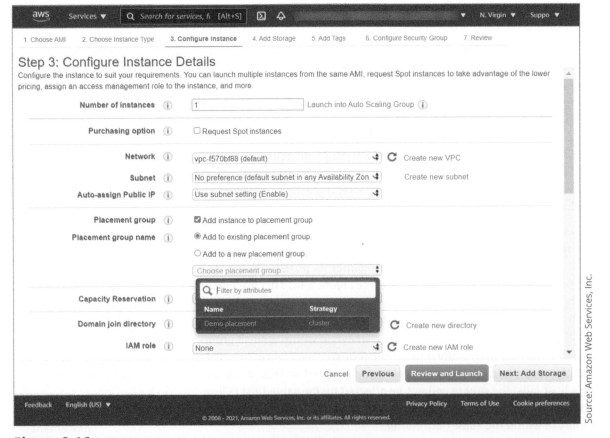

Figure 2-16 This demo placement group uses the cluster strategy

Allocation Factors

While cloud technology can support huge deployments of virtual hardware resources, budget and other considerations impose certain limitations on these deployments. Many factors directly affect the cost efficiency of virtualized CPU and memory resources for a particular deployment. Let's examine a few of these factors:

- *Security*—As you learn about CPU and memory virtualization technologies, you can see there are many efficiency advantages to relying on a shared compute environment in the cloud. This arrangement sometimes creates complications for security concerns, however. Organizations might be required to keep some types of data completely on-prem. In other cases, the data can be stored in the cloud but only on dedicated equipment that is not shared with other tenants. Although more expensive, a dedicated compute environment can also be kept more secure.

- *High availability*—Availability of a network or service is calculated as total uptime over a given period and is expressed as a percentage, such as 99.9%. HA (high availability) is a network's or service's maximized potential for being available consistently over time and is often referred to as the number of nines referenced in the percentage. For example, 99.99% HA is called "four nines availability." For virtualized systems, HA features are often built into the hypervisor to manage VMs and their resources. The hypervisor can restart a failed VM or move a VM to another host in the event of hardware failure. In large data centers, multiple host machines working together in a cluster provide failover coverage for guest VMs. The hosts collectively offer more CPU and memory capacity than is needed to run the virtual infrastructure, allowing for sufficient resources to support the VMs if a host fails. Similar configurations can be deployed in the cloud.

- *Disaster recovery*—DR (disaster recovery) strategies tend to be greatly simplified with virtualized systems. Copies of virtual servers, including all their installed components, can be easily stored off-site and brought online within minutes. Compared to physical systems, whose backups are expensive to store and maintain in hot site, warm site, and cold site arrangements, copies of virtual systems can be stored online (in a different cloud from the active system), automatically updated, and quickly activated if needed. When designing backup solutions as part of a DR plan, consider additional processing capacity needed for VMs to maintain these backups.

- *Energy savings*—On-prem virtualization provides significant energy savings for an organization compared to running an on-prem data center with no virtualization, as less hardware is needed to support a complex infrastructure. Expanding into the cloud further increases energy savings as the hardware power and cooling burdens are shouldered by the CSP. However, this energy savings can be offset by the increased need for ISP bandwidth or dedicated lines to CSP data centers.

- *Cost considerations*—The rates charged for VM instances in the cloud are often determined by the number and type of vCPUs as well as the amount of allocated RAM. Other factors include storage type and size, payment schedules, and added features:
  - *Storage*—Storage fees are calculated according to disk type (such as SSD or HDD) and provisioned space, multiplied by time. With storage costs, you pay for the *provisioning* of space, not the actual space used. So if you create a 2 TB virtual SSD (solid-state drive) for a VM instance, you pay for the 2 TB the entire time that SSD exists, even if you have no data stored in that space.
  - *Features*—Added features such as burstable processing, attached GPUs to accelerate processing, or static public IP addresses affect overall rates for an instance type.
  - *Network placement*—Data coming into your cloud's instances, called ingress traffic, generally is free unless using particular services such as a load balancer. Traffic leaving an instance's network, called egress traffic, might be charged, depending on where that traffic is going. For example, if the traffic is leaving the CSP's own infrastructure onto the public Internet, typically this traffic incurs charges. Position instances carefully to minimize the cost of network traffic.
  - *Cost model*—Most of the major CSPs are moving toward per-second billing, although calculations vary (such as requiring a minimum of one minute billing before counting to the nearest second).
  - *Commitment-based discounts*—Committing to a service for a longer period allows for discounted rates. Some commitment plans allow for early cancellation or shifts to different services, and varying levels of ease for accomplishing those changes.
  - *Payment schedule*—Some CSPs offer discounts for full payment upfront.

You're Ready

You're now ready to complete the following projects:

- Project 2-2: Deploy a VM in AWS
- Project 2-3: Deploy a VM in Azure
- Project 2-4: Deploy a VM in GCP

You can complete these projects now or wait until you've finished all the readings for this module.

Remember This

- When deploying VM instances in the cloud, CSPs offer preconfigured instance types where CPU and memory capacity are automatically allocated in a fixed ratio.
- When launching many instances of the same configuration, you can use a template to ensure every instance is configured the same way.
- Guest VMs residing on the same host are part of an affinity group, while an anti-affinity rule will ensure VMs do *not* share the same physical host.
- Factors that directly affect the cost efficiency of virtualized CPU and memory resources for a particular deployment include security considerations, HA (high-availability) requirements, DR (disaster recovery) strategies, energy savings, and cost considerations.

Self-Check

7. Which selection determines the amount of RAM a cloud VM can use?

    a. Instance type

    b. Image

    c. Storage volume

    d. Network bandwidth

8. Which configuration parameter can ensure all the VMs for a deployment reside on the same physical host?

    a. Partition

    b. Cluster

    c. Affinity

    d. Template

9. Which principle ensures you can consistently access your cloud resource?

    a. Placement

    b. HA

    c. DR

    d. Cluster

○ Check your answers at the end of this module.

Section 2-4: VM Alternatives

Certification

1.1 Compare and contrast the different types of cloud models.

1.3 Explain the importance of high availability and scaling in cloud environments.

3.1 Given a scenario, integrate components into a cloud solution.

4.3 Given a scenario, optimize cloud environments.

5.3 Given a scenario, troubleshoot deployment issues.

5.5 Given a scenario, troubleshoot common performance issues.

No discussion of virtualization in the cloud would be complete without some coverage of alternatives to VMs for hosting applications and other services. Let's first consider serverless functions.

Serverless Computing

A cloud-native, streamlined technology for hosting cloud-based applications is serverless computing ("serverless" for short). Despite the name, servers are still involved with serverless computing. However, the cloud customer doesn't have to bother with configuring or managing the server—the CSP does this part.

When running a serverless application, the CSP offers short-term use of a server only when the application or other code needs to run. For example, running code in Lambda can be measured in microseconds. This reduces overall costs to the consumer and transfers responsibility for managing the server (such as provisioning, patching, and maintenance) to the CSP. This paradigm is sometimes called FaaS (Function as a Service), which refers to managing individual processes or functions in the cloud rather than managing an entire OS environment.

Examples of serverless services include the following:

- *AWS*—Lambda for running code, S3 (Simple Storage Service) for object storage, and DynamoDB for NoSQL databases
- *Azure*—Cosmos DB for databases, Bot Service for intelligent serverless bots, and Azure Blob for object storage
- *GCP*—Cloud Functions for running code, App Engine for hosting web and mobile apps, and Cloud Run for managed container deployment

Serverless computing is ideal for many databases, backup or data transfer tasks, and apps or code that doesn't need to run continuously, such as IoT. Serverless is often used for backend tasks behind the scenes of complex websites or applications.

Containers

VM technology has been around for several years and has become the operating standard for most data centers. A VM relies on an underlying hypervisor of some kind to manage communication between the VM's OS and the host's physical hardware. Then applications of various types are installed inside the VM's OS. This stack is portrayed on the left side of Figure 2-17.

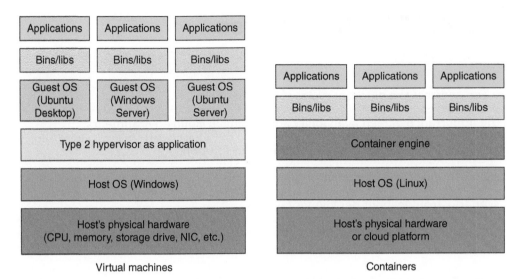

Figure 2-17 A container engine creates a lightweight, self-contained environment that provides only the files and services needed to run an application

However, the overhead created by installing and then booting an entire OS on a full VM to host applications can be problematic. Suppose you're only hosting one or a few applications on the VM. You have an entire OS with much of its potential sitting unused by the apps. You also have the processing, memory, and storage resources allocated to the VM that are rarely used to full capacity and, in fact, must maintain some buffer of allocated resources beyond the maximum amounts used at any time.

What if, instead, you could take the parts of the OS you need for that specific application and package them into a container with the app itself? What if you could use exactly the amount of hardware resources you need at any given time, and nothing more, without having to boot up an operating system? This is the essence of a container, which is a lightweight, self-contained environment that provides the services needed to run an application in nearly any OS environment. As shown on the right side of Figure 2-17, the OS layer is run by a software platform called a container engine. The market-leading container engine is Docker Engine, and many cloud platforms include services that support Docker containers. In this scenario, the app draws on exactly the hardware resources it needs and, as it is moved from one environment to another, takes with it exactly the OS resources that it needs and nothing more; essentially, this is OS virtualization. It abstracts the application's processes outside of the traditional OS. This makes the app more portable to be hosted in different operating environments in a more predictable way, and it makes the container more lightweight than an entire VM with its OS and apps.

An advantage to this arrangement is that multiple containers can run on multiple hardware resources to achieve high availability and load balancing objectives. Suppose you break down a large application into its smaller parts, called microservices. For example, you might separate the ordering processes of an application from the inventory process or the sales history process. Each microservice communicates with other microservices using APIs (application programming interfaces). Next, you design each part of the application to run in a separate container. Then, a cluster of physical servers can support a high number of containers where the application's microservices spread throughout several containers can pull on physical resources (such as CPU, memory, or storage) throughout the cluster.

One of the most significant factors in an organization's adoption of containers is that software can be developed, tested, and deployed in a more stable environment when each application is essentially packaged with its own environment inside the container. Developers can test changes to the underlying code and accurately predict the effect of those changes on the application, no matter the environment where it's used.

Supporting Containers

When you write code for an application to be run in a container, you include with the code some information about the dependencies needed for that application to work. These dependencies are created from a specific OS, such as Ubuntu or Windows Server. For example, an environment variable determined by dependency information is the file path. Windows systems use a different file path configuration than do Linux systems, so one environment variable might convert the Windows paths to a Linux configuration. Another environment variable might indicate the location of a **secrets** file the container needs to do its job, such as passwords or API keys. The most secure way to do this is to store a secrets file in a volume mount. A volume mount connects a container to **persistent storage**, which is a storage device that continues to exist even when the container is terminated. And one of the environment variables might give the container information on how to connect with that storage device. Alternatively, some orchestration tools contain built-in secrets storage, and the container would need to know how to find the information listed there.

Once the code and all its variables and dependencies are defined, you then package this information into a fairly small file called a Docker image. This image will serve as a template for all the containers that will run this code.

Next, you deposit the image in a repository so the image can be accessed by a container management service. The Docker repository is called Docker Hub, although there is a cost to use this repository beyond the very limited free option. (The storage space for images is free but the number of times you can access those images is limited.) In AWS, this repository is created in the AWS ECR (Elastic Container Repository) service, which offers more free options and native compatibility with other AWS services. As shown in Figure 2-18, a repository might be public if the images it contains are intended to be shared freely, or it might be private if the included images are proprietary.

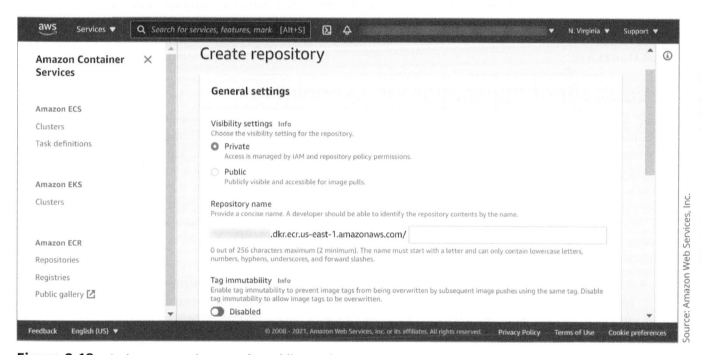

Figure 2-18   An image repository can be public or private

When you deploy VM instances, you need a hypervisor, whether that's a type 1 or type 2 hypervisor. For containers, however, you need a container management service. One very popular option is **Kubernetes**, also called K8s, where the middle eight letters, *-ubernete*, are replaced by the number *8*. Kubernetes (kubernetes.io) is an open-source container management service developed by Google and now available in other major cloud platforms such as AWS and Azure. K8s works to optimize management of container workloads and services.

To run the containers, you need underlying hosts, whether physical or virtual, to support the container management tool. AWS's ECS (Elastic Container Service) can be used to deploy, schedule, scale, and manage containers on top of EC2 instances. ECS creates multiple EC2 instances, collectively called a cluster, to provide the services needed to manage your containers. Alternatively, you could create several EC2 instances yourself directly in EC2 and install something like Docker Swarm on top of those instances to manage your containers. However, ECS creates instances that are optimized as members of a host cluster, and AWS provides some additional automated services that make container management easier for the customer. To accomplish this goal, each instance contains an ECS agent and a Docker agent for monitoring and communication.

When using ECS, the customer maintains certain responsibilities for managing these EC2 instances, such as the following:

- Create the EC2 instances and join them to the ECS cluster.
- Monitor resource usage and scale resources as needed.
- Manage each host instance's OS, including security and updates.

An alternative to EC2 for hosting containers is Fargate, which automates some of these host cluster responsibilities. When using Fargate, it will create the needed instances for your containers. Essentially, Fargate is a serverless service because the customer is not responsible for managing the underlying servers for their containers. As the customer's containers need additional resources, Fargate provisions sufficient EC2 instances to handle the demand. Fargate is more expensive than the customer-managed instances in EC2, but it's also more responsive to shifting demand, which can be less expensive for a customer whose workload is less predictable.

When managing containers, you can also orchestrate container management to ensure automated deployment, scaling, and management. You'll learn more about orchestration later, but for now, know that container orchestration tools can help ensure high availability of applications running in containers. A high percentage of companies use Kubernetes for container orchestration. You can then incorporate Kubernetes directly into your AWS infrastructure using EKS (Elastic Kubernetes Service). This enables a smooth migration from any K8s deployment into AWS because EKS is designed to natively support K8s. One drawback, however, is that EKS is less cooperative with other AWS services than ECS is.

Troubleshoot Applications in Containers

Transitioning to containers doesn't solve all application-related problems. For example, CPU and memory management can be a particular challenge with containers. When originally creating a Docker image, you can set hard limits on the access a container has to its hosts' CPU cycles or memory. Otherwise, the container management system will control CPU and memory resource distribution according to the available resources in the host cluster. Embedding limits within the container image can help avoid host limitations causing a shutdown of the entire container system. However, these hard-coded limits might also restrict an application's performance under high demand.

As with any application infrastructure, container-based applications can suffer from service overload where one or more services within the overall system becomes inundated with requests and slows or crashes the entire system. The following list describes two potential solutions for this problem:

- *Rate limiting*—Allows for a constant flow of traffic or requests to the service regardless of the rate of incoming requests or the service's capacity. When more traffic arrives than the rate allows, those excessive requests are delayed and tend to back up until the service can work through earlier requests.
- *Concurrency control*—Applies an upper limit of traffic or requests based on the service's capacity and denies traffic or requests that exceed that threshold, which is called back pressure. Clients detecting back pressure identify the service overload and can adaptively adjust their rate of requests.

While service overload is a common problem regardless of application design, this issue is particularly relevant to the microservice design used in conjunction with containers.

Remember This

- When running a serverless application, the CSP offers short-term use of a server only when the application or other code needs to run.
- A container is a lightweight, self-contained environment that provides the services needed to run an application in nearly any OS environment.
- When you write code for an application to be run in a container, you include with the code some information about the dependencies needed for that application to work.
- When originally creating a Docker image, you can set hard limits on the access a container has to its hosts' CPU cycles or memory.

Self-Check

10. Who manages the server behind a serverless compute service?
    a. The end user
    b. The CSP
    c. The cloud customer
    d. The ISP

11. Which component does a container virtualize?
    a. The CPU
    b. The storage device
    c. The memory card
    d. The OS

12. Which file contains the information needed to create a container instance?
    a. Secrets file
    b. Volume mount
    c. File path
    d. Docker image

○ Check your answers at the end of this module.

Module Summary

Section 2-1: Virtualization Technologies

- Each VM (virtual machine) can have its own OS (operating system), and all the VMs on a physical computer share the same hardware resources.
- A type 1 hypervisor is installed directly on the firmware of a physical machine while a type 2 hypervisor is installed as an application in an existing OS.
- Each VM can be configured to network with other machines on the physical network or only to its host and other VMs on the same host.
- When configuring VMs inside of a hypervisor, you're given options for the number and size of CPUs and GPUs, amount and type of memory, storage type and space, and access to device drivers.

Section 2-2: Virtualized Processing and Memory

- Whether building VMs in the cloud or on a hypervisor, a technician will need to decide how many vCPUs to give the VM.
- Most type 1 hypervisors allow you to configure various RAM settings for each VM: minimum memory, maximum memory, and start-up memory.

Section 2-3: VMs in the Cloud

- When deploying VM instances in the cloud, CSPs offer preconfigured instance types where CPU and memory capacity are automatically allocated in a fixed ratio.
- When launching many instances of the same configuration, you can use a template to ensure every instance is configured the same way.
- Guest VMs residing on the same host are part of an affinity group, while an anti-affinity rule will ensure VMs do *not* share the same physical host.
- Factors that directly affect the cost efficiency of virtualized CPU and memory resources for a particular deployment include security considerations, HA (high availability) requirements, DR (disaster recovery) strategies, energy savings, and cost considerations.

Section 2-4: VM Alternatives

- When running a serverless application, the CSP offers short-term use of a server only when the application or other code needs to run.
- A container is a lightweight, self-contained environment that provides the services needed to run an application in nearly any OS environment.
- When you write code for an application to be run in a container, you include with the code some information about the dependencies needed for that application to work.
- When originally creating a Docker image, you can set hard limits on the access a container has to its hosts' CPU cycles or memory.

Key Terms

For definitions of key terms, see the Glossary.

affinity	guest	serverless computing
AMD-V (AMD virtualization)	HA (high availability)	SMT (simultaneous multithreading)
anti-affinity	host	template
ballooning	HT (hyperthreading)	thread
cluster	hypervisor	type 1 hypervisor
container	ingress traffic	type 2 hypervisor
core	instance	vCPU (virtual CPU)
DHCP (Dynamic Host Configuration Protocol)	Kubernetes	VDI (virtual desktop infrastructure)
	memory bursting	virtual memory
DR (disaster recovery)	microservice	VM (virtual machine)
driver	overcommitment ratio	vNIC (virtual NIC)
egress traffic	persistent storage	volume-based licensing
elasticity	placement group	vRAM (virtual RAM)
FaaS (Function as a Service)	resiliency	VT (Virtualization Technology)
GPU (graphics processing unit)	secret	

Acronyms Checklist

The acronyms in Table 2-2 are listed in the Cloud+ objectives and could appear on the Cloud+ exam. This means that exam questions might use any of these acronyms in context so that you must know the meaning of the acronym in order to answer the question correctly. Make sure you're familiar with what each acronym stands for and the general concept of the term itself. All these acronyms are used in context in this module.

Table 2-2 Module 2 acronyms

Acronym	Spelled out	Acronym	Spelled out
CPU	central processing unit	OS	operating system
DHCP	Dynamic Host Configuration Protocol	SMT	simultaneous multithreading
GPU	graphics processing unit	SSD	solid-state drive
HA	high availability	vCPU	virtual central processing unit
IPC	instructions per cycle	VDI	virtual desktop infrastructure
KVM	Kernel-based Virtual Machine	vGPU	virtual graphics processing unit
KVM	keyboard, video, and mouse	vNIC	virtual network interface controller
NAT	network address translation	vRAM	virtual random access memory
NIC	network interface controller	vSwitch	virtual switch

Review Questions

1. Which of the following functions most like a typical operating system?

   a. Type 1 hypervisor
   b. Type 2 hypervisor
   c. Kubernetes
   d. Docker

2. Which rule would ensure two VMs are always hosted on different physical machines?

   a. Required affinity rule
   b. Preferred affinity rule
   c. Required anti-affinity rule
   d. Preferred anti-affinity rule

3. What CSP cost-saving strategy can you overcome by using a dedicated host?

   a. Oversubscription
   b. Overcommitment
   c. Tenancy
   d. High availability

4. Which driver type will most likely provide the most functionality for a device?

   a. Generic
   b. Vendor
   c. Pass-through
   d. Open source

5. Which is largest?

   a. 1 GB
   b. 1 GiB
   c. 1 MB
   d. 1 MiB

6. What resource can provide file access to several containers over a long period of time?

   a. Image repository
   b. Secrets file
   c. Microservice
   d. Persistent storage

7. Which technology enables a CPU core to function as two threads?

   a. Affinity
   b. Elasticity
   c. SMT
   d. IPC

8. Where does an AWS VM instance find its OS files?

   a. AMI
   b. Template
   c. Boot volume
   d. SAN

9. Which technique enables a client service to adjust its rate of requests to accommodate service overload?

   a. Hard-coded memory limitations
   b. Concurrency control
   c. Container orchestration
   d. Rate limiting

10. What kind of service do you need to store and access container images?

    a. Persistent storage volume
    b. Microservice
    c. Hypervisor
    d. Repository

Scenario-Based Questions

Question 2-1

Vicki works from home developing apps for managing highly regulated data, such as patients' medical history or customers' payment information. She's always concerned with prioritizing data security and ensuring that no programming loopholes would allow hackers access to data managed by one of her apps. During the development process, Vicki performs some initial, lightweight testing of her apps in a few OS environments running in VMs on her home computer, and then she passes each app along to a team at another location for more intense and thorough testing. Which hypervisor is Vicki most likely using?

   a. ESXi
   b. VirtualBox
   c. Windows Server 2016
   d. XenServer

Question 2-2

Brian is moving his network's backup DHCP server to a VM running Ubuntu Server. The VM will provide a couple of other network services as well, including DNS. Which networking mode should Brian assign to the Ubuntu VM?

   a. NAT mode
   b. DHCP mode
   c. Host-only mode
   d. Bridged mode

Question 2-3

Douglas is setting up VM instances on a Hyper-V server to host some basic web server and legacy software workloads along with some light app testing. He needs to know how many vCPUs to allocate to each VM. The server's motherboard has two CPU sockets, both populated with eight-core processors, and hyperthreading is enabled. He's decided that the VMs' workloads can easily handle a 3:1 overcommitment ratio. He plans on creating 15 VMs at first and eventually increasing to 25 VMs as he fine-tunes the workloads and resource allocations. How many vCPUs should Douglas initially allocate to each VM?

   a. 1
   b. 6
   c. 32
   d. 96

Note 10

Websites, applications, public cloud platforms, and related account options change often. While the instructions given in these projects were accurate at the time of writing, you might need to adjust the steps or options according to later changes.

Hands-On Projects

Note to Instructors and Students: A rubric is provided for evaluating student performance on these projects. Please see Appendix D.

Project 2-1: Create a VM in a Hypervisor

Estimated time: 45 minutes
Objective 3.4: Given a scenario, configure the appropriate compute sizing for a deployment.
Resources:

- Internet access
- An installation of VirtualBox or administrative rights on a computer to install VirtualBox
- ISO file to install Windows or Linux on a VM

Context:
You need to understand how to create a VM in a local hypervisor before you begin managing VM instances in the cloud. VirtualBox (virtualbox.org) is a type 2 hypervisor that works on various host OSs, including Windows, macOS, and many Linux distros. It's also free and easy to learn. Using any current edition of Windows, macOS, or Linux (Ubuntu, Debian, openSUSE, Fedora, and many others), you can download and install Oracle VirtualBox and then use this free hypervisor to create virtual machines and a virtual network.

Note 11

VirtualBox is free and easy to use and works well on many OS platforms. However, if you have a different hypervisor you'd rather use (such as Hyper-V or VMware Workstation), you can complete this project using that hypervisor instead by adjusting the steps as necessary.

Complete the following steps:

1. Make sure HAV (hardware-assisted virtualization) is enabled in UEFI/BIOS setup. If you are not sure it is enabled, power down your computer, turn it on again, press a key during start-up to access UEFI/BIOS setup (check the motherboard's documentation to know which key), and make sure the virtualization feature is enabled. For the system shown earlier in Figure 2-5, that's done on the Advanced CPU Configuration screen. Also make sure that any subcategory items under HAV are enabled. Save your changes, exit UEFI/BIOS setup, and allow the system to restart to Windows.

2. Go to **virtualbox.org** to download and install the appropriate **VirtualBox platform package** for your host machine. Accept all default settings during the installation. The Oracle VM VirtualBox Manager window opens.

3. To create a virtual machine using VirtualBox, click **New** on the toolbar, and follow the wizard to create a VM. Give your VM a name, such as VM1 or VM_Lab_A (or something more creative), and select the OS you will install in it.

4. For Memory size, consider increasing the amount of RAM allocated to the VM. For example, 64-bit Windows installs more easily with 4 GB of RAM (which is 4096 MB) rather than the minimum 2 GB.

5. You can accept the default settings for the VM's storage unless directed otherwise by your instructor. Notice that the default settings create a dynamically allocated VDI (VirtualBox Disk Image) of 50 GB.

6. After the VM is created, select it in the left pane. Click **Settings**, and answer the following questions about your VM:
   a. How much base memory is allocated to your VM?
   b. What's the VM's boot order?
   c. How many processors are allocated to the VM?
   d. What network connection type is currently configured for your VM?

7. In the VM's Settings box, click **Storage** in the left pane.

8. In the Storage Tree area, to the right of *Controller: SATA*, click the **Adds optical drive** icon, which looks like a CD with a plus (+) symbol, as shown in Figure 2-19.

Figure 2-19 Storage Tree options allow you to mount an ISO image as a virtual CD in the VM

9. In the Optical Disk Selector dialog box, select your ISO file or click **Add Disk Image** to add a new one. Click **Choose** and then click **OK**. You return to the VirtualBox Manager window.

Hands-On Projects Continued

> **Note 12**
>
> If you have any empty disks attached to your VM, you might need to remove those before it will find your bootable ISO file during start-up.

10. Click **Start** on the toolbar. Your VM starts up and begins installing the operating system. Follow the prompts on-screen and make any adjustments to default settings as directed by your instructor.

> **Note 13**
>
> Hyper-V and VirtualBox don't play well together on the same machine, especially if your computer uses an Intel CPU. If you get an error message that VT-x is not available when trying to start a VM, consider that Hyper-V might be enabled on your machine, and you'll need to disable it. This is done in Windows Features (press **Win+R** and enter **optionalfeatures**). Make sure you disable all Hyper-V components.

11. After you have installed the OS in your VM, open its browser to confirm the VM has a good Internet connection. **Take a screenshot** showing your running VM; submit this visual with your answers to this project's questions.

Project 2-2: Deploy a VM in AWS

Estimated time: 30 minutes
Objective 3.4: Given a scenario, configure the appropriate compute sizing for a deployment.
Resources:

- Internet access
- AWS account (either a standard account or an AWS Academy account)

Context:
Each of the major public cloud providers works similarly when deploying VM instances in the cloud. In this project, you will deploy a VM in AWS. In the next two projects, you'll see how that process varies slightly in Azure and GCP.

AWS VM instances are deployed in the EC2 service. Other than a few minimal choices such as OS image and VM size, most of the typical settings are configured by default. While you can change them if you want to, the default settings work well while you're still learning what you're doing.

Recall that in Project 1-2, you surveyed available AWS account options and created an AWS account. In your AWS console, complete the following steps:

1. Go to the **EC2** dashboard. Go to the list of running instances and click **Launch instances**.
2. Give your instance a name. Choose a free-tier-eligible **Windows Server** AMI. Which AMI did you choose?
3. Choose an instance type, again being careful to choose a free-tier-eligible option if needed. Instance types offer various combinations of capacity for CPU, memory, storage, and networking resources. Click **Compare instance types** to see other options and how the types vary from family to family. Which instance type did you choose? The naming convention gives you significant clues as to the instance type:
   - Instance types start with a letter and a number, such as T2 or C5, where the letter represents the instance class (for example, T is general purpose and C is compute optimized), and the number represents the generation.
   - Within a class and generation, varying sizes of resources can be selected while retaining the originally designated ratios of those resources. For example, doubling the vCPUs will also double the RAM. This sizing scheme is represented by words such as nano, micro, small, medium, large, xlarge, or 2xlarge.

4. To connect to your instance, you'll need a key pair. A key pair acts like a lock and a key. AWS holds the public key, similar to a lock on a door. You save the private key, similar to a key that fits the lock. When you present the private key, it's like using a custom key to unlock the front door to your house. Key pairs are more secure than passwords because the lock and the key must match—this is harder than a password for a hacker to crack. Key pairs are also encrypted when stored, so it's harder for a hacker to discover this information.

   Create a new key pair, give the key pair a name, and then download the key pair as a .pem file. Be sure to save your key pair in a safe place, as anyone with that file can access your VM instance. Where did you save your key pair file?

   CAUTION: Do NOT proceed with this step until you confirm you have downloaded your key pair. You will not have another opportunity to do so.

5. Scroll through the additional configuration options to familiarize yourself with what options are available. For now, stick with the default settings. When you're ready, click **Launch instance** to proceed with default settings. When the VM is launched, click **View all instances**.

6. You might need to refresh your list to see your instance. When the VM reaches a running state, explore information about this VM on the Instances page by selecting the check box next to the instance—this generates information in the lower pane. There's a lot of important information on this screen, such as the availability zone, security group, VPC (virtual private cloud), and subnet. You'll learn more about these items in later modules. What is your VM's private IP address? What is its public IP address?

Now you're ready to remote into your Windows Server instance using RDP (Remote Desktop Protocol). If you're working from a macOS computer, you'll need to use the Microsoft Remote Desktop app from the Mac App Store. Research this online for more specific steps. If you're using a Linux computer, many Linux distros come with an RDP tool to connect to a Windows computer. If you're using a Windows computer, the tools you'll need are built into the OS.

Note 14

Had you created a Linux VM, you could instead use SSH (Secure Shell) to remote into the instance.

These instructions apply to a Windows computer. Complete the following steps:

7. At the top of the Instances page, click **Connect**. Click the **RDP client** tab.
8. Click **Download remote desktop file**. Save the file and then open it.
9. On the Remote Desktop Connection window, click **Connect**.
10. The username defaults to Administrator. To get the password, return to the Connect to instance page, and click **Get password**. Browse to the location of your key pair file, and open it. Click **Decrypt Password**. Copy the password and paste it in the Windows Security dialog box. Click **OK**.
11. You will likely get a warning that the identity of the remote computer cannot be verified and asking if you want to connect anyway. Click **Yes**.

Note 15

If the connection with your VM is not successful, you'll need to do some troubleshooting. For example, make sure your local firewalls (both on your network and on your physical computer) allow RDP traffic, and make sure your VM instance allows RDP traffic from the local IP address of your physical network or from all IP addresses (i.e., from 0.0.0.0/0). Make sure you used the correct private key file and that it was formatted using the correct file type.

(continues)

Hands-On Projects Continued

12. When the RDP connection is established, interact with your Windows Server VM's apps, utilities, or other resources. **Take a screenshot** showing your VM in an RDP window on your local computer; submit this visual with your answers to this project's questions.

13. Close the Remote Desktop Connection window, and click **OK** to disconnect from the VM.

14. Return to the list of running instances. Select your instance, click **Instance state**, choose **Terminate instance**, and then click **Terminate**. Note that stopping the instance is not sufficient as this is analogous to shutting down a physical server—the VM will continue to exist and could accrue charges. Terminating the instance deletes all related resources to prevent ongoing charges. Wait a few minutes, and then refresh the list of running instances. Confirm your instance is removed from the list or is listed as terminated.

> ### Note 16
>
> It's important to develop good cloud hygiene habits and delete any resources you no longer need. This is an important habit that will help you minimize cloud expenses.

Project 2-3: Deploy a VM in Azure

Estimated time: 30 minutes

Objective 3.4: Given a scenario, configure the appropriate compute sizing for a deployment.

Resources:

- Internet access
- Microsoft account and Azure subscription

Context:

Creating a VM instance in Azure works similarly to AWS and other cloud platforms. There are a few significant differences, which you'll learn about in this project.

Recall that in Project 1-3, you surveyed available Azure subscription options and created an Azure subscription for your Microsoft account. Sign into your Azure portal, and complete the following steps:

1. Click **Virtual machines** to manage and create VM instances. On the Virtual machines page, click **Create** and then click **Virtual machine** to begin the creation process.

2. Check that you're using the correct subscription. An Azure subscription identifies a payment method or some other crediting account. If you signed up for a free trial account with Azure, then you automatically have a Free Trial subscription. In a business environment, subscriptions allow costs to be tracked to specific departments or organizations. Subscriptions can also be transferred so that billing ownership can be reassigned to a different user.

3. Next to Resource group, click **Create new** and give the resource group a name. Resource groups organize various resources with the same life cycle, permissions, and policies. For example, each VM instance can be related to many resources such as network interfaces, storage disks, IP addresses, security groups, and a virtual network. Together, the resources that make the VM function are part of a resource group. Resource groups may contain many VMs and their associated resources. Resource groups also provide a quick and easy way to delete all resources associated with a VM when you're finished with the VM. What is the name of your resource group?

4. Name your VM, and then choose an image. Images are offered from the Marketplace, including several BYOL (bring your own license) options, or you can use your own images. Choose a **Windows Server** image, such as Windows Server 2019 Datacenter. Which image did you choose?

5. Next to Size, click **See all sizes**. Like AWS, Azure offers options for number of vCPUs and allocation of memory, storage disks, storage space, and more. At the time of this writing, the Azure free trial includes 750 hours of Azure B1S General Purpose VMs for Windows Server and Linux. Choose the **B1s** size, and then click **Select**.

6. Specify a username and password, and then confirm the password. Save this information to use later in this project.

7. Next to Public inbound ports, confirm that RDP (Remote Desktop Protocol) is allowed. You'll need this access to connect to your instance soon.

8. Click **Next: Disks >** and explore the other configuration options through the other pages while keeping the default settings. When you're ready, click **Review + create**. If the validation fails, troubleshoot any missing information or configurations. Once the VM passes validation, click **Create**.

9. Return to the Virtual machines page and examine available information on your VM. What is your VM's public IP address?

Now you're ready to remote into your Windows Server instance using RDP (Remote Desktop Protocol). If you're working from a macOS computer, you'll need to use the Microsoft Remote Desktop app from the Mac App Store. Research this online for more specific steps. If you're using a Linux computer, many Linux distros come with an RDP tool to connect to a Windows computer. If you're using a Windows computer, the tools you'll need are built into the OS. This process is particularly simple and straightforward when using Azure from a Windows computer.

Note 17

Had you created a Linux VM, you could instead use SSH (Secure Shell) to remote into the instance.

Complete the following steps:

10. Wait until your instance is listed as running. Click the instance name, and then click **Connect**. Choose the **RDP** option.

11. Download and then open the RDP file. If required, click **Connect** and then click **Yes** to continue. Sign in using the credentials you created earlier in this project.

12. You will likely get a warning that the identity of the remote computer cannot be verified and asking if you want to connect anyway. Click **Yes**.

Note 18

If the connection with your VM is not successful, you'll need to do some troubleshooting. For example, make sure your local firewalls (both on your network and on your physical computer) allow RDP traffic, and make sure your VM instance allows RDP traffic from the local IP address of your physical network or from all IP addresses (i.e., from 0.0.0.0/0). Make sure you used the correct RDP file.

13. When the RDP connection is established, interact with your Windows Server VM's apps, utilities, or other resources. **Take a screenshot** showing your VM in an RDP window on your local computer; submit this visual with your answers to this project's questions.

14. Close the Remote Desktop Connection window, and click **OK** to disconnect from the VM.

15. Return to the VM's page in Azure. Click **Overview** and then click the name of the resource group you created in Step 3. Delete the resource group. Wait a few minutes for the task to complete. Click the menu icon in the upper-right corner, and click **Resource groups**. Confirm the resource group deletion has completed. If the notification icon still shows activity in the upper-left corner, wait a few more minutes, and refresh the Resource groups list until your resource group is removed from the list.

(continues)

Hands-On Projects Continued

> **Note** 19
>
> It's important to develop good cloud hygiene habits and delete any resources you no longer need. This is an important habit that will help you minimize cloud expenses.

Project 2-4: Deploy a VM in GCP

Estimated time: 30 minutes

Objective 3.4: Given a scenario, configure the appropriate compute sizing for a deployment.

Resources:

- Internet access
- GCP account

Context:

In GCP, you create VMs using the Compute Engine service. As with AWS and Azure, you can choose CPU, memory, storage, and networking configurations.

Recall that in Project 1-4, you surveyed available GCP account options and created a GCP account. Sign into Google Cloud and complete the following steps:

1. First check which project you're using. Google projects allow you to organize related resources for easy access. For example, projects can group a set of users with billing, authentication, and resource monitoring settings. Projects can be used to target billing activities so specific departments or programs within an organization can track their GCP expenses separately. When you create a VM in Compute Engine, you must create the VM within a project. When you first create your GCP account, a default project called "My First Project" is created for you. Click the scope picker at the top of the window to see the list of projects in your account.
2. Click **NEW PROJECT**. Give the project a name, and then click **CREATE**. What name did you give your project?
3. After the project is created, click the scope picker again, and select your new project.
4. Click the Navigation menu icon, and then click **Compute Engine**. There might be a delay while GCP initializes Compute Engine for your new project. If you get an error, watch the notifications list, and try again in a few minutes.
5. Click **CREATE INSTANCE** and give the instance a name. What name did you give this VM?
6. You choose a machine type by the number of vCPUs, which then determines the amount of memory the VM will have and gives an initial indication of how much it will cost to run the machine. At the time of this writing, the GCP free tier includes use of the e2-micro machine type within certain limits. Under Machine type, choose **e2-micro**. The e2-micro instance type is only available in a few regions, so if you do not see this instance type as an option, research the current regions where the type is available, and change to that region. You might need to research current free-tier services for GCP.
7. The boot disk holds the OS image for the VM. GCP supports several varieties of Linux and Windows operating systems. Under Boot disk, click **Change**. Choose an **Ubuntu** operating system, and click **SELECT**. Which version did you choose?
8. Click **NETWORKING, DISKS, SECURITY, MANAGEMENT, SOLE-TENANCY**, and explore the other configuration options, but leave all defaults in place. When you're ready, click **CREATE**.
9. Wait for the instance to reach a running state. Click the instance and explore its configuration information. What is this VM's private IP address? What is its public IP address?

Although it's possible to use a separate SSH (Secure Shell) client to connect to your GCP instance, it's easy to connect directly through your browser.

Note 20

Had you created a Windows VM, you could instead use RDP (Remote Desktop Protocol) to remote into the instance.

Complete the following steps:

10. Make sure your instance is running. Click the **SSH** drop-down arrow to see the options you have, and then click **Open in browser window**. Note that in the future, you can click SSH to go straight to the new tab in your browser. When prompted, click **Connect** to confirm.
11. When the VM's connection opens, interact with it by running some Linux commands. Which commands did you run?
12. With the VM connection still active, **take a screenshot** showing your VM in an SSH window on your local computer; submit this visual with your answers to this project's questions.
13. End the connection by entering the **exit** command.
14. On the GCP navigation pane, point to **IAM & Admin**, and then click **Manage Resources**. Select the project you created in Step 2 and delete it.

Note 21

It's important to develop good cloud hygiene habits and delete any resources you no longer need. This is an important habit that will help you minimize cloud expenses.

Capstone Project 2: Create a Serverless Function

Note 22

Websites, applications, public cloud platforms, and related account options change often. While the instructions given in these projects were accurate at the time of writing, you might need to adjust the steps or options according to later changes.

Note to Instructors and Students: A rubric is provided for evaluating student performance on these projects. Please see Appendix D.
Estimated time: 1 hour
Objective 3.1: Given a scenario, integrate components into a cloud solution.
Group work: This project includes enhancements when assigned as a group project.
Resources:

- Internet access
- An account for a public cloud platform, such as AWS, Azure, or GCP

Context:
In the module and Hands-On Projects, you learned how to deploy VM instances in the cloud. You also learned about serverless compute, which is a way to run code directly in the cloud without having to manage underlying server instances. In this Capstone, you will teach yourself to deploy a sample serverless function in your chosen public cloud platform using resources made available by the cloud provider.

(continues)

Hands-On Projects Continued

Complete the following steps:

1. Choose one of the public cloud platforms where you have an account, such as AWS, Azure, or GCP. Research that platform's serverless services, and choose one of the more popular and mainstream services to practice with in this project. For example, in AWS, you might choose Lambda. Comparable services in other platforms include Azure Functions and Google Cloud Functions. Do some basic research on this service so you understand its purpose and the big picture of how it works. Which service did you choose?

2. Most of the large CSPs provide extensive training and practice activities to help customers learn how to use their cloud services. Some of this material can be found on the CSP's website. Other materials are embedded within the platform itself. For example, to create an AWS Lambda function, you have the option to use a pre-built blueprint that lets you practice with the process before authoring your own function. Find online training materials or embedded practice activities for your selected service. Which resource do you think will be the most helpful as you practice deploying a function in your chosen serverless service?

3. Work through the steps to deploy a resource in this service and troubleshoot any problems or error messages you encounter. For example, if you're working with AWS Lambda, you would create a function using a blueprint, which is allowed with an AWS Academy account if you choose an existing IAM role instead of creating a new role. If you're using AWS Academy or another education-based account, you might encounter permission limitations. If the limitations are too restrictive, consider switching to a different service. Work through the process as far as you can, and document your progress and limitations. When you've created the resource or worked as far as you can before running into insurmountable permissions issues, **take a screenshot** of your progress; submit this visual with your answers to this project's questions.

4. If you were able to create the resource, test the function. For example, in AWS Lambda, you create a test event, run it, and then view the execution results. What outcome do you observe?

5. **For group projects:** Each member of the group should choose a different platform or serverless service for this project. Group members should share what they learned about their selected serverless service, including what the service does, common use cases, and the results of their practice using the service.

6. Delete all resources you created—good cloud hygiene will help protect you from unwanted cloud charges.

Solutions to Self-Check Questions

Section 2-1: Virtualization Technologies

1. When starting a VM in a type 1 hypervisor, which component starts first?

   Answer: b. The hypervisor

   Explanation: With type 1 hypervisors, the motherboard's BIOS or UEFI firmware hands the start-up process to the installed hypervisor, which then boots any VMs it's configured to start up automatically.

2. Which network mode requires a VM to receive an IP address from the physical network's DHCP server?

   Answer: c. Bridged

   Explanation: In bridged mode, a vNIC obtains its own IP address, default gateway, and subnet mask information from the physical LAN's DHCP (Dynamic Host Configuration Protocol) server.

3. Your hypervisor can allocate use of the host's GPU to only one VM at a time. Which deployment technique is the hypervisor using?

   Answer: b. Pass-through

   Explanation: With pass-through GPU deployment, the GPU can only be used by one VM at a time.

Section 2-2: Virtualized Processing and Memory

4. How many threads does an SMT-enabled, 16-core CPU offer?

    Answer: b. 32

    Explanation: Using the formula, # of threads = # of CPUs × # of physical cores × 2 if using SMT, a 16-core, SMT-enabled CPU offers 32 threads: 1 × 16 × 2.

5. Which of the following license types do you use when you purchase and install Microsoft Office on your personal computer?

    Answer: d. Client access license

    Explanation: A CAL (client access license) is a software license provided per user or per device.

6. Which memory management technique borrows memory from one VM for another VM?

    Answer: a. Ballooning

    Explanation: Ballooning is a way to trick the guest OS into releasing some of its RAM so the hypervisor can allocate it elsewhere.

Section 2-3: VMs in the Cloud

7. Which selection determines the amount of RAM a cloud VM can use?

    Answer: a. Instance type

    Explanation: The instance type determines the instance's virtual hardware resources, including vCPUs, RAM, and storage space.

8. Which configuration parameter can ensure all the VMs for a deployment reside on the same physical host?

    Answer: c. Affinity

    Explanation: Guest VMs residing on the same physical host are part of an affinity group.

9. Which principle ensures you can consistently access your cloud resource?

    Answer: b. HA

    Explanation: HA (high availability) is a resource's maximized potential for being available consistently over time and is often referred to as the number of nines referenced in the percentage.

Section 2-4: VM Alternatives

10. Who manages the server behind a serverless compute service?

    Answer: b. The CSP

    Explanation: Despite the name, servers are still involved with serverless computing. However, the cloud customer doesn't have to bother with configuring or managing the server—the CSP does this part.

11. Which component does a container virtualize?

    Answer: d. The OS

    Explanation: A container is a self-contained environment that provides the OS services needed to run an application—essentially, this is OS virtualization.

12. Which file contains the information needed to create a container instance?

    Answer: d. Docker image

    Explanation: Once the code and all its variables and dependencies are defined, the information is packaged into a Docker image. This image will serve as a template for all the containers that will run this code.

Module 3

Migration to the Cloud

Module 3 Objectives

After reading this module, you will be able to:

1 Describe cloud migration phases and strategies.

2 Explain cloud migration types and tools.

3 Compare deployment testing types.

4 Explain agility in the cloud.

5 Apply business continuity planning.

Module 3 Outline

Study the module's outline to help you organize the content in your mind as you read.

Module 3 Scenario

"I think I get it now!" quips Nigel as he walks into Kendra's office. You and Kendra had been discussing an upcoming audit, and you're both more than happy to talk about something else—anything else.

"What's up, Nigel?" asks Kendra with an amused and quizzical look on her face.

"VMs. A machine within a machine or, really, lots of virtual machines running on one physical machine. It's like lots of apartments in one apartment building, or lots of stores in a mall, or maybe the way we use a bus system where people ride together instead of driving their own cars. Oh! Maybe it's like a party tray with lots of sandwiches for everyone to share. By the way, I'm hungry."

Kendra laughs as she pushes away from her desk, stands up, and grabs her jacket. "Come on, let's get some lunch."

At the restaurant, as you all settle in to eat your tacos (because it's Tuesday and you always eat tacos on Tuesday), Nigel adds a little more detail to his revelation. "So each VM on a physical server shares resources with other VMs. That makes sense now. But the VM also is its own system, so it can live on just about any server to use shared resources. That makes it easy to move VMs from one system to another."

"Right," you say as you jump in on the conversation. "We can move VMs from one server or hypervisor to another, so long as the VM is configured with the right file type. If it's the wrong type, it has to be converted first—if that's possible."

"Okay," says Nigel. "So it sounds like this cloud migration thing is going to be easy. Convert all our VMs to the right file format. Then save them in the cloud and use them. Right?" he asks.

"Well, it's not quite that simple," sighs Kendra. "For one thing, the VMs have to be configured for the right network settings and connections to network resources. And all the right resources need to *be* there in the cloud, or *accessible* from the cloud. Most of these systems—they're all interrelated. They depend on each other, or they depend on the same core resources. Another issue is that not everything we'd need to move lives in a VM. There are applications that might work better if run in a different kind of environment, like in a container or as a stand-alone service. And other applications really won't work well in the cloud at all. And then there are directory services and databases and other stuff, too. Moving large amounts of data to the cloud—such as our student database—can be really expensive." She puts down her taco. "It makes my stomach churn to think about it all."

"Okay," you say, "remember our mantra—one step at a time." You hold up one finger to emphasize your point. "This process could take months or even years, and we don't have to make all the decisions up front."

"True," says Kendra, picking up her taco again. "We don't even know yet how *much* of our network we'll move to the cloud. Will it be a few applications, or the whole 'kit and caboodle,' or something in between? Let's work on answering a few more questions." She jots down a few notes on a clean napkin:

- What should we move to the cloud first?
- What tools can help us make the migration process easier?
- How will this migration affect the applications we have and need?
- How can we make changes later?
- What problems should we expect?

Section 3-1: Migration Planning

Certification

1.2 Explain the factors that contribute to capacity planning.

1.4 Given a scenario, analyze the solution design in support of the business requirements.

At this point, you've already learned in earlier modules many concepts related to assessment and planning, and you'll learn more in this module. You'll also explore the actual process of migrating into the cloud and how to validate the outcomes, prepare for problems, and adapt to changing needs. The remainder of the course will dig deeper into areas that will help you maintain and optimize a cloud deployment, including topics such as security, automation, and troubleshooting.

Cloud Migration Phases

When moving an organization's IT resources to the cloud—whether a single application, a few servers, a database, or the entire network—you complete five major phases of the project: assess, plan, migrate, validate, and manage. Figure 3-1 shows the phases in a cycle because a cloud migration is never fully complete.

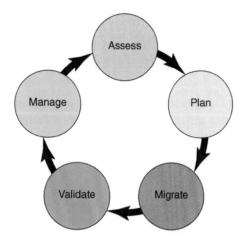

Figure 3-1 The five phases of cloud migration

Your cloud migration might be performed in layers, beginning with a simple application and continuing with more complex projects. You might find that, at some point, one cloud provider no longer meets your needs and then decide to migrate to another cloud provider. You might choose to extend the scope of your deployment to include additional providers and services. The accelerating growth of cloud technologies, fluctuating prices for services, and constant demand for quality improvement impel organizations to continually evolve their cloud deployments. For these and other reasons, you'll likely revisit each migration phase repeatedly throughout your engagement with the cloud.

Transition Assessment

Before beginning a cloud migration, you must first assess whether the cloud is a good fit for your company. Not every application, service, or database will perform well in the cloud. Legacy software, especially, might not be compatible with the cloud environment. Latency is the delay between the transmission of a signal and its receipt, and this physical reality might make certain cloud-hosted services unreasonably slow. In fact, latency is the most often-cited reason for a company's return to its own data center after trying a cloud deployment. Thorough research and testing are required before migration to avoid costly mistakes in moving workloads to the cloud that don't really belong there.

Even if you've determined a move to the cloud is the right choice for your company, you have many other decisions to make:

- Which cloud is the *right* cloud for you? Among the countless CSPs (cloud service providers), which is the best fit for your needs?
- What are your needs? Is your focus more on developing and hosting applications, running servers, storing accessible databases, or something else?
- How well will your existing applications and processes work in the cloud? Will they need to be retooled or replaced entirely?

- What new skills does your staff need to learn before tackling this migration? How can you train existing staff, and what new expertise might you need to hire?

- What will all of this cost? You can't find an accurate price tag for your cloud on a simple chart. You'll need to factor in expenses based on your geographical location relative to your CSP's location, your backup and load balancing needs, and bandwidth availability, among many others. As with an on-prem data center, hidden costs for using the cloud are easy to overlook when projecting your initial budgets. Examples include required adjustments to licensing fees, backup and archive services, and the expense of running cloud services outside of normal business hours for updates, backups, or off-hours access. All these expenses—both obvious and hidden—are collectively called TCO (total cost of ownership or total cost of operations). Many CSPs provide sophisticated TCO calculators to help you anticipate the cloud expenses you'll need to include in your budget. You'll need to compare this projected budget with your existing costs, which also include hidden expenses you might not initially consider, such as the electric bill to cool your data center or expenses for physical security and insurance coverage.

- Who in the company might champion the cause? Which users can serve as test subjects as you introduce new and improved applications? Who can advocate for patience and understanding as you navigate the necessary growing pains?

Considering all these questions takes a significant amount of time in the initial assessment phase. All the information you gather during this phase, however, will continue to serve you throughout the process. Guard against analysis paralysis—you don't want to get so bogged down in considering all possible factors that you can't make a decision and move forward.

Migration Plan

Probably the most challenging phase of a migration to the cloud is the planning stage. However, a well-laid plan will help to ensure the migration proceeds smoothly and the outcome meets the organization's goals. The plan should consider the type of migration you're undertaking, whether you are moving data, databases, applications, or network functions. An effective plan contains thorough information on the following topics:

- *Baselines*—Collect robust baselines before beginning any transition, which will indicate current functioning and configuration of the systems in your network. This includes collecting information on KPIs (key performance indicators) such as CPU and RAM usage, page load time and error rates, storage and network usage, and patch and application versions.

- *Business continuity*—Consider the effects of any anticipated downtime and how to minimize or avoid it. Also consider user training that can be performed before the migration occurs. Will the migration affect how users interact with the network or applications? Will they notice any significant changes in their work processes? Do they need training on any new applications? You might need to temporarily increase your service desk staff hours immediately following the transition to support users throughout the process. Keeping users informed and helping them understand the benefits that will be achieved once the migration is complete will more effectively manage expectations so everyone can cooperate and be patient.

- *Existing systems*—Thoroughly understand and document existing systems and dependencies that will be affected by the cloud migration. Recognize that systems and resources are highly interrelated—systems to migrate interact with many components and services such as databases, network services, or applications. Sometimes these dependencies can also be moved to the cloud. Other times, the other systems relying on these same resources require that the entire web of interdependencies stay on-prem, such as when several applications (both modern and legacy) pull from a single, monolithic database. A dependency diagram shows which components rely on what other components. This diagram will help you decide which components should be migrated and in what order. Be sure to investigate how the transition will affect the systems left behind. Also include a discovery process to identify so-called shadow IT components, which refers to resources or services running outside the knowledge or oversight of the IT department. These rogue components might have been instituted by users outside of the appropriate approval processes. However, changing systems that these shadow components rely on can interrupt work activities for the people who use them. By discovering who is using what, you can more likely bypass angry complaints from co-workers and related work delays.

- *Target hosts*—Initially, resources begin the migration process on the source host, which is whatever system—physical, virtual, or cloud based—that currently supports the resource. Any resource being moved is headed toward a target host. Configure this target host carefully to match the needs and anticipated growth of the transitioned resources.

- *Cloud architecture*—A cloud deployment is made up of many components, not just VMs. These cloud elements (also called target objects) include applications, databases, servers, processes, virtual appliances (such as a firewall), logs, and storage blocks or volumes. In addition, the overall cloud architecture includes the interfaces between these elements, the networking architecture that manages these interfaces, and the connections to your on-prem data center or users. In developing your migration plan, consider all these aspects to the degree they'll be incorporated into your cloud deployment and integrated throughout all portions of your network, both on-prem and in the cloud. Provide the appropriate structure in your target cloud for the resources and workloads it will support.

- *Legal restrictions*—Countries and states have different laws for data protection. For example, some countries require that travelers entering their territory report the password to their phone or laptop to pass customs. These laws might require that the government be able to access stored data. For similar reasons, some types of data cannot be stored at data centers located inside countries with laws against certain kinds of data security. Some types of regulated data are required to be stored only within the geographical borders of an organization's own country or a customer's resident country. This poses a challenge for cloud-based data storage, and you'll need to be aware of these issues before signing a contract. In other cases, there are limitations on what software can run on machines hosted in certain countries. An organization should have formal processes for evaluating contracts before signing them and ensure that both legal and IT experts weigh in on the terms of the agreement.

- *Order of operations*—Consider the order in which you want to move elements to the cloud. Most often, you'll want to start with an easy application, something simple and well defined without a lot of interdependencies on other systems. Ideally, this first migration will also involve a low-priority resource so that if something goes wrong, your organization doesn't lose significant amounts of revenue or productivity while you troubleshoot the problem. As you tackle more complex systems, you'll need to carefully consider which parts of each system should be moved first so the timing of data synchronization and DNS (Domain Name Service) record transitions will flow smoothly.

As you and your team hash out your migration plan, continue to fine-tune it even as the migration proceeds. Also revisit your plan after the migration is complete. Migration is not a one-time event. Whether you're migrating only parts of your data center at a time or migrating between CSPs as technologies mature, what you learn from this experience can inform future endeavors. Document the process and use this information to create your own SOPs (standard operating procedures) for workload migration. SOPs help ensure consistent performance across multiple migrations and staff members. You might also be able to use your SOPs as the starting point for automating parts of the migration process. Continue to explore improvements and document what you learn.

Migration Strategies

Each organization will take its own unique approach to its cloud migration, depending on the scope of elements being migrated and the company's intent in making the transition. Intentions can range from wanting to save money to overhauling their entire IT infrastructure and anything in between. Throughout the industry, some general categories have emerged for cloud migration strategies that reveal a spectrum of organizational investment in the cloud. These categories have been defined by the research company Gartner (gartner.com), AWS, and others along the following lines:

- *Rehost*—Also called *lift-and-shift* or *forklift*, this migration strategy refers to moving the application, server, or data into the cloud as it is. The process is often automated for high efficiency. One disadvantage is that weaknesses in the resource are retained. However, the speed of making this transition is appealing and can save money quickly, and then the resource can be further adapted or eventually replaced.

- *Revise or replatform*—Also called *lift-tinker-and-shift*, this approach makes some relatively minor changes to the application or data before moving it to the cloud, such as adding a management layer or incorporating auto-scaling features.

- *Repurchase or replace*—This strategy refers to replacing the product with an existing cloud-native product. This can be a quick, easy, and inexpensive solution, especially considering the increasing variety of options in the cloud marketplace.
- *Refactor, rearchitect, or rebuild*—In this approach, the changes are more significant, such as recoding portions of an application.
- *Retain*—Also called the *do-nothing* option, this is a low-complexity strategy that means the organization keeps using an application or data as it is, without any changes. The company might revisit the resource later as circumstances continue to evolve.
- *Retire*—This is also a low-complexity strategy that basically means the organization stops using the application or data.

Figure 3-2 shows how the migration process varies among the different strategy options. Study this diagram carefully, as many CSPs and related vendors use similar diagrams to help customers consider their options.

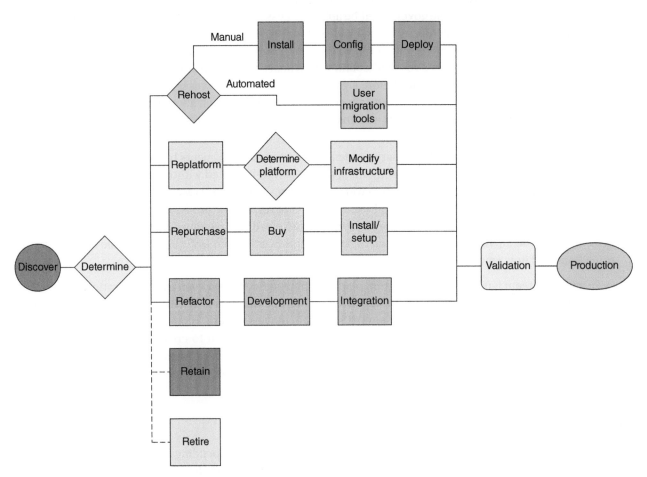

Figure 3-2   Cloud migration strategies

In choosing which approach to take for a specific resource, consider relevant factors both from a business perspective and from a technical perspective. For example, does the application generate income, or does it support ongoing business processes? An app that generates income justifies greater financial investment in adapting it for migration. Initial expenses for developing or updating an app like this might be classified as CapEx (capital expenditures), where the benefits are experienced over a longer time period (more than one year). In contrast, the costs of maintaining a simple app that supports basic business functions should be minimized. This is an OpEx (operational expenditure), where benefits are used up in about the same period as when the expenses are paid for those benefits. Another factor to consider is technical compatibility. Is the app compatible with a cloud environment? Can it easily be adapted to the cloud, or is it too old or have dependencies too complex to be moved? When the app can't reasonably be adapted, it might need to stay where it is or be replaced entirely.

Timing

Once the decision is made to migrate to the cloud and your overall migration plan is coming together, you'll need to consider the timing of the actual workload migration. Environmental constraints require careful scheduling to minimize the impact of downtime and maximize the available network bandwidth for the migration. Factors to consider include the following:

- ***Impact of downtime***—Some types of migrations can avoid downtime altogether, although overall performance might be affected. To some degree, you can choose how much downtime will be involved with your cloud migration. For example, if a small amount of downtime is acceptable, this could allow for the migration process to be completed in one fell swoop. However, if downtime must be avoided at all costs, the migration might need to occur in smaller increments over a period of several days or longer. How much downtime you can allow might fluctuate in balance with other factors, such as efficiency of the migration, overall migration time, bandwidth dedicated to the migration, and migration strategy.

- ***Work hour restrictions***—Schedule any anticipated downtime to avoid normal user work hours. For example, evenings and weekends lend themselves well to scheduled maintenance tasks. However, also consider any unique schedules kept by your organization. For example, a hospital emergency department—which tends to be busier on the weekends—might benefit from minimal downtime in the middle of a weekday instead of on a Saturday night. Many organizations keep a regularly scheduled maintenance window that might be sufficient for your cloud migration.

- ***Time zones***—Consider the impact of varying time zones on your planned migration schedule. One model used in customer support or software development is called FTS (follow the sun), where staff in one time zone hand off work at the end of their day to staff in a time zone several hours west to maximize work hours throughout a 24-hour day. The convenience of this model also works in reverse when making major changes to an organization's data center resources and scheduling downtime. For organizations spread across time zones, carefully choose your migration window, and consider migrating in phases to avoid prime work times for users in each time zone.

- ***Peak time frames and costs***—The time and money invested in a migration are not constant from beginning to end. Anticipate that demand on both these resources will follow a bell-shaped curve, as shown in Figure 3-3.

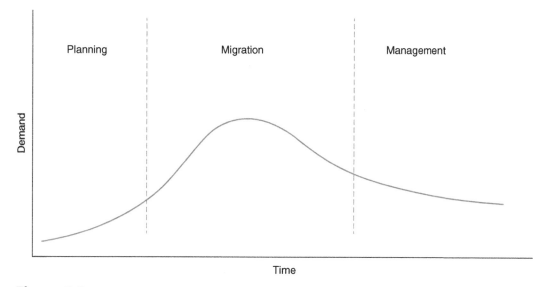

Figure 3-3   Time and money resources are most in demand in the middle of the migration process

You're Ready

You're now ready to complete Project 3-1: Research Cloud Migration Success Stories. You can complete the project now or wait until you've finished all the readings for this module.

Remember This

- When moving an organization's IT resources to the cloud, you complete five major phases of the project: assess, plan, migrate, validate, and manage.
- Before beginning a cloud migration, a thorough assessment will evaluate whether the cloud is a good fit for business needs and which part of the company's data center might work well in a cloud environment.
- An effective migration plan contains thorough information on network baselines, business continuity needs, dependencies between existing systems, needed target hosts, cloud architecture design, relevant legal restrictions, and planned order of operations.
- Cloud migration categories include the following: rehost; revise or replatform; repurchase or replace; refactor, rearchitect, or rebuild; retain; and retire.
- Environmental constraints require careful scheduling to minimize the impact of downtime and maximize the available network bandwidth for the migration.

Self-Check

1. What physical restriction might make the cloud unreasonable for certain types of workloads?
   - a. Latency
   - b. Order of operations
   - c. Business continuity
   - d. Shadow IT

2. Which cloud migration strategy requires the most work to perform?
   - a. Retain
   - b. Revise
   - c. Refactor
   - d. Rehost

3. What kind of expense is an electric bill?
   - a. KPI
   - b. OpEx
   - c. CapEx
   - d. TCO

○ Check your answers at the end of this module.

Section 3-2: Migration Execution

Certification

3.1 Given a scenario, integrate components into a cloud solution.

3.5 Given a scenario, perform cloud migrations.

4.2 Given a scenario, maintain efficient operation of a cloud environment.

5.3 Given a scenario, troubleshoot deployment issues.

Because resources on a network—either on-prem or in the cloud—are so deeply interconnected, changes to network wiring, device configuration, IP addressing, resource provisioning and availability, and more must be carefully considered, implemented, and documented. Even a seemingly minor change can have serious repercussions for resource security and availability. Most medium and large organizations have formal, documented business processes; these process documents describe in detail each step of a business-related process, including customer support procedures, product development activities, incident response procedures, and the change management process. A formal change management process gives specific procedures for requesting, planning, and making changes on a network, and clearly defined standards for how to categorize the significance and priority of a proposed change. You'll need to incorporate this change management process into your cloud migration.

Change Management

Change management provides carefully defined processes to evaluate the need for a change, the cost of the change, a plan for making the change with minimal disruption, and a backup plan if the change doesn't work as expected. Change management processes rely on extensive documentation. At each step, be sure to refer to documentation frequently, following standard operating procedures for your organization and factoring in documentation and guidelines from the CSP. It's easy to forget a small step that can fail the entire migration, such as updating DNS records. For example, when migrating email services to the cloud, you'll need to update MX (mail exchange) records on your DNS servers on the day of your migration. Notably, most of the migration process itself will be performed using CLI-based commands or, more likely, will be automated through automation scripts or migration tools from CSPs or third-party vendors. These tools can help you perform the migration, check configurations along the way, and troubleshoot problems that arise. Additionally, automation scripts and logs from migration tools will provide documentation for troubleshooting issues or for future reference.

Your company might rely on any of several theoretical models to guide its change management process. The best-known model is the standards set forth by ITIL (IT Infrastructure Library), which is a collection of publications that defines many kinds of best practices in IT. These models typically follow steps that define the change, consider its implications, implement the change, and evaluate the outcome. Many of these models emphasize the human factor as well, including steps for inviting user input and helping those affected to understand the need for the change to ensure user acceptance before the change is implemented.

Note 1

ITIL (IT Infrastructure Library) publications are currently produced by Axelos (axelos.com), which is a joint venture between the OGC (Office of Government Commerce) in the United Kingdom and Capita Plc (capita.com), a BPO (business process outsourcing) company based in London. The latest version, ITIL 4, was released in early 2019 and overhauls the entire framework with a greater emphasis on agility, DevOps, and collaboration across an organization. Axelos offers a handful of highly respected ITIL certifications, starting with the ITIL 4 Foundation certification.

The following are highlights of a typical change management process:

1. *Change request*—A change initiator determines the need for a change and submits a formal change request that covers details about the requested change—including the purpose and scope of the change, its importance, and how to implement the change. You can download a copy of a sample change request form from the CDC (Centers for Disease Control and Prevention) at www2a.cdc.gov/cdcup/library/templates/CDC_UP_Change_Request_Form_Example.doc, or search for "cdc change request form" to find an updated link.

2. *Change assessment*—The change coordinator reviews change requests and processes those requests to create a change proposal. The proposal includes a thorough explanation of the change and the need for that change, a priority rating, a plan for the change as if it will proceed (including timeline and needed resources), a risk analysis detailing how the change will impact various business processes and resources (such as network availability or revenue losses), a backout plan in the event the change is not successful,

and an explanation of risks involved in *not* making the change. The change coordinator also conducts a small-scale test of the change, if possible. To complete the approval process, the approver accepts or rejects change requests or, if the change coordinator determines the change is needed but also brings high risks to business resources, a CAB (change advisory board) reviews the change request and makes a final determination of whether to proceed with the change. If necessary, an ECAB (emergency change advisory board) can meet quickly, such as in an online conference call, to make decisions on changes classified as emergencies.

3. *Change implementation*—If approvals are obtained from all appropriate decision makers, the change is performed by the change implementation team, which might consist of one or more managers, specialists, and technicians. Scheduling is carefully managed to minimize disruptive impact on users and interrelated systems.

4. *Change review*—Reviewing the change after it's completed and its effects on the business is an essential step to determine whether the change was successful, what unexpected effects might have occurred, and how the change management process can be fine-tuned for future use.

5. *Change documentation*—The change is thoroughly documented, including timeline, expenses, troubleshooting, and results. As the final validation and analyses of the migration results are performed, any lessons learned should be documented to inform efforts on the next migration. Finally, any configuration changes, hardware upgrades, or software adjustments should also be well documented. These items might be tracked in a simple spreadsheet or in a more sophisticated CMDB (configuration management database). Configuration management is a critical component of asset management, which tracks valuable resources throughout their respective life cycles.

> ## Grow with Cengage Unlimited!
>
> If you'd like more information about managing changes on a network, use your Cengage Unlimited subscription to go to *CompTIA Network+ Guide to Networks*, 9th edition, Module 2, and read the section titled "Change Management."
> If you don't have a Cengage Unlimited subscription, you can find more information at cengage.com/unlimited.

Deployment Automation

As mentioned earlier, some parts of a migration plan might be automated; collectively, these steps are called a workflow. Figure 3-4 shows an amusing example of a workflow for the simple process of how to handle a spam caller. Notice the various symbols used. The diagram begins with some kind of input presented in an oval, change occurs through decisions (diamonds) and processes (rectangles), and then the result of the workflow is the output.

Automation reduces the overall time and cost of the migration as well as the potential for mistakes or unplanned downtime. Automation also affects the efficiency of the sync between the source and target hosts. As your resources are spread across both the old and new network during the migration process, a differentiation between the on-prem data and the cloud-hosted data is created if the data continues to change during the migration. The difference between the two is called a delta, like the Greek letter Δ that in math represents a change in some value. This difference must be accounted for so the cloud data is completely up to date with the latest changes to the on-prem data before decommissioning your on-prem services. Differences are minimized by completing the migration as quickly as possible. This is one area where automation can have a significant impact.

Technicians will orchestrate the many interrelated automated processes ahead of time. A detailed workflow diagram shows the order of tasks performed as well as the reports that will be generated. These automated processes should then be tested before relying on them in a live migration. If this is part of your migration process, execute each workflow in an orderly manner, and validate the results before moving on. Orchestration and automation continue to be a significant part of cloud management after each migration project is complete. A later module will discuss automation concepts more extensively.

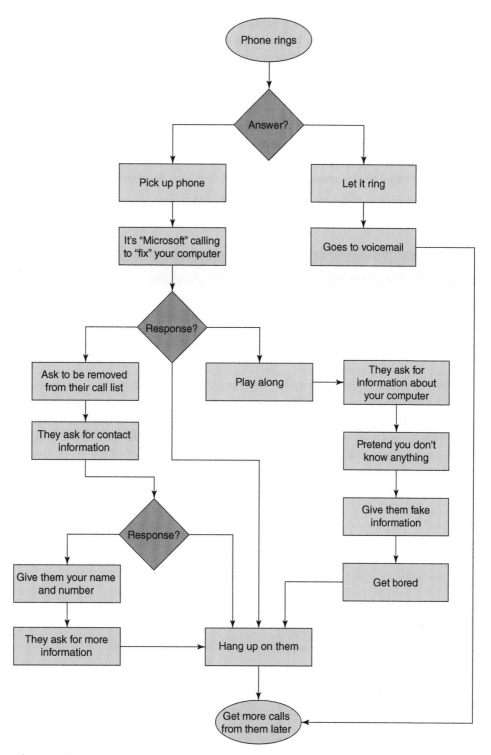

Figure 3-4   A simple workflow for handling spam calls

Data Transfer

Besides timing issues, getting your data from your data center into the cloud presents additional challenges related to both security and bandwidth. Organizations can choose from several data transfer methodologies, depending on how much data they need to migrate and how quickly, including the following:

- *Public Internet*—Online transfers over the public Internet can support small or slow data migrations. For example, over a 1 Gbps connection, it would take about 12 days to upload 100 TB of data—*if* there's no throttling, interference, or interruption.

- *Private connection*—Online transfers over a private connection can offer more dedicated bandwidth, cutting upload to a fraction of the cheaper, public Internet options. However, a private connection often requires a long-term contract with an ISP and paying for a direct connection into the CSP's POP (point of presence), which is typically located at an IX or IXP (Internet exchange point) facility or some other colocation facility ("col" or "colo" for short) shared by multiple providers of various types. The capital investment required for this method is most cost-effective when there will be a steady stream of data over a long period of time, there's one data center, and all the data is destined for one cloud location. However, this arrangement also can result in vendor lock-in, which refers to the ominous expense of changing vendors that often prevents customers from considering competitors' products once they've reached a level of commitment with an existing vendor. This means it could be expensive to transfer to a different CSP later. Further, adding services from another CSP for a multi-cloud infrastructure might not allow you to take full advantage of the expensive private connection unless that other CSP also has a presence at the same colocation facility.

Grow with Cengage Unlimited!

If you'd like more information about private WAN (wide area network) connections, use your Cengage Unlimited subscription to go to *CompTIA Network+ Guide to Networks*, 9th edition, Module 9, and read the section titled "WAN Connectivity." If you don't have a Cengage Unlimited subscription, you can find more information at cengage.com/unlimited.

- *Offline transfer*—An offline transfer consists of loading encrypted data onto a storage appliance and then physically shipping that appliance to the CSP, either by a common package-delivery service or via a dedicated transport. Upon arrival, the CSP uploads the data to the cloud, where the client can configure the data as needed. These appliances are appropriate for terabyte- or petabyte-scale data migrations. Examples include AWS's Snowball, Azure's Data Box, and Google's Transfer Appliance. AWS offers an exabyte-scale data transport service called Snowmobile (see Figure 3-5) that relies on a secure 45-foot ruggedized shipping container carried by a semitrailer truck. If you ever attend an AWS conference, you might be lucky enough to catch this truck on display.

Source: Amazon Web Services, Inc.

Figure 3-5   Snowmobile can transfer up to 100 PB per trip

Note 2

One of the first customers to use AWS Snowmobile was Maxar Technologies (formerly called DigitalGlobe), a provider of satellite imagery. You can watch a video about its transfer experience on YouTube at youtu.be/iB86NtOyw4E or search for "AWS Snowmobile DigitalGlobe".

For context, an exabyte equals a little over one quintillion (10^{18}) bytes, or one billion gigabytes. Five exabytes would approximately equal the text of all the words ever spoken by human beings. Common data units are listed in Table 3-1 to help you visualize the relative scale of each unit.

Table 3-1   Common units of data

Unit	Size	Example
Byte (B)	8 bits	One unit of information, such as a single character in ASCII (American Standard Code for Information Interchange)
Kilobyte (KB)	1024 bytes	Two or three paragraphs of text
Megabyte (MB)	1024 kilobytes	Almost 900 pages of text
Gigabyte (GB)	1024 megabytes	Almost 4500 books, or about 640 webpages
Terabyte (TB)	1024 gigabytes	More than 650,000 webpages, or about 40 25-GB Blu-ray discs
Petabyte (PB)	1024 terabytes	Almost 42,000 25-GB Blu-ray discs
Exabyte (EB)	1024 petabytes	Almost 43,000,000 25-GB Blu-ray discs

Note 3

Recall that kilobytes, megabytes, and so on are calculated based on multiples of 10. So 1 KB is 1000 bytes. Kibibytes (KiB), mebibytes (MiB), and so on are calculated based on powers of 2. Therefore, 1 KiB is 1024 bytes. The same holds true for megabytes and mebibytes, where 1 MB is 1000 KB, and 1 MiB is 1024 KiB.

Not many people are aware of this distinction, much less in the habit of using the binary prefixes Ki, Mi, and others as the unit of measurement when referring to the power of 2 system. Common usage allows for referring to, for example, KB as the unit of measurement when really the actual number would be more accurately represented by KiB. However, you will likely see the more accurate units (KiB, MiB, etc.) when configuring resources in common cloud platforms, such as AWS and Azure.

VM Migrations

Common types of data that might need to be migrated to the cloud—or between clouds—are server images, data files, and databases. While you can create new VMs from scratch, as you've seen, you can also migrate an existing physical machine to a VM. Migrating VMs is a fairly common task, especially when transitioning to the cloud, and many tools are available to help you with this process. The following list describes some common migration types:

- *P2V (physical to virtual)*—P2V (physical to virtual) is the process of migrating an OS and its dependencies (configurations, applications, and data) from a physical machine to a virtual one. The physical machine is saved as a snapshot or image, the VM is created with the appropriate resources (including vCPUs, memory, storage space, and network configurations), and the snapshot is installed on the new VM. This process is commonly used, for example, to salvage a system from an aging physical server or to consolidate several physical servers onto a single host managed by a hypervisor.

- *V2V (virtual to virtual)*—V2V (virtual to virtual) is the migration of a VM from one host system to another. Often the transition is made because of the need to upgrade host hardware, the host OS, or the hypervisor, or for the purpose of transitioning to a cloud-based host. V2V also plays a role in disaster recovery. In some cases, migrations can be done while the VM is still running, which is called online migration or live migration. Most of the time, this process is handled internally by the hypervisor. The primary challenges in a live migration are matching the CPU architecture between hosts (such as number of cores and advanced CPU features) and matching virtual network configurations.

- *V2P (virtual to physical)*—V2P (virtual to physical) is the process of migrating an OS and its dependencies from a virtual machine to a physical one. The V2P tool (not a hypervisor) confirms the physical hardware is compatible with the VM, creates the VM image, and installs it on the physical machine along with the needed device drivers. V2P might be used when recovering a physical system from a VM backup.
- *P2P (physical to physical)*—While it seems out of place in a discussion on virtualization and cloud, you also need to know about P2P (physical to physical), which is the migration of an OS and its dependencies from one physical machine to another. This is especially useful when upgrading hardware. Some of the tools that can perform P2V or V2P can also perform P2P.

Note 4

Although not included in the Cloud+ exam, some organizations use "C" to refer to cloud-hosted machines instead of generically referring to both virtual machines and cloud-hosted instances with "V." For example, C2C is a migration from one cloud to another. V2C is a migration from virtual instances on your own network to cloud-hosted instances.

When moving VMs to the cloud, you'll need to consider the source and destination format of the workload. This includes operating systems, VM sizes, infrastructure services, application and data portability, and application licensing. Many of these details will be explored further as you dig deeper into the migration process. Specific to the VM migration itself, however, consider these factors:

- *Platform*—Different CSPs support various OSs for VMs. You might run into problems if you need an older, obscure, or customized OS.
- *Virtualization format*—Two primary components of a VM must be considered when migrating machines from one system to another: the VM's system image or snapshot, and the VM's virtual hard drive or storage space. Each of these parts is managed using different file formats:
  - *VM image*—The most common file format of a VM's image is OVF (Open Virtualization Format), which is an open-source standard for VM images consisting of multiple files in a single package. In contrast, CSPs often use their own VM image file type. For example, AWS uses AMIs (Amazon Machine Images) and includes a conversion tool that allows the user to import and export VM images between AWS and an existing virtualization environment.
  - *Storage drive*—The storage drive image is a single, large image file. VM storage drive file formats include VMDK (Virtual Machine Disk), VDI (Virtual Disk Image), and VHD (Virtual Hard Disk). VMDK, an open file format originally developed by VMware, is the most common. VDI is used by default in VirtualBox, and VHD is commonly used by Microsoft. It's possible to convert between these file formats using a tool such as qemu-img, which is part of the QEMU (Quick Emulator) project (qemu.org).
  - *Both*—A file format that packages both these pieces and any other dependencies into a single, compressed file is OVA (Open Virtual Appliance). The OVA file must be extracted before it can be imported into a hypervisor.
- *Connection types*—Network connections from a system to its network can affect connectivity to resources or to the machine itself after migration. For example, if either SSH's (Secure Shell) port 22 or RDP's (Remote Desktop Protocol) port 3389 is not enabled on the new VM, you won't be able to access it remotely. IP addressing must be carefully configured, other network options set correctly (such as DNS and gateway information), and firewalls configured with necessary allow or deny permissions.

Grow with Cengage Unlimited!

If you'd like more information about protocols used to create remote connections, use your Cengage Unlimited subscription to go to *CompTIA Network+ Guide to Networks*, 9th edition, Module 4, and read the section titled "Remote Access Protocols."

If you don't have a Cengage Unlimited subscription, you can find more information at cengage.com/unlimited.

Storage Migration

Expensive data transfer options are most relevant when migrating a large amount of storage data to the cloud. Storage migration is the process of moving blocks or volumes of data from one storage medium to another. A VM migration might include storage migration if the VM's storage drive must be moved along with the VM's configuration data. Storage migration can also be performed unrelated to VM migration. An organization might choose to move stored data, such as file repositories or large databases, from one physical medium to another, from older hardware to newer machines, or from a physical storage network to a virtual one, or it might choose to combine data from multiple sources. The data itself typically is not changed during migration. The process requires consideration of several factors, including the following:

- *Streamlining*—Before beginning any migration, unneeded data should be removed. For example, orphaned records can be cleared from a database, or archived data separated from active data and stored in a different location. Streamlining is especially helpful when data is stored in the cloud, as archive storage is significantly cheaper than storage types that must be more accessible.
- *Capacity*—Sufficient space for existing data should be provisioned with additional capacity available for anticipated growth over the next three to five years.
- *Migration path*—A migration path determines how data will be transferred from the old location to the new one. This includes providing sufficient bandwidth and transfer time, especially if the data will be transmitted over a WAN connection.
- *Security*—Data must be protected in transit to the new storage location, and it might need a different form of protection once it's in place. This is especially important for cloud-based storage. Carefully consider any relevant compliance regulations, depending on the type and sensitivity of the data. Also consider any changes or updates needed for a disaster recovery plan.
- *Scheduling*—If the system will be taken offline at any point during the migration, plans should be made to allow downtime when it will be least disruptive to users. Online migrations might still involve a small amount of downtime, while offline migrations could require several hours to days of downtime for users.
- *Rollback plan*—Problems happen. It's easier to plan for them than to be surprised when they happen. An established rollback plan before beginning the migration process will identify what events would trigger the rollback plan and what steps are needed to restore the original storage configuration.

Cloud-to-Cloud Migrations

Once a company creates a cloud presence, its migration journey is not complete. There are times when a company might need to migrate from one cloud platform to another, from one vendor to another. For example, another cloud provider might offer better financial incentives, increased security measures, better scalability options, or resource types that better fit the company's objectives. Similarly, a cloud customer might decide to migrate their application, data, or other function from one cloud service to another within the same platform. For example, a company using EC2 in AWS to host a database might decide to migrate its database to AWS's Aurora service, which is designed to provide a native, cloud-hosted database experience. This is called a cross-service migration and can often be performed more easily using a cloud provider's in-platform migration tools. One example is AWS's DMS (Database Migration Service), as shown in Figure 3-6.

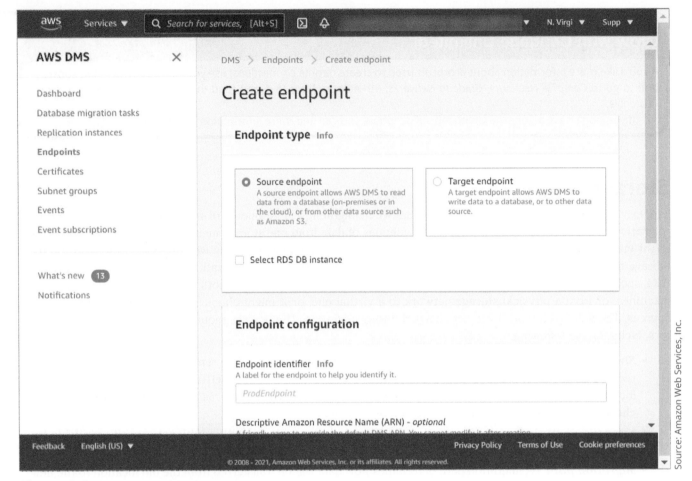

Figure 3-6   A cross-service migration tool

The simplest migrations shift resources from one vendor's platform or cloud service to another without requiring significant changes to the application's or data's underlying structure. For example, migrating an application from one SaaS vendor to another is typically simpler than refactoring an IaaS-hosted application for a SaaS deployment.

The following list describes some common concerns when migrating from one SaaS to another SaaS or from one PaaS to another PaaS:

- *Compatibility*—Some SaaS and PaaS providers offer standardized compatibility that eases a migration into or out of the provider's platform. But not all of them do. Some providers intentionally create a proprietary environment where the components of a system cannot be migrated from one platform to another. It's important to consider this factor before committing to a vendor. Similarly, your company has likely applied some customizations to its existing service. Consider whether these customizations will transfer, what modifications might have to be made, how long that will take, and what effect those changes will have on users' experience of the application or data.

- *Porting data*—Usually, one of the components you'll want to migrate is data. Sometimes a SaaS or PaaS provider offers the ability to export data in a standardized format, such as a .csv file or a .xlsx file. Again, this is a factor to consider before choosing the initial vendor to allow for the possibility of changing platforms in the future. When shopping vendors, also consider whether the export format from the current provider's platform can be imported to the new provider's platform.

- *Compliance*—Federal and industry regulations are designed to protect certain kinds of data, and many of these compliance issues apply when moving data from one location to another. Protected data must be protected when in use, in motion, and at rest.

- *Tenancy*—Whether a service is currently hosted on-prem or in the cloud, the target system might offer a different tenancy structure. For example, some cloud-to-cloud migrations involve a shift from single tenancy, where the application is hosted on a dedicated server or a single cloud, to multitenancy, where the application will be distributed across multiple physical hosts or even multiple clouds. A change in tenancy can affect how an application functions and might require some refactoring.

- *Security*—Security configurations can be distributed throughout a cloud deployment in ways the customer might not completely be aware of. When migrating to another cloud provider, it's important to evaluate all relevant security settings to ensure traffic is blocked where it should be and also that access is allowed where it should be. For example, firewall rules or ACLs (access control lists) are often not ported automatically during a migration, especially for PaaS and SaaS migrations.

- *Downtime*—During any planned or possible downtime, users should be kept informed, and the migration should be scheduled at a time when it will have the least impact on users. Keep in mind you might face downtime not just for the service being migrated but also for other services that rely on this service's processes or data.

- *Performance comparisons*—After the migration, KPIs from before and after the migration should be compared to confirm the new service is performing as expected. Additional fine-tuning of the deployment after migration will help to achieve target KPIs.

One of the reasons for a cloud-to-cloud migration is often to save money. Monitor costs going forward and determine if your new deployment is sufficiently optimized for cost benefits. Any cost or billing issues and concerns should be raised with the vendor to ensure you're getting the benefits you were promised.

Remember This

- Change management provides carefully defined processes to evaluate the need for a change, the cost of the change, a plan for making the change with minimal disruption, and a backup plan if the change doesn't work as expected.
- Automation reduces overall time and cost of the migration as well as potential for mistakes or unplanned downtime.
- Organizations can choose from several data transfer methodologies, depending on how much data they need to migrate and how quickly, including the public Internet, a private connection, or an offline transfer.
- Common VM migration processes include P2V (physical to virtual), V2V (virtual to virtual), V2P (virtual to physical), and P2P (physical to physical).
- Storage migration is the process of moving blocks or volumes of data from one storage medium to another.
- A cross-service migration is the migration of a resource from one service type in a cloud platform to a different service type in the same platform and often can be performed more easily using a cloud provider's in-platform migration tools.

Self-Check

4. Who submits a change request?
   - **a.** Change coordinator
   - **b.** Change advisory board
   - **c.** Change initiator
   - **d.** Change implementation team

5. Which data transfer methodology requires a long-term commitment?
   - **a.** Offline transfer
   - **b.** Private connection
   - **c.** Dedicated transport
   - **d.** Public Internet

6. Which migration type is most likely used to restore a physical server from backup?
   - **a.** P2P
   - **b.** V2V
   - **c.** P2V
   - **d.** V2P

○ Check your answers at the end of this module.

Section 3-3: Deployment Testing and Validation

Certification

1.2 Explain the factors that contribute to capacity planning.

1.3 Explain the importance of high availability and scaling in cloud environments.

1.4 Given a scenario, analyze the solution design in support of the business requirements.

2.4 Given a scenario, apply data security and compliance controls in cloud environments.

2.5 Given a scenario, implement measures to meet security requirements.

3.1 Given a scenario, integrate components into a cloud solution.

4.3 Given a scenario, optimize cloud environments.

5.3 Given a scenario, troubleshoot deployment issues.

5.4 Given a scenario, troubleshoot connectivity issues.

During and after the migration, extensive testing is needed to ensure the migration goes smoothly and the outcome meets business requirements. Formal testing strategies define various approaches to the testing process to validate different aspects of the deployment. This section discusses testing types and considerations as well as some of the problems this testing might reveal.

Testing Types

You might have performed some testing during the planning stage to help ensure that any component moved to the cloud—such as a database, application, or server—would work well in the cloud environment. Testing is often done by cloning the resource or environment into the cloud and then running tests on this temporary copy. On the upside, this approach allows you to experiment with changes to the resource being tested and to try out different CSPs to determine which works best for you before you commit to one. On the downside, the cloned resource is not synced with its source data and might not have live data streams to work with. Still, this step can be highly informative.

Two additional rounds of testing occur after the data has made it to your cloud: both before and after going live in your cloud environment. There are a variety of testing techniques used to explore a new deployment, including the following:

Exam Tip ✔

The CompTIA Cloud+ exam is known to ask questions requiring you to differentiate between testing techniques, when each is appropriate to use for a specific objective, or what issue a particular test type might reveal.

- *Functional testing*—Functional testing ensures that predefined system requirements are met. Basically, this process confirms everything works as it should. Some approaches to functional testing test an individual component, which is called component testing or module testing. Further, some kinds of functional testing include initial checks during development, called smoke testing (based on the saying, "Where there's smoke, there's fire," and implies a small problem early on could cause a serious issue later).

- *Performance testing*—Performance testing checks for compatibility issues, especially for any programs that rely heavily on each other to perform complex tasks.

- *Load testing*—Load testing pushes the limits of the cloud environment to ensure that it can handle the anticipated workload and to see how well the environment auto-scales as user demand increases and decreases. Load testing can be done manually or automatically and often involves both methods. The data collected during load testing informs auto-scaling threshold configurations. Carefully plan and monitor this phase of testing to avoid accruing unnecessary costs from auto-scaled resources.

- *Regression testing*—When you change one system, this can affect other systems in unexpected ways. **Regression testing** confirms that changes to one system haven't negatively impacted other functions within that system or other systems in the network. This type of testing is not necessarily limited to the system under development—interdependent systems might also be tested to determine if the new system's changes will have unintended effects throughout the network.

- *Usability testing*—During the development process, **usability testing** asks users to test the system while developers observe the users and the system. This is a form of black-box testing and might also be called acceptance testing or UAT (user acceptance testing). The acquired information helps developers identify problems that might cause confusion for users. For example, are instructions clear? Do components function the way users expect? Does the system perform well when nontechnical users, who don't have knowledge of the background design and processes of the system, interact with it? Phases of usability testing might include alpha testing or beta testing.

- *Security testing*—Security testing includes both **vulnerability testing** or vulnerability assessment, which looks for application liabilities or gaps in protection of sensitive data, and **pen (penetration) testing**, which attempts to take advantage of vulnerabilities. Either of these testing types might result in a VRR (vulnerability remediation request). Before performing any security testing in the cloud, be sure to study the CSP's guidelines and restrictions on testing and get any necessary approvals from the CSP, as unauthorized security testing could result in loss of use from the provider or severe financial penalties.

Grow with Cengage Unlimited!

If you'd like more information about vulnerability and penetration testing, use your Cengage Unlimited subscription to go to *CompTIA Security+ Guide to Network Security Fundamentals*, 7th edition, Module 2, and read the sections titled "Penetration Testing" and "Vulnerability Scanning."

If you don't have a Cengage Unlimited subscription, you can find more information at cengage.com/unlimited.

Testing in the cloud often requires a different set of tools from what is used for testing in a physical environment, especially for load testing that is designed to ensure **auto-scaling**, which is the automatic increase or decrease of capacity as needed. Many CSPs offer testing tools optimized for their platforms.

Testing might also require help from users who are familiar with the resources being evaluated. For example, an accounting application is best understood by the accountants on staff and so can best be evaluated and challenged by a tech-savvy accountant. Coordinate testing efforts so the appropriate migration team members are available to process feedback as it comes in from these users.

Testing Considerations

Imagine you work for a company named Sisko Enterprises that owns and manages long-term care facilities. Sisko began its migration with a test run moving a simple application to the cloud, one that tracked travel expenses for some of its medical staff. The migration went well, and with increased confidence, IT next transitioned the company to Office 365 for email, office productivity applications, and basic file storage. Their most recent migration effort is currently in progress: transitioning the home office's server infrastructure to the cloud with plans to migrate all satellite office networks to the cloud in the future. But first, the migration team must perform validation testing before going live with the newly migrated servers.

As part of the migration team, your job is to help identify all the components and characteristics of your cloud deployment that should be validated before going live with the new migration. Items on your list include the following:

- *Proper functionality*—Simply put, make sure everything works as it should. For example, directory names and file sharing shouldn't have changed unless you intended for them to. Interactions between the server and applications it hosts should perform as expected, and, if relevant, applications should present to users the same as before the migration. Verify logging is functioning well, capturing all activities as desired.

- *Data integrity*—Migrated data should not show any indications of errors or incomplete transition, whether that data is being moved to the cloud or being replicated in the cloud as a backup. You might use testing tools to help with this process. With a database, you can run queries on both the source and the target databases to see if both yield the same results; also check that both have the same number of records. Remember to check for any changes to the source data since the time the data was copied to the cloud.

- *Connectivity*—Test the quality of connections between your location and your cloud, as well as between shared components within the cloud, such as compute, network, and storage components. Network latency is one of the biggest obstacles to a well-functioning cloud, so be sure to confirm connectivity performance is within acceptable parameters. Also check that all interfaces are configured correctly and that users can access all resources as expected from the geographical locations where these resources are needed.

- *Availability*—Any redundancies that are part of your high-availability plan should be tested, such as redundant CPUs, network connections, servers, or storage connections. Simulate a failure by shutting down one of the redundancies and evaluate the performance of the other parts of the system. How quickly does the system compensate for the loss? Is any data lost in the interim? Also check any data replication system to ensure that data can be recovered and restored from backup.

- *Security*—Check that data is adequately encrypted both at rest and in transit, and possibly in use as well (some modern encryption methods can encrypt data in use while it resides in RAM). Check virtual firewall configurations, and make sure all default usernames and passwords have been changed. Ensure that authentication and access control mechanisms are functioning properly.

- *Sizing*—The physical hardware supporting your cloud should be sized appropriately to meet your needs in balance with your budget, which is called rightsizing. When hosting your own private cloud, this is your responsibility. When using a CSP's cloud, they'll take care of this part. You also need to check sizing of allocated virtual resources, such as vCPUs, vRAM, and storage space.

- *Monitoring*—Check that all systems are reporting to monitoring services in ways that yield expected information. You might need to reconfigure dashboards, adjust log filters, or fine-tune reporting thresholds.

Test Analysis

As you design your testing plan, anticipate how to analyze the results that you'll obtain. The information you gather can be compared to any standards defined by your change management documentation and the SLA provided by your CSP. This document identifies minimum performance benchmarks and maximum downtimes for specific services. You'll need to refer back to this document occasionally during the course of any service subscription you maintain, so be sure you thoroughly understand the commitments made by the vendor and your options for recourse should performance fall short of guaranteed minimums or maximums.

You'll also need to compare test results to baselines collected before the migration began. Check your baselines for KPIs such as CPU usage, RAM usage, storage utilization, network utilization, and application and patch versions. Thoroughly document these results. Also confirm that auditing is enabled so logs are properly collected. You want to target actions and events that will give you an accurate picture of what's happening with your cloud resources without overwhelming your logs with useless information. Certain management tools involved in monitoring resources can send live data feeds to your dashboard. Ensure these dashboards are well configured to show the metrics you need to monitor.

> **You're Ready**
>
> You're now ready to complete Project 3-2: Research Third-Party Migration Tools and Services. You can complete the project now or wait until you've finished all the readings for this module.

Common Deployment Issues

Despite the best-laid plans, things still go wrong during cloud migrations. Knowing more about what to expect and how to handle the more common issues will prepare you to manage problems quickly and minimize disruption of services. Common issues in cloud deployments include the following:

- *Resource contention*—Resource contention refers to the demand many workloads make on limited resources, such as processing power, memory, or network bandwidth. On-prem, it's your responsibility to provide sufficient hardware and network support for the workloads you're running. In the cloud, you rely on the CSP to provide sufficient resources so that other customers' workloads don't interfere with your own ability to receive reliable and dependable service. If your CSP is not providing this level of service, you might find yourself needing to migrate to a different CSP. Benchmark testing before, during, and after migration can help minimize the likelihood of resource contention being an issue.

- *Template misconfiguration*—When creating or migrating servers, template misconfigurations can have serious implications for security, in addition to concerns about functionality and connectivity. Leaving remote access channels such as SSH or RDP open to the Internet makes servers vulnerable to attack, as does missing software updates or leaving wide-open permissions. There are many tools available to help monitor and audit server configurations, such as AWS's CloudTrail. Server images should be scanned when first created and again any time a change is made. Regular configuration audits after migration are also essential. Image management services, such as AWS's EC2 Image Builder, can help with building, testing, and updating images used to deploy servers.

- *CSP or ISP outage*—Widely reaching CSP outages, which could affect a single service or even the entire platform, are somewhat rare but, when they happen, can deeply disrupt your organization's ability to do business. Similarly, while a CSP outage can affect your customers directly, an ISP outage can interfere with your own ability to reach your cloud services. Larger companies likely have redundancies, such as multiple ISP connections to their premises and multiple cloud-based resources for critical functions, and they possibly even have cyber-insurance to cover unavoidable losses. Smaller businesses, however, are more vulnerable to outages. Redundancies across platforms and across regions within a platform, as well as backups stored in a location separate from your primary CSP (such as in another platform or on-prem), can reduce the negative impact of an outage.

- *Platform integration issue*—While a hybrid or multi-cloud can help reduce risks related to a CSP outage or vendor lock-in, integrating services across multiple platforms also introduces compatibility issues. Many CSPs and other vendors offer products that help address these issues. The reliance of cloud services on APIs helps open communication between platforms, and new tools are being developed to take advantage of this interactive layer. Staff training is also a crucial component of an organization's ability to take full advantage of the features and tools offered by various cloud platforms.

- *Licensing outage*—Many kinds of licenses, such as subscription licenses for Office 365 or pay-as-you-go licenses for AWS services, require ongoing payments to maintain the license. If the bill doesn't get paid, the licenses expire. This might seem like a minor thing, and yet it can cause major problems. SLM (software license management) can help minimize license expenses by eliminating unneeded licenses and renewing licenses before expiration, thereby avoiding fees or legal fines. Keep license documents and receipts in a central repository (not your email inbox) and set reminders or appointments in your calendar or schedule email reminders to yourself to renew or update licenses periodically.

Note 5

Subscription licensing requires the customer to pay a monthly or annual fee per user or per device for as long as they use the license. Essentially, the customer is leasing a license rather than purchasing it. If they stop paying the regular fee, they can no longer use the software or service covered by the subscription. Many cloud services are covered by this type of subscription-based payment, such as the following:

- Email and messaging services
- File storage services
- VoIP (Voice over IP) services
- A SaaS that provides collaboration tools (such as project scheduling or instant messaging) to support remote team members
- VDI or DaaS (Desktop as a Service) services that offer access to different OSs or various configurations of installed applications

- *Time synchronization issue*—Due to irregularities in Earth's rate of rotation, occasionally an extra second must be added to UTC (Coordinated Universal Time), which is called a leap second. These leap seconds can offset the accuracy of network and system clocks. To increase synchronization accuracy across cloud-based resources, many CSPs offer a time service, such as AWS's Amazon Time Sync Service, which operates by default on all EC2 instances and connects through the internal IP address 169.254.169.123. Time services rely on NTP (Network Time Protocol) to sync clocks across a network and smooth out these leap seconds in a process called leap smearing.

Note 6

The abbreviation UTC for universal time was agreed upon as a compromise between English and French authorities. English speakers wanted the abbreviation CUT (coordinated universal time), and French speakers wanted TUC (*temps universel coordonné*).

Note 7

Most CSPs offer troubleshooting support in multiple languages. The list of available languages continues to expand.

Remember This

- Common testing techniques include functional testing, performance testing, load testing, regression testing, usability testing, and security testing.
- Rightsizing balances performance requirements and capacity needs with budgetary restrictions.
- An SLA (service level agreement) identifies minimum performance benchmarks and maximum downtimes for specific services and defines options for recourse should performance fall short of guaranteed minimums or maximums.
- Common deployment issues include resource contention, template misconfiguration, CSP or ISP outages, platform integration issues, licensing outages, and time synchronization issues.

Self-Check

7. What kind of testing would detect unintended changes to an interdependent system?
   - **a.** Usability testing
   - **b.** Regression testing
   - **c.** Vulnerability testing
   - **d.** Performance testing

8. Which feature ensures a resource adjusts size to meet demand?
   - **a.** Rightsizing
   - **b.** Online migration
   - **c.** Orchestration
   - **d.** Auto-scaling

9. Which problem can result in an inappropriately opened RDP port?
   - **a.** Licensing outage
   - **b.** Template misconfiguration
   - **c.** Platform integration issue
   - **d.** Resource contention

○ Check your answers at the end of this module.

Section 3-4: Cloud Agility

Certification

2.3 Given a scenario, apply the appropriate OS and application security controls.

3.1 Given a scenario, integrate components into a cloud solution.

4.4 Given a scenario, apply proper automation and orchestration techniques.

As you've learned, cloud computing relies heavily on virtualization technologies. Cloud-hosted, software-defined infrastructure can therefore be configured and managed using techniques more common to software development than to hardware management. Many of the processes that support adaptive, agile software development are now being applied to cloud deployments. This section discusses some of these overlapping approaches and innovations.

Project Management

Now that you've seen how cloud migration works, you might realize that your role in this project relies on more than the technical skills of how to deploy a VM or how to configure a network interface. Many IT professionals in the thick of a cloud migration find themselves leaning less on their technical knowledge and more on project management skills.

A **project** is an effort that has a clearly defined beginning and ending. A project involves many processes that are generally grouped into five categories: initiating, planning, executing, monitoring and controlling, and closing (see Figure 3-7). **Project management**, then, is the application of specific skills, tools, and techniques to manage these processes in such a way that the desired outcome is achieved.

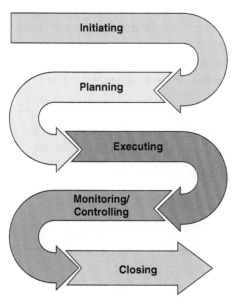

Figure 3-7   The five project management process groups

There are several popular certifications related to project management, including the following:

- PMP (Project Management Professional) by PMI (Project Management Institute at pmi.org)
- CSSBB (Certified Six Sigma Black Belt) by ASQ (American Society for Quality at asq.org)
- CSM (Certified ScrumMaster) by the Scrum Alliance (scrumalliance.org)
- Project+, an entry-level project management certification by CompTIA (comptia.org/certifications/project)

One or more project management certifications is a nice feather in any IT professional's cap. Nearly any undertaking in IT benefits from good project management skills, and cloud computing is an excellent example of why this is true. Let's take a brief look at some key project management skills:

- *Communication*—For an industry built upon the need for communication technology, IT professionals sometimes lack in this so-called "soft skill." When asked which one skill a potential employer most wants in a new hire, the ability to communicate well often rises to the top of the list. When managing a project, good communication is even more critical, as many people are involved in various levels and phases of the project. Consistent and thorough communication also involves making good decisions in specific scenarios about communication channels used, such as emails, social media, face-to-face meetings, and online conferencing.

- *Negotiation*—Negotiating with vendors creates the opportunity to expand the reach of a limited budget. Knowing how to write good **RFPs (requests for proposal)** and negotiate favorable contractual terms will help protect your organization not if, but when, something goes wrong during a project.

- *Task and time management*—Deadlines are often the driver for pushing things through and getting people to finish what they start. Time management is the art of learning how to set realistic deadlines that ensure the project will be completed on time while not overly stressing your team. Project management can teach you how to schedule phases of a project as well as smaller, more incremental steps so the work is well paced, and everyone knows what they should be doing next.

- *Cost and quality management*—In many cases, budgets place nonnegotiable limits on a project. A team that regularly exceeds its budget will not be allowed to continue operations for long. What's more, a budget isn't a number you can set at the beginning of a project and not look at it again until you near the end. Ongoing expenses and projected costs must be continuously and closely monitored and revised. Like steering an airplane onto a landing strip, it takes a lot of planning, skill, and practice to learn how to manage costs and budgets for large projects while maintaining high quality standards.

- *Risk management*—Accepting some risks in a project will increase the likelihood that your endeavor is relevant and innovative, while minimizing unhealthy risks will prevent detrimental surprises that undermine confidence in your goals. Effective risk management, to a great degree, requires experience and maturity. Project management training will teach you how to identify the most relevant factors when considering a particular risk and propel you toward greater skill in choosing risks wisely.

- *Leadership*—The value of the ability to inspire and guide others can't be overstated. Whether you're the type of person who loves being out in front of the crowd and energizing people or you prefer to offer a quieter, more subtle form of influence, you can still be a strong leader. In fact, you don't even have to be in charge to be a leader. Anyone on the team can set the pace for focus, creativity, resourcefulness, and productivity. Project management skills help you understand how to balance the details of a project with the big picture, and how to organize communications and activities to help everyone maximize the potential of what they have to offer your team.

Application Life Cycle

A specific use of project management is in ALM (application lifecycle management). Cloud deployment design often revolves around applications hosted in the cloud. Similarly, due to its software-defined nature, much of a cloud deployment's configuration itself is managed through ALM phases, which follow the progression of an application or software-defined deployment from its conception through its retirement. The various phases are shown in Figure 3-8.

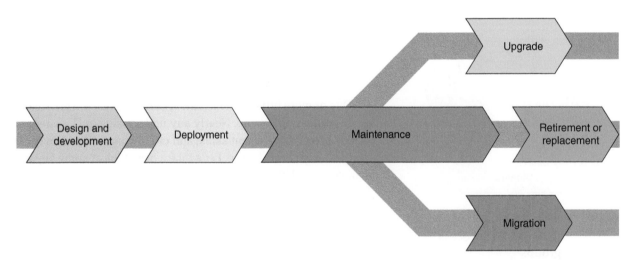

Figure 3-8 ALM (application lifecycle management) phases

The most active portion of the ALM is the software development phase, which is referred to as the SDLC (software development life cycle). In the past, organizations took a linear path to SDLC called the waterfall method. As shown in Figure 3-9, software development begins with an evaluation of the requirements, followed by work on the design, coding the application, testing functionality, and deploying the software. As with the project management process groups mentioned earlier, the waterfall method has a clearly defined beginning and ending, which can occur several months or even years apart.

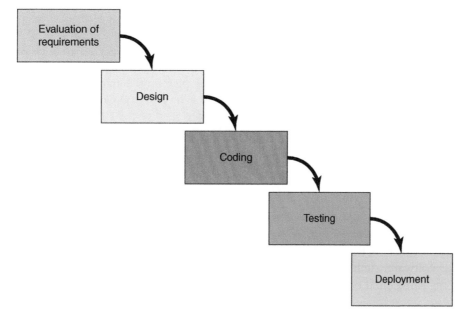

Figure 3-9   Waterfall method

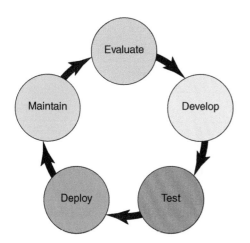

Figure 3-10   A cyclical approach to software development

With the increasing speed of technology advancement, organizations are finding the waterfall method can no longer keep up with demand. The need for more efficiency and faster response times has resulted in a continuous or cyclical software development approach that offers increased agility, which is the ability to adapt quickly to market demands according to increased or decreased feature use within an app. Figure 3-10 shows the software development cycle more commonly in use today. With this approach, software development is never finished. It keeps going. As soon as changes are deployed, new changes are already underway. Organizations accomplish this feat by making smaller changes much more frequently, sometimes as quickly as every 24 hours.

The streamlining and built-in repetition of the application life cycle, along with increased collaboration among the teams working on each app, has come to be known as DevOps (development and operations). Once an application is deployed, the data gathered from monitoring the application's use can immediately inform efforts to develop new features for the application, as shown in Figure 3-11. Continuous collaboration between development teams and operations teams brings highly responsive updates to application or software-defined deployments.

Due to the software-defined nature of cloud deployments, the DevOps culture and the emphasis on agility results in a focused effort toward collaboration among teams, automation of processes, and continuous integration and continuous delivery (often referred to together as CI/CD) of improvements and other changes.

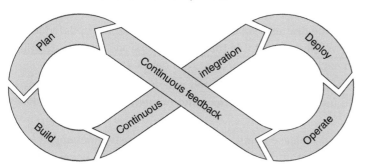

Figure 3-11   DevOps blends development and operations functions

The inherent agility of cloud technologies allows cloud admins to adjust quickly to the changing needs of an organization and its customers.

Exam Tip ✔

CI/CD generally refers to continuous integration/continuous delivery. However, the acronym occasionally refers to continuous integration/continuous deployment, which is slightly different. **Continuous deployment** is a DevOps practice that deploys new code as soon as it passes testing, rather than waiting for a scheduled release. Be sure you're familiar with all three of these terms—and the distinctions among them—for the CompTIA Cloud+ exam.

Builds

In the process of making changes to your application or other parts of your cloud deployment, you'll manage several builds, or releases, that help users identify the types of changes and stability they can expect. A **build** assembles a working application, website, or other system from source code files. Build automation in a DevOps environment can streamline releases and increase agility, which is critical for CI/CD. You might have noticed various build types released by makers of popular software, such as Microsoft Edge, Google Chrome, and Linux or Android operating systems. System iterations of the same build type are called a **channel**, as illustrated in Figure 3-12.

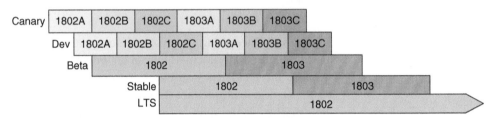

Figure 3-12 Timeline for various release channels

These different channels reflect varying degrees of previous testing, incorporation of new features, and dependability over time, as follows:

- *Canary*—A **canary build** incorporates all new changes but tends to be very unstable, despite having been tested by development teams before release.
- *Dev*—A **dev (developer) build** is released often, such as weekly, as bugs in the canary version are addressed. This build is intended for app developers who need to test their own software's compatibility with anticipated changes to a browser or OS.
- *Beta*—The **beta** release benefits from user testing on the dev and canary builds and is generally updated less often than earlier releases, such as every six weeks. While more stable than earlier versions, beta users still expect to encounter some bugs in a beta release in exchange for earlier access to new features.
- *Stable*—The **stable release** incorporates features that have been fully tested and, hopefully, is free of bugs or security gaps. The stable release is appropriate for use in a production environment. It will also receive regular updates from the developer.
- *LTS (long-term support)*—An **LTS (long-term support)** release is intended to remain mostly unchanged for two years or longer. The LTS build does not receive regular updates to features or new features because it is intended to be used in an environment where regular changes are undesirable.

Remember This

- Project management is the application of specific skills, tools, and techniques to manage a project in such a way that the desired outcome is achieved.
- Due to its software-defined nature, much of a cloud deployment's configuration is managed through ALM (application lifecycle management) phases, which follow the progression of an application or software-defined deployment from its conception through its retirement.
- Build automation in a DevOps environment can streamline releases and increase agility, which is critical for CI/CD (continuous integration/continuous delivery).

Self-Check

10. Which of the following is NOT a category of project management processes?

    a. Closing
    b. Executing
    c. Planning
    d. Securing

11. Which of the following is accomplished by a circular approach to SDLC?

    a. Latency
    b. Waterfall
    c. Agility
    d. Stability

12. Which channel incorporates user testing?

    a. Dev
    b. Stable
    c. Canary
    d. Beta

○ Check your answers at the end of this module.

Section 3-5: Planning for Problems

Certification

1.2 Explain the factors that contribute to capacity planning.

1.3 Explain the importance of high availability and scaling in cloud environments.

1.4 Given a scenario, analyze the solution design in support of the business requirements.

2.6 Explain the importance of incident response procedures.

3.1 Given a scenario, integrate components into a cloud solution.

4.3 Given a scenario, optimize cloud environments.

4.5 Given a scenario, perform appropriate backup and restore operations.

4.6 Given a scenario, perform disaster recovery tasks.

5.3 Given a scenario, troubleshoot deployment issues.

Development, testing, and troubleshooting a deployment don't end after a system is fully migrated to the cloud. In later modules, you'll learn more about the types of problems you might encounter in the cloud and the kinds of tools available to you to address these issues. This section discusses capacity-related issues and steps you can take to ensure your cloud services can continue functioning even when something goes wrong.

Capacity Limitations

While the cloud itself might be capable of supporting almost unlimited capacity for compute, storage, and networking resources, your budget might not be so flexible. Additionally, there are other limits on how far a cloud service can expand to support increased demand. Limitations on cloud capacity might be imposed by any of the following sources:

- ***CSP quotas and throttles***—As you've been completing projects throughout this course, you might have noticed limits defined on various services. For example, EC2 allows 20 on-demand t2.micro instances and 20 reserved t2.micro instances, although limits for other instance types vary. Typically, you can request an increase to these limits by contacting the CSP. With SaaS products, such as Salesforce, you'll also see limits on API requests. Recall that APIs allow for standards-based communication between different services, and a product such as Salesforce might be integrated via API with other custom applications. In that case, an API request limit throttles communications with the provider so they're not overwhelmed by one customer's API activities and can maintain optimal performance for all customers.

- ***Account owner caps***—As the account owner, you can cap usage and expenditures within your account across users. Some cloud platforms will allow you to configure budget restrictions according to service, while others will only allow you to set overall spending limits. Figure 3-13 shows configuration options for a cost budget in AWS. Budget requirements might also dictate a limit on license purchases, which restricts the number of users who can use software or other services. As the number of users varies, either the budget must be increased or users will feel the pain of not having access to the resources they need.

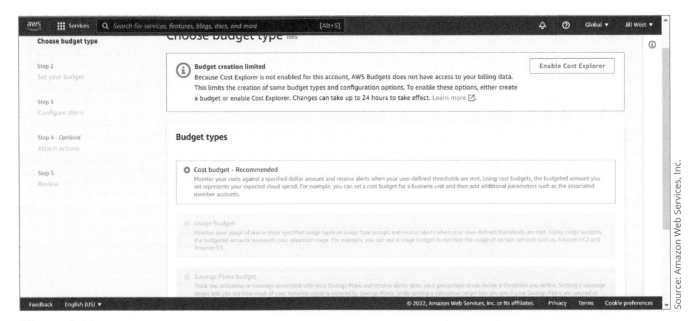

Figure 3-13   AWS offers four budget types: cost budget, usage budget, savings plans budget, and reservation budget

- ***Technology limitations***—While many limitations are set due to the cloud consumer's budgetary restrictions or the CSP's need to balance resources among customers, many other limitations are simply due to physics. For example, bandwidth limitations increase latency. Throwing money at this problem won't change the speed of light, the geographical distance between data centers, or the amount of data that can be carried across a cable at any given time. Similarly, IP address limitations require careful planning of IP address spaces, and choosing a particular VM type limits the capability of the hardware (virtual and physical) supporting that instance.

Capacity Planning

As you can see, usable cloud capacity does have its limitations. This reality requires planning and prioritizing on your part. You can then avoid problems such as VM sprawl, where forgotten instances are left running, and misappropriated or underutilized resources, such as unassigned public IP addresses or storage volumes that aren't holding much data. The following resource balancing techniques can help you better plan for cloud capacity allocations:

- Refer to your SLAs. Whether you're working under a commitment to your organization or to your customers, plan for your cloud's capacity to exceed expectations defined by the SLA. This can be accomplished partially through business continuity planning and high-availability configurations. You can also moderately overprovision resources for optimal performance and schedule auto-scaling in response to increasing demand.

- Balance reserved services, which provide stable performance, with on-demand services, which start in response to increasing demand. For example, AWS and Azure both allow you to reserve VM instances, meaning you can commit to pay for an instance over a one- or three-year period of time at a lower rate than on-demand instances that you start only as needed. This arrangement can save you as much as 70 percent of the cost of an instance and is especially useful with workloads that have a predictable minimum resource demand. However, subscribing to more reserved instances than you need during that time will reduce or eliminate the potential savings. In some cases, you're also locking yourself into a specific level of technological sophistication (such as a processor's generation) or resource utilization (such as the number of processors). Subscribing to reserved instances reduces your ability to adapt to new technologies (such as new processor generations) or changing workload needs (such as needing a different instance type) during that time frame. It also locks you into that price point even as cloud service costs continue to fall.

- Establish utilization baselines and refer to these standards when determining initial resource allocation as well as when analyzing performance trends over time as your resources deviate from the original baselines. These trends can help you forecast future resource capacity needs so you can tune cloud target objects such as compute, network, storage, and service/application resources. You can upsize, or increase, resources in anticipation of this increasing demand. Alternatively, you might find that shifting trends indicate a need to downsize, or decrease, resources. Upsizing and downsizing might look like any of the following, as illustrated in Figure 3-14:

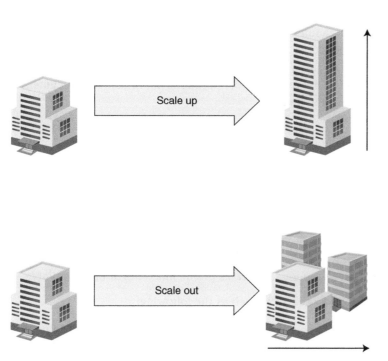

- Scale up (called **vertical scaling**) by increasing resources such as vCPUs or IOPS (input/output operations per second) allocated to an existing instance or storage container

- Scale down by reducing resources allocated per instance or container

- Scale out (called **horizontal scaling**) by increasing the number of running instances or the number of available storage containers

- Scale in by reducing the number of running instances or available storage containers

Due to the convenience of scalability in the cloud, it's easy to fall into a pattern of asymmetrical provisioning of resources. You scale up or out when you feel the pain of slow or underprovisioned resources, but then you forget to scale down or in when resources are overprovisioned. Elastic services (those that scale up/down or out/in automatically) can help with this problem; however, elasticity is

Figure 3-14   Scaling up increases the size of an existing resource while scaling out increases the number of resource instances

sometimes charged as a premium feature. Habitually configure checkpoint alarms or alerts that will identify unused or underused resources. You can also use budget alarms or spending limits that will help prevent unexpected charges, either from unplanned expansions where resources are auto-scaling beyond budgetary allowances or from resources that are running without being used. Some CSPs also offer features such as auto shutdown for VMs, which can prevent ongoing charges for instances no longer in use.

> **Exam Tip** ✔
>
> Vertical and horizontal scaling is a topic commonly covered by questions on the CompTIA Cloud+ exam. Be sure you thoroughly understand these concepts, the differences between them, and when to use one versus the other.

Business Continuity Planning

The worst disaster is the one you didn't prepare for. A disaster could be anything from a localized disruption, such as a break-in or building fire, to a regional crisis such as a flood, hurricane, or act of terrorism. While you hope that none of these things will interfere with your business activities, chances are, you'll have to face one or more significant crises at some point in your career.

At the same time, it doesn't take a disaster to interfere with your IT systems' abilities to function and meet the demands of your business. Even a small failure, if not compensated for, can "break" the system and cost your company money or even cost you your job. To protect your company's IT resources—and to protect your employment—do the work ahead of time to prepare for these eventualities.

BC (business continuity) refers to a company's ability to weather a failure, crisis, or disaster of some kind while maintaining continuity of operations, especially for critical services to customers and income-generating activities. Part of the BC planning process is developing a BIA (business impact analysis) that evaluates how different departments and components of an organization's business would, if lost, affect the company's bottom line. Corporate guidelines will help in the decision-making process to determine what services should be prioritized for BC protection and how much money should be invested in protecting those resources. These terms might be spelled out in an OLA (operational level agreement), which is a document that supports the standards defined by the SLA. While simple redundancies and replication will account for many of the lower-grade incidents, such as a failed server or the proverbial backhoe cutting your connection to the Internet, more extensive planning is required in preparation for larger-scale crises.

A BCP (business continuity plan), sometimes called a COOP (continuity of operations plan), contains documentation to support these standards and might include the following details:

- Contact names and phone numbers for emergency coordinators who will execute the response in case of disaster, as well as roles and responsibilities of other staff
- Details on which data and servers are being backed up, how frequently backups occur, where off-site backups are kept, and (most importantly) how backed-up data can be recovered in full
- Details on network topology, redundancy, and agreements with national service carriers, in case local or regional vendors fall prey to the same disaster
- Regular strategies for testing the BCP
- A plan for managing the crisis, including regular communications with employees and customers, taking into consideration the possibility that regular communication modes (such as phone lines) might be unavailable

Organizations employ many different strategies as part of their BCP, such as the following:

- *Roles and responsibilities*—Assigning roles and responsibilities to specific people ensures that everyone knows what is expected of them and how to perform those tasks. For example, the team leader is expected to serve as the final decision maker during an incident while the BC planner is responsible for developing and maintaining plan documentation. These assignments can also help identify gaps in coverage of tasks or gaps in skills or knowledge needed by everyone.

- *Call trees*—You've already learned that part of BC planning involves keeping a list of contact names and information for emergency coordinators. A more formal structure for this information is a call tree, which defines who should be contacted, in what order, and how to contact them. Automated call tree systems can perform these calls, texts, or emails automatically.

- *Incident types and categories*—Although you can't anticipate every possible event, you can develop categories of incident possibilities to inform your plans and preparations. Categories might be organized by the type of response needed, the severity of the event, or the resources affected.

- *Training*—Regular training ensures affected people know what to do and how whenever an incident occurs for which they must respond. This training doesn't necessarily apply only to IT personnel. For example, an emergency security alert system for instructors at a school requires training to ensure faculty know how to use the system and under what circumstances. A localized incident, such as a medical emergency for a student in a classroom, might require a different response from affected faculty and security personnel than a more global incident, such as someone bringing an unauthorized weapon onto campus.

- *Backup services*—A company might team up with partners or hire third parties to help with organizing backup resources. A backup service can manage data backups, or a business partner might arrange a sharing agreement where each partner could provide backup equipment or other IT services should the other partner suffer a severe loss. These strategies hinge on redundancy, such as duplicate or triplicate connectivity to the Internet and other off-site resources, or backup and restore policies to compensate for loss of availability of other services, such as communications or power. Some forms of redundancy include alternate sites, such as company-owned edge sites where services are located at remote offices or in data centers closer to customers to reduce latency. These edge sites often could serve as backups if needed. Outsourcing to third-party services or sites is also an option. Backup locations host backup hardware, data, and services in preparation for use during an emergency.

Different types of backup storage offer various options for ease and timeliness of restoration. The following three categories provide a general description of the options (also shown in Figure 3-15):

- *Cold site*—Computers, devices, and connectivity necessary to rebuild a replacement network exist, but they are not appropriately configured, updated, or connected. Therefore, restoring functionality from a cold site could take a long time.

- *Warm site*—Computers, devices, and connectivity necessary to rebuild a replacement network exist, with some pieces appropriately configured, updated, or connected. Recovery using a warm site can take hours or days, compared with the weeks a cold site might require. Maintaining a warm site costs more than maintaining a cold site, but not as much as maintaining a hot site.

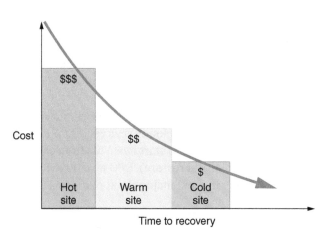

Figure 3-15   The most expensive option also provides the fastest recovery

- *Hot site*—Computers, devices, and connectivity necessary to rebuild a replacement network exist, and all are appropriately configured, updated, and connected to match your active network's current state. For example, you might use server mirroring to maintain identical copies of your servers at two locations. In a hot site contingency plan, both locations would also contain identical connectivity devices and configurations and thus would be able to stand in for the other at a moment's notice. As you can imagine, hot sites are expensive and potentially time-consuming to maintain. For organizations that cannot tolerate downtime, however, hot sites provide the best disaster recovery option.

Disaster Recovery

"Business continuity" and "disaster recovery" are two related but distinct terms. While BC (business continuity) refers to an organization's ability to continue doing business *during* a crisis, DR (disaster recovery) refers to the process of getting back to normal *after* the crisis is over. Typically, DR is considered to be a subset of BC planning. Two concepts commonly used to measure disaster recovery effectiveness are RPO (recovery point objective) and RTO (recovery time objective). Consider the diagram in Figure 3-16.

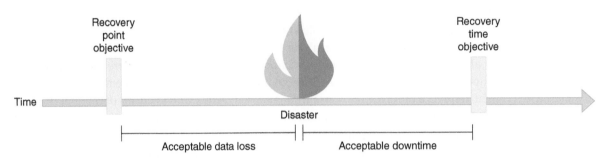

Figure 3-16   RPO defines how much data loss is acceptable, whereas RTO defines how much downtime is acceptable

The RPO shows at what point in the past data will be recovered from. Data that was created or changed since that point will be lost because data backups were not copying data in real time. For example, relying on a full backup that's created only once a week will result in multiple days' worth of lost data if the disaster happens later in the week. However, if you're also keeping incremental or differential backups each day, your RPO would lose less than a day's worth of data.

In contrast, the RTO shows at what point in the future full functionality will be restored (less any lost data). If you're creating a full backup each month and differential backups each day, you can apply the full backup and one differential backup and you're done. If, however, you're creating an incremental backup each day, then you'll have to apply every incremental backup since the last full backup, which will take more time. While incremental backups take up less space and take less time to create, they require more time to recover and therefore result in more recovery time needed after a loss.

RPOs and RTOs in the cloud have the potential to reach near-zero numbers. Cloud DR options open many new avenues of preparedness with much lower costs due to the pay-as-you-go nature of public cloud services. DRaaS (Disaster Recovery as a Service) can greatly reduce RTO because it doesn't take nearly as long to start new VMs from existing images as it does to reinstall OS images on physical servers (called BMR, or bare metal restore). RPO also benefits due to inexpensive data replication and storage options. DRaaS is available natively in most major cloud platforms and is also widely available from third-party providers.

When planning for your cloud RTO, however, also consider bandwidth or ISP limitations and costs for transferring files from backup locations back into your main data center.

Figure 3-17 shows the spectrum of recovery tiers available in AWS to illustrate the relationship among RPO, RTO, and cost. These tiers are described as follows:

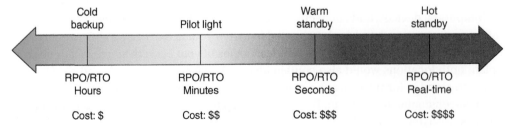

Figure 3-17   Various tiers of recovery services

- Cold backup services are relatively inexpensive. Perhaps you're storing regular snapshots of VMs and databases, but none of these resources is running in duplicate. This means you'll need hours to recover from a loss.

- AWS developed a new DR approach called pilot light that allows you to design the backup resources you need and leave them in a stopped state so you're not charged as much as what you would pay for running services. You might keep the database running so it's regularly updated, and you might periodically update server images, but they're not left running indefinitely. Recovery requires the amount of time needed to start these replacement services.

- Warm standby means copies are designed and created, and a scaled-down version of the environment is left running for immediate failover. This arrangement might buy you enough time to start the remaining resources for full backup services if needed.

- Hot standby provides real-time failover with no significant data loss. For example, site mirroring copies the current version of your website to a duplicate web server cluster. A load balancer or DNS server can transfer traffic over to the mirrored site instantly if the original web service becomes overloaded or goes down completely. Ideally, you would use an active-active, multi-site configuration so that both sites are working and productive at all times. However, each site is large enough to handle the entire workload if the other site fails.

Deciding which of these DR tiers is most appropriate for your cloud services will be determined by corporate guidelines and by existing SLAs for disaster recovery scenarios, which will define different expectations for service during a crisis. Make sure users understand the limitations of your DR arrangements, especially according to what is defined in the relevant SLAs. Consider the CSP's guidelines for DR planning, and incorporate other techniques as needed. Whatever BCP or DRP (disaster recovery plan) your organization develops, be sure to test it thoroughly two or three times a year, or more often if required by relevant compliance regulations. These tests might look like any of the following scenarios:

- *Tabletop exercise*—Involves a team of representatives from each department reviewing the plan together and looking for gaps

- *Structured walk-through*—Requires each department to walk through the plan in detail, usually with a specific disaster scenario in mind

- *Disaster simulation testing*—More involved and requires the presence and participation of all personnel, including business partners and vendors

Various models identify core phases of incident response. Some of these systems consist of four or five phases while others list six or even seven phases. Furthermore, the phases listed vary slightly from model to model. A common distinction between these models is whether preparation before the incident is included as a distinct phase.

Preparation tasks include planning for possible incidents and gathering the resources you would need to handle those issues. For example, a BCP (business continuity plan) tends to be lengthy and detailed in its written preparations and plans. However, this unwieldy document might not provide the most usable guidance in a moment of crisis. Instead, a playbook provides succinct, organized information that is easy to access and follow during the stress of an emergency. You might create a different playbook for each major type of incident, such as for a cybersecurity breach, a terror attack, a weather crisis, or a customer or employee protest.

Similarly, you'll need to think through what resources should be collected before an incident occurs. For example, you might gather a DR kit (disaster recovery kit), which includes items that will be needed during a crisis and is already organized and accessible before the emergency occurs. Some DR kits a company might need include the following:

- BCP records for restoring access and backups of core systems

- Essential tools for addressing common and critical problems

- Grab-and-go kits for employee safety during a crisis

Even a small company should maintain a handful of DR kits designed for certain types of emergencies. These kits might contain access information (such as passwords), backup restoration information, emergency contact devices (such as a satellite phone), and cash funds.

In addition to these preparation tasks, the following incident response phases are identified in the CompTIA Cloud+ exam objectives and begin when an incident occurs:

- *Identification*—This phase begins when an incident is identified, such as a security breach. Initial identification of the incident includes defining the scope of the incident and activating a response. An automated response might include failover to backup systems where services are transferred to backups if their primary systems suffer problems.

- *Investigation*—The investigation phase involves determining the initial trigger of the incident, tracing the effects of the incident, and evaluating the details of the incident, such as listing items that were stolen, data that was compromised, services that are down, and so on.

- *Containment, eradication, and recovery*—The focus of this phase is to minimize the impact of the incident and restore services as soon as possible. Affected systems are isolated, services are restored to their primary systems (called a failback), and evidence is gathered. When acquiring and managing evidence, be sure to maintain a legally defensible chain of custody. All collected data must be carefully processed and tracked so it does not leave official hands at any point in the forensics process. Typically, documentation used to track chain of custody describes exactly what the evidence is, when it was collected, who collected it, its condition, and how it was secured. If at any point in the process you have custody of evidence, be sure to sign off on a chain of custody document and obtain a signature from the next person in line when you hand over custody of the evidence.

- *Post-incident and lessons learned*—The saying "hindsight is 20/20" refers to the fact that looking back on what happened provides a clearer perspective than trying to foresee what *might* happen in the future. The post-incident phase, sometimes called the "lessons learned phase," takes advantage of this insight. After the incident is handled and services are restored, this phase requires a review of processes to determine how the incident happened and, most importantly, how to prevent similar problems in the future. Part of this process includes a root cause analysis, which is a formal procedure that identifies all the contributing factors that allowed the incident to happen. Some root cause analysis techniques include the following:

  - *Five whys*—Dig deeper into each possible explanation by repeatedly asking why; this helps determine if the suspected cause is instead a symptom of a deeper issue.
  - *Cause map*—List what happened and, for each item, identify its cause, which might also have a cause, which might have a deeper cause, and connect all these items in a map to identify the root cause of the incident.

These discussions should also include reviews of the incident response procedures and evaluation of any needed changes to these processes.

You're Ready

You're now ready to complete the following projects:

- Project 3-3: Use the AWS Pricing Calculator
- Project 3-4: Use the Azure Pricing Calculator
- Project 3-5: Use the Google Cloud Pricing Calculator

You can complete these projects now or wait until you've finished the other projects for this module.

Remember This

- Limitations on cloud capacity might be imposed by CSP quotas and throttles, account owner caps, or technology limitations.
- Vertical scaling increases resources allocated to an existing instance or storage container, while horizontal scaling increases the number of running instances or available storage containers.
- BC (business continuity) refers to a company's ability to weather a failure, crisis, or disaster of some kind while maintaining continuity of operations, especially for critical services to customers and income-generating activities.
- The RPO (recovery point objective) shows at what point in the past data will be recovered from, while the RTO (recovery time objective) shows at what point in the future full functionality will be restored (less any lost data).

Self-Check

13. Adding more RAM to a web server is what kind of capacity adjustment?
    - **a.** Scaling in
    - **b.** Vertical scaling
    - **c.** Scaling down
    - **d.** Horizontal scaling

14. Which kind of backup site provides the fastest RTO?
    - **a.** Hot site
    - **b.** Pilot site
    - **c.** Cold site
    - **d.** Warm site

15. What kind of DR test involves the most people?
    - **a.** Structured walk-through
    - **b.** Tabletop exercise
    - **c.** Disaster simulation testing
    - **d.** Playbook

○ Check your answers at the end of this module.

Module Summary

Section 3-1: Migration Planning

- When moving an organization's IT resources to the cloud, you complete five major phases of the project: assess, plan, migrate, validate, and manage.
- Before beginning a cloud migration, a thorough assessment will evaluate whether the cloud is a good fit for business needs and which part of the company's data center might work well in a cloud environment.
- An effective migration plan contains thorough information on network baselines, business continuity needs, dependencies between existing systems, needed target hosts, cloud architecture design, relevant legal restrictions, and planned order of operations.
- Cloud migration categories include the following: rehost; revise or replatform; repurchase or replace; refactor, rearchitect, or rebuild; retain; and retire.
- Environmental constraints require careful scheduling to minimize the impact of downtime and maximize the available network bandwidth for the migration.

Section 3-2: Migration Execution

- Change management provides carefully defined processes to evaluate the need for a change, the cost of the change, a plan for making the change with minimal disruption, and a backup plan if the change doesn't work as expected.
- Automation reduces overall time and cost of the migration as well as potential for mistakes or unplanned downtime.
- Organizations can choose from several data transfer methodologies, depending on how much data they need to migrate and how quickly, including the public Internet, a private connection, or an offline transfer.
- Common VM migration processes include P2V, V2V, V2P, and P2P.
- Storage migration is the process of moving blocks or volumes of data from one storage medium to another.
- A cross-service migration is the migration of a resource from one service type in a cloud platform to a different service type in the same platform and often can be performed more easily using a cloud provider's in-platform migration tools.

Section 3-3: Deployment Testing and Validation

- Common testing techniques include functional testing, performance testing, load testing, regression testing, usability testing, and security testing.
- Rightsizing balances performance requirements and capacity needs with budgetary restrictions.
- An SLA (service level agreement) identifies minimum performance benchmarks and maximum downtimes for specific services and defines options for recourse should performance fall short of guaranteed minimums or maximums.
- Common deployment issues include resource contention, template misconfiguration, CSP or ISP outages, platform integration issues, licensing outages, and time synchronization issues.

Section 3-4: Cloud Agility

- Project management is the application of specific skills, tools, and techniques to manage a project in such a way that the desired outcome is achieved.
- Due to its software-defined nature, much of a cloud deployment's configuration is managed through ALM (application lifecycle management) phases, which follow the progression of an application or software-defined deployment from its conception through its retirement.
- Build automation in a DevOps environment can streamline releases and increase agility, which is critical for CI/CD (continuous integration/continuous delivery).

Section 3-5: Planning for Problems

- Limitations on cloud capacity might be imposed by CSP quotas and throttles, account owner caps, or technology limitations.
- Vertical scaling increases resources allocated to an existing instance or storage container, while horizontal scaling increases the number of running instances or available storage containers.
- BC (business continuity) refers to a company's ability to weather a failure, crisis, or disaster of some kind while maintaining continuity of operations, especially for critical services to customers and income-generating activities.
- The RPO (recovery point objective) shows at what point in the past data will be recovered from, while the RTO (recovery time objective) shows at what point in the future full functionality will be restored (less any lost data).

Key Terms

For definitions of key terms, see the Glossary.

agility
ALM (application lifecycle management)
asset management
auto-scaling
baseline
BC (business continuity)
beta
build
CAB (change advisory board)
call tree
canary build
CapEx (capital expenditures)

chain of custody
change management
channel
CMDB (configuration management database)
colocation facility
continuous delivery
continuous deployment
continuous integration
cross-service migration
dev (developer) build
DevOps (development and operations)

DR kit (disaster recovery kit)
failback
failover
FTS (follow the sun)
functional testing
horizontal scaling
ITIL (IT Infrastructure Library)
IX or IXP (Internet exchange point)
KPI (key performance indicator)
load testing
LTS (long-term support)
online migration
OpEx (operational expenditures)

P2P (physical to physical)
P2V (physical to virtual)
pen (penetration) testing
performance testing
playbook
POP (point of presence)
project
project management
regression testing
RFP (request for proposals)

rightsizing
root cause analysis
SDLC (software development life cycle)
shadow IT
SOP (standard operating procedure)
stable release
storage migration
subscription

usability testing
V2P (virtual to physical)
V2V (virtual to virtual)
vendor lock-in
vertical scaling
vulnerability testing
waterfall method
workflow

Acronyms Checklist

The acronyms in Table 3-2 are listed in the Cloud+ objectives and could appear on the Cloud+ exam. This means that exam questions might use any of these acronyms in context so that you must know the meaning of the acronym in order to answer the question correctly. Make sure you're familiar with what each acronym stands for and the general concept of the term itself. All these acronyms are used in context in this module.

Table 3-2 Module 3 acronyms

Acronym	Spelled out
BCP	business continuity plan
BIA	business impact analysis
CAB	change advisory board
CD	continuous deployment or continuous delivery
CI	continuous integration
CMDB	configuration management database
COL	colocation facility
COOP	continuity of operations plan
DNS	Domain Name Service
DR	disaster recovery
DRP	disaster recovery plan
IOPS	input/output operations per second
LTS	long-term support
NTP	Network Time Protocol

Acronym	Spelled out
OLA	operational level agreement
P2P	physical to physical
P2V	physical to virtual
RDP	Remote Desktop Protocol
RPO	recovery point objective
RTO	recovery time objective
SDLC	software development life cycle
SLA	service level agreement
SSH	Secure Shell
TCO	total cost of ownership or total cost of operations
UAT	user accepting testing
V2P	virtual to physical
V2V	virtual to virtual
VHD	Virtual Hard Disk

Review Questions

1. What kind of expense is the purchase of a new firewall device?

   a. CapEx
   b. OpEx
   c. Shadow
   d. Standard

2. What type of migration would support the transition of an application from a VM instance to a container instance?

   a. Storage migration
   b. VM migration
   c. Storage migration
   d. Cross-service migration

3. You're moving your application server from AWS Lightsail to AWS EC2. What kind of migration is this?

    a. Database migration

    b. Cloud migration

    c. Storage migration

    d. Cross-service migration

4. A larger delta results in reduced data _____.

    a. security

    b. integrity

    c. latency

    d. connectivity

5. You've just deployed an update to an HR application that is widely used throughout your company. Which type of testing should you conduct to ensure your scheduling and shift planning software has not been adversely affected by the HR application update?

    a. Progressive testing

    b. Regression testing

    c. Beta testing

    d. Usability testing

6. Why might you NOT want to use an LTS release of an application?

    a. Increased integrity

    b. Early access

    c. Lack of updates

    d. Increased consistency over time

7. You work as a software developer and require early access to an operating system's updates so you can recode your application before OS updates are released to the public. Which OS channel are you most likely getting access to?

    a. Beta

    b. Dev

    c. Stable

    d. Canary

8. Which channel would provide the most stable release of an application to be deployed in a branch office with minimal technical staff?

    a. Beta

    b. Stable

    c. LTS

    d. Canary

9. During which incident response phase are backup systems activated?

    a. Identification

    b. Recovery

    c. Post-incident

    d. Investigation

10. Which resource might you use to quickly determine how to respond to a physical security breach?

    a. Chain of custody

    b. Call tree

    c. Playbook

    d. DR kit

Scenario-Based Questions

Question 3-1

Corin works in the IT department of a law firm specializing in real estate closings. The firm is already using G Suite (web-based Google apps) productivity software for office staff, and it recently acquired a company-wide license for Zoom, an online video conferencing app. The next, more audacious target is their billing software. The company has been using an antiquated program for more than 20 years—longer than most of their staff has been employed. One accountant has been with the firm for nearly 30 years and remembers when the firm first started using this billing software. She says everyone hated it even then. Corin has been asked to make a recommendation as to how to proceed with this phase of the migration. Given these conditions, what is the best approach to migrating the billing functions to the cloud?

    a. Rehost

    b. Replatform

    c. Retire

    d. Replace

Question 3-2

Mia's company is moving their video database—about 34 TB—to a cloud-based storage solution. The company is located in a fairly small town, at least an hour's drive from the nearest large city, and doesn't do a great deal of data transfer online for normal business operations other than regular contact with customers through email or video conferences. Which data transfer option is the best fit for Mia's company?

a. Private connection through a colocation facility
b. Storage appliance shipped via UPS
c. Existing public Internet connection
d. Data transport service such as Snowmobile

Question 3-3

Mykel and his team recently completed a major migration of several business-critical applications to the AWS public cloud, and they're performing some final tests before going live. While taking a short break at a nearby coffee shop, Mykel decides to remote into one of the primary servers from his personal laptop so he can make additional configuration changes. As he's completing the changes, it occurs to him that this particular server is supposed to be locked down to provide access only from his computer back at his desk. He pokes around in the account to see how much access he has with this user account and then returns to the office to address the problem. What kind of testing did Mykel use to identify this issue?

a. Vulnerability testing
b. Penetration testing
c. Performance testing
d. Load testing

Hands-On Projects

Note 8

Websites, applications, public cloud platforms, and related account options change often. While the instructions given in these projects were accurate at the time of writing, you might need to adjust the steps or options according to later changes.

Note to Instructors and Students: A rubric is provided for evaluating student performance on these projects. Please see Appendix D.

Project 3-1: Research Cloud Migration Success Stories

Estimated time: 30 minutes
Objective 3.5: Given a scenario, perform cloud migrations.
Resources:
• Internet access

Context:
It's been said that a wise person learns from other people's mistakes. To build on that idea, entrepreneur and author Jim Rohn said, "It's important to learn from your mistakes, but it is *better* to learn from other people's mistakes, and it is *best* to learn from other people's successes. It accelerates your own success." In this project, you'll explore cloud migration success stories. As you research, notice the benefits realized by each company as they moved to the cloud. How did their business model change? How was their bottom line affected?

(continues)

Hands-On Projects Continued

Complete the following steps:

1. Using your favorite search engine, search for "cloud migration success stories".
2. Many CSPs list success stories on their websites to promote the benefits of the cloud. Choose one of these success stories and read about it. Then summarize the story in a short paragraph, including challenges the company faced and how it solved the problems it encountered. Be sure to provide source information.
3. Other media organizations and experts also report on cloud success stories in blogs, articles, and case studies. Choose a success story from one of these other sources (not a CSP) and read about it. Then summarize the story in a short paragraph, including challenges the company faced and how it solved the problems it encountered. Be sure to provide source information.
4. Lessons learned from these stories can inform your own exploration into transitioning to the cloud. Find a list of keys to a successful migration, or make your own list based on what you read in your research. Include at least three items and provide your source information.

Project 3-2: Research Third-Party Migration Tools and Services

Estimated time: 30 minutes
Objective 5.3: Given a scenario, troubleshoot deployment issues.
Resources:

- Internet access

Context:
When migrating to the cloud, a company rarely relies solely on tools provided by the CSP—or on their own skills to operate those tools most effectively. Often, the migration can be performed more quickly, efficiently, and accurately when incorporating third-party tools or services. As the popularity of the cloud continues to rise, many vendors have developed tools and services to make migrating to the cloud easier and more effective. Some of these providers help cloud consumers find the best prices or plan their migration, while others walk clients through the entire process and continue providing maintenance services indefinitely. In this project, you'll research some of these providers so you can be familiar with the types of services and other options that they offer.

Complete the following steps:

1. Using your favorite search engine, look for a current list of "best cloud migration tools," "leading cloud migration service providers," or something similar. Read through a couple of lists to understand what makes one tool or service better than another. Then choose one of these tools or providers for further research. What criteria did you use to make your selection?
2. Which cloud platforms does this provider work with?
3. What is this provider's philosophy for calculating the cost of and best approach to a particular organization's cloud migration?
4. "Free" isn't always cost-effective. What are some limitations of this provider's free-tier option?

Project 3-3: Use the AWS Pricing Calculator

Estimated time: 20 minutes
Objective 1.4: Given a scenario, analyze the solution design in support of the business requirements.
Group work: This project includes enhancements when assigned as a group project.
Resources:

- Internet access

Context:
When planning a new cloud deployment, you'll need to do some research on anticipated costs of the resources you intend to use. All the major CSPs offer calculator tools to help customers explore their options for meeting their

business needs while staying within the restrictions of their budgets. In this project, you will use the AWS Pricing Calculator to create an estimate for a fictional cloud deployment. Complete the following steps:

1. Go to **calculator.aws** and click **Create estimate**.
2. Notice you can choose a service to calculate prices for resources within each service. On the Amazon EC2 tile, click **Configure**.
3. The quick estimate will be sufficient for this project. In a real-world scenario, you might need the advanced estimate to provide more accurate numbers. Make sure **Quick estimate** is selected.
4. Complete Table 3-3 as you make selections.

Table 3-3   EC2 pricing

Factor	Your selections
Operating system	
Instance type	
Quantity	
Utilization	
Pricing strategy*	
EBS volume type	
Storage amount	
Total monthly cost	

*Pricing strategy refers to the price model you use. Committing to long-term use and paying more upfront offers lower prices.

5. Click **Add to my estimate**.

When running a cloud deployment for, say, a web server, the server and its storage volume are not the only costs of the deployment. There are many other services you might include to expand functionality, add security, increase performance, or provide monitoring options. To expand your estimate, complete the following steps:

6. Click **Add service**.
7. Choose an AWS service that you think might be helpful for your deployment. For example, you might add a database, a key management service, a load balancer, or DNS management options. What service did you choose?
8. Make selections for that service's configurations that make sense to you. What total monthly cost will this service configuration add to your overall estimate?
9. Add this total to your estimate. **Take a screenshot** of your estimate summary information; submit this visual with your answers to this project's questions.
10. **For group projects:** Each group member should compare their estimate information with estimates from at least one other group member. Is your estimate higher or lower than the other estimate? What factors resulted in your estimate being so different from the other estimate?

Project 3-4: Use the Azure Pricing Calculator

Estimated time: 20 minutes
Objective 1.4: Given a scenario, analyze the solution design in support of the business requirements.
Group work: This project includes enhancements when assigned as a group project.
Resources:
- Internet access

Hands-On Projects Continued

Context:

When planning a new cloud deployment, you'll need to do some research on anticipated costs of the resources you intend to use. All the major CSPs offer calculator tools to help customers explore their options for meeting their business needs while staying within the restrictions of their budgets. In this project, you will use the Azure Pricing Calculator to create an estimate for a fictional cloud deployment. Complete the following steps:

1. Go to azure.microsoft.com/**calculator**.
2. Notice you can choose a service to calculate prices for resources within each service. Click the **Virtual Machines** tile.
3. Scroll down to the Your Estimate tab. Complete Table 3-4 as you make selections.

Table 3-4   Virtual Machines pricing

Factor	Your selections
Region	
Operating system	
Type	
Tier	
Instance	
Quantity of VMs	
Utilization	
Savings options*	
Managed disks tier	
Disk size	
Number of disks	
Any other selections (You do not need to choose additional storage transactions, bandwidth, support, or licensing options— you can keep the default settings for all of these.)	
Estimated monthly cost	

*Savings options refer to the pricing model you use. Committing to long-term use and paying more upfront offer lower prices.

When running a cloud deployment for, say, a web server, the server and its storage volume are not the only costs of the deployment. There are many other services you might include to expand functionality, add security, increase performance, or provide monitoring options. To expand your estimate, complete the following steps:

4. Choose an Azure service that you think might be helpful for your deployment. For example, you might add a database, a key management service, a load balancer, or DNS management options. What service did you choose? Click that tile at the top, and scroll down to the Your Estimate tab.
5. Make selections for that service's configurations that make sense to you. What monthly cost will this service configuration add to your overall estimate?
6. **Take a screenshot** of your total estimated upfront and monthly costs, as shown below the last service included in the estimate; submit this visual with your answers to this project's questions.
7. **For group projects:** Each group member should compare their estimate information with estimates from at least one other group member. Is your estimate higher or lower than the other estimate? What factors resulted in your estimate being so different from the other estimate?

Project 3-5: Use the Google Cloud Pricing Calculator

Estimated time: 20 minutes

Objective 1.4: Given a scenario, analyze the solution design in support of the business requirements.

Group work: This project includes enhancements when assigned as a group project.

Resources:

- Internet access

Context:

When planning a new cloud deployment, you'll need to do some research on anticipated costs of the resources you intend to use. All the major CSPs offer calculator tools to help customers explore their options for meeting their business needs while staying within the restrictions of their budgets. In this project, you will use the Google Cloud Pricing Calculator to create an estimate for a fictional cloud deployment. Complete the following steps:

1. Go to **cloud.google.com/calculator**.
2. Notice you can choose a service to calculate prices for resources within each service. Confirm **COMPUTE ENGINE** is selected.
3. Complete Table 3-5 as you make selections.
4. Click **ADD TO ESTIMATE** to see the total estimated cost.

Table 3-5 EC2 pricing

Factor	Your selections
Number of instances	
Operating system	
Machine class	
Machine family	
Series	
Machine type	
Boot disk type	
Boot disk size	
Datacenter location	
Other options selected	
Committed usage, hours per day, and days per week*	
Total estimated cost	

*Committing to long-term use and paying more upfront offer lower prices.

When running a cloud deployment for, say, a web server, the server and its storage volume are not the only costs of the deployment. There are many other services you might include to expand functionality, add security, increase performance, or provide monitoring options. To expand your estimate, complete the following steps:

5. Choose a GCP service that you think might be helpful for your deployment. For example, you might add a database, a key management service, a load balancer, or DNS management options. What service did you choose?
6. Make selections for that service's configurations that make sense to you. Add this total to your estimate. What total monthly cost will this service configuration add to your overall estimate?

(continues)

Hands-On Projects Continued

7. Find the Total Estimated Cost with all selected services included. **Take a screenshot** of your Total Estimated Cost; submit this visual with your answers to this project's questions.

8. **For group projects:** Each group member should compare their estimate information with estimates from at least one other group member. Is your estimate higher or lower than the other estimate? What factors resulted in your estimate being so different from the other estimate?

Note 9

Websites, applications, public cloud platforms, and related account options change often. While the instructions given in these projects were accurate at the time of writing, you might need to adjust the steps or options according to later changes.

Capstone Project 3: Compare Cloud Platform Costs

Note to Instructors and Students: A rubric is provided for evaluating student performance on these projects. Please see Appendix D.

Estimated time: 30 minutes

Objective 4.3: Given a scenario, optimize cloud environments.

Resources:

- Internet access

Context:

When comparing cloud platforms for a potential cloud deployment, it can be challenging to get a so-called "apples-to-apples" comparison in which you're looking at the corresponding products in each platform. For example, none of the platforms use the same instance type names. So how are you supposed to know you're comparing the same kind of instance to get an accurate picture of how costs compare? This is the question you will explore in this project. Complete the following steps:

1. In each of the three CSPs covered in this course (AWS, Azure, and GCP), use their pricing calculators to determine the cost of a robust Windows server and a lightweight Linux server with 100 percent utilization for one month. Try to find an instance type for each platform that is as close to identical as possible to each other for each of these servers. For example, if your Windows server in AWS has 16 vCPUs and 96 GiB of RAM, make sure you choose an instance type in Azure and in GCP with an identical ratio of resources. Similarly, if the AWS Windows instance is compute optimized, choose a compute-optimized instance in Azure and GCP as well. Also make sure the storage volume for each Windows comparison and for each Linux comparison match across cloud platforms. Complete Table 3-6 and Table 3-7. Adjust your selections as needed to try to get all three instances in each table closely matched in price as well as resource configuration.

Table 3-6   Robust Windows instance comparison

Windows instance	AWS	Azure	GCP
Instance type			
vCPUs			
RAM			
Storage volume			
Storage amount			
Total monthly cost			

Table 3-7   Lightweight Linux instance comparison

Linux instance	AWS	Azure	GCP
Instance type			
vCPUs			
RAM			
Storage volume			
Storage amount			
Total monthly cost			

Solutions to Self-Check Questions

Section 3-1: Migration Planning

1. What physical restriction might make the cloud unreasonable for certain types of workloads?

   Answer: a. Latency

   Explanation: Latency is the delay between the transmission of a signal and its receipt, and this physical reality might make certain cloud-hosted services unreasonably slow.

2. Which cloud migration strategy requires the most work to perform?

   Answer: c. Refactor

   Explanation: Refactoring requires the most significant changes to a resource, such as recoding portions of an application.

3. What kind of expense is an electric bill?

   Answer: b. OpEx

   Explanation: The benefits of OpEx, such as an electric bill, are experienced in about the same period as when the expenses are paid, such as on a monthly or quarterly basis.

Section 3-2: Migration Execution

4. Who submits a change request?

   Answer: c. Change initiator

   Explanation: A change initiator determines the need for a change and submits a formal change request that covers details about the requested change.

5. Which data transfer methodology requires a long-term commitment?

   Answer: b. Private connection

   Explanation: A private connection often requires a long-term contract with an ISP and paying for a direct connection into the CSP's POP (point of presence).

6. Which migration type is most likely used to restore a physical server from backup?

   Answer: d. V2P

   Explanation: A V2P (virtual to physical) migration might be used when recovering a physical system from a VM backup.

(continues)

Section 3-3: Deployment Testing and Validation

7. What kind of testing would detect unintended changes to an interdependent system?

    Answer: b. Regression testing

    Explanation: Regression testing confirms that changes to one system haven't negatively impacted other functions within that system or other systems in the network.

8. Which feature ensures a resource adjusts size to meet demand?

    Answer: d. Auto-scaling

    Explanation: Auto-scaling is the automatic increase or decrease of capacity as needed.

9. Which problem can result in an inappropriately opened RDP port?

    Answer: b. Template misconfiguration

    Explanation: When creating or migrating servers, template misconfigurations can have serious implications for security, such as leaving remote access channels like SSH or RDP open to the Internet.

Section 3-4: Cloud Agility

10. Which of the following is NOT a category of project management processes?

    Answer: d. Securing

    Explanation: A project involves many processes that are generally grouped into five categories: initiating, planning, executing, monitoring and controlling, and closing.

11. Which of the following is accomplished by a circular approach to SDLC?

    Answer: c. Agility

    Explanation: A continuous or cyclical software development approach offers increased agility, which is the ability to adapt quickly to market demands according to increased or decreased feature use.

12. Which channel incorporates user testing?

    Answer: d. Beta

    Explanation: The beta release benefits from user testing on the dev and canary builds.

Section 3-5: Planning for Problems

13. Adding more RAM to a web server is what kind of capacity adjustment?

    Answer: b. Vertical scaling

    Explanation: Scaling up, called vertical scaling, increases resources such as vCPUs or IOPS allocated to an existing instance or storage container.

14. Which kind of backup site provides the fastest RTO?

    Answer: a. Hot site

    Explanation: A hot site contains identical resources to the original site and can take over functionality nearly instantaneously.

15. What kind of DR test involves the most people?

    Answer: c. Disaster simulation testing

    Explanation: Disaster simulation testing requires the presence and participation of all personnel, including business partners and vendors.

Module 4

Cloud Networking

Module 4 Objectives

After reading this module, you will be able to:

1 Explain how common networking concepts apply to cloud networking.

2 Manage IP address spaces in the cloud.

3 Configure basic AWS networking resources.

4 Configure basic Azure networking resources.

5 Configure basic GCP networking resources.

Module 4 Outline

Study the module's outline to help you organize the content in your mind as you read.

Module 4 Scenario

"What won't work?" Kendra asks as you realize she's standing beside your desk.

"Huh?" You drag your thoughts away from the gadget you were fiddling with and attempt to focus on what Kendra is saying.

"You just muttered something about, 'This is not going to work!' Is everything okay?"

"Oh, I must have been talking to myself. Sorry about that." You turn your attention back to the access point device on your desk. "I was trying to configure this access point so any preapproved computer or smartphone that connects to it will automatically authenticate to the network *and* recognize this network printer. But something's not working, and the printer keeps showing up as an unknown device."

"Ah, networking," she replies. "My favorite topic. Need some help?"

"No, I'll mess with it again after I take a break. I'm not even sure what I want it to do is possible." You slide the access point to a side table and look up at Kendra. "I do have a question, though. I've been thinking…"

"That's a dangerous activity!" Kendra says. "What's on your mind?"

"Networking. Except in the cloud." As Kendra settles into a chair, you continue to muse aloud. "How do devices in the cloud talk to each other? I mean, here in our own data center, we have routers and switches and cables and access points. But in the cloud, we won't be able to get to any of those devices. Do we remote into the cloud provider's devices so we can configure them? How does that work?"

At that moment, Nigel finishes a phone call, hears the word "cloud," and wheels his chair to your makeshift meeting space to join the conversation. "This I've gotta hear," he says as he reaches to his desk to grab his cup of coffee.

Kendra props one foot on a nearby box and starts explaining. "No, we can't access the cloud provider's equipment directly. Remember how we talked about VMs that run on top of a virtualization layer? Those VMs are configured separately from the host hardware underneath the hypervisor. It's the same idea with the cloud. The network functions are all managed at a software layer through a cloud console of some kind. Like … if you want a new subnet, you go into the console and create one. Tell it what IP address range to use, maybe configure some routes in a route table, and then spin up VMs inside your virtual network."

"That sounds easy," says Nigel. "But then when I think about it, it also sounds really complicated. How does it all work?"

"Let's do some more research," suggests Kendra. She grabs a sticky notepad and pen from your desk and scribbles the following questions:

- Where do networking functions fit in the big picture of cloud computing?
- How are cloud networks created and configured?
- What IP addresses do cloud resources use?
- What kinds of default connections are included in a cloud network?

Section 4-1: Networking Concepts in the Cloud

Certification

1.3 Explain the importance of high availability and scaling in cloud environments.

3.3 Given a scenario, deploy cloud networking solutions.

4.3 Given a scenario, optimize cloud environments.

Networking in the cloud works similarly to networking in a physical data center, except at more of a logical level rather than a physical one because you do not need to rely directly on the configurations of physical hardware. Due to the virtualization layer provided by the cloud platform, you have freedom to build the components you need in the ways you need them without many of the restrictions of working with physical infrastructure. To a great degree, if you can imagine it, you can build it. This module discusses how networking concepts work in the cloud and covers networking configurations in AWS, Azure, and GCP.

Networking Concepts

The IT industry has been shifting toward more virtualized, abstracted networking for some time. Initially, SDN (software-defined networking) technologies separated the control plane, or management layer, of the network from the data plane where transmissions on the network actually traverse physical devices. This separation allows for centralized control of network devices from an SDN controller. Figure 4-1 shows how this works at a conceptual level.

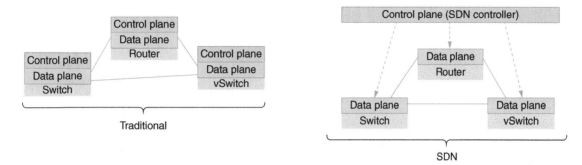

Figure 4-1   Individual control planes in a traditional network versus a centralized control plane in an SDN network

NFV (network functions virtualization) takes this idea a step further by virtualizing network devices and services, much like VMs are virtualized computers. Most of the technologies are the same but abstracted to the virtual platform. For example, cloud networks still use firewall technologies. Similar security features apply firewall rules, such as the AWS security group shown in Figure 4-2 that allows inbound SSH traffic to manage a Linux instance. However, these firewalls are virtual appliances or logical configurations running on a virtual network. Messages are directed through invisible hardware according to rules enforced by tags added to message headers.

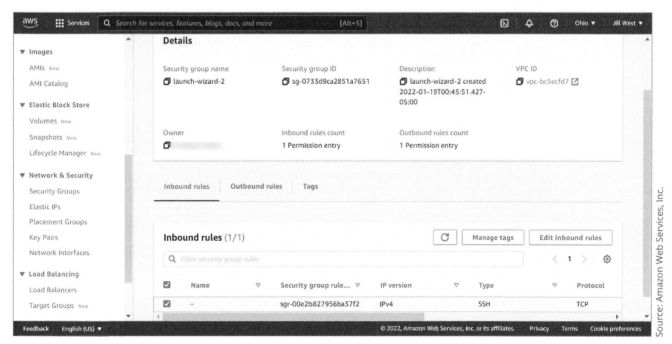

Figure 4-2   Inbound rule in an AWS security group

When your data lives in the cloud, accessing your data and securing your data must be discussed simultaneously. As a result, this course's modules on cloud networking might at times look more like modules on cloud security. Nearly every networking decision you make for your cloud will need to consider the security implications of each option available to you.

Note 1

What you already know about physical networking will serve you well when working with cloud-based networks. You'll recognize familiar network components such as routers, switches, firewalls, load balancers, authentication servers, and DNS (Domain Name System) and DHCP (Dynamic Host Configuration Protocol) servers. This course focuses on how these components work when used in the cloud, and it won't cover that content as if it's the first time you've seen it. If you've not yet completed a networking course, you might need to do some additional research on some networking concepts to help you understand the big picture of what's being discussed. Some ways to find this information include searching online for helpful articles and videos, which is often the way IT professionals keep their own knowledge up to date after completing their formal education. You might also buy a networking textbook—even a used one can be a handy resource. If you have a Cengage Unlimited subscription, you can bookmark the *CompTIA Network+ Guide to Networks*, 9th edition, for quick reference throughout the next few modules.

Grow with Cengage Unlimited!

If you'd like more information about SDN (software-defined networking), use your Cengage Unlimited subscription to go to *CompTIA Network+ Guide to Networks*, 9th edition, Module 7, and read the section titled "Software-Defined Networking (SDN)."

If you don't have a Cengage Unlimited subscription, you can find more information at cengage.com/unlimited.

From OSI Model to Cloud Stack

If you've spent time in networking, you're familiar with the OSI model and its cousin the TCP/IP model. Figure 4-3 shows the OSI and TCP/IP layers as a brief refresher. Both models present theoretical representations of what happens during network communication.

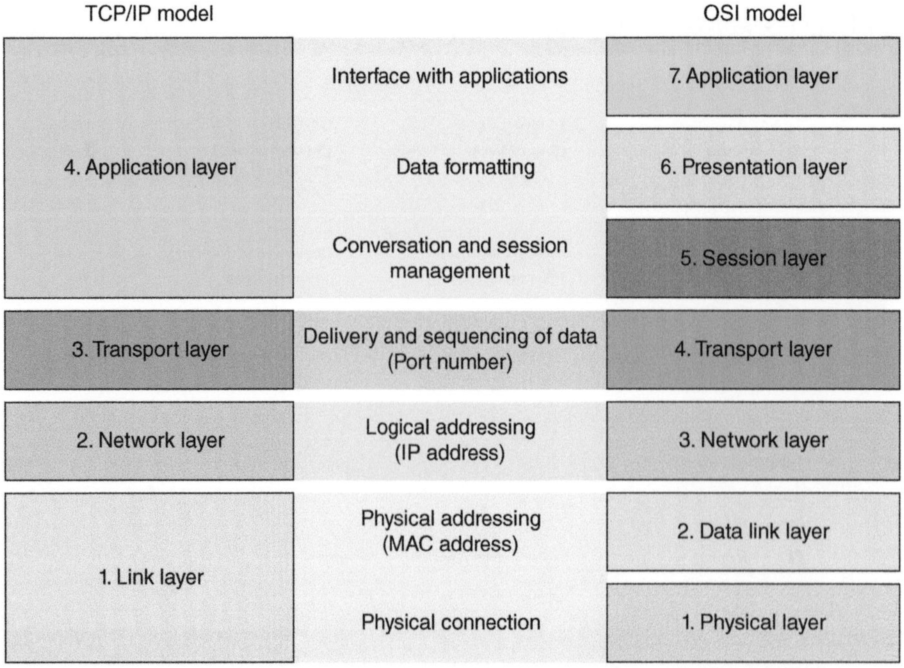

Figure 4-3   The OSI and TCP/IP models of networking communications

Note 2

The names of the TCP/IP layers are not as tightly standardized in the industry as the names of the OSI layers are. Many organizations and other sources take the liberty to alter the names of the TCP/IP layers to make them easier to understand or more informative in a certain context. For example, the lowest TCP/IP layer might be called "network," "network access," or "host to network." The second layer is often called "Internet" even though it does not necessarily refer to the public Internet. The third layer might be called "host-to-host," and the top layer might be called "process application." To minimize confusion between the two models and to simplify references to each layer, this text uses the layer names as shown in Figure 4-3.

Imagine that a web browser is requesting information from a distant web server about a webpage the user has requested access to. The browser application creates the information request and sends it along to the computer's operating system so the information can be transmitted across the network. The message then progresses downward through the layers as various tasks are accomplished to manage the communication, as follows:

- The OS first formats the request and encrypts it, if necessary. This process is handled at the application layer (or, according to the OSI model, in the application, presentation, and session layers).
- At the transport layer, the computer communicates across the network with the web server to create a connection, thereby starting the conversation. This process includes handling information about the applications involved on each end, which are identified to each computer by a port number (such as port 80 or port 443 for a conversation between a web browser and a web server).
- At the network layer, addressing information is added to ensure the message gets to the right destination. These addresses are defined by IP (Internet Protocol) and so are called IP addresses.
- At the link layer (the data link and physical layers in the OSI model), the physical connection is managed between the computer and the network infrastructure. A physical address called a MAC (media access control) address identifies each device on an interface and is part of the link (TCP/IP model) or data link (OSI model) layer.

Grow with Cengage Unlimited!

If you'd like more information about the OSI model, use your Cengage Unlimited subscription to go to *CompTIA Network+ Guide to Networks*, 9th edition, Module 1, and read the section titled "Seven-Layer OSI Model."

If you don't have a Cengage Unlimited subscription, you can find more information at cengage.com/unlimited.

At each layer, information is added to the message that various devices along the way will need. For example, the port number at the transport layer is added at the front of the message in a section called a header. At the network layer, another header is added to the front of the first header and contains IP addressing information for the source device and the destination device. At the link layer, yet another header is added to provide the MAC address for the next device on the path that will receive the message. This process of adding headers to carry various layers of information is called encapsulation. Figure 4-4 shows an example of a message with data and three headers containing addressing information.

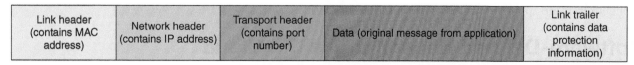

| Link header (contains MAC address) | Network header (contains IP address) | Transport header (contains port number) | Data (original message from application) | Link trailer (contains data protection information) |

Figure 4-4   The transport layer first adds a header to the message, followed by the network layer, and finally the link layer's header and trailer on the outermost edges

To get the message from the source computer to the web server, the message must traverse several other devices. Initially, the message crosses the local network's router at the MDF (main distribution facility) onto the Internet. The message then encounters many routers and other devices along the way. When it reaches its destination network, the message might cross that network's router first and then probably a firewall (or the firewall first), followed by a switch and possibly several other devices. Each device reads only deeply enough into the message's headers to know where to send the message next (or, in the case of a firewall, to check the message content for security issues).

These models are helpful in troubleshooting network problems and in understanding how networking protocols relate to one another because different protocols function at different layers. While cloud computing brings some creative modifications of the models, the overall structure and logic remains somewhat the same in that each layer builds on another to create a stack of functions, with hardware at the bottom of the stack and applications at the top. Let's explore how the cloud stack compares to the network layers.

Various versions of the cloud stack model show five to seven layers performing different functions from those described in the traditional network models for physical data centers. With the OSI model, layers are defined by where information is found within a message's headers. But cloud layers are better defined by who has access to the configurations of that layer. While the layers are not yet standardized because cloud technologies are still in flux, in general, these layers can be described as shown in Table 4-1.

Table 4-1   Cloud stack theoretical model

Layer	Name	Description
1	Physical layer	Contains the physical infrastructure, including cables, servers, networking devices, cooling systems, and power systems. In a public cloud, the physical layer is the CSP's responsibility and is not accessible by the cloud consumer, who often does not know where these components are geographically located.
2	Virtualization layer	Abstracts virtual hardware from the physical hardware through virtualization software. This might be a hypervisor, such as VMware's ESXi, or a cloud platform, such as OpenStack, or a combination of these tools, such as Azure's modified form of Hyper-V. In a public cloud, the virtualization layer is the CSP's responsibility.
3	Network or management layer	Provides "infrastructure as code" where APIs allow IaaS customers to create and manage virtual networks in what is called an **SDDC (software-defined data center)**. This layer is where resources, access control, costs, security, and other services are managed. From a cloud customer's perspective, the options here include the major CSPs: AWS, Azure, and GCP.
4	Image or OS layer	Provides instances or native services that support features at the application layer. Workloads, data storage, and data processing happen at this layer. Here, PaaS customers can manipulate various OS environments for development, testing, and hosting.
5	Application layer	Hosts many traditionally lower-layer functions such as load balancing and firewalls. Also presents applications to SaaS users.

It's helpful to think about cloud computing in these layers because, as with the OSI model in networking, the layers can help you organize information in your mind as you're learning it and help with troubleshooting later, when something goes wrong. This module—and the next few modules—focuses primarily on the network layer, where IaaS configurations are applied to achieve networking and security services.

Software-Defined Networking in the Cloud

As you've learned, SDN separates the control plane where decision making occurs from the data plane where bits are transferred from device to device. This is the basis on which the cloud works—the underlying physical infrastructure that supports the cloud is not accessible to the cloud customer. However, the cloud customer can configure networking infrastructure, such as routing and switching, at a software-defined level using tools in a cloud platform. For example, when you configure a static route in AWS, you're not configuring a physical router, but many physical routers will have access to your route's information so traffic is properly handled.

Not only can SDN make network infrastructure configuration easier, it also can make it more highly available. When you design and implement a physical network, you need routers and switches. To ensure HA (high availability), you need multiple routers and switches at key intersections of network media and segments to avoid any single point of failure. This way, if one device fails, another can take over.

In the public cloud, you as the customer are not responsible for ensuring there are enough physical devices to guarantee availability—the cloud provider is. In fact, you don't have to configure routers and switches at all. Instead, you might configure static routes and you'll assign IP address ranges to your subnets. As you know, these functions (routing and subnetting) are handled by physical or virtual routers and switches in the on-prem network. But in the cloud, they're configured through the cloud platform's SDN-backed interface.

What steps should you take, then, to ensure availability for your routes and subnetting in the cloud? While you don't need to add duplicate configurations for these structures, you will likely need redundant virtual devices in your cloud. Just like on-prem, you need to avoid any single point of failure. For example, Figure 4-5 shows a deployment in AWS with duplicate web servers and a load balancer to distribute traffic between both servers. Notice you do not need to duplicate the load balancer because it's inherently redundant due to AWS's design for load balancers.

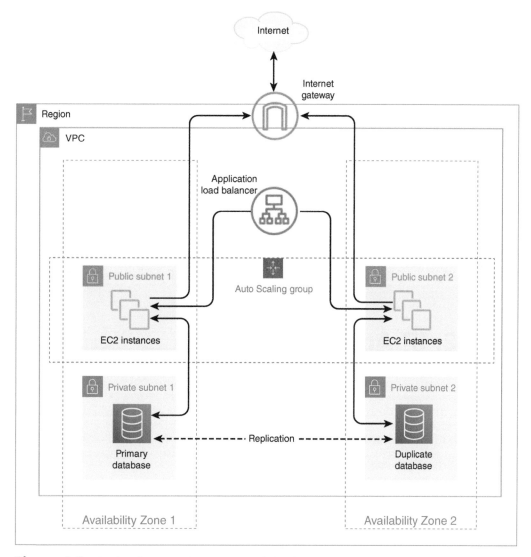

Figure 4-5   Redundant EC2 instances and databases

You might configure the servers to auto-scale in response to increasing demand or to compensate for a failed server instance. You might also configure database replicas in multiple regions. For each of these redundancies, you'll need to make sure IP address configurations will carry over to replacement resources as they're needed. In that case, duplicating IP address configurations across redundant servers or databases is a form of HA for switching. Similarly, if you duplicate a subnet and copy route tables to redundant subnets, this is a form of HA for routing.

Remember This

- SDN (software-defined networking) separates the control plane, or management layer, of the network from the data plane where transmissions on the network actually traverse physical devices; similarly, NFV (network functions virtualization) virtualizes network devices and services.
- Various versions of the cloud stack model show five to seven layers that are defined by who has access to the configurations of that layer.
- When configuring cloud networking services, you will likely need redundant virtual devices in your cloud to ensure HA (high availability) and avoid any single point of failure.

Self-Check

1. Which SDN plane moves traffic from switch port to switch port?
   - **a.** Application plane
   - **b.** Data plane
   - **c.** Control plane
   - **d.** Management plane

2. At which cloud layer are user access accounts managed?
   - **a.** Virtualization layer
   - **b.** Image layer
   - **c.** Physical layer
   - **d.** Network layer

3. Who configures physical devices hosting the cloud?
   - **a.** The IaaS user
   - **b.** The SaaS user
   - **c.** The CSP
   - **d.** The PaaS user

○ Check your answers at the end of this module.

Section 4-2: IP Address Spaces

Certification

1.4 Given a scenario, analyze the solution design in support of the business requirements.

- -

3.1 Given a scenario, integrate components into a cloud solution.

- -

3.3 Given a scenario, deploy cloud networking solutions.

- -

At the network layer of the TCP/IP or OSI model, IP addresses are used to identify devices across networks. This system is also used in the cloud. Cloud resources are given one or both of two kinds of IP addresses: public and private. **Public IP addresses** provide access to a resource from the Internet. **Private IP addresses** are only accessible from within the cloud-based network where that resource is located.

Most of the time, private IP addresses are automatically assigned to a resource if it needs one to communicate. Some cloud platforms—such as AWS, Azure, and GCP—also assign a public IP address to many cloud resources by default. However, these public IP addresses are dynamic, meaning the address could change at any time without warning, especially when the resource is power cycled (shut down and restarted). Assigning a static public IP address to a resource typically incurs charges.

As you might guess, there is much more to the process of managing network connections in the cloud than choosing between public and private IP addresses. This section explains IP addressing, subnetting, segmentation, and interface management in the cloud.

IP Addressing

In an on-prem network, the process of assigning private IP addresses is normally managed by a DHCP server. In the cloud, IP address assignment is more automatic. Private IP addresses are assigned chronologically from specific IP address ranges that are defined when you create the virtual network and its subnets. The IETF (Internet Engineering Task Force) published **RFC (Request for Comments) 1918** in February 1996 to specify best practices for address allocation on private networks. RFC 1918, which you can read at https://datatracker.ietf.org/doc/html/rfc1918, identifies three blocks of IP address space reserved by IANA (Internet Assigned Numbers Authority) for use on private networks, including private networks hosted in the cloud. See Table 4-2.

Table 4-2   RFC 1918 address blocks

Start address	End address	Prefix	Subnet mask
10.0.0.0	10.255.255.255	10.x.x.x/8	255.0.0.0
172.16.0.0	172.31.255.255	172.16.x.x/12	255.240.0.0
192.168.0.0	192.168.255.255	192.168.x.x/16	255.255.0.0

Note 3

The addresses in Table 4-2 are written using IPv4 (IP version 4). IPv4 has been around for a long time. When it was first defined, no one realized how many devices would eventually be connected to the Internet, and so the numbering system used by IPv4 is not expansive enough to support the demand for IP addresses today. A newer version, IPv6, was developed to solve this problem. Although IPv6 has been around for several years, it has not yet been widely adopted due to the lengthy addresses it uses, the updates required to other network protocols to support it, and the way it changes the rules used to direct traffic across a network. Still, IPv6 offers increased security and greater efficiency for network traffic. Here's an example of an IPv6 link-local address (that is, an address used on a local network, not across the Internet) so you can see how it's formatted differently. Notice the address begins with FE80, which indicates it only works on the local network:

```
FE80::64D2:BD2E:FA62:B911
```

IPv6 is supported to some degree by many CSPs, but its use is still considered optional in most cases.

Grow with Cengage Unlimited!

If you'd like more information about IP addresses, use your Cengage Unlimited subscription to go to *CompTIA Network+ Guide to Networks*, 9th edition, Module 3, and read the section titled "IP Addresses."

If you don't have a Cengage Unlimited subscription, you can find more information at cengage.com/unlimited.

Subnetting

IPv4 address blocks, such as 192.168.0.0/16, are written using **CIDR (classless interdomain routing) notation** so that subnet masks, such as 255.255.255.0, don't have to be written as well. The number after the slash, such as /16 or /24, indicates how many bits in the IP address are used to indicate the network portion of the IP address, which is the network ID. For example, 192.168.4.1 is written in binary as

```
11000000.10101000.00000100.00000001
```

Notice that each set of bits between the decimals contains 8 bits and is called an octet. If this IP address is part of a /24 CIDR block of addresses, then the first 24 bits are used to identify the network, and here are written in bold:

```
11000000.10101000.00000100.00000001
```

Every host on this network will have the same first 24 bits and share the same first three octets: 192.168.4. The last octet will be different for each host. Only the last eight bits can be used to identify different hosts, and so are called host bits or the host ID. However, the number of bits committed to identifying the network can be adjusted. For example, the IP address 192.168.4.1/25 has 25 network bits:

```
11000000.10101000.00000100.00000001
```

Because more of the bits are used to identify the network, fewer of the bits can be used to identify the hosts. This means that you have more networks and fewer hosts on each of these networks. The process of calculating address spaces in this manner is called subnetting.

Subnetting helps manage IP address spaces in the cloud, so it's important that you're comfortable with choosing subnets and identifying subnet-related problems. Most of the time, you'll see IPv4 subnets listed in CIDR blocks, such as 192.168.0.0/24. For ease of use, most default settings will use classful subnets, where the network bits take up complete octets with no splits in the middle of an octet:

- Class A subnets use the first octet for the network ID, such as **10**.0.0.0/8.
- Class B subnets use the first and second octets for the network ID, such as **172.16**.0.0/16.
- Class C subnets use the first, second, and third octets for the network ID, such as **192.168.100**.0/24.

Grow with Cengage Unlimited!

If you'd like a more detailed explanation of how to calculate subnets, use your Cengage Unlimited subscription to go to *CompTIA Network+ Guide to Networks*, 9th edition, Module 8, and read the section titled "Calculating Subnets."
If you don't have a Cengage Unlimited subscription, you can find more information at cengage.com/unlimited.

In adjusting subnet settings, recall that increasing the number after the slash (/) effectively increases the number of subnets you have—and decreases the number of hosts on each subnet—by increasing the number of IP bits used for the network ID and decreasing the number of bits used for the host ID. Consider the following example.

Suppose you're given a network ID of 192.168.89.0/24 for an entire network and you want to create *eight* smaller subnets. The 192.168.89 portion of the network ID represents the 24 bits (**11000000 10101000 01011001**) dedicated to the host portion of the IP addresses used in this network. The .0 portion at the end of the CIDR block represents the eight bits (00000000) that can be used to identify individual hosts within the network. To create eight smaller subnets, you need to use some of the bits from the host portion to instead identify these different subnets. How many bits should become part of the network ID?

Considering that each bit represents two possible numbers—1 or 0—think through your options:

- 192.168.89.0/25 would adopt one of the host bits for the network portion (**11000000 10101000 01011001** ?0000000), giving you two subnets:
  - 192.168.89.0 (**11000000 10101000 01011001** 00000000)
  - 192.168.89.128 (**11000000 10101000 01011001** 10000000)

That's not enough, so try again:

- 192.168.89.0/26 adopts two host bits for the network portion, yielding four subnets ($2^2 = 4$):
  - 192.168.89.0 (**11000000 10101000 01011001 00**000000)
  - 192.168.89.64 (**11000000 10101000 01011001 01**0000000)
  - 192.168.89.128 (**11000000 10101000 01011001 10**0000000)
  - 192.168.89.192 (**11000000 10101000 01011001 11**0000000)

That's still not enough, so take one more bit from the host portion:

- 192.168.89.0/27 adopts three host bits for the network portion, yielding eight possible subnets ($2^3 = 8$):
  - 192.168.89.0 (**11000000 10101000 01011001 000**00000)
  - 192.168.89.32 (**11000000 10101000 01011001 001**00000)
  - 192.168.89.64 (**11000000 10101000 01011001 010**00000)
  - 192.168.89.96 (**11000000 10101000 01011001 011**00000)
  - 192.168.89.128 (**11000000 10101000 01011001 100**00000)
  - 192.168.89.160 (**11000000 10101000 01011001 101**00000)
  - 192.168.89.192 (**11000000 10101000 01011001 110**00000)
  - 192.168.89.224 (**11000000 10101000 01011001 111**00000)

The range for each subnet begins at the subnet address and ends at the address immediately preceding the next subnet address. For example, the range of IP addresses for the first subnet in this example is 192.168.89.0 through 192.168.89.31.

Within each subnet's IP address range are reserved addresses that cannot be used for hosts in the subnet. In the typical on-prem data center, these reserved addresses include the first address (192.168.89.0) for the network ID and the last address (192.168.89.31) for broadcast traffic. Other reserved addresses might include the router, a printer, or some other network service. Cloud-based subnets also have reserved IP addresses. For example, AWS reserves five addresses in each subnet, as shown in Table 4-3.

Table 4-3 Reserved IP addresses on each AWS subnet

Location within range	Example	Purpose
First	192.168.89.0	Network address
Second	192.168.89.1	Reserved for virtual router
Third	192.168.89.2	Reserved for DNS server or other service
Fourth	192.168.89.3	Reserved by AWS for future use
Last	192.168.89.31	Reserved by AWS even though broadcasting is not supported

Note 4

A quick way to determine how many subnets you create with each borrowed bit is to skip-count by powers of two (such as $2 \times 2 \times 2$, which is 2^3) while holding up an additional finger each time you count up. At the end, count how many fingers you're holding up, and that's how many bits you need to borrow to get the number you counted to.

For example, imagine that your network uses a /24 CIDR block, and you want eight subnets. You already have 24 bits allocated to the network ID. How many bits do you need to borrow from the host ID to get eight subnets? Say "two" and hold up one finger. Say "times *two* is four" and hold up a second finger. Say "times *two* is eight" and hold up a third finger. You reached your goal of eight (which is 2^3), so stop counting and notice that you're holding up three fingers. This means you need to borrow three bits from the host ID to get eight subnets.

Now try this yourself. Say you have a /20 network and you want 32 subnets. How many bits do you need to borrow from the host ID? Lift another finger each time you say "two": *Two* times *two* is four, times *two* is eight, times *two* is 16, times *two* is 32. How many fingers are you holding up?

If you're familiar with subnetting calculations from the CompTIA Network+ exam or in a networking course, you'll remember using formulas or subnet tables to calculate subnets. While these tools are necessary for extensive, precise calculations, subnetting in the cloud doesn't always have to be quite so precise. In fact, you'll generally want to include significant room for growth. At the same time, however, you'll find situations where your subnets should be carefully sized, identified, and/or mapped across multiple networks. Consider carefully which address ranges are used for various segments of a network or for different networks that will be connected, as connected address ranges should not overlap. In these cases, like most networking professionals, you can use a subnet calculator to help eliminate potential calculation errors. For your convenience, Table 4-4 shows a CIDR chart, which shows a breakdown of network bits and host bits for each CIDR block from /16 through /28. These are the block sizes most commonly available for use in a public cloud. Remember to allow for the number of host addresses the CSP will reserve in each subnet in addition to the number of host addresses needed for your purposes.

Table 4-4   CIDR chart

CIDR	# of host bits	# of IP addresses	Subnet mask
/16	16	65,536	255.255.0.0
/17	15	32,768	255.255.128.0
/18	14	16,384	255.255.192.0
/19	13	8,192	255.255.224.0
/20	12	4,096	255.255.240.0
/21	11	2,048	255.255.248.0
/22	10	1,024	255.255.252.0
/23	9	512	255.255.254.0
/24	8	256	255.255.255.0
/25	7	128	255.255.255.128
/26	6	64	255.255.255.192
/27	5	32	255.255.255.224
/28	4	16	255.255.255.240

Exam Tip ✔

While you're not likely to be required to calculate subnets on the CompTIA Cloud+ exam, you should still review the steps involved in these calculations. You might be given a scenario that requires you to analyze appropriate subnet sizing or positioning when considering specific factors. For example, you should be able to identify smaller CIDR blocks within a larger CIDR block. You should also know how to identify overlapping CIDR blocks, which can cause problems with IP address spaces. And you should be able to determine whether a specific IP address falls within a given IP address range.

You're Ready

You're now ready to complete Project 4-1: Practice Subnetting. You can complete the project now or wait until you've finished all the readings for this module.

Cloud Network Interfaces

When you plug an Ethernet cable into the RJ-45 port on your computer's motherboard, you probably don't think about that port as being anything other than an integral part of the computer. In networking, however, each interface on a computer or other network device is, in a way, its own entity. Each interface has its own address(es) and can be configured with different rules. You can see this more clearly on a Linux computer than on a Windows computer. When you run `ipconfig` on a Windows computer, you see a list of all interfaces on the computer and configuration information about each. However, when you run `ifconfig` (or the more modern `ip` command) on a Linux computer, you see that each interface has a name. Examples include eth0 for Ethernet 0, wlan0 for wireless LAN 0, or enp0s3 for a network interface on an Ubuntu machine, as shown in Figure 4-6.

> **Note 5**
>
> The `ifconfig` command has been deprecated, or retired, in some Linux distros. Instead use the `ip` command, which is part of the iproute2 suite of tools, to display and configure settings on network interfaces in Linux.

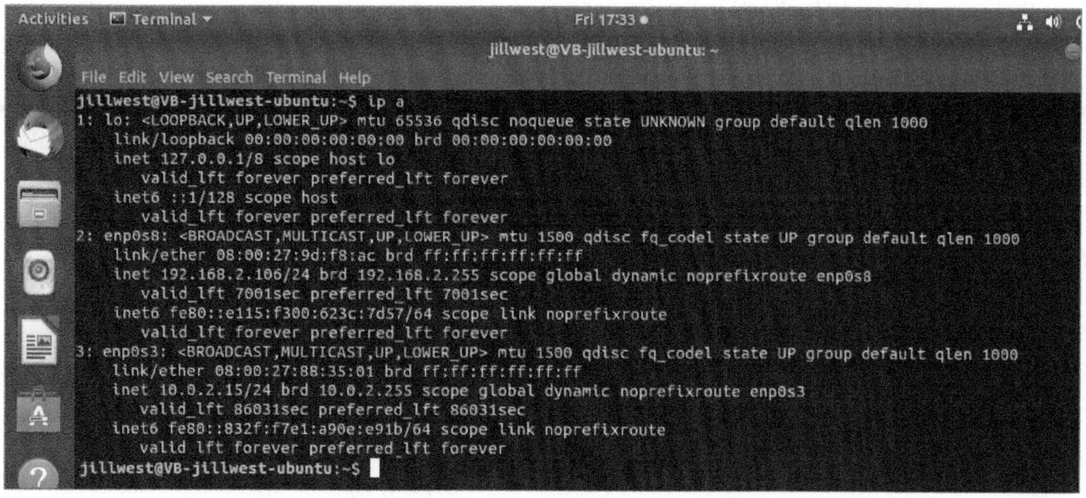

Figure 4-6 This Ubuntu VM has three network interfaces: a loopback interface, a connection to the host machine's Ethernet interface, and a wireless interface to the local network

Source: Canonical Group Limited

Interfaces are also separate entities, or resources, in cloud networking. When you create a VM, you also create a virtual network interface resource with its own ID number and configuration settings. This vNIC provides a connection between the VM and its subnet in a virtual network. You can create and delete vNICs separately from VMs, and you can move vNICs between VMs or subnets. Keep in mind that you must power down a VM before attaching or detaching its vNIC.

Some of the available configurations for a vNIC can affect that interface's potential performance. When configuring a VM's network interface, many cloud platforms offer the option of accelerated networking or enhanced networking. Improved network performance is achieved using a technology called **SR-IOV (single root input/output virtualization)**, which alters the way the host distributes use of its physical NICs. Essentially, the host passes network traffic directly to its NIC hardware rather than processing that traffic through the internal, virtual switch created by the hypervisor. This increases data throughput and reduces demand on the host's CPU.

To enable SR-IOV, you'll need to make some specific selections that support this option. For example, in AWS, you can use an ENA (Elastic Network Adapter) that offers up to 100 Gbps connections or an Intel 82599 VF (Virtual Function) interface that offers up to 10 Gbps throughput. To get an idea of how this works, consider the following restrictions for an ENA:

- Each option is available only on certain, relatively expensive instance types, but the enhanced networking option itself does not incur additional charges.
- You must use a Linux distribution that supports SR-IOV network configurations. Popular distros for this purpose include Amazon's Linux 2, Ubuntu 14.04 or later, and RHEL (Red Hat Enterprise Linux) 7.4 or later.
- ENA configuration can only be managed at a CLI, such as AWS's CloudShell or the AWS CLI tool. It cannot be managed directly through the management console.

If all these requirements are met, ENA is enabled by default on the instance. There are similar restrictions for using the VF option. For example, this feature is only available on certain instance types, and it can only be managed from a CLI.

Remember This

- Public IP addresses provide access to a resource from the Internet, and private IP addresses are only accessible from within the cloud-based network where that resource is located.
- In the cloud, private IP addresses are assigned chronologically from specific IP address ranges that are defined when the virtual network and its subnets are created.
- Subnetting helps manage IP address spaces in the cloud; within each subnet's IP address range are reserved addresses that cannot be used for hosts in the subnet.
- When a VM is created, a virtual network interface resource is also created with its own ID number and configuration settings; this vNIC provides a connection between the VM and its subnet in a virtual network.

Self-Check

4. What kind of address is 8.8.8.8?

  a. RFC 1918 address   **c.** IPv6 address

  b. Private IP address   **d.** Public IP address

5. If a VM is assigned the address 172.16.18.10/24, what is its network ID?

  a. 172.16   **c.** 192.168.18

  b. 172.16.18   **d.** 192.168

6. SR-IOV bypasses which component?

  a. The virtual switch   **c.** The hypervisor

  b. The VM   **d.** The IP address

                                              ○ Check your answers at the end of this module.

Section 4-3: Networking in AWS

Certification

2.2 Given a scenario, secure a network in a cloud environment.

2.4 Given a scenario, apply data security and compliance controls in cloud environments.

3.1 Given a scenario, integrate components into a cloud solution.

3.3 Given a scenario, deploy cloud networking solutions.

4.3 Given a scenario, optimize cloud environments.

4.6 Given a scenario, perform disaster recovery tasks.

The cloud has necessitated the development of many new segmentation concepts. Most notable is the concept of the VPC (virtual private cloud). When you create a network in a public cloud, you're reserving your own space within that larger cloud environment to configure as you choose. This is your VPC (also called a VNet in Azure). It's essentially a software-defined portion of a larger, cloud-based network. Each CSP conceptualizes the VPC a little differently, allocating various segmentation and configuration options, but the overall idea is the same. To get a good idea of how this works, you will first learn about VPCs in AWS. Then you'll discover some of the differences with VPCs in Azure and GCP.

When you first create an account, AWS creates a default VPC for you. When you create a VM instance in AWS, the instance is automatically configured to work within your default VPC unless you change this setting. When adding new resources, you can create a new VPC, or you can use a nondefault VPC that you've already created. Within the VPC, you can configure subnets, route tables, network gateways, and network connections, as well as many other options. To understand what all this means, this section discusses the networking components used to segment and connect cloud resources in AWS, beginning with the largest segment type: regions.

Regions in AWS

AWS offers services in more than two dozen geographical regions around the world, with many more slated for release in the next few years. Each region is named for the geographic location of AWS's physical data centers in that area and has an identity code, such as us-east-2, which is US East (Ohio), or eu-west-3, which is EU (Paris). Figure 4-7 shows AWS's public North American regions. Cloud consumers typically can create resources in any region, such as when placing web servers near customers or complying with data residency restrictions.

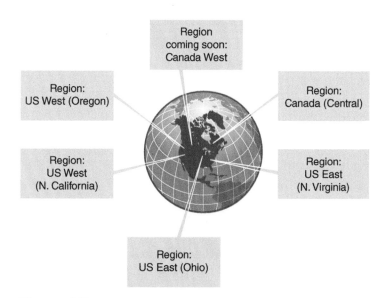

Figure 4-7   AWS public regions in North America

When you create an AWS account, you're assigned a default region. You can later choose a different region near you in which to create your AWS resources. You might instead choose a region farther away from you according to the following factors:

- Cost estimates of the resources you intend to use, as costs can vary considerably among regions
- Inherent latencies for a specific region, as some regions perform better than others
- Available features in a region, as not all services are available in all regions

Availability Zones in AWS

Each region has two or more **AZs (availability zones)**, as shown in Figure 4-8 (this diagram will be developed further as you read through this section, adding more layers of information). Availability zones address HA requirements by providing multiple isolated zones within each region. For the most part, an event that causes an outage in one AZ should not affect services in a different AZ, even if both AZs are in the same region. While some communication between regions crosses the public Internet, communication between AZs in the same region never leaves the AWS infrastructure.

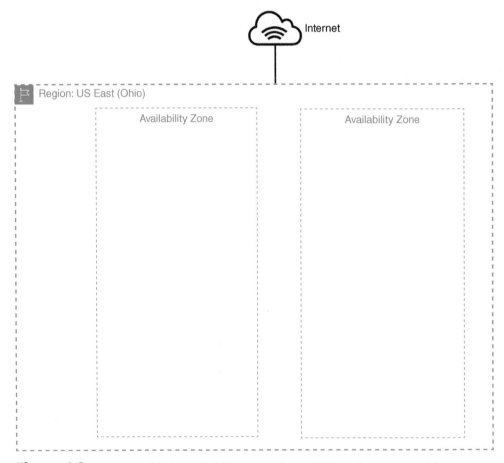

Figure 4-8   Using multiple availability zones in an AWS region can provide redundancy for cloud resources

VPCs in AWS

When you create an AWS account, a default VPC is created for you in each region that is available to you. Each default VPC is automatically assigned a /16 IPv4 CIDR range, though you can assign smaller spaces to your custom VPCs (as small as /28). Every VPC spans all AZs in its region, as shown in Figure 4-9. Also, DNS and DHCP options are initially set at the VPC level. Most AWS resources must be associated with a VPC.

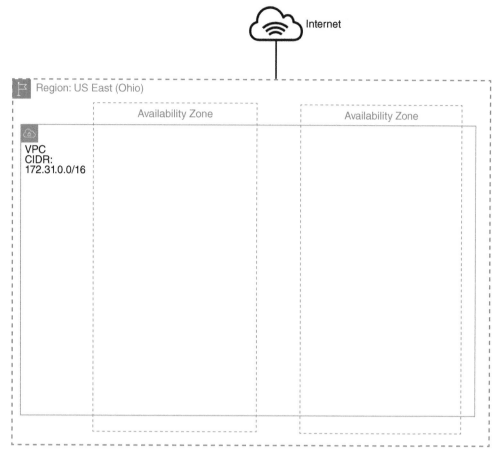

Figure 4-9   An AWS VPC spans all AZs in a region

Note 6

The default IPv4 CIDR block range for a default VPC is /16. However, you can instead use any CIDR block size from /16 (i.e., 65,536 IP addresses) to /28 (i.e., 16 IP addresses) when setting this configuration manually. The same restriction on CIDR block size applies to a VPC's subnets.

Figure 4-10 shows a default VPC. Notice the /16 CIDR range and the options associated with the VPC such as DHCP, DNS, route table, and the network ACL. (You learn more about network ACLs later.) All these settings will, by default, carry over to any VM instances created within the VPC. You can change many of these settings for the default VPC, as shown in Figure 4-11, create nondefault VPCs, or replace the default VPC with a new one. When you create a new VPC, you also have the option to assign CIDR ranges using the Amazon VPC IP Address Manager tool. **IPAM (IP address management)** gives a bird's-eye view of an organization's IP address space for more efficient and organized distribution of these spaces across VPCs and subnets or organizational departments and projects.

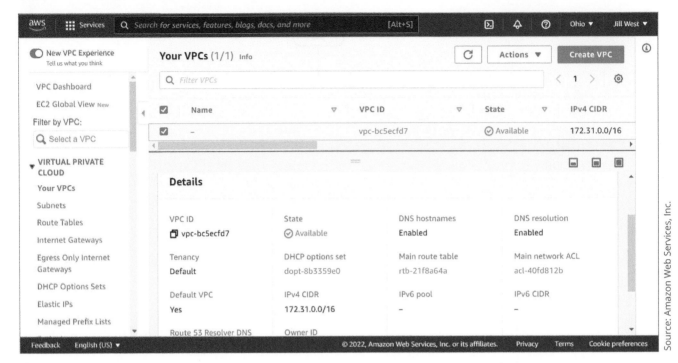

Figure 4-10   A VPC's configurations apply settings to subnets and VM instances within the VPC

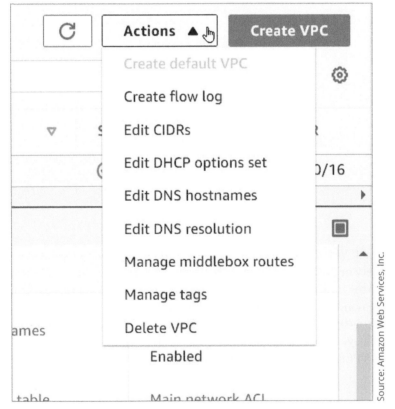

Figure 4-11   Change a VPC's CIDR range, DHCP options, or DNS settings

Note 7

You can also enable IPv6 within a VPC, but you cannot disable IPv4. The configurations for IPv4 and IPv6 operate independently of each other.

Subnets in AWS

By default, each default VPC in each region contains one /20 subnet in each AZ for that region. That's 4096 IPv4 addresses per subnet, with five of those addresses reserved for use by AWS, leaving 4091 available host addresses. In Figure 4-12, the default subnets are the green-colored, public subnets. Default subnets have access to the Internet, which is why they are called public subnets. You'll see in a moment how this is accomplished. Private subnets, such as the blue ones shown at the bottom of Figure 4-12, do not have direct access to the Internet. You can create multiple subnets within each AZ, and you can choose whether these subnets are public or private. Subnets cannot span AZs.

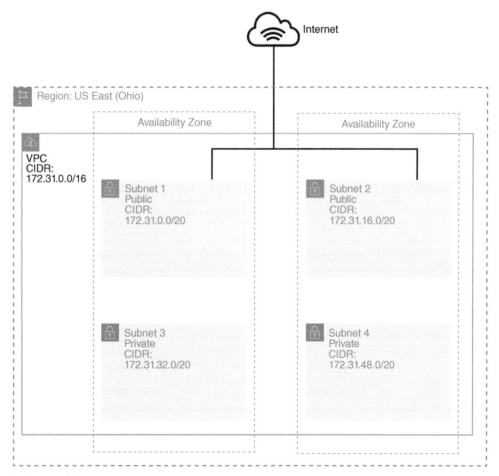

Figure 4-12   Public subnets in AWS have access to the Internet, whereas private subnets do not

Note 8

CIDR block ranges for VPCs and subnets conform to the RFC 1918 specifications for private IP addressing. While you *can* use publicly routable IP addresses for your CIDR block ranges, it's not recommended and will not result in Internet access for instances within those VPCs or subnets. Internet access is only provided through an Internet gateway, which is discussed next.

Gateways and Route Tables in AWS

As you just read, an Internet gateway is required to allow any of your AWS resources to communicate with the Internet. In addition to this gateway, common virtual network devices you'll need in your VPCs include those shown in Figure 4-13 and described next:

- An **IG or IGW (Internet gateway)** is analogous to the cable modem on a home network in that it provides a path to the Internet for resources hosted within the VPC. IGs support both IPv4 and IPv6 traffic and provide **NAT (network address translation)** services for instances that have a public IP address within your public subnets.
- A **route table** is analogous to a router on a physical network and determines where traffic within and from the VPC is routed. Route tables provide one layer of segmentation and security.
- An **NGW (NAT gateway)** device situated in a public subnet gives resources in a connected private subnet egress-only access to the Internet. This arrangement allows protected resources to communicate through the Internet without being exposed to public Internet traffic.

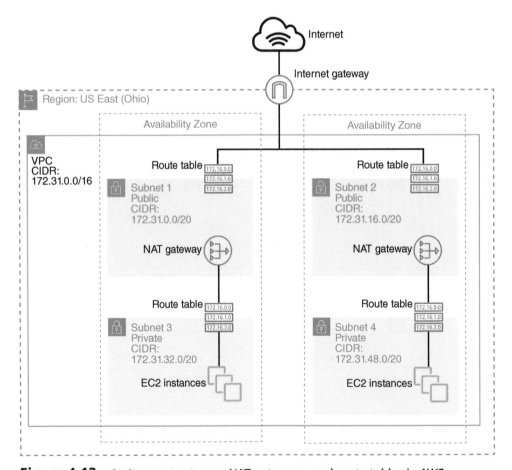

Figure 4-13   An Internet gateway, NAT gateways, and route tables in AWS

Routing to the Internet Gateway

A VPC's route table decides what traffic is directed where. By default, each VPC has a main route table, which is the default route table for all subnets in the VPC. You can make changes to this route table, or you can create new route tables for one or more subnets in your VPC. Many subnets can use the same route table, and each subnet must be associated with exactly one route table.

When a default VPC is created, an IG is also created and is connected to each public subnet within the VPC. This virtual device acts as a bridge, giving each public subnet and its instances access to the Internet. Each time you create a new subnet within a VPC that has an attached IG, the subnet by default is configured as a public subnet and is given a connection to the IG. Resources within a public subnet can communicate through the IG because a rule in the route table allows this communication. You can instead make a subnet private by associating a new route table with that subnet, one that does not include a route to the IG.

Figure 4-14 shows the default route table for a default VPC. As you can see, it lists two routes: one that directs local traffic to the local subnet (enabling instances on the same subnet to talk to each other) and another one that directs all other traffic to the IG. The wildcard address 0.0.0.0/0 can be used to direct all unspecified traffic to the Internet.

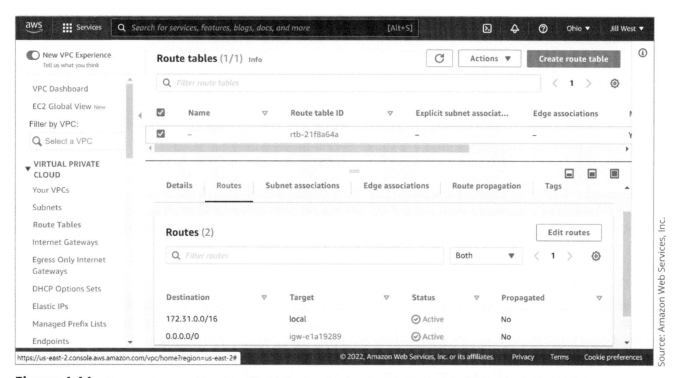

Figure 4-14   Two routes send local traffic to the local subnet and all other traffic to the Internet gateway

Consider the following details of these routes:

- The Destination field identifies the destination IP address or CIDR range the destination IP belongs to.
- The Target field identifies the IP address of the device the traffic should be sent to for it to reach its destination. For example, the CIDR range 0.0.0.0/0 refers to all traffic not otherwise defined. The target for that traffic (that is, traffic not already sent somewhere else) is the IG, which connects to the Internet.

This route table is designed to be used by a public subnet that allows all traffic between the subnet and the Internet. While you can delete the route allowing traffic to and from the IG (effectively making this subnet a private subnet), you can't delete or change the route allowing local traffic.

Applying Routes

Routes are applied to traffic not by a ranked order like what you normally see on physical routers but by matching the traffic to the most specific route applicable to that traffic. For example, consider a route table with the routes shown in Table 4-5, which shows a route to an Internet gateway and a peering connection between two VPCs that allows resources in the VPCs to communicate via private IP addresses (as opposed to requiring public IP addresses). VPC peering is analogous to adding a switch to connect physical networks. (You learn more about VPC peering in a later module.)

Table 4-5   Sample route table

Destination	Target
172.31.0.0/16	Local
(This is the local subnet's CIDR range.)	(This traffic is directed to the local subnet.)
10.0.0.0/16	pcx-1a2b1a2b
(This is the CIDR range of a peered VPC.)	(This traffic is directed to the peering connection, whose ID starts with *pcx*.)
0.0.0.0/0	igw-11aa22bb
(This CIDR range covers all remaining traffic.)	(This traffic is directed to the IG, whose ID starts with *igw*.)

Communications coming from an instance on the local subnet and directed to an instance with the destination IP 10.0.0.25 most closely match the route going to the peering connection pcx-1a2b1a2b. Therefore, this traffic would be sent to the peering connection. However, traffic from the local subnet directed to the destination IP 8.8.8.8 doesn't match any of the more specific routes and would therefore be sent to the IG.

NAT Gateways

Instances running in a private subnet might need to communicate across the Internet while still being protected from Internet-initiated communication. This can be accomplished by creating an NGW in a public subnet and then routing Internet-bound traffic from the private subnet to the NGW instead of going directly to the IG.

Looking back at Figure 4-13, you can see an NGW running on each of the public subnets. A route table on each of the private subnets connects EC2 instances in those subnets to one or the other NGW, which, in turn, can communicate with the Internet. This arrangement accomplishes multiple goals:

- Instances in the private subnets remain protected from Internet-initiated traffic.
- Instances in the private subnets can communicate outward to the Internet.
- Fewer public IP addresses are required to allow this Internet-directed traffic.
- Traffic can be more tightly monitored and filtered.

Unlike IGs, NGWs cost money to use, both for the time the NGW is running and for the data processed over the connection. NGWs require an Elastic IP address, and the EC2 instances also incur data transfer charges.

Note 9

Alternatively, you can create a NAT instance, which is a VM instance hosting NAT services. Typically, however, the NAT gateway is the better option.

Three-Tier Architecture in the Cloud

As you've learned, some degree of segmentation is achieved through disbursing resources in various geographies, such as regions and availability zones. Cloud platforms also use subnets to segment network portions and determine the type of access the resources within the subnet have to the public Internet. An additional approach to segmentation, often used in conjunction with subnets, is called a three-tier architecture, or tiering. While there are a wide variety of interpretations and implementations of this model, the one most commonly used in cloud environments places virtual devices such as the gateways you just read about to divide a customer's cloud space into three logical areas called the presentation tier, the logic tier, and the data tier. Figure 4-15 illustrates the tiers, which are described next.

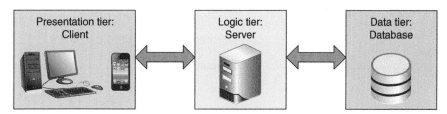

Figure 4-15   Basic three-tier architecture

- *Presentation tier*—The presentation tier is represented by the client devices used to access the application or website. It also incorporates the available connectivity into a company's cloud for users to access the application or website. For example, a load balancer or Internet gateway is part of this tier and is publicly accessible from the Internet.
- *Logic tier*—The logic tier is represented by the server that hosts the application or website. The server sits in a private subnet that does not have direct access to the Internet. However, it can communicate with Internet-based clients through a gateway or proxy device, such as a NAT gateway.
- *Data tier*—The data tier contains one or more databases that are not accessible from the Internet and only communicate with resources in the logic tier.

This approach helps cloud architects decide what resources are needed and where to place them within network segments to accurately control access to those resources. For example, the presentation tier should be publicly accessible for a web app used by customers or website visitors, while the database should be stored in a highly protected subnet that does not have direct access to the Internet. Figure 4-16 shows a sample layout of AWS resources designed to conform to this three-tier architecture model. IP address space is distributed among the subnets.

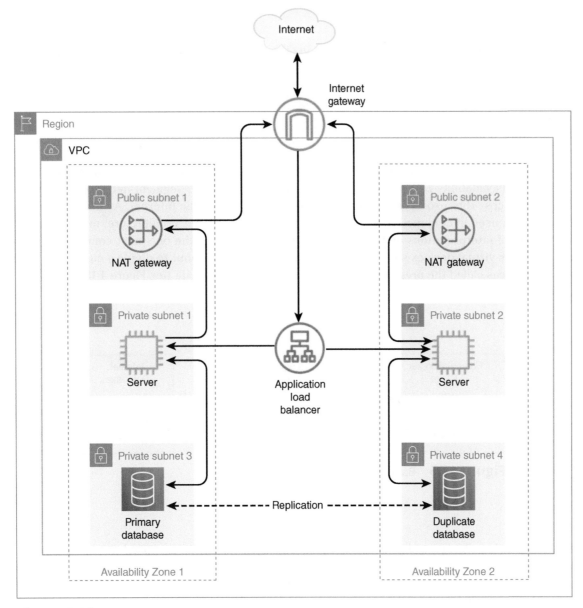

Figure 4-16   Tiered segmentation in AWS

You're Ready

You're now ready to complete Project 4-2: Configure a VPC and Subnets in AWS. You can complete the project now or wait until you've finished all the readings for this module.

Remember This

- A VPC (virtual private cloud, or VNet in Azure) is a software-defined portion of a larger, cloud-based network.
- Each AWS region is named for the geographic location of AWS's physical data centers in that area and has an identity code.
- Availability zones address HA (high availability) requirements by providing multiple isolated zones within each region.
- VPC settings, such as DHCP, DNS, route table, and the network ACL, carry over to any VM instances created within the VPC.
- Resources in public subnets have access to the Internet, whereas resources in private subnets do not have direct access to the Internet.
- A VPC's route table decides what traffic is directed where; an IG (Internet gateway) provides a path to the Internet for resources hosted within the VPC; and an NGW (NAT gateway) gives resources in a connected private subnet egress-only access to the Internet.

Self-Check

7. Which AWS segment type is largest?
   - **a.** Availability Zone
   - **b.** Region
   - **c.** Subnet
   - **d.** VPC

8. Availability zones provide _____.
   - **a.** increased throughput
   - **b.** decreased latency
   - **c.** decreased complexity
   - **d.** increased availability

9. Which AWS device's configuration options determine whether a subnet is public or private?
   - **a.** NGW
   - **b.** Route table
   - **c.** IG
   - **d.** Region

○ Check your answers at the end of this module.

Section 4-4: Networking in Azure

Certification

2.4 Given a scenario, apply data security and compliance controls in cloud environments.

3.1 Given a scenario, integrate components into a cloud solution.

3.3 Given a scenario, deploy cloud networking solutions.

4.3 Given a scenario, optimize cloud environments.

4.6 Given a scenario, perform disaster recovery tasks.

Now that you've seen how networks are set up in AWS, you're ready to explore some of the variations you'll encounter in other cloud platforms. By seeing what tends to change between platforms, you'll develop a deeper understanding of the networking types and the resources used to manage these network spaces.

As you've already read, Azure calls its virtual networks VNets instead of VPCs. You'll find there are more similarities than differences, however, between AWS's and Azure's networking services. As with AWS, you'll start with geographical regions and then work your way into smaller and smaller segmentation components.

Regions and Availability Zones in Azure

At the time of this writing, Microsoft offers nearly 60 Azure regions worldwide with many more regions in the works. Each region offers different services, so it's important to check service availability in any region you're considering before you commit to it. Costs also vary by region, as do data residency compliance standards.

Regions are grouped into a larger category called geographies. A geography is a geographic area containing multiple Azure regions to provide data residency and compliance boundaries for discrete markets. For example, the United States geography contains 10 regions (plus additional government regions), such as West US in California and East US in Virginia. Other geographies include Canada, Australia, Europe, UK, India, and Asia Pacific.

Not all of Azure's regions currently offer availability zones. The ones that do contain at least three AZs where each AZ consists of one or more completely separate physical data centers with independent power, cooling, and networking infrastructure. See Figure 4-17 (this diagram will be developed further as you read through this section, adding more layers of information). Microsoft guarantees at least 99.99 percent uptime when VM resources are backed up across at least two AZs. While there's no cost to deploy VMs in multiple AZs, there is a charge for data transfer between VMs in different AZs.

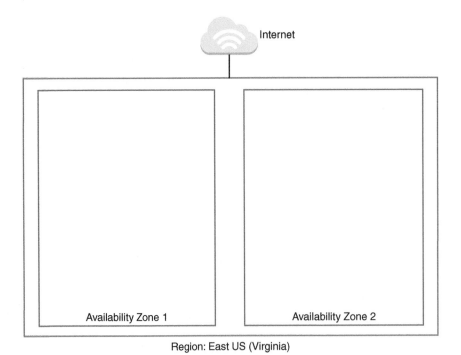

Figure 4-17   Availability zones in Azure reduce the risk of loss due to failures or problematic updates

VNets and Subnets in Azure

Within each of your Azure subscriptions, you can create multiple VNets. Every Azure VM in your account must be associated with one VNet, even if it has multiple network interfaces. As with AWS's VPCs, each VNet can span multiple AZs within a region (see Figure 4-18), which means the VNet can support resources residing in those different AZs.

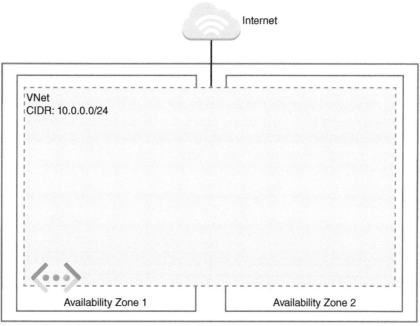

Figure 4-18   Azure VNet resources can be distributed across multiple availability zones

Each VNet contains one or more subnets, as shown in Figure 4-19. Subnets must use an IP address space contained within the VNet's IP range, and each subnet must have a unique IP address range without overlapping any other subnets in the same VNet. By default, all subnets within a VNet can communicate with one another and with the Internet. You can change this setting if you need to restrict access to resources within a subnet.

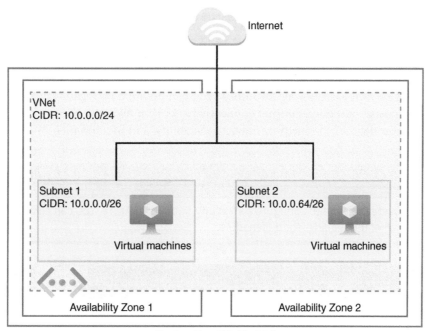

Figure 4-19   Subnets in an Azure VNet can communicate with one another by default

Route Tables in Azure

When you first create a VNet, Azure automatically generates system routes that enable communication between all resources within the VNet, regardless of subnet, and allow for access to the Internet. These system routes can't be changed because you don't have access to them. However, you can create a route table with routes that will override the default system routes, as shown in Figure 4-20. These custom routes might be defined by the user, which is called UDR (user-defined routing), or learned from nearby gateways, such as a VPN gateway. Like AWS, Azure chooses the route to apply to traffic by how closely the destination IP address matches a route's address prefix. Notice that Azure does not provide private subnets as AWS does. To control traffic between a subnet and the Internet, other solutions must be configured. You learn more about those options in later modules.

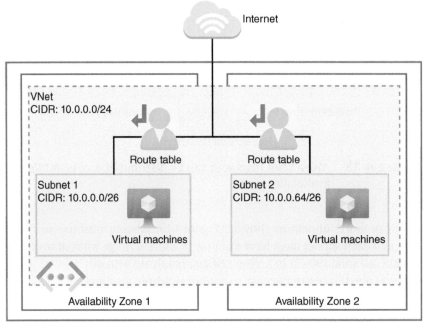

Figure 4-20   Each Azure subnet can be associated with a custom route table

While Azure does not rely on IGs the way AWS does, you can create a NAT gateway through the Azure Virtual Network NAT service to manage outbound Internet connectivity. As with AWS, the NAT gateway instance is not a free resource and offers a greater degree of security, resiliency, scalability, and performance.

> ## You're Ready
>
> You're now ready to complete Project 4-3: Configure a VNet and Subnets in Azure. You can complete the project now or wait until you've finished all of the readings for this module.

> ## Remember This
>
> - Azure regions are grouped into a larger category called geographies, where each geography contains multiple Azure regions to provide data residency and compliance boundaries for discrete markets.
> - Each VNet can span multiple AZs within a region, and each VNet contains one or more subnets.
> - Azure system routes enable communication between resources within a VNet, regardless of subnet, and allow for access to the Internet.

Self-Check

10. Which Azure segment type is largest?
    a. Availability zone
    b. Region
    c. Geography
    d. VNet

11. How does Azure choose which route to apply to traffic crossing a route table?
    a. First match
    b. Best match
    c. Priority rating
    d. Privacy setting

○ Check your answers at the end of this module.

Section 4-5: Networking in GCP

Certification

2.4 Given a scenario, apply data security and compliance controls in cloud environments.

3.1 Given a scenario, integrate components into a cloud solution.

3.3 Given a scenario, deploy cloud networking solutions.

4.3 Given a scenario, optimize cloud environments.

4.6 Given a scenario, perform disaster recovery tasks.

GCP is set up very similarly to AWS with regions, VPCs, zones, and subnets. However, there are some significant differences. For example:

- A GCP VPC is global, meaning it spans all regions by default.
- A GCP VPC does not have an IP range assigned to it. CIDR ranges are defined only at the subnet level.
- IPv6 traffic is only supported to external resources, not between resources internal to a GCP VPC.

In this section, you explore the various components of networking in GCP.

Regions and Zones in GCP

At the time of this writing, GCP has nearly 30 regions worldwide, and most of those regions have at least three zones with independent power, cooling, networking, and control planes (which is the management layer of a software-defined infrastructure). See Figure 4-21. (This diagram will be developed further as you read through this section, adding more layers of information.) Because GCP VPCs span regions as well as zones, backing up resources and applications around the globe can be accomplished without leaving Google's private infrastructure. In other words, a VM in one region can communicate with a VM in another region without relying at all on the public Internet infrastructure. As you might imagine, this provides a layer of security as well.

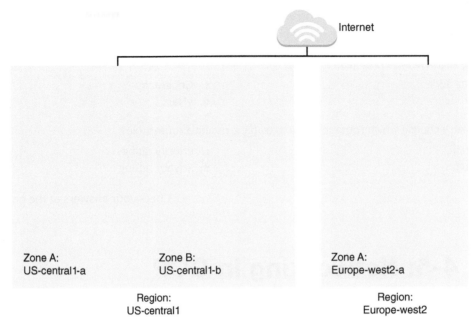

Figure 4-21   Most GCP regions have at least three zones

When choosing regions and zones to host your resources, select options that keep those resources geographically close to the users who will need to access them regularly. You might also choose a specific region or zone based on the services available there, the costs for those services, and the hardware available to support those services (such as CPU platforms, available machine types, and GPU availability).

VPCs and Subnets in GCP

As already mentioned, a GCP VPC spans multiple regions (see Figure 4-22). When you create a VPC using auto mode, you automatically get a subnet in each region for that VPC. If a new region is added, auto mode adds a new subnet to your VPC for that region. Auto mode networks use preconfigured IP address ranges. You could instead use custom mode and choose where your subnets are located, or even whether to create any subnets at all.

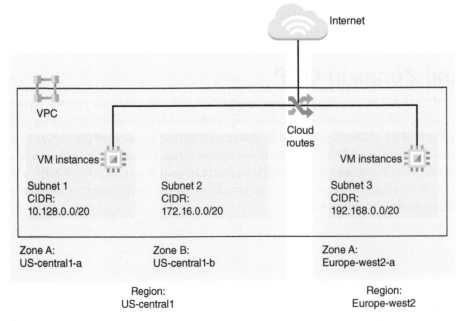

Figure 4-22   A single VPC can span all of GCP's regions

A significant advantage of global VPCs is that you can access distant regions from on-prem resources through a single VPC connection. In cloud platforms where virtual networks are limited to a single region, you would need a different connection from your on-prem data center to each region where you host resources, or you would need some other kind of transitory connection. (You learn more about network-to-network connections in a later module.) Much of the cost of networking in the cloud is related to connecting resources across regions. With GCP, you can avoid much of this expense due to the global access provided by a single VPC. Although there is still a fee for egress traffic (i.e., traffic moving out of the VPC) across zones or regions, the rate is much lower than the cost for egress traffic to the Internet. In contrast, ingress traffic, or traffic entering a VPC, is not charged.

Routes in GCP

Routes in GCP are applied at the VPC level, not at the subnet level. Instances within the subnet maintain their own copy of applicable routes. When a route table is first created, two types of routes are automatically generated by the system. Additional, custom-defined routes can also be added. The different types of routes are as follows:

- System-generated
  - Subnet routes direct traffic between all the VPC's subnets.
  - The default route sends all other traffic to the default Internet gateway.
- Custom
  - Dynamic routes are created automatically by a Cloud Router service.
  - Static routes are created manually by a cloud user.

While GCP does direct Internet-bound traffic to the default Internet gateway, this gateway is not a device you can access, reconfigure, delete, or create. You control a VPC's access to the Internet by managing the default route. You can prevent all Internet traffic between a VPC and the Internet by deleting the default route that connects to the Internet gateway. Routes in GCP are applied first by how closely a rule applies to traffic and then by the priority rating of the route.

You're Ready

You're now ready to complete Project 4-4: Configure a VPC in GCP. You can complete the project now or wait until you've finished all the readings for this module.

Remember This

- Because GCP VPCs span regions as well as zones, backing up resources and applications around the globe can be accomplished without leaving Google's private infrastructure.
- A significant advantage of global VPCs is that you can access distant regions from on-prem resources through a single VPC connection.
- While GCP does direct Internet-bound traffic to the default Internet gateway, this gateway is not a device you can access, reconfigure, delete, or create; instead, you control a VPC's access to the Internet by managing the default route.

Self-Check

12. Which GCP resource type is assigned CIDR ranges?

   a. Region

   b. Zone

   c. VPC

   d. Subnet

13. Which GCP route type is created by a Cloud Router?

   a. Static routes

   b. Dynamic routes

   c. Subnet routes

   d. Default routes

○ Check your answers at the end of this module.

Module Summary

Section 4-1: Networking Concepts in the Cloud

- SDN (software-defined networking) separates the control plane, or management layer, of the network from the data plane where transmissions on the network actually traverse physical devices; similarly, NFV (network functions virtualization) virtualizes network devices and services.

- Various versions of the cloud stack model show five to seven layers that are defined by who has access to the configurations of that layer.

- When configuring cloud networking services, you will likely need redundant virtual devices in your cloud to ensure HA (high availability) and avoid any single point of failure.

Section 4-2: IP Address Spaces

- Public IP addresses provide access to a resource from the Internet, and private IP addresses are only accessible from within the cloud-based network where that resource is located.

- In the cloud, private IP addresses are assigned chronologically from specific IP address ranges that are defined when the virtual network and its subnets are created.

- Subnetting helps manage IP address spaces in the cloud; within each subnet's IP address range are reserved addresses that cannot be used for hosts in the subnet.

- When a VM is created, a virtual network interface resource is also created with its own ID number and configuration settings; this vNIC provides a connection between the VM and its subnet in a virtual network.

Section 4-3: Networking in AWS

- A VPC (virtual private cloud, or VNet in Azure) is a software-defined portion of a larger, cloud-based network.

- Each AWS region is named for the geographic location of AWS's physical data centers in that area and has an identity code.

- Availability zones address HA requirements by providing multiple isolated zones within each region.

- VPC settings, such as DHCP, DNS, route table, and the network ACL, carry over to any VM instances created within the VPC.

- Resources in public subnets have access to the Internet, whereas resources in private subnets do not have direct access to the Internet.

- A VPC's route table decides what traffic is directed where; an IG (Internet gateway) provides a path to the Internet for resources hosted within the VPC; and an NGW (NAT gateway) gives resources in a connected private subnet egress-only access to the Internet.

Section 4-4: Networking in Azure

- Azure regions are grouped into a larger category called geographies, where each geography contains multiple Azure regions to provide data residency and compliance boundaries for discrete markets.
- Each VNet can span multiple AZs within a region, and each VNet contains one or more subnets.
- Azure system routes enable communication between resources within a VNet, regardless of subnet, and allow for access to the Internet.

Section 4-5: Networking in GCP

- Because GCP VPCs span regions as well as zones, backing up resources and applications around the globe can be accomplished without leaving Google's private infrastructure.
- A significant advantage of global VPCs is that you can access distant regions from on-prem resources through a single VPC connection.
- While GCP does direct Internet-bound traffic to the default Internet gateway, this gateway is not a device you can access, reconfigure, delete, or create; instead, you control a VPC's access to the Internet by managing the default route.

Key Terms

For definitions of key terms, see the Glossary.

AZ (availability zone)
CIDR (classless interdomain routing) notation
IG or IGW (Internet gateway)
IPAM (IP address management)
NAT (network address translation)
NFV (network functions virtualization)
NGW (NAT gateway)

peering connection
private IP address
private subnet
public IP address
public subnet
region
RFC (Request for Comments) 1918
route table

SDDC (software-defined data center)
SDN (software-defined networking)
SR-IOV (single root input/output virtualization)
subnetting
tiering
VNet
VPC (virtual private cloud)

Acronyms Checklist

The acronyms in Table 4-6 are listed in the Cloud+ objectives and could appear on the Cloud+ exam. This means that exam questions might use any of these acronyms in context so that you must know the meaning of the acronym in order to answer the question correctly. Make sure you're familiar with what each acronym stands for and the general concept of the term itself. All these acronyms are used in context in this module.

Table 4-6   Module 4 acronyms

Acronym	Spelled out
DHCP	Dynamic Host Configuration Protocol
HA	high availability
IPAM	IP (Internet Protocol) address management
MDF	main distribution facility
NAT	network address translation
SDN	software-defined networking
SR-IOV	single root input/output virtualization
VPC	virtual private cloud

Review Questions

1. What type of cloud network traffic incurs fees?

   a. Traffic between two VMs in the same subnet
   b. Ingress traffic to a storage bucket
   c. Egress traffic from a database
   d. Traffic between two VMs in the same VPC

2. Which of the following is a legitimate CIDR block for a subnet? Choose TWO.

   a. 172.300.7.0/25
   b. 192.168.4.0/24
   c. 10.10.10.0/33
   d. 192.168.168.0/10

3. Which of the following concepts is ensured by redundant routers and switches?

   a. VPC
   b. HA
   c. SDN
   d. AZ

4. Which IP address belongs within the CIDR block 172.25.1.0/23?

   a. 172.25.2.10
   b. 192.25.1.100
   c. 172.25.0.254
   d. 192.24.1.0

5. Which tier is most protected?

   a. Logic tier
   b. Subnet tier
   c. Data tier
   d. Presentation tier

6. Which cloud stack layer corresponds to IaaS services?

   a. Physical layer
   b. Network layer
   c. Virtualization layer
   d. Image layer

7. Which technology is used to improve vNIC performance?

   a. SDDC
   b. NFV
   c. RFC 1918
   d. SR-IOV

8. How do you change applicable routes in an Azure VNet?

   a. Delete system routes.
   b. Edit system routes.
   c. Create a new VNet with different system routes.
   d. Override system routes with custom routes.

9. What factor is improved by SR-IOV?

   a. Security
   b. Performance
   c. Availability
   d. Adaptability

10. Which cloud platform's VPC or VNet can extend beyond a single region?

   a. Azure
   b. VMware
   c. GCP
   d. AWS

Scenario-Based Questions

Question 4-1

Ginny is building a series of subnets in her AWS cloud that will host VMs used to test applications her company is developing. The applications are tested by a team of users who are specialists in their respective industries. Ginny establishes the subnets, spins up a few experimental VMs, and starts testing her connections. She realizes there's a misconfiguration in one of the VMs and needs to remote into it to make some changes. What piece of information does Ginny need to collect from AWS first?

   a. The VM's user password
   b. The subnet's private IP address
   c. The VM's public IP address
   d. The AWS account's key pair

Question 4-2

Adan is mapping out address pools for the subnets he plans to create in his Azure account. He has determined the network will use a CIDR /24 address space, and he needs 16 small subnets within this space. How many bits should Adan borrow from the host ID to create these subnets?

    a. 1
    b. 2
    c. 3
    d. 4

Question 4-3

Tim is troubleshooting a problem with his VM in AWS. He created a new VPC and a new subnet, enabled auto-assign public IPs, added an IG and a VM, and attached the VM's interface to a subnet within the VPC. This is where he ran into problems. Tim has been trying for 30 minutes to open an RDP connection to the VM, and it's not working. He confirmed the VM is set to allow RDP traffic, and the VPC and subnet both also allow RDP traffic. He also confirmed the VM is running. What is the next step Tim must take to solve the problem?

    a. He should install RDP in the VM.
    b. He should configure a route to the IG.
    c. He should assign the VM a public IP address.
    d. He should create a new subnet in the VPC.

Hands-On Projects

Note 10

Websites, applications, public cloud platforms, and related account options change often. While the instructions given in these projects were accurate at the time of writing, you might need to adjust the steps or options according to later changes.

Note to Instructors and Students: A rubric is provided for evaluating student performance on these projects. Please see Appendix D.

Project 4-1: Practice Subnetting

Estimated time: 30 minutes
Objective 1.4: Given a scenario, analyze the solution design in support of the business requirements.
Group work: This project includes enhancements when assigned as a group project.
Resources:

- Internet access

Context:
You can find many handy shortcuts online for calculating subnets quickly and easily. On the job, it would probably be best to use a subnet calculator, such as the one at subnet-calculator.com, to better ensure you don't make any time-consuming mistakes in your calculations. However, on certification exams, subnetting shortcuts can help you get to an answer quickly without wasting your limited exam time.

(continues)

Hands-On Projects Continued

> **Note 11**
>
> At the time of this writing, you are allowed to use a dry-erase board for calculations during the exam if you take the exam at a testing center. However, if you take the exam remotely from home, you are not allowed to use any writing instruments at all.

To use this shortcut method, you'll first draw a series of numbers. This might look confusing at first but hang in there. It should make sense by the end. Complete the following steps:

1. Write one row of eight numbers from right to left, starting with 1 on the right, then 2, then 4, and so on, doubling each number as you move left. See the top row in Figure 4-23.

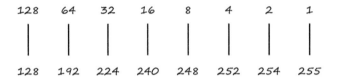

Figure 4-23 Write these numbers and connect the number in each column

2. Below this first row, write another row of eight numbers from right to left, this time starting with 255 on the right. Subtract the number directly above 255 to get the next number, 254. Subtract the number directly above 254 to get 252, and so on. You know you've done it correctly if the leftmost number in both rows is 128. (After you've done this a few times, you'll likely have these numbers memorized.) When you're finished, draw a line connecting the corresponding numbers in each row, as shown in Figure 4-23.
3. Above the top row, write another row of eight numbers, but this time, work left to right. Start with 2 on the left and double each number as you move to the right. See the top row in Figure 4-24.

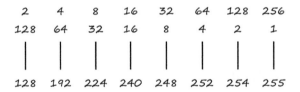

Figure 4-24 If you have trouble memorizing these numbers, just memorize the pattern of how to get them and where to write them

You're now ready to use your shortcut to calculate subnets. Let's start with the class C network at 192.168.15.0 and create as many subnets as possible with at least 10 hosts each, as follows:

4. On the second row (the row immediately above the vertical lines), find the smallest number that covers the needed hosts and circle it, as shown in Figure 4-25. This is your magic number. In Figure 4-25, the magic number is 16, which is the smallest number that will provide at least 10 hosts as required by the scenario.

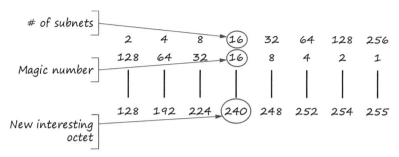

Figure 4-25   Circle the magic number, the number of subnets,
and the new subnet octet

5. Circle the number directly above the magic number, as shown in Figure 4-25. This tells you how many subnets you'll be creating.

6. Circle the number directly below the magic number, as shown in Figure 4-25. This is the new interesting octet in the subnet mask. What is the subnet mask for the subnets in this scenario?

7. To calculate the subnets' network IDs, start with the original network IP address 192.168.15.0 for the first subnet, as shown in Table 4-7. In the fourth octet, skip-count by the magic number as high as you can go without going over 255. Add this information to Table 4-7 in the Network ID column. The second subnet is done for you.

Table 4-7   Subnetting practice

Network ID	Host IP range	Broadcast address
192.168.15.0	192.168.15.1 – 192.168.15.14	192.168.15.15
192.168.15.16	192.168.15.17 – 192.168.15.30	192.168.15.31

8. Fill in the rest of Table 4-7. Recall that you can subtract 1 from a network ID to get the previous subnet's broadcast address. The host IP address range consists of all numbers between the network ID and the broadcast address. Be sure to submit your completed table with your answers to this project's questions.

Hands-On Projects Continued

How well did this shortcut help you? If it clicked for you, great! Keep practicing with this method, and you might even learn it well enough to do most of it in your head. If it didn't work for you, do a Google search for *subnetting shortcuts* and find a method that does work for you.

Several good websites and apps can give you a variety of practice subnet questions so you can become especially comfortable with calculating subnets. Do a Google search for *subnetting practice*, or try an app on your phone, such as /24 Subnetting Practice, available on both Android and iPhone. A good subnetting practice app like /24 Subnetting Practice will give you options on the types of problems to work with, will tell you the correct answer, and will explain why that answer is correct.

9. **For group assignments:** Share with your group the subnetting shortcut method that makes the most sense to you. As you listen to other group members explain their shortcut methods, take notes of any formulas, shorthand calculations, or memorized facts required for each of their methods. Give a short description of each method according to what information must be memorized, what formulas are used, and any other significant details required to make that method work in a testing environment where no calculators are allowed.

Project 4-2: Configure a VPC and Subnets in AWS

Estimated time: 45 minutes
Objective 3.3: Given a scenario, deploy cloud networking solutions.
Resources:

- AWS account
- Drawing app, such as Visio or app.diagrams.net
- Internet access

Context:

For security purposes, it's important to know the difference between public and private subnets in AWS and how to manage the traffic that can enter or exit each subnet. In this project, you will create a VPC and subnets and configure those subnets as either public or private. Complete the following steps:

1. In your AWS Management Console, go to the **VPC dashboard**. The VPC service is listed in the **Networking & Content Delivery** category.
2. In the left pane, click **Your VPCs** to see what VPCs you currently have. Click **Create VPC**. Give the VPC a name, such as MyVPC. Make sure **IPv4 CIDR manual input** is selected, and then specify an IPv4 CIDR block such as 192.168.0.0/24. You don't need an IPv6 CIDR block, and make sure you use the **Default** tenancy. You also do not need to add any new tags in this project (you'll learn more about tags later). Click **Create VPC**. Return to your list of VPCs to confirm your new nondefault VPC is listed along with any other VPCs you already had in your account. What CIDR block did you use?
3. AWS created a default route table for your new VPC. To see what routes are included, in the new VPC's Details pane, click the main route table's ID, and then click the **Routes** tab. The route table should only include one route for local traffic to the VPC you just created and no other routes. What is the destination range for the local traffic route?
4. You do not yet have a subnet in this new VPC. To create a subnet, click **Subnets** in the left pane, and then click **Create subnet**. Select the VPC you created in Step 2. Give the subnet a name, such as MyPrivateSubnet. You do not need to specify an AZ. Assign a CIDR block that is contained within and is smaller than the VPC's CIDR range, such as 192.168.0.0/26. Click **Create subnet**. You should now see the new subnet listed with any other subnets you already had in your account. What CIDR block did you use?
5. Your new subnet adopted the main route table from your VPC configurations. In the new subnet's Details pane, click the route table's ID, and check the routes to confirm this information matches what you saw in Step 3. Instances created within this private subnet will not be able to reach the Internet with the current configuration, as there is no route to the Internet.

6. For VM instances within a public subnet to reach the Internet, you'll need to add an IG (Internet Gateway). In the left pane, click **Internet Gateways**. While you likely already have an IG here, for this project, you'll create a new IG. Click **Create internet gateway**. Give the IG a name, such as MyIG, and click **Create internet gateway**. What is the state of your new IG?

7. Attach the IG to your VPC. To do this, on the IG's page, click **Actions**, and then click **Attach to VPC**. Choose your VPC from the list and click **Attach internet gateway**. What is the state of your IG now?

8. Now you're ready to add a new subnet that will have access to the Internet through your new IG. Create a new subnet. This time, name it something like MyPublicSubnet. Add it to the same VPC as the first subnet, and use an adjacent CIDR block, such as 192.168.0.64/26. What CIDR block did you use?

9. Check the route table for your second subnet. This subnet also adopted the VPC's main route table and so only allows for local traffic. To route Internet traffic through the IG, you could either change this route table (which would affect all resources using this route table, including your private subnet) or create a new route table. For this project, you'll create a new route table so the private subnet will stay private. To do this, go to the list of route tables and click **Create route table**. Give the route table a name, such as MyPublicRT, select the VPC you created earlier in this project, and then click **Create route table**. Go to the full list of route tables. You now have two route tables using the same VPC ID. Which route table is the main route table for that VPC?

10. Check the routes for your new route table. This new route table still only allows local traffic because you've not yet added a route to the IG. Click **Edit routes** and then click **Add route**. Traffic destined for the Internet can be described with the CIDR range **0.0.0.0/0**. Add this destination to your new route. For the target, choose **Internet Gateway** and then click your IG. Click **Save changes**. Confirm the new route was added to your public route table. How can you tell the target for Internet traffic is an IG?

11. Now you need to add the new route table to the public subnet. Return to your list of subnets and select your public subnet. Click **Actions** and then click **Edit route table association**. Select your public route table, confirm the routes are listed as expected, and click **Save**. How can you confirm your subnet is now connected to the IG?

12. Unless you change this setting, nondefault subnets do not auto-assign a public IP address even if there's an IG attached to it. To change this setting, on the **Subnets** page, select your public subnet, click **Actions**, and click **Edit subnet settings**. Enable auto-assignment of public IPv4 addresses, and then save your change.

13. To test your configuration of the public subnet, create a new VM instance. Under Network settings, click **Edit**. Select your new VPC and the public subnet you created. Launch the instance (you do not need to download the key pair). Did your machine receive a public IPv4 address? If so, what is it? What is the VM's private IP address?

14. Use a drawing app, such as Visio or app.diagrams.net, to **draw the VPC and its resources** that you created in this project, showing logical connections and the relative position of each resource. Submit this visual with your answers to this project's questions.

15. Delete all the resources you created in this project, including the VM instance, the VPC, both subnets, both route tables, and the IG. In what order did you delete these resources? What error messages did you encounter? How did you handle these problems? Check through your account to confirm that all related resources have been deleted.

Note 12

Depending on the status of your account and the selections you made during this project, the resources you created can deplete your credits or accrue charges. Double-check to make sure you've terminated all resources you created in this project.

(continues)

Hands-On Projects Continued

Project 4-3: Configure a VNet and Subnets in Azure

Estimated time: 30 minutes
Objective 3.3: Given a scenario, deploy cloud networking solutions.
Resources:

- Azure account
- Internet access

Context:
Each VM connects to a subnet through an interface. Given multiple interfaces, the VM can connect to multiple subnets. In this project, you'll create a VNet and two subnets and practice managing VM interfaces. Complete the following steps:

1. In your Azure portal, go to the **Resource groups** page. Create a new resource group. You don't need to use tags in this project (you learn more about tags in a later module). What did you name your new resource group?

> **Note 13**
>
> Be sure to use this same resource group for all resources created in this project, and then delete the entire resource group at the end of the project.

2. Go to the **Virtual networks** dashboard. Click **Create virtual network**. Choose the resource group you just created, and give the network a name, such as MyVnet1. Click **Next: IP Addresses**.
3. Assign an IPv4 address space, such as 192.168.0.0/24. What address space did you use?
4. In Azure, you create a new subnet at the same time you create a new VNet. Click **Add subnet**. Give the subnet a name, such as Subnet1. Delete the existing IPv4 address space, and then create a new address range within the VNet's CIDR range, such as 192.168.0.0/26. How many addresses are included in the subnet's CIDR block? Click **Add**.
5. Keep the remaining default settings for your new VNet and click **Create**.
6. Create a new VM in the VNet using the same resource group. On the Networking page, be sure to select the VNet you created and its subnet. Then create the VM.
7. After the VM is deployed, click the VM, and then click **Networking** in the left pane. What is the VM's private IP address? What is the name of this network interface?
8. Under the name of the network interface, click **Topology** and describe the information given in this diagram.
9. Now you're ready to add a second network interface to this VM. Power down the machine (but don't delete it). Make sure the VM is completely stopped, then return to the VM's Networking page and click **Attach network interface**. Click **Create and attach network interface**. Give the network interface a name, such as MyNewInt. What options do you have for selecting a VNet? Why do you think this is?
10. Leave the default settings in place and click **Create**. On the Attach network interface pane, click **OK**.
11. When complete, the VM's Networking page should show two interfaces. Click the second interface's tab. What IP address is assigned to this interface?
12. Click **Topology** and describe the information given in this diagram.

Both interfaces are included in the same subnet, and you were not able to add the new interface to a different VNet than the first interface was already attached to. Can you place the second interface in a different *subnet* from the first interface? To determine the answer to this question, complete the following steps:

13. Create a second subnet in the first VNet. Give the subnet a name and an address space within the first VNet's CIDR block, such as 192.168.0.64/28. What address space did you use?

14. After the subnet is created, return to the VM's Networking page. Associate the second network interface with the new subnet. What is the new IP address for this interface?

15. What changed on the topology? **Take a screenshot** of the topology; submit this visual with your answers to this project's questions.

16. Delete all the resources you created in this project, including the VM instance, the VNet, both subnets, both interfaces, and the entire resource group. In what order did you delete these resources? What error messages did you encounter? How did you handle these problems? Check through your account to confirm that all related resources have been deleted.

Note 14

Depending on the status of your account and the selections you made during this project, the resources you created can deplete your credits or accrue charges. Double-check to make sure you've terminated all resources you created in this project.

Project 4-4: Configure a VPC in GCP

Estimated time: 30 minutes
Objective 3.3: Given a scenario, deploy cloud networking solutions.
Resources:

- GCP account
- Drawing app, such as Visio or app.diagrams.net
- Internet access

Context:
GCP VPCs are unusual in that the subnets within a VPC do not need to use a CIDR block within the VPC's address space because the VPC doesn't have an address space assigned to it. In this project, you'll explore VPC configuration options in GCP. Complete the following steps:

1. To make cleanup easier at the end of this project, first click the scope picker at the top of your GCP console, as shown in Figure 4-26, to create a new project. Click **NEW PROJECT** and give this project a name. Click **CREATE**.

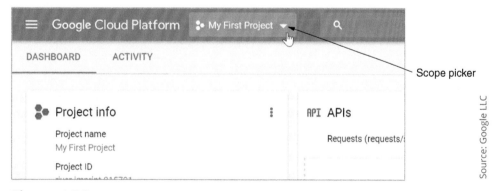

Figure 4-26   Creating a new project makes it easier to clean up everything later

2. Make sure you're in the new project you just created. Then go to the VPC networks dashboard. Click **CpREATE VPC NETWORK**. Give the network a name, such as myautovpc. Under Subnet creation mode, click **Automatic**. Leave all other default settings and click **Create**.

(continues)

Hands-On Projects Continued

3. On your VPC networks page, scroll down to find your new VPC. After it's fully deployed, how many subnets are included in your new VPC?

4. Click the VPC name, and then click **Routes**. What is the next hop for most of the routes? What is the next hop for the Internet route?

5. Return to your list of VPC networks, and then create a new VPC. This time, use the **Custom** subnet creation mode. Name the subnet and select a region. (Do not select a region in Asia, as it will cause an error later in the project.) Assign a private IP address range to the subnet, such as 192.168.0.0/24. Notice the subnet receives an IP address range but the VPC does not. What CIDR range did you choose?

6. Create a second subnet in a different region. (Do not select a region in Asia, as it will cause an error later in the project.) Try to give it the same CIDR range as the first subnet and create the VPC. What happens?

7. Try creating your custom VPC again, and this time give the second subnet a CIDR range that is not in the same class as the first subnet's CIDR range. For example, if you used 192.168.0.0/24, try 172.16.0.0/16 for the second subnet. What happens?

8. After the VPC is fully deployed, how many subnets are included in the newest VPC? Which two regions did you use?

9. Check the routes for this VPC. How many routes are included? Where do they each go?

10. Use a drawing app, such as Visio or app.diagrams.net, to **draw the custom VPC and its resources** that you created in this project, showing logical connections and the relative position of each resource. Submit this visual with your answers to this project's questions.

11. Delete all the resources you created in this project, including both VPCs and all subnets. In what order did you delete these resources? What error messages did you encounter? How did you handle these problems? Check through your account to confirm that all related resources have been deleted. To delete the project in GCP, click the **Settings and utilities** icon in the top right of your console, and then click **Project settings**. Click **SHUT DOWN** to delete all resources created in this Hands-On Project. Enter the project ID and then click **SHUT DOWN**. Click **OK** and return to your GCP console.

Note 15

Depending on the status of your account and the selections you made during this project, the resources you created can deplete your credits or accrue charges. Double-check to make sure you've terminated all resources you created in this project.

Capstone Project 4: Deploy a Cloud Network

Note 16

Websites, applications, public cloud platforms, and related account options change often. While the instructions given in these projects were accurate at the time of writing, you might need to adjust the steps or options according to later changes.

Note to Instructors and Students: A rubric is provided for evaluating student performance on these projects. Please see Appendix D.

Estimated time: 45 minutes

Objective 1.4: Given a scenario, analyze the solution design in support of the business requirements.

Resources:

- Public cloud account (such as AWS, Azure, or GCP)
- Drawing app, such as Visio or app.diagrams.net
- Internet access

Context:

You've now learned how to deploy compute and networking resources in the cloud. In this Capstone, you will choose a cloud platform and create resources for a cloud deployment. Complete the following steps:

1. Sign into your chosen cloud platform. Using the tools and services available to you in this platform, create resources needed for the following cloud deployment:

    a. One VPC or VNet

    b. Two subnets in the VPC or VNet using the CIDR blocks 172.16.0.0/24 and 172.16.1.0/24.

    c. A VM instance in each subnet with access to the Internet

Consider the order of steps you should take to create these resources and think about which resources require which configurations to meet the deployment requirements (for example, what CIDR block should be assigned to your VPC or VNet, if any?).

2. Use a drawing app, such as Visio or app.diagrams.net, to **draw the VPC or VNet and its resources** that you created in this project, showing logical connections and relative position of each resource.

3. When your deployment is complete and fully running, **take screenshots** to document the configurations required in Step 1.

4. Delete all the resources you created in this project. Check through your account to confirm that all related resources have been deleted.

> **Note 17**
>
> Depending on the status of your account and the selections you made during this project, the resources you created can deplete your credits or accrue charges. Double-check to make sure you've terminated all resources you created in this project.

Solutions to Self-Check Questions

Section 4-1: Networking Concepts in the Cloud

1. Which SDN plane moves traffic from switch port to switch port?

    Answer: b. Data plane

    Explanation: The data plane is where transmissions on the network actually traverse physical devices.

2. At which cloud layer are user access accounts managed?

    Answer: d. Network layer

    Explanation: The network layer is where resources, access control, costs, security, and other services are managed.

3. Who configures physical devices hosting the cloud?

    Answer: c. The CSP

    Explanation: The underlying physical infrastructure that supports the cloud is not accessible to the cloud customer and can only be configured by the CSP.

Section 4-2: IP Address Spaces

4. What kind of address is 8.8.8.8?

    Answer: d. Public IP address

    Explanation: Public IP addresses provide access to a resource on the Internet and are not found within a private IP address range.

(continues)

5. If a VM is assigned the address 172.16.18.10/24, what is its network ID?

    Answer: b. 172.16.18

    Explanation: The /24 says the first three octets identify the network ID, which are 172.16.18.

6. SR-IOV bypasses which component?

    Answer: a. The virtual switch

    Explanation: When using SR-IOV (single root input/output virtualization), the host passes network traffic directly to its NIC hardware rather than processing that traffic through the internal, virtual switch created by the hypervisor.

Section 4-3: Networking in AWS

7. Which AWS segment type is largest?

    Answer: b. Region

    Explanation: Each AWS region contains multiple AZs and multiple physical data centers. Subnets are contained within AZs and VPCs, which are contained within regions.

8. Availability zones provide _____.

    Answer: d. increased availability

    Explanation: Availability zones address HA (high availability) requirements by providing multiple isolated zones within each region.

9. Which AWS device's configuration options determine whether a subnet is public or private?

    Answer: c. IG

    Explanation: Resources within a public subnet can communicate through the IG because a rule in the route table allows this communication.

Section 4-4: Networking in Azure

10. Which Azure segment type is largest?

    Answer: c. Geography

    Explanation: Azure regions are grouped into a larger category called geographies. A geography is a geographic area containing multiple Azure regions to provide data residency and compliance boundaries for discrete markets.

11. How does Azure choose which route to apply to traffic crossing a route table?

    Answer: b. Best match

    Explanation: Like AWS, Azure chooses the route to apply to traffic by how closely the destination IP address matches a route's address prefix.

Section 4-5: Networking in GCP

12. Which GCP resource type is assigned CIDR ranges?

    Answer: d. Subnet

    Explanation: A GCP VPC does not have an IP range assigned to it. CIDR ranges are defined only at the subnet level.

13. Which GCP route type is created by a Cloud Router?

    Answer: b. Dynamic routes

    Explanation: Dynamic routes are created automatically by a Cloud Router service.

Module 5

Cloud Connectivity and Troubleshooting

Module 5 Objectives

After reading this module, you will be able to:

1 Describe technologies used to connect hybrid and multi-cloud networks.

2 Explain how common network services can be extended across hybrid and multi-clouds.

3 Use common troubleshooting commands to solve common cloud connectivity problems.

Module 5 Outline

Study the module's outline to help you organize the content in your mind as you read.

Section 5-1: Hybrid Cloud and Multi-Cloud Networking
  Connecting Networks
  Virtual LANs (VLANs)
  Virtual Extensible LAN (VXLAN)
  Generic Network Virtualization Encapsulation (GENEVE)

Section 5-2: Extending Network Services
  DHCP Services
  DNS Services
  Routing
  Load Balancing

Section 5-3: Troubleshooting Cloud Connectivity
  Common Troubleshooting Commands
  Common Connectivity Problems

Module 5 Scenario

"Doodles!" squawks Liz, as she rounds the corner into the IT Department's lobby area. Liz is the school's HR director and a close friend of Kendra's. A couple of years ago, Liz started calling Kendra *Doodles* because she always drew little pictures on the back of her notes during staff meetings. Kendra returned the favor with a nickname for Liz…

"Sunshine! You're all bright and happy today, as usual. What's in the box?" Kendra asks.

"Doughnuts for you and your gang," replies Liz. "They're running a fundraiser upstairs. I can't eat these rings of sugary goodness because of my diet, but I can live vicariously through you! Here, Nigel, pass them around." Liz hands the box of doughnuts to a drooling Nigel.

"That's so *sweet* of you!" Kendra smirks as she scoops up a warm doughnut.

"Ha-ha, aren't you the clever one," Liz says. "Lunch today? Our usual time?" Liz and Kendra always go to lunch together on Fridays.

"Absolutely! See you then," Kendra mumbles through a mouthful of doughnut.

As Liz walks out, Kendra swallows then lets out a long sigh.

"What's wrong?" you ask as you wipe a few crumbs off your desk and take a sip of coffee to put the finishing touch on your own doughnut. "Don't you want to go to lunch with Liz?"

"Oh, it's not that," replies Kendra. "Seeing Liz just reminded me of something. HR uses an old, custom program to manage contacts with alumni and other school supporters. It's so old and so convoluted that we haven't even been able to migrate it to an updated Windows server. There's no way we'll be able to put that thing in the cloud."

"Can we move the data to a SaaS solution?" you ask. "Surely there's something out there that would work."

"Maybe," says Kendra. "But this software is pretty customized. The school had someone build it from scratch back in the early '90s. Migrating the data to a different system will be a nightmare."

Nigel heard the last part of Kendra's statement as he walked in with an empty doughnut box. "What happens if we can't move everything to the cloud? Is this an all-or-nothing deal?"

"No," says Kendra. "We can certainly run a hybrid cloud. That means we'll have some of our systems in the cloud, and some things will just have to stay on-prem."

"So how does that work?" you ask. "Do we have to find a dividing line, or can those systems communicate with each other somehow?"

"That's a good question," replies Kendra. "There are ways to allow communication between our cloud and our on-prem network. Some options are better than others, and there are limitations on how seamlessly we can blend resources across that gap. Let's look into this some more." She scribbles some notes on the back of yesterday's staff meeting agenda. She hands the sheet to you, doodle side up, where you can read the following questions:

- How does the on-prem network connect with the cloud?
- What network services can be extended across a hybrid cloud?
- What problems are likely to crop up in managing these connections?

Section 5-1: Hybrid Cloud and Multi-Cloud Networking

Certification

1.1 Compare and contrast the different types of cloud models.

1.3 Explain the importance of high availability and scaling in cloud environments.

2.2 Given a scenario, secure a network in a cloud environment.

3.3 Given a scenario, deploy cloud networking solutions.

4.3 Given a scenario, optimize cloud environments.

5.4 Given a scenario, troubleshoot connectivity issues.

Recall that a hybrid cloud is an organization's network that exists both on-prem and in the cloud. Similarly, a multi-cloud is an organization's network that spans two or more cloud platforms, such as AWS and GCP or Azure and Salesforce. It seems this architecture would introduce significant complexity in getting the various network services and resources to talk to and support each other. So why would an organization create this metaphorical monster?

The reality is that hybrid and multi-clouds are becoming more reasonable and popular due to their flexibility and potential cost benefits. A hybrid cloud is a typical transition phase as companies migrate to the cloud, and many companies ultimately decide to continue indefinitely with a hybrid infrastructure. This often makes sense financially because, while many cloud services such as compute are extremely inexpensive, other cloud services, such as data transfer, can be quite costly. Where it might make good sense to run web servers in your cloud, it might be more cost-effective to keep media storage on-prem for cheaper access by the company or its customers. In other cases, the reverse might be true. Whereas application development might benefit from cloud adaptability, application hosting might work better in your own data center's production environment, and cloud storage could be used for inexpensive archival storage that is rarely accessed. Consider the following use cases for a hybrid cloud:

- *Application development*—Develop and test applications in the cloud, and then move to the on-prem production environment for stable releases of the application.
- *Market testing*—Determine the demand for a new application before investing on-prem infrastructure into hosting that application.
- *Cloud bursting*—Temporarily extend a workload that has exceeded its on-prem capacity until the short-term demand decreases to a normal range.
- *High availability and disaster recovery*—Inexpensively establish redundancy that can share workloads with on-prem resources or that can take over in an emergency.
- *Compliance*—Retain regulated data storage on-prem to comply with relevant restrictions while off-loading less sensitive applications, servers, or other resources to the cloud.
- *Archives*—Store archived data that is not likely to be accessed often, thereby greatly reducing the cost of data storage.

Reasons for deploying a multi-cloud infrastructure are similar in nature to those of a hybrid cloud along with additional benefits, including:

- *Features*—Choose services from different platforms that best fit the organization's needs, and maintain portability where possible to benefit from emerging cloud technologies.
- *Cost optimization*—Negotiate for the best prices from each vendor, and then avoid vendor lock-in to continue to take advantage of potential cost savings offered by various CSPs.
- *Edge locations*—Leverage regional availability and proximity of various CSPs to maximize performance and minimize latency.
- *Disaster recovery*—Spread redundancy across multiple CSPs to minimize the effects of one CSP's outage by having another CSP host part of the network.

Hybrid and multi-clouds do present significant challenges, however. For example, not all services are portable across CSPs. For that matter, not all skill sets are portable across cloud platforms, either. Additional cross-network connections will need to be created and maintained, and additional security measures are needed to protect data in and between the various cloud platforms. While the debate continues as to whether it's better to focus an organization's resources on deeply integrating a single cloud platform (such as AWS) or spread its interests across multiple platforms, you as an IT professional can offer your company more options if you understand how to blend network services across hybrid and multi-clouds.

Connecting Networks

When extending your network to the cloud, the connection between your on-prem data center and your cloud becomes a crucial factor in the overall success of your cloud deployment. Three major categories of options to make these connections include the following:

- Use the public Internet as you've done in this course's projects.
- Rely on VPN (virtual private network) connections.
- Subscribe to some variety of direct connect or interconnect option.

Clearly, relying on the open, public Internet with no added layers of security or encryption is the least secure of these options. It can also be the least predictable in terms of performance because many Internet connections run over broadband where network oversubscription (i.e., overcommitment of network bandwidth by the ISP) can result in slower throughput when many customers access the Internet at the same time. The direct connect option is more secure, yet the characteristics and service features differ depending on the cloud provider. This also tends to be the most expensive option. Between these options is using a VPN, which might run over the public Internet infrastructure or over a private WAN (wide area network) connection. In this section, you examine the issues to consider when using a VPN, and then you explore direct connect and interconnect options from some of the major CSPs.

Virtual Private Network (VPN)

VPNs (virtual private networks) are an inexpensive and relatively secure mode of connection to your cloud resources. Regardless of what other options you use, many organizations rely on VPNs to give remote workers, traveling sales-people, and contract partners access to their cloud resources. AWS, for example, calls this service Client VPN. Some organizations use VPNs as the primary connection between the on-prem data center and their cloud-based VPC. AWS calls this service Site-to-Site VPN.

A VPN creates an encrypted tunnel for traffic to safely traverse the public Internet, which means that latency can be an issue depending on Internet "weather conditions." Availability of the connection might not be covered by an SLA (service level agreement), or high availability might be guaranteed only if you establish and maintain multiple VPN connections. Alternatively, a VPN tunnel can be established across a private, ISP-provided MPLS (Multiprotocol Label Switching) connection, although this is more expensive.

To support cloud-based VPN connections from individual users, such as remote workers, you need a VPN endpoint resource configured in your VPC. You then send a client configuration file to your users, who need a VPN client application installed on their computers. The VPN service scales automatically as user demand increases or decreases. Your organization is typically charged by connection-hours.

To create a VPN connection from a VPC to another VPC or to an on-prem data center, you need a VPN gateway (also called VPN endpoint) in each network. For example, if you're connecting your data center in Memphis to your VPC on AWS, you need a CGW (customer gateway) appliance in your Memphis network and a VGW (virtual gateway) service running on your VPC, as shown in Figure 5-1. The CGW might be a hardware VPN gateway device or a virtual VPN gateway application hosted on a server. The VGW is hosted in a specific VPC and provides access to resources running within that VPC.

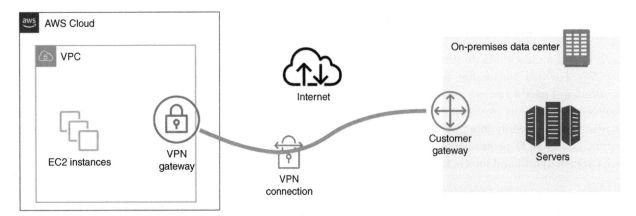

Figure 5-1   A VPN tunnel carries encrypted traffic over the Internet between two VPN gateways

To increase availability of the connection, you can create multiple VPN tunnels hosted on each VPN endpoint. In most cases, you'll also need a separate tunnel (or set of tunnels) for each VPC in your cloud.

Grow with Cengage Unlimited!

If you'd like more information about VPN technologies, use your Cengage Unlimited subscription to go to *CompTIA Network+ Guide to Networks*, 9th edition, Module 4, and read the section titled "VPNs (Virtual Private Networks)."
If you don't have a Cengage Unlimited subscription, you can find more information at cengage.com/unlimited.

VPN Tunneling Protocols

To ensure a VPN can carry all types of data in a private and secure manner over any kind of connection (including the public Internet), special VPN protocols encapsulate higher-layer protocols in a process known as tunneling. This process creates a virtual connection, or tunnel, between two VPN endpoints.

To understand how a VPN tunnel works, imagine a truck being transported across a river on a ferry. The truck is carefully loaded, tethered, and covered, and then it's carried across the water to its destination. At its destination, the cover and tethers are removed, and the cargo is unloaded. The truck can then drive down the road as it was originally designed to function. Similarly, with VPN tunneling protocols, a message with all its headers and trailers (called a frame) is encrypted, encapsulated, and transported inside a new frame that masks the original message's information and headers. In other words, a frame travels across the network as the payload inside another frame. Once the frame is released on the other side of the tunnel, it acts as it would have on the network where it originated, allowing the user to access network resources as if they were locally signed into the network.

Many VPN tunneling protocols operate at the data link layer (OSI layer 2) to encapsulate the VPN frame. Some VPN tunneling protocols work instead at the network layer (OSI layer 3), which enables additional features and options, especially for S2S (site-to-site) VPN traffic. Most tunneling protocols rely on an additional encryption protocol, such as **IPsec (Internet Protocol Security)**, to provide data security. Figure 5-2 shows an IPsec encrypted frame encapsulated inside a VPN frame.

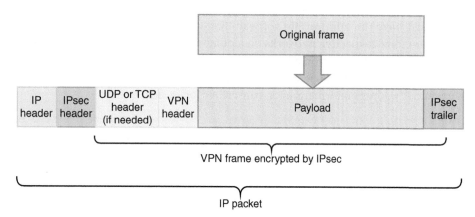

Figure 5-2   The VPN frame, such as GRE or L2TP, is encapsulated inside the network layer packet

When you configure a VPN connection on a physical appliance, you're often given options for which protocols to use. Some of these protocols provide tunneling, some encryption, some work only on IP networks, and some are more versatile. You'll need to carefully choose the best protocol(s) for your situation. Some common VPN tunneling protocols are described in the following list:

- PPTP (Point-to-Point Tunneling Protocol) is an older, data link layer protocol developed by Microsoft that encapsulates VPN data frames. You might often find PPTP in use simply because it's commonly preinstalled in the OS, such as Windows. However, PPTP itself is outdated and is no longer considered secure.

- L2TP (Layer 2 Tunneling Protocol) is a VPN tunneling protocol based on technology developed by Cisco and standardized by the IETF. L2TP encapsulates data in a similar manner to PPTP but differs in a few significant ways. Unlike PPTP, L2TP is a standard accepted and used by multiple vendors, so it can connect a VPN that uses a mix of equipment types—for example, a Juniper router, a Cisco router, or a NETGEAR router. Also, L2TP can connect two routers, a router and a remote access server, or a client and a remote access server. Typically, L2TP is implemented with IPsec for security, and this L2TP/IPsec combination is considered secure and acceptable for most situations.

- GRE (Generic Routing Encapsulation), developed by Cisco, is a layer 3 protocol. Like L2TP, GRE is used in conjunction with IPsec to increase the security of the transmissions. Some public cloud platforms, such as GCP, support the termination of GRE traffic through a VPN so cloud customers can use SASE (Secure Access Service Edge) or SD-WAN (software-defined WAN) solutions to seamlessly manage remote networks.

- OpenVPN is an open-source VPN protocol that uses a custom security protocol called OpenSSL for encryption. OpenVPN has the ability to cross many firewalls where IPsec might be blocked. It is both highly secure and highly configurable, but it can be difficult to set up.

- IKEv2 offers fast throughput and good stability when moving between wireless hotspots. It's compatible with a wide variety of devices and is often recommended by VPN providers as the most secure option among the VPN protocols they support.

- Wireguard, a recent and open-source addition to the list of VPN options, offers faster and more efficient connections than what older protocols can support. A major emphasis for Wireguard's developers was security. It uses modern cryptographic techniques with streamlined code that allows for easy auditing by security personnel. Still, being so new to the VPN market, Wireguard has some limitations and presents some concerns. For example, without additional configurations, Wireguard doesn't provide privacy protection. In other words, someone monitoring network traffic could determine identifying information (such as an IP address) for a device connected to a VPN using Wireguard.

VPN Topologies

VPNs are commonly used to connect on-prem and cloud resources. But different types of VPNs are needed for various purposes. Based on the kinds of endpoints they connect, VPNs can be loosely classified according to three models:

- *Point-to-point*—Two devices create a point-to-point VPN tunnel directly between them, as shown in Figure 5-3. Both computers must have the appropriate software installed, and they don't serve as a gateway to other hosts or resources on their respective networks. In a point-to-point VPN, usually the device that receives the VPN connection (such as a computer on a home network) needs a static public IP address. Another option, however, is to subscribe to a service such as Oracle DNS (oracle.com/cloud/networking/dns), which automatically tracks dynamic IP address information for subscriber locations.

Figure 5-3   A point-to-point VPN tunnel connects two computers

- *Site-to-site*—Site-to-site tunnels connect two networks, as shown in Figure 5-4, creating a many-to-many relationship with multiple devices on each side of the connection. On the edge of each site's network, a VPN gateway (called the VPN headend) establishes the secure connection. Each gateway is a router, firewall, or remote access server with VPN software installed, and it encrypts and encapsulates data to exchange over the tunnel. Meanwhile, clients, servers, and other hosts on the protected networks communicate through the VPN gateways as if they were all on the same, private network without needing to run VPN software themselves. Traffic is bidirectional, meaning hosts on each side of the connection can communicate with hosts on the other side of the connection. Site-to-site VPNs require that each location have a static public IP address, and the connection is persistent, meaning it's intended to always stay up.

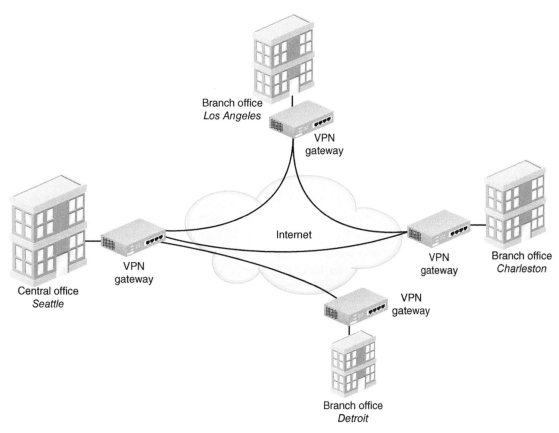

Figure 5-4   A site-to-site VPN gateway connects each site to one or more other sites

- *Point-to-site*—A remote client, server, or other host establishes a point-to-site tunnel with a private network through a VPN gateway, as shown in Figure 5-5. The tunnel created between the client and the gateway encrypts and encapsulates data. The connection is not persistent and must be created manually by the user on the remote client. Also, the VPN gateway needs a static public IP address. If the client device is restarted, the connection is lost and must be reestablished. As with site-to-site VPNs, clients and hosts on the protected network communicate with remote clients by way of the VPN gateway and are not required to run VPN software. However, each remote client on a point-to-site VPN must either run VPN software to connect to the VPN gateway or establish a more limited, web-based connection called a clientless VPN, which uses a browser and is secured by SSL/TLS.

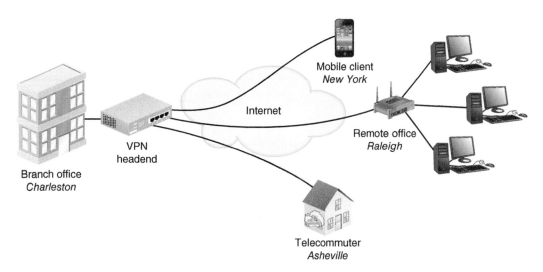

Figure 5-5   Point-to-site remote clients connect to the network through the VPN headend device

> **Note** 1
>
> Although you are connecting two devices or networks across the Internet when you use a VPN, you still generally don't need NAT (network address translation) for communications across this connection. However, if you are trying to communicate across a NAT device in your on-prem network, you must ensure UDP port 4500 is open. This port carries **NAT-T (NAT-Traversal)** information, which provides a means to communicate IP addresses and port numbers that would otherwise be encrypted through the VPN.

Direct Connection

In the context of cloud networks, VPNs are often used to connect a single device to cloud resources or to connect a cloud network to an on-prem network over the public Internet. In contrast, a direct connection uses dedicated, private infrastructure to connect an on-prem network with a cloud provider's infrastructure. Creating a direct connection from your data center to your public cloud can be accomplished by meeting the CSP in a common location called a col or colo (colocation). The colo is a data center facility dedicated to interconnecting service providers (both ISPs and CSPs) with their business partners and customers. For example, Equinix (equinix.com) currently offers more than 200 colocation facilities on five continents and offers direct connect options for AWS, Azure, GCP, Oracle, Zoom, and many other service providers.

By connecting to the colo, a cloud customer has the option to request direct connections within that facility to any number of service providers to support a hybrid or multi-cloud deployment (see Figure 5-6). Each of these connections offers low latency and assured bandwidth that don't rely on public Internet conditions. Although direct connect options are more expensive than relying on the Internet, customers maintain much greater control of the connections and related costs while maximizing availability and performance. AWS calls its direct connection service Direct Connect. In Azure, the service is ExpressRoute. And in GCP, it's called Cloud Interconnect. These direct connections are managed by VLAN (virtual local area network) technology, which you learn more about later in this module.

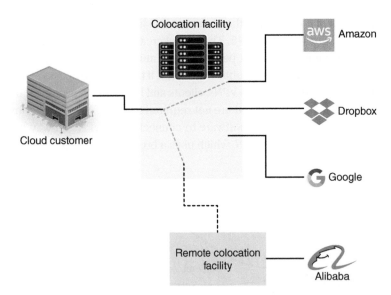

Figure 5-6   A colocation facility for creating direct connections between service providers and their customers

Cloud Peering

In the context of cloud computing, cloud peering refers to connecting multiple VPCs to each other in such a way that ensures traffic between the networks can communicate via private IP addresses (as opposed to requiring public IP addresses). This is not the same arrangement as network peering used between ISPs (Internet service providers), where the peering organizations are equal parties with equal needs for the network peering connection. ISP network peering creates a "settlement-free" relationship where neither party pays the other.

Module 5 Cloud Connectivity and Troubleshooting 177

Instead, cloud peering allows for fast and secure connections between an organization's VPCs, or between VPCs owned by different organizations, than what they could get by traversing the Internet. The customer is not truly a "peer" to the CSP, and the CSP charges the customer for the peered connection. Peering is similar in concept to VPN connections, but this technology is native to cloud platforms and is simpler and more straightforward to create and manage. This service is built into the major IaaS platforms—such as AWS, Azure, and GCP—and involves creating a simple connection that bridges the gap between each virtual network.

Cloud peering gives instances within each VPC access to instances in the peered VPC. In effect, you're blending the routes available to instances in each VPC. Because routes rely on distinct CIDR ranges, the CIDR blocks of peered VPCs can't overlap.

In the interest of security, a cloud peering relationship is typically not transitory (although there are exceptions). For example, consider Figure 5-7. Imagine that VPC A is peered to VPC B, and VPC B is also peered to VPC C. Because this peering is not transitory, VPC A is not automatically peered with VPC C. You would need a direct peering relationship between VPC A and VPC C for instances in those two VPCs to communicate directly.

Peering arrangements are not limited to connecting two VPCs with each other. In many cloud platforms, you can instead deploy a central device (such as AWS's Transit Gateway) or a central network (such as Azure's hub virtual network) to connect many VPCs to each other. This architecture is called **hub-and-spoke**, or just hub-spoke, and is illustrated in Figures 5-8 and 5-9. The hub in each case can be used to

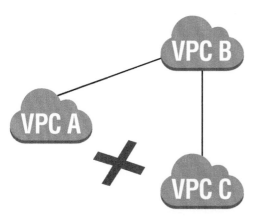

Figure 5-7 VPC A's peer connection with VPC B does not give VPC A access to VPC C's instances

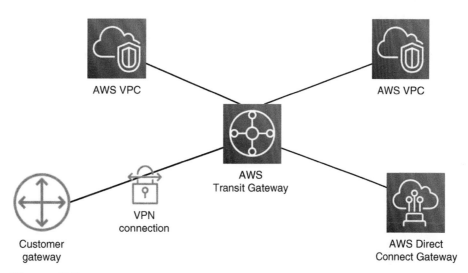

Figure 5-8 Hub-and-spoke VPC peering architecture using AWS Transit Gateway

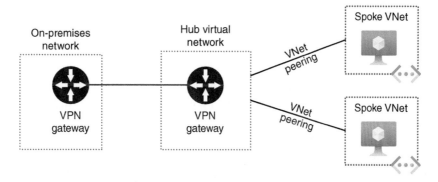

Figure 5-9 Hub-spoke VPC peering architecture using an Azure hub virtual network

connect large numbers of VPCs in the cloud to each other as well as connect on-prem networks or individual users to resources contained within many VPCs.

You're Ready

You're now ready to complete the following projects:

- Project 5-1: Explore VPN Options in AWS
- Project 5-2: Explore VPN Options in Azure
- Project 5-3: Explore VPN Options in GCP

You can complete these projects now or wait until you've finished all the readings for this module.

Virtual LAN (VLAN)

In the on-prem data center, **VLANs (virtual LANs)** play a significant role in segmenting the network for both security and efficiency purposes. A VLAN groups ports on a switch so that some of the local traffic on the switch is forced to go through a router to reach ports in a different VLAN, even if those ports are on the same switch. This allows a network admin to limit which network clients can communicate with other network clients without having to install a different switch for each group. Specifying a VLAN is accomplished by adding a tag, called a VLAN tag, to the data link header of each message. The VLAN tag identifies which VLAN the message belongs to, and that message can only be delivered to other ports in the same VLAN.

Figure 5-10 shows what happens when ports on a switch are partitioned into two VLANs. Traffic within each VLAN still goes through the switch as normal to reach other devices on the same VLAN. Traffic to hosts on other networks still goes through the router. However, traffic between hosts on VLAN 1 and VLAN 2 must now also go through the router, which is called inter-VLAN routing. This simple VLAN configuration, where one router connects to a switch that supports multiple VLANs, is sometimes called a ROAS ("router-on-a-stick").

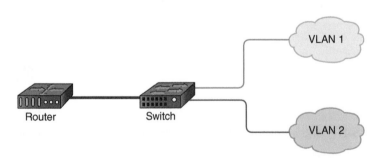

Figure 5-10   A switch with its ports partitioned into two groups, each belonging to a different VLAN

You've seen that a switch can support more than one VLAN. Similarly, a VLAN can include ports from more than one switch. Suppose you add a couple more switches to the LAN, as in Figure 5-11. In this example network, Switch B's ports can be configured with the same or different VLANs as the ports on Switch A. Traffic from one device on VLAN 1 connected to Switch A can travel to another device on VLAN 1 connected to Switch B as local traffic (using private IP addresses). However, devices on separate VLANs—even if they're connected to the same switch—can't talk to each other without going through the router. Therefore, transmissions from a device on VLAN 1 connected to Switch B must go through the router to reach a device on VLAN 3, even though both devices are plugged into the same switch.

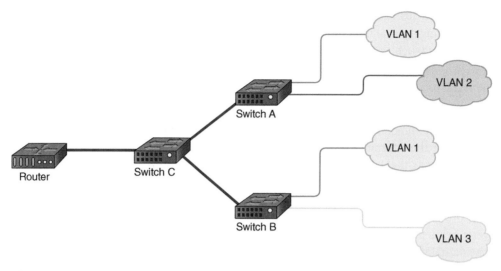

Figure 5-11   Three switches on a LAN with multiple VLANs

Where you'll likely see VLANs in cloud computing is on direct connections with a CSP. VLAN configurations are used to manage direct connections between an organization's on-prem data center and its cloud hosted by a public cloud provider. You can configure the VLANs on this connection with your CSP to manage access to various subnets within your VPC. For example, one VLAN might host traffic for an Internet-facing subnet in your VPC, while a different VLAN would host traffic for a private subnet in your VPC, thereby maintaining traffic segmentation over the interconnect. However, once you get traffic into the cloud, other technologies are used to blend or segment traffic and IP address spaces, as you've already learned.

Exam Tip ✔

The CompTIA Cloud+ exam likely will not expect you to configure or manage VLANs on a network. However, you might be given a scenario that requires you to identify symptoms related to a misconfigured VLAN. Having a basic understanding of how VLANs work and how to deploy them on-prem will help you to recognize these symptoms.

Grow with Cengage Unlimited!

If you'd like more information about VLANs and how they work, use your Cengage Unlimited subscription to go to *CompTIA Network+ Guide to Networks*, 9th edition, Module 8, and read the section titled "Virtual LANs (VLANs)." To practice configuring VLANs on a switch, complete that course's Hands-On Project 8-4, "Configure VLANs Using a Switch's GUI," or Simulation Lab 8.2 of the same title.

If you don't have a Cengage Unlimited subscription, you can find more information at cengage.com/unlimited.

Virtual Extensible LAN (VXLAN)

With this brief review of VLANs and how they work, let's consider the limitations of using VLANs in cloud computing:

- A VLAN is, by definition, an OSI layer 2 technology, which means VLAN-to-VLAN traffic never leaves the local network. VLAN tags exist in the data link layer header and are not designed to traverse layer 3 networks (like the Internet). While there are ways around this limitation, doing so is more of a hack than a best practice.

- VLANs are limited to 4096 subnets. While this sounds like a lot, it's not sufficient for large data centers, especially considering the scalability for virtual data centers provided by the cloud. An organization providing multitenant services (such as a CSP) must often manage more subnets than what VLANs offer.
- VLANs define broadcast domains. Extending broadcast traffic over a WAN connection can be expensive and significantly reduces available bandwidth for other traffic.

A newer technology, called **VXLAN (virtual extensible LAN)**, addresses these weaknesses. VXLANs rely on UDP (User Datagram Protocol) to function at OSI layer 4, which works much better for managing extended infrastructure across networks and over the Internet. Like VLANs, VXLANs identify network hosts by MAC address (an OSI layer 2 addressing scheme). However, that information is inserted immediately after the UDP header at layer 4 instead of residing in the layer 2 header. This functionality is called MAC-in-UDP. The following description unravels this mystery a bit.

At an abstract level, a VXLAN creates a layer 2 network that overlays, or lays on top of, a layer 3 network (such as a WAN connection). More concretely, VXLAN information is added to messages between the network layer's header and the transport layer's header. Figure 5-12 shows how a VXLAN functions at an abstract level. Figure 5-13 shows what's happening with the actual messages holding VXLAN information.

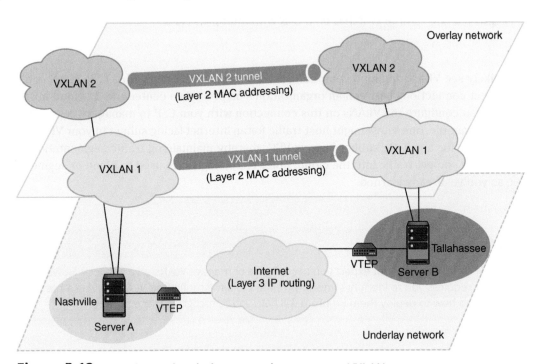

Figure 5-12   Overlay and underlay networks to support VXLANs

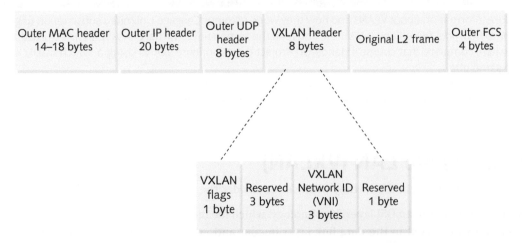

Figure 5-13   The VXLAN header is inserted next to the UDP header

A normal, physical network lies on the lower yellow plane and is called the underlay network. This network is made up of all the familiar components, such as switches, routers, and cables. The underlay network relies on layer 3 IP addressing to route packets across the Internet. A VTEP (VXLAN Tunnel Endpoint) device manages VXLAN communications between the physical LAN locations.

The overlay network is represented on the upper blue plane. VMs in VXLAN1 on Server A in Nashville can communicate with VMs in VXLAN1 on Server B in Tallahassee, and the vSwitches for VXLAN1 track all these VMs through MAC addresses on their ARP (Address Resolution Protocol) tables, a layer 2 mechanism.

This technique of overlaying the layer 2 network on top of the physical layer 3 network is made possible by encapsulating the VXLAN messages in a new, VXLAN-tagged header that includes information for layers 2, 3, and 4, as you saw in Figure 5-13. VXLANs offer a couple of other advantages as well:

- The VNI or VNID (VXLAN network ID) is 3 bytes long, offering up to 16 million VXLANs within one organization's network—a reasonable scenario when deploying large numbers of VMs and other instance types in the cloud, especially when supporting multitenancy cloud services.
- VXLANs rely on multicasting instead of broadcasting to handle all BUM (broadcast, unknown-unicast, and multicast) traffic, which are messages sent to many or unknown destinations, often in the service of maintaining ARP tables. This reduces the amount of bandwidth required of a WAN-based connection supporting VXLANs.

At the same time, the enlarged headers needed to support VXLANs require a much larger message on the network than the normal 1500-byte message, which is defined by the MTU (maximum transmission unit). To account for these larger headers, networks supporting VXLANs must be configured with a larger MTU, such as 1600 bytes.

Exam Tip ✔

A misconfigured MTU can cause connectivity issues, as messages larger than the MTU are fragmented, or broken up into smaller messages. Similarly, an MSS (maximum segment size) misconfiguration results in dropped messages. The MSS refers to the maximum size of the payload before any headers and trailers are added to the message for transmission over a network interface. Knowing these common causes of problems with VXLAN communications can help you identify VXLAN misconfigurations in a given scenario.

In the context of cloud computing, VXLANs are typically implemented by CSPs who host multiple tenants on their physical architecture or by large organizations who host their own private cloud. Cloud tenants, such as an organization renting cloud space from AWS or GCP, likely won't need to configure VXLANs in their normal course of business.

Exam Tip ✔

The CompTIA Cloud+ exam likely will not expect you to configure or manage VXLANs on a network. However, you might be given a scenario that requires you to identify symptoms related to a misconfigured VXLAN. Having a basic understanding of how VXLANs work will help you to recognize these symptoms.

Generic Network Virtualization Encapsulation (GENEVE)

A newer alternative to VXLAN technology is GENEVE (Generic Network Virtualization Encapsulation), which is pronounced "gen-ĕv." GENEVE is a similar overlay network technology that uses a slightly longer header design to provide more adaptable configurations across the underlay network. Because of the longer header, the network's MTU must also be adjusted when supporting GENEVE packets.

Like VXLAN, GENEVE encapsulates each message with MAC, IP, and UDP fields and inserts its own header as well. Part of the GENEVE header, however, is variable in nature and can be used in many ways to serve many use cases. See Figure 5-14.

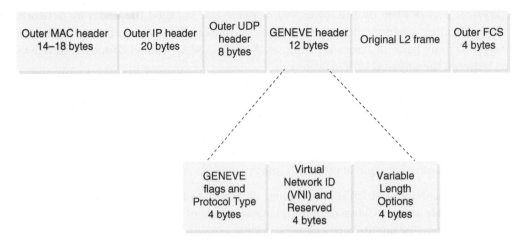

Figure 5-14   The GENEVE header contains a variable field for adaptive uses

Common problems with GENEVE configuration include properly enabling GENEVE and adjusting the network's MTU:

- Only newer virtualization systems are designed to support GENEVE, so ensure GENEVE is supported and enabled.
- Because the GENEVE header is longer than the VXLAN header, the network's MTU must be adjusted to accommodate the longer header or fragmentation must be enabled on all connected devices.

Like VXLAN, GENEVE is supported by UDP at the transport layer. UDP incorporates a basic checksum function, and with IPv4 networks, this checksum can be disabled if packet integrity is provided at another layer. When using IPv6, the UDP checksum must be enabled.

A common concern when using any network protocol is security. GENEVE does not include any security features of its own and must rely on other protocols' security mechanisms. For example, when transporting GENEVE messages across the Internet, encryption should be employed through VPNs to prevent snooping. Within a single company's network, VLAN-based isolation can help protect GENEVE traffic.

Note 2

You can learn more about GENEVE as defined by RFC 8926 at https://datatracker.ietf.org/doc/html/rfc8926.

Remember This

- Three major categories of options to connect the on-prem data center with a cloud deployment include the public Internet, VPN (virtual private network) connections, and a direct connect or interconnect option.
- In the on-prem data center, a VLAN (virtual LAN) helps segment a network for both security and efficiency purposes by grouping ports on a switch so that some of the local traffic on the switch is forced to go through a router to reach ports in a different VLAN.
- VXLAN (virtual extensible LAN) addresses VLAN weaknesses by inserting MAC addressing information in a UDP header at layer 4 to better manage extended infrastructure across networks and over the Internet.
- GENEVE (Generic Network Virtualization Encapsulation) is a similar overlay network technology to VXLAN that uses a slightly longer header design to provide more adaptable configurations across the underlay network.

Self-Check

1. Which protocol is used to secure VPNs?

   a. GRE

   b. IPsec

   c. OpenVPN

   d. PPTP

2. Which cloud connection type is the most expensive for the cloud customer?

   a. Public Internet

   b. Direct connection

   c. OpenSSL

   d. VPN

3. Which protocol provides checksum functions for VXLAN and GENEVE headers?

   a. MTU

   b. TCP

   c. UDP

   d. MAC

4. What characteristic allows GENEVE to support a wider variety of use cases than VXLAN?

   a. Variable header field

   b. Higher MTU

   c. Message encapsulation

   d. Built-in security

○ Check your answers at the end of this module.

Section 5-2: Extending Network Services

Certification

1.3 Explain the importance of high availability and scaling in cloud environments.

1.4 Given a scenario, analyze the solution design in support of the business requirements.

2.2 Given a scenario, secure a network in a cloud environment.

3.3 Given a scenario, deploy cloud networking solutions.

5.4 Given a scenario, troubleshoot connectivity issues.

When you extend a network's infrastructure to the cloud, several network and security-related services are involved in bridging the gap between on-prem and cloud-based resources. Making the connection between the two locations, which you just learned about, is only the first step. For example, you've already seen how IP address spaces cannot overlap across a VPN, interconnect, or peered connection. Therefore, it's important to manage your address spaces efficiently. This section begins with a discussion of DHCP services across hybrid and multi-clouds. The section also covers DNS (Domain Name System) services, routing, and load balancing across platforms.

DHCP Services

Consider where a computer on a traditional network gets its IP address. A static IP address is manually assigned by a network administrator, while a dynamic IP address is assigned by the DHCP (Dynamic Host Configuration Protocol) server each time a computer connects to the network. To enable DHCP, a network admin configures specific IP address pools from which the DHCP server can assign addresses to clients (see Figure 5-15). Along with the IP address comes additional information called scope options, including the following:

- A time limit called a lease time, after which the DHCP client must request an IP address renewal from the server
- The IP address of the network's router interface, which is called the default gateway
- Primary and secondary DNS server addresses, which the DHCP client can use to resolve IP addresses

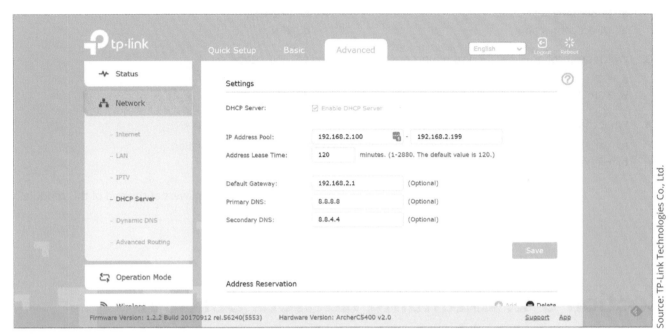

Figure 5-15   DHCP options on a small network router

In addition to allocating one or more address pools for DHCP to use, the network admin might also configure reserved or excluded addresses. For example, a network printer might have a static IP address. If that IP address is included in the range of addresses in the DHCP pool, then the IP address should be listed as an exclusion so it won't be used for another client. Alternatively, the network admin might configure an IP reservation based on the printer's MAC address so the DHCP server reserves that address only for the printer. The server then assigns the printer that reserved address any time the printer connects to the network.

DHCP in the Cloud

DHCP in the cloud accomplishes many of the same tasks but not necessarily from a single resource. For example, consider how instances in AWS receive dynamic IP addresses. When you create a VPC, you define an address space from which addresses are allocated to new VM interfaces in the VPC. This address allocation process happens in the background. Other than setting the CIDR block, you don't need to do anything else to ensure that your instances receive a private IP address along with all the other information they need to communicate with other resources in the VPC. By design, each interface keeps its private IP address indefinitely until the interface is deleted (although this is not necessarily true in other cloud platforms).

If desired, however, you can change some of the DHCP options that a VM instance receives when its interface is created. This might be important, for example, if you need to use your own DNS servers instead of relying on AWS's. In AWS, changing DHCP options is accomplished by creating a new DHCP options set from the VPC dashboard and then editing the options set associated with an existing VPC, as shown in Figure 5-16. If instances already exist using a previous options set, you must restart the instances for the new settings to take effect. Figure 5-17 shows the options you can configure in the DHCP options set.

Your VPCs (1/2) Info
Actions
Create VPC
Filter VPCs
Create default VPC
Create flow log
Edit CIDRs
Edit DHCP options set
Edit DNS hostnames
Edit DNS resolution
Manage middlebox routes
Manage tags
Delete VPC
Name
VPC ID
MyVPC
vpc-0f3c112a2f6b9bf31
vpc-bc5ecfd7
Source: Amazon Web Services, Inc.

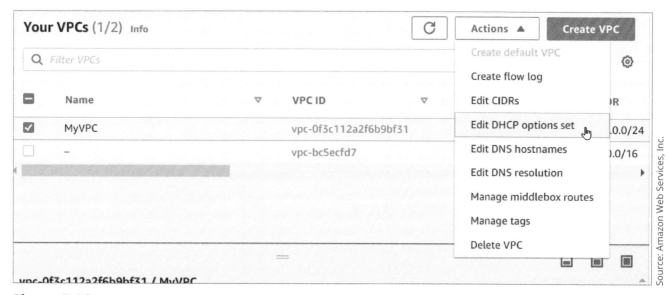

Figure 5-16 You can change the DHCP options set associated with a VPC

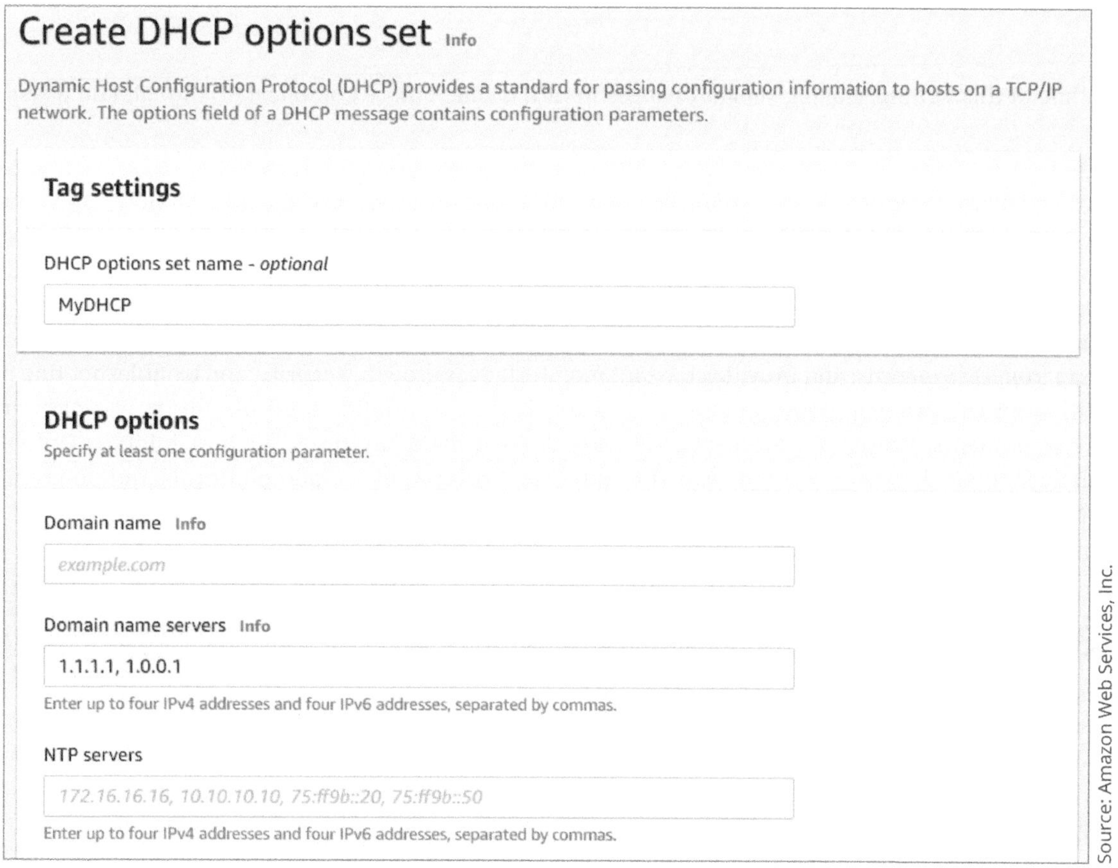

Create DHCP options set Info
Dynamic Host Configuration Protocol (DHCP) provides a standard for passing configuration information to hosts on a TCP/IP network. The options field of a DHCP message contains configuration parameters.
Tag settings
DHCP options set name - optional
MyDHCP
DHCP options
Specify at least one configuration parameter.
Domain name Info
example.com
Domain name servers Info
1.1.1.1, 1.0.0.1
Enter up to four IPv4 addresses and four IPv6 addresses, separated by commas.
NTP servers
172.16.16.16, 10.10.10.10, 75:ff9b::20, 75:ff9b::50
Enter up to four IPv4 addresses and four IPv6 addresses, separated by commas.
Source: Amazon Web Services, Inc.

Figure 5-17 Set one or more of these options

In Azure, you can, of course, choose the address space for a VNet. You can also change the DNS servers the VNet's instances use. To change DNS servers, go to the VNet's page, as shown in Figure 5-18, click DNS servers in the left pane, and change the setting to Custom. Then enter the DNS server addresses you want to use.

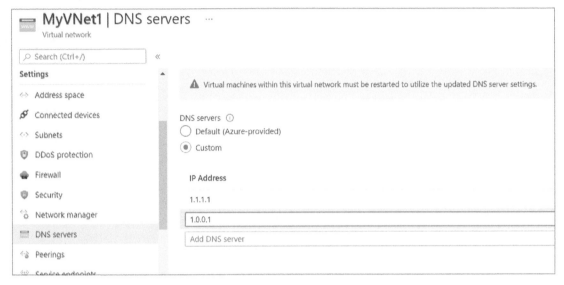

Figure 5-18   You can choose custom DNS server addresses for instances in an Azure VNet

At the time of this writing, making similar changes in GCP is much more complicated, though still possible.

DHCP Across a Hybrid Cloud

Now that you've figured out how to adjust your cloud's DHCP options, the next question is, how can you configure DHCP across a hybrid cloud so that one system manages DHCP services both on-prem and in the cloud? The solution is IPAM (IP address management), which is a stand-alone product or an application embedded in another product, such as Windows Server. IPAM provides a way to plan, deploy, and monitor a network's IP address space. IPAM tools can automatically detect and manage IP address ranges, assignments, reservations, and exclusions; integrate this information with data from DNS records; and provide constant monitoring for growth, security, and troubleshooting purposes.

At the time of this writing, IPAM functionality is not built into public cloud platforms like AWS and Azure for hybrid deployments. However, third-party, software-defined IPAM solutions, such as Infoblox (infoblox.com) and FusionLayer (fusionlayer.com), are designed to integrate with popular cloud platforms and on-prem network resources to provide a unified interface for managing address spaces across hybrid and multi-clouds.

DNS Services

You read earlier that DHCP scope options can be used to define a virtual network's DNS servers. Why is this an important capability? And how does this feature apply to a hybrid or multi-cloud environment? A quick review of what DNS is will help answer these questions.

You might have noticed that VM instances are typically assigned a host name in the cloud. For example, Figure 5-19 shows an example of an instance in AWS with its auto-generated public and private host names along with their corresponding IP addresses.

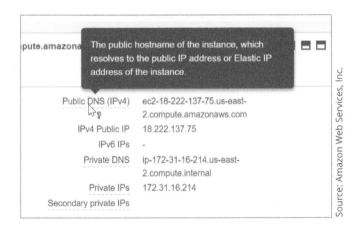

Figure 5-19   Each host name corresponds to an IP address

Host names, such as the ones in Figure 5-19, and domain names, such as google.com, were created because character-based names are easier for humans to remember than numeric IP addresses. While domain names are convenient for humans, a computer must convert the domain name to an IP address before it can find the referenced machine. This is where DNS (Domain Name System or Domain Name Service) comes in. Through a process called name resolution, DNS associates computer names with IP addresses.

Each organization that provides host services (for example, websites or email) on the public Internet is responsible for providing and maintaining its own DNS authoritative servers. An authoritative server is the authority on computer names and their IP addresses for computers in their domains. An organization also uses DNS servers for network clients to access public DNS data for resolution of domain names across the Internet.

When a computer requests name resolution of a particular domain, the computer first reaches out to its designated DNS server, whether that's a private DNS server managed locally by the organization or a public DNS service offered by an ISP or organization like Google. (For example, Google's public DNS server addresses are 8.8.8.8 and 8.8.4.4.) If that DNS server already has the requested information cached, it will return that information to the DNS client. Otherwise, the DNS server will query other DNS servers that function at higher layers of the name server hierarchy until it locates the authoritative name server for that domain name. The authoritative name server can then report the associated IP address for the domain. The entire process might take a few seconds, at most.

DNS servers collect lists of computer names and their associated IP addresses in namespace databases. These databases are stored on thousands of servers around the world rather than being centralized on a single server or group of servers. In other words, DNS doesn't follow a centralized database model but a distributed database model across a hierarchy of servers. Because data is distributed over thousands of servers, DNS will not fail catastrophically if one or a handful of servers experiences errors.

The information in the databases is organized in various types of records, each designed to hold specific pieces of information:

- *A (Address) record*—Stores the name-to-address mapping for a host. This record type provides the primary function of DNS, which is to match host names to IPv4 addresses.
- *AAAA (Address) record* (called a "quad-A record")—Holds the name-to-address mapping for IPv6 addresses.
- *CNAME (Canonical Name) record*—Holds alternative names for a host. These names can be used in place of the canonical name, which is the complete and properly formatted name, such as www.mycompany.com. An alternative to this canonical name might be mycompany.com.
- *PTR (Pointer) record*—Used for reverse lookups, which provide a host name when you know its IP address.
- *NS (Name Server) record*—Indicates the authoritative name server for a domain.
- *MX (Mail Exchanger) record*—Identifies an email server and is used for email traffic.
- *SRV (Service) record*—Identifies the host name and port of a computer that hosts a specific network service besides email, such as FTP (File Transfer Protocol) or SIP (Session Initiation Protocol), which is a signaling protocol used to establish a video or voice connection between hosts.

Each resource record begins with a TTL (Time to Live) field that identifies how long the record should be saved in a cache on a server. Administrators can set the TTL based on how volatile the DNS data is (in other words, how often the administrator expects the IP addresses to change). This is the field that determines the shelf-life of information in a DNS server's cache, and this is the reason that it can take several minutes for DNS record changes to proliferate globally through the Internet.

DNS in the Cloud

Major public cloud platforms offer DNS services for resources hosted in their cloud. For example, by default, all AWS VPCs are configured to use the Amazon DNS server by default. You can set the VPC's instances to use your own DNS servers or public DNS servers by creating a new DHCP options set, as discussed earlier. Many organizations run their own DNS servers to have more control over their network's traffic and to provide name resolution for internal network traffic.

AWS also offers its Route 53 DNS service (DNS's default TCP/IP port is 53, thus the name). Organizations can use the highly available and scalable Route 53 as its authoritative DNS service for domains that it owns.

DNS Across a Hybrid Cloud

Recently released functionality in AWS's Route 53 service can allow an organization's on-prem resources to access cloud-based DNS services through a VPN or Direct Connect connection. This enables fully integrated DNS across the entire hybrid cloud without the use of a third-party service provider. Azure offers similar functionality by running Active Directory on Azure-hosted VMs. In GCP, you can use Cloud DNS forwarding capability for hybrid cloud DNS management.

Grow with Cengage Unlimited!

If you'd like more information about DNS and how DNS servers work, use your Cengage Unlimited subscription to go to *CompTIA Network+ Guide to Networks*, 9th edition, Module 3, and read the section titled "Domain Names and DNS."
If you don't have a Cengage Unlimited subscription, you can find more information at cengage.com/unlimited.

Routing

You've already learned how route tables are used to manage a virtual network's access to the Internet. When you create connections between on-prem and cloud networks, routing plays a key role in determining how traffic flows between resources across the connection. However, establishing and maintaining those routes works a little differently in the cloud than it does for a traditional, on-prem network.

You might have studied routing protocols in a networking class. These routing protocols are categorized in two major groups: interior and exterior gateway protocols. Interior gateway protocols propagate routes within an autonomous system, while exterior gateway protocols communicate routes between autonomous systems. An **AS (autonomous system)** is a group of networks, often on the same domain, that are operated by the same organization. For example, Cengage, the company that published this course, might have several LANs that all fall under its domain. Each LAN is connected to the others by routers. An AS is sometimes referred to as a trusted network because the entire domain is under the organization's control. The AS is also identified by a globally unique ASN (autonomous system number). Interior gateway protocols managing routes within an AS include the following:

- *RIP (Routing Information Protocol) and RIPv2*—An outdated routing protocol that is limited to 15 hops (each jump from one router to the next is called a "hop").
- *OSPF (Open Shortest Path First)*—An open standard routing protocol designed for large, multivendor networks by eliminating the hop limit imposed on RIP.
- *IS-IS (Intermediate System to Intermediate System)*—A routing protocol designed for large enterprise and ISP networks. It was originally codified by ISO, which referred to routers as "intermediate systems," thus the protocol's name.
- *IGRP (Interior Gateway Routing Protocol)*—A proprietary routing protocol developed by Cisco and designed for small or medium-sized networks.
- *EIGRP (Enhanced Interior Gateway Routing Protocol)*—Another Cisco routing protocol but designed for larger, enterprise networks.

While your CSP likely relies on one or more interior gateway protocols, you typically won't manage these protocols directly for configuring public cloud services (although you do need to be familiar with their acronyms for the Cloud+ exam). The only routing protocol you'll work with in the cloud is **BGP (Border Gateway Protocol)**, which is the only modern exterior gateway protocol.

VPN Routing

Routing for VPNs can be configured using static routes set by the cloud admin (which do not automatically adapt to route outages) or using dynamic routing, where routes are configured automatically by the cloud platform. When configuring traditional VPNs, you often have many routing protocol options to choose from. However, in the cloud, you most often are required to use BGP. BGP dynamically manages routes between autonomous systems, such as across the Internet. A router using BGP calculates the best path between two locations and accumulates this information in its route table. If congestion or failures affect the network, a router can detect the problems and reroute messages through a different path. To use BGP, it must be supported by the device (physical or virtual) on each end of the connection.

When configuring a VPN, you also have the option to enable route propagation between the connected networks. For example, if VPC A is connected by VPN to VPC B, route propagation will allow VPC A to learn all the routes that VPC B already knows. This can be helpful in some circumstances and problematic in others.

Direct Connect Routing

Direct connection services require BGP routing on each virtual interface. A virtual interface is basically a subinterface on the connection that allows different connections to access various cloud services. This feature functions similarly to VRF (virtual routing and forwarding), which is a technology that allows a single router to maintain multiple route tables instead of only one. A single direct connection can have many virtual interfaces, and each one has its own VLAN. Recall that VLANs are used to segment a network into smaller subnets. The direct connection is a small network, and each subinterface represents a smaller portion of that network. Segmenting a direct connection in this way allows a single connection to be used for many purposes, which provides significant cost savings for the cloud customer.

> ### Grow with Cengage Unlimited!
>
> If you'd like more information about routers and how routing works, use your Cengage Unlimited subscription to go to *CompTIA Network+ Guide to Networks*, 9th edition, Module 9, and read the section titled "Routing Protocols."
> If you don't have a Cengage Unlimited subscription, you can find more information at cengage.com/unlimited.

Load Balancing

Routed cloud traffic doesn't always go directly to a single destination. It's common for organizations to establish multiple servers to take turns performing essentially the same task so that a failure with one server won't disrupt the service itself. For example, consider a typical web server setup for a popular website. A single web server can't possibly handle all the website's traffic, and so the company runs multiple web servers to spread the demand of traffic across several machines. However, DNS still might point to only a single IP address. How does this work? The secret ingredient is a load balancer.

Load balancing is the distribution of traffic over multiple components to optimize performance and fault tolerance. Basically, the load balancer stands between the Internet traffic and a cluster of web servers and then distributes that traffic to all the servers in the cluster according to rules defined by the administrator. Examine Figure 5-20, which shows Internet traffic on the left (called the frontend) and the organization's web server cluster on the right (called the backend).

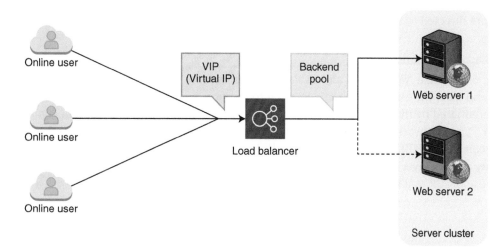

Figure 5-20 A load balancer distributes traffic to multiple destinations

The public IP of the website, called a VIP (virtual IP), represents the entire cluster and directs traffic to the load balancer, not to any single web server. The load balancer uses NAT to send traffic to one of the web servers at a time, where each web server is part of the cluster identified by a backend pool, or list of private IP addresses belonging to the servers.

Load-Balancing Algorithms

The load balancer chooses a server according to one or more load-sharing algorithms. For example, the load balancer might use a round-robin rule (see Figure 5-21), where each server in the cluster gets a turn in a particular order. However, this method does not take into consideration how much work a server is already doing. Web server 1 might receive a large, time-consuming request. Then web servers 2 and 3 each get a quick and easy request and are finished with their tasks long before web server 1 has completed its task. In the meantime, the next request comes in. Using a round-robin rule, the load balancer would send the newest request to web server 1 even if that server is still busy from the first request.

Other algorithms can be used to balance workloads more efficiently across a cluster. For example, the load balancer might instead send the next request to the least busy server. Collecting information about the servers' activity levels and health might be achieved by installing a small piece of monitoring software called an agent on the server, or the load balancer might periodically probe the server for health information. A server that is experiencing problems will be removed from the load balancer's queue until that server is up and running again. More complex algorithms might be handled though a PAC (proxy automatic configuration or proxy auto config) file so traffic is balanced according to various characteristics of the traffic itself.

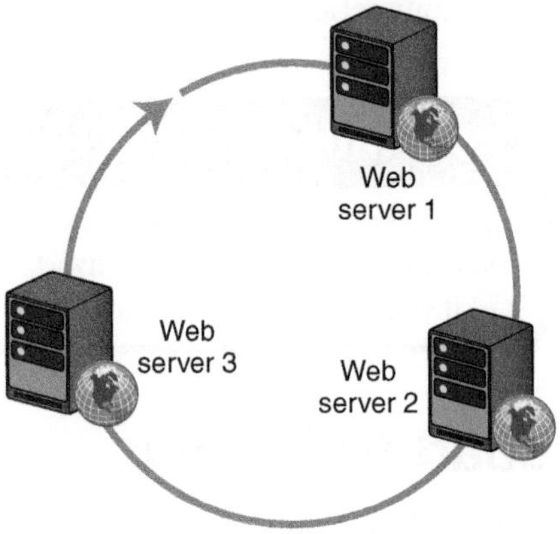

Sticky Sessions

Load balancers can also maintain session information so a client communicating with a server can continue with the same server until the session is complete. For example, consider an online shopper who has added a few items to the website's shopping cart. If the session is suddenly transferred to a different server by a load balancer, that server wouldn't have access to the live data on the initial server from when the items were first placed in the cart because the order has not yet been completed—this information doesn't yet exist in any official records.

Figure 5-21   Using a round-robin algorithm, each server takes a turn in a set order

It's the responsibility of the load balancer to ensure the shopper's session continues to be handled by a single server so that temporary data (such as items in a shopping cart) isn't lost. The load balancer might use PAT (port address translation) to accomplish this goal. When the session is first created, it's assigned to a port on a single server. Further communications between the web client and the web server are tracked by this port number, ensuring that future messages are directed to the one server while the session is active. This is called a sticky session.

Load Balancing in the Cloud

The major public clouds like AWS, Azure, and GCP offer various load balancer services. These load balancers can handle traffic to and from the Internet or traffic internal to the organization's cloud. Specific load balancer services are typically differentiated by the OSI layer in which they function. For example, as shown in Figure 5-22, AWS offers application (layer 7) and network (layer 3) load balancers, where the network load balancer is the more robust of the two. In GCP, you can use an HTTP/HTTPS (layer 7), TCP (layer 4), or UDP (layer 4) load balancer. At the time of this writing, Azure only offers a layer 4 load balancer. In AWS, load balancer options are accessed through the EC2 service category. In Azure and GCP, you'll find load balancing under the Networking category.

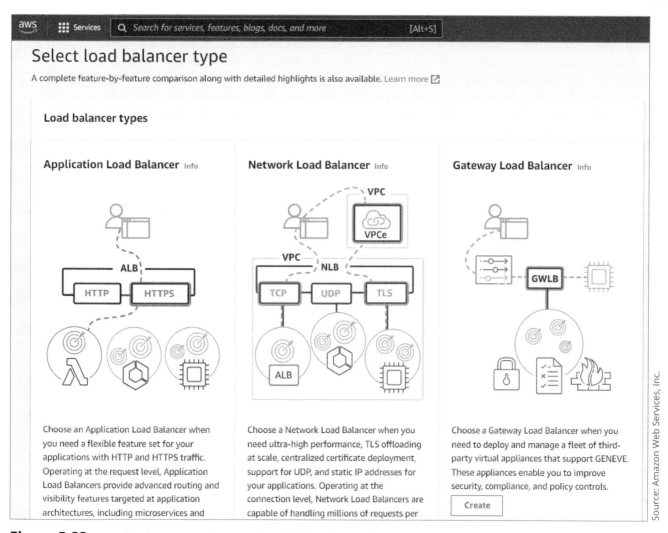

Figure 5-22 Load balancer services are classified by the OSI layer on which they function

---

Note 3

TCP (Transmission Control Protocol) is a connection-oriented protocol, meaning it makes a connection with the host on the other end, checks whether the data is received, and resends it if it is not. UDP (User Datagram Protocol) is a connection-less protocol or best-effort protocol. It does not guarantee delivery and does not check to see if the data was received.

Load Balancing Across a Hybrid Cloud

Now that you understand the basics of how load balancing works, the relevant question here is, how do load balancers work across a hybrid or multi-cloud? As it turns out, CSPs have already thought about this. Most cloud-based load-balancing services can be extended to cover resources hosted on-prem and in other clouds, which is helpful for disaster recovery and business continuity planning. In fact, GSLB (global server load balancing), also called multi-site load balancing, can be configured to direct traffic to servers based on their proximity to users, which minimizes latency as users are accessing cloud-based resources.

For example, suppose a user wants to sign into the AWS cloud console. AWS runs servers all around the world. Global load balancing allows the user's traffic to be directed to servers hosted geographically near the user's own location. The user's traffic is directed to other locations only if needed to complete the requests. This is similar in concept to what happens when you place an order with Amazon for a book. Amazon has warehouses distributed throughout the United States. If you place an order for a book that is stored in multiple warehouses, the book will be shipped from the warehouse closest to you, thereby minimizing transit time.

Remember This

- IP address spaces are managed by DHCP (Dynamic Host Configuration Protocol) services, both on-prem and in the cloud; IPAM (IP address management) tools can be used to manage IP spaces across hybrid and multi-clouds.
- DNS (Domain Name System) servers collect lists of computer names and their associated IP addresses in namespace databases, and some CSPs can allow an organization's on-prem resources to access cloud-based DNS services through a VPN or direct connection.
- Routing can be configured using static routes set by the cloud admin (which do not automatically adapt to route outages) or using dynamic routing, where routes are configured automatically by the cloud platform.
- A load balancer stands between the incoming traffic sources and a cluster of servers and distributes that traffic to all the servers in the cluster according to rules defined by the administrator.

Self-Check

5. Which of the following devices is least likely to need a static IP address?

    a. Web server

    b. Web client

    c. DNS server

    d. Default gateway

6. Which DNS record must be updated when changing email servers?

    a. A record

    b. NS record

    c. CNAME record

    d. MX record

7. Which routing protocol is used across the Internet?

    a. OSPF

    b. BGP

    c. RIPv2

    d. EIGRP

8. Which device helps ensure HA for a web server?

    a. DNS server

    b. DHCP server

    c. Router

    d. Load balancer

○ Check your answers at the end of this module.

Section 5-3: Troubleshooting Cloud Connectivity

Certification

2.2 Given a scenario, secure a network in a cloud environment.

5.3 Given a scenario, troubleshoot deployment issues.

5.4 Given a scenario, troubleshoot connectivity issues.

5.5 Given a scenario, troubleshoot common performance issues.

One of the most common ways to troubleshoot network connections is to use CLI-based commands, such as ping and traceroute. You can use many of the same commands when troubleshooting cloud network connections, though some of these commands might produce different results than normally expected, or the command's protocol might be blocked by the CSP. In this section, you learn about how to use common CLI troubleshooting tools with cloud resources. You also explore common connectivity problems you might face.

Common Troubleshooting Commands

When establishing connectivity within the cloud or between your cloud and your on-prem network, you'll use many of the same CLI tools you've come to rely on within a physical data center. The following list discusses many of these common commands and how they can be used in the cloud:

- *ping*—You can ping a cloud server, gateway interface, or similar resource just as you would your on-prem interfaces. When using ping in the cloud, carefully consider which two interfaces are supposed to be able to communicate, and then ping from one to the other. If it doesn't work, consider first that the problem could be as simple as enabling ICMP (Internet Control Message Protocol) on an intervening firewall somewhere along the route. Also consider that some cloud platforms place limits on which devices you can ping. For example, in Azure, you can't ping the VNet's default router. Figure 5-23 shows the results of pinging a running VM instance's public IP address from a physical Windows computer in an on-prem network.

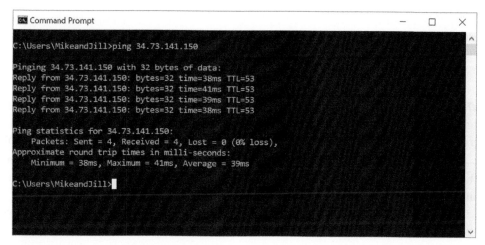

Figure 5-23   The physical Windows computer reports connectivity with the running VM instance

- *tracert/traceroute*—Tracert (Windows systems) and traceroute (Linux systems) help identify bottlenecks causing latency issues, which is a common concern when hosting resources in the cloud. Like ping, both utilities rely on ICMP, so check that it is enabled across the route when using these tools for troubleshooting. Know that not all cloud platforms support tracert or traceroute within virtual cloud networks. For example, tracert and traceroute can't be used to diagnose connectivity issues in Azure.
- *ipconfig/ip/ifconfig*—The ipconfig (Windows systems) utility and the ip and ifconfig (Linux systems) utilities identify interface configurations such as IP address. While the most used of this information is typically listed in the cloud platform's console, you'll still use these tools from within a VM to check or manage interfaces. Figure 5-24 shows the results of running ifconfig on a VM running in AWS.

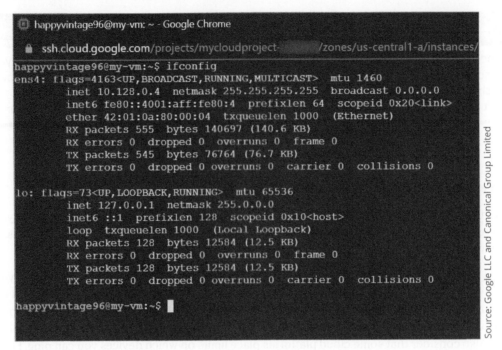

Figure 5-24   This VM instance in GCP has one active interface (ens4) and the loopback interface (lo)

> **Note** ④
>
> The newer ip is slowly replacing ifconfig in Linux. While ifconfig will continue to be available for some time, the ip utility is more robust. To see a Linux system's IP address, enter `ip addr show`.

- *ipconfig /flushdns*—A popular switch to use with the `ipconfig` command is `/flushdns`. This command flushes, or clears, the name resolver cache, which might solve a problem when the browser cannot find a host on the Internet or when a misconfigured DNS server has sent incorrect information to the resolver cache.

- *ss/netstat*—The ss (socket statistics) and netstat (network statistics) utilities list current connections, ports used, and the state of each connection. This is helpful when troubleshooting connectivity to a running service and determining whether the server is listening on the correct port. Figure 5-25 shows some of the output for the `netstat -a` command on a VM running in GCP. You can see where the VM is hosting an SSH connection over its public IP address.

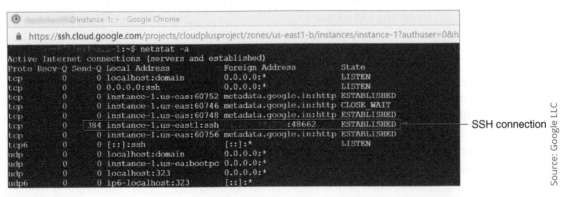

Figure 5-25   Several active connections on this VM are running to support its connections with Google-hosted services

Note 5

The netstat utility has been deprecated in most Linux distributions, although it's still often included in the distribution by default. While the versatile ss (socket statistics) utility is designed to replace netstat, the CompTIA Cloud+ exam expects you to know how to use both. Furthermore, both utilities use many of the same parameters.

- **arp**—ARP (Address Resolution Protocol) works in conjunction with IPv4 to discover MAC addresses of devices on a network. The arp utility provides a way of obtaining information from and manipulating a device's ARP table, where these IPv4 addresses and MAC addresses are mapped and stored. For example, `arp -a` on your local computer lists devices on your network. ARP is a layer 2 protocol and only works within a local network. Because cloud functions are only available to cloud consumers from layer 3 and above, the arp utility isn't as helpful in the cloud. You can, however, use arp to troubleshoot problems with a direct connection between your data center and your cloud.

- **nslookup/dig**—Both nslookup (name server lookup) and dig (domain information groper) can be used to check the FQDN (fully qualified domain name) for an IP address and vice versa. This is especially helpful when troubleshooting problems with DNS server configurations, such as when using Route 53 in AWS. While the dig utility is newer and more robust, there are some cases where nslookup is simply easier to use. Figure 5-26 shows the public DNS and public IP address of an instance running on AWS. Figure 5-27 shows where nslookup on a remote computer was able to resolve the public IP address to the instance's public DNS.

Source: Amazon Web Services, Inc.

Figure 5-26   This AWS instance was automatically given a public IP address and an FQDN

Figure 5-27   This physical Windows computer resolved the VM instance's public IP address to its FQDN

- *tcpdump*—The tcpdump utility is a free, command-line packet sniffer that runs on Linux and other Unix operating systems. It captures packets that cross a computer's network interface. The output can be saved to a file that you can filter or play back to look for problems. The tcpdump utility is especially helpful when troubleshooting VPN connections. A similar, GUI-based tool is Wireshark, which can be used in Windows as well. Wireshark and other packet sniffers might also be called packet analyzers. While tcpdump and Wireshark typically aren't used directly in the cloud, CSPs offer similar tools for monitoring cloud traffic, such as flow logs. You learn more about these cloud-native tools in later modules.

- *route*—The route utility allows you to view a host's route table. Route tables on a user's computer typically contain no more than a few unique entries, including the default gateway and loopback address. However, route tables on Internet routers, such as those operated by ISPs, maintain hundreds of thousands of entries. While the route tables of cloud resources are readily accessible through the cloud console, the route utility is useful for troubleshooting routes on the on-prem data center side of a connection.

- *curl*—The curl utility is used to transfer data to or from a server. It's often used for automation processes and can support many protocols, including HTTP, FTP, SFTP, TFTP, and LDAP.

- *ssh*—SSH (Secure Shell) is the go-to tool for remoting into Linux instances in the cloud. If you're having trouble creating an SSH connection with an instance, check the username and password or key pair, and check any intervening firewalls to ensure they allow SSH traffic in both directions. For SSH to work, TCP port 22 must be enabled. The ssh command is used to manage SSH connections. Remote access alternatives to SSH include the open-source and cross-platform VNC (Virtual Network Computing), the Windows-based RDP (Remote Desktop Protocol) using port 3389, and the insecure Telnet, which uses port 23.

Exam Tip ✔

Be sure to memorize the ports for SSH, RDP, and Telnet. On the Cloud+ exam, you might be given a scenario that requires you to know which ports to enable for these remote access protocols to work.

Common Connectivity Problems

When troubleshooting cloud connectivity issues, whether a connection isn't happening at all or traffic isn't traversing the connection as expected, you'll encounter several common issues. For example, incorrectly managing IP address spaces can often cause connectivity issues. As you read earlier in this module, peered VPCs cannot use overlapping IP address ranges. Other common causes of peering issues are incorrect or missing route tables or firewall rules. In this section, you further explore cloud connectivity issues you might encounter.

Unreachable Instance

When you can't connect to a VM instance, it could be a problem with the VM's OS or connectivity settings internal or external to the VM. Some cloud platforms allow you to access task logs for the instance. For example, to access logs for an EC2 instance in AWS, select the instance, click Actions, Instance Settings, and Get System Log. Use the logged data for further troubleshooting.

When connectivity is slow, consider that you might have insufficient bandwidth at your location for the quantity of communication you're attempting to support. Latency can also be caused by Internet "weather conditions" or poor routing configurations.

Each cloud platform provides additional tools for troubleshooting running instances and their connections. It helps first to understand some of the typical underlying causes of network connectivity issues. Consider the following:

- *Incorrect IP address or incorrect subnet*—Mistyping a static IP address into an instance interface can result in no connectivity to that interface. Similarly, mistyping a virtual network's or subnet's CIDR range can prevent communications. If you're trying to reach an instance across the Internet, make sure you're targeting the instance's public IP address. If it doesn't have one, you'll need to give it one.

- **DNS errors**—You might instead attempt to use the instance's public DNS host name, if available. DNS host names should be enabled in the account, network, or VPC where the instance resides. Also check any relevant DNS records to ensure there are no typos or other errors.

- **Misconfigured firewall rule**—Check to make sure the connection protocol's traffic is allowed through any firewalls, both at the on-prem computer's location and the cloud instance's location. For example, if using Remote Desktop to connect to a Windows VM, make sure RDP's port 3389 is enabled on all intervening firewalls. For Linux instances, make sure SSH's port 22 is enabled.

- **Incorrect routing or incorrect gateway**—A missing route in a route table is a common cause of broken connections in the cloud. For example, suppose your AWS VPC has an IG (Internet gateway), but instances in the VPC still can't reach the Internet. Check to make sure the static route to the VPC's IG is properly configured in the route table. If the VPC is instead using a NAT gateway, again, check to make sure the route is pointing to the correct gateway.

- **Tunneling issues**—Unused VPN tunnels might time out, causing tunneling issues. You can configure a host or some VPN endpoints to send a message every so often to keep the tunnel active.

- **Misconfigured proxy**—A proxy server acts as an intermediary between external and internal networks, screening all ingress and egress traffic. This helps increase security of the internal network (called network hardening) by masking information about internal resources from outside Internet systems and by providing some degree of content filtering. Proxies are commonly used to protect web servers from external threats. Due to the proxy's role on the network, a misconfigured proxy can prevent or delay network communications.

- **QoS issues**—QoS (Quality of Service) is a group of techniques for adjusting the priority a network assigns to various types of transmissions. QoS configurations don't work across the open Internet. However, QoS can be configured within a cloud network or across a direct connection with your cloud. This is often done for IoT (Internet of Things) traffic or sometimes for UC (unified communications) traffic, such as VoIP (voice over IP). With IoT, QoS settings are used with the MQTT (Message Queuing Telemetry Transport) protocol, which is a simple messaging protocol designed for communicating basic commands and status updates between small mobile devices and a message broker across low-bandwidth, high-latency network conditions. Three QoS-level options for messages are the following:

  ○ **QoS 0**—The message is delivered once at most and is most likely to be dropped if network conditions are poor.

  ○ **QoS 1**—The message is delivered at least once and expects an ACK (acknowledgment) response from the target device.

  ○ **QoS 2**—The message is delivered exactly once.

The correct QoS level must be set for each message type; confusing, duplicate communications can cause misconfigurations of the devices being controlled.

NAT Issues

Earlier in this course, you learned that you can use either a NAT gateway or a NAT instance in AWS to establish communications between the Internet and resources in a private subnet. While AWS recommends using a NAT gateway because the NAT instance feature is being deprecated, you can still manually configure a NAT instance in EC2 using the latest Amazon Linux 2 AMI. By default, an EC2 instance performs source/destination checks to confirm that any traffic it receives lists that instance as either the source or the destination before it accepts that traffic. A NAT instance, however, will need to send and receive traffic that does not list itself as the source or destination. For this reason, you'll need to disable the SrcDestCheck attribute on the NAT instance. Figure 5-28 shows how to access this option from the listed instance in EC2, and Figure 5-29 shows the source/destination option disabled.

Figure 5-28   Use the Action menu to change the source/destination check option in AWS

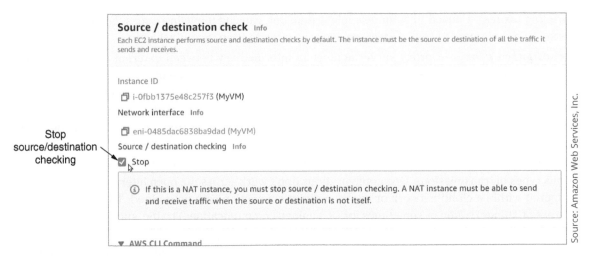

Figure 5-29   Disable source/destination checks

Load-Balancing Issues

Most load-balancing issues result from incorrectly configured load balancers or failed devices somewhere along the load-balanced path. Consider the following possibilities:

- *Method*—Typically, load balancers use a round-robin approach so traffic is distributed evenly across targets. Another popular method is weighted round robin where traffic is distributed according to varying weights (such as sending 80 percent of traffic to one target and 20 percent of traffic to another target). Or traffic might be sent to the target currently handling the fewest connections, which is called least connection. Using an inappropriate method for the network can result in one or more targets being overloaded with traffic while other targets are underutilized. In this case, consider changing the load-balancing method or adjusting weights to better distribute traffic across targets.

- *Persistence*—To maintain the integrity of a conversation between a load-balanced server and a client, the persistence option might be enabled on the load balancer, which you read earlier is called a sticky session. This ensures that communication from a single client IP address continues to be sent to the same server. If the client–server communications require consistency throughout the conversation, enabling persistence might be necessary. However, this might also result in a target server being overwhelmed with too much traffic during a session. If this becomes a problem, you can use HTTP cookies to support conversations between a client and different servers in the load-balanced cluster.

- *Headers*—Load balancers require that message headers include necessary information for directing traffic, and these headers must be edited in the process of being redirected so that source and destination IP addresses are properly handled. Common header issues include headers that are too long, that are missing key information, and that include too much, irrelevant, or invalid information. When there's a problem with a header, the load balancer will generate an error code. Refer to the load balancer's vendor documentation to interpret the error code and resolve the issue.

- *Health check protocol*—Load balancers rely on health checks to ensure target systems are functioning within expected parameters. Confirm the required port is open to allow this protocol's traffic to pass any security groups or ACLs (access control lists) protecting the targets—this information will vary by platform and vendor, so check load balancer documentation. In many cases, the health check port will be the same as the port used for other traffic to target servers, but not always.

- *Unhealthy backend server*—A failed health check on a backend server may or may not indicate a problem with the server itself. Confirm that traffic is supported through the entire route from the load balancer to the server, such as checking security groups or NACLs (network access control lists), which you learn more about in a later module. Also confirm that health messages from the load balancer are being monitored by the servers and that these servers are responding appropriately. If it's clear that the servers themselves are experiencing issues, you'll need to troubleshoot these VM instances or replace them.

- *Unreachable frontend*—Confirm the load balancer has access to the Internet. For example, in AWS, a load balancer must be attached to a subnet. If it's attached to a private subnet, Internet traffic cannot reach the load balancer. Ensure the IP address assignment is correct and that no security devices are blocking legitimate traffic to this device. Also check relevant DNS records. If the frontend is being overloaded with traffic, you might need to configure a pool of public IP addresses, add a backup load balancer appliance, or scale up the load balancer's resources.

- *Security of data in transit*—You can increase the security of data contained in load-balanced traffic by employing encryption protocols, such as HTTPS and TLS. You can reduce processing demands on the back-end servers by terminating encrypted connections at the load balancer, which requires the load balancer to perform encryption and decryption of traffic before reaching the backend servers.

Remember This

- Many popular CLI-based commands are useful when troubleshooting cloud network connections; however, some of these commands might produce different results than normally expected, or the command's protocol might be blocked by the CSP.
- When troubleshooting cloud connectivity issues, whether a connection isn't happening at all or traffic isn't traversing the connection as expected, common issues include unreachable instances, NAT issues, and load-balancing issues.

Self-Check

9. Which protocol requires port 22 be open on a firewall?

   a. RDP   **c.** ICMP

   b. SSH   **d.** ARP

10. Which utility would best be used to list all current connections on a Linux system?

    a. ping   **c.** arp

    b. ip   **d.** ss

11. Which device is used to camouflage internal network resources from the outside world?

    a. Load balancer   **c.** DNS server

    b. Proxy server   **d.** Default gateway

12. Which protocol can secure load-balanced traffic?

    a. TLS   **c.** DNS

    b. HTTP   **d.** NACL

○ Check your answers at the end of this module.

Module Summary

Section 5-1: Hybrid Cloud and Multi-Cloud Networking

- Three major categories of options to connect the on-prem data center with a cloud deployment include the public Internet, VPN (virtual private network) connections, and a direct connect or interconnect option.
- In the on-prem data center, a VLAN (virtual LAN) helps segment a network for both security and efficiency purposes by grouping ports on a switch so that some of the local traffic on the switch is forced to go through a router to reach ports in a different VLAN.
- VXLAN (virtual extensible LAN) addresses VLAN weaknesses by inserting MAC addressing information in a UDP header at layer 4 to better manage extended infrastructure across networks and over the Internet.
- GENEVE (Generic Network Virtualization Encapsulation) is a similar overlay network technology to VXLAN that uses a slightly longer header design to provide more adaptable configurations across the underlay network.

Section 5-2: Extending Network Services

- IP address spaces are managed by DHCP (Dynamic Host Configuration Protocol) services, both on-prem and in the cloud; IPAM (IP address management) tools can be used to manage IP spaces across hybrid and multi-clouds.
- DNS (Domain Name System) servers collect lists of computer names and their associated IP addresses in namespace databases, and some CSPs can allow an organization's on-prem resources to access cloud-based DNS services through a VPN or direct connection.
- Routing can be configured using static routes set by the cloud admin (which do not automatically adapt to route outages) or using dynamic routing, where routes are configured automatically by the cloud platform.
- A load balancer stands between the incoming traffic sources and a cluster of servers and distributes that traffic to all the servers in the cluster according to rules defined by the administrator.

Section 5-3: Troubleshooting Cloud Connectivity

- Many popular CLI-based commands are useful when troubleshooting cloud network connections; however, some of these commands might produce different results than normally expected or the command's protocol might be blocked by the CSP.
- When troubleshooting cloud connectivity issues, whether a connection isn't happening at all or traffic isn't traversing the connection as expected, common issues include unreachable instances, NAT issues, and load balancing issues.

Key Terms

For definitions of key terms, see the Glossary.

AS (autonomous system)

BGP (Border Gateway
Protocol)

DNS (Domain Name System or
Domain Name Service)

GENEVE (Generic Network
Virtualization Encapsulation)

hub-and-spoke

IPsec (Internet Protocol security)

load balancing

NAT-T (NAT-Traversal)

QoS (Quality of Service)

VLAN (virtual LAN)

VXLAN (virtual extensible
LAN)

Acronyms Checklist

The acronyms in Table 5-1 are listed in the Cloud+ objectives and could appear on the Cloud+ exam. This means that exam questions might use any of these acronyms in context so that you must know the meaning of the acronym to answer the question correctly. Make sure you're familiar with what each acronym stands for and the general concept of the term itself. All these acronyms are used in context in this module.

Table 5-1   Module 5 acronyms

Acronym	Spelled out
ARP	Address Resolution Protocol
BGP	Border Gateway Protocol
col or colo	colocation
DHCP	Dynamic Host Configuration Protocol
DNS	Domain Name System or Domain Name Service
FTP	File Transfer Protocol
GENEVE	Generic Network Virtualization Encapsulation
GRE	Generic Routing Encapsulation
ICMP	Internet Control Message Protocol
IGRP	Interior Gateway Routing Protocol
IPAM	IP address management
IPsec	Internet Protocol Security
L2TP	Layer 2 Tunneling Protocol
LAN	local area network
MPLS	Multiprotocol Label Switching

Acronym	Spelled out
MTU	maximum transmission unit
OSPF	Open Shortest Path First
PAT	port address translation
PPTP	Point-to-Point Tunneling Protocol
QoS	Quality of Service
SIP	Session Initiation Protocol
TCP	Transmission Control Protocol
TTL	Time to Live
UDP	User Datagram Protocol
VLAN	virtual LAN
VNC	Virtual Network Computing
VoIP	voice over IP
VPN	virtual private network
VXLAN	virtual extensible LAN
WAN	wide area network

Review Questions

1. Which VPN topology is the best fit for a connection between an on-prem database and a cloud-based application?

   a. Point-to-point
   b. Site-to-point
   c. Site-to-site
   d. Point-to-site

2. Which network configuration must be adjusted to support VXLAN and GENEVE?

   a. MTU
   b. UDP
   c. NAT
   d. MPLS

3. What type of virtual network can peer many other virtual networks to allow communication between all connected networks?

   a. Private
   b. Spoke
   c. Public
   d. Hub

4. Why are VLANs restricted to layer 3 communications?

   a. VLANs must use MAC addresses.
   b. VLANs rely on UDP.
   c. VLAN tags are added at layer 2.
   d. VLANs define broadcast domains.

5. Suppose you have a large cluster of web servers in one availability zone and a much smaller cluster in a different availability zone. You want to make sure your larger cluster takes a larger portion of the website traffic. Which load-balancing method is the best fit?

   a. Least connection
   b. Round robin
   c. Persistent
   d. Weighted round robin

6. What would you need to change in your VPC configurations to ensure VM instances use DNS servers hosted by your organization?

   a. DNS records
   b. Scope options
   c. Default gateway
   d. CIDR block

7. At what level is an IP address space typically defined in the public cloud? Choose TWO.

   a. VPC
   b. Region
   c. Subnet
   d. Gateway

8. What misconfiguration will result in failed health checks from a load balancer's server cluster?

   a. Incorrect IP address
   b. DNS error
   c. Incorrect gateway
   d. Misconfigured firewall rule

9. Which load-balancing method is the best fit for a server cluster where workloads can be highly unpredictable in the time required to complete each series of tasks?

   a. Least connection
   b. Round robin
   c. Persistent
   d. Weighted round robin

10. Which utility will help you identify the port a network service is using?

   a. flushdns
   b. ss
   c. ipconfig
   d. curl

Scenario-Based Questions

Question 5-1

Marc has configured two VLANs on his office network: VLAN A and VLAN B. He has three switches: Switches 1, 2, and 3. As shown in Figure 5-30, Switch 1 on the first floor of Marc's office building is connected to his router. It's also connected to Switch 2 on the first floor and to Switch 3 on the second floor. VLAN A handles traffic for the Accounting Department, and VLAN B handles traffic for Sales. Both VLANs have network clients on each floor.

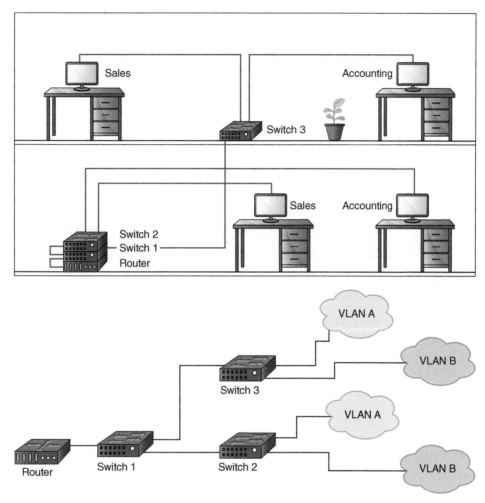

Figure 5-30   Marc's office network

Marc is having trouble getting clients on different VLANs to talk to each other, even when they're on the same floor. For example, the sales computer on the first floor can't connect to the accounting computer sitting right next to it. It's the same problem on the second floor. Which device is most likely the source of the problem?

  a. Switch 1
  b. Switch 2
  c. Switch 3
  d. The router

Question 5-2

Luca is configuring a VPN connection to her company's new cloud network. She has web server instances deployed in the cloud, and she's using the VPN to connect those instances to a database that will remain in her on-prem network. Luca has decided to use dynamic routing in the VPN. Which routing protocol will she most likely be using?

  a. RIP
  b. EIGRP
  c. IPsec
  d. BGP

Question 5-3

Sami is trying to ping between instances in her newly created VNet, but it's not working. She's double-checked the IP addresses she's using, and she's confirmed the instances are running. She decides to check the network's firewall settings to ensure that the ping protocol is allowed. Which protocol should she look for?

   a. BGP
   b. SSH
   c. IPsec
   d. ICMP

Hands-On Projects

Note 6

Websites, applications, public cloud platforms, and related account options change often. While the instructions given in these projects were accurate at the time of writing, you might need to adjust the steps or options according to later changes.

Note to Instructors and Students: A rubric is provided for evaluating student performance on these projects. Please see Appendix D.

Project 5-1: Explore VPN Options in AWS

Estimated time: 30 minutes
Objective 3.3: Given a scenario, deploy cloud networking solutions.
Resources:

   • AWS account
   • Drawing app, such as Visio or app.diagrams.net
   • Internet access

Context:
A VPN connection, with all its protocols and configuration options, seems like an abstract concept until you start building your own VPNs. Once you see and build the various components yourself, the whole idea starts to make more sense. In this project, you'll configure a VPN connection to a VPC. The VPN will connect a virtual gateway device in your VPC to a customer gateway device in your on-prem network. If you have an actual VPN gateway device at your location, you can use the real information for that device and establish a real VPN connection to AWS. The instructions in this project assume that you don't have a VPN gateway device at your location. You'll configure the VPN connection without activating it.

Data transfer across a VPN and use of the related gateways incur charges in AWS. To avoid these charges, the steps indicate at what point further progress in the project is optional. If you have plenty of free credit in your account or if spending a few dollars is not problematic for you, you might want to complete the project for the sake of the experience. However, these last few steps are not required to earn full credit for the project.

Complete the following steps:

1. In your AWS Management Console, create a VPC, which you learned to do in Project 4-2. What CIDR block did you use?
2. From the list of VPCs, click your new VPC's main route table. Give this route table a name that you can easily identify later, such as MyVPN-RT. To add the name, click the pencil icon that appears when you point to the route table's name field. What did you name your route table?

(continues)

3. Before creating the VPN resources in AWS, you need your public IP address for your local network. Using a search engine, search **what is my ip**. Copy your public IP address from the search results.

4. Now you're ready to create the VPN gateways. In the navigation pane, scroll down and click **Customer Gateways**. Recall that the CGW is a VPN appliance in the customer's on-prem network. This process does not create a new resource in AWS—it simply informs AWS of how to find your VPN device in your on-prem network. Click **Create customer gateway**. Give the CGW a name and paste your public IP address in the IP Address field. Click **Create customer gateway** and then click **Close**. What is your CGW's type?

5. Now you're ready to create a virtual gateway in AWS, which will provide access to the VPN connection on the VPC's side. In the navigation pane, click **Virtual Private Gateways**, and then click **Create virtual private gateway**. Give the VGW a name. Leave the ASN selection as **Amazon default ASN**, click **Create virtual private gateway**, and then click **Close**. What did you name your VGW?

6. Click to select your new VGW and attach it to the VPC you created in Step 1.

7. If you were creating this VPN connection for use with a real CGW, you would also need to make some changes to the security group for this VPC. Like allowing traffic through a firewall, this would enable RDP, SSH, and ICMP traffic into the VPC from the on-prem network. You learn more about security groups in a later module. For now, because you won't activate the VPN connection in this project, you can skip this step. However, if you're planning to configure the VPN connection on an actual VPN gateway at your physical location, be sure to search online for the changes you need to make to the VPC's security group.

8. You're now ready to create the VPN connection between these two gateways. In the navigation pane, click **Site-to-Site VPN Connections**. Click **Create VPN connection**. Give the VPN a name, and then select the VGW and CGW that you created earlier in this project. Change the routing option to **Static**. In the Static IP Prefixes field that appears, enter a private CIDR range that you might be using in your on-prem network. If you were establishing this VPN connection for real, you would need to ensure that your on-prem network's private CIDR ranges and your VPC's CIDR range don't overlap. What private CIDR range did you list for your on-prem network?

9. *WARNING: Do not complete the next few steps in this project if you need to avoid incurring any charges in your AWS account.*

- If you are using AWS Academy and you have available credits, you should be able to complete this project using only a small amount of credit and without encountering any permissions restrictions. Therefore, continue with the next step.

- If you are using a standard AWS account and you must avoid any charges, click **Cancel**, read the next few steps, and complete Step 14. You can read the remaining steps instead and watch the video for this project to see the project's completion. Otherwise, continue with the next step.

10. If you have credits in your account or if you're comfortable with paying a few dollars to complete this project, click **Create VPN connection**, and then click **Close**.

11. The VPN connection will take a few minutes to reach an available state. In the meantime, click the **Tunnel details** tab. Notice the VPN has two tunnels to provide redundancy. Each of these tunnels can be configured separately when you first configure the VPN.

12. Instances in your VPC will need routes in the VPC's route table to find the CGW and to know what IP addresses exist on the other side of the VPN connection. You can configure these routes manually or enable route propagation so this is done automatically. To enable route propagation, in the navigation pane, click **Route Tables** and then select the route table you identified in Step 2. Click the **Route propagation** tab, and then click **Edit route propagation**. Click the box to enable route propagation, and then click **Save**.

13. Return to the Site-to-Site VPN Connections page. By now, your VPN connection should be available; if not, give it a few more minutes. Select your VPN and click the **Tunnel details** tab. Notice that both tunnels are still down. To complete the VPN configuration, you'll need to download a configuration file from AWS and use it to configure the customer gateway device in your local network. If you don't have a real VPN gateway, you can still download the configuration file to see what information it includes. Click **Download**

(continues)

Hands-On Projects Continued

configuration. For the Vendor, select **Generic** (or use the correct information for your device); then keep the default settings that appear (unless you're using an actual device and have more specific information). Which IKE version is selected by default? Click **Download**.

14. After the file downloads, open it and explore the information given. Particularly important pieces of information used to complete the configuration on the customer's side include the preshared key and the outside IP addresses for the CGW and VGW, as shown in Figure 5-31. If you have an actual VPN gateway at your location, you can configure it with the provided information from the download and then activate the VPN connection.

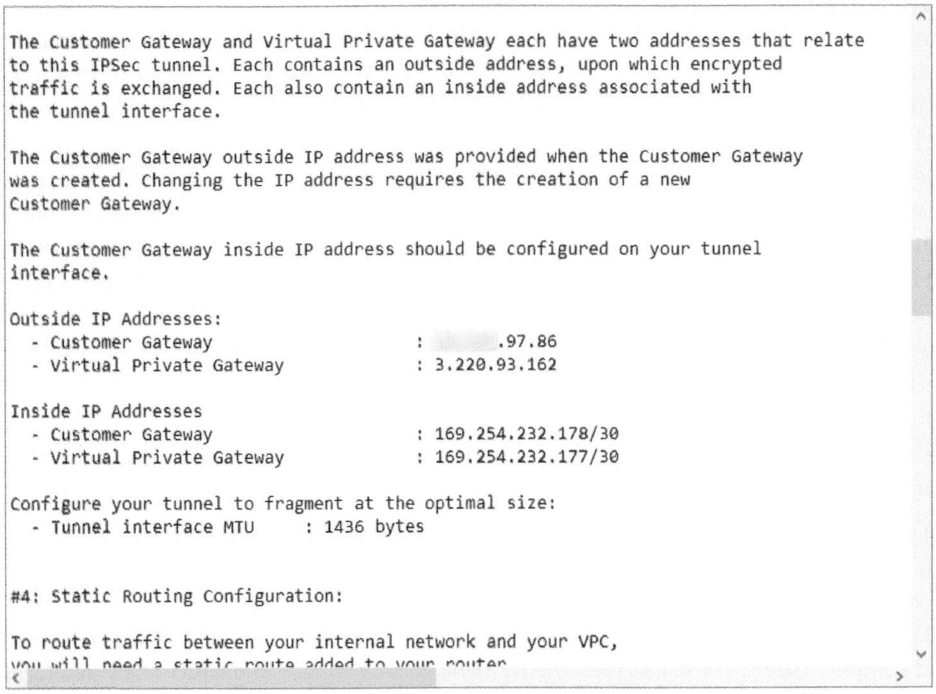

```
The Customer Gateway and Virtual Private Gateway each have two addresses that relate
to this IPSec tunnel. Each contains an outside address, upon which encrypted
traffic is exchanged. Each also contain an inside address associated with
the tunnel interface.

The Customer Gateway outside IP address was provided when the Customer Gateway
was created. Changing the IP address requires the creation of a new
Customer Gateway.

The Customer Gateway inside IP address should be configured on your tunnel
interface.

Outside IP Addresses:
  - Customer Gateway           :      .97.86
  - Virtual Private Gateway    : 3.220.93.162

Inside IP Addresses
  - Customer Gateway           : 169.254.232.178/30
  - Virtual Private Gateway    : 169.254.232.177/30

Configure your tunnel to fragment at the optimal size:
  - Tunnel interface MTU       : 1436 bytes


#4: Static Routing Configuration:

To route traffic between your internal network and your VPC,
you will need a static route added to your router.
```

Source: Amazon Web Services, Inc.

Figure 5-31   These public IP addresses allow the VPN gateway devices to find each other across the Internet

15. Use a drawing app, such as Visio or app.diagrams.net, to **draw a diagram of the resources used to create this VPN**. Include the VPC, the on-prem network, both gateways, and the VPN connection using official AWS diagram symbols, such as those you saw in this module. Submit this visual with your answers to this project's questions.

16. Delete all the resources you created in this project, including the VPC, both gateways, and the VPN connection (if you created it). In what order did you delete these resources? What error messages did you encounter? How did you handle these problems? Check through your account to confirm that all related resources have been deleted.

Note 7

Depending on the status of your account and the selections you made during this project, the resources you created can deplete your credits or accrue charges. Double-check to make sure you've terminated all resources you created in this project.

Project 5-2: Explore VPN Options in Azure

Estimated time: 1 hour (including 30 minutes' wait time at the end of Step 4)
Objective 3.3: Given a scenario, deploy cloud networking solutions.
Resources:

- Azure account
- Drawing app, such as Visio or app.diagrams.net
- Internet access

Context:

A significant difference between Azure's VPN options and AWS's VPN services is that Azure allows you to create a VPN between two VNets. While you can do this in AWS, it takes more finagling. In this project, you'll create a VPN connection between two VNets in the same subscription. Although it's possible to connect VNets in different subscriptions, that process is much more complicated.

A VPN connection to a VNet in Azure relies on a special subnet called a gateway subnet, which holds two VM instances that manage traffic through the gateway subnet. In this project, you'll see how to configure and connect these gateway subnets.

At the time of this writing, VNet-to-VNet VPN connections within the same region are free. Unless something has changed more recently, you should be able to complete this entire project without incurring charges so long as you follow the steps correctly—watch for updated information in your Azure portal. Complete the following steps:

1. In your Azure portal, create two VNets; you learned how to create VNets in Project 4-3:
   a. Create a new resource group for each VNet.
   b. Take note of the region and use the same region for both VNets.
   c. Use a different CIDR block for each VNet that do not overlap each other. What CIDR blocks did you use?
   d. Use a smaller CIDR block for the subnet in each VNet, as you'll need some of the available address range for the gateway subnets. What CIDR block did you use for each subnet?
2. Create a new gateway subnet in each VNet. You learned how to add a second subnet to a VNet in Project 4-3. However, this time you need to create a gateway subnet, not a regular subnet (see Figure 5-32). The process is similar except that you won't be able to change the name of the subnet. You should also use a smaller CIDR block, such as /27 or /28. Don't change any other default settings. What CIDR block did you use for each gateway subnet?

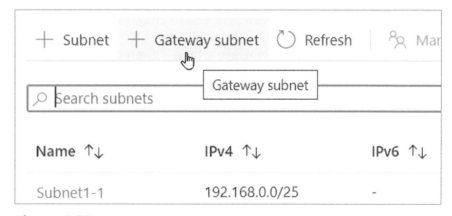

Figure 5-32   A gateway subnet gives a VNet access to a VPN connection

(continues)

Hands-On Projects Continued

3. Now you're ready to create a virtual network gateway for each VNet. In the portal menu, click **Create a resource**. In the Search services and marketplace field, enter **virtual network gateway**. Click **Virtual network gateway** when it appears as a suggestion. On the Virtual network gateway blade that appears, click **Create**.

4. Configure the following settings:
   a. Give the VGW a name and make sure you add it to the same region where you created your VNets. What did you name the VGW?
   b. Select **VPN** gateway type and **Route-based** VPN type.
   c. Under SKU, choose **Basic**. The basic VPN supports fewer users, less security, and no BGP routing. However, this option is sufficient for this project.
   d. Assign the VGW to a VNet.
   e. Make sure **Create new** is selected for the public IP address, and then give the IP address a name.
   f. Click **Review + create** and then click **Create**.
   g. Repeat Steps 4a through 4f for the second VGW.
   h. Make sure you've created a VGW for each VNet before continuing with the next step, and make sure all deployments are complete. It might take quite a while—perhaps 30 minutes or more—for the VGWs to fully deploy. Grab a cup of coffee or tea while you wait.

5. You're now ready to create the connection between the VGWs. Go to your list of virtual network gateways. One way to do this is to click **All services** in the portal menu, click **Networking**, and then click **Virtual network gateways**. After all deployments have completed, click the first VGW.

6. Click **Connections** and then click **Add** to create a VPN connection.
   a. Give the connection a descriptive name, such as MyVNet1toMyVNet2.
   b. Make sure that **VNet-to-VNet** is selected for the connection type.
   c. The first VGW is selected for you because it's already associated with the VNet where you're creating the connection.
   d. Select the second VNet for the other end of the connection.
   e. Create a shared key (PSK) for the connection (this is basically a password), and write it down where you can get to it easily in the next step.
   f. Click **OK**.

7. Create a connection in reverse from the second VGW. Be sure to use the same shared key.

8. Watch the Connections blade for one of the VGWs until the status for each connection changes to Connected (this might take several minutes).

9. Click one of the connections to open its overview page. How much data in and data out is reported? What IP addresses are being used at each end of the connection?

10. Use a drawing app, such as Visio or app.diagrams.net, to **draw a diagram of the resources used to create this VPN**. Include both VNets, all subnets, both gateways, and the VPN connections using official Azure diagram symbols, such as those you saw in this module. Submit this visual with your answers to this project's questions.

11. Delete all the resources you created in this project, including both VNets, both resource groups, all related subnets and gateway subnets, both VGWs, and all connections. In what order did you delete these resources? What error messages did you encounter? How did you handle these problems? Check through your account to confirm that all related resources have been deleted.

> ## Note 8
>
> Depending on the status of your account and the selections you made during this project, the resources you created can deplete your credits or accrue charges. Double-check to make sure you've terminated all resources you created in this project.

Project 5-3: Explore VPN Options in GCP

Estimated time: 30 minutes

Objective 3.3: Given a scenario, deploy cloud networking solutions.

Resources:

- GCP account
- Drawing app, such as Visio or app.diagrams.net
- Internet access

Context:

As with Azure, GCP allows you to create a VPN connection between two VPCs. In this project, you'll create a VPN connection between two VPCs in the same region. Data transfer across a VPN and use of the related gateways incur charges in GCP. *Unfortunately, not all these charges can be avoided to complete any significant portion of this project.* However, if you follow the steps carefully and quickly (complete in less than an hour), the total charge should not be more than a few cents.

Complete the following steps:

1. To make cleanup easier at the end of this project, first click the scope picker at the top of your GCP console to create a new project. Click **NEW PROJECT** and give this project a name. Click **CREATE**.

2. Make sure you're in the new project you just created. Then create two custom-mode VPCs with one subnet each—you might be prompted to enable Compute Engine API first. You learned how to create VPCs in Project 4-4. Place each VPC's subnet in the same region, and make sure the CIDR blocks for the VPCs' subnets don't overlap. What region did you use? What CIDR blocks did you use?

3. In the navigation menu, scroll down to the **Networking** category and point to **Hybrid Connectivity**; then click **VPN**. Click **CREATE VPN CONNECTION**. Configure two VPN gateways with one in each VPC:

    a. Under VPN options, make sure **High-availability (HA) VPN** is selected and click **CONTINUE**.

    b. Give the VPN gateway a name, such as vpn-gw-1.

    c. For Network, select the first VPC you created in Step 2.

    d. Select the first VPC's region

    e. Click **CREATE & CONTINUE**. You're not ready to create VPN tunnels until after you create the second VPN gateway, so in the navigation pane, click **VPN**.

    f. Click **CREATE VPN GATEWAY** to add a second VPN gateway resource.

    g. Add this VPN gateway to the second VPC you created in Step 2.

4. You need a Cloud Router in each VPC to manage communications across the VPN:

    a. In the navigation pane, click **Cloud Routers**, and then click **CREATE ROUTER**.

    b. Give the router a name, place it in the first VPC you created in Step 2, and use that VPC's region. For Google ASN (autonomous system number), enter **65400**. Leave the other default settings and click **CREATE**.

    c. Create a second Cloud Router in the second VPC you created in Step 2 and use Google ASN **65500**.

5. Now you're ready to configure the tunnels:

    a. In the navigation pane, click **VPN**. Click the **CLOUD VPN TUNNELS** tab, and then click **CREATE VPN TUNNEL**.

    b. Choose the first VPN gateway you created earlier and click **CONTINUE**.

    c. Under Peer VPN gateway, select **Google Cloud** to choose your other VPC for the VPN connection. Choose the project you created in Step 1, and then choose the second VPN gateway you created in this project.

    d. Select **Create a single VPN tunnel** to minimize expense. Choose the first cloud router you created earlier.

    e. Give the tunnel a name, such as my-vpn-1.

(continues)

Hands-On Projects Continued

   f. Generate and copy an IKE preshared key. Paste this key into a text document so you can use it again in a moment.

   g. Click **CREATE & CONTINUE**. You do not need to configure BGP sessions for this project, so click **CONFIGURE BGP SESSIONS LATER**.

6. Create a second VPN tunnel from the second VPN gateway to the first one and be sure to use the same IKE preshared key from Step 5.

7. To use this VPN connection for communication between the VPCs, you would need to create firewall rules on both sides of the VPN to allow traffic through the gateways. You learn how to configure firewall rules in a later module, and this step is not necessary for the purposes of this project. For now, return to the **CLOUD VPN TUNNELS** tab and check that both tunnels show as Established. *Note: VPN tunnels incur a per-hour charge, although this fee is not large. For example, in a test where these tunnels were left running overnight, the total fee was less than $1. Still, you don't want to leave the tunnels running any longer than necessary for this project.*

8. Click the **Settings and utilities** icon at the top right of your console, and then click **Project settings**. Click **SHUT DOWN** to delete all resources created in this project. Enter the project ID and then click **SHUT DOWN**. Click **OK** and return to your GCP console for a different project.

9. Use a drawing app, such as Visio or app.diagrams.net, to **draw a diagram of the resources used to create this VPN**. Include both VPCs, both subnets, both gateways, both cloud routers, and both tunnels using official GCP diagram symbols, such as those you saw in this module. Submit this visual with your answers to this project's questions.

> **Note 9**
>
> Depending on the status of your account and the selections you made during this project, the resources you created can deplete your credits or accrue charges. Double-check to make sure you've terminated all resources you created in this project.

Capstone Project 5: Configure Cloud Peering

> **Note 10**
>
> Websites, applications, public cloud platforms, and related account options change often. While the instructions given in these projects were accurate at the time of writing, you might need to adjust the steps or options according to later changes.

Note to Instructors and Students: A rubric is provided for evaluating student performance on these projects. Please see Appendix D.

Estimated time: 45 minutes

Objective 5.4: Given a scenario, troubleshoot connectivity issues.

Group work: This project includes enhancements when assigned as a group project.

Resources:

- Public cloud account (such as AWS, Azure, or GCP)
- Internet access

Context:

VPN connections are the traditional method for connecting networks across the Internet. However, for network connections within the cloud, you have the option to use a more streamlined configuration to connect VPCs or VNets to each other. This service is called peering, which you read about in the module. Cloud peering, for what it does, is a significant improvement over using VPNs when connecting virtual networks to each other. Peering is simpler to set up and is typically cheaper than a VPN. Because of your experience at this point with configuring VPNs, peering connections should be easy for you to figure out. In fact, this is an excellent opportunity for you to practice teaching yourself a new skill in the cloud.

In this project, you'll use one or more cloud platforms to practice researching and teaching yourself how to peer virtual networks. Complete the following steps:

1. Choose a cloud platform: AWS, Azure, or GCP. You can repeat these steps with a second or third platform later. Check with your instructor on the requirements for this Capstone Project.
2. Research the platform's peering service and answer the following questions:
   a. How much does peering cost?
   b. Can you peer with a virtual network in another account?
   c. Is peering transitive?
   d. Where is peering configured in the cloud platform?
   e. What resources must already exist before peering can be established?
   f. What are the basic steps to create the peering connection?
   g. What significant limitations exist on the peering service for this platform?
3. In your selected cloud platform, create two virtual networks with nonoverlapping CIDR blocks, such as 192.168.0.0/24 and 192.168.1.0/24. Create a peering connection between these virtual networks. **Take a screenshot** showing the peering connection; submit this visual with your responses to this project's questions.
4. In your selected cloud platform, create two virtual networks with overlapping CIDR blocks, such as 192.168.0.0/24 and 192.168.0.128/24. Attempt to create a peering connection between these virtual networks. What happens?
5. Suppose you wanted to peer three virtual networks in a mesh network. List three /24 CIDR blocks that would work for this scenario.
6. **For group projects:** Each group member should create a VPC or VNet in their chosen cloud platform. Work together to try to create a peering connection between your VPC or VNet and another group member's VPC or VNet. What information did you have to share with each other? What problems did you run into? Were you successful in establishing an active peering connection?
7. Delete any cloud resources you created for this project. Repeat the project with another cloud platform if desired or if required by your instructor.

Note 11

Depending on the status of your account and the selections you made during this project, the resources you created can deplete your credits or accrue charges. Double-check to make sure you've terminated all resources you created in this project.

Solutions to Self-Check Questions

Section 5-1: Hybrid Cloud and Multi-Cloud Networking

1. Which protocol is used to secure VPNs?

    Answer: b. IPsec

    Explanation: Most tunneling protocols rely on an additional encryption protocol, such as IPsec (Internet Protocol Security), to provide data security.

2. Which cloud connection type is the most expensive for the cloud customer?

    Answer: b. Direct connection

    Explanation: The direct connect option is more secure, and yet the characteristics and service features differ depending on the cloud provider. This also tends to be the most expensive option.

3. Which protocol provides checksum functions for VXLAN and GENEVE headers?

    Answer: c. UDP

    Explanation: VXLAN and GENEVE are supported by UDP at the transport layer, which incorporates a basic checksum function.

4. What characteristic allows GENEVE to support a wider variety of use cases than VXLAN?

    Answer: a. Variable header field

    Explanation: Part of the GENEVE header is variable in nature and can be used in many ways to serve a wider variety of use cases than VXLAN.

Section 5-2: Extending Network Services

5. Which of the following devices is least likely to need a static IP address?

    Answer: b. Web client

    Explanation: Devices such as web clients can use dynamic IP addresses assigned from a DHCP server because they do not need to be located at the same address over time.

6. Which DNS record must be updated when changing email servers?

    Answer: d. MX record

    Explanation: An MX (Mail Exchanger) record identifies an email server and is used for email traffic.

7. Which routing protocol is used across the Internet?

    Answer: b. BGP

    Explanation: BGP (Border Gateway Protocol) dynamically manages routes between autonomous systems, such as across the Internet.

8. Which device helps ensure HA for a web server?

    Answer: d. Load balancer

    Explanation: A load balancer distributes traffic over multiple components to optimize performance and fault tolerance, thereby increasing HA (high availability).

Section 5-3: Troubleshooting Cloud Connectivity

9. Which protocol requires port 22 be open on a firewall?

    Answer: b. SSH

    Explanation: For SSH to work, TCP port 22 must be enabled on any intervening firewalls.

10. Which utility would best be used to list all current connections on a Linux system?

Answer: d. ss

Explanation: The ss (socket statistics) and netstat (network statistics) utilities list current connections, ports used, and the state of each connection.

11. Which device is used to camouflage internal network resources from the outside world?

Answer: b. Proxy server

Explanation: A proxy server acts as an intermediary between external and internal networks, screening all ingress and egress traffic. This helps increase security of the internal network (called network hardening) by masking information about internal resources from outside Internet systems and by providing some degree of content filtering.

12. Which protocol can secure load-balanced traffic?

Answer: a. TLS

Explanation: Data carried by load-balanced traffic can be secured by employing encryption protocols, such as HTTPS and TLS.

Module 6

Securing Cloud Resources

Module 6 Objectives

After reading this module, you will be able to:

1 Describe common threats to and configurations for cloud security.

2 Secure cloud networks.

3 Secure cloud compute resources.

4 Secure cloud-hosted data.

5 Troubleshoot cloud security issues.

Module 6 Outline

Study the module's outline to help you organize the content in your mind as you read.

Section 6-1: Cloud Security Configurations
Threats to Cloud Security
Scanning Tools
Cloud-Based Approaches to Security
Supporting Shadow IT

Section 6-2: Virtual Network Security
Allow and Deny Rules
AWS VPCs and Subnets
Azure Virtual Networks
GCP VPCs
Securing Hybrid and Multi-Clouds

Section 6-3: Compute Security
Device Hardening
Application Security

Section 6-4: Data Security
Encrypting Data
Securing Protocols

Section 6-5: Troubleshooting Cloud Security
Security Misconfigurations
Data Misclassification
Key Management

Module 6 Scenario

"What's up, man? Did you catch the game last night?" Nigel gives Henry a fist bump as the two of you walk into the guard station at the front entrance of your school's campus, which also hosts the security department's main office.

"Aw, man, that game was brutal," groans Henry. "I bet Kendra's giving you a hard time today! But there's still time to make the playoffs." Henry and Nigel, both Cubs fans, show tireless optimism the entire baseball season. Kendra, a Cardinals fan, enjoys bantering with them. But they insist the Cubs' World Series win has fueled their hope for another hundred years, if that's what it takes. You've not yet decided if this is a sign of admirable loyalty or mild delusion.

You spot two large monitors on Henry's desk, each with several camera feeds that slowly rotate among different cameras throughout campus. "Hey, so this is where the security camera feeds go?" you ask him.

"Yep, this is the grand view of the whole campus," replies Henry. "We've got cameras in and around every building, even the football field."

"You said you're having a problem with some of them, right?" asks Nigel.

"Right," Henry says. "The new cameras in the science building—we're not getting a feed from those here at this station. When I plug my laptop into the system there in the building, I see everything fine. But back here, we're not getting anything. Any idea what's wrong?"

"We'll look into it and get it fixed for you," you reply with a little more confidence than you actually feel. It seems like security cameras should be such a simple thing, and yet those new cameras were tough to install.

After you and Nigel get back to the IT office, the two of you check in with Kendra for a little advice on how to troubleshoot the security cameras before heading to the science building. As she gears up to gloat over the Cardinals' win last night, Nigel cuts her off with a question: "You know, I've been wondering about how to keep our stuff safe in the cloud. We keep everything behind a firewall here on campus. What happens when we start moving stuff to the cloud?"

"Ah, yeah. That's a good question," muses Kendra. "Well, it's kind of like security here on campus," she begins. "We have the guard station at the front that is kind of like a firewall. And like with on-prem firewalls, there are ways to control what traffic gets into your cloud network. But a *lot* of people come onto this campus, and not everyone can be closely and always tracked. We need good security throughout campus to alert us if something goes wrong."

"Oh, like the security cameras?" you suggest.

"Right," says Kendra. "And locked doors, and passwords on computers, and security personnel patrolling the campus. At your home, you don't need such dense security because it's a private space—you have more control over who is in your house. But our campus is more communal, like the cloud. There are security measures throughout campus, just like in the cloud. We can add different layers of security that protect our cloud resources in different ways."

"What are some of those other security tools?" you wonder out loud.

"I smell a research project coming on," quips Nigel.

"You read my mind!" grins Kendra. "Here ya go—do a little research on these questions," she adds as she scribbles a few notes on her notepad:

- What kinds of threats do cloud users face?
- What techniques can keep cloud networks, VM instances, and data secure?
- What tools can help in troubleshooting problems with cloud security?

Section 6-1: Cloud Security Configurations

Certification

1.1 Compare and contrast the different types of cloud models.

1.4 Given a scenario, analyze the solution design in support of the business requirements.

2.1 Given a scenario, configure identity and access management.

2.2 Given a scenario, secure a network in a cloud environment.

2.3 Given a scenario, apply the appropriate OS and application security controls.

2.4 Given a scenario, apply data security and compliance controls in cloud environments.

2.5 Given a scenario, implement measures to meet security requirements.

5.2 Given a scenario, troubleshoot security issues.

When considering a move to the cloud, technical and nontechnical professionals alike often list security concerns as their number one reason for hesitating. Cloud consumers face both familiar and new threats to their data and other cloud resources. While their concerns are warranted to a degree, the technologies supporting cloud security continue to evolve and mature. By understanding the nature of the relevant threats and the tools used to protect the cloud, IT professionals can make informed and effective decisions as their reliance on the cloud continues to increase. This section explores these common threats and popular tools used to mitigate related risks. Later in this module, you learn about ways to protect cloud networks, compute resources, and cloud-hosted data.

Threats to Cloud Security

To begin, let's first examine a few of the most common internal and external threats to cloud security:

- **Data breaches**—Any data accessible from the Internet, no matter where it's stored, is inherently at risk. Data stored in the cloud has some unique vulnerabilities, however, including risks due to shared hardware resources and vulnerabilities to CSP personnel or third-party providers. Cloud consumers also have no control over physical security or little influence on configuration of the physical infrastructure supporting their cloud-hosted data. For example, when deleting data in the cloud, the consumer has no way of knowing whether the data continues to exist on hardware outside their control, and this data could be recovered in an attack. The outcome of a data breach, regardless of the cause, can be devastating to a business, its customers, and its employees due to loss of privacy, risk of fraud, and resulting fines, lawsuits, and possibly criminal charges.

- **DoS and DDoS attacks**—A DoS (denial of service) attack is any kind of attack that affects the availability or performance of services or data. For example, an economic DoS attack might artificially escalate the demand on a start-up company's auto-scaled cloud resources, increasing the company's bills beyond its ability to pay. Sometimes multiple attackers (or bots) are used in a DDoS (distributed denial of service) attack, such as flooding a web server with traffic until the server is no longer able to respond.

- **Insecure interfaces**—Whether a UI (user interface) or an API (application programming interface), points of transition from one system to another can leave security vulnerabilities. Designed for access and interactivity, UIs and APIs are both prime targets for hackers attempting to gain entry.

- **Advanced persistent threats**—APTs (advanced persistent threats) are attacks that clear the way for future attacks, essentially gaining a foothold in the target's IT systems and infrastructure. APTs are long-term projects where the infiltration blends with normal network traffic so as not to raise red flags. These efforts are more commonly undertaken by large enterprises or government organizations due to the complexity of the attack, the required resources, and the type of data that is targeted.

- **Account hijacking**—While account hijacking is not a unique cloud computing risk, having a cloud account hijacked can result in some cloud-specific damage due to the software-defined nature of cloud resources. The cloud environment allows a hacker greater leverage for eavesdropping on activities, manipulating data, redirecting customer traffic, and reconfiguring cloud resources.

- **Poor account management**—Poorly managed identity and account systems increase the likelihood of an account being compromised. Weak password rules; lack of multifactor authentication; improper storage of account credentials; inadequate account life cycle oversight; and sloppy handling of keys, passwords, and certificates all put a company and its users at risk.

- **User error**—People make mistakes. Whether from lack of knowledge, carelessness, or willful sloppiness, simple mistakes can create huge problems. Specific to the cloud, file oversharing, storing protected information in insecure file storage accounts, and designing problematic file names (such as naming a password spreadsheet "passwords") are all examples of user carelessness that could create some serious legal and economic consequences for their employer.

- *Insider threats*—Beyond user error, malicious users pose an even greater threat. This threat could come from current or former employees, contractors, or business partners who intentionally use company resources beyond acceptable-use standards in a way that damages confidentiality, integrity, or availability of company data and services.
- *Data loss with no backups*—Just because data lives in the cloud doesn't mean it's being backed up. With the current trend toward relying on the cloud to store backups, it's easy to overlook the need to back up cloud-hosted data. Several things can go wrong in this scenario: There could be problems with backup syncing, a cloud service could crash, accounts that access the data could be compromised, or accounts can be deleted for inactivity.
- *CSP changes or outages*—Capabilities and conditions change, and SLAs (service-level agreements) are occasionally adapted to keep up with the changes. However, this isn't always in a cloud customer's favor, which can affect the ways they manage their data and other cloud resources. When relying on a service provider, the organization is susceptible to changes and outages experienced by the CSP. For example, a December 2021 power outage at an AWS data center in the North Virginia region affected services for many popular websites and companies, including the workplace communications site Slack and the media streaming site Hulu. Due to the reliance of so many services and websites on a few major CSPs, a single cloud outage can have ripple effects throughout many industries.

Note 1

Most CSPs provide a service monitoring site to check availability reports for their platform. For example, status.aws.amazon.com shows current status of all services across the AWS platform in all regions. Broad coverage monitoring sites, such as Downdetector (downdetector.com), report on outages for hundreds of ISPs, CSPs, SaaS providers, social media platforms, and more. Some of these reporting sites are more accurate or timely than others.

You're Ready

You're now ready to complete Project 6-1: Research Data Breaches. You can complete the project now or wait until you've finished all the readings for this module.

Scanning Tools

Whether you're securing on-prem or cloud-based resources, you should know how to use common scanning tools to produce popular scan types and track risks. This section discusses port scanners and vulnerability scanners. It also compares types of scans and describes how to track the vulnerabilities found in network scanning and monitoring activities.

Scanning tools provide hackers—and you—with a simple and reliable way to discover crucial information about your network, including but not limited to the following:

- Every available host
- Each host's available services and software, including operating systems, applications, and their versions
- Software configurations
- Open, closed, and filtered ports on every host
- Existence, type, placement, and configuration of firewalls
- Unencrypted or poorly encrypted sensitive data

Used intentionally on your own network, scanning tools improve security by pointing out insecure ports, software and firmware that must be patched, permissions that should be restricted, and so on. They can also contribute valuable data to asset management and audit reports. The following list describes three popular scanning tools you can use:

- *Nmap*—The scanning tool Nmap and its GUI version, Zenmap, are designed to scan large networks quickly and provide information about a network and its hosts. Nmap began as a simple port scanner, which is an application that searches a device for open ports indicating which insecure service might be used to craft an attack. For example, if a server's port 23 is open, Telnet can be used to remote into the target device and take control of it. Developers later expanded Nmap's capabilities to include gathering information about hosts and their software. When running Nmap, you can choose what type of information to discover, thereby customizing your scan results.

- *Nessus*—Developed by Tenable Security (tenable.com), Nessus is a vulnerability scanner that performs even more sophisticated scans than Nmap. Among other things, Nessus can identify unencrypted, sensitive data (such as credit card numbers) saved on your network's hosts. The program can run on your network or from off-site servers continuously maintained and updated by the developer.

- *Metasploit*—This popular penetration testing tool combines known scanning and exploit techniques to explore potentially new attack routes. For example, Figure 6-1 shows a Metasploit scan using HTTP, SMTP, and SMB probes; the application also employs Nmap, Telnet, FTP, and UDP probes. Notice that the scan successfully identified the administrative username and password transmitted in plaintext for this home network's SOHO (small office home office) router. You can download an open-source version of the Metasploit framework from their website at metasploit.com.

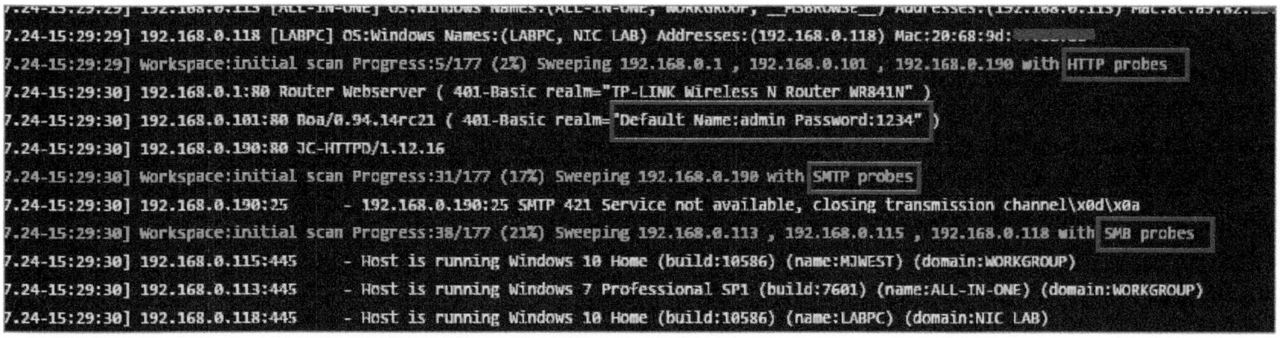

Figure 6-1   Metasploit detected a SOHO router's administrative username and password

Scan Types

Many scanning tools, such as Nessus, can perform deeper scans of a network if provided with account credentials for one or more systems on the network, which is called a credentialed scan. Sometimes, these tools use only default credentials or common credentials, such as using "admin" for the username and "password" for the password. Other times, tools might be given actual credentials for sensitive accounts to determine, from a trusted user's perspective, the sophistication and security of other kinds of configurations in a system. For example, a credentialed scan can reveal missing patches or configured routes that provide open access from the Internet.

Most of these scans are network-based scans, which are applications that scan devices connected to the network to check configurations and identify network security gaps. In contrast, some networks might incorporate agent-based scans. For this to work, agents, or small applications, are installed on various devices that collect information about the individual devices and send that information to a central location for analysis. Agent-based scanning can be especially useful for legacy devices or devices that are not constantly connected to the network. Cloud instances often incorporate agent software as well to increase visibility into cloud configurations and performance.

Tracking Risks

All these tools can provide useful insights into a network's weaknesses that need attention. Used by hackers—or more likely, by bots—these tools can instead lead to compromised security. In other words, each of these tools can be used for legitimate purposes as well as illegal ones. However, even if scanning tools are used against you, you can learn from them. For example, a properly configured firewall will collect information about scanning attempts in its log. By reviewing the log, you will discover what kinds of exploits could be—or have been—attempted against your network.

As you collect information on the vulnerabilities in your network, you will likely need to track this information in a risk register. A **risk register** is a project management tool that can be used to document cybersecurity risks, background information on these risks, mitigation strategies specific to each risk, plans for responding should a vulnerability be attacked, and team members with responsibilities related to each risk. Risks are rated according to the likelihood of the threat happening, the expected impact to the business, and the cost to fix the problem. Documentation will also include historical data on previous attacks and the related responses and outcome.

Cloud-Based Approaches to Security

With new challenges come new innovations. Cloud computing provides a prime example of how security innovations are solving new problems. Cloud security works according to the **shared responsibility model**, meaning the CSP is partially responsible for a cloud's security, and the customer is responsible for the rest of it. Figure 6-2 shows how this shared responsibility breaks down according to the type of cloud deployment.

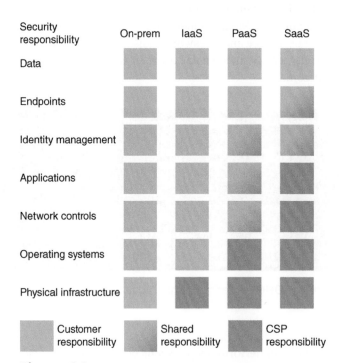

Figure 6-2   Shared responsibility model

Working in the cloud highlights the need for adaptive technology, quick response times, and creative thinking. Two significant security approaches have emerged as core techniques for maximizing cloud security: DevSecOps and micro-segmentation.

DevSecOps

Traditionally, the application life cycle began with a development team, passed through a security team, and went on to be deployed and maintained by the operations team. You've already learned how a DevOps culture blends development and operations workflows into a single, unending cycle, thereby increasing feature agility to reflect the shifting demands of an application's market more quickly. The natural evolution of this culture—in the interest of more reliable, built-in security—is to invite the security team to participate earlier and more flexibly as well. This cultural shift has been dubbed DevSecOps, as shown in Figure 6-3. Essentially, the DevSecOps mantra is, "Security is everyone's responsibility."

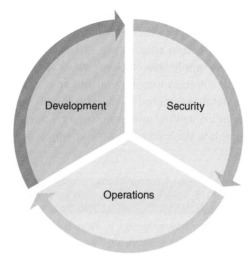

Figure 6-3 DevSecOps involves input from all three teams throughout the application's life cycle

This cultural standard applies to cloud computing as well. Where there's a need to continually adapt and innovate to meet the demands of a shifting market, there's also the need to consider security throughout every phase of any change being made. With available automation technologies and the software-defined nature of the cloud, security strategies can be embedded across the entire cloud deployment and throughout the process of developing and maintaining that deployment. Nearly every cloud service type offers cloud-native security features. These technologies require proactive, security-focused skills from cloud developers and architects rather than handing off the responsibility for security to a separate team. If you think about this pipeline of development as a progression from left to right (see Figure 6-4), you can see how the principle of "shift-left" security describes the DevSecOps approach to securing cloud architecture sooner in the design and development process.

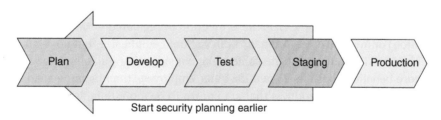

Figure 6-4 Shift-left security

Micro-Segmentation

Network segmentation in general is used for many purposes, including increasing both efficiency and security of network communications. You're already familiar with traditional segmentation techniques for on-prem networks, such as VLANs and firewalls, and cloud-centric segmentation techniques, such as VPCs and gateways. In the remainder of this module, you learn about more cloud-centric security tools, such as security groups and network ACLs (access control lists). To put these tools in context, you need to first learn about micro-segmentation.

Micro-segmentation techniques allow for more granular control of security for traffic and workflows within the cloud. In traditional, on-prem networks, you primarily secure the perimeter by closely monitoring traffic into and out of the network. This traffic travels in what's called a north–south direction. Because you must assume a zero-trust security model in the cloud—where nothing is trusted and every system, communication, and user is considered a threat until proven otherwise—you also need a way to secure communication *within and between* your cloud resources. This traffic is said to travel in a lateral or east–west direction. Micro-segmentation helps monitor and restrict this east–west activity and applies security measures specifically to workloads, VMs, or network connections. This way, security policies travel with the resource. For example, if you move a VM from one subnet to another or even from one cloud to another, it can still have its own security policies in place.

Micro-segmentation tools are often application-aware. This allows for fine-tuned control of exactly what kinds of information can flow between two systems, applications, or networks. Furthermore, applications themselves often comprise multiple components residing in different locations within an organization's cloud. For example, a web app running on a web server might rely on a database hosted in an entirely different geographical location. The communications between these components can be controlled and monitored by micro-segmentation tools.

As you work through this module, notice the various layers at which security can be applied to many kinds of cloud components.

Grow with Cengage Unlimited!

If you'd like more information about how to use network design to increase security, use your Cengage Unlimited subscription to go to *CompTIA Network+ Guide to Networks*, 9th edition, Module 11, and read the sections titled "Network Hardening by Design" and "Network Security Technologies."

If you don't have a Cengage Unlimited subscription, you can find more information at cengage.com/unlimited.

Supporting Shadow IT

With all the work to secure a cloud network from external attacks, it's easy to miss the internal threats. For example, the high accessibility of cloud services makes it easy for shadow IT to flourish in an organization. Significant benefits to shadow IT include increased efficiency and productivity when employees can get the tools and software features they need quickly and easily. However, unmonitored IT resources can create significant security gaps and blind spots, as well as organization-wide inefficiency when IT resources are not managed on a larger scale.

Organizations often find that cloud-hosted applications are the most common component of shadow IT. Other components might include other cloud services (PaaS and even IaaS), installed software, and hardware such as Wi-Fi hotspots, servers, and tablets or other mobile devices. One of the most effective ways to manage shadow IT sprawl is to establish clear company security policies and educate users about the need for and scope of these policies. For example, the company might explicitly allow shadow IT for peripheral functions, such as social media, productivity, or time tracking, while disallowing shadow IT for business-critical functions.

One of the biggest concerns with shadow IT is the protection of regulated data, such as customers' PII (personally identifiable information) or medical data. Company policy should emphasize that no regulated data can be stored or processed through shadow IT solutions. At the same time, consider that guidelines for how best to use shadow IT products might be more beneficial both for IT and for other employees than banning shadow IT altogether. These guidelines can provide direction toward products that are known to be more reliable, such as Office 365, rather than blocking well-known apps only for employees to resort to less secure options. An approved application list (previously known as whitelisting) can give employees options that have already been reviewed by IT staff. Opening those lines of communication so that employees feel supported in finding the solutions they need will enable IT to provide both support and protection more effectively.

Remember This

- Common internal and external threats to cloud security include data breaches, DoS and DDoS attacks, insecure interfaces, APTs (advanced persistent threats), account hijacking, poor account management, user error, insider threats, data loss with no backups, and CSP changes or outages.
- Scanning tools such as Nmap, Nessus, and Metasploit provide a simple and reliable way to discover crucial information about a network.
- Cloud security works according to the shared responsibility model, meaning that the CSP is partially responsible for a cloud's security, and the customer is responsible for the rest of it.
- One of the most effective ways to manage shadow IT sprawl is to establish clear company security policies and educate users about the need for and scope of these policies.

Self-Check

1. Which of these threats could be mitigated with good backups?
   - **a.** Data loss
   - **b.** Insider threat
   - **c.** Account hijacking
   - **d.** Data breach

2. Which type of scan requires software installation on the monitored resource?
   - **a.** Vulnerability scan
   - **b.** Credentialed scan
   - **c.** Network-based scan
   - **d.** Agent-based scan

3. Which cloud service model places the greatest responsibility on the cloud customer for cloud security?
   - **a.** RaaS
   - **b.** PaaS
   - **c.** IaaS
   - **d.** SaaS

○ Check your answers at the end of this module.

Section 6-2: Virtual Network Security

Certification

1.3 Explain the importance of high availability and scaling in cloud environments.

2.2 Given a scenario, secure a network in a cloud environment.

2.4 Given a scenario, apply data security and compliance controls in cloud environments.

3.3 Given a scenario, deploy cloud networking solutions.

5.2 Given a scenario, troubleshoot security issues.

5.4 Given a scenario, troubleshoot connectivity issues.

Computing in the cloud presents a slew of new security challenges. In response to these changing needs, many technologies have emerged to help protect cloud resources from external attacks. If you think about cloud resources in layers—platform, network, instances, applications, and data—you can see where DiD (defense-in-depth) strategies can be applied at each of these layers.

There are various perspectives on how best to cover each layer. Many organizations end up with a patchwork system that uses pieces of one security tool and pieces of another. This is dangerous in that it can leave gaps in coverage. It's also difficult to monitor feedback from multiple security systems. Often, a better approach is to use a unified, end-to-end cloud security system. This often means relying on a CSP's built-in security tools, which helps eliminate compatibility issues, increases visibility into your cloud infrastructure, collects monitoring activities in a central location, and scales more efficiently as business needs expand. New challenges arise when blending multiple cloud platforms, but even in these circumstances, CSPs are catching on and providing security solutions that bridge the gaps for hybrid and multi-clouds.

In these next few sections, you explore some of the built-in tools for securing cloud resources hosted in AWS, Azure, and GCP. In a later module, you learn more about how to secure access to the cloud platform itself through identity and access management. Let's begin with an analysis of how to secure cloud networks.

Allow and Deny Rules

You learned about some layers of VPC (virtual private cloud) security when you studied techniques for controlling a subnet's access to the Internet. For example, in AWS, you learned that a private subnet is logically isolated from the Internet in that it does not have direct access to an Internet gateway. You can also control whether an instance has a public IP address and what routes allow traffic between subnets or other gateways (such as a VPN gateway). VPNs themselves can control traffic that reaches a subnet and encrypt traffic as it crosses a WAN connection. Additionally, load balancing can filter the traffic allowed to reach a subnet from the open Internet.

Cloud platforms also typically offer built-in security at the platform level that provides significant protection to your cloud resources. For example, Azure includes DDoS (distributed denial of service) protection that the cloud consumer does not need to configure, and yet your Azure resources reside in an environment that is covered by these protective measures.

At the same time, there are many security techniques that you, as the cloud consumer, must apply, configure, and manage. Although not a true perimeter, traffic to and from a virtual network can be managed using various techniques, depending on the platform. A common component used by many of these security techniques is allow or deny rules like what you might have seen on a firewall device in an on-prem network. Before digging into the ways each platform configures and uses these rules, it's helpful to understand on a basic level how these rules work.

When a message crosses a firewall (physical or virtual), the firewall checks its rules to determine whether the message is allowed to pass. In Module 5, you learned that routes are applied to a message according to which route in a route table most closely matches the message's destination. With firewalls, however, rules are usually applied in order of priority. The highest-priority rule is checked first. If the message is allowed or denied according to that rule, no further rules are checked. If the rule doesn't apply to that message, the firewall continues to the next rule. This process continues until no rules remain. Figure 6-5 shows a diagram for how this process plays out.

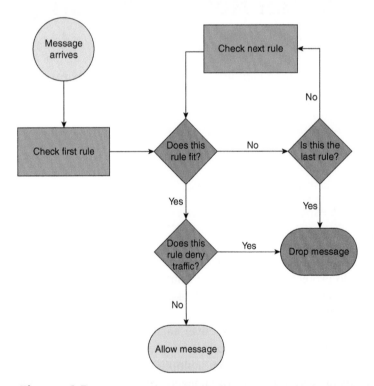

Figure 6-5   Firewall rules are checked in order of priority to determine whether a message is allowed to pass

These rules check for information such as port, protocol, and IP address or CIDR range. If the information matches, the message is allowed or denied according to the matched rule. An **allow list** lets traffic through while a **block list** or **deny list** prevents traffic from passing. Firewall rules are configured differently for inbound and outbound traffic. In other words, there's a different list of rules for inbound traffic, which is typically more restrictive, than there is for outbound traffic. Security rules configured in various resources also provide high availability in that you don't have to manage firewall instances or devices and provide backups for those firewalls.

In this section, you learn about the primary security techniques for virtual networks in AWS, Azure, and GCP. In the next section, you see security techniques for instances within those virtual networks. While there are significant similarities between each platform, there are also differences that will help you better understand the purposes and limitations of these various technologies. Notice how security can be applied at multiple layers, and each CSP has different recommendations for which layers provide the best security in their platform.

AWS VPCs and Subnets

NAC (network access control) balances the need for network access with the demands of network security by employing a set of network policies that determine the level and type of access granted. For example, adding a NAT gateway to a private subnet in AWS allows that subnet's VMs to access the Internet without exposing them directly to Internet traffic. In addition to the segmentation provided by public and private subnets, AWS offers more techniques for securing VPCs and the resources contained within them, as described next.

Network Access Control List (NACL)

Essentially a virtual, network firewall, a **NACL (network access control list;** informally pronounced "nackle") can limit or allow traffic into and out of a VPC's subnets. Every subnet in a VPC is initially associated with the default NACL, which by default allows all traffic. You can change these rules or create custom NACLs. You can use one NACL for multiple subnets, but each subnet must have exactly one NACL associated with it. Figure 6-6 shows the default NACL inbound rules near the bottom of the screen. Some specific NACL characteristics include the following:

- NACL rules can either allow or deny traffic.
- NACL rules are numbered for priority, starting with the lowest number. When a rule is found that applies to a message, that rule is enacted immediately without looking at any other rules.
- NACL rules are stateless, meaning inbound and outbound traffic are evaluated by separate rules.

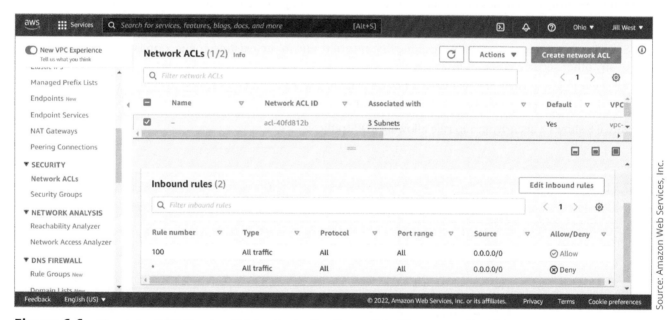

Figure 6-6 The default NACL rule of highest priority allows all traffic to enter the VPC

Security Groups

A security group serves as a virtual firewall at the host level. Like NACLs, security groups have rules that control whether traffic can cross a network interface. Unlike NACLs, security groups function on the instances within a subnet, not on the subnet itself. You can associate up to five security groups per instance, and instances within a subnet don't have to use the same security groups. The diagram in Figure 6-7 shows the relationship of NACLs, VPCs, security groups, and instances in AWS.

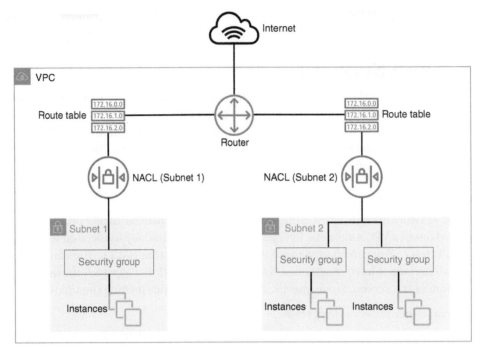

Figure 6-7   NACLs apply to subnets, and security groups apply to instances

AWS best practices state that security groups and NACLs should be used together to secure EC2 instances because each of these security techniques offers different strengths. Some key characteristics of security groups are as follows:

- Security group rules only allow traffic—you can't create deny rules for security groups.
- Security group rules are stateful, meaning that return traffic for an existing connection is allowed regardless of any other security group rules.
- All security group rules are evaluated when determining whether to allow traffic to enter an instance's interface, and the most specific rule to the type of traffic is applied.

Figure 6-8 shows a security group rule allowing RDP traffic.

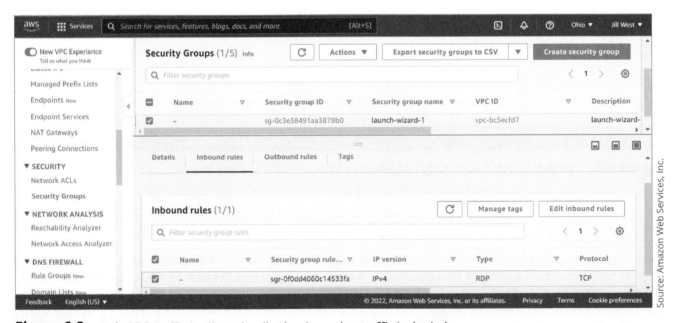

Figure 6-8   Only RDP traffic is allowed—all other incoming traffic is denied

Flow Logs

VPC flow logs monitor traffic that crosses an individual network interface. When you create a flow log for a VPC or subnet, all interfaces within that VPC or subnet are monitored. Log data is directed to the CloudWatch Logs service or to an Amazon S3 storage bucket, and this activity accrues charges to your account. Fields within flow log records include information such as source and destination IP addresses (IPv4 or IPv6), source and destination ports, number of packets and bytes, start and end times, and whether the traffic was accepted or rejected. Because flow logs collect traffic data for a period of time (such as 15 minutes) before publishing each new record, there is a delay from when the traffic occurs until that information is available for review. Figure 6-9 shows where to find flow logs in a VPC's configuration information, and Figure 6-10 shows how to create a flow log.

Figure 6-9   Find a VPC's flow logs

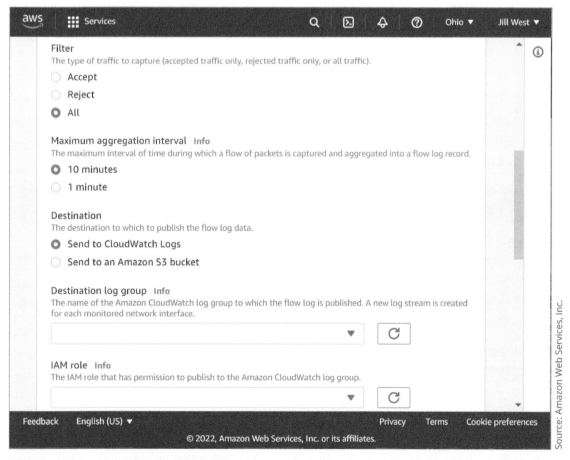

Figure 6-10   Choose an Accept, Reject, or All filter, then choose a log destination and IAM role to create a flow log

Traffic Mirroring

Traffic mirroring in AWS provides deeper insight into captured traffic than what flow logs offer, and it's similar to the packet capture and analysis functions you can do with Wireshark. For example, flow logs indicate allowed or denied traffic, but with traffic mirroring, you can examine the packets of denied traffic. This information can be used to reverse-engineer a network attack and identify the vulnerabilities that allowed the attack to happen. You can also use this information to identify the root cause of a performance issue. Captured packets can also be exported to out-of-band monitoring and packet analyzer tools for filtering and examination.

To use traffic mirroring, create a source network interface (which can be attached to an EC2 instance or some other resource), a target (such as another network interface or a network load balancer), and a traffic mirroring session. Traffic mirroring sessions incur a small fee per hour per interface. Figure 6-11 shows the traffic mirror session settings requesting a mirror source and a mirror target.

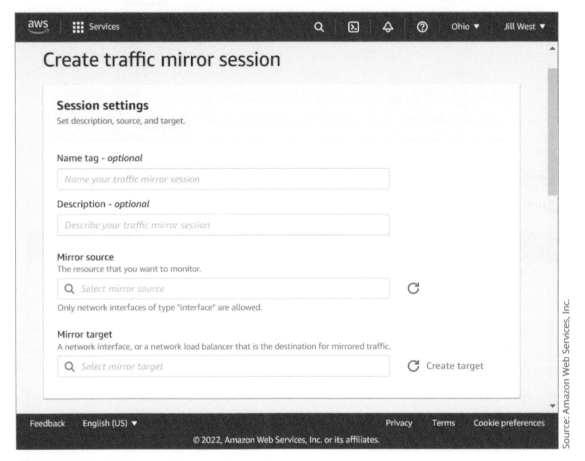

Figure 6-11   Create a traffic mirroring session

> ### Note 2
>
> AWS NACLs, security groups, flow logs, and traffic mirroring sessions don't filter or monitor traffic to or from link-local addresses (169.254.0.0/16) or AWS-reserved IP addresses. These addresses are used to support DNS, DHCP, instance metadata, license management services, and subnet routing.

Network Firewalls

While each of the tools you've read about so far incorporate firewall rules such as allowing or denying traffic, you also have the option to add virtual firewall devices to your cloud networks. For this purpose, AWS offers Network Firewall.

AWS Network Firewall is a managed firewall, which is a PaaS resource that includes built-in high availability and unrestricted scalability. You might choose to incorporate a managed firewall to gain fine-tuned control of traffic flows and greater visibility of network traffic and to create a central point of control for firewall policies across all your cloud networks. For example, recall that NACL rules are stateless and are evaluated in order of priority. In contrast, security group rules are stateful and are applied according to which rule provides the best match. However, AWS Firewall policies can be either stateful or stateless. Stateless rules are evaluated in order of priority. Stateful rules can be formatted and applied with more granular control, as shown in Figure 6-12.

Figure 6-12   Choose how to apply stateful firewall rules to traffic

You're Ready

You're now ready to complete Project 6-2: Configure Security in AWS. You can complete the project now or wait until you've finished all the readings for this module.

Azure Virtual Networks

Similar to AWS's public subnets, Microsoft recommends that you establish a perimeter network in your Azure cloud to restrict and manage Internet traffic to your protected resources. A perimeter network is a subnet within a VNet that functions as a **screened subnet** (also called a DMZ, or demilitarized zone) between your private resources and the open Internet by standing between the Internet and your other subnets. Figure 6-13 shows how this architecture is laid out conceptually.

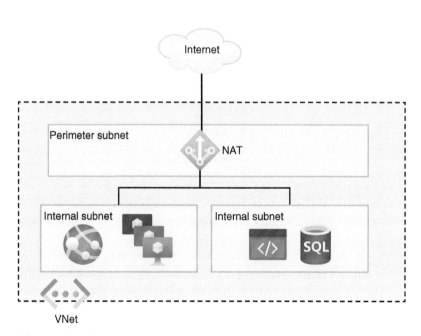

Figure 6-13   The perimeter network provides a level of isolation for internal subnets from the Internet

Additionally, Azure offers several security devices you can configure to provide protection on and within your VNets, as described next.

Network Virtual Appliance (NVA)

An NVA (network virtual appliance) is a VM running in the perimeter network that controls traffic between the perimeter network and your other subnets. It's similar in concept to the IG (Internet gateway) in an AWS public subnet except that it connects the internal subnets with the perimeter network and not directly to the Internet. Third-party NVAs are available in the Azure Marketplace that can provide additional security features and traffic management capabilities, such as the following:

• *Firewalling*—Firewalls filter what traffic is allowed to enter the network based on defined rules.

- **IDS/IPS**—An IDS (intrusion detection system) identifies activity that appears suspicious and reports on that activity. An IPS (intrusion prevention system) acts to mitigate malicious activity.
- **Antivirus**—Antivirus and anti-malware products identify, block, and remove malware infections.

An NVA can be configured to manage incoming (ingress) traffic, outgoing (egress) traffic, or both and can work at OSI layer 4 (transport layer) or OSI layer 7 (application layer). You can also configure NVAs to manage traffic to and from the on-prem network. To provide high availability, Microsoft recommends you deploy multiple NVAs.

Network Security Group (NSG)

Similar to AWS's NACL, the Azure NSG (network security group) provides firewall-style protection at the subnet level. Although an NSG can be applied to a single interface on a VM instance, Microsoft recommends using an NSG for an entire subnet instead. This arrangement applies the NSG to all instances in the subnet rather than creating complexity from using a different NSG for every instance.

Azure creates six default rules for every NSG: three for inbound traffic (see Table 6-1) and three for outbound traffic (see Table 6-2). These rules cannot be removed or altered, but you can override them by creating higher-priority rules. Lower numbers represent higher priorities. For example, the first rule in Table 6-1 has a priority of 65,000 and allows all traffic within the VNet. The last rule in Table 6-1 has a priority of 65,500 and denies all traffic, regardless of where it comes from or where it's going. But this rule has the lowest priority rating (i.e., 65,500), which is a much lower priority than the first rule listed (i.e., 65,000). If traffic matches the AllowVNetInBound rule, meaning it *comes from* a resource within the VNet and is *sent to* a resource also inside the VNet, the traffic is allowed, even though a lower-priority rule would deny that traffic.

Table 6-1   Default inbound rules in an Azure NSG

Name	Priority	Source	Destination	Access
AllowVNetInBound	65,000	VirtualNetwork	VirtualNetwork	Allow
AllowAzureLoadBalancerInBound	65,001	AzureLoadBalancer	0.0.0.0/0	Allow
DenyAllInBound	65,500	0.0.0.0/0	0.0.0.0/0	Deny

Table 6-2   Default outbound rules in an Azure NSG

Name	Priority	Source	Destination	Access
AllowVNetOutBound	65,000	VirtualNetwork	VirtualNetwork	Allow
AllowInternetOutBound	65,001	0.0.0.0/0	Internet	Allow
DenyAllOutBound	65,500	0.0.0.0/0	0.0.0.0/0	Deny

Priority ratings for custom rules that you create can range from 100 to 4096. This means, for example, you could create a rule with a priority rating of 4000 that denies HTTP (Hypertext Transfer Protocol) traffic between VNet resources, and this rule would trump the lower-priority rule, AllowVNetInBound whose priority rating is 65,000, which would have allowed that traffic.

NSG rules are stateful, meaning that once a message is allowed to cross the NSG, later messages in that conversation continue to be allowed. For example, imagine an incoming HTTP message on port 80 requesting webpage information is allowed through to a subnet that holds a web server. The web server can then reply to the request even if outgoing rules don't specify that traffic is allowed on port 80. The same is true in reverse. If a subnet's NSG allows an instance inside the subnet to send traffic on port 80 to external websites, inbound responses from those websites are allowed even if port 80 is not explicitly allowed by an inbound NSG rule. Figure 6-14 shows how this works to support a connection between a web client and a web server.

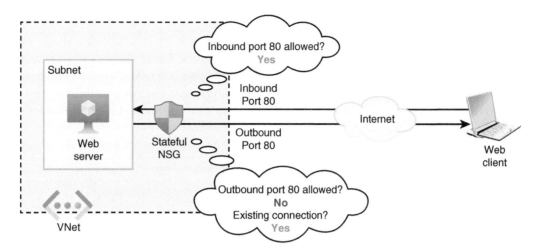

Figure 6-14   Return traffic on an existing connection is allowed by the NSG

Application Security Group (ASG)

An ASG (application security group) is a subgrouping of an NSG, allowing for micro-segmentation of your security policies according to application and workload type within the VNet. You can associate one or more ASGs to each network interface. For example, you might configure one group of VM interfaces to allow access to an application's database, while another ASG in the VNet might not have this access. ASGs can also be identified as a source or destination for NSG rules.

Other Azure Security Tools

Azure offers many other tools for securing cloud traffic, including the following:

- Azure Firewall for highly available threat protection
- Azure Network Watcher for capturing and monitoring traffic logs
- MS Defender for Cloud to provide anti-malware for cloud instances
- VNet TAP (Terminal Access Point) for network capture and analysis

---

You're Ready

You're now ready to complete Project 6-3: Configure Security in Azure. You can complete the project now or wait until you've finished all the readings for this module.

GCP VPCs

Segmentation of GCP resources is first achieved at the project level. Resources that are logically related, such as the various components of an application or the resources used by a specific team, should be contained in the same project. However, resources that have no need to communicate with each other, such as the HR database and the sales team's CRM (customer relationship management) database, should be hosted in different projects within the organization.

Other techniques and tools are available for managing and monitoring traffic into and out of a VPC, including virtual firewalls, VPC flow logs, and packet mirroring, described next.

Virtual Firewall

GCP's Firewall, as shown in Figure 6-15, is set at the network level to manage IPv4 traffic into and out of the VPC. Additionally, Firewall works within the VPC between the VPC's own resources. These rules can be set to target specific protocols, ports, sources, or destinations. Some traffic within a VPC is always blocked, such as the tunneling protocol GRE (generic routing encapsulation), regardless of what the firewall rules say, and other traffic is always allowed, such as DHCP and DNS traffic. Set firewall rules to allow or deny specific types of traffic. Consider carefully which traffic needs to be allowed so you can minimize the traffic allowed into or out of the VPC.

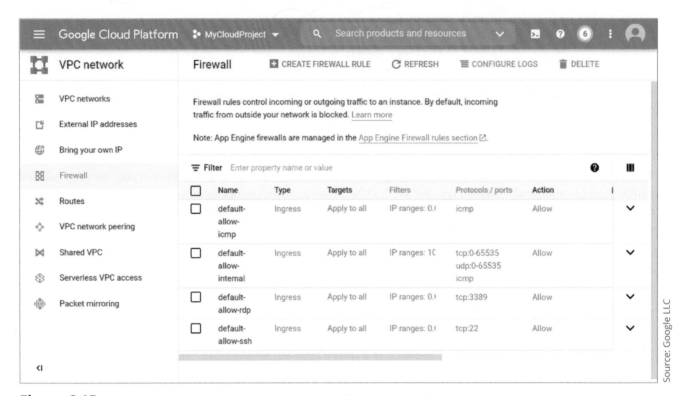

Figure 6-15   Firewall rules can apply to one, some, or all instances within a VPC

Firewall rules are applied first according to priority and then by how specifically the rule matches the traffic. Firewall rules are also stateful, meaning that traffic allowed in one direction automatically allows traffic in the other direction for an active connection. As long as there is at least one message going in either direction within 10 minutes, the connection is kept active. You can enable firewall logging to monitor the effects of specific rules on your VPC traffic.

VPC Flow Logs

The VPC flow logs service is enabled at the subnet level, as shown in Figure 6-16. Once enabled, flow logs track TCP and UDP traffic for all instances in that subnet. Each log record contains two types of fields:

- Base fields are common to all log records, such as connection type, start time, and bytes sent.
- Metadata fields are specific to the type of log record and, for VPC flow logs, contain information such as source and destination instance and source and destination location. To save storage space (which reduces cost), metadata fields can be excluded from flow log records.

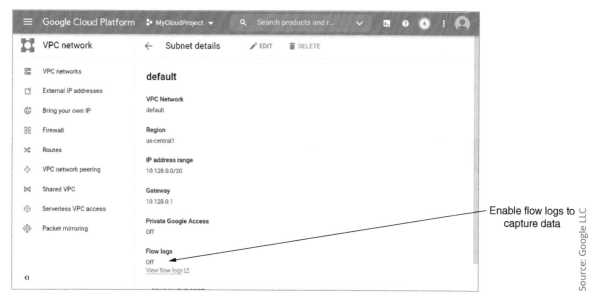

Figure 6-16   Enable flow logs in the subnet settings

While not every message crossing a VM's interfaces is captured in a flow log record, log record captures still take up a great deal of storage space. Sampled messages are collected into a single flow log record at various time intervals as short as 5 seconds (the default configuration) or as long as 15 minutes. These records are stored in a GCP storage service, such as Cloud Logging, which incurs charges after a basic, free allotment. Flow logs are helpful for trouble-shooting connectivity issues and monitoring network performance, and they're also used for network forensics when investigating an incident or for real-time security monitoring using third-party solutions.

Packet Mirroring

GCP also offers a Packet Mirroring service that copies traffic involving specified instances for further analysis—this capture can include incoming traffic, outgoing traffic, or both. The captures also include message headers and payloads, similar to what Wireshark can do. Messages can then be analyzed by security software or evaluated for performance issues.

You're Ready

You're now ready to complete Project 6-4: Configure Security in GCP. You can complete the project now or wait until you've finished all the readings for this module.

Securing Hybrid and Multi-Clouds

Securing resources across a hybrid or multi-cloud presents the challenge of needing to blend different security tools into a unified system for both simplicity and effectiveness. Cloud security techniques must auto-scale, while on-prem security tools must have deep access within the network perimeter. Furthermore, as you've seen in this module, cloud security tools in each platform can vary widely in technique, applicable layer, and output types.

Many of the same best practices apply for hybrid and multi-clouds as for other cloud structures, such as encrypting data, monitoring activity on the network, and using segmentation and micro-segmentation to isolate certain resources. Some tools have been developed specifically to help bridge the security gap between the on-prem and cloud portions of an organization's network or between different cloud platforms. One of the most commonly used is a **CASB (cloud access security broker)** solution. Examples include Bitglass's Zero-day CASB (bitglass.com) or Masergy's Managed CASB (masergy.com).

A CASB (pronounced "cas-b") is designed to detect applications and other resources running within a domain—even resources IT staff don't know about—and monitor those resources according to policies set by the organization. A CASB product increases transparency on the network, both on-prem and in the cloud, and provides a central dashboard, sometimes called a "single pane of glass," for managing security across the cloud and on-prem environments. Gartner (gartner.com) defines a CASB's purposes as providing visibility, compliance, data security, and threat protection.

Remember This

- Security rules check for information such as port, protocol, and IP address or CIDR range—an allow list lets traffic through while a block list or deny list prevents traffic from passing.
- AWS provides subnet-level security with NACLs (network ACLs), instance-level security with security groups, VPC traffic monitoring with flow logs, packet analysis with traffic mirroring, and managed firewall services with Network Firewall.
- Azure provides VNet-level security with NVAs (network virtual appliances), subnet-level security with NSGs (network security groups), interface-level security with ASGs (application security groups), and many other security tools for threat protection, traffic capture, anti-malware, and traffic analysis.
- GCP provides VPC-level security with firewall rules, subnet-level traffic monitoring with VPC flow logs, and traffic capture and analysis with packet mirroring.
- A CASB (cloud access security broker) is designed to detect applications and other resources running within a domain—even resources IT staff don't know about—and monitor those resources according to policies set by the organization.

Self-Check

4. A stateless rule applies to _____.
   a. incoming traffic
   b. outgoing traffic
   c. traffic in one direction
   d. traffic in both directions

5. What cloud security tool functions similar to Wireshark?
   a. Virtual firewalls
   b. Traffic mirroring
   c. Flow logs
   d. Security groups

6. Security at which of these levels provides the most fine-tuned traffic filtering?
   a. Subnet
   b. Interface
   c. Instance
   d. Virtual network

○ Check your answers at the end of this module.

Section 6-3: Compute Security

Certification

2.2 Given a scenario, secure a network in a cloud environment.

2.3 Given a scenario, apply the appropriate OS and application security controls.

2.5 Given a scenario, implement measures to meet security requirements.

Typical cloud compute resources include instances (an IaaS resource) and applications (a PaaS or SaaS resource). While you've already learned about some security functions that apply to instances (such as AWS security groups) in conjunction with network security, other techniques help secure instances from within the instance. Similarly, security functions must be configured on applications running in the cloud. This section explores compute security for instances and applications.

Device Hardening

In Module 3, you learned about collecting baselines before beginning a cloud migration. Baselining is also important in securing cloud resources. For example, when you first install an OS on a server, you'll need to create a hardened baseline that documents all configuration changes needed to secure the system and its OS. Whenever the OS is updated or upgraded, you'll need to update the hardened baseline configuration.

VM instances, like physical workstations, require patches, updates, and anti-malware measures to protect them from external threats. Firmware upgrades and OS upgrades play an important role in keeping on-prem systems up-to-date and securely hardened against potential attack vectors. The standard methods for securing a VM instance (or physical machine) on-prem apply to VM instances running in the cloud. For example, restrict access and privileges to the minimum required for each instance, and monitor for deviations in performance. The cloud offers additional security options, depending on the specific tools available in a cloud platform. Consider the following techniques:

- *Plan subnet placement*—Carefully choose the subnet for each instance so that it has only the necessary access to the outside world. For example, place in a public subnet only the AWS EC2 instances that need direct access to the Internet.

- *Disable unnecessary ports and services*—Just like with a physical machine, only enable ports and services that are needed. For example, don't allow RDP (port 3389) or SSH (port 22) traffic from all Internet addresses using the wildcard 0.0.0.0/0 except during initial testing. To remote into VMs in a production environment, use VPN or direct connect options instead, or at the very least, specify the public IP address for the computer you're working from.

- *Enforce account management policies*—You've seen how Linux distros are configured with default user accounts, which you've used to remote into your VMs. To further protect these virtual systems, deactivate any default user accounts and require other, best-practice account management policies such as password complexity and least privilege access.

- *Install antivirus/anti-malware software and keep it updated*—Windows Server 2016 and beyond comes with Microsoft Defender Antivirus preinstalled, which provides robust anti-malware protection for the VM itself. For other OSs, make sure sufficient antivirus/anti-malware software is installed. This might be accomplished through the VM's OS, or it might be available as a service from the cloud platform. For example, the Microsoft Antimalware for Azure extension service can be added to a VM to provide real-time protection, remediation, and reporting. Microsoft Antimalware provides an excellent application of this technology for VMs running OSs besides Windows Server.

- *Install host-based/software firewalls and IDS/IPS*—While your virtual network should already have firewall rules protecting VMs within all its subnets, each VM should also have a host-based, software firewall installed on it. Again, this might be accomplished through the VM's OS or via a cloud service, such as AWS's security groups, which you learned about earlier in this module. Another option is to add a host-based IPS (HIPS) or host-based IDS (HIDS), which monitors the VM for signs of malicious behavior and, in the case of a HIPS solution, can activate protective measures in response.

- *Create single-function resources*—In the cloud, especially considering the flexibility and elasticity in choosing appropriately sized resources, you can create single-function resources that are optimally designed to perform a specific task. This limited scope offers the ability to create a hardened baseline specific to each function and leaves a much smaller attack surface for each resource.

Considering how convenient it is to create, or "spin up," new instances, keep in mind how easy it is to forget about unused instances as well. These running systems, if they're not monitored and maintained, eventually become outdated and vulnerable to infiltration. From there, hackers can access other resources in your network. Consider using an EDR (endpoint detection and response) solution that detects and monitors endpoints in your cloud to increase visibility of attack surfaces from forgotten or outdated instances.

Application Security

The security of compute resources can be placed at risk by the applications that run in them. Application security also applies to SaaS applications and to the PaaS components used to build those applications. A policy called an application approved list (also known as whitelisting) can restrict which applications can run on an endpoint, whether physical or virtual. This policy can cause problems with users, however, if they already rely on a wide variety of applications to do their jobs. A deny-by-default approach increases security but can also increase user frustration and slow their work progress. Consider the tradeoffs carefully, and thoughtfully incorporate application restrictions that prioritize company goals.

A special kind of firewall to protect SaaS applications is a **WAF (web application firewall)**. WAFs can be installed either on-prem or in the cloud and are designed specifically to protect web apps, which are applications accessible over the Internet. (Google Docs is an example of a web app.) A WAF can inspect, monitor, and filter messages coming into a web app to protect it from attack. Many cloud platforms offer WAF services, or you can use a third-party product such as Cloudflare WAF (cloudflare.com) or Imperva WAF (imperva.com).

You've learned that a load balancer has basic capabilities to filter traffic allowed to reach a subnet from the open Internet. A more sophisticated evolution of a load balancer is an **ADC (application delivery controller)**. In addition to load-balancing services, an ADC can:

- Provide granular filtering of traffic
- Handle encryption to reduce the load on servers
- Incorporate traffic shaping and monitoring techniques

The ADC serves as the entry point for users' access to SaaS applications, including managing authentication processes and preventing DDoS attacks. To do this work, the ADC is typically placed in a screened subnet. Considering that today's users rely heavily on cloud-based applications, an ADC can help improve application responsiveness across the Internet.

Remember This

- A hardened baseline documents all configuration changes needed to secure a system and its OS.
- Application security refers to applications running on compute resources, SaaS applications, and PaaS components used to build applications and other services.

Self-Check

7. Which security technique will increase the number of running resources while decreasing the attack surface?

    a. Disable unnecessary ports and services
    b. Create single-function resources
    c. Install host-based firewalls
    d. Plan subnet placement

8. Which security appliance can perform encryption to reduce the processing load on protected servers?

    a. WAF
    b. IDS
    c. IPS
    d. ADC

○ Check your answers at the end of this module.

Section 6-4: Data Security

● **Certification**

2.2 Given a scenario, secure a network in a cloud environment.

2.3 Given a scenario, apply the appropriate OS and application security controls.

2.4 Given a scenario, apply data security and compliance controls in cloud environments.

3.3 Given a scenario, deploy cloud networking solutions.

5.2 Given a scenario, troubleshoot security issues.

5.4 Given a scenario, troubleshoot connectivity issues.

As you've already learned, data sitting in the cloud is not protected by a secure perimeter the same way data in the on-prem network can be. Security measures need to travel with the data, no matter where it's stored or what hardware it transits. Data can exist in three states:

- *At rest*—Data at rest, whether stored on a device or in the cloud, includes data in file storage, block storage, or object storage.
- *In use*—Data in use is temporarily stored in memory or is being used in calculations by a processor. The data might be visible to a user, who might be making changes to it. Or the data might be used in an underlying compute process.
- *In motion*—Data in motion is being transported between locations, whether that's within a single server along its motherboard's bus lines, between devices on a single network, or between networks and possibly across the Internet.

Robust cloud security can reliably protect data in all three of these states—*if* the security measures are correctly configured. In fact, DLP (data loss prevention) solutions, such as CASBs and SWGs (secure web gateways), specifically target data in all three states to provide comprehensive protection. A DLP solution identifies sensitive data on the network and prevents it from being copied (such as downloading to a flash drive) or transmitted off the network (such as emailing or posting to cloud storage).

Encrypting Data

Unfortunately, a slight misconfiguration can undermine even the most advanced cloud security technologies. However, encrypted data can still be protected so that damage caused by a breach is minimized. For example, consider what would happen if you store sensitive data on a laptop and the laptop is stolen. If that data is encrypted, such as by using an SED (self-encrypting drive) enabled by TPM (Trusted Platform Module) hardware authentication, the data might still be safe from discovery, as the thief would not be able to read the data. Many of the worst cloud-based data breaches could have been significantly reduced or even avoided had the organizations involved used reliable encryption technologies.

Encryption is the use of an algorithm to scramble data into a format that can be read only by reversing the algorithm—that is, by decrypting the data. Data that has not been encrypted is called plaintext and can be read without any special decoding. However, encrypted data looks like gibberish. For example, Figure 6-17 shows the phrase "Cloud computing rocks!" encrypted using AES (Advanced Encryption Standard) encryption and the key "Cengage." The encrypted output in the right box doesn't reveal any pattern that would indicate the original text in the left box.

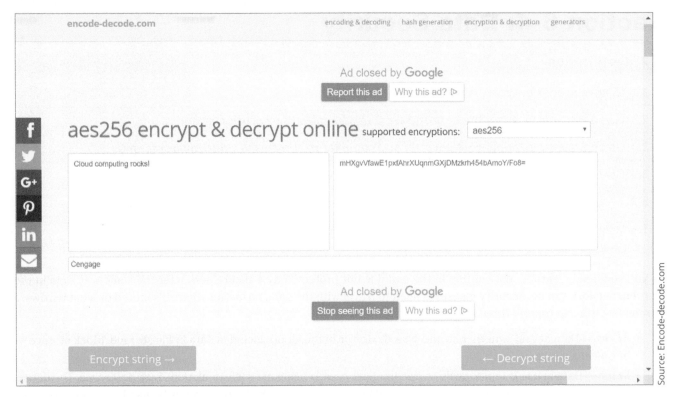

Figure 6-17   AES encryption is considered secure

Encryption of data stored in the cloud can be performed by the company who owns the data before that data leaves the company's network, by the CSP where the data is stored, or by a third-party encryption service. These options add new layers of complexity to encryption of cloud data beyond what you would encounter in on-prem data encryption processes. The following tasks must be completed to deploy encryption in the cloud:

- Learn about and work with the encryption capabilities, policies, and techniques of the CSP.
- Determine where the encryption keys are stored. Keys stored with the data might be more convenient—both for you and for any hackers. Therefore, in most cases, keys should be stored in a location that is isolated from the data those keys encrypt.
- Consider the costs involved with each of the available options. Performing encryption in-house before sending data to the cloud might be more cost-effective as well as more secure if this works for a particular situation. There are trade-offs in functionality, however, such as not being able to search or edit files stored in the cloud without first downloading and decrypting them. (However, some services are beginning to offer the ability to search encrypted files.)

Encryption Techniques

Encryption can be used to protect data in all three of its primary states, such as in the following examples:

- ***At rest***—Storage volumes attached to a VM instance can be encrypted, either in part or in whole. For example, in AWS, you can encrypt an EBS (Elastic Block Storage) volume attached to an EC2 instance. Figure 6-18 shows the option to encrypt a new instance's boot volume (i.e., the volume on which the OS files are stored) during EC2 instance creation.

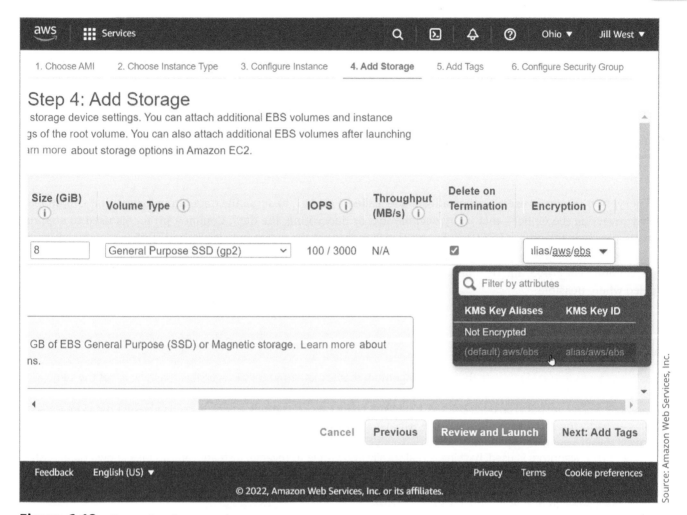

Figure 6-18   Encrypt a storage volume

- *In use*—Rather than encrypting data only after it is stored, a cloud application can encrypt data while it is being used. For example, when incorporating client-side encryption, data is encrypted on the client device before it is transmitted back to the app server in the cloud. AWS offers the Encryption SDK to handle data encryption, decryption, and related key transmission for applications or scripts.
- *In motion*—When building cloud solutions, APIs enable communication between various resources that work together for an application, network, or other system. Data carried by these API messages can be encrypted by HTTPS to protect information such as passwords, private keys, and credit card information. For example, AWS's API Gateway only supports HTTPS endpoints, which ensures API communications are encrypted between endpoints.

To protect data at rest, in use, and in motion, encryption methods are primarily evaluated by three benchmarks, and together, these principles form the standard security model called the CIA (confidentiality, integrity, and availability) triad, as follows:

- *Confidentiality*—Data can only be viewed by its intended recipient or at its intended destination.
- *Integrity*—Data is not modified in the time after the sender transmits it and before the receiver picks it up.
- *Availability*—Data is accessible to the intended recipient when needed, meaning the sender is accountable for successful delivery of the data.

Exam Tip ✔

You might already be familiar with some common protocols used to support encryption. For example, when setting up your home Wi-Fi network, you can choose between the older and less secure WPA (Wi-Fi Protected Access) security, which uses TKIP (Temporal Key Integrity Protocol) and RC4 (Rivest Cipher 4), or the newer and more secure WPA2, which relies on AES (Advanced Encryption Standard) for encryption. Although you don't need to understand the underlying mechanics of encryption for the Cloud+ exam, you do need to be able to identify which protocols are used to support encryption processes and which options are considered more secure than others.

Encryption protocols use a mathematical code, called a **cipher**, to scramble data into a format that can be read only by reversing the cipher—that is, by deciphering, or decrypting, the data. Common protocols used to support encryption include the retired DES (Data Encryption Standard) or the newer but also retired 3DES (pronounced "triple dez"), more current ciphers such as RC5 (Rivest Cipher 5) or RC6, hashing functions such as SHA-2 (Secure Hash Algorithm, version 2) or SHA-3, and the popular AES (Advanced Encryption Standard). Weaker, insecure ciphers should be disabled where possible.

Note 3

Hashing means to transform data through an algorithm that is mathematically irreversible. Hashing is not the same as encryption, though it's often listed as a type of encryption and does, in a similar manner, transform data from one format to another. Encrypted data can be decrypted, but hashed data cannot. Hashing is mostly used to ensure data integrity— that is, to verify the data has not been altered, which is similar to the purpose of a checksum. However, hashes can play a critical role in a good encryption protocol.

If a secure algorithm is used, hashing is realistically impossible to reverse. Instead, you can take known data, hash it using the same hashing function, and compare the new hash with the stored, hashed data. If the hashes match, this indicates the known data is exactly the same as the original data. If the output does not match, this indicates the data has likely been altered. In fact, this is often the most secure way to store and use passwords.

Many forms of encryption exist, with some being more secure than others. Even as new forms of encryption are developed, new ways of cracking their codes emerge, too. The most secure forms of encryption encode the original data's bits using a long and complex **key**—sometimes several times in different sequences—to scramble the data and, from it, generate a unique and consistently sized data block called ciphertext. The key is created and used according to a specific set of rules, or algorithms.

You've used keys before, most commonly on your Wi-Fi network. WPA-Personal and WPA2-Personal Wi-Fi security rely on a PSK (preshared key) that is generated from your Wi-Fi passphrase, the name of your network, and other information so that each device has its own unique key. More complex and randomized keys can be generated by techniques such as ECC (elliptic curve cryptography), which uses elliptic curves like what you might have seen in algebra, to generate a public and private key pair that are mathematically related in a way that is impossible to predict.

Key encryption can be divided into two categories:

- *Private key encryption*—Data is encrypted using a single key that only the sender and receiver know. Private key encryption is also known as symmetric key encryption because the same key is used during both the encryption and decryption processes. A potential problem with private key encryption is that the sender must somehow share the key with the recipient without it being intercepted.

- *Public key encryption*—Data is encrypted with a private key known only to the user, and it's decrypted with a mathematically related public key that can be made available to the public through a third-party source. This ensures data integrity, as the sender's public key will only work if the data has not been tampered with. Alternatively (and more commonly), data can be encrypted with the public key and then can only be decrypted with the matching private key. This ensures data confidentiality, as only the intended recipient (the owner of the keys) can decrypt the data. The combination of a public key and a private key is known as a key pair. Because public key encryption requires the use of two different keys, one to encrypt and the other to decrypt, it is also known as asymmetric encryption.

Exam Tip ✔

On the CompTIA Cloud+ exam, you might be given a scenario where you must choose whether it would be better to use a public key or a private key to encrypt data, and then which key (public or private) would be used to decrypt that data. In short, if you use one to encrypt, you'll use the other to decrypt.

More specifically, if the owner of the keys is encrypting the data so everyone will know who performed the encryption, the owner will use their private key to encrypt, and everyone else could use the owner's public key to decrypt. Only the key owner's public key will successfully decrypt that data, and this confirms the data owner's identity. If, instead, someone else is encrypting data that only the owner of the keys should be able to read, that person would use the owner's public key to encrypt the data. Then, only the key owner's private key could decrypt the data, ensuring its confidentiality. This last example is more common and the one you'll likely see on the Cloud+ exam.

With the abundance of private and public keys, not to mention the number of places where each may be kept, organizations need simple and secure key management. On-prem, this is often handled by a KMS (key management system), such as Key Orchestration KMS by Fornetix (fornetix.com) or qCrypt by Quintessence Labs (quintessencelabs.com). Many cloud providers offer KMS (key management services) as well, such as AWS's KMS, Azure's Key Vault, and GCP's Cloud KMS.

Grow with Cengage Unlimited!

If you'd like more information about how key encryption works, use your Cengage Unlimited subscription to go to *CompTIA Security+ Guide to Network Security Fundamentals*, 7th edition, Module 7, and read the section titled "Public Key Infrastructure (PKI)."

If you don't have a Cengage Unlimited subscription, you can find more information at cengage.com/unlimited.

Securing Protocols

SSL (Secure Sockets Layer) and TLS (Transport Layer Security) are two public key encryption protocols commonly used to encrypt communications across the Internet. The two protocols can work side by side and are widely known as SSL/TLS or TLS/SSL. All browsers today support SSL/TLS to secure transmissions of website traffic, which is what makes the difference between HTTP (Hypertext Transfer Protocol) traffic and the more secure HTTPS (HTTP Secure) traffic, or the difference between FTP (File Transfer Protocol) and FTPS (FTP Secure or FTP over SSL). Note, however, that SFTP (Secure FTP) relies on SSH, not SSL/TLS.

SSL was originally developed by Netscape and operates in the application layer. Since that time, the IETF (Internet Engineering Task Force), which is an organization of volunteers who help develop Internet standards, has standardized the similar TLS protocol. TLS operates in the transport layer and uses slightly different encryption algorithms from SSL but, otherwise, it's essentially the updated version of SSL. SSL has now been deprecated and should be disabled whenever possible, as shown in Figure 6-19, leaving the more secure TLS to provide protection. In reality, you'll often see them both enabled for backward compatibility.

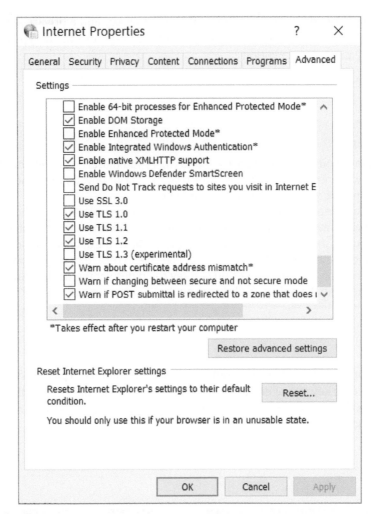

Figure 6-19 TLS is a more secure option for encryption

> **Note 4**
>
> When requiring the more secure versions of network protocols, you might run into compatibility issues with older technology that does not support newer forms of encryption. When facing the problem of unsupported, secure protocols, consider upgrading the older equipment rather than compromising network security.

Each time a client and server establish an SSL/TLS connection, they generate a unique session, which is an association between the client and server that is defined by an agreement on a specific set of encryption techniques. The session allows the client and server to continue to exchange data securely as long as the client is still connected to the server. A session is created by a handshake protocol, one of several protocols within SSL/TLS and perhaps the most significant. As its name implies, the handshake protocol allows the client and server to introduce themselves to each other and establishes terms for how they will securely exchange data.

Given the scenario of a browser accessing a secure website, the SSL/TLS handshake works as follows:

1. The browser, representing the client computer in this scenario, sends a client_hello message to the web server, which contains information about what level of security the browser is capable of accepting and what type of encryption the browser can decipher.

2. The server responds with a server_hello message that confirms the information it received from the browser and agrees to certain terms of encryption based on the options supplied by the browser. Depending on the web server's preferred encryption method, the server might choose to issue to the browser a public key or a digital certificate.

3. If the server requests a certificate from the browser, the browser sends it. Any data the browser sends to the server is encrypted using the server's public key. Session keys used only for this one session are also established.

After the browser and server have agreed to the terms of encryption, the secure channel is in place, and they begin exchanging data.

You can use the versatile CLI utility **OpenSSL** to troubleshoot issues with SSL/TLS encryption and related certificates. The s_client command offers options for testing secure connections, gathering information on security configurations, and managing certificates. For example, Figure 6-20 shows output from running s_client from a local computer to the Cengage website where the web server provided its certificate information. OpenSSL is included by default in most Linux distros. It must be installed to use in Windows.

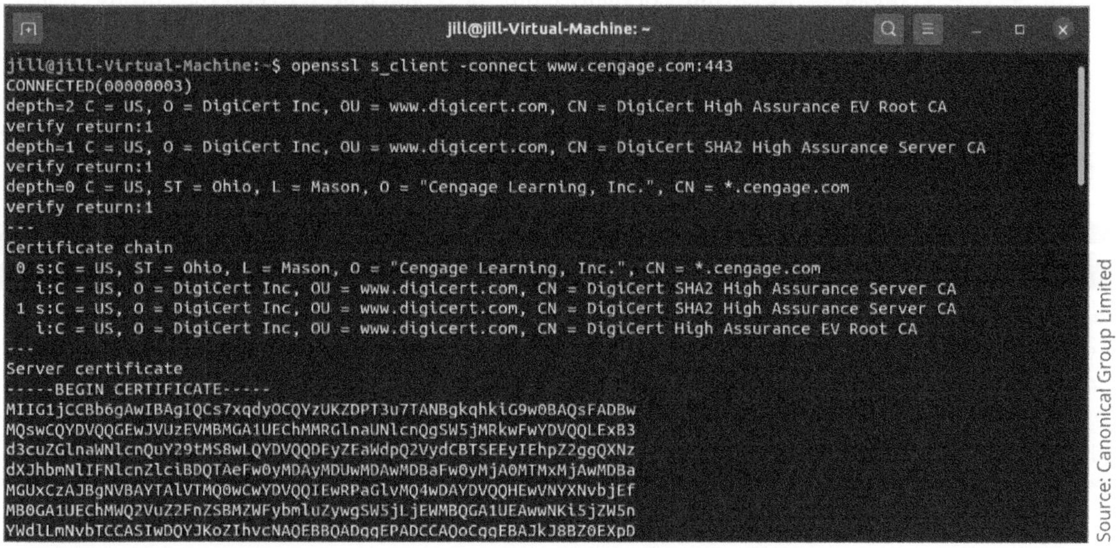

Figure 6-20 OpenSSL client collects web server certificate information

DNS Security

By default, DNS messages are sent unencrypted and unauthenticated. This creates some serious security issues that have been widely exploited by attackers. Whether you're configuring DNS records in the cloud or on-prem, you'll need to employ some security measures to protect your DNS-guided traffic. The following technologies can help with this requirement:

- *Authentication*—Authenticating sources of DNS records can help prevent attacks such as DNS cache poisoning, where cached DNS records at a DNS server are falsified. **DNSSEC (DNS Security Extensions)** requires verification of DNS records using public key cryptography. When DNSSEC is enabled, browsers look for embedded digital signatures and will not display a website if those signatures do not match. Note that not all cloud platforms currently support DNSSEC. Check with your provider before you commit to a specific platform for hosting DNS records.

- *Encryption*—Encryption protocols can be used to encrypt DNS messages to protect users' privacy as these messages traverse networks and the Internet. Two alternatives include the following:

  ○ With **DoT (DNS over TLS)**, TLS encrypts traditional, UDP traffic used for DNS. This traffic uses port 853.
  ○ With **DoH (DNS over HTTPS)**, encrypted DNS messages are sent using HTTPS instead of UDP. While HTTPS is also encrypted by TLS, the traffic uses HTTPS port 443.

NTP Security

As you learned in Module 4, NTP (Network Time Protocol) is used to provide time synchronization across a network. The genius of NTP is how it can almost completely account for the variable delays across a network, even on the open Internet. It does this through a hierarchy of time servers where stratum-1 servers communicate directly with a primary time source, such as GPS (global positioning system) or Galileo (Europe's version of GPS). These servers track UTC (Coordinated Universal Time) and provide this information to lower-strata servers. Each hop between NTP servers increases the stratum number by 1 up to 16. NTP servers at any stratum can then convert the provided UTC into its local time zone. Not every network has its own time server, but those that do can maintain accuracy for its NTP clients to within a millisecond of each other and are closely synced to the UTC. NTP communicates over port 123.

Many cloud platforms provide NTP services native to the platform. For example, the Amazon Time Sync Service is available to all EC2 instances at no charge using the IPv4 address 169.254.169.123 or the IPv6 address fd00:ec2::123. One benefit of this type of service is that you don't need to provide Internet access for your EC2 instances simply to support NTP synchronization. Many network admins set their network clocks according to UTC rather than local time, as local time zones experience some fluctuations due to users being located in different time zones or from shifts required by daylight savings time. Using UTC provides consistent timing for all users and in all logs. In AWS Windows AMIs, the Amazon Time Sync Service is configured by default. For many Linux AMIs, you'll need to edit the chrony configuration file.

As with DNS, lack of authentication for NTP servers leaves a network vulnerable to attack. Also like DNS, NTP can be secured using TLS as an authentication mechanism in a standard called **NTS (Network Time Security)**. NTP clients use TLS's handshake and public key infrastructure to authenticate NTP servers and to encrypt communications with these servers, ensuring NTP messages have not been tampered with. While an attacker might still be able to delay or prevent the delivery of NTP messages, the messages themselves maintain integrity.

Remember This

- Data can exist in three states: at rest, in use, and in motion.
- Encryption is the use of an algorithm to scramble data into a format that can be read only by reversing the algorithm—that is, by decrypting the data.
- SSL (Secure Sockets Layer) and TLS (Transport Layer Security) are two public key encryption protocols commonly used to encrypt communications across the Internet.

Self-Check

9. Which AWS service provides client-side encryption to increase application security?

    a. Encryption SDK

    b. API Gateway

    c. EBS (Elastic Block Store)

    d. Trusted Advisor

10. How many keys are required for asymmetric encryption?

    a. None

    b. One

    c. Two

    d. Three

11. What port should you open in your firewall to allow DoT traffic?

    a. 22

    b. 853

    c. 53

    d. 443

○ Check your answers at the end of this module.

Section 6-5: Troubleshooting Cloud Security

Certification

2.1 Given a scenario, configure identity and access management.

2.5 Given a scenario, implement measures to meet security requirements.

5.2 Given a scenario, troubleshoot security issues.

5.4 Given a scenario, troubleshoot connectivity issues.

Security issues carry significant risks to a company, both from a technological standpoint and from financial, reputational, and legal perspectives. This section discusses some common security troubleshooting scenarios you might face when managing cloud resources.

Security Misconfigurations

Clearly, security technologies must adapt quickly to the demands of cloud computing and the cloud environment. Where the public in general and IT professionals in particular were long skeptical of the potential for securing data and workloads in the cloud, the development of new security techniques and the adaptation of tried-and-true security technologies has, in many cases, made the cloud more secure than other environments rather than less so.

However, all these cloud security techniques rely on proper configurations and consistent maintenance. When traffic fails to arrive at its intended destination, often the problem is one of the following:

- A misconfigured or misapplied security policy or ACL in a firewall or network security group
- A misconfigured or failed security appliance (such as an IPS, IDS, NAC, or WAF)
- Incorrectly administered micro-segmentation

Similarly, these misconfigurations can result in access that should not exist, thereby potentially opening a resource to attack. These problems are common vulnerabilities that inadvertently allow data exploits.

Tools within cloud platforms can help to protect your cloud resources by confirming best practices are applied to resource configurations. For example, AWS offers Trusted Advisor, which checks resources for security and availability configurations that do not conform to best-practice standards. It also checks for performance issues, cost optimization configurations, and relevant service limits. Figure 6-21 shows recommended actions in a student's AWS account hosted in an AWS Academy Learner Lab environment. Following the recommended actions would help improve security for the student's AWS resources.

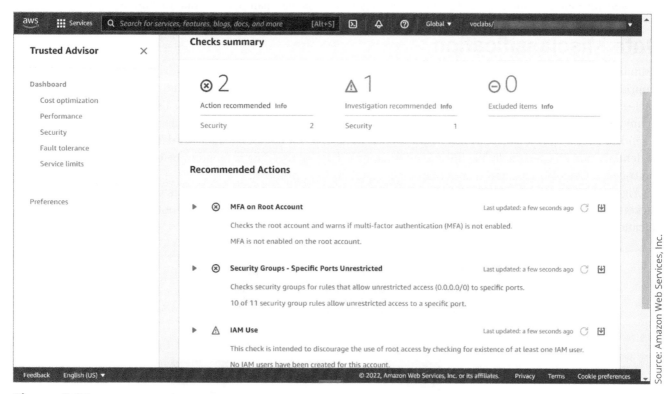

Figure 6-21   Trusted Advisor recommended actions

A huge majority of security failures result from user or administrative error. With this reality in mind, the following is a list of common security weak spots you'll want to be mindful of and watch for:

- *Unencrypted data and unencrypted communications*—Breaches happen. When they do, encrypted data can mean the difference between a learning opportunity and a career-breaking crisis. Make sure that all sensitive data, whether at rest, in motion, or in use, is securely encrypted using reliable encryption protocols.

- *Weak or obsolete security technologies*—As an IT professional, keep your own knowledge up-to-date on the latest developments in security techniques relative to your work.

- *Incorrect hardening settings*—Most default system hardening settings at the instance level are pretty effective. For example, Windows Server on a VM benefits from built-in defenses that typically don't need adjusting from their default settings. However, hardening settings within the cloud platform can be problematic. Oftentimes, default settings allow for maximized access while you're setting up your resources. Watch for warnings in your console indicating you need to tighten security settings and be wary of areas where cloud admins tend to leave blind spots or backdoors so you can close these gaps.

- *Security device failure*—Security devices do fail sometimes. Failovers and redundant systems can minimize the impact of these events.

- *Insufficient security controls and processes*—Poorly designed networks can leave gaps and blind spots where intruders can enter, or data might be exposed to the open Internet. When a security event occurs, insufficient logging can prevent you from learning what went wrong and how to fix the problem. Consider network design carefully, and employ logging, monitoring, and alerts where needed. You'll learn more about monitoring and alerts later in this course.

- *Unauthorized physical access*—Although the cloud consumer is not responsible for managing physical access to hardware supporting a public cloud, you and the other employees at your organization still need to be aware and vigilant of risks involving an attacker's physical access to the organization's trusted endpoint devices, such as workstations and mobile devices, and an attacker's ability to use social engineering to collect sensitive information that could be used to illegally access and manipulate cloud resources.

Data Misclassification

A similar problem to security misconfigurations is when data is misclassified and, as a result, is configured with inappropriate access permissions. Many cloud providers offer a service to help with this issue, as well. For example, AWS's Macie service works in partnership with AWS SecurityHub to validate data classifications using ML (machine learning) techniques, which search for sensitive data in S3 (Simple Storage Service) buckets. Macie regularly scans all S3 buckets and can accurately identify sensitive data such as bank account numbers, credit card information, authentication credentials, and PII (personally identifiable information). If any of this data is found to be improperly exposed, Macie can trigger a CloudWatch alarm that notifies cloud admins of the problem.

Figure 6-22 shows a possible validation system where data is classified in S3 buckets using tags. Macie scans the buckets and triggers a Lambda function to send an SNS (Simple Notification Service) notification if a data misclassification is found.

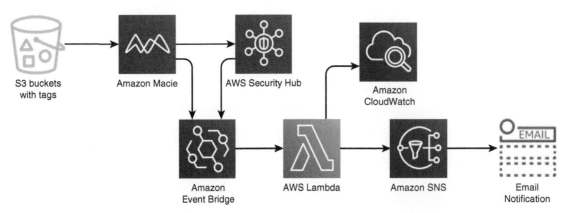

Figure 6-22 A validation system where data is classified in S3 buckets using tags

Key Management

Good key management can make encrypting and decrypting data more convenient. However, problems arise if the keys are too convenient, such as being stored in the same location as the data or when storing keys temporarily in memory while they're being used. Keys should be kept in a protected, isolated environment with current backups stored securely in yet another location, and keys should be regularly rotated. (Don't forget to update backups when rotating keys.)

To support public key encryption in the cloud, you must store private keys either on-prem (and provide access to those keys where needed) or in the cloud through a key management service. While cloud-based key stores are highly available and resilient, you might still encounter certain issues, such as:

- Unavailable keys
- Failed connections
- Encryption operation failure

To fix common key store problems, confirm that needed keys are configured as available instead of unavailable or deleted. Also check the configuration of resources attempting to access stored keys and the configuration of network connections between these resources and the key store.

Remember This

- Common cloud security weak spots include unencrypted data, unencrypted communications, weak or obsolete security technologies, incorrect hardening settings, security device failure, insufficient security controls and processes, and unauthorized physical access.
- Many cloud providers offer a service to help with data misclassification that, if left unchecked, can result in inappropriate access permissions.
- Keys should be kept in a protected, isolated environment with current backups stored securely in yet another location, and keys should be regularly rotated.

Self-Check

12. What security technique can protect inappropriately exposed data?

   a. Device hardening
   b. Encryption

   c. Device failovers
   d. Physical access controls

13. Which of the following service types can help with rotating encryption keys?

   a. WAF
   b. NAC

   c. TLS
   d. KMS

○ Check your answers at the end of this module.

Module Summary

Section 6-1: Cloud Security Configurations

- Common internal and external threats to cloud security include data breaches, DoS and DDoS attacks, insecure interfaces, APTs (advanced persistent threats), account hijacking, poor account management, user error, insider threats, data loss with no backups, and CSP changes or outages.
- Scanning tools such as Nmap, Nessus, and Metasploit provide a simple and reliable way to discover crucial information about a network.
- Cloud security works according to the shared responsibility model, meaning that the CSP is partially responsible for a cloud's security and the customer is responsible for the rest of it.
- One of the most effective ways to manage shadow IT sprawl is to establish clear company security policies and educate users about the need for and scope of these policies.

Section 6-2: Virtual Network Security

- Security rules check for information such as port, protocol, and IP address or CIDR range—an allow list lets traffic through while a block list or deny list prevents traffic from passing.
- AWS provides subnet-level security with NACLs (network ACLs), instance-level security with security groups, VPC traffic monitoring with flow logs, packet analysis with traffic mirroring, and managed firewall services with Network Firewall.
- Azure provides VNet-level security with NVAs (network virtual appliances), subnet-level security with NSGs (network security groups), interface-level security with ASGs (application security groups), and many other security tools for threat protection, traffic capture, anti-malware, and traffic analysis.
- GCP provides VPC-level security with firewall rules, subnet-level traffic monitoring with VPC flow logs, and traffic capture and analysis with packet mirroring.
- A CASB (cloud access security broker) is designed to detect applications and other resources running within a domain—even resources IT staff don't know about—and monitor those resources according to policies set by the organization.

Section 6-3: Compute Security

- A hardened baseline documents all configuration changes needed to secure a system and its OS.
- Application security refers to applications running on compute resources, SaaS applications, and PaaS components used to build applications and other services.

Section 6-4: Data Security

- Data can exist in three states: at rest, in use, and in motion.
- Encryption is the use of an algorithm to scramble data into a format that can be read only by reversing the algorithm—that is, by decrypting the data.
- SSL (Secure Sockets Layer) and TLS (Transport Layer Security) are two public key encryption protocols commonly used to encrypt communications across the Internet.

Section 6-5: Troubleshooting Cloud Security

- Common cloud security weak spots include unencrypted data, unencrypted communications, weak or obsolete security technologies, incorrect hardening settings, security device failure, insufficient security controls and processes, and unauthorized physical access.
- Many cloud providers offer a service to help with data misclassification that, if left unchecked, can result in inappropriate access permissions.
- Keys should be kept in a protected, isolated environment with current backups stored securely in yet another location, and keys should be regularly rotated.

Key Terms

For definitions of key terms, see the Glossary.

ADC (application delivery controller)
agent-based scan
allow list
block list
CASB (cloud access security broker)
CIA (confidentiality, integrity, and availability) triad
cipher
credentialed scan
DDoS (distributed denial of service) attack
deny list

DLP (data loss prevention)
DNSSEC (DNS Security Extension)
DoH (DNS over HTTPS)
DoS (denial of service) attack
DoT (DNS over TLS)
EDR (endpoint detection and response)
encryption
hardened baseline
hashing
key
micro-segmentation
NAC (network access control)

network-based scan
NTS (Network Time Security)
OpenSSL
port scanner
risk register
screened subnet
shared responsibility model
SSL (Secure Sockets Layer)
stratum
TLS (Transport Layer Security)
vulnerability scanner
WAF (web application firewall)
zero-trust security model

Acronyms Checklist

The acronyms in Table 6-3 are listed in the Cloud+ objectives and could appear on the Cloud+ exam. This means that exam questions might use any of these acronyms in context so that you must know the meaning of the acronym to answer the question correctly. Make sure you're familiar with what each acronym stands for and the general concept of the term itself. All these acronyms are used in context in this module.

Table 6-3   Module 6 acronyms

Acronym	Spelled out
ACL	access control list
ADC	application delivery controller
AES	Advanced Encryption Standard
CASB	cloud access security broker
DDoS	distributed denial of service
DLP	data loss prevention
DMZ	demilitarized zone
DNSSEC	Domain Name System Security Extensions
DoH	Domain Name System over Hypertext Transfer Protocol Secure
DoT	Domain Name System over Transport Layer Security
EDR	endpoint detection and response
FTPS	File Transfer Protocol Secure or File Transfer Protocol over Secure Sockets Layer

Acronym	Spelled out
HIDS	host-based intrusion detection system
HIPS	host-based intrusion prevention system
HTTPS	Hypertext Transfer Protocol Secure
IDS	intrusion detection system
IPS	intrusion prevention system
NAC	network access control
NTS	Network Time Security
SFTP	Secure File Transfer Protocol
SHA	Secure Hash Algorithm
SSL	Secure Sockets Layer
TKIP	Temporal Key Integrity Protocol
TLS	Transport Layer Security
TPM	Trusted Platform Module
WAF	web application firewall

Review Questions

1. Which type of scan provides the most in-depth view of system misconfigurations?

    a. Network-based scan
    b. Credentialed scan
    c. Port scan
    d. Default scan

2. Your credentialed scan revealed a known vulnerability in a recently updated application that is widely used across the company. Where can you get information on your company's policies for how to reconfigure the application to close the vulnerability?

    a. Network-based scanner
    b. Scanning agent
    c. Port scanner
    d. Risk register

3. How should you decide which security configurations to apply in a cloud deployment?

    a. Apply security first to the virtual network level, then to the instance level.
    b. Apply security first to the instance level, then to the virtual network level.
    c. Check CSP best practices.
    d. Use all available security tools for each layer.

4. What security technique can you use to control traffic to a web server separately from traffic control for the website database?

    a. Zero-trust
    b. Micro-segmentation
    c. Shadow IT
    d. DevSecOps

5. Which of the following security rules would allow an incoming Echo Reply on a stateful firewall?

    a. Outbound rule: ICMP Allow to 0.0.0.0/0
    b. Inbound rule: HTTP Allow from 0.0.0.0/0
    c. Outbound rule: HTTPS Allow to 0.0.0.0/0
    d. Inbound rule: ICMP Deny from 0.0.0.0/0

6. Which security appliance can be used to secure an LMS (learning management system) application with some components deployed in a public cloud platform and some components deployed on-prem?

    a. ADC
    b. WAF
    c. APT
    d. CASB

7. Which protocol provides the best encryption for data in transit over a Wi-Fi network?

    a. TKIP
    b. AES
    c. SHA-3
    d. PSK

8. Which security tool can you use to find security vulnerabilities in forgotten EC2 instances?

    a. ACL
    b. NTS
    c. EDR
    d. DLP

9. Which device would be best to provide traffic shaping services on your network?

    a. CASB
    b. Firewall
    c. ADC
    d. Port scanner

10. Suppose you are running an application secured by client-side encryption and you receive an error stating CLUSTER_NOT_FOUND. Which of the following problems is most likely the source of the issue?

    a. Deleted key store
    b. Encryption failure
    c. Invalid credentials
    d. Connection misconfiguration

Scenario-Based Questions

Question 6-1

Krista runs a website that reports on current events in IT security. She recently noticed a huge spike in traffic that has caused several new web server instances to spin up in her AWS cloud. What kind of attack is Krista most likely experiencing?

  a. User error
  b. Data breach
  c. Account hijacking
  d. DDoS

Question 6-2

Roxie has created a Windows Server VM instance in Azure so she can test a new application she's developing. She'll need to remote into the VM from her home computer so she can install the app and run it through its paces. What port will Roxie most likely need to enable in the NSG so she can connect with the VM?

  a. 3389
  b. 443
  c. 80
  d. 22

Question 6-3

Zane is troubleshooting a problematic connection between a web server and a load balancer. The load balancer had reported the server was shut down, but when Zane checked it, the server instance was running fine. He suspects there's a routing problem or possibly an interface configuration problem. Where can he look for more information about the traffic that has been crossing this connection before the problem occurred?

  a. Firewall rules
  b. Flow logs
  c. Security group settings
  d. Load balancer configuration options

Hands-On Projects

Note 5

Websites, applications, public cloud platforms, and related account options change often. While the instructions given in these projects were accurate at the time of writing, you might need to adjust the steps or options according to later changes.

Note to Instructors and Students: A rubric is provided for evaluating student performance on these projects. Please see Appendix D.

Project 6-1: Research Data Breaches

Estimated time: 30 minutes
Objective 5.2: Given a scenario, troubleshoot security issues.
Group work: This project includes enhancements when assigned as a group project.

(continues)

Hands-On Projects Continued

Resources:
- Internet access

Context:
In this module and the next, you're learning about cloud-based access control methods and some of the risks, concerns, and technologies involved in controlling access to cloud networks, data, and other resources. Unfortunately, these methods don't always work as intended, especially when improperly implemented. That's one way that data breaches happen. These breaches can be costly to the organizations involved and can cause significant damage to customers, clients, patients, and users.

Many websites report on major breaches throughout the world. One website in particular allows you to look up your own email address to determine if it's been posted along with other hacked data on the web: Have I Been Pwned (haveibeenpwned.com). "Pwned" is an Internet slang term for having been taken advantage of, and it's pronounced "powned." (The term supposedly came from a frequent mistyping of the word "owned" because of the proximity of the o and the p on the keyboard.) This website also keeps an ongoing list of the websites whose data has been hacked, along with a brief historical description of the breach. To learn more about recent data breaches, complete the following steps:

1. Visit the webpage at **haveibeenpwned.com/pwnedwebsites** and read the list of breaches. Choose three of these breaches that most interest you.
2. In your own words, describe what happened in each breach.
3. For each breach you chose, suggest one or more ways similar breaches can be prevented in the future. Give at least one different suggestion for each breach. The grading rubric in Table 6-4 shows what is expected of you for your responses in this project. Note that your instructor might choose to adjust the point distribution in this rubric.
4. **For group projects:** Each member of the group should share details of one of the breaches they researched and their suggestions for mitigating the risk that led to this breach. Group members evaluate the proposed solution and provide additional suggestions for improved security or other concerns that should be researched. Each group member provides an improved evaluation of their breach and their suggestions for mitigation.

Table 6-4   Grading rubric for Project 6-1

Task	Novice	Competent	Proficient	Earned
Coverage of breaches	Generalized statements describing three breaches **15 points**	Specific statements describing three breaches **25 points**	Detailed and thoughtful description of three breaches **35 points**	
Proposed protections	Three generalized suggestions for breach prevention **15 points**	Three specific suggestions for breach prevention with realistic details **25 points**	Three thoughtful suggestions for breach prevention with supporting evidence **35 points**	
Organization	Little cohesiveness to presentation **5 points**	Logical organization of ideas from beginning to end **10 points**	Clear organization of ideas, showing logical connections between thoughts **15 points**	
Mechanics	Several grammar and spelling errors **5 points**	Occasional grammar and spelling errors **10 points**	Appropriate grammar and spelling throughout **15 points**	

Total

Project 6-2: Configure Security in AWS

Estimated time: 45 minutes

Objective 2.2: Given a scenario, secure a network in a cloud environment.

Resources:

- AWS account
- Internet access

Context:

AWS uses NACLs and security groups to manage traffic to and from resources in a VPC. In this project, you'll explore how to configure these tools to manage SSH and RDP traffic. Complete the following steps:

1. In your AWS Management Console, go to the **VPC** dashboard. In the navigation pane, scroll down and click **Network ACLs** in the Security category. You should have at least one NACL listed here as a default. Select that NACL (or if you have multiple NACLs listed, choose the one with active subnet associations). Click the **Inbound rules** tab for that NACL. Two rules should be listed here, one that allows all traffic and one that denies all traffic. Considering that these rules seem to accomplish exactly opposite purposes, what net effect do you think these rules have on traffic into this VPC? Why do you think this is?

2. Click the **Outbound rules** tab and notice that it also shows two similar rules with similar configurations. Click the **Subnet associations** tab. How many subnets are listed here?

3. In the navigation pane, click **Security Groups**. Unless you've been deleting security groups along the way, you should have a few groups listed here. Select a default security group and examine the inbound and outbound rules. Notice that there is no setting for "Allow" or "Deny." Any traffic referenced by a rule is allowed. Traffic not referenced by a rule is not allowed. What traffic is allowed in this security group?

4. Deselect the default security group and select a security group created by a launch wizard. Launch-wizard security groups are created when you create a new VM. You've probably deleted the relevant VMs, but the security groups are still present unless you've been deleting these along the way. The traffic that is allowed in a launch-wizard security group is determined by the permission settings you configured on that VM, such as allowing SSH or RDP for remoting into the VM. What inbound traffic type is allowed for this launch-wizard security group? Based on this information, what OS do you think that VM had (or has, if it still exists)?

5. Create a new VPC, a subnet within that VPC, and a VM instance in that subnet. Check the following details as you create the VM:

   - Under Network settings, make sure to associate the VM with your new VPC, not your account's default VPC.
   - Also under Network settings, choose to select an existing security group instead of creating a new security group. Select the default security group for your new VPC.

6. While the VM is initializing, return to the VPC dashboard and check the rules created by default for your new subnet's NACL and the new VPC's default security group. It might be helpful to write down the last few digits of the subnet ID and VPC ID to identify the correct NACL and security group later. What traffic is currently allowed to this VPC, its subnet, and its instance?

Now you're ready to create a higher-priority NACL rule that will specifically allow inbound RDP or SSH traffic, depending on the OS you chose for your VM. Complete the following steps:

7. Select the NACL assigned to the VPC you created earlier in this project. On the NACL's Inbound rules tab, note the priority for the existing rule, and then click **Edit inbound rules**. Click **Add new rule**. For the new rule, choose a higher priority rating than what the existing rules have—remember that higher priorities use lower numbers. What priority did you choose?

8. Under Type, what are two protocols you recognize in this list? Choose **SSH** or **RDP**, depending on the OS you chose for your instance. Save your changes.

(continues)

Hands-On Projects Continued ───────────────────────────

Next, you'll need to create a new security group that only allows inbound RDP or SSH traffic, depending on the OS you chose for your VM. Complete the following steps:

9. On the Security Groups page, click **Create security group**. Give the security group a name, such as MySG-1, and a description, such as *RDP traffic only* or *SSH traffic only*. Assign the security group to the VPC you created earlier in this project.

10. Under Inbound rules, click **Add rule**. Under Type, select SSH or RDP, depending on your instance's OS. Under Source, select **My IP**. What happens?

11. Give the rule a description that would help you identify its purpose in a long list of security rules. This is good practice for later when you'll be managing many NACL and security rules, and you won't necessarily remember why you created any specific rule. What description did you give the rule? Finish creating your security group.

12. Return to the EC2 dashboard, and check the detailed information for your instance, which should be running by now. What is the instance's private IP address?

13. Does the instance have a public IP address? Thinking back to what you've learned over the past few modules, why do you think this is?

14. Change the instance's security group to the one you just created. To do this, click **Actions**, click **Security**, and click **Change security groups**. What security group is currently assigned to the VM?

15. Select and assign the new security group. Are you able to assign both security groups to this one VM? Save your changes.

16. Scroll through the navigation pane for the EC2 Dashboard. Of the security resources you used in this project, which one can you manage from the EC2 Dashboard?

17. Delete all the resources you created in this project—including the VPC, subnet, VM, the VPC's default NACL, and both security groups. In what order did you delete these resources? What error messages did you encounter? How did you handle these problems? Check through your account to confirm that all related resources have been deleted.

> ### Note 6
>
> Depending on the status of your account and the selections you made during this project, the resources you created can deplete your credits or accrue charges. Double-check to make sure you've terminated all resources you created in this project.

Project 6-3: Configure Security in Azure

Estimated time: 45 minutes

Objective 2.2: Given a scenario, secure a network in a cloud environment.

Resources:

- Azure account
- Internet access

Context:

Azure uses NSGs and ASGs to manage traffic to and from resources in a VNet. In this project, you'll explore how these tools relate to each other and how to configure NSG rules to allow SSH traffic. Complete the following steps:

1. In your Azure portal, create a VNet using the following details:

   - Create a new resource group.
   - Give it a /24 CIDR range, such as 192.168.0.0/24.
   - Add a subnet with a /26 CIDR range, such as 192.168.0.0/26.

2. In the portal menu, click **All services**. Select the **Networking** category and click **Network security groups**. Click **Create network security group**. Place the NSG in your project's resource group that you created in Step 1.

3. After the NSG is created, go to the resource to see information about it. Answer the following questions:
   - What inbound and outbound security rules are listed in your NSG?
   - How many network interfaces are associated with this NSG?
   - What subnets are currently associated with this NSG? Why do you think this is?

4. Notice that NSGs are associated either with network interfaces or with subnets. Microsoft recommends using subnets rather than network interfaces as a general rule, so now you're ready to associate your subnet with this NSG. On the NSG's subnets list, click **Associate**. Choose your VNet and then choose the subnet. Click **OK**.

Note 7

If your VNet is not at first available in the Virtual network dropdown list, wait a few minutes and refresh the page, and then try again.

---

5. Return to the Virtual networks page and click your VNet. Do you see your NSG listed here?
6. Click **Subnets** and then scroll to the right to see all the information about your subnet. Do you see your NSG listed here?
7. In the portal menu, click **All services**. Select the **Networking** category and click **Application security groups**. Click **Create application security group**. Place the ASG in your project's resource group that you created in Step 1 and create the ASG.
8. Create a new Linux VM using the following details:
   - Add the VM to the resource group you created for this project.
   - Use the **Standard_B1s** size.
   - Use a password authentication type for simplicity in this project.
   - Under Inbound port rules, select **Allow selected ports** and choose **SSH (22)**.
   - Confirm the VM will be added to your project VNet and subnet.
   - On the Networking tab, what does Azure say about the VM's NSG?
   - Review and create the VM.
9. Open the VM's information page and click **Networking** on the left under Settings. What NSG is associated with this VM? How many inbound port rules are currently listed? Why do you think this is?
10. Click **Topology**. What is the NSG connected to?
11. Close the Topology blade. On the VM's Networking blade, click the **Application security groups** tab. Click **Configure the application security groups**. Select the ASG you created in Step 7 and save your changes.
12. Return to the details page for your NSG and click **Inbound security rules**, and then click **Add**. Configure a new inbound security rule using the following details:
    - Allow traffic from any source.
    - Leave the Source port ranges as * because port filtering is typically performed on the destination port in Azure, not the source port. If you're feeling adventurous, change the Source port ranges to 22, and read the caution message at the bottom of the blade. Then change the Source port ranges field back to *.
    - For Destination, notice that you can choose an IP address, VNet, or ASG as the destination for traffic covered by this rule. Select **Application security group** and select the ASG you created in Step 7.
    - Change the Service to **SSH**.
    - Allow traffic with priority **100** and name **SSH_traffic**.
    - Click **Add**.
13. Return to the details page for your VM and, if needed, refresh the page. How many inbound port rules are listed now?
14. Click the **SSH_traffic** rule. What warning does Azure give you about this rule?

(continues)

Hands-On Projects Continued ────────────────────────────

15. Delete all the resources you created in this project, including the VNet, subnet, NSG, ASG, VM, and resource group. In what order did you delete these resources? What error messages did you encounter? How did you handle these problems? Check through your account to confirm that all related resources have been deleted.

> **Note 8**
>
> Depending on the status of your account and the selections you made during this project, the resources you cre-ated can deplete your credits or accrue charges. Double-check to make sure you've terminated all resources you created in this project.

Project 6-4: Configure Security in GCP

Estimated time: 45 minutes

Objective 2.2: Given a scenario, secure a network in a cloud environment.

Resources:

- GCP account
- Internet access

Context:

GCP uses firewall rules to manage traffic to and from resources in a VPC. In this project, you'll explore how to config-ure these tools to allow you to connect to resources in a custom VPC and ping between those resources. Complete the following steps:

1. In your GCP console, create a new project. In that project, create a new, custom-mode VPC and one subnet within that VPC.
2. Create a new Linux VM in the VPC you just created. Use the same region as the VPC you created in Step 1. If you need to avoid accruing charges, use the e2-micro machine type in one of the free regions. (Search online for a current list of regions that support free instances in GCP.) Be sure to expand the **Networking** section to select the VPC you created in Step 1.
3. Once the VM is running, attempt to console into it by clicking **SSH** on the VM instances page. What happens? Why do you think this is?
4. In the navigation menu, point to **VPC network** and click **Firewall**. What ingress rules are listed here, and what are their purposes?
5. Click **CREATE FIREWALL RULE**. Configure the following details:
   - Give the rule a name, such as ssh-myvpc, and a good description.
   - Select your network that you created in Step 1.
   - Leave the priority at **1000**, the direction of traffic as **Ingress**, and the action as **Allow**.
   - Under Targets, select **All instances in the network**.
   - Under Source IPv4 ranges, enter **0.0.0.0/0**, which is a wildcard that allows traffic from any source.
   - Under Protocols and ports, select **Specified protocols and ports**, select **tcp:**, and enter **22**. Why do you think 22 is the appropriate number for this field? Click **CREATE**.
6. Return to your VM instance and try again to console into it. What happens this time? Why do you think that is?
7. Create a second VM in the same region, VPC, and subnet. Attempt to console in to that VM. Does it work? Why do you think this is?
8. Attempt to ping from one VM to the other. Wait several seconds, then press **Ctrl+C** to see the results. What happens? Why do you think this is?
9. Create a new firewall rule that allows ICMP in your custom VPC. ICMP does not have a TCP or UDP port, so you'll have to enter **icmp** in the *Other protocols* field. Otherwise, use the same settings as in Step 5.
10. Try again to ping from one VM to the other. Does it work? Why do you think this is?

11. Delete all the resources you created in this project, including the VPC, subnet, both VMs, and both firewall rules. In what order did you delete these resources? What error messages did you encounter? How did you handle these problems? Check through your account to confirm that all related resources have been deleted.

Note 9

Depending on the status of your account and the selections you made during this project, the resources you created can deplete your credits or accrue charges. Double-check to make sure you've terminated all resources you created in this project.

Capstone Project 6: Configure Security Across VPCs

Note 10

Websites, applications, public cloud platforms, and related account options change often. While the instructions given in these projects were accurate at the time of writing, you might need to adjust the steps or options according to later changes.

Note to Instructors and Students: A rubric is provided for evaluating student performance on these projects. Please see Appendix D.

Estimated time: 1 hour

Objective 5.2: Given a scenario, troubleshoot security issues.

Resources:

- One or two public cloud accounts (This project can be completed entirely in one public cloud platform, or the instructor can require that students set up each VM on a different public cloud platform and establish communication across clouds.)
- Internet access

Context:

In the Hands-on Projects for this module, you created security rules that allowed traffic from any source to help with initial testing. In this project, you will restrict the traffic source to a single VM instance.

Imagine you work for a small company that is building its first website hosted in the cloud. The company will have one VM as a web server and a second VM in a different VPC or VNet as a database server. The web server should be accessible from the open Internet, but the database server should only allow communication with the web server.

Before opening ports for web traffic and database traffic, you want to ensure you have your security rules set appropriately. You decide to start with pings, which use ICMP and are easy to test. You'll need a source VM (your web server instance) and a target VM (your database server instance) in two separate VPCs or VNets. You need to prove that you can ping your target VM from your source VM but not from your local computer. While there are more secure ways to do this, in this scenario, you will place the target VM in a public subnet so that you can determine how to use security rules to control traffic to the target VM.

Complete the following steps:

1. Create two VPCs with one subnet each, either in the same cloud platform or in two different cloud platforms. (Your instructor might require that you use the same cloud platform for this project or two cloud platforms—check with your instructor for specific requirements.) Make sure both subnets have access to the Internet. For example, in AWS, you'll need to add an Internet gateway to each subnet and add an Internet route to each subnet's route table.

(continues)

Hands-On Projects Continued

2. Create a VM instance in each subnet. Make sure each VM receives a public IP address. What public IP address is assigned to your VMs?

3. Configure security rules that allow ICMP traffic from any source to your target VM so you can confirm the target VM will respond successfully to pings. Get a working ping from your local computer to your target VM before proceeding.

4. Configure security rules that allow SSH or RDP connections to your source VM. Remote into the source VM.

5. Configure security rules that only allow ICMP traffic from your source VM to your target VM. What rules did you add? What effect do you expect each rule to have on traffic to and from each VM?

6. Run a ping from the source VM to the target VM that shows ICMP traffic is reaching the target VM. **Take a screenshot** showing the output; include this visual with your answers to this project's questions.

7. Run a ping from your local computer to your target VM that shows ICMP traffic from other sources cannot reach the target VM. **Take a screenshot** showing the output; include this visual with your answers to this project's questions.

8. Delete all resources created in this Capstone project. Check through your account to confirm that all related resources have been deleted.

Note 11

Depending on the status of your account and the selections you made during this project, the resources you created can deplete your credits or accrue charges. Double-check to make sure you've terminated all resources you created in this project.

Solutions to Self-Check Questions

Section 6-1: Cloud Security Configurations

1. Which of these threats could be mitigated with good backups?

   Answer: a. Data loss

   Explanation: Data loss can generally be avoided by keeping good backups.

2. Which type of scan requires software installation on the monitored resource?

   Answer: d. Agent-based scan

   Explanation: For an agent-based scan to work, agents (or small applications) are installed on monitored devices to collect information about the devices and send that information to a central location for analysis.

3. Which cloud service model places the greatest responsibility on the cloud customer for cloud security?

   Answer: c. IaaS

   Explanation: With an IaaS cloud service model, the customer maintains a higher degree of responsibility for the management, configuration, and security of a cloud deployment.

Section 6-2: Virtual Network Security

4. A stateless rule applies to _____.

   Answer: c. traffic in one direction

   Explanation: Stateless security rules apply to either inbound traffic or outbound traffic but not both at the same time.

5. What cloud security tool functions similar to Wireshark?

    Answer: b. Traffic mirroring

    Explanation: Traffic mirroring or packet mirroring provides deeper insight into captured traffic than what flow logs offer, and it's similar to the packet capture and analysis functions that Wireshark offers.

6. Security at which of these levels provides the most fine-tuned traffic filtering?

    Answer: b. Interface

    Explanation: Virtual networks can contain several subnets, each of which can contain several instances, each of which can contain several interfaces. Security configured at the interface level provides the most fine-tuned traffic filtering.

Section 6-3: Compute Security

7. Which security technique will increase the number of running resources while decreasing the attack surface?

    Answer: b. Create single-function resources

    Explanation: Creating single-function resources increases the number of smaller-sized resources while leaving a much smaller attack surface for each resource.

8. Which security appliance can perform encryption to reduce the processing load on protected servers?

    Answer: d. ADC

    Explanation: An ADC (application delivery controller) can handle encryption to reduce the load on servers.

Section 6-4: Data Security

9. Which AWS service provides client-side encryption to increase application security?

    Answer: a. Encryption SDK

    Explanation: AWS offers the Encryption SDK to handle client-side data encryption, decryption, and related key transmission for applications or scripts.

10. How many keys are required for asymmetric encryption?

    Answer: c. Two

    Explanation: Asymmetric encryption, also called public key encryption, requires the use of two different keys, one to encrypt and the other to decrypt.

11. What port should you open in your firewall to allow DoT traffic?

    Answer: b. 853

    Explanation: With DoT (DNS over TLS), TLS (Transport Layer Security) encrypts traditional, UDP (User Datagram Protocol) traffic used for DNS. This traffic uses port 853.

Section 6-5: Troubleshooting Cloud Security

12. What security technique can protect inappropriately exposed data?

    Answer: b. Encryption

    Explanation: Encrypting data can mean the difference between a learning opportunity and a career-breaking crisis.

13. Which of the following service types can help with rotating encryption keys?

    Answer: d. KMS

    Explanation: Many cloud providers offer KMS (key management services) that can securely store keys and help with regular key rotation.

Module 7

Identity and Access Management

Module 7 Objectives

After reading this module, you will be able to:

1 Describe how accounts are managed in the cloud.

2 Explain authentication processes used in the cloud.

3 Apply IAM (identity and access management) policies in the cloud.

4 Explain technologies used for hybrid cloud IAM.

5 Identify common IAM issues.

Module 7 Outline

Study the module's outline to help you organize the content in your mind as you read.

Module 7 Scenario

"Nigel, did you put these coffee beans on my desk?" Mika, the cybersecurity specialist, walks out of her office carrying a small package of chocolate-covered coffee beans.

"Nope, wasn't me," replies Nigel. "And you know *I'm* not your secret pal because *I* know you don't like coffee."

"Well, I did list chocolate on my questionnaire. Maybe I should have specified coffee-less chocolate." Mika hands Nigel the coffee beans and says, "Here, you can have them," as her phone begins to ring and she darts back into her office.

The departments in your building are running a secret pal event this month, and you drew Mika's name. You're also aware she doesn't like coffee, but you're hoping the coffee beans will throw her off your trail because she was beginning to suspect her secret pal was someone in IT. She's a former police detective, and her nose for finding clues is legendary throughout campus. No one wants Mika's name for a secret pal because no one has successfully kept the secret from her for more than 16 days. You're determined to set a new record, maybe even get through the whole month.

Nigel glances over at you and says, "She knows."

"She doesn't know!" you whisper back. "How could she know? She thought it was you!"

"No, she wants you to *think* she thought it was me," says Nigel. "She's playing you."

"Whatever," you reply. "We're only eight days into the month. There's no way she could know already."

"She knows," repeats Nigel as he pops a coffee bean into his mouth. "You gave it away when you gave her those *Star Wars* stickers. Only us IT geeks know she likes *Star Wars* and she knows I'm a full-blood Trekkie. You're so busted."

Just then, Kendra walks in and says, "Okay, team. I've set up accounts in two public clouds, and I'm going to give each of you an admin user account so you can play around with this stuff. What thoughts do you have on where you'd like to start?"

"I want to spin up some VMs," says Nigel. "I've not worked much with Windows Server yet."

"I'd like to look at the networking services," you reply, "and maybe see how to set up users, too. How does that work in the cloud? Do users sign into their workstations like they do now, or do they go to AWS or Azure or whatever and sign in there?"

"That's a good question," says Kendra. "It really depends on what the user needs to be able to do."

"How do we know who is who?" asks Nigel. "Do we have, maybe, an HR account that all of HR uses, and they share the password? Or do we have a different account for each person?"

"Each person typically has their own account," explains Kendra. "We won't use only passwords, though. That's not secure enough. I'll check with Mika on what kind of authentication we'll want to set up." Then she adds, "Each user gets a different kind of role, depending on their job duties and the kinds of information they need. It's kind of like our secret pal thing—it's almost like you can tell who a person is based on what they know about you."

Nigel gives you "the look," and you try not to roll your eyes. Kendra pretends not to notice.

"Let's find out a little more about how identity management works in the cloud," says Kendra. "Here are some more questions for you two," as you make some notes on your notepad:

- How can users prove their identity in the cloud?
- How do admins choose what resources users can access?
- How is access control managed across a hybrid cloud?

Section 7-1: Cloud Accounts

Certification

2.1 Given a scenario, configure identity and access management.

2.3 Given a scenario, apply the appropriate OS and application security controls.

2.5 Given a scenario, implement measures to meet security requirements.

When you first create a cloud account, this account takes the role of the root account in that platform. For example, when you created an account in AWS for Project 1-2, the account you created was configured as a root account. As you've been completing projects in AWS in later modules, you've performed most of these tasks from the root account. From a security perspective, this is a bad idea. It's okay for the practice activities you've been doing in this course, but you don't want to use this approach in the work world.

When working for an organization, you'll instead use less privileged user accounts. These user accounts can also allow other users in your organization to access and interact with cloud resources. You can set up these accounts using the IAM (identity and access management) services built into most major cloud platforms. AWS, Azure, and GCP all offer many IAM services for free. Once these user accounts are established, the root account should not be used again except when absolutely necessary.

Note 1

Keep in mind that each VM instance also has one or more default accounts in its OS, including privileged root accounts. As you create new VMs, you'll need to deactivate default accounts in each VM's OS or, at the very least, change default credentials to use secure authentication methods.

IAM works at multiple levels to control users' access to resources: identification, authentication, authorization, and accounting. You read about each of these levels of access management throughout this module. Let's begin with identification.

Identity

IAM services work at multiple levels to control users' logical access to resources. Logical access control contrasts with physical access control, such as door locks, and often refers more specifically to remote access, which is especially relevant to accessing cloud resources. IAM policies and tools provide directory and identity services that are applied broadly to all users who are given any kind of logical access to resources, both on-prem and in the cloud. Logical access control is managed through permissions granted to identities.

Both users and resources (such as an application) can have an identity, which is a digital entity to which you can attach roles and permissions. A user is given permissions based on what job responsibilities the user needs to fulfill. A resource such as a server or application might need an identity, for example, to access information in a database or to access data stored in logs. Accounts assigned to resources (such as a server instance) are sometimes called service accounts, while a human user is given a user account.

You can create accounts through the IAM dashboard in your cloud platform (see Figure 7-1). Here, you set the username, password, and permissions or create some other kind of credentials such as access keys or a certificate. You might require that users reset their passwords when they first sign in, and you might require certain standards for those passwords, such as length and complexity rules. Afterward, every time a user signs in with those credentials, the user is identified with the permissions and roles assigned to the user account.

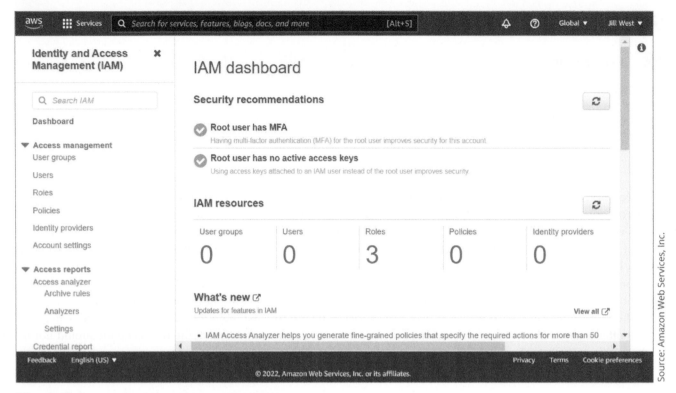

Figure 7-1   Create user accounts in AWS IAM

These identities and their credentials are stored in a repository called an identity vault, which might draw information from other authoritative sources (called sources of truth) and becomes the centralized source of truth for authentication and authorization functions in that cloud platform.

Account Management

Account management plays a key role in a successful IAM deployment. People come and go in an organization, and the existing user accounts at any given time should accurately reflect the people who can legitimately access digital resources. For example, when an employee leaves an organization for another job, that person's user account(s) should be disabled as a matter of course. Effective account management policies can help ensure that the following tasks occur reliably and consistently:

- Accounts are set up, or provisioned, in a timely manner for new users.
- Compromised accounts are locked out for protection.
- Privilege creep, the gradual increase of disorganized and unmonitored privileges, is limited.
- Unused accounts are closed to further activity, or deprovisioned.

Figure 7-2 shows the life cycle of user accounts from creation through deletion. An active account might be modified or deactivated and sometimes deleted. Typically, it's better to deactivate an account when an employee leaves the company in case there are resources only that account can access. That way, an admin could still access those protected resources, if needed.

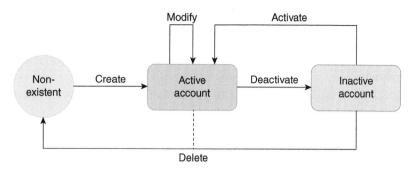

Figure 7-2   Once an account is created, it can be modified, deactivated, or possibly deleted

Another consideration in managing accounts is whether and when users should be given multiple accounts. For example, a user who needs administrative privileges to create new accounts might not need access to those privileges for day-to-day use. Using a different account for each level or type of privilege can help minimize inherent vulnerabilities from those privileges. Other reasons to generate multiple accounts per user include the need to limit visibility of workloads between groups or teams, to limit the so-called **blast radius** of a critical event such as a security breach, and to comply with strict regulations on data isolation and auditing activities.

Privileged Access Management (PAM)

PAM (privileged access management) is a subset of IAM that applies stricter rules and safety precautions specifically to users who are given elevated permissions to do their jobs. These users might have backend access to databases or other critical systems containing highly sensitive information. They can perform more sensitive tasks, such as viewing or changing financial information, making configuration changes, or adjusting access privileges for other users. These users are also more likely to be targeted by cyber criminals.

Security precautions that might be taken for these accounts include the following:

- *Limited use*—These accounts should only be used when higher privileges are necessary to accomplish a task. Employees who have a privileged user account should also have a lower-level account for normal activities. In fact, anyone who has a user account of any kind should be given only the least privilege, or least amount of access, needed to do a specific job.

- *Limited location*—Many companies require access to the privileged account only on premises so that no one, not even a legitimate network administrator, can access the device remotely and make high-level changes from outside the protected network.

- *Limited duration*—Privileged accounts should be carefully accounted for and disabled as soon as they're not needed, such as when an employee is terminated or transferred.

- *Limited access*—The passwords for these accounts should be especially secure and difficult to crack. Passwords should also be stored securely, and when possible, multifactor authentication should be required.

- *Limited privacy*—A privileged account can be used for destructive activity, whether malicious or not. For that reason, every user action in these accounts should be logged and monitored by someone other than the owner of that account.

PAM software is available from companies such as Imperva (imperva.com), ManageEngine (manageengine.com), and Splunk (splunk.com).

> ## Remember This
>
> - Both users and resources (such as an application) can have an identity, which is a digital entity to which you can attach roles and permissions.
> - Effective account management policies can help ensure that accounts are provisioned and deprovisioned in a timely manner, compromised accounts are locked out, and privilege creep is limited.
> - PAM (privileged access management) is a subset of IAM that applies stricter rules and safety precautions specifically to users who are given elevated permissions to do their jobs.

Self-Check

1. A user account is a(n) _____.

   a. root

   b. privileged account

   c. vault

   d. identity

2. What is a goal of successful account management?

   a. Limit users to one account each

   b. Expand a blast radius

   c. Limit privilege creep

   d. Increase time for account provisioning

3. When would a technician most likely need to use a privileged account?

   a. To store a report

   b. To create a user account

   c. To update a database record

   d. To check email

○ Check your answers at the end of this module.

Section 7-2: Authentication

> ### ● Certification
>
> 2.1 Given a scenario, configure identity and access management.
> -
> 2.3 Given a scenario, apply the appropriate OS and application security controls.
> -
> 2.4 Given a scenario, apply data security and compliance controls in cloud environments.
> -
> 3.1 Given a scenario, integrate components into a cloud solution.
> -
> 4.4 Given a scenario, apply proper automation and orchestration techniques.
> -
> 5.2 Given a scenario, troubleshoot security issues.

Once a user or service has an identity, there must be a way to validate that account before allowing access to resources. This is where authentication comes in. Authentication is part of a three-tiered approach to NAC (network access control) called AAA (authentication, authorization, and accounting) and pronounced "triple-A." Put simply:

- Authentication gets you into a system.
- Authorization lets you do things while you're there.
- Accounting tracks what you're doing for later review.

This section discusses authentication; you learn about authorization in the next section and you explore accounting techniques (logging and monitoring) in a later module.

Authentication Processes

Authentication is a process usually managed by a server that proves the identity of a client (which could be a user, service, or application) and determines whether that client is allowed to access a secured system. Essentially, it answers the question, "Who are you?" To confirm a client's identity, some sort of directory service must maintain a database of account information such as usernames, passwords, and any other authentication credentials. Often this is accomplished in AD (Active Directory), a Microsoft product that relies on the older NTLM (NT LAN Manager) authentication protocol or the newer and open-source Kerberos authentication protocol, or something more Linux focused such as OpenLDAP (openldap.org) or 389 Directory Server (directory.fedoraproject.org).

All these options are built to be LDAP compliant. LDAP (Lightweight Directory Access Protocol) is a standard protocol for accessing an existing directory. The mechanisms of LDAP dictate some basic requirements for any directory it accesses. Therefore, directory servers are configured and function in similar ways, regardless of the software used. LDAP can query the database, which means to draw information out of the database. It can also be used to add new information or edit existing data.

Authentication in the cloud also often relies on REST APIs. Let's break this down. An API (application programming interface), as you've already learned, is a request made in a specific format to an application or platform. It's a standardized means of communicating data between applications and services. For example, you might have an app that needs 360-degree panoramas of specific locations on a map. You can program the app to collect map data from Google's Street View Static API, knowing the data will be available as pure data that your app can easily incorporate into its algorithms.

REST (REpresentational State Transfer) is a kind of architecture standard that requires certain characteristics for HTTP or HTTPS communications over the web. A REST-compliant system, called a RESTful system, will conform to the following characteristics:

- Client and server systems run independently of each other. You can replace one or change the code on one without being concerned about how it will affect the other. This creates a modular separation of duties that allows for each to evolve separately.

- The server saves no client data. Session information is stored only on the client system. This means that either side can respond to a single message without having seen any earlier messages.

Now you can put API and REST concepts together in the context of authentication: RESTful APIs can be used to perform basic, standardized functions across the web to interact with an authentication directory. This allows organizations to set up relationships between various services or apps and the authentication service, knowing the communication standards will allow these different systems to reliably understand each other.

Password Policies

One way to increase security of user authentication is through a well-designed password policy. Password policies can require that passwords meet certain requirements, such as the following:

- *Complexity*—Password complexity can be increased by requiring a certain combination of character types, such as uppercase and lowercase letters, numbers, or non-alphanumeric characters.

- *Length*—According to many cybersecurity experts, password length is the factor most predictive of password security. Statistically, a long but simple password trumps a short but complex password almost every time.

- *Expiration*—Requiring users to change their passwords somewhat frequently increases password resistance to hacking. Often, you can also configure the policy to remember previous passwords and prevent users from reusing an earlier password.

- *Lockout*—An account lockout policy locks down an account after a specified number of failed attempts to sign in. A low lockout threshold (such as five attempts) reduces the risk of an attacker succeeding in guessing the right password. Some systems will also generate an alert for IT staff even after one or two failed login attempts.

Figure 7-3 shows the password policy options for AWS, and Figure 7-4 shows similar options for Azure, although these Azure options require a paid license to alter.

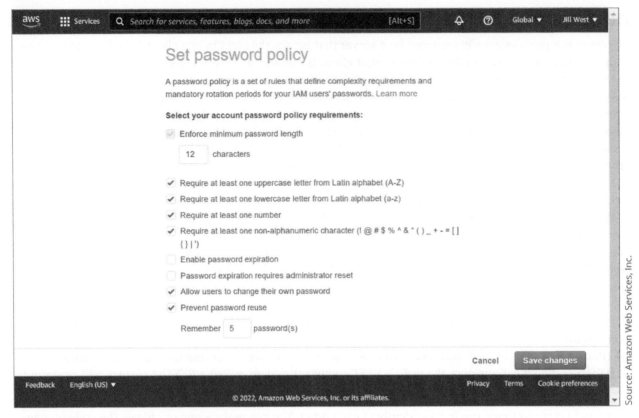

Figure 7-3 Set a password policy in AWS

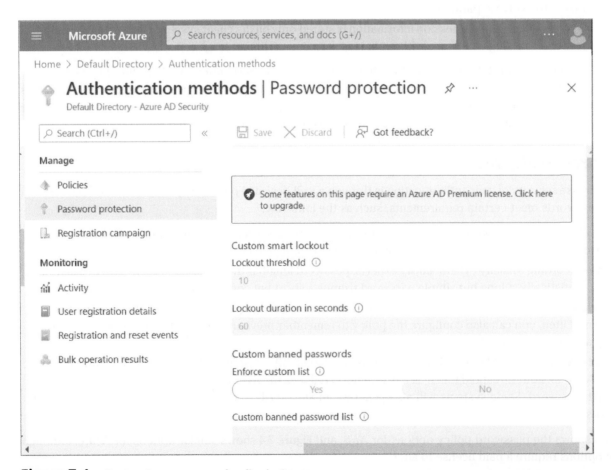

Figure 7-4 Customize a password policy in Azure

Note 2

One way to increase password security and also increase convenience is to use a password manager. A password manager such as LastPass (lastpass.com) or KeePass (keepass.info) securely stores passwords and other credentials in a **password vault**. The user enters a long, complex master password to sign into the password manager vault, which then auto-fills passwords in websites and can even generate highly complex and very long passwords. Password information for other resources can also be stored, such as application passwords or server credentials. Relying on a password manager can help users create longer, more complex passwords and avoid reusing passwords, both of which increase password security. Although no password manager can guarantee complete protection, using additional security methods such as multifactor authentication (described next) can provide a layer of assurance.

You're Ready

You're now ready to complete Project 7-1: Install and Use a Password Manager. You can complete the project now or wait until you've finished all the readings for this module.

Multifactor Authentication (MFA)

A simple form of authentication is providing a username and password. Most people are familiar with this process, and most people (especially IT professionals) are aware that this kind of authentication is readily cracked if the password is compromised. A major weakness of passwords is their susceptibility to social engineering attacks. Social engineering doesn't require a great deal of technical skill at all. In fact, "playing dumb" is often the best way to convince people to give out their information. Search on YouTube for examples of social engineering attacks and notice the techniques attackers use to successfully gain the trust of the person they're talking with.

One way to increase authentication security is by requiring MFA (multifactor authentication), which requires two or more pieces of information—called factors—from across two or more categories of authentication factors. The following is a list of the primary MFA factor categories with examples of each:

- *Something you know*—A password, PIN (personal identification number), or biographical data (such as first elementary school)

Figure 7-5
A smartphone 2FA app

- *Something you have*—An ATM card, ID badge, key, or smartphone with an authentication app
- *Something you are*—Your fingerprint, facial pattern, or iris pattern
- *Somewhere you are*—Your location in a specific geopolitical area (such as a country), a company's building, or a secured closet
- *Something you do*—The specific way you type, speak, or walk

MFA requires at least one factor from at least two different categories. For example, signing into a network might require a password (something you know), a fingerprint scan (something you are), plus a code generated by an app on your smartphone (something you must have with you to find the code). Figure 7-5 shows an app called Authy. A website-generated QR (quick response) code is requested to set up a new account for 2FA (two-factor authentication), such as a QR code provided by a social media site. Once established, a random six-digit code is generated every 30 seconds that must be entered on the secured site in addition to the user's password to access the account.

Google Authenticator, Google's number generator service, also provides free, software-based 2FA. You can use either of these apps to establish MFA in cloud platforms such as AWS. In fact, if you've not yet done so, this is a good time to set up MFA in your cloud accounts.

Certificate-Based Authentication

One example of a "something you have" authentication factor can be a digital certificate. You've already learned about how a key pair can be used to support secure encryption services. Public key encryption can also be used to prove the identity of a person, business, or server. This is accomplished through digital certificates.

A digital certificate is a small file containing verified identification information and the public key of the entity whose identity is being authenticated. If the public key can successfully decrypt data contained within the certificate, the entity has proven possession of both the public and private keys. Other information contained within the digital certificate provides additional identity information, which is validated by a third party called a CA (certificate authority). CAs issue, maintain, and validate digital certificates. CAs also maintain a CRL (certificate revocation list) to identify which certificates have been withdrawn prior to their expiration date and should not be trusted. The use of certificate authorities to associate public keys with certain users is known as PKI (public key infrastructure).

Digital certificates are primarily used to certify and secure websites where financial and other sensitive information is exchanged, but they're also used for other types of websites and to secure email communications, to authenticate client devices in a domain, or to authenticate users to a network. When surfing the web, at some point you might have gotten an error that said the website's SSL certificate was untrusted. This means the website's digital certificate used by the encryption protocol SSL (which was formerly used to secure HTTP) or TLS was not signed by a trusted CA or associated with a trusted root certificate.

Establishing and maintaining an organization's PKI can be expensive and complicated. Doing this on-prem requires significant infrastructure investment, and then the PKI services are limited to authentication of on-prem resources. By moving to a cloud-based PKI solution, companies can reduce overall expenditure while simplifying the work required to support PKI services and extending the reach of those services to cover both on-prem and cloud-based resources. Effective certificate management also includes monitoring certificates for compromise, revocation, or expiration and renewing certificates in a timely manner.

Grow with Cengage Unlimited!

If you'd like more information about digital certificates and PKI, use your Cengage Unlimited subscription to go to *CompTIA Security+ Guide to Network Security Fundamentals*, 7th edition, Module 7, and read the sections titled "Digital Certificates" and "Public Key Infrastructure (PKI)."

If you don't have a Cengage Unlimited subscription, you can find more information at cengage.com/unlimited.

Single Sign-On (SSO)

Security is always a tug-of-war between convenience and safety (see Figure 7-6). As you increase security functions to lock down a resource, convenience decreases. Conversely, as you increase the convenience of authentication or other security concerns, you sacrifice some of the assurance that your resources are secure.

This conflict isn't just theoretical. If security measures are too inconvenient, people won't use them and will find ways to get around security protocols. On the flip side, if you focus more on making these processes convenient for users, your resources won't truly be secure. The secret to good security is to find and use tools that increase both convenience (so people will use them correctly) and safety (so they keep your resources secure) and avoid sacrificing safety to increase convenience.

Single sign-on is one part of the solution to this conundrum. SSO (single sign-on) is a form of authentication in which a client signs in one time to access multiple systems or resources. This way,

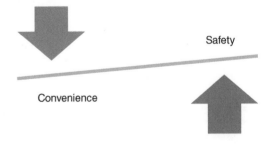

Figure 7-6 Convenience versus safety

users don't have to remember several passwords and, depending on the system configuration, might not need to complete the authentication process multiple times in a single work session for every new resource they need to access.

Many applications are designed to support SSO functionality through the use of standards such as SAML (Security Assertion Markup Language) or OpenID Connect, which relies on authentication by OAuth2 (Open Authorization). These standards bridge the connection between IdPs (identity providers) and SPs (service providers). SP websites can subscribe to managed directory and identity services offered by an IdP so the service provider does not have to manage identities and authentication themselves.

For example, you've likely seen the option on some websites to "Continue with Google," as shown in Figure 7-7, or "Sign in with Facebook." In these cases, Google and Facebook are acting as IdPs, offering a validated authentication of the user so the person can access whatever service the SP is offering (such as information, media, or retail access). To make applications readily compatible with these authentication mechanisms, developers often use pre-coded PAMs (pluggable authentication modules). A PAM is an authentication API designed to work with standardized input and output.

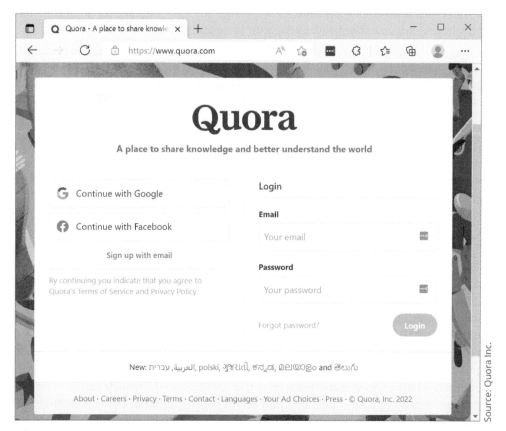

Source: Quora Inc.

Figure 7-7   Google and Facebook both function as identity providers

SSO offers the simplicity of using a single source of truth so user data isn't duplicated through multiple systems and the users themselves don't have to keep track of so many different sets of credentials. SSO can be implemented within a single organization that allows their users to access multiple services, or it might bridge services across multiple organizations. In this case, federation services create a trust relationship between organizations. Federation is the process of managing user identities across organizations on the foundation of this trust relationship.

Grow with Cengage Unlimited!

If you'd like more information about password security and SSO, use your Cengage Unlimited subscription to go to *CompTIA Security+ Guide to Network Security Fundamentals*, 7th edition, Module 12, and read the section titled "Authentication Solutions."

If you don't have a Cengage Unlimited subscription, you can find more information at cengage.com/unlimited.

Digital Signatures

When participating in financial or legal transactions, you often prove your identity through a handwritten signature or by entering a PIN (personal identification number). But how can you prove your identity when signing an electronic document so that later, you and others can know it is the document you signed, that you are the one who signed it, and that it has not been altered since you signed it?

To authenticate electronic documents as yours, you need to create a digital signature. A **digital signature** is a security procedure that uses public key cryptography and assigns a code to a document for which you alone have the key. The process involves the following steps:

1. The document is hashed using a hashing algorithm such as SHA-3. If either the document or the hash is altered, they will not match, and others will know the document is not yours or that it has been altered.
2. The hash is encrypted using your private key. The encrypted hash becomes the digital signature and is either stored with the document or transmitted with the document (or both).
3. Later, when someone needs to verify this is the document you signed, a new hash is created from the document. The original hash, which was encrypted with your private key, is decrypted with your public key, and the two hashes are compared. If the two hashes agree, the data was not tampered with, and the user's digital signature is valid. If they do not match, the document's integrity must be questioned.

One drawback to this system is that if someone discovers your private key, a digital signature could be forged. Another challenge involves the complexity of creating and managing key pairs. What if someone doesn't have a public key and private key pair, or doesn't have the resources to post the public key as needed? While the digital signature technique requires a key pair, an e-signature does not. An e-signature can be a digital version of a handwritten signature or, alternatively, it might consist of any electronic sound, symbol, or process intended by the user to approve or accept the terms of an agreement. It is typically associated with other identifying information, such as the user's device IP address.

In 2000, the U.S. government approved the ESIGN (Electronic Signatures in Global and National Commerce) Act, and similar legislation has long been in place for many other countries as well. This legislation grants digital signatures and e-signatures in electronic documents the same legal standing as that of handwritten signatures on pieces of paper. It is important to note, however, there are restrictions and exceptions. For example, although home loans and mortgages may be digitally signed, documents such as divorce agreements, wills, and adoption contracts still need old-fashioned, pen-and-paper signatures.

While a digital signature is different from a digital certificate used in PKI (public key infrastructure), it does play an integral role in public key encryption. Recall that a digital certificate is an electronic document similar to a passport that establishes your credentials when you are performing transactions on the web. It can contain your name, a serial number, expiration dates, a copy of your public key, and the digital signature of the certificate-issuing authority (to allow you to verify that the certificate is legitimate). Certificates are usually kept in a registry so that other users may look up a user's public key information.

Securing Secrets

Information such as private keys and certificates must be carefully managed to ensure they are available when legitimately needed but not vulnerable to discovery by attackers or unauthorized users. Let's explore some of the technologies used in safely storing and using these sensitive files.

Secrets Management

Secrets management systems handle the security and distribution of keys, passwords, authorization tokens, and other files used to secure access to resources. Many cloud platforms include native tools for handling these kinds of secrets. For example, AWS offers Secrets Manager, which supports the secure storage, retrieval, rotation, and retirement of secrets such as database credentials, API keys, and OAuth tokens. Figure 7-8 shows some of the options for storing a new secret in Secrets Manager.

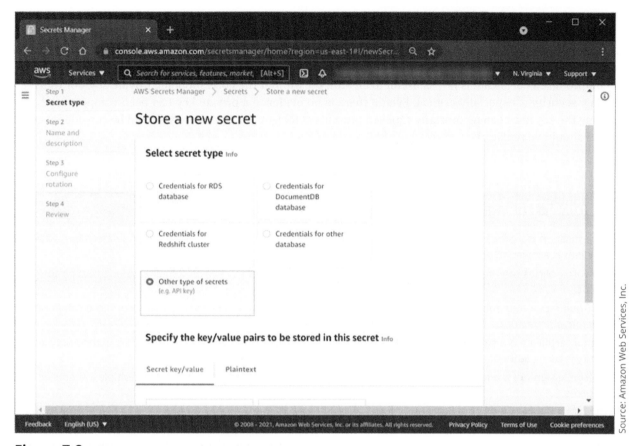

Figure 7-8   Store a secret as a key-value pair

Securely storing secrets in password vaults and similar services avoids the need to hard-code this sensitive information into applications, configuration management scripts, and other cloud resources. For example, an application might expose an API endpoint that other applications can use to allow both applications to interact with each other. This connection requires some kind of authentication, such as providing an authorization token or a private key. Instead of storing these secrets in the code of the application requesting authentication, they are encrypted in storage or generated only when needed. An application, script, or other resource can request access to the secret at the time of use, which is then securely transmitted to the authorized service or process. Access to these secrets is also logged for live monitoring and retroactive analysis, as needed.

Status of Certificates

Part of the management of secrets, such as keys and certificates, includes identifying trusted or revoked certificates. The following list describes various certificate statuses:

- **Good**—A secret is good, or trusted, during the timeframe when it was approved (i.e., it has not yet reached its expiration date), and there is no indication it has been compromised.
- **Retired**—Once a certificate reaches its expiration date, it is retired and can no longer be used.
- **Revoked**—If there is any indication the secret has been compromised or destroyed, or if the secret is no longer needed (such as when an employee leaves a company), the secret must be revoked.

To revoke a certificate, the CA (certificate authority) that issued the certificate requires submission of a revocation request, and sometimes supporting evidence will need to be included. Once revoked, the certificate is added to a CRL (certificate revocation list), which other entities can check to confirm whether a certificate has become invalidated. However, these lists are not consistently checked because they are long, flat files that take a while to download and search. Therefore, a revoked certificate might still sometimes be used successfully to perform unauthorized access or to impersonate someone else. Alternatively, a revoked certificate might be identified with OCSP (Online Certificate Status Protocol), which offers an updated and scalable method of tracking certificate revocation. The OCSP server collects CRLs from multiple CAs and can respond to requests for a certificate's status.

A compromised certificate is not as useful to an attacker without the corresponding private key. For this reason, private key security is especially critical. Even if there is no evidence a private key has been compromised, simply discovering the key has been temporarily exposed presents sufficient risk that the key should be considered compromised and should be replaced.

Remember This

- Authentication is a process usually managed by a server that proves the identity of a client and determines whether that client is allowed to access a secured system.
- Password policies can require that passwords meet certain requirements, such as complexity, length, expiration, and lockout.
- MFA (multifactor authentication) requires two or more pieces of information from across two or more categories of authentication factors.
- A digital certificate is a small file containing verified identification information and the public key of the entity whose identity is being authenticated.
- SSO (single sign-on) is a form of authentication in which a client signs in one time to access multiple systems or resources.
- A digital signature is a security procedure that uses public key cryptography and assigns a code to a document for which only the signer has the key.
- A secrets management system handles the security and distribution of keys, passwords, authorization tokens, and other files used to secure access to resources.

Self-Check

4. Which protocol defines how most authentication directories work?

   a. LDAP
   b. OCSP

   c. HTTPS
   d. MFA

5. If a certificate is included in a CRL, what is its status?

   a. Retired
   b. Revoked

   c. Trusted
   d. Renewed

6. Which authentication technique bridges the gap across IdPs and SPs?

   a. Secrets management
   b. Active Directory

   c. Federation
   d. Password vault

○ Check your answers at the end of this module.

Section 7-3: Authorization to Cloud Objects

Certification

2.1 Given a scenario, configure identity and access management.

2.3 Given a scenario, apply the appropriate OS and application security controls.

2.4 Given a scenario, apply data security and compliance controls in cloud environments.

3.1 Given a scenario, integrate components into a cloud solution.

While authentication gets you into a system, authorization determines what you can do while you're there. For example, if you sign into the AWS Management Console as the root user, you're then authorized to do pretty much anything with the resources, services, and processes contained in that account. However, if you're using a different user account, such as a web developer user or a network admin user, you're only authorized for limited actions.

Each cloud platform manages IAM permissions in different ways. For example, all three of the major public cloud platforms that you're learning about in this course (AWS, Azure, and GCP) control access to system resources—such as compute services, storage, or virtual networks—by managing requests to access those resources. However, each platform uses different terminology and access control architecture. This section evaluates these variations.

AWS Identity and Access Management (IAM)

AWS, like the other platforms mentioned, creates a user object to represent a human or another resource. That user is given permissions, and each permission allows the user to access a certain resource or service and perform a certain action on that resource or service. Meanwhile, AWS can track each user's activities and collect that information in a logging system that can be used during an audit or investigation to account for changes made within the AWS cloud. The following list details IAM terms as used in the AWS environment:

- *User*—A user is an identity that represents a person or an application that needs to interact with AWS resources. The user itself is also an AWS resource and is limited to the account in which it was created. A user has a name, an ARN (Amazon Resource Number), and credentials such as a password, access keys (including an access key ID and a secret access key), or a server certificate.

- *Root user*—The root user is the original identity from when you first create an AWS account. It has all access to all services and resources in your account. When using AWS in your work outside of school, you should never use the root user for typical day-to-day activities. Amazon recommends that you use the root user only long enough to create the first IAM user, and then store the root user credentials in a secure location for emergency access only.

- *Group*—A group is an identity that represents a collection of users. You can assign permissions to multiple users at one time by making them part of a group. A user can belong to multiple groups, but groups cannot contain other groups.

- *Permission*—A permission defines a specific action that an identity (i.e., a user, group, or role) is allowed to take. For example, a user might be permitted to create a new VM.

- *Policy*—A policy is a collection of permissions and is assigned to an identity (user, group, role), as shown in Figure 7-9. There are different kinds of policies. For example, an identity-based policy grants permissions to an identity. An ACL (access control list), on the other hand, is assigned to a resource to identify who from outside the account can access that resource. In AWS, you assign policies to users or roles to manage permissions. That way, you can add or take away permissions without having to manage each permission or user account separately. For example, imagine you run a bank with 12 tellers who need certain permissions to perform actions for their jobs. You can create a Teller policy that gives all teller users the same permissions. If the tellers later need a new permission, you can change the permissions assigned to the Teller policy, and all teller users will receive the updated permission. If one employee who worked as a teller is later promoted to a different position, you can change the policy attached to that employee's user account without having to reconfigure each individual permission.

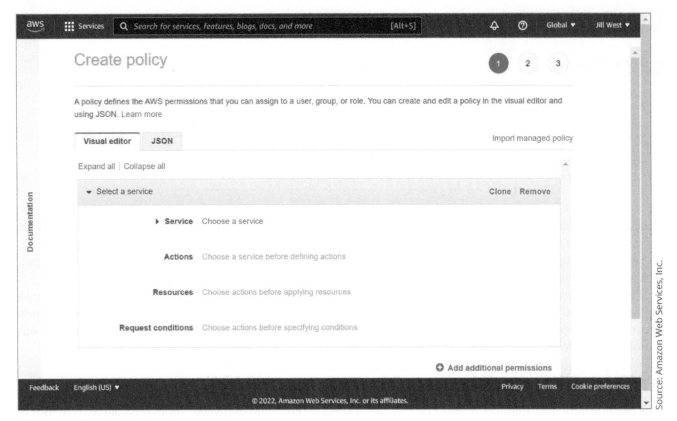

Figure 7-9 A policy defines an action that can be performed

- *Role*—A role is an identity that provides a way to assign policies to other resources for a short duration. In some ways, a role is an identity similar to a user except it's used to assign policies to other resources based on temporary credentials that are rotated automatically. This is helpful, for example, when you want to give a mobile app short-term access to a resource without having to store long-term user credentials (such as access keys) in the app. You can also use roles to temporarily assign permissions to a user, such as when an engineer is working on a short-term project or when a network administrator needs to temporarily access higher permissions to execute an approved change.

Note 3

In short, a user or group is given access permissions through attachment to a policy or through temporary assignment of a role. A resource (such as an EC2 instance) is given permissions by being assigned a role.

When setting permissions in a policy for a user, group, or role, be sure to limit access to the least privilege needed. For example, if a group of users needs to be able to read data in a database, don't also give that group the ability to write data to the database. This is called the **principle of least privilege**. Give only the minimum permissions needed for the users in that group to be able to perform their job duties.

You're Ready

You're now ready to complete Project 7-2: Manage Users and Permissions in AWS. You can complete the project now or wait until you've finished all the readings for this module.

Azure Identity and Access Management (IAM)

Azure manages IAM services through Azure AD (Active Directory). Azure AD is the cloud-native cousin of Active Directory found in Windows Server for on-prem networks. Active Directory offers many services for the on-prem network, including the following:

- *Domain Services (AD DS)*—Provides authentication and authorization support for users and devices on an organization's network
- *Certificate Services (AD CS)*—Creates, distributes, and manages secure certificates
- *Lightweight Directory Services (AD LDS)*—Supports applications that rely on LDAP
- *Federation Services (AD FS)*—Supports SSO
- *Rights Management Services (AD RMS)*—Provides IRM (information rights management) protection of data by enforcing data access policies

One of the defining aspects of AD is its hierarchical structure, as shown in Figure 7-10. The all-encompassing container is the forest. Within a forest, you can have many domains branching out to multiple layers. A root domain along with its branch domains collectively is called a tree. Within each domain, you might have multiple OUs (organizational units). Inside the OUs is where you'll find leaf objects, such as users, computers, or printers.

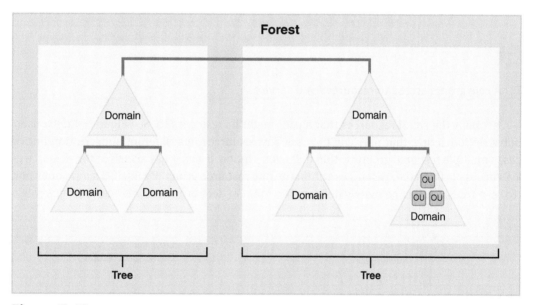

Figure 7-10   A forest contains trees, which contain domains, which contain OUs

In contrast, Azure AD uses a flat-file structure. This means there is no container hierarchy like OUs or forests. Azure AD does use a domain, but this is more of a naming system and not designed to hold OUs or leaf objects. Azure AD relies instead on groups, such as resource groups or user groups. The following is a list of terms you need to know for working with Azure AD:

- *User*—A user is an identity associated with a person's profile.
- *Group*—A group is a collection of users.
- *Service principal*—A service principal is an identity for an application or a service.
- *Permission*—A permission defines an action an identity is allowed to take.
- *Role*—A role definition, or role for short, is a collection of permissions. See Figure 7-11. Four of Azure's built-in roles include:
    - *Owner*—The owner has complete access to all resources and can give access to others.
    - *Administrator*—An administrator has full access to resources within that role.

○ ***Contributor***—A contributor can create and manage resources but can't give access to others.

○ ***Reader***—A reader can view existing resources but can't make changes.

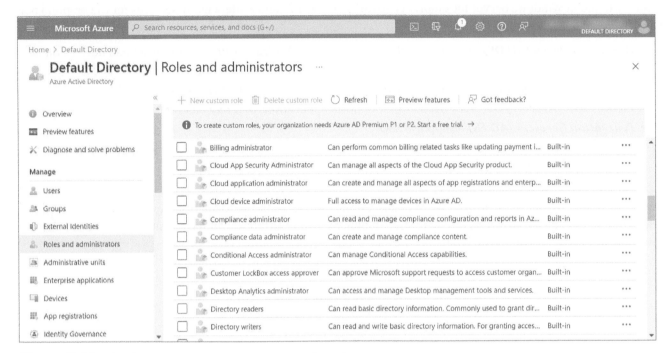

Figure 7-11   A role grants access to resources and services

- ***Scope***—A scope is the set of resources that a user might have access to. See Figure 7-12. If a user has access at the subscription scope, that user can't access any resources in a different subscription but could access resources in multiple resource groups within that subscription. If a user has access at the resource group scope, that user's access is limited to resources within the one resource group. By itself, a scope does not give a user access to resources. The scope merely defines the extent of access a user *can* receive from a role assignment.

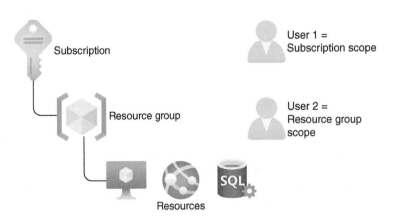

Figure 7-12   A scope defines which resources a user might have access to

- ***Role assignment***—A role assignment defines the connection of a user to a role within that user's scope and must be completed for access to be granted to a user.

Azure relies on **RBAC (role-based access control)** to manage users' access to resources. With RBAC (also called nondiscretionary access control), a network administrator receives from a user's supervisor a detailed description of the roles or jobs the user performs for the organization. The admin is responsible for assigning exactly the privileges and permissions necessary for the user to perform these roles. The admin creates a role with the needed privileges and permissions for each job, and then the admin creates a user group associated with one or more roles. Users are assigned to groups that match the roles they need to do their jobs. RBAC in Azure is additive, so each additional role given to a user increases that user's access to resources.

In contrast to RBAC, other popular access control methods you need to know about include the following:

- DAC (discretionary access control) is the least secure of these methods. With DAC, users decide for themselves who has access to their resources. You might have used DAC when setting share permissions on a Windows computer to determine who on your home network has access to your files.

- MAC (mandatory access control) is the most restrictive of these methods. In this case, resources are organized into hierarchical data classifications, such as "confidential" or "top secret." Resources are also grouped into categories—for example, by department. Users, then, are also classified and categorized. If a user's classification and category match those of a resource, then the user is given access.

Note 4

Another access control type you might encounter—which can be confusing because it reuses one of the same acronyms—is rule-based access control. This method relies on access rules, such as time of day or source IP address. When users present their credentials to authenticate, they are then given access to the protected resource only if the defined rules are met.

Grow with Cengage Unlimited!

If you'd like more information about access control models, use your Cengage Unlimited subscription to go to *CompTIA Network+ Guide to Networks*, 9th edition, Module 11, and read the section titled "Authentication, Authorization, and Accounting (AAA)."

If you don't have a Cengage Unlimited subscription, you can find more information at cengage.com/unlimited.

You're Ready

You're now ready to complete Project 7-3: Research Azure Active Directory. You can complete the project now or wait until you've finished all the readings for this module.

GCP Identity and Access Management (IAM)

GCP uses many of the same terms as Azure does and with very similar definitions, as listed here:

- *User*—A user is a GCP member who has a Google account associated with their email account.
- *Service account*—A service account is an account associated with an application or other resource instead of a person's email. Note that a service account is given its own email address when the account is created.
- *Group*—A Google group is a collection of Google accounts (users) and service accounts, and the group has its own email address.
- *Permission*—A permission defines an operation allowed on a resource, such as a VM instance or a storage bucket. You can grant permissions at the project level or, in some cases, on a specific resource. Permissions are defined in the form <service>.<resource>.<verb>, such as compute.instances.delete.
- *Role*—A role is a collection of permissions and can be granted to a user, service account, or group. You can grant a predefined role that allows granular access control or create a custom role to tailor permissions, as shown in Figure 7-13.

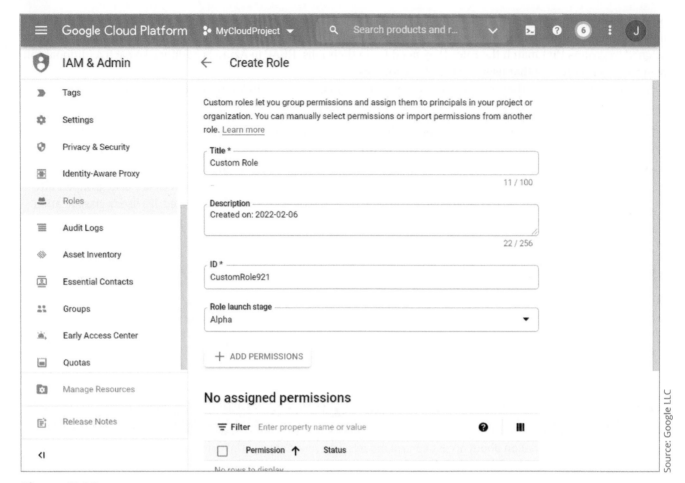

Figure 7-13 Customize permissions added to a role

- *Policy*—A policy contains a collection of statements that define who has what type of access. The policy grants, or binds, a role to a user. It's also attached to a resource, such as a project or VM instance, to enforce access control on that resource.

You're Ready

You're now ready to complete Project 7-4: Manage Users in GCP. You can complete the project now or wait until you've finished all the readings for this module.

Remember This

- AWS creates a user object to represent a human or another resource, which is given permissions, and each permission allows the user to access a certain resource or service and perform a certain action on that resource or service.
- Azure manages IAM services through Azure AD (Active Directory), which is the cloud-native cousin of Active Directory found in Windows Server.
- A GCP user has a Google account associated with their email account, while a service account is an account associated with an application or other resource.

Self-Check

7. AWS users receive long-term permissions through an attached _____.
    a. service
    b. policy
    c. root
    d. role

8. What access control method does Azure use?
    a. AD
    b. RBAC
    c. DAC
    d. MAC

9. What resource defines a set of permissions in GCP?
    a. Group
    b. Policy
    c. Service account
    d. Role

○ Check your answers at the end of this module.

Section 7-4: IAM for Hybrid Clouds

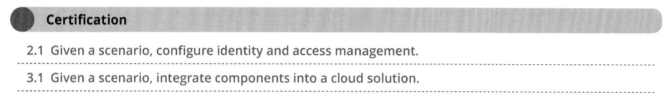

Certification

2.1 Given a scenario, configure identity and access management.
- -
3.1 Given a scenario, integrate components into a cloud solution.
- -

With so many organizations camping out somewhere in the middle of the spectrum between all-cloud and everything on-prem, managing identity and access across a hybrid cloud becomes essential. One way to do this is to adapt on-prem AAA methods to the cloud environment. For example, you might install Active Directory on a VM server in the cloud. As you've seen throughout this course, however, much of the advantage of moving to the cloud is only realized when deploying cloud-native solutions. IAM is no different in this regard.

Consider each of the elements of identity management that you've been reading about in this module: identification, authentication, authorization, federation, certificate services, and multifactor authentication. Let's examine some of the available hybrid solutions in the AWS, Azure, and GCP clouds.

AWS IAM in a Hybrid or Multi-Cloud

AWS offers AWS Managed Microsoft AD, also called AWS Directory Service for Microsoft Active Directory (or just Directory Service for short). This service is essentially Active Directory in the AWS cloud.

Directory Service is a managed directory service in AWS and can apply AD features, such as Group Policy and SSO, to other AWS services, such as EC2 or RDS (Relational Database Service). Directory Service can also support traditional AD applications such as Remote Desktop, SharePoint, and SQL Server. The AWS Directory Service coverage area can extend beyond AWS-hosted resources, as shown in Figure 7-14.

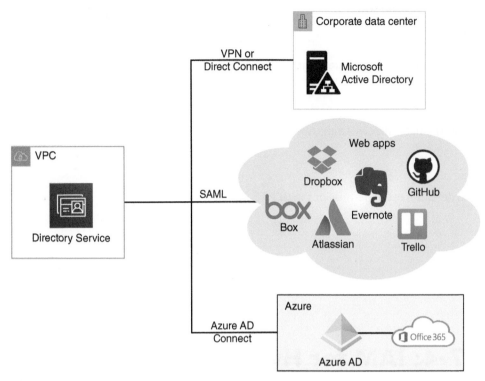

Figure 7-14   Use AWS Directory Service with many kinds of services

Specifically relevant to extending AAA from an on-prem AD to AWS, an AD trust relationship can be established between AWS Directory Service and the on-prem AD, as shown in Figure 7-15.

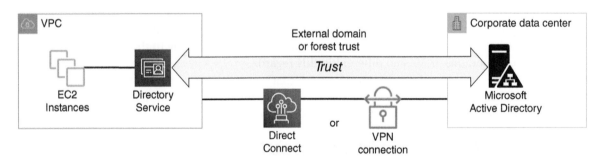

Figure 7-15   Extend AAA from on-prem Active Directory to AWS

Alternatively, user credentials can authenticate to web apps such as Dropbox or Salesforce using SAML. For organizations running Azure AD, the Azure AD Connect service can provide pass-through authentication to AWS Directory Service, which is particularly relevant with Azure-hosted Office 365.

Azure IAM in a Hybrid Cloud

Azure offers three options for integrating IAM services in the cloud with on-prem workloads, as shown in Figure 7-16 and described next.

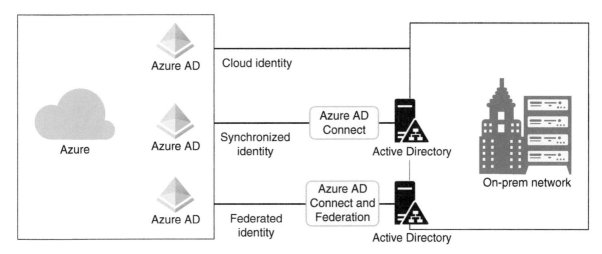

Figure 7-16   Azure hybrid cloud options

- *Cloud identity*—The pass-through authentication option consists of all IAM services residing in the cloud and includes limited synchronization of passwords or other credentials.
- *Synchronized identity*—With the synchronized authentication option, identities exist both on-prem and in the cloud, and password hashes are shared between the two locations. As changes are made in one place, that information is synced to the other location. However, there can be a delay of up to three hours when disabling a user on-prem, leaving cloud resources vulnerable to that user's credentials during the delay.
- *Federated identity*—Federated authentication is the more complicated and expensive option, offering more complete SSO functionality and immediate synchronization between locations so that approvals or deletions propagate throughout both the on-prem and cloud portions of the network simultaneously. This arrangement maintains a more consistent access policy.

GCP IAM in a Hybrid Cloud

Google suggests using one of two approaches to extend identity services across a hybrid cloud, as follows:

- Extend the existing IdP (such as Active Directory) to GCP. Figure 7-17 shows an example of an on-prem Active Directory that has been extended across a Cloud VPN or an Interconnect connection to an AD domain controller running in a GCP VM.

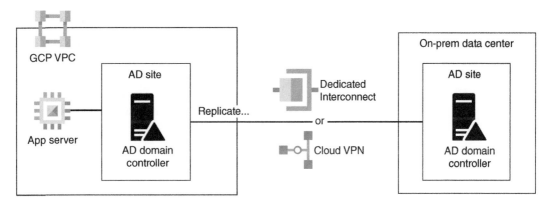

Figure 7-17   The GCP-hosted AD domain controller services GCP resources

- Federate the existing IdP with GCP's Cloud Identity service. Cloud Identity is a robust, paid service within Cloud IAM that includes app and device management in addition to identity and access management. In Figure 7-18, GCP's Cloud Identity serves as an IdP for GCP resources, and a trust relationship is established between Cloud Identity and the on-prem Active Directory.

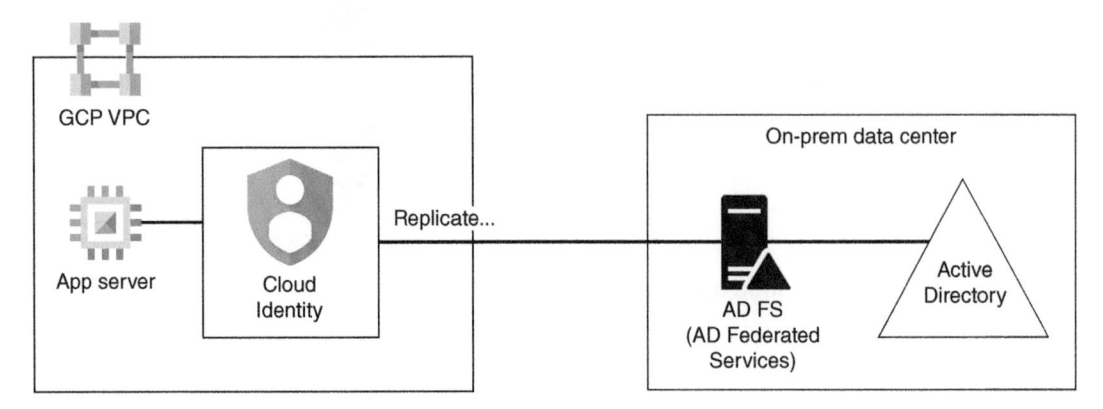

Figure 7-18   GCP's Cloud Identity service provides IAM functions for GCP resources

Remember This

- Directory Service is a managed directory service in AWS and can apply AD features, such as Group Policy and SSO, to other AWS services, such as EC2 or RDS (Relational Database Service).
- Azure offers three options for integrating IAM services in the cloud with on-prem workloads: cloud identity, synchronized identity, and federated identity.
- Google suggests using one of two approaches to extend identity services across a hybrid cloud: extend the existing IdP to GCP or federate the existing IdP with GCP's Cloud Identity service.

Self-Check

10. True or False: Active Directory can only be run on-prem.

    a. True

    b. False

11. Which of the following is the most difficult configuration for extending IAM across a hybrid cloud?

    a. Synchronization

    b. Federation

    c. Pass-through (i.e., authentication occurs in the cloud)

    d. Extension

○ Check your answers at the end of this module.

Section 7-5: Troubleshooting Cloud IAM

Certification

5.2 Given a scenario, troubleshoot security issues.

5.4 Given a scenario, troubleshoot connectivity issues.

Most IAM problems you face when you begin working in the cloud are the responsibility of more qualified cloud administrators. However, there are some symptoms that, if you know what to look for, can indicate where the problem is located and what kind of action will be needed to fix the problem. Having these kinds of insights can help you ask better questions as you're initially investigating a problem, even if it will likely be elevated to a higher support tier.

Common IAM Issues

Consider the following common authentication and authorization issues:

- *Authentication issues*—Authentication issues can be caused by expired credentials, mistyped passwords, misconfigured certificates, or misconfigured trust relationships. Repeatedly attempting to access an account with wrong or expired credentials can cause it to lock out, which protects the account from brute force attacks. If a user is locked out, an admin with sufficient privileges will need to reset the account's credentials. Specific examples of issues and their solutions include the following:
  - *Expired certificate*—Most certificates renew automatically, or the system prompts an admin to approve the renewal process. An expired certificate error could be caused by an incorrect time on your local computer. If the certificate truly is expired, you might need to replace it with a new one.
  - *Misconfigured certificate*—First confirm you're attempting to use the correct certificate. If that doesn't work, replace it with a new one with the correct configurations.
  - *Federation and single sign-on issues*—SSO issues are often caused by mistyping the username (such as entering an email address instead of the username, or vice versa). Double-check the credentials being used. Also check the trust configuration between the SSO service (such as AWS SSO) and the service provider's application.
- *Authorization issues*—Authorization issues are often caused by misconfigured permissions, groups, or roles. Read the error message carefully for clues, and check permissions, policies, and resource levels for referenced policies or permissions. Also consider that switching to a different internal role (within your organization's account) or an external role (in a business partner's account) changes your permissions. You can only use one set of permissions at a time, so if you're not able to access the resources you think you should be seeing, check that you're using the correct role.

Troubleshooting Privilege Issues

When distributing privileges for activities in the cloud, it's important to limit privileges to the minimum required for someone to do their job. As you learned earlier, this is called the principle of least privilege. In the interest of minimizing each person's permissions, however, you might find that someone doesn't have permissions they need for their job. Missing or incomplete privileges can be resolved by confirming the person does, in fact, need the identified privileges, and then assigning those privileges to that person's account. In AWS, for example, these privileges might be assigned by attaching a new policy to the user's account or by giving the user access to a new role. Figure 7-19 shows where you can assign policies to a new user.

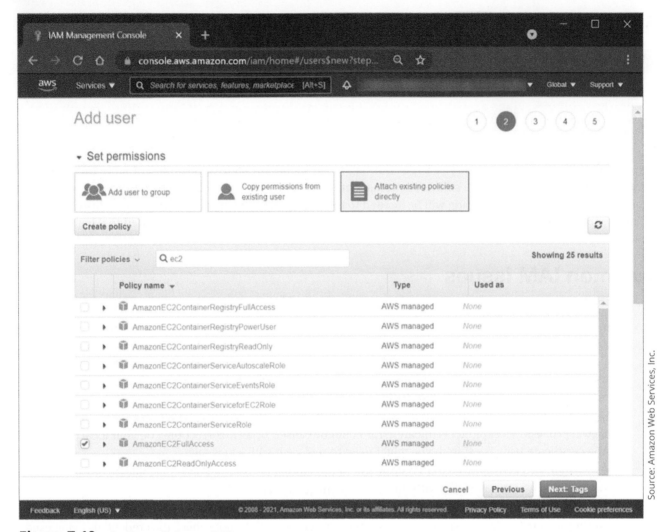

Figure 7-19   Assign policies to AWS user

In contrast to missing or incomplete privileges, attackers can also use existing privileges—or even just basic, unprivileged access—to perform a privilege escalation attack. There are two types of privilege escalation attacks:

- *Horizontal*—In a horizontal attack, the attacker uses typical user privileges to access information available to the compromised account, such as information about other users. This attack type is typically used for reconnaissance.

- *Vertical*—In a vertical attack, the attacker escalates privileges by manipulating privileges granted to the account being used or using the current account to gain access to more privileged accounts. This attack type requires more sophisticated skills to manipulate privilege assignments.

A system is vulnerable to these attacks through misconfigurations or system loopholes. For example, a user with permission to attach a role to a user group could give themselves a role with full administrative access. The following best practices can help reduce a cloud system's vulnerability to privilege escalation attacks:

- Use wildcards sparingly when creating permission policies because these wildcards can inadvertently grant permissions beyond the minimum required for a user to perform their job duties.

- Design permission policies as specifically as possible to avoid giving more privileges than intended.

- Design an overall IAM approach that clearly identifies the purpose of each policy and role.

- Use directory security groups to logically organize users according to the permissions they should have and to provide better oversight of each user's permissions.

- Watch for inherited permissions where membership in one group provides access that is denied in another group or in a subgroup.
- Require MFA for every user account.
- Enable logging as well as tools that monitor these logs, and frequently check the logs yourself to identify signs of unapproved changes to users, groups, roles, and policies.
- Use platform-specific tools designed to monitor IAM access and configurations.

Remember This

- Authentication issues can be caused by expired credentials, mistyped passwords, misconfigured certificates, or misconfigured trust relationships, whereas authorization issues are often caused by misconfigured permissions, groups, or roles.
- Missing or incomplete privileges can be resolved by first confirming the person does, in fact, need the identified privileges, and then assigning those privileges to that person's account.

Self-Check

12. An expired certificate is a(n) _____ issue.
    - **a.** authorization
    - **b.** accounting
    - **c.** authentication
    - **d.** privilege

13. What kind of attack causes changed account privileges?
    - **a.** External
    - **b.** Internal
    - **c.** Horizontal
    - **d.** Vertical

○ Check your answers at the end of this module.

Module Summary

Section 7-1: Cloud Accounts

- Both users and resources (such as an application) can have an identity, which is a digital entity to which you can attach roles and permissions.
- Effective account management policies can help ensure that accounts are provisioned and deprovisioned in a timely manner, compromised accounts are locked out, and privilege creep is limited.
- PAM (privileged access management) is a subset of IAM that applies stricter rules and safety precautions specifically to users who are given elevated permissions to do their jobs.

Section 7-2: Authentication

- Authentication is a process usually managed by a server that proves the identity of a client and determines whether that client is allowed to access a secured system.
- Password policies can require that passwords meet certain requirements, such as complexity, length, expiration, and lockout.

- MFA (multifactor authentication) requires two or more pieces of information from across two or more categories of authentication factors.
- A digital certificate is a small file containing verified identification information and the public key of the entity whose identity is being authenticated.
- SSO (single sign-on) is a form of authentication in which a client signs in one time to access multiple systems or resources.
- A digital signature is a security procedure that uses public key cryptography and assigns a code to a document for which only the signer has the key.
- A secrets management system handles the security and distribution of keys, passwords, authorization tokens, and other files used to secure access to resources.

Section 7-3: Authorization to Cloud Objects

- AWS creates a user object to represent a human or another resource, which is given permissions, and each permission allows the user to access a certain resource or service and perform a certain action on that resource or service.
- Azure manages IAM services through Azure AD (Active Directory), which is the cloud-native cousin of Active Directory found in Windows Server.
- A GCP user has a Google account associated with their email account, while a service account is an account associated with an application or other resource.

Section 7-4: IAM for Hybrid Clouds

- Directory Service is a managed directory service in AWS and can apply AD features, such as Group Policy and SSO, to other AWS services, such as EC2 or RDS (Relational Database Service).
- Azure offers three options for integrating IAM services in the cloud with on-prem workloads: cloud identity, synchronized identity, and federated identity.
- Google suggests using one of two approaches to extend identity services across a hybrid cloud: extend the existing IdP to GCP or federate the existing IdP with GCP's Cloud Identity service.

Section 7-5: Troubleshooting Cloud IAM

- Authentication issues can be caused by expired credentials, mistyped passwords, misconfigured certificates, or misconfigured trust relationships, whereas authorization issues are often caused by misconfigured permissions, groups, or roles.
- Missing or incomplete privileges can be resolved by first confirming the person does, in fact, need the identified privileges, and then assigning those privileges to that person's account.

Key Terms

For definitions of key terms, see the Glossary.

AD (Active Directory)	IAM (identity and access management)	password vault
authentication		PKI (public key infrastructure)
blast radius	identity	principle of least privilege
DAC (discretionary access control)	logical access control	privilege escalation attack
digital certificate	MAC (mandatory access control)	RBAC (role-based access control)
digital signature	MFA (multifactor authentication)	root
federation	PAM (privileged access management)	secrets management
		SSO (single sign-on)

Acronyms Checklist

The acronyms in Table 7-1 are listed in the Cloud+ objectives and could appear on the Cloud+ exam. This means that exam questions might use any of these acronyms in context so that you must know the meaning of the acronym to answer the question correctly. Make sure you're familiar with what each acronym stands for and the general concept of the term itself. All these acronyms are used in context in this module.

Table 7-1   Module 7 acronyms

Acronym	Spelled out
AAA	authentication, authorization, and accounting
CRL	certificate revocation list
DAC	discretionary access control
LDAP	Lightweight Directory Access Protocol
MAC	mandatory access control
MFA	multifactor authentication
NAC	network access control
PKI	public key infrastructure
SAML	Security Assertion Markup Language
SSO	single sign-on

Review Questions

1. Which of the following employees will most likely need a cloud privileged user account?

   a. A sales manager who trains sales reps on how to use a new application
   b. A custodian who needs access to every office for cleaning
   c. A new hire who must submit employment documents to HR
   d. A technician who helps users reset passwords

2. Which part of AAA lets you perform the creation of an EC2 instance?

   a. Accounting
   b. Authentication
   c. Authorization
   d. Auditing

3. When signing an electronic document, what secret must you keep?

   a. The other party's public key
   b. Your identity
   c. Your private key
   d. The other party's private key

4. Which of the following combinations is MFA?

   a. ATM card and smartphone
   b. Fingerprint and password
   c. Password and PIN
   d. Fingerprint and facial pattern

5. When Lisa needs access to make edits to the tables in a database, her boss gives her user account the same role he has. What tenet of IAM security has been compromised?

   a. Privilege escalation
   b. Password complexity
   c. Mandatory access control
   d. Least privilege

6. Which key is used to decrypt information contained within a server's digital certificate?

   a. The server's private key
   b. The server's public key
   c. The client's private key
   d. The client's public key

7. Which access control method is controlled by individual users?

   a. DAC
   b. MAC
   c. RBAC
   d. NAC

8. Which technology ensures a cluster of servers can handle incoming requests without having to track individual conversations?

   a. HTTPS
   b. LDAP
   c. API
   d. REST

9. Haphazardly adding permissions every time someone needs to do a new task causes increased _____.

   a. inheritance drift
   b. privilege creep
   c. privilege escalation attacks
   d. blast radius

10. Which standard supports SSO?

   a. SAML
   b. LDAP
   c. REST
   d. PKI

Scenario-Based Questions

Question 7-1

Kason works for a real estate company that owns and manages apartment complexes. He recently deployed a new application designed to track maintenance calls for apartments across three of his company's larger properties. The information is stored in an AWS RDS (Relational Database Service) database. Kason designed the database with the intent of expanding this app to track much more information than just maintenance calls. However, he's currently experiencing problems with the connection between the app and the database. It seems the database is not yet aware that the app is allowed to work with the information stored there. What kind of IAM account should Kason check to confirm its permissions are configured correctly?

   a. Service account
   b. Root user
   c. User account
   d. Application account

Question 7-2

Paulo has configured multifactor authentication on his AWS account using a virtual MFA application on his phone. When he signs into his account on a computer in his school's computer lab, he is prompted to enter his password, and then he's asked for a code from his phone's app. Which category of MFA does the code represent?

   a. Something you are
   b. Something you know
   c. Something you have
   d. Something you do

Question 7-3

Alicia and her two business partners have been steadily building their homegrown company that sells custom-embroidered bags and other accessories. They've recently received a few large contracts that required them to invest in new machinery, and they want to expand their customer base to help keep that machinery working at full capacity. Alicia, the IT specialist in her company, decided to invest in a Salesforce subscription so that she, her business partners, and their sales reps can better track their sales efforts. She already has a website running in AWS and wants to set up SSO from her AWS account to her Salesforce account. Which protocol makes this possible?

   a. AAA
   b. SSH
   c. PKI
   d. SAML

Hands-On Projects

Note 5

Websites, applications, public cloud platforms, and related account options change often. While the instructions given in these projects were accurate at the time of writing, you might need to adjust the steps or options according to later changes.

Note to Instructors and Students: A rubric is provided for evaluating student performance on these projects. Please see Appendix D.

Project 7-1: Install and Use a Password Manager

Estimated time: 30 minutes
Objective 2.3: Given a scenario, apply the appropriate OS and application security controls.
Group work: This project includes enhancements when assigned as a group project.
Resources:
- Internet access

Context:
Security experts recommend that you use long, complex passwords and use a different password for every account. A password manager is a free and secure way to store passwords so it's easier to observe these security recommendations. All you need to remember is a single, complex master password.

In this project, you create a LastPass account. LastPass is a password manager and offers a free subscription option. With LastPass, you can store account information for your school and personal accounts, and with a paid account, you can access your information from any device. Just remember to always keep your master password secure and never share it with anyone.

Complete the following steps to create your password manager account online:

1. Go to **lastpass.com** and click **Log In**. If you already have an account, log in here. Otherwise, on the Log In page, click **CREATE AN ACCOUNT**. Create a new account with a master password (the longer, the better—just make sure you can remember it because there is only one, somewhat unreliable way to recover the account if you forget the password). You can then install the free extension in your browser or explore more ways to download. Complete your preferred method of download. For consistency, for the remaining steps in this project, work with your LastPass account from the website rather than from an extension or the installed app. Make sure you're logged into the LastPass website.
2. In your vault on the LastPass website, take the tour or click through each menu option in the left pane. What is your current security score? What is the purpose of the emergency access?
3. When you get to Account Settings, scroll down to SMS Account Recovery and click **Update Phone**. Add a phone number where you can receive a recovery text message should you forget your master password. The phone must be in your possession to complete this step. Complete the verification process, and then close the Account Settings dialog box.

Note 6

Whenever you change your phone number, be sure to update this information in LastPass right away.

4. Return to the **All Items** page. Click the **Add Item** button (the plus sign in a circle), and then click **PASSWORD**. Enter information for a site you visit often, such as a social media site or an email service.
5. Move the mouse pointer over the site's tile and click **Launch** to open and sign into that site. If you want, you can add more sites. What other kinds of items can you add?

(continues)

Hands-On Projects Continued

6. **For group assignments:** Each group member should share one secure resource, such as a secure note, with one or more other group members using the Sharing Center in LastPass. Create a shared folder between the group members, then each group member adds at least one item to the shared folder. Each group member should **take a screenshot** showing the shared items in the shared folder and **take another screenshot** showing the shared folder's settings; submit these visuals with your answers to this project's questions.

7. Sign out of LastPass in your browser. Always remember to sign out of your account before walking away from your computer. Store a copy of your master password in a very secure place, such as a lockbox in your home, a safe deposit box at a bank, or a securely encrypted file on your computer or in the cloud.

Note 7

You can download and install LastPass as an extension in your favorite browser on a computer that you own. LastPass is compatible with Chrome, Firefox, Safari, Opera, and Edge. You can also install the LastPass app on your smartphone (Android or iPhone). However, you must upgrade to a paid account to use LastPass on multiple devices at the same time. Also, there is a limit on the number of times you can switch your LastPass account to other devices. Consider carefully which device you prefer to keep your LastPass account attached to.

Caution !

No password manager is 100 percent reliably secure. Hackers target these services, and occasionally they're successful. LastPass, however, is one of the most reliable password managers currently available for free. KeePass is another good one. No password manager is secure if you leave your account open on a computer or device you're not using or if you write your master password where someone else can find it. Follow these guidelines consistently:

- Always sign out of your password manager account and any other secure account when you're not using it.
- Always close browser windows where you have been signed into a secure account of any kind, even though you have signed out of that account.
- Always lock or sign out of the OS before walking away from your computer.

Project 7-2: Manage Users and Permissions in AWS

Estimated time: 45 minutes
Objective 2.1: Given a scenario, configure identity and access management.
Resources:

- AWS account
- Internet access

Context:
Creating a user in AWS IAM allows you to give other people limited access to your AWS resources. In this project, you'll create a new user and experiment with different permissions settings. Because you'll be signed in both as the root user and as an IAM user at the same time, you'll need to perform parts of the project in two different browsers, such as Chrome and Edge. Before you begin, make sure you have at least two browsers installed on your computer, or you can use two different devices (such as two laptops).

Note 8

If you're using the same computer on which you installed LastPass in Project 7-1, you'll need to perform the steps for this project in an incognito window in your browser or sign out of LastPass while you work on this project. This is because LastPass wants to record the passwords you create for your users, and it also tries to auto-fill the new users' password fields with an existing password from your account. In Chrome, click the ellipsis icon in the top-right corner of your browser window, and then click **New incognito window**. In Edge, click the ellipsis icon in the top-right corner, and then click **New InPrivate window**. In Firefox, click the menu icon in the top-right corner, and then click **New private window**.

Note that if you're using an AWS Academy account instead of a standard AWS account, there will be limitations on the changes you can save. Complete the following steps:

1. In your AWS Management Console, go to the **IAM** dashboard. IAM is listed under the **Security, Identity, & Compliance** service category. What security recommendations are listed here?
2. In the navigation pane on the left, click **Account settings**. What is the current password policy?
3. Click **Change password policy**, and select the following rules:

   - **Enforce a minimum password length** of **12** characters
   - Require at least one uppercase letter from Latin alphabet (A–Z)
   - Require at least one non-alphanumeric character
   - **Enable password expiration** with a period of **60** days
   - Allow users to change their own password
   - **Prevent password reuse** for the latest **8** passwords

If you're using a standard AWS account, click **Save changes**. If you're using an AWS Academy account, you do not have permission to save these changes, so click **Cancel**.

4. Now you're ready to add a user. In the navigation pane on the left, click **Users**, and then click **Add users**. Give the user a name, such as TestUser.
5. Under Select AWS access type, you have two options: programmatic access and console access. Programmatic access is used to allow access to AWS resources through the AWS API, CLI, SDK, and other tools. To authenticate for programmatic access, you would need to create an access key ID and a secret access key. However, this option is not needed for the current project. For the purposes of this project, select **Password – AWS Management Console access**, which relies on a password instead of an access key and gives AWS access through the GUI-based management console.
6. Select **Custom password**. Enter the password **password** and select **Show password**. What happens?
7. Set a different password that conforms to the password policy. What password did you set?
8. Deselect the option **User must create a new password at next sign-in**. Click **Next: Permissions**.
9. Under Set permissions, click **Attach existing policies directly**. Search for **EC2**. Read through some of the EC2 policy options, and then select **AmazonEC2ReadOnlyAccess**.
10. Click **Next: Tags**. Tags are key-value pairs used to add information that doesn't fit in existing fields for the user, such as an email address or job title. You define a key (such as Department or Office Location) and then add a value for that key (such as Human Resources or Nashville). Add the key **Job** and the value **ITstaff**.
11. Click **Next: Review**. If you're using a standard AWS account, click **Create user**. If you're using an AWS Academy account, you do not have permission to save these changes, so click **Cancel**. Because you're using a password and not access keys for this user, you do *not* need to download the user credentials. Click **Close**.

(continues)

Hands-On Projects Continued

If you're using an AWS Academy account, you will not be able to complete the following steps. Confirm you have not created any resources (and if you did, be sure to delete them), and then watch this project's video to see the rest of the project's steps. If you're using a standard AWS account, continue with the following steps:

12. Click the user you just created, and then click the **Security credentials** tab. Copy and paste the console sign-in link into a different browser's window (make sure the browser is not signed into LastPass). Sign in with the username you created in Step 4 and the password you configured in Step 7.
13. Explore the user's console and answer the following questions:
    - In the Storage category, click **S3**, which is a simple storage service in AWS that you'll learn about in a later module. Can you access S3 information?
    - Go to the **VPC** dashboard. Can you see a list of existing VPCs?
    - Can you create a new VPC?
    - Go to the **EC2** dashboard. Can you see a list of existing instances, key pairs, security groups, or any other resource listed in this dashboard?
    - Can you create a new EC2 instance?
14. Return to your root user's console. Give the new user the permissions policy called **AmazonEC2FullAccess**.
15. Return to your new user's console and try again to create a new EC2 instance. Does it work?
16. Delete all the resources you created in this project, including the user and the VM. Check through your account to confirm that all related resources have been deleted.

> **Note 9**
>
> Depending on the status of your account and the selections you made during this project, the resources you created can deplete your credits or accrue charges. Double-check to make sure you've terminated all resources you created in this project.

Project 7-3: Research Azure Active Directory

Estimated time: 30 minutes
Objective 3.1: Given a scenario, integrate components into a cloud solution.
Resources:
- Internet access

Context:
If you used your school account to create your Azure subscription, most likely you will not be able to create new users in Azure AD. The Azure domain holding your account is managed by your school, and you don't have permission to do much in Azure AD. Because so many students are expected to be using their school accounts, this project will focus on researching information about Azure AD rather than using it. Complete the following steps:

1. Search online for three articles, blogs, or videos that discuss the differences between Active Directory and Azure AD. List your resources.
2. Based on what you learned from your research, what are three defining differences between AD and Azure AD?
3. Describe an example of a situation where using AD would be a better choice and explain your reasoning.
4. Describe an example of a situation where using Azure AD would be a better choice and explain your reasoning.

The rubric in Table 7-2 shows how your responses for this project will be evaluated. Note that your instructor might choose to adjust the point distribution in this rubric.

Table 7-2   Rubric for Project 7-3

Task	Novice	Competent	Proficient	Earned
Three resources	Three resources loosely related to the topic **5 points**	Three reputable resources directly related to the topic **10 points**	Three reputable resources directly related to the topic with rich, clearly articulated information **15 points**	
Three differences between AD and Azure AD	Three vague or superficial differences **10 points**	Three specific differences **15 points**	Three specific and fundamental differences **20 points**	
AD example	Vague example with little detail and no supporting explanation **15 points**	Clearly explained example with contextual details and supporting explanation **20 points**	Thoughtful and clearly explained example with specific contextual details and logical supporting explanation **25 points**	
Azure AD example	Vague example with little detail and no supporting explanation **15 points**	Clearly explained example with contextual details and supporting explanation **20 points**	Thoughtful and clearly explained example with specific contextual details and logical supporting explanation **25 points**	
Mechanics	Several grammar and spelling errors **5 points**	Occasional grammar and spelling errors **10 points**	Appropriate grammar and spelling throughout **15 points**	
			Total	

Project 7-4: Manage Users in GCP

Estimated time: 45 minutes

Objective 2.1: Given a scenario, configure identity and access management.

Resources:

- GCP account
- Internet access

Context:

To add a new user who can access your GCP resources, you must provide their Google account. All you need is their email address, not their password or other information. If you have an extra Google account, or if a friend or family member will allow you to use their email address (you won't need access to their email account or any other information), you can complete this project. Considering that not everyone will have easy access to a second Google account, the project indicates which steps are optional. After that portion of the project, you will continue with the steps using your original Google account.

(continues)

Hands-On Projects Continued

To gather some initial information, complete the following step:

1. In the GCP navigation menu, point to **IAM & Admin** then click **IAM**.

   - How many principals are listed?
   - How many of these are service accounts?
   - What is the name of each of these service accounts?
   - Do you have any role recommendations listed under Security insights? If so, what are they?

Some service accounts might show as having excessive permissions. The IAM recommender tool uses ML (machine learning) to identify excessive permissions and to identify permissions a principal might need but doesn't yet have. GCP officially recommends not changing these service accounts' roles unless specifically advised to do so by the relevant role recommendations. In a production environment where you have accurate use history for these service accounts, you might want to reduce these accounts' permissions by changing their roles. In these projects, you are not yet using these service accounts to the full extent required for this course. Therefore, it's not needed to make any adjustments to these service accounts at this time. To create a new role, complete the following step:

2. In the navigation pane, scroll down and click **Roles**, and then click **CREATE ROLE**. Give your role a name, such as ReadCompute. Click **ADD PERMISSIONS**. Filter the permissions by the role **Compute Viewer**, and then select **compute.instances.get** and **compute.networks.list**. Click **ADD**, and then click **CREATE**. Where does your role appear in the list of roles? Why do you think this is?

To add a new principal, you can use another Gmail address that you own or (with permission) that belongs to a friend or family member. You do *not* need their password or any other information, and you will be removing the account from your IAM list at the end of this project. Alternatively, you can create a new service account. To create a new service account, complete the following steps:

3. In the navigation pane, click **Service Accounts**, and then click **CREATE SERVICE ACCOUNT**. Give the service account a name, such as server. Click **CREATE AND CONTINUE**. You will grant the service account a role in a later step. Click **DONE**.

4. In the list of service accounts, what is your new service account's email address?

Now you're ready to create a new principal. Complete the following steps:

5. Click **IAM** to return to the list of principals. Click **ADD** to create a new principal.

6. Enter a Gmail address (a second Gmail address you own or someone else's address if they have agreed to let you use this information), or enter the email address for the service account you created in Step 3.

7. In the Role field, click **Custom** and click the role you created in Step 2. Click **SAVE**.

8. Examine the list of principals again. How can you tell the difference between a user account and a service account?

9. Delete all the resources you created in this project, including the role, principal, and service account (if you created one). Check through your account to confirm that all related resources have been deleted.

Note 10

Depending on the status of your account and the selections you made during this project, the resources you created can deplete your credits or accrue charges. Double-check to make sure you've terminated all resources you created in this project.

Capstone Project 7: Assign Permissions to Resources

Note 11

Websites, applications, public cloud platforms, and related account options change often. While the instructions given in these projects were accurate at the time of writing, you might need to adjust the steps or options according to later changes.

Note to Instructors and Students: A rubric is provided for evaluating student performance on these projects. Please see Appendix D.

Estimated time: 45 minutes

Objective 5.2: Given a scenario, troubleshoot security issues.

Resources:

- Public cloud account (such as AWS, Azure, or GCP)
- Internet access

Context:

In the Hands-on Projects for this module, you assigned access permissions to users. In this project, you will assign access permissions to VM instances. Complete the following steps:

1. Depending on the platform used, create one role or policy that provides read-only access to a popular file system storage service in that platform. For example, you might choose EFS or FSx in AWS. **Take a screenshot** of the configurations that ensure this access is enabled and all other access is blocked; submit this visual with your answers to this project's questions.

Note 12

If you're not sure which service in a cloud platform can be used to accomplish a certain type of task or create a certain type of resource, you can use a search engine to look for the cloud platform's name and the type of service you need, and then examine the results for a service that would be a good fit for your use case. For example, if you need file system storage in Azure, you might search for "azure file system storage." Azure Files might be the first result, or you might instead find a page that lists Azure's core storage services. Read through the service descriptions to find the best fit for your needs. You learn more about cloud storage types in a later module.

---

2. Create one role or policy that provides full access to the same storage service and full access to the cloud platform's most popular relational database service; for example, that would be RDS or Aurora in AWS. **Take a screenshot** of the configurations that ensure this access is enabled and all other access is blocked; submit this visual with your answers to this project's questions.
3. Create two VMs: one with read-only access to storage buckets and one with full access to both storage buckets and VMs. **Take a screenshot** of the configurations that ensure this access is enabled and all other access is blocked; submit this visual with your answers to this project's questions.
4. Delete all resources created in this Capstone project. Check through your account to confirm that all related resources have been deleted.

Note 13

Depending on the status of your account and the selections you made during this project, the resources you created can deplete your credits or accrue charges. Double-check to make sure you've terminated all resources you created in this project.

Solutions to Self-Check Questions

Section 7-1: Cloud Accounts

1. A user account is a(n) _____.

    Answer: d. identity

    Explanation: Both users and resources (such as an application) can have an identity, which is a digital entity (such as a user account) to which you can attach roles and permissions.

2. What is a goal of successful account management?

    Answer: c. Limit privilege creep

    Explanation: Account management policies can help ensure that privilege creep is limited and monitored.

3. When would a technician most likely need to use a privileged account?

    Answer: b. To create a user account

    Explanation: A privileged account is required when performing sensitive tasks, such as creating other user accounts or adjusting access privileges for other users.

Section 7-2: Authentication

4. Which protocol defines how most authentication directories work?

    Answer: a. LDAP

    Explanation: The mechanisms of LDAP (Lightweight Directory Access Protocol) dictate some basic requirements for any directory it accesses. Therefore, directory servers are configured and function in similar ways, regardless of the software used.

5. If a certificate is included in a CRL, what is its status?

    Answer: b. Revoked

    Explanation: Once revoked, a certificate is added to a CRL (certificate revocation list), which other entities can check to confirm whether a certificate has become invalidated.

6. Which authentication technique bridges the gap across IdPs and SPs?

    Answer: c. Federation

    Explanation: Federation is the process of managing user identities across organizations on the foundation of an established trust relationship.

Section 7-3: Authorization to Cloud Objects

7. AWS users receive long-term permissions through an attached _____.

    Answer: b. policy

    Explanation: A user or group is given long-term access permissions through an attachment to a policy.

8. What access control method does Azure use?

    Answer: b. RBAC

    Explanation: Azure relies on RBAC (role-based access control) to manage users' access to resources. The admin creates a role with the needed privileges and permissions for each job, and then the admin creates a user group associated with one or more roles. Users are assigned to groups that match the roles they need to do their jobs.

9. What resource defines a set of permissions in GCP?

    Answer: d. Role

    Explanation: A role is a collection of permissions and can be granted to a user, service account, or group.

Section 7-4: IAM for Hybrid Clouds

10. True or False: Active Directory can only be run on-prem.

    Answer: b. False

    Explanation: Active Directory can be run in a VM instance on the cloud. Many CSPs also offer managed AD services in the cloud.

11. Which of the following is the most difficult configuration for extending IAM across a hybrid cloud?

    Answer: b. Federation

    Explanation: Establishing a trust relationship for federated authentication is the more complicated and expensive option of all typical approaches for extending IAM across a hybrid cloud.

Section 7-5: Troubleshooting Cloud IAM

12. An expired certificate is a(n) _____ issue.

    Answer: c. authentication

    Explanation: An expired certificate can result in an authentication failure.

13. What kind of attack causes changed account privileges?

    Answer: d. Vertical

    Explanation: In a vertical privilege escalation attack, the attacker escalates privileges by manipulating privileges granted to the account being used or using the current account to gain access to more privileged accounts.

Module 8

Cloud Storage

Module 8 Objectives

After reading this module, you will be able to:

1   Compare storage technologies.

2   Explain storage optimization techniques.

3   Configure common cloud storage services.

4   Describe options for creating and storing backups.

5   Identify storage security techniques.

Module 8 Outline

Study the module's outline to help you organize the content in your mind as you read.

Module 8 Scenario

"Someone stole my snack again!" you exclaim, feeling frustrated as you dig through your desk drawer looking for a stray granola bar or something else edible.

"What happened?" asks Kendra as she leans against the doorway to her office.

"I brought some leftover quesadillas to hold me over until our late lunch meeting this afternoon. I put them in the refrigerator in the snack room *with my name on the box*," you emphasize. "But now they're gone! Some people have no manners."

"I have some extra yogurt and a brownie you can have," offers Nigel. "I made the brownies myself!"

"I guess it's important to have backups," laughs Kendra.

As you rummage through your desk drawer a little more, you mumble, "I thought I had an old granola bar in here... where *is* that thing?"

"A stale granola bar in your desk drawer hardly qualifies as a good backup," she points out.

Kendra turns to go back into her office and then stops and comes back. "Hey, can you two take these file boxes to the storage unit for me? That'll get you out of the office for 20 minutes or so—it's a beautiful day, and you can hit the drive-through for a snack while you're out."

"Yeah, sure," you say as you stand up and grab your jacket. Then you add, "Thanks."

"No problem," says Kendra. "It's good timing anyway—when you get back, we need to talk about how to design some storage space in our cloud."

"What kind of storage space do we need?" asks Nigel. "Files and folders?"

"Not exactly," replies Kendra. "We'll need a file system to support a couple of applications, but mostly we'll use block storage and object storage."

"What are those?" you ask, genuinely intrigued.

"Well, block storage is kind of like our storage unit where you're taking these boxes. Each box on the shelf is like a block of storage space. You can put a certain amount of stuff in there, and you track the location of the stuff based on the name of the box."

"What about object storage?" Nigel asks.

"That's a little different," says Kendra. "That's more like...well, that's kind of like the stuff stored on your desk," she laughs.

"Hey, I like my desk! I can find everything I need," Nigel says, as you all three glance over his desk piled with papers, boxes, bottles, electronics, books, and all kinds of other things. You're pretty sure you saw a rubber chicken staring out at you from one of the piles last week.

"This is true," Kendra says. "*You* can always find exactly what you need because, in your mind, you know where everything is. But from the outside, it just looks like piles of *stuff*. Object storage is the same idea: You pile lots of different kinds of things together in whatever amount of space it takes. It's a very flexible system that can handle massive amounts of data."

"Okay, that kind of makes sense," you nod. "I guess we won't need to back up anything we move to the cloud, right? I mean, the cloud provider keeps everything backed up already, don't they? It's kind of like going to a restaurant—there's always food there."

"Ah, well, that's a common misconception," explains Kendra. "Not everything in the cloud is backed up. Just like your favorite restaurant can be out of your favorite food, or they can be closed, or maybe you can't eat out every time you're hungry, you need to have backup plans for food when something goes wrong. And with the cloud, you still need to back up your data."

"Tell you what," Kendra adds. "Let's do a little research..." she says, as she pulls a spare notepad off Nigel's desk.

- How is data organized and optimized in the cloud?
- What cloud services store data?
- How is data backed up in the cloud?
- What can be done to keep cloud data safe?

Section 8-1: Storage Types

2.3 Given a scenario, apply the appropriate OS and application security controls.

2.4 Given a scenario, apply data security and compliance controls in cloud environments.

3.2 Given a scenario, provision storage in cloud environments.

3.4 Given a scenario, configure the appropriate compute sizing for a deployment.

3.5 Given a scenario, perform cloud migrations.

Whether you're working on-prem or in the cloud, managing an enterprise-scale network, or typing a research paper on a home computer, you're creating, saving, and accessing data. If you think about it, all of IT exists to manage data. The companies that do this well have an edge in their respective industries. Nearly every business decision hinges on the quality of data made available to decision makers.

Knowing the key role data plays in business highlights the need for good data storage methodologies. Compromised data can destroy an organization. Therefore, as companies move their data centers to the cloud, it's the responsibility of IT professionals to ensure that data is kept both safe and accessible.

Consider the many kinds of workloads that rely on data. A CRM (customer relationship management) application draws on data stored in a database. Media services access what are often very large media files, such as videos or high-resolution images. Office staff create documents, spreadsheets, and presentations that are stored on their workstations or in file shares accessed across their company's network. All these examples of data might be stored on-prem or in the cloud. Examples of data types stored in the cloud include the following:

- **Office and media files**—Probably the most recognizable type of data, office files include file types such as documents, spreadsheets, and presentations. These files might be created in an Office app (such as Word, Excel, or PowerPoint) or created in a web app (such as Google Docs, Google Sheets, or Google Slides). Media files include file types such as photos or videos. Files are then typically stored in a hierarchical file system, as shown in Figure 8-1. This file system might live on a local computer or in the cloud, such as in Microsoft OneDrive or Google Drive. Files are grouped within folders (also called directories), and a folder can also hold other folders (also called subfolders or subdirectories). Common file systems you might be familiar with include the old FAT32 (File Allocation Table), the newer NTFS (New Technology File System), the even newer ReFS (Resilient File System), the long-time default Linux file system ext4 (fourth extended file system), and the newer Linux file systems BTRFS (B-Tree File System, pronounced "butter f-s") and ZFS (Z File System, pronounced "zed f-s").
- **Applications**—Applications can be made up of many parts stored in various places on a network. These parts interact as needed to generate requested output. An application might run inside an operating system, in a container, inside another application, or across the web. Applications often rely on data supplied by other sources, such as a database, an operating system, or another application.
- **Websites**—Websites usually consist of many files stored on a web server. Each webpage lives in a different file and often collects data from many files. A webpage might also pull data from other sources, such as APIs from another website, a database, or an application.
- **Logs**—A log file, or log for short, is a special kind of file that collects information on events associated with a system or application. For example, a log might show information about traffic crossing a network interface. The information could include data about the time a particular network message was received, where it came from, where it was going, and whether it was allowed to pass. Keeping logs generates a tremendous amount of data in a short period of time and can take up a lot of storage space. But logs are important for troubleshooting problems or investigating security issues.
- **Databases**—A database is a large collection of data that is organized for quick retrieval of information. A phone directory is a kind of database, where information on thousands of people is organized by name, address, and phone number. The information for each person listed in the phone directory is contained within a single

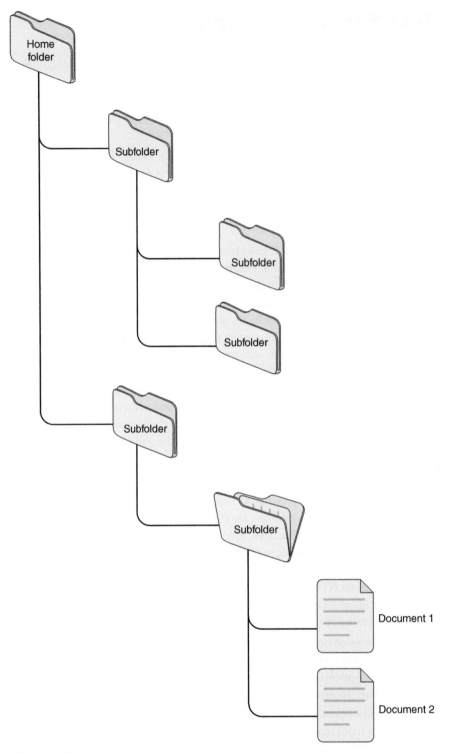

Figure 8-1   A file system consists of folders within folders

record. Those records can be filtered or sorted to investigate patterns of data, guide business endeavors, or interact with other databases. In general, there are two kinds of databases, as follows:

○ ***Flat file database***—A basic phone directory is an example of a flat file database. All the records are contained within one large table, and all the records contain the same kinds of information (such as name, address, and phone number) about each person. You could store a flat file database in a basic spreadsheet.

○ *Relational database*—A relational database contains many tables with different kinds of information, and it can show the relationship between those tables. For example, imagine you own a cupcake bakery. You might have one table for customer records, one table for all orders placed, another table showing a list of all the food products you create along with a list of ingredients, and another table showing the supplies you must keep in stock for your business to operate smoothly. A relational database shows the meaningful connections between these tables. Using a relational database, you could determine which customers are most likely to visit the store on National Chocolate Day in October because they've ordered many chocolate cupcakes in the past. From that list, you can determine how much more chocolate you should order to be prepared after running an email campaign advertising to those customers. In other words, the relational database shows the relationship between customers who like chocolate and your chocolate supplies to help you determine how much extra chocolate you'll need in preparation for the holiday special. A relational database requires more sophisticated DBMS (database management system) software such as SQL Server or MySQL. SQL (Structured Query Language and pronounced "see-quel") is a programming language designed specifically for communication with databases.

○ *Nonrelational databases, also called NoSQL (not-only SQL) databases*—In many situations, the enforced consistency of a relational database (with the same kinds of information in every record in a table) is an advantage. However, this consistency comes with the limitation that data must generally be represented by text or numbers rather than images, videos, or other file types. As the Internet—and particularly web applications—became more popular, this restriction led to the emergence of more powerful database technologies better suited to managing less consistent data types. Nonrelational databases resolve many of the weaknesses of relational databases. NoSQL originally stood for non-SQL, but more recently has been called not-only SQL because some of these systems do support SQL-based languages. Popular, cloud-based, nonrelational database services include AWS's DynamoDB and Azure's Cosmos DB. These unstructured databases use a variety of approaches to store many kinds of data. One simple example is a key-value database. Key-value databases (also called key-value stores) create any number of key-value pairs for each record. You've seen key-value pairs when creating tags for cloud resources.

As you can see, data is integral to running a business, whether that's a small, one-person shop or a global organization. As an IT professional managing data in the cloud, you'll need to know how to keep data safe while also ensuring that it's accessible by those authorized to use it.

Grow with Cengage Unlimited!

If you'd like more information about the kinds of logs collected when monitoring a network, use your Cengage Unlimited subscription to go to *CompTIA Network+ Guide to Networks*, 9th edition, Module 12, and read the section titled "Traffic Monitoring Tools."

If you don't have a Cengage Unlimited subscription, you can find more information at cengage.com/unlimited.

On-Prem Storage Technologies

While cloud-based technologies are the focus of CompTIA Cloud+, on-prem storage technologies that use similar principles are also covered in the exam objectives. It's important that you understand how the principles of cloud computing can apply to on-prem technologies, and vice versa. This portion of the module explores on-prem storage types, data redundancy techniques, and some recent advances in storage technologies.

On-Prem Storage Types

There are three basic networking approaches to storing data on-prem, as described next:

- DAS (direct attached storage), the most familiar storage type to the typical user, is directly connected to the computer or server that uses it. For example, the hard drive in a laptop is typically accessed only by that laptop. Even if a volume on the drive is shared with other computers on the network, those files are only accessible if the host computer is turned on. Attaching several disks (called "just a bunch of disks," or JBOD) to a server is also an example of DAS. These disks might be shared among several servers, but each server has its own connection directly to the disks and does not rely on a switched network to access the data stored on the disks. These disks must initially be formatted using a partitioning system, such as the older MBR (Master Boot Record) or the newer GPT (GUID Partition Table), before installing a file system on it, such as NTFS.

- **NAS (network attached storage)** relies on network infrastructure to provide file access. NAS is most often provided by a NAS device containing multiple disk drives and accessed by any device over the network. The NAS device is attached to a network switch, which allows access from network servers and other networked devices. It relies on access protocols such as CIFS (Common Internet File System) or SMB (Server Message Block) for Windows systems, or NFS (Network File System) for Linux or UNIX systems. NAS often incorporates RAID (redundant array of inexpensive disks) to provide data redundancy, which would protect data in the event one or more disks fail. NAS works well for SMBs (small or medium-sized businesses) that need to make data available to several users on the network but can't afford an expensive SAN, described next.

Note 1

Although NFS (Network File System) has "file system" in its name, it's really a DFS (distributed file system) protocol used to give file server clients access to files across a network. A related technology is HDFS (Hadoop Distributed File System), where Hadoop is a framework for distributing **big data** across a network and efficiently processing that data in parallel functions.

- A **SAN (storage area network)** is a portion of an organization's network dedicated entirely to supporting storage hardware (collectively called a storage array). Data in a SAN array is stored in blocks rather than in a file system hierarchy. Each block is a specified size, much like storage lockers in a U-Haul (uhaul.com) storage facility, and each block contains data that is referenced by the block's LUN (logical unit number). A server sees each block as a separate volume and can treat that volume as an attached drive, even installing a file system on it if the block size is large enough. The server then adds data to the block over time. Here are a few helpful points to consider when learning about SANs:
  - SAN devices don't communicate by Ethernet like the rest of the network does—at least, not directly. The SAN relies on different kinds of access protocols, such as FC (Fibre Channel), SCSI (Small Computer Systems Interface), SAS (Serial Attached SCSI), SATA (Serial Advanced Technology Attachment or Serial ATA), or NVMe (nonvolatile memory express).
  - Variations of these protocols and other supporting protocols can make SAN devices more accessible to other networked devices, such as FCoE (Fibre Channel over Ethernet), FCIP (Fibre Channel over IP), IFCP (Internet Fibre Channel Protocol), iSCSI (Internet Small Computer Systems Interface), and ISNS (Internet Storage Name Service).
  - Nodes on an FC network are identified by WWNN (World Wide Node Name)—which is similar to a MAC address on an Ethernet network—and by WWPN (World Wide Port Name) for individual ports. On an iSCSI network, nodes are identified by an IQN (iSCSI Qualified Name).
  - A VSAN (virtual SAN) is a SAN infrastructure existing on top of a virtualization layer provided by a hypervisor, such as VMware ESXi or Microsoft Hyper-V.

SANs are more complex and expensive to set up and maintain than other storage options. As shown in Figure 8-2, a SAN requires specialized switches that connect to servers using HBAs (host bus adapters) instead of NICs. However, more recent SAN technologies use CNAs (converged network adapters) or UTAs (unified target adapters), which can use typical, multipurpose LAN Ethernet devices in service of the SAN (see Figure 8-3).

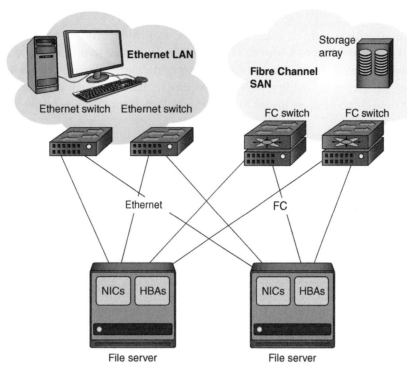

Figure 8-2   A Fibre Channel SAN connected to an Ethernet LAN

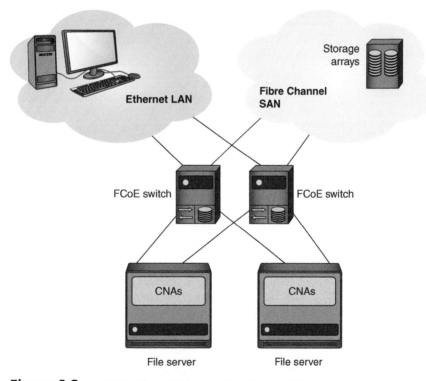

Figure 8-3   A SAN using FCoE to connect to a LAN

Grow with Cengage Unlimited!

If you'd like more information about network storage technologies, use your Cengage Unlimited subscription to go to *CompTIA Network+ Guide to Networks*, 9th edition, Module 7, and read the section titled "Storage Area Network (SAN)." If you don't have a Cengage Unlimited subscription, you can find more information at cengage.com/unlimited.

Redundant Array of Independent Disks (RAID)

Servers are often configured with a form of redundant storage to protect from catastrophic disk failure. **RAID (Redundant Array of Independent Disks or Redundant Array of Inexpensive Disks)** is a collection of storage drives (called an array) interfaced in a way to ensure one or more layers of redundant copies of data across the drive array. There are many forms of RAID. Except for the first RAID technique explained next, which is called RAID 0, RAID offers the ability to recover lost data if one or more drives in the array is lost. Figure 8-4 illustrates some of the more common RAID techniques, as follows:

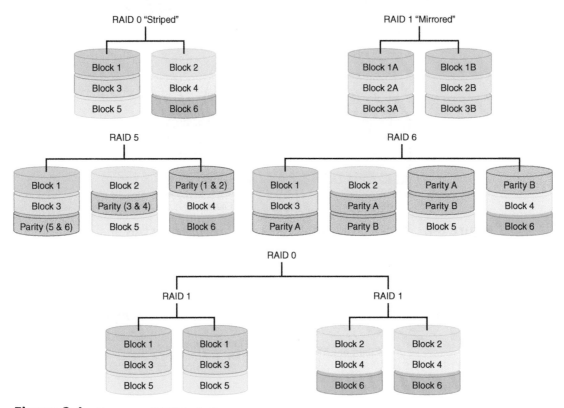

Figure 8-4   Common RAID techniques

- **RAID 0**—Data is broken into pieces, and each consecutive piece is stored on a different drive. This technique is known as striping. There is no redundancy of data in this RAID technique: if one drive fails, data is lost. The advantage of this technique, however, is the high speed at which data can be read or written across multiple drives at once. RAID 0 requires at least two disks.

- **RAID 1**—Data is stored on at least two drives, in duplicate, to provide a level of redundancy (or fault tolerance) should one drive become corrupted. This technique is also known as disk mirroring. RAID 1, however, does not provide protection against certain risks to data such as ransomware or a virus, as those kinds of attacks would affect data on both drives. Therefore, RAID 1 is not considered a reliable data backup method. RAID 1 requires at least two disks.

- **RAID 5**—Data is broken into pieces (stripes) and stored across three or more drives. Parity information (error-checking code) is interleaved with the striped data. This configuration maximizes performance while minimizing cost and still provides reliable data recovery if a drive is lost. RAID 5 is the most popular of these RAID techniques in corporate environments. Keep in mind, however, that RAID 5 by itself is also not a complete backup strategy. RAID 5 requires at least three disks.

- **RAID 6**—Similar to RAID 5, RAID 6 stripes data across multiple disks and interleaves parity information to assist in data recovery. However, parity information is calculated in two different ways, and each portion of parity data is distributed across multiple disks. RAID 6 requires at least four disks.

- *RAID 10*—More correctly referred to as RAID 1+0 (and pronounced "RAID one-oh," not "RAID ten"), RAID 10 combines RAID 0 and RAID 1 techniques by mirroring data and then striping it. It's sometimes called a "stripe of mirrors." A similar technique, RAID 01, reverses these techniques and stripes the data first, then mirrors it. This technique is sometimes called a "mirror of stripes." RAID 10 requires at least four disks.

Several more RAID techniques exist. They are essentially variations on and combinations of the preceding techniques, providing various speed and redundancy benefits while also requiring more disks.

Note 2

As you just read, RAID 0 provides no data redundancy. There are situations, however, where RAID 0 is the preferred technique, especially when performance is more important than redundancy. For example, consider the data stored in blockchains. Blockchain data is typically distributed across many servers, which provides inherent data redundancy. When configuring a blockchain server, therefore, performance is by far the higher priority. As a result, RAID 0 is commonly used for blockchain servers to increase their write-to-disk speeds.

On-Prem Storage Performance

Many developments have emerged over the past decade or so to support increased performance of on-prem storage. The following list explains three of these technologies you'll need to know for the CompTIA Cloud+ exam:

- *High-speed connections*—Within a single computer, you can choose from several standards to connect a storage device with the CPU: SCSI, SAS, SATA, or NVMe. Adjustments to these protocols are needed for them to work in a SAN. For example, iSCSI applies the basic principles of SCSI to SAN connections. Similarly, NVMe-oF (nonvolatile memory express over fabrics) applies NVMe technology to connections between servers and the SAN. Improvements in storage technology led to the transition from hard disks to SSDs (solid-state drives), thus improving performance of the disks themselves. However, the connection technologies at the time imposed a bottleneck that reduced experienced performance of storage devices. NVMe-oF offers connectivity performance capable of matching the data read and write performance of SSDs in the SAN.

- *Virtualization*—SDS (software-defined storage) virtualizes the storage infrastructure to provide highly scalable, manageable storage space on top of generic (as opposed to proprietary) and diverse hardware. SDS can even run on top of virtual servers, and some SDS products can run across containers. SDS offers flexibility and versatility not available through traditional SAN and NAS systems. Figure 8-5 shows the basic structure of an SDS-connected network.

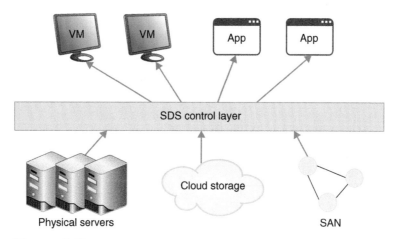

Figure 8-5   SDS (software-defined storage)

- *Hyperconvergence*—SDS is an integral part of HCI. HCI (hyperconverged infrastructure) is an implementation of software-defined compute, networking, and storage services all in one solution, typically provided by a single vendor and managed through a single interface that, like public cloud, relies on API calls. While HCI might be seen as an on-prem competitor to the public cloud, it's not truly private cloud technology. Additionally, one HCI provider, Nutanix, now offers their HCI technology through the AWS cloud. Nutanix Clusters can run on AWS EC2 instances, which allows current Nutanix customers to lift-and-shift their on-prem clusters to the public cloud. This type of blending between on-prem and cloud-based technologies provides one of many paths to a hybrid cloud deployment.

Note 3

A special application of SDS developed by VMware is called VMFS (virtual machine files system). It applies the advantages of block storage to the virtualized environment to provide efficient storage of VM images.

Cloud Storage Technologies

You've learned that one of the primary differences between NAS and a SAN is that NAS relies on a file system hierarchy while a SAN stores data in consistently sized blocks. Although you won't set up NAS or SAN storage in the cloud per se, these storage structures continue to provide helpful categories of storage services available in the cloud. Cloud storage services also offer one more type of storage: object storage. Figure 8-6 shows how these storage categories compare to each other. Let's explore a more detailed comparison of these three storage types.

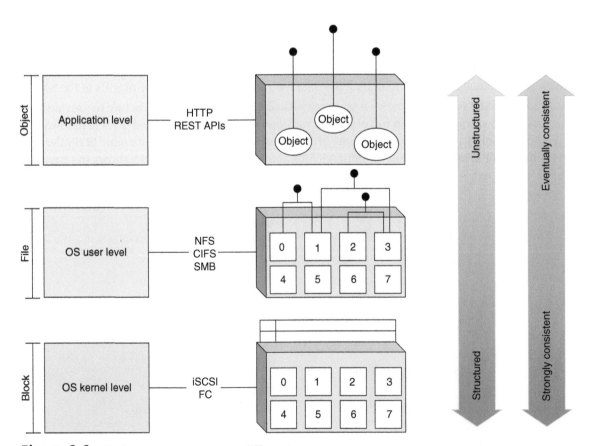

Figure 8-6 Each storage type serves different purposes

File System Storage

File system storage is easy to visualize if you think about putting papers in folders inside a file cabinet. You might have folders within folders, which are then organized by hanging folders. In a digital environment, you can theoretically create many more layers of subfolders than would be reasonably accessible.

File system storage lends itself well to organizing a single person's or small department's files, but it does not scale well for large amounts of different kinds of data used by many people. An additional advantage of file system storage, however, is the metadata that can be stored with each file. Metadata is data about the file, such as creation date, author, and permissions. This can be helpful when you're searching for a particular file or need to sort files by creation date, last edited date, or file size.

Block Storage

Block storage scales up more easily for massive amounts of data because the data is stored in a flat namespace. Each block is addressed by a unique number rather than being organized within other blocks. This is similar to the difference between your street address versus your email address. Your home address is identified by a number on a street in a zip code that's in a city within a state. The street name represents a group of dwellings; that group is part of a larger group represented by a zip code; and that zip code is part of a larger group of zip codes in a city, which is joined by many cities in your state. These are groups within groups within groups. With your email, however, you're identified only by your account name. Every other email account by the same provider (such as Gmail) also has a unique name, and they're not grouped within groups in a hierarchical structure. The namespace is said to be flat.

Block storage works much the same way as an email provider's namespace. Every block in the storage network is addressed by a unique number called a LUN. This avoids the complexity from multiple layers of nested folders and allows for low-latency access to databases, virtual machines, and boot drives. This flat namespace can decrease latency, but as the overall volume of data stored in the block service increases, latency increases again. A newer initiative called **block zoning** can help organize block storage for decreased latency and more efficient use of storage space. Each zone on the disk can be dedicated to different types of data, such as read-intensive data or write-intensive data. Still, block storage provides no metadata, and it requires specialized protocols, such as FC (Fibre Channel), that are expensive and complicated to manage.

Object Storage

Object storage is a more cloud-native storage infrastructure—it takes some of the best characteristics of file and block storage and reimagines storage in a way that capitalizes on the cloud's auto-scaling functionality. An object packages stored data with metadata about the object. This metadata can give extensive information about the object and about the data stored within the object. This metadata is also optimized for quick search and retrieval functions. Where file systems keep basic metadata about a file, such as creation date and author, object metadata can contain extensive and customized information about the data itself. This is especially useful when the data can't be easily searched, such as photos, videos, or complex CAD (computer-aided design) 3-D images.

Object storage also relies on a flat namespace; however, this space is not organized into consistently sized blocks. Objects are held in a single repository, or pool of storage. This space can be expanded indefinitely, even across geographies. However, the expansiveness and flexibility of the space also results in higher latency. Object storage lends itself well to unstructured data storage (such as massive collections of images or video), archival storage, or big data storage (such as IoT raw data stored in a data lake).

Object storage offers one more benefit specific to the cloud environment: simpler protocols. Where block storage relies on complex protocols such as FC, object storage uses REST APIs and HTTP.

Choosing Between File, Block, and Object Storage

Whereas block storage in a SAN is the Cadillac of on-prem storage options, object storage maximizes the potential of storage capabilities in the cloud. To be fair, each storage type best supports different use cases, no matter where the storage is located. Object storage is generally less expensive and more flexible, while block storage provides faster performance at a higher price point.

Another difference between storage types is consistency of data. Data consistency refers to how well copies of data stored in a particular environment are consistent with each other. In block storage, the most current version of data is immediately available after a change is made. This is called "strongly consistent." In object storage, however, more time is required for data modifications to propagate through the system. This is said to be "eventually consistent." Data that is infrequently updated is better suited to object storage than is data that is changed often.

Object storage lends itself well to data that is written once and then left alone or only read, such as log files. This data type is referred to as WORM (write once read many) and is similar in concept to the on-prem data center's CAS (content addressed storage), where content is written once and then referenced by its content rather than by its location on a disk. The data goes in and then it stays put and doesn't have to be changed. This kind of storage is highly scalable but not easy to plan for how to organize it (such as a log file that will increase in size almost indefinitely). And it's not as well suited to more organized data, such as a database, unless it's only hosting backup or archived data.

Block storage works well for hosting databases, operating systems, and VM-attached storage. This is data that changes frequently and must provide low-latency performance.

File system storage provides managed file system organization of data and can often be mounted to multiple VM instances, unlike block storage. Again, the focus with file system storage is on data organization rather than storage capacity.

Storage Migrations

When a company has hosted its data in its on-prem data center, the company's storage resources have typically been designed around the needs of the data itself. When moving to a cloud provider's infrastructure, the company might need to make some changes to the data, such as its format, structure, or even the way it is labeled. For example, the cloud platform might not support all file types, or there might be certain symbols that the cloud provider does not allow in file names or file paths.

Shifting data storage to the cloud is a popular migration type among today's cloud users. You might have performed a similar step if you've shifted your photos, files, or contacts from a local hard drive or storage device (such as a storage card in a camera) to cloud-based storage, such as Google Drive or Microsoft OneDrive. With a batch of photos, the process is relatively simple—copy the photo files from one location to the other. You might also perform some basic reorganization. In a corporate environment, the process is more complicated, but the basic idea is the same: move data from one place to the other.

The following list explores some of the factors to consider when migrating data from on-prem to cloud storage:

- *Migration plan*—Most companies don't migrate all their data at once. You'll need to identify the data to transfer first, either because it's the easiest to migrate or because it will offer the most savings. How much is it costing you to store the data on-prem? How will this data integrate with other on-prem or cloud-based resources? How often is it accessed or modified? What storage regulations apply to this data, and how can you ensure compliance throughout the migration process? You might also want to tackle a data cleansing process to reduce the overall volume of data to be migrated, such as deleting duplicated data or removing data that is no longer needed.

- *Data transfer costs*—Many cloud providers allow unlimited data ingress for free. You can transfer data into your cloud storage at no cost from the cloud provider unless you use a special migration service (such as AWS's Snowball or Snowmobile services). Still, you'll likely need to pay for the ISP's service that supports the data transfer. In addition to your usual demand on your ISP service, you'll be moving large volumes of data over your Internet or other WAN connections, and this might incur additional charges from the ISP.

- *Data transfer time*—Similarly, the time it takes to move large amounts of data can cause synchronization issues between the data that arrives at the cloud and the data that has continued to change on-prem during the migration. You'll need to plan to resync the migrated data before your cloud storage deployment goes live. You'll also need to plan for how much time this transfer can require. If you've ever tried to upload many large files from your home computer to a cloud backup service, you know it can take days or even weeks to complete the transfer. In many cases, an extended delay is not acceptable, and you'll need to see what options the cloud provider can offer for speeding up the data transfer.

- *Data types*—Data might require different target storage services depending on its type, including:
  - ○ Files arranged in hierarchical file systems
  - ○ Volumes that are handled by block storage
  - ○ Unorganized data collected in an object storage service

Migration requirements and processes for relational and nonrelational databases depend significantly on the combination of source and target database services. For example, migrating from an on-prem MySQL server to a cloud-based MySQL server is relatively straightforward. Converting from an on-prem relational database to a cloud-based nonrelational database is more complex. Some of these migration types can be performed live with no downtime for the applications and other services that depend on these databases. Other times, there will be some—perhaps a lot—of downtime. Many cloud providers offer database migration services that can ease the transition and reduce or eliminate downtime.

Remember This

- Data types stored in the cloud include office and media files, applications, websites, logs, and databases.
- Common RAID techniques include RAID 0 (striping), RAID 1 (mirroring), RAID 5 (parity), RAID 6 (double parity), and RAID 10 (a stripe of mirrors).
- Cloud storage services generally fall into three categories: file system storage, block storage, and object storage.
- When moving data to a cloud provider's infrastructure, the company might need to make some changes to the data, such as its format, structure, or even the way it is labeled.

Self-Check

1. Which file system is specific to Linux?
   - a. FAT32
   - b. BTRFS
   - c. NTFS
   - d. ReFS

2. What type of storage is the hard drive in your laptop?
   - a. SAN
   - b. NAS
   - c. DAS
   - d. SDS

3. Which protocol supports object storage communications?
   - a. CAD
   - b. FC
   - c. HTTPS
   - d. LUN

○ Check your answers at the end of this module.

Section 8-2: Storage Optimization Techniques

● **Certification**

1.3 Explain the importance of high availability and scaling in cloud environments.

1.4 Given a scenario, analyze the solution design in support of the business requirements.

2.3 Given a scenario, apply the appropriate OS and application security controls.

2.4 Given a scenario, apply data security and compliance controls in cloud environments.

3.1 Given a scenario, integrate components into a cloud solution.

3.2 Given a scenario, provision storage in cloud environments.

3.3 Given a scenario, deploy cloud networking solutions.

4.2 Given a scenario, maintain efficient operation of a cloud environment.

4.3 Given a scenario, optimize cloud environments.

Clearly, storage options can be compared with each other based on several factors. For example, the organization of data, expandability of the storage space, and required durability of the data all factor into storage decisions. Storage performance can be evaluated based on several measurable factors, three of which are described here:

- *Transfer rate or read/write throughput*—This metric specifies the speed at which data is moved through the storage infrastructure and is measured in MB/s.
- *IOPS (input/output operations per second)*—This number details how many read and write operations can be completed per second. It's typically given as an integer, such as 500 for an HDD (hard disk drive) in the cloud or 16,000 for a cloud-hosted SSD. In some cases, you can request an IOPS-optimized configuration to improve database operations. For example, AWS offers Provisioned IOPS storage that allows for more predictable database performance.
- *Latency*—Latency results from bottlenecks in technology, geographical distances, or subpar optimization of data. It can be measured by TTFB (time to first byte), RTT (round-trip time), or similar metrics. You can decrease the latency of a storage solution by turning on data caching and by carefully choosing where data is located geographically.

Storage Capacity

When provisioning storage resources, sufficient storage space must be allocated to host the data. In Module 2, you read about dynamic storage for VMs and storage overcommitment, or oversubscription, that allocates more storage space to a host's VMs than what the underlying hardware actually has available. This is possible based on the assumption that most VMs won't use all their allocated space, and certainly not all at the same time. Much the same approach can be used for an on-prem SAN, where users are allocated more space than what is collectively available in the storage array. This oversubscription is called a TP (thin provisioning) model and is cheaper than the more predictable FP (fat provisioning) model, which is also called thick provisioning, where only existing physical storage space can be allocated.

In the traditional, on-prem data center, an IT admin must anticipate the organization's increasing needs well ahead of when those needs are realized. It can take months to get approval for new file servers, order the equipment, install the new infrastructure hardware, and provision higher-capacity storage spaces. This process incurs significant bulk expenses and work time, and results in frequent mismatches between used space and available space. Thin provisioning offers some flexibility in this process, but the admin must carefully monitor when needed storage space is anticipated to approach available physical storage space.

In the cloud, these storage provisioning models are mostly irrelevant from the customer's perspective, although this varies by cloud service. For example, when attaching a storage volume to a VM, most public cloud platforms require full allocation of the storage space even if you're not yet using it. You saw this in earlier modules where you're charged for the entire volume's storage space even if it's mostly empty. Therefore, when deleting a VM, you must ensure the associated storage volume is also deleted to avoid accruing charges. When using elastic storage services, however, most public cloud platforms charge you only for the storage space you use. Costs increase or decrease immediately and granularly, eliminating the budget cushion required for an on-prem storage solution.

Data Optimization

One way to maximize storage performance is to optimize the data itself. Some cloud storage services—especially if they target specific kinds of storage, such as databases or websites—offer data compression. For example, AWS Redshift (which is designed to warehouse massive databases) and AWS CloudFront (a high-speed CDN service) both offer data compression options. Compression reduces the number of bits needed to store data by recoding the data in a more efficient manner. You might have used compression when you zipped large files into a smaller attachment to send by email. Many compression technologies exist, such as the following:

- Zip compressors like 7-Zip (7-zip.org), xz (tukaani.org/xz), and gzip (gnu.org/software/gzip)
- RAR (Roshal Archive Compressed) compressors like WinRAR in Windows or the aforementioned 7-Zip

Figure 8-7 shows a folder of photos being compressed in Windows.

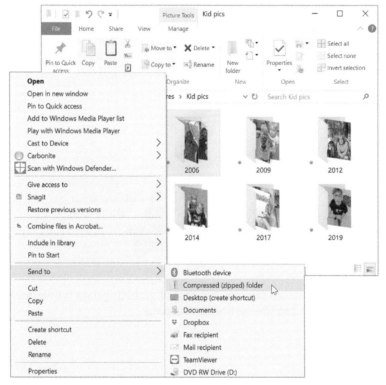

Figure 8-7   Compress a group of files to take up less storage space

Another option for reducing the sheer volume of stored data is data deduplication, which eliminates multiple copies of the same data. For example, suppose you email a video file to several members of a project team, and everyone saves their own copy of the file to the company network. Data deduplication stores only one copy of the video and tracks metadata references for all other copies back to that one file instance.

Data Lifecycle

Stored data progresses through a series of states in its lifetime. For example, recent data might need to be accessed frequently while older data is rarely if ever accessed. With some data, you need to keep older versions in addition to current versions. Sometimes, data is placed under legal protection and must be saved for a period. And other times, data must be destroyed according to legal guidelines. In some cases, you can configure storage services to automatically transition data through these various stages.

Tiering

Storage tiers, also called storage classes, can decrease the cost of storing data in exchange for increasing the cost and time of retrieving it. For example, data that is accessed frequently can be stored using a cloud service that charges more for the space used and less for the number of times you access it, as shown in Figure 8-8. This allows for frequent access while paying a premium for the storage space itself. In contrast, data that doesn't require regular access, such as archived data or backups that need to be kept long term, can be kept in cold storage where storage space is cheaper but each request for data costs more (and takes longer). This system replicates the on-prem process of transferring old data from active systems, such as fast flash storage, to cheaper but less accessible storage media, such as tapes.

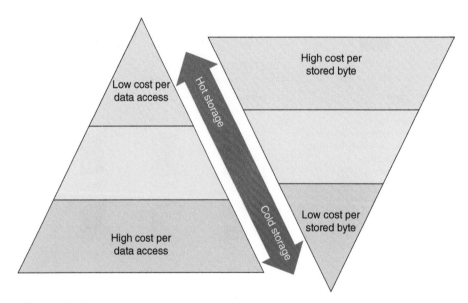

Figure 8-8   With tiered storage, the cost of accessing data is inversely related to the cost of storing data

Lifecycle Rules

Adaptive optimization of storage costs can shift data from one tier to another based on criteria the customer defines. These adaptive optimization settings are called **lifecycle rules** or lifecycle management. For example, in AWS's S3 (Simple Storage Service), you can set lifecycle rules that apply to one or more objects stored in a bucket. Available lifecycle rules can move current or previous versions of objects between storage classes (such as frequent access, infrequent access, archive, or deep archive) a certain number of days after the object was created or last accessed. See Figure 8-9.

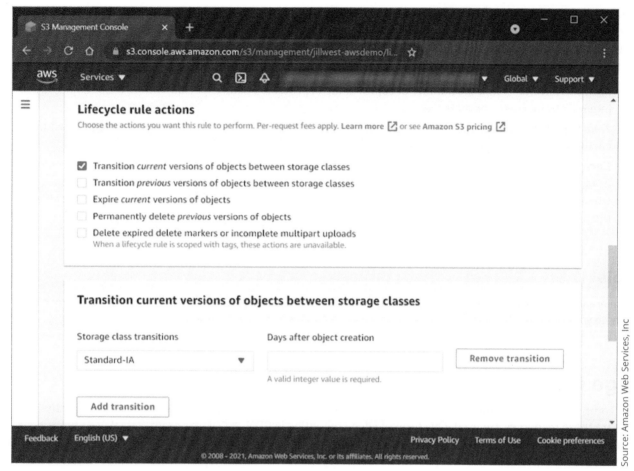

Figure 8-9   AWS lifecycle rule configuration

Versioning

While not all data justifies paying for storing its older versions, versioning is an option where needed. **Versioning** refers to keeping older versions of the data as a backup or to document changes in the data, such as for compliance or regulatory purposes. In many cases, versioning is enabled automatically if data is identified as a record. A **record** is an item whose content provides evidence of communications, decisions, and actions during business activities. When an item is marked as a record, certain retention-based restrictions are automatically enabled that ensure the record cannot be deleted or changed by users.

Legal Hold

Records management refers to the entire process of identifying and protecting items that qualify as records and is an important component of administrating storage services. For example, in most cases, records must be protected by retention policies that prevent deletion or alteration. Records might also fall under additional restrictions imposed by a **legal hold**, which is a court-ordered notification preventing the deletion of identified data. At some point, records might also be covered under data destruction policies that require secure disposal of the data at the end of the retention period.

Data Destruction

When handling physical documents and devices on-prem, companies will often hire professional disposal services that thoroughly destroy hard copies of documents (such as by shredding) and adequately sanitize or destroy devices so no data can be recovered. Reputable vendors provide end-to-end insurance coverage from the moment they take possession of a device.

Destroying cloud-hosted data can present additional complications, however. Many customers also use services that duplicate data to personal devices or to on-prem storage for convenience, which is called **hybrid cloud storage**. Cloud providers also will often make redundant copies of data to ensure its high durability. Even the providers themselves might not know where all these so-called "zombie" copies of data reside within their platforms, and they can continue to exist undetected for years. With replicated and backed-up data stored across cloud providers' data centers, how can a customer ensure their data is destroyed in a manner that meets regulatory requirements?

The following options can help increase the security of cloud-based data disposal:

- *Use restrictions*—Limit the number of copies made of protected data, especially where those copies are only intended to increase convenience.
- *Tenancy*—Limit data storage to a single host device dedicated to a single customer or even owned by that customer.
- *Encryption*—Encrypt all records stored in the cloud. Encryption can protect the data even if it's recovered from a backup storage location. Whereas this process presents other difficulties (such as key management when some of the data must be destroyed but not all of it), encryption ensures the data is irrecoverable once the private key is destroyed.

Note

In reference to hosting cloud services, the term "tenant" can refer to the physical host device. However, the term can also refer to your customer that accesses data you've stored in an object storage service.

Edge Computing

Edge computing is an evolution of cloud computing that places compute power, data storage, and connectivity closer to where these resources are used. One form of edge computing is CDN. A CDN (content delivery network) is a distributed storage structure that allows customers to store files in locations closer to where their users are located. For example, suppose you run a video repository website. If your users in India try to stream a video that is stored on a server located in Virginia, those users will experience significant latency. A CDN such as AWS CloudFront allows you to cache a copy of your video at an edge location that is physically located in India. The proximity to your users will decrease latency and increase user satisfaction.

The CDN service routes user traffic to the closest edge location with the best performance at the time of the request. It also manages the TTL (time to live) of files cached at those edge locations according to parameters you define. These parameters are usually determined by factors such as the following:

- Resistance of the data to becoming stale (i.e., becoming outdated over time)
- Sensitivity of the data to customization for the user (such as caching data used by many users but not caching data specific to only one user)

When cached files expire (i.e., they have exceeded their TTL) or have not been used within a given period, they are discarded at the edge location. If the files are requested again from a user near that edge location, the CDN will refer to the data's origin point to retrieve updated files.

Remember This

- Storage performance can be evaluated based on transfer rate or read/write throughput, IOPS (input/output operations per second), and latency.
- Provisioning storage capacity in the cloud is most often performed automatically in direct response to needed space.
- One way to maximize storage performance is to optimize the data itself through techniques such as compression and deduplication.
- Stored data needs to progress through various states in its lifetime, including transitioning to different tiers according to access needs, possibly keeping past versions of the data, possibly being placed under a legal hold, and eventually being thoroughly destroyed.

Self-Check

4. Which data optimization technique eliminates unnecessary copies of data?

   a. Tiering

   b. Deduplication

   c. Compression

   d. Versioning

5. Which of these storage tiers would be most appropriate for archived data?

   a. Glacier

   b. Frequent access

   c. Infrequent access

   d. Standard

6. Which feature of CDN files helps ensure customers get current copies of cached data?

   a. Tier

   b. Version

   c. TTL

   d. CAS

○ Check your answers at the end of this module.

Section 8-3: Cloud Storage Services

Certification

1.3 Explain the importance of high availability and scaling in cloud environments.

2.3 Given a scenario, apply the appropriate OS and application security controls.

3.1 Given a scenario, integrate components into a cloud solution.

3.2 Given a scenario, provision storage in cloud environments.

Each of the major public cloud providers offers several options for meeting storage needs. Most of these services can be categorized according to file, block, or object storage. Some services are targeted specifically to databases or VM instances or other specific use cases. Some services are also designed for cost optimization by reducing the prices on colder storage tiers while allowing increased data retrieval latency.

Let's explore some of the primary file, block, and object storage services offered by AWS, Azure, and GCP. As you read about these services, also notice different options for creating backups, which you learn more about later in this module.

AWS Storage Services

AWS continues to release new storage services to meet a variety of needs, including file system, block, object, and database storage options. AWS also offers a Backup service, which provides fully automated backup processes across multiple services—including block storage, file system storage, and database services—and can also back up on-prem data. Another popular service is AWS Storage Gateway, which can be used to bridge the gap between on-prem and AWS storage, even offering a VTL (virtual tape library) feature that presents virtual tape drives to an on-prem backup application. The following is a description of some of AWS's other popular storage services.

Object Storage

S3 (Simple Storage Service) is AWS's most popular and flexible cloud storage service, able to host just about any kind of data. AWS offers 11 nines durability (that's 99.999999999% guarantee of not losing a stored object) for data contained in S3 when stored across multiple AZs (availability zones). Also, data can be encrypted by the cloud customer (called client-side encryption) or by AWS (called server-side encryption). Figure 8-10 shows some of the options available when creating a new bucket in S3. A storage bucket is essentially a container for files, logs, static websites, or other objects.

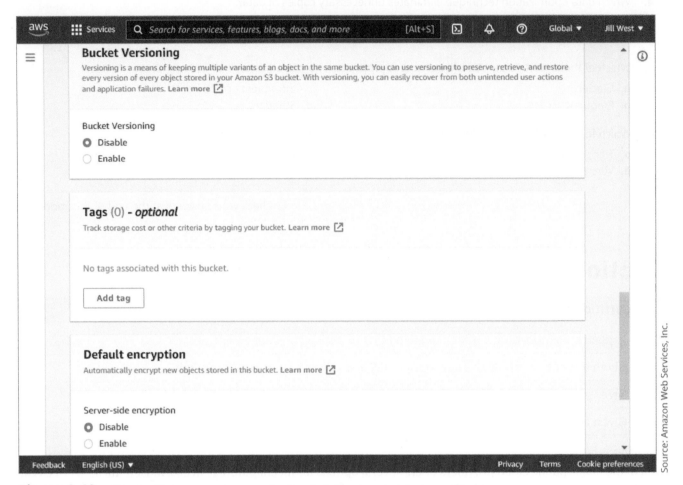

Figure 8-10   Choose features such as versioning, logging, tags, and encryption

There's no minimum fee to use S3, and costs are calculated based on actual storage space used, data requests (such as retrieving, scanning, or deleting data), and data transfers. S3 classes provide different storage tiers and rates to better meet customers' needs. For example, the Standard class allows for high durability, availability, and performance of data that is accessed frequently. However, data that does not need to be accessed often could be stored in the cheaper Infrequent Access class, and data that is archived for long-term storage could use the even cheaper Glacier Deep Archive storage class. This archival service is ideal for highly regulated data that must be stored for many years but is rarely accessed, such as financial or medical records. Retrieval for the coldest storage type might take up to 12 hours.

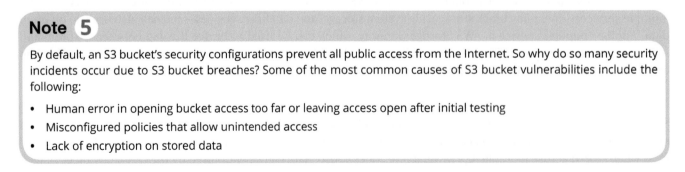

Note 5

By default, an S3 bucket's security configurations prevent all public access from the Internet. So why do so many security incidents occur due to S3 bucket breaches? Some of the most common causes of S3 bucket vulnerabilities include the following:

- Human error in opening bucket access too far or leaving access open after initial testing
- Misconfigured policies that allow unintended access
- Lack of encryption on stored data

File System Storage

AWS's EFS (Elastic File System) and FSx (third-party file system) both provide managed file system storage. EFS supports Linux-based workloads while FSx for Windows File Server provides a native Windows file system built on Windows Server. These file systems can be mounted to many cloud-hosted VM instances or on-prem servers using NFS. This capability makes it easy to lift and shift applications that require file system access and to share files across a hybrid cloud network. The file system space can also be expanded as needed rather than being limited by the size of the physical disks hosting the file system.

As with on-prem file systems, access to files can be managed through file system policies that grant read, write, or root user access to files. Using file system policies, you can also enforce secure transport when moving files or allow access by approved accounts only when using approved endpoints. File system policies are configured using JSON (JavaScript Object Notation). In a project at the end of this module, you have the opportunity to practice editing JSON policies to manage access to stored data.

VM-Attached Storage

AWS EBS (Elastic Block Store) is designed to work with EC2 to provide instance-level storage volumes. An EBS volume exists as a separate resource from an EC2 instance, similar to how you can remove or attach a hard drive in a computer. This is called persistent storage because it doesn't necessarily cease to exist when you terminate the EC2 instance. In contrast, EC2 Instance Storage provides a temporary drive called an ephemeral drive that exists only while the EC2 instance exists. Ephemeral instance storage is not available for all instance types. For example, the t2.micro instance type uses only EBS storage. Figure 8-11 shows a t2.micro instance being created with its default root volume plus a new EBS volume.

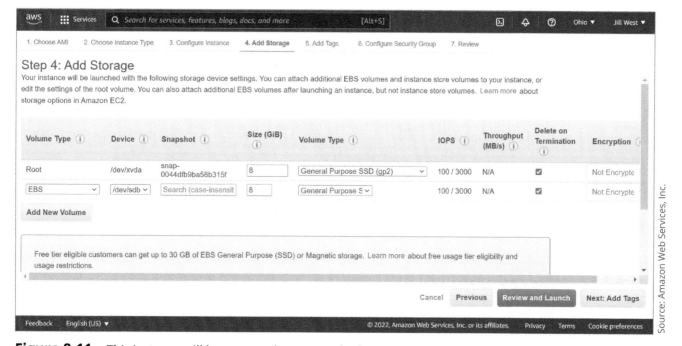

Figure 8-11   This instance will have two volumes attached

You're Ready

You're now ready to complete Project 8-1: Manage Storage in AWS. You can complete the project now or wait until you've finished all the readings for this module.

Azure Storage Services

Azure also offers object, file system, and VM-attached block storage. To use most of Azure's storage services, you must first create a storage account. This storage account contains all your Azure Storage data, including blobs, file shares, and disks. The storage account also defines a unique namespace in the Azure cloud, meaning that you must choose a name for your storage account that is not already being used by anyone else in Azure. You can associate a storage account with an existing subscription and even include it within a specific resource group for easy management. Figure 8-12 shows some of the options you have when creating a storage account. In a project at the end of this module, you use the redundancy option LRS (locally-redundant storage) to conform to the free-tier requirements in Azure.

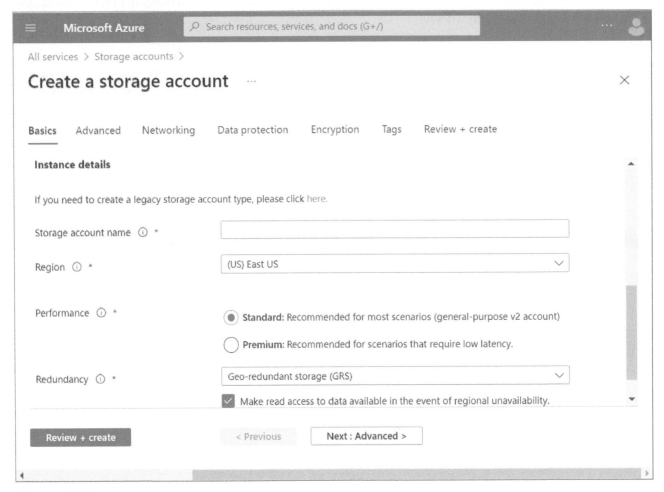

Figure 8-12   Create a storage account

Object Storage

When managing a database, there are times when large files, such as photos or audio files, must be included with other, more structured data. Over time, these kinds of unstructured, opaque files came to be known as BLOBs (binary large objects). Microsoft borrowed this concept in naming its object storage service, which is called Azure Blob storage. Like other object storage services, Blob storage supports storage of massive amounts of unstructured data.

You create storage containers from within an existing storage account, as shown in Figure 8-13, and choose public access at the blob level or container level as you create the container. In Azure, storage containers are analogous to AWS S3's buckets, and blobs are like S3 objects. You create a container, and then you upload blobs to it.

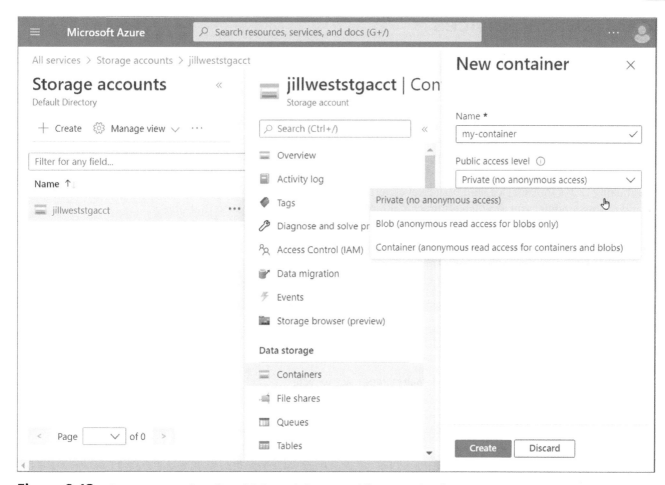

Figure 8-13   Create a container for a blob, and choose public access level

There are three blob types:

- **Block blob**—Block blobs are designed for binary data, such as text, photos, or other binary files.
- **Page blob**—Page blobs support frequent read/write operations, such as VM disks or persistent database storage.
- **Append blob**—Append blobs work best for files where data is frequently added, or appended, to the file (such as log files).

File System Storage

Azure Files provides cloud-hosted file share services. File shares can be mounted from Azure to Windows, Linux, or macOS systems either in the cloud or on-prem, acting as a file server or NAS device on your network. File Share can also support applications that have been shifted to the cloud from the on-prem data center, or hybrid applications that run on-prem while their data resides in the cloud.

VM-Attached Storage

Azure Disk storage offers VM-attached storage, like a hard disk attached to a physical computer. An Azure disk can provide an organized file system to the VM but can only be attached to one VM at a time. An Azure disk is a VHD (Virtual Hard Disk) stored as a page blob in Azure Blob Storage.

You're Ready

You're now ready to complete Project 8-2: Manage Storage in Azure. You can complete the project now or wait until you've finished all the readings for this module.

GCP Storage Services

GCP, like the other platforms, offers object storage as its primary storage solution, file system storage to support apps and file sharing, and VM-attached storage to provide persistent storage to VM and container instances.

Object Storage

Cloud Storage is GCP's object storage solution. It offers 99.999999999% (that's 11 nines) annual durability and TTFB (time to first byte) measured in milliseconds. To use Cloud Storage, you create a bucket and then upload objects to the bucket, similar to how AWS's S3 works. Cloud Storage supports popular features such as lifecycle management and object versioning; however, some of these features are only available through the CLI. Bucket-level permissions are set using GCP's IAM service, and object-level permissions are set using an ACL (access control list). In a project at the end of this module, you practice editing an object's ACL to control access to that object.

GCP's object storage is categorized by four storage classes, as shown in Figure 8-14 and described next.

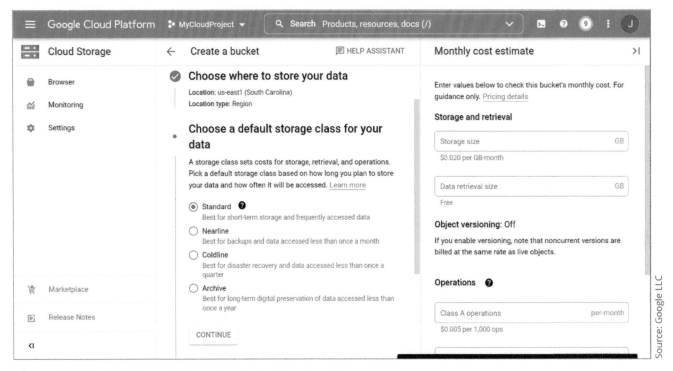

Figure 8-14   GCP's free trial includes limited Standard-class storage

- Standard storage provides a balance of inexpensive storage for data that needs to be accessed frequently without requiring a minimum storage duration.
- Nearline Storage is designed for moderate frequency access, such as less than once a month, and requires storage duration of at least 30 days.
- Coldline Storage is designed for data that is accessed less than once or twice a year and requires storage duration of at least 90 days.
- Archive Storage is optimized for long-term storage that is rarely accessed and requires a minimum storage duration of at least 365 days.

File System Storage

Cloud Filestore is a managed file storage service designed to support cloud-hosted applications that rely on a shared file system, similar to adding a NAS to a network. Filestore file shares can attach to Compute Engine instances or Kubernetes Engine instances. Use IAM permissions to control access to Filestore operations, such as creating a

Filestore instance. Use Linux permissions to control access to the file share itself, such as read, write, and execute. Filestore supports any NFSv3 client.

VM-Attached Storage

Persistent Disk offers high-performance block storage for attaching virtual SSDs or HDDs to Compute Engine or Kubernetes Engine instances. You can resize, back up, or snapshot these disks, and you can even mount a disk to multiple readers, which means several VMs can read from the same Persistent Disk. This enables easy content sharing between VMs.

You're Ready

You're now ready to complete Project 8-3: Manage Storage in GCP. You can complete the project now or wait until you've finished all the readings for this module.

Remember This

- S3 (Simple Storage Service) is AWS's most popular and flexible cloud storage service, able to host just about any kind of data.
- To use most of Azure's storage services, you must first create a storage account.
- GCP's Cloud Storage supports popular features such as lifecycle management and object versioning; however, some of these features are only available through the CLI.

Self-Check

7. AWS file system policies are configured using _____.
   a. NFS
   b. JSON
   c. S3
   d. VTL

8. An object stored in Azure is called a _____.
   a. storage account
   b. container
   c. bucket
   d. blob

9. GCP object-level permissions are set using _____.
   a. IAM
   b. ACLs
   c. policies
   d. records

○ Check your answers at the end of this module.

Section 8-4: Creating and Storing Backups

Certification

1.3 Explain the importance of high availability and scaling in cloud environments.

2.3 Given a scenario, apply the appropriate OS and application security controls.

3.2 Given a scenario, provision storage in cloud environments.

As you've already learned, cloud platforms such as AWS, Azure, and GCP include built-in durability and availability features for many of their services, including keeping multiple copies of your data across hardware stacks to allow for their data recovery efforts should something go wrong. In this case, durability is something the CSP provides and manages.

That said, durability is not the same thing as a backup. Durability refers to the resistance of data to errors due to corruption or loss. A high durability rating reduces the likelihood you'll need a backup. However, critical business data still warrants backup protection. Whether data is lost through user error, such as deleting needed files or not paying a data storage bill, or through an attack or disaster, backups provide a layer of protection managed by the cloud consumer that is not covered by durability ratings.

Backup professionals suggest, at the minimum, following the 3-2-1 Rule for backups. This rule states, as shown in Figure 8-15, that you should have at least three copies of your data (that's one production copy and two backup copies), stored on at least two different kinds of media (such as disk and tape), with one copy stored in an alternate location geographically separate from the original data.

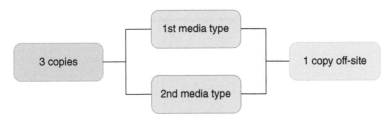

Figure 8-15 Three copies of data, stored on two different kinds of media, with one copy stored off-site

For an on-prem network, this means that storing one backup copy locally is acceptable; however, the other backup should be stored in a remote location, preferably in a different geographic area where a natural disaster that affects the local network would not endanger the remote backup. For more sophisticated backup strategies that rely more natively on the cloud, consider the following variations of this rule, such as 3-1-2 (Figure 8-16) or 4-2-3 (Figure 8-17).

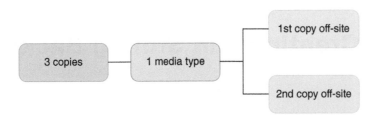

Figure 8-16 Three copies of data, stored on one kind of media (such as SSD), at two geographically isolated locations in the cloud

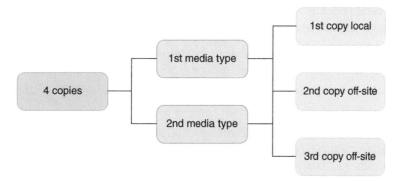

Figure 8-17   Four copies of data, stored on two different kinds of media, with one backup stored locally and two in geographically isolated locations in the cloud

It's also important to understand the difference between archived data and backup data. Archived data is cold data that is no longer used. It might be an earlier version of data that is in use, or it might be the master copy of old data that is no longer accessed (such as medical records for former patients). Typically, archived data is stored in cheap cold storage that is not easily accessible. It's not synced to any active systems. While backup data is not regularly accessed, it must be frequently updated to match active data, and it should be quickly accessible should something bad happen to the active data store. Backups might include versioning, which keeps different versions of a file that has been changed multiple times.

Protection Capabilities

Storing backups is a common use of storage space in the cloud. Various backup types can protect a network's data. However, not every failure wipes your data. Other items in the network should be backed up as well. Some common backup objects include the following:

- *Applications*—Applications might rely on many components: databases, object or block storage, code, VMs, and containers. Application-level backup ensures that none of the infrastructure resources (such as VMs or code resources) rely on a single point of failure and that all resource configurations are saved for future reference.

- *File systems*—Cloud-based file systems, such as those created in AWS's EFS, can incorporate built-in backup features such as redundancy across regions or create automatic backups on a set schedule. In most cases, these backups consist of data that has changed since the previous backup and include the file organizational structure.

- *Configuration files*—You might have used TFTP (Trivial File Transfer Protocol) to back up configuration files for on-prem network devices, such as a router or switch, to a TFTP server. These files can be used to restore a device's configuration if the device experiences a failure or reset. Similarly, cloud resource configurations, such as EC2 instance configurations, should be backed up. You might accomplish this goal by creating a snapshot or image file or by using a backup solution designed for this purpose.

- *Databases*—Some cloud-based database services automatically back up stored data and database configuration information. Other database services require that you opt into the backup feature, or you can perform a manual update. For example, if you're running Amazon RDS (Relational Database Service), you can create a database dump file and restore the database to a different DB instance later. A database dump file is created using the database software's export facility and can contain the database's metadata, the database's content, or both.

How long should you retain backup files? In some cases, backup retention length is dictated by regulatory standards. In other cases, you can choose what makes the most sense in your situation. Factors to consider include:

- *How extensively data changes from backup to backup*—At some point, older backup data is no longer relevant or useful.
- *How expensive backup storage is in comparison to overall budget*—Backup storage places demands on the IT budget that can be reduced by deleting older backups.

Deleting old backups can help reduce storage costs and, if using physical media for those backups, can increase available space for newer data. Using cheaper storage media, such as hard disk drives (also called spinning disks), can also reduce costs of backup storage. Many cloud platforms offer cheaper storage rates when using these slower storage devices. For example, Figure 8-18 shows the option to use HDDs (hard disk drives) for the EBS volumes attached to an EC2 instance. Some automated tiering features can help automate, taking advantage of this cheaper storage option for older backup files.

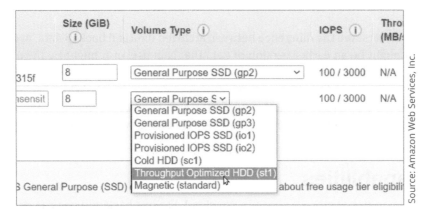

Figure 8-18   Storage volume options in EC2

> **Note 6**
>
> You can also reduce data storage and backup costs by restricting the amount of data stored. For example, you might implement **user quotas** on file system storage to limit how much storage space any individual user can consume. As a user approaches their limit, they will receive a warning message. When they have reached their limit, they are no longer allowed to write new files to the storage space until they delete other files or obtain special permission for exceeding the configured limits.

Many of the cloud services consumers configure and manage offer options for backups. Consider the following protection capabilities:

- *Network redundancy*—HA (high availability) refers to having reliable access to data. In contrast, durability refers to protection from loss. Durability is achieved by keeping multiple copies of data. If one copy is damaged, another copy can be used to restore the data. HA, however, is achieved with hardware redundancy—such as having multiple servers, cables, power supplies, and cooling solutions—so that if one of these components fails, a redundant component can take over. You've seen how CSPs provide failover AZs where you can replicate virtual hardware across multiple physical data centers. If one data center experiences a crisis, your workloads can failover to a different AZ. This is an example of how to optimize data availability.
- *Cloning*—Cloning is the act of creating a new copy of existing data. The clone can replace the original with a simple swap and no further configuration. A similar concept for copying a disk drive is called imaging, where the copy is more compressed.

- ***Storage replication***—Storage replication supports data durability. Data is replicated across multiple data centers in a region or, for a higher price tag, across data centers in multiple regions. Where cloning creates a new copy of existing data, storage replication to the backup target can occur immediately or periodically, as follows:

  - Synchronous replication writes data to the replica at the same time the data is written to primary storage. If a failure occurs with the primary data, the replica provides an exact, updated copy. Synchronous replication requires more bandwidth, however, because data is written to two locations at the same time.

  - Asynchronous replication writes data to primary storage first and then periodically copies these updates to the replica. Asynchronous replication requires less bandwidth but can also result in some data loss due to the delay in writing to the replica, depending on when a failure occurs.

- ***Storage mirroring***—Storage mirroring is similar in concept to storage replication in that it creates two copies of your data. However, with storage mirroring, the mirror copy (or shadow copy) is an exact copy of the original data source, meaning it reflects any structural changes made to the data, not just adding or editing the data itself. A mirror copy is also not intended to be used side by side with the active copy, in contrast to storage replication where the replica can sometimes be used simultaneously. In reality, however, these two terms are often used interchangeably.

Backup Types

Notice that cloning creates a complete copy of the data at a single PIT (point in time) whereas data replication makes changes to the replica as or soon after the data itself changes. A clone represents a single, historical point in time and is not continually updated. In contrast, a replica is synced with the original data as that data changes and so represents the *current* point in time. Different backup types take different approaches to copying data, which affects the point in time represented by the backup. Working with these various options can help maximize the use of available storage space and minimize the cost of storing backups. Consider the following backup types:

- ***Full backup***—Backs up everything every time a backup is performed
- ***Incremental backup***—Backs up only data that has changed since the last backup of any kind
- ***Differential backup***—Backs up data that has changed since the last *full* backup

Figure 8-19 shows the conceptual differences between these backup types. It might help to imagine the different file sizes if you were to look at a full backup file, an incremental backup file, and a differential backup file side by side. The full backup would be the largest because it copies all the original data, even old data that hasn't changed in a long time. The time to recover data from a full backup, called RTO (recovery time objective), would be fairly short because all the copied data exists in one place. In other words, full backups allow for a low RTO. However, full backups take up a lot of space and require a lot of time to create.

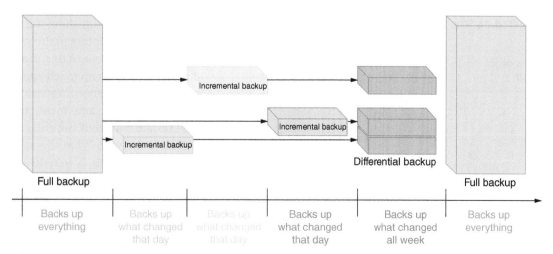

Figure 8-19   Incremental and differential backups require fewer resources than do full backups

The incremental backup would be the smallest file. It only includes data that has changed since the last backup of any kind. For example, if you perform a full backup on Sunday, then an incremental backup would copy whatever changed on Monday, the next incremental backup would copy whatever changed on Tuesday, and then the next incremental backup would include whatever changed on Wednesday. You have one full backup from early in the week, with several smaller files containing changes for each day. To recover this data to its RPO (recovery point objective), you would need to start with the full backup, then apply changes from Monday, then changes from Tuesday, and finally, changes from Wednesday. This creates a series of dependencies between backup files. Incremental backups don't take up much space and don't require much time to create. However, you must make them frequently and allow more time to recover when relying on incremental backups.

The size of a differential backup (also called a delta backup or delta differential backup) falls between the other two. It includes all data changed since the last full backup (this changed data is called the delta) regardless of any other smaller backups performed since then. For example, suppose you make a full backup on Sunday. On Monday, you would make a differential backup for changes made that day. On Tuesday, you would make a new differential backup of all changes made since Sunday's full backup. On Wednesday, you would create an even larger differential backup that includes all changes made since Sunday's full backup. To recover this data, you would need to start with the full backup made on Sunday, and then apply only the latest differential backup, which would contain all changes since the latest full backup was performed. VMware uses a similar technology called Changed Block Tracking to back up only changed blocks of VMs on the network.

Note 7

Some backup systems can create a **synthetic full backup**, which is created from the most recent full backup and any applicable incremental or differential backups. Functionally, a synthetic full backup is equivalent to a full backup and can reduce the processing load to create the backup. As with all backup types, confirm the completion of backup generation and regularly test restoration processes.

Snapshots

As you've already learned, a clone is a complete copy of data, a VM, or another system. A **snapshot**, however, is a temporary copy at a particular point in time. There's a lot of variety in how vendors define and use snapshot technology and terminology. When working with VMs, for example, you can create a snapshot to capture a specific VM state at that point in time. Then as you make changes to the VM, such as when testing a new application, the snapshot files record the differences, or delta, to track what's changing. When you're finished with your experimentations, you can revert to the snapshot to bring the VM back to its earlier state or simply delete the snapshot. Snapshots aren't intended to be kept for very long and are only useful if the VM itself still exists because the snapshot's files don't contain enough information to recreate the VM from scratch.

Similarly, a storage snapshot records the state of a storage system at a particular point in time, as determined by the system's metadata. The snapshot does not include the stored data itself—just information about the states of that data, including pointers to the various blocks or volumes. Because of this, a storage snapshot does not take up much space or require much time for creation. You can save storage snapshots in the same location as the data itself because without the data, the snapshot is useless anyway. What the snapshot does accomplish, though, is to reduce the RTO, or time required to recover from a loss or revert back to a specific point in time. As changes are made to the protected data, the snapshot continues to point to the old data, which still exists in the storage block or volume, while the active metadata is updated through a redirect-on-write process to redirect its pointers to the new data. See Figure 8-20.

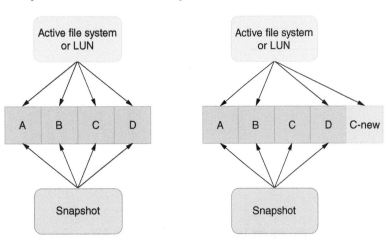

Figure 8-20   The snapshot continues to point to the old data while the active metadata points to the new data

Redundancy Levels

Backups and HA both rely on some amount of redundancy. To further understand the importance of redundancy, let's discuss redundancy levels. Redundancy, as you've read, refers to having multiple copies of a resource. This is similar in concept to having a spare tire in your car. Suppose N refers to the resources required for operation, such as having four functional tires. N by itself means you have no backup and refers to the minimum resources needed to support day-to-day operations. But if you have a spare tire in your car's trunk, then you have a redundancy level of N+1. You could get one flat tire and you'd be okay.

Have you ever had two flat tires at the same time? If you happened to have two spare tires in your car, which is a redundancy level of N+2, then you could handle this situation, too. Similarly, having three spare tires would give you a redundancy level of N+3. As in algebra, you can use X to refer to any number of redundancies, such as N+X, although it's unusual to implement redundancy of more than N+2.

As with tires, the redundant resources on your network aren't always as good as the resources you use most of the time. For example, your spare tire might be rated for a much lower maximum speed than your normal tires, and will suffer wear and tear much more quickly, with a life expectancy of only about 70 miles. These spare tires, as shown in Figure 8-21, are called temporary or donut spare tires, and using one for extended periods can cause additional wear and tear on your other tires as well. Similarly, your UPS (uninterruptible power supply) might not be able to provide backup power for more than a few minutes to a few hours, and the number of devices it can power will likely be reduced. So, when you are forced to resort to using your backup, you get subpar performance that can also cause damage if relied on for too long. Even if you have a full-size spare tire, the difference in wear and tear between the new tire and old tires can cause all the tires to wear more quickly. That's why you're usually advised to replace all four tires at the same time.

Figure 8-21 A spare tire is usually smaller and less capable than a full-size tire

Source: iStock.com/MichaelSvoboda

However, suppose you have a complete set of four full-size tires as your backup rather than keeping just a donut spare tire in the car. A redundancy that provides equal performance to the component it's replacing is referred to with a redundancy level of 2N. For example, if you have two ISPs providing Internet access to your business when you only need one for day-to-day operations, you have 2N redundancy. Suppose you have four full-size spare tires plus a donut spare tire. This redundancy level would be represented as 2N+1.

Note 8

Redundancy level is similar in concept to RF (redundancy factor). RF1 refers to the minimum resources required for operation. RF2 indicates you have enough excess resources operating that you could tolerate one resource failure, such as getting one flat tire on an off-road vehicle that uses six tires and can function with only five. Notice this is a subtractive concept rather than additive: RF measures how much you can take away and still be okay, while redundancy levels measure how much extra you have on hand. RF3 indicates you could tolerate the loss of two redundant resources and still function, such as a specialized, off-road military vehicle getting two flat tires and continuing to be operational.

Grow with Cengage Unlimited!

If you'd like more information about redundancy on networks, use your Cengage Unlimited subscription to go to *CompTIA Network+ Guide to Networks*, 9th edition, Module 7, and read the section titled "Network Availability."

If you don't have a Cengage Unlimited subscription, you can find more information at cengage.com/unlimited.

Backup Considerations

Several factors contribute to decisions about what backup strategy best fits your company's situation. Consider the following points:

- *SLA (service-level agreement)*—You've already learned that CSPs offer SLAs to guarantee a certain level of performance and recourse options for the customer if service falls below or above certain thresholds. An IT department might also have a written SLA with the organization it belongs to. Ideally, management will play a role in defining the terms of this SLA and will budget for sufficient funds to meet those expectations. These factors will be determined by thresholds such as RTO, which is the maximum tolerable outage time, and RPO, which defines how much data loss is tolerable (a day's worth? an hour's worth?). This kind of information will factor into decisions on backup types and backup schedule. This will also determine whether backups should be stored online and configured for automatic failover, or stored offline, which requires more time for retrieval and recovery. Many backup systems use a mixture of both.

- *Resource configurations*—The types of resources on your network, whether on-prem or in the cloud, will also dictate some of the available options and decisions that must be made. For example, backing up a database or object storage will require different backup methodologies than backing up a large collection of VMs and their connected storage.

- *Authentication backups*—As with device configurations, authentication directories and configurations should also be backed up.

- *Backup rotation*—Recall that a full backup backs up everything. So how many full backups should you keep? For that matter, how many iterations of any backup files should you keep? To a degree, this decision will be made at an organizational level and, in many cases, this decision will be affected by applicable government regulations or industry standards. Make sure you know and implement the appropriate policy for rotating backup files. On a similar note, when deleting backup files, make sure you follow any relevant standards or guidelines for adequately destroying this data. You don't want deleted backups to be recoverable by an attacker.

- *Security*—Where and how data is stored must be considered in the context of industry security standards and regulations. Data residency restrictions might dictate that data—even backup copies of data—be stored within certain geopolitical regions. Compliance standards might also require certain kinds of encryption, including the encryption of stored databases, file systems, volumes, or objects. The next section explores storage security more thoroughly.

- *Practice backup restoration*—Creating backups is only part of the story. Those backups will do you no good if you can't restore from the backups when data is lost. For example, if your backup files are corrupted or if the storage medium is damaged, the backup will fail. Another major problem is needing the backup and then finding you haven't been creating backups of the data you thought you were protecting. Some professionals call this a resume-generating event in that you might find yourself unemployed and searching for another job as a result of this failure. Regularly test restoring from backups to ensure your team is familiar with the process and to make sure the backup system works reliably and is doing what it should.

Remember This

- Whether data is lost through user error, such as deleting needed files or not paying a data storage bill, or through an attack or disaster, backups provide a layer of protection managed by the cloud consumer that is not covered by durability ratings.
- Common objects that require backup include applications, file systems, configuration files, and databases.
- Common backup types include a full backup, an incremental backup, and a differential backup.
- Redundancy refers to having multiple copies of a resource and can be measured by the number and effectiveness of those copies, such as N+1 or 2N.
- Factors to consider in developing a backup strategy include any applicable SLAs, relevant resource configurations, and needed security standards.

Self-Check

10. What data characteristic ensures the data continues to exist?
    - **a.** Consistency
    - **b.** Availability
    - **c.** Redundancy
    - **d.** Durability

11. What type of copy ensures the latest changes are always included in the backup?
    - **a.** Incremental backup
    - **b.** Differential backup
    - **c.** Synchronous replication
    - **d.** Asynchronous replication

12. Which backup type creates the largest backup file?
    - **a.** Incremental
    - **b.** Full
    - **c.** Differential
    - **d.** Delta

○ Check your answers at the end of this module.

Section 8-5: Storage Security

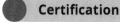

Certification

1.3 Explain the importance of high availability and scaling in cloud environments.

1.4 Given a scenario, analyze the solution design in support of the business requirements.

2.3 Given a scenario, apply the appropriate OS and application security controls.

Stored data security can benefit from concepts of segmentation just like the rest of the network can. The software-defined environment of the cloud, including SDS (software-defined storage), especially lends itself to segmentation security techniques. Two additional approaches to securing data stored in the cloud are classification and obfuscation.

Data Classification

When designing a storage infrastructure and access rights to the data, it's easy to initially think in terms of classifying data by data type or by department or team. This kind of data classification might seem convenient at first but will create security-related headaches as you try to protect that data going forward. Instead, it might be more beneficial to think of and categorize data along different axes. For example, consider each axis listed here, how it could affect the organization of data in a storage system, and how proper organization could increase security around the data:

- *Sensitivity*—Who should have access to the data? Should the data be accessible from outside the organization or only from within the organization? Grouping data objects together that require similar levels of access control or monitoring makes it easier to manage that data effectively and securely.
- *Compliance*—What kinds of restrictions and regulations dictate how the data should be stored? Encryption requirements might include whether data must be encrypted at rest, in motion, in use, or all of these. Relevant regulations might also list acceptable encryption protocols or restrictions on where keys are stored. There might be standards for determining who can see the data versus who can change it.
- *Lifecycle*—How long will the data be active, and at what point should it be transitioned to colder storage, archived, or deleted? Use data compression and data tags to help manage large chunks of similarly life-cycled data more efficiently and enable versioning only on the data sets that need it. Also, situate data in regions that put it close to where it's being used or migrated to other storage types, such as archival storage. This will speed up data transfer times and minimize the complexity of applicable governance requirements.
- *Visibility*—How should data be tracked? Logs can be configured on organized data sets that best reveal the information needed without over- or undermonitoring.

Data Obfuscation

You've already learned about security configurations in AWS, Azure, and GCP platforms, including ACLs, zones, and user or host authentication and authorization. These security tools can apply to storage services as well. For example, AWS S3 buckets can be protected by ACLs that determine which AWS accounts can access data in which buckets and what those accounts can do with that data. Data objects or volumes can reside in security zones best suited to the data's security needs. A security zone refers to the level of protection in place, for example, whether there's an emphasis on preventative controls (which provide active mitigation of threats) or on detective controls (which passively report signs of potential problems). Grouping data sets, applications, and other resources by security zone can simplify security settings.

You've also already learned about encryption, which is a form of data obfuscation. Obfuscation refers to techniques that make data difficult or impossible to understand even if it is discovered or stolen. For example, data that is encrypted looks like gibberish and must either be decrypted using the right key, or you must have knowledge of encryption technology as well as significant processing power to break the encryption and convert the data back into plaintext. One weakness of encryption, however, is that it is reversible.

An alternative to encryption is tokenization. With this technique, sensitive data is replaced by a token, which is random data unrelated to the original data. It might be in the same format as the original data; for example, it might have 16 digits like a credit card number does. This is called a format-preserving token; it can be presented to the DBMS in a way that doesn't cause data validation issues. Alternatively, a nonformat-preserving token doesn't resemble the original data at all.

The token, then, sits in place of the sensitive data so that, if the company's stored data is hacked, the attacker won't obtain the sensitive data itself and would have no way of reversing the tokenization, even with very powerful tools. For example, suppose the company has stored tokens in place of credit card numbers for purchases from customers. The company sends the tokens to the payment processor, who can then exchange the token with the tokenization service that provided the token to retrieve the sensitive data. That data is stored in the tokenization service's data vault, which is the only place where it is associated with the token.

This process is similar to checking baggage when flying on an airliner. Each passenger receives a tag associated with their luggage. The luggage is managed and transported by airline staff while each passenger holds the tag associated with their bag. As passengers arrive at their destinations, they can exchange their tags for their luggage. Similarly, the data itself is stored at the tokenization provider's site in a way that would be useless to an attacker. Only when redeemed by the token and placed back into its original context does the data provide any valuable information.

You're Ready

You're now ready to complete Project 8-4: Research Database Concepts. You can complete the project now or wait until you've finished other projects for this module.

Remember This

- Data can be classified by its sensitivity, relevant compliance requirements, lifecycle, or needed tracking visibility.
- Obfuscation refers to techniques that make data difficult or impossible to understand even if it is discovered or stolen.

Self-Check

13. Which of the following classification factors would be most secure?

   a. Classify by department   **c.** Classify by sensitivity
   b. Classify by data type   **d.** Classify by project

14. Which of the following is the most effective form of data obfuscation?

   a. Classification   **c.** Authorization
   b. Encryption   **d.** Tokenization

○ Check your answers at the end of this module.

Module Summary

Section 8-1: Storage Types

- Data types stored in the cloud include office and media files, applications, websites, logs, and databases.
- Common RAID techniques include RAID 0 (striping), RAID 1 (mirroring), RAID 5 (parity), RAID 6 (double parity), and RAID 10 (a stripe of mirrors).
- Cloud storage services generally fall into three categories: file system storage, block storage, and object storage.
- When moving data to a cloud provider's infrastructure, the company might need to make some changes to the data, such as its format, structure, or even the way it is labeled.

Section 8-2: Storage Optimization Techniques

- Storage performance can be evaluated based on transfer rate or read/write throughput, IOPS (input/output operations per second), and latency.
- Provisioning storage capacity in the cloud is most often performed automatically in direct response to needed space.

- One way to maximize storage performance is to optimize the data itself through techniques such as compression and deduplication.
- Stored data needs to progress through various states in its lifetime, including transitioning to different tiers according to access needs, possibly keeping past versions of the data, possibly being placed under a legal hold, and eventually being thoroughly destroyed.

Section 8-3: Cloud Storage Services

- S3 (Simple Storage Service) is AWS's most popular and flexible cloud storage service, able to host just about any kind of data.
- To use most of Azure's storage services, you must first create a storage account.
- GCP's Cloud Storage supports popular features such as lifecycle management and object versioning; however, some of these features are only available through the CLI.

Section 8-4: Creating and Storing Backups

- Whether data is lost through user error, such as deleting needed files or not paying a data storage bill, or through an attack or disaster, backups provide a layer of protection managed by the cloud consumer that is not covered by durability ratings.
- Common objects that require backup include applications, file systems, configuration files, and databases.
- Common backup types include a full backup, an incremental backup, and a differential backup.
- Redundancy refers to having multiple copies of a resource and can be measured by the number and effectiveness of those copies, such as N+1 or 2N.
- Factors to consider in developing a backup strategy include any applicable SLAs, relevant resource configurations, and needed security standards.

Section 8-5: Storage Security

- Data can be classified by its sensitivity, relevant compliance requirements, lifecycle, or needed tracking visibility.
- Obfuscation refers to techniques that make data difficult or impossible to understand even if it is discovered or stolen.

Key Terms

For definitions of key terms, see the Glossary.

application-level backup
big data
block zoning
CDN (content delivery network)
compression
DAS (direct attached storage)
database dump
deduplication
durability
edge computing
HCI (hyperconverged infrastructure)

hybrid cloud storage
key-value database
legal hold
lifecycle rule
NAS (network attached storage)
NVMe-oF (nonvolatile memory
    express over fabric)
RAID (Redundant Array of
    Independent Disks or
    Redundant Array of
    Inexpensive Disks)

record
records management
SAN (storage area network)
SDS (software-defined storage)
snapshot
storage tier
synthetic full backup
tokenization
user quota
versioning

Acronyms Checklist

The acronyms in Table 8-1 are listed in the Cloud+ objectives and could appear on the Cloud+ exam. This means that exam questions might use any of these acronyms in context so that you must know the meaning of the acronym to answer the question correctly. Make sure you're familiar with what each acronym stands for and the general concept of the term itself. All these acronyms are used in context in this module.

Table 8-1 Module 8 acronyms

Acronym	Spelled out
CAS	content addressed storage
CDN	content delivery network
CIFS	Common Internet File System
CNA	converged network adapter
DAS	direct attached storage
DBMS	database management system
DFS	distributed file system
FC	Fibre Channel
FCoE	Fibre Channel over Ethernet
GPT	GUID Partition Table
HBA	host bus adapter
IFCP	Internet Fibre Channel Protocol
IQN	iSCSI Qualified Name or Initiator Qualified Name
iSCSI	Internet Small Computer Systems Interface
ISNS	Internet Storage Name Service
JBOD	just a bunch of disks
LUN	logical unit number
MBR	Master Boot Record
NAS	network attached storage
NFS	Network File System

Acronym	Spelled out
NTFS	New Technology File System
NVMe	nonvolatile memory express
NVMe-oF	nonvolatile memory express over fabrics
PIT	point in time
RAID	redundant array of inexpensive disks
ReFS	Resilient File System
SAN	storage area network
SAS	Serial Attached Small Computer Systems Interface
SATA	Serial Advanced Technology Attachment
SCSI	Small Computer Systems Interface
SDS	software-defined storage
SMB	Server Message Block
UPS	uninterruptible power supply
VMFS	virtual machine file system
VSAN	virtual storage area network
VTL	virtual tape library
WWNN	World Wide Node Name
WWPN	World Wide Port Name
ZFS	Z File System

Review Questions

1. Which RAID type performs parity calculations using two different algorithms?

   a. RAID 5
   b. RAID 6
   c. RAID 10
   d. RAID 11

2. Which type of cloud storage would be the best fit for storing medical X-rays?

   a. File system
   b. Database
   c. Block
   d. Object

3. Which language is used to ask questions of a database?

   a. SQL
   b. HTTP
   c. SMB
   d. JSON

4. What effect does enabling versioning have on your cloud storage?

   a. Decreases durability
   b. Increases retention-based restrictions
   c. Increases cost
   d. Requires secure data disposal

5. Which data lifecycle state is complicated by data redundancies?

   a. Frequent access
   b. Archival
   c. Destruction
   d. Creation

6. What cloud technology can increase the speed of compute processes in smart cars?

   a. Storage versioning
   b. Edge computing
   c. Lifecycle rules
   d. Content delivery network

7. What kind of data is best stored in a nonrelational database?

   a. Metadata
   b. Unstructured data
   c. Versioned data
   d. Encrypted data

8. What kind of storage volume exists only in connection with a VM instance?

   a. Distributed
   b. Persistent
   c. Ephemeral
   d. Elastic

9. If you only need one ISP connection to support your network's regular Internet communications, which of the following redundancy levels would reflect your having two ISP connections? Choose TWO.

   a. N
   b. 2N
   c. N+1
   d. N+2

10. Suppose you make a full backup the first Sunday of each month, a differential backup on each of the other Sundays, and an incremental backup every Tuesday and Thursday. Today is the 12th, which is the second Wednesday of this month. Which files (using the latest version available for each) would need to be combined to create a current synthetic full backup?

   a. One full backup
   b. One full backup and two differential backups
   c. One full backup, one differential backup, and one incremental backup
   d. One full backup, one differential backup, and two incremental backups

Scenario-Based Questions

Question 8-1

Emile works for a startup tech firm that caters to financial advisors and consultants in a thriving metropolis. His firm's existing network architecture worked fine for a two-person team forming the concept of their business and wooing investors. Now they're ready to expand to a fully functional virtual environment that hosts applications on several VM and container instances and supports shared storage among all the instances. However, Emile must keep in mind that his company still cannot afford specialized expertise for managing their network storage. Which storage architecture is the best fit for Emile's needs?

   a. SAN
   b. DAS
   c. JBOD
   d. NAS

Question 8-2

Amber is restoring a database backup after a server failure caused by flood damage from a leaky pipe. Her company creates a full backup on the first weekend of each month, a differential backup each weekend between those full backups, and an incremental backup each weeknight. Today is Wednesday in the third week of the month. Which backup files will Amber need to apply to this month's full backup to restore all backed-up data?

   a. The most recent differential backup and the most recent incremental backup
   b. The second differential backup and the two most recent incremental backups
   c. Both differential backups and the most recent incremental backup
   d. Both differential backups and the two most recent incremental backups

Question 8-3

Terrence and Natasha are passing notes during their fifth-grade math class. To keep their information secure, the note writer prints a letter two spaces further along the alphabet than the letter he or she intends to write. For example, to write a letter *A*, the note writer prints *C*. The word *DOG*, then, is printed as *FQI*. Which of the following terms do *not* describe their secret note method? Choose TWO.

    a. Obfuscation

    b. Hashing

    c. Tokenization

    d. Encryption

Hands-On Projects

Note 9

Websites, applications, public cloud platforms, and related account options change often. While the instructions given in these projects were accurate at the time of writing, you might need to adjust the steps or options according to later changes.

Note to Instructors and Students: A rubric is provided for evaluating student performance on these projects. Please see Appendix D.

Project 8-1: Manage Storage in AWS

Estimated time: 45 minutes

Objective 4.5: Given a scenario, perform appropriate backup and restore operations.

Group work: This project includes enhancements when assigned as a group project.

Resources:

- AWS account
- A photo or screenshot saved as a .jpg file on the local computer
- Internet access

Context:

Storage management responsibilities include controlling who has access to data and what kind of access they have. It also includes keeping sufficient backups to restore any data that is lost or accidentally deleted. In this project, you'll practice working with access policies for storage buckets and objects in S3. You'll also practice restoring an object after deletion.

Note 10

At the time of this writing, all the services used in this project offered sufficient free tier limits to complete this project with no fees so long as the following are true:

- You stay within 5 GB of monthly storage space used.
- You are within the first 12 months of when your account was created.

  To see a current list of what services are included for free during your AWS free trial, visit aws.amazon.com/free. All project steps can also be completed using an AWS Academy account with no additional fees.

Complete the following steps:

1. In your AWS Management Console, go to the **S3** dashboard. S3 is listed under the **Storage** service category. Click **Create bucket** to create a storage bucket. Give the bucket a unique name. This name must be unique across all of AWS S3, so you might have to get a little creative with the bucket name. What name did you give your bucket?

(continues)

Hands-On Projects Continued

2. In the public access settings section, leave all default public access restrictions in place. Notice that, by default, your bucket's configurations will prevent any public access to your bucket or its contents.

3. In the bucket versioning section, enable versioning. Leave all other default settings and click **Create bucket**.

4. In your list of buckets, click the bucket you just created. Upload to your bucket a photo from your local computer. If you don't have a photo on your computer, you can take a screenshot of part of your screen. Save the screenshot as a .jpg file, and then upload the image to your bucket. Scroll through the available options for destination, permissions, and properties, but don't change any default settings for the upload.

5. Return to the Objects tab for your bucket and click the file you just uploaded. Copy and paste the object URL in a new tab in a different browser or in an incognito window for your current browser. What output do you get on the new tab? Keep this tab open, as you will refresh it throughout this project to test public access to the object.

6. Return to the bucket's page and go to the **Permissions** tab for the bucket. In the Block public access section, click **Edit**. Click to deselect all the public access restrictions for your bucket and save your changes. Confirm the changes.

7. Return to your browser tab with the Object URL and refresh the page. Does it show the image this time? Why do you think this is?

AWS has recently changed the way public access is granted to a bucket and its objects. Previously, users would create ACLs to manage access to the bucket or to individual objects. While this functionality is still available in S3 at the time of this writing, AWS recommends avoiding the use of ACLs when possible and, instead, managing access to objects at the bucket level using bucket policies. At the time of this writing, bucket policies are managed using JSON. To change the bucket policy, you'll need to edit the Policy JSON Document. Complete the following steps:

8. On the object's Properties tab, copy the object's Amazon Resource Number (ARN).

9. On the bucket's Permissions tab in the Bucket policy section, click **Edit**. In the *Edit statement* pane on the right, under *1. Add actions*, select **S3**. Under *Access level – read or write*, select **GetObject**. Notice the JSON code changing in the Policy pane as you make your selections. What code lines reflect the selections you've made so far?

10. Next to *2. Add a resource*, click **Add**. The S3 service should be preselected. For resource type, select **object**. For resource ARN, paste your object's ARN that you copied in Step 8. Click **Add resource**. What code line reflects this selection?

11. To make the object accessible to the public (i.e., to all principals), you'll need to edit the Principal field manually. In the line that defines the Principal, replace the curly brackets { } with **"*"** to use the wildcard * in reference to all principals. The line should read

```
"Principal": "*",
```

without changing any other lines.

12. At the bottom of the page, click **Save changes**. If you get any error messages, troubleshoot the problem. When the bucket policy is successfully edited, **take a screenshot** of your bucket name showing the bucket is publicly accessible.

13. Try again to access the file through the Object URL on your incognito tab. Does it work? Why do you think this is?

14. **For group assignments:** Each group member should edit access to their object so only one other group member, using their AWS account, can access the object over the Internet. **Take a screenshot** of the access settings that allow access to your group member but no one else; submit this visual with your answers to this project's questions.

Now you're ready to practice deleting the object and recovering it. Complete the following steps:

15. Return to the bucket's Objects tab where you can see the file listed in the bucket. Click the check box to select the file, and then click **Delete**. Confirm the deletion. How many objects are listed on your bucket's Objects tab now?

16. Toggle the switch next to *Show versions*. Now how many items are listed in your bucket?

17. One of these items is the file itself, and the other is a delete marker on the object that suppresses the file so it won't show up in a list of objects contained in the bucket. The file itself is not deleted, only hidden. To recover the file, click to select the Delete marker item in the list and click **Delete**. Confirm the deletion of the delete marker (not the object itself), and then return to the bucket's Objects tab. Toggle off the *Show versions* switch. How many items are listed in your bucket now? Why do you think this is?

18. Return to the S3 dashboard; empty and delete the bucket.

Note 11

Depending on the status of your account and the selections you made during this project, the resources you created can deplete your credits or accrue charges. Double-check to make sure you've terminated all resources you created in this project.

Project 8-2: Manage Storage in Azure

Estimated time: 30 minutes
Objective 3.2: Given a scenario, provision storage in cloud environments.
Resources:

- Azure account
- Internet access

Context:
Storage management responsibilities include controlling who has access to data and what kind of access they have. It also includes keeping sufficient backups to restore any data that is lost or accidentally deleted. In this project, you'll practice working with storage accounts, containers, and blobs. You'll also create and restore a blob snapshot.

Note 12

At the time of this writing, all the services used in this project offered sufficient free limits to complete this project with no fees so long as the following are true:

- You stay within 5 GB of monthly storage space used.
- You are within the first 12 months of when your account was created.
- You choose the LRS (locally-redundant storage) option when creating your storage account.

To see a current list of what services are included for free during your Azure free trial, in the navigation pane, click All services and search for Free services.

Complete the following steps:

1. First, you need to create a text file to upload and edit later in the project. These instructions are written for Windows and can be adapted for other OSs. Create a text document in Notepad. Type some text, such as This is a test. Save the document and name it something easily identifiable, such as BlobProject.txt. Close the document. What is the name of your document, and where did you save it?

2. You need a storage account to manage storage in Azure. In your Azure portal on the portal menu, click **Storage accounts**. Click **Create storage account**. Select the desired subscription, and then click **Create new** to create a new resource group. Give the resource group a name. Name your storage account something that is unique across all of Azure and choose a location. Change Redundancy to **Locally-redundant storage (LRS)**—this setting is required to stay within free tier service limits. Leave all other options at their default selections. Click **Review + create**, and then click **Create**.

(continues)

Hands-On Projects Continued

3. After deployment is complete, on the Storage accounts page, click your new storage account. What types of data storage are available, as listed in the blade's navigation pane?

Note 13

Recall that containers in Azure are similar in concept to buckets in AWS and GCP.

4. In the blade's navigation pane, click **Containers**. Create a new container and give it a name, such as mycontainer. Without changing the Public access level setting, look to see what other settings are available. What options are listed? Leave the Public access level set to **Private (no anonymous access)**. Click **Create**.

5. Click the container you just created. To upload the text file you created in Step 1, click **Upload** and select the file. Click the **Advanced** dropdown menu. By default, the blob type is set to Block blob. Without changing the setting, look to see what other types are available. What options are listed? Leave the Blob type set to **Block blob**, and then click **Upload**.

6. Close the Upload blob blade, and then click the file you just uploaded. Copy the URL and paste it into a new tab in your browser. What happens?

7. Close the tab and return to your Azure portal. Close the blob blade. On the container blade, click **Change access level**. Change the Public access level selection to **Blob (anonymous read access for blobs only)** and click **OK**. Click the filename again, and then try again to open the text file's URL in a new tab in your browser. What happens this time?

8. Close the tab and return to your Azure portal. On the blob's blade, click the **Snapshots** tab, and then click **Create snapshot**. The new snapshot appears in the list.

9. Click the **Edit** tab. Change the text to something noticeably different, such as Beam me up, Scotty. Save your changes. Return to the **Overview** tab, and open the blob's URL in a new tab. What happens this time?

10. Close the tab and return to your Azure portal. On the blob's blade, click the **Snapshots** tab. Select the snapshot and click **Promote snapshot**. Open the blob's URL in a new tab again. What happens this time?

11. Delete the resource group you created for this project.

Note 14

Depending on the status of your account and the selections you made during this project, the resources you created can deplete your credits or accrue charges. Double-check to make sure you've terminated all resources you created in this project.

Project 8-3: Manage Storage in GCP

Estimated time: 30 minutes
Objective 3.2: Given a scenario, provision storage in cloud environments.
Resources:

- GCP account
- A photo or screenshot saved as a .jpg file on the local computer
- Internet access

Context:
Storage management responsibilities include controlling who has access to data and what kind of access they have. It also includes keeping sufficient backups to restore any data that is lost or accidentally deleted. In this project, you'll practice working with storage buckets and objects in Cloud Storage. You'll also practice setting up lifecycle rules.

Note 15

At the time of this writing, all the services used in this project offered sufficient free tier limits to complete this project with no fees so long as the following are true:

- You stay within 5 GB of monthly storage space used.
- You create storage buckets in the us-east1, us-west1, or us-central1 regions.

  To see a current list of what services are included for free during your GCP free trial, visit cloud.google.com/free.

Complete the following steps:

1. In your GCP console, create a new project. In that project, in the navigation menu, scroll down to the STORAGE category, point to **Cloud Storage**, and click **Browser**. If it opens, close the LEARN pane on the right. To create a bucket, click **CREATE BUCKET**. Give the bucket a name that is unique across all of Cloud Storage and click **CONTINUE**.
2. Change the location type to **Region**. Make sure the Location is set to one of the regions that supports free tier services: us-east1, us-west1, or us-central1. Click **CONTINUE**.
3. Leave the default storage class as **Standard** and click **CONTINUE**.
4. Change the access control settings to **Fine-grained** and click **CONTINUE**.
5. Leave Protection tools at **None**. Click **CREATE**.
6. On your new bucket's page, click **UPLOAD FILES**. Select a photo file from your local computer to add to your bucket. If you don't have a photo on your computer, you can take a screenshot of part of your screen. Save the screenshot as a .jpg file, and then upload the image to your bucket. Click **Open**. The object is added to the list near the bottom of your screen. What is the Public access setting for your object?
7. Click the ellipsis icon for your object, and then click **Edit access**. How many permissions are listed here?
8. To make the object publicly accessible, click **ADD ENTRY**. Change the Entity field to **Public**. The Name field should auto-populate with **allUsers**. Leave the Access field as **Reader**. Click **SAVE**. What is the Public access setting for your object now? Point to the question mark icon next to the Public access column and read the information for Public to internet.
9. To truly test public access to this object, you'll need to attempt to open the URL in a browser where you're not signed in to GCP or any other Google site or browser. Copy the object's URL. Open a different browser where you're not signed into Google, or open an incognito window in your current browser and paste the link in that window. What happens? Do not close this browser tab or window.
10. Test your control over the permission settings for this object by "breaking" the public access configuration. Edit access to this object again, and then delete the **Public** item you created in Step 8. Save your changes.
11. The paper clip icon next to the object's access setting disappears; however, you should still have the URL showing in the other browser's tab or window. Return to that page, copy the URL, and then close the browser. Open a new browser window where you're not signed into Google and paste the link in that window. What happens?
12. Click the bucket's **PROTECTION** tab and turn on object versioning. Notice that GCP recommends configuring lifecycle rules to limit the number of file versions saved in your account. Click **MANAGE RULES** and click **ADD A RULE**.
13. Suppose objects in this bucket will be accessed maybe three or four times a year. Which lifecycle action would be the best fit for this lifecycle rule?
14. The wait time for a lifecycle rule to take effect is longer than what is appropriate for this project. Therefore, click **CANCEL**.
15. Delete all the resources you created in this project, including the bucket and the GCP project. Check through your account to confirm that all related resources have been deleted.

Note 16

Depending on the status of your account and the selections you made during this project, the resources you created can deplete your credits or accrue charges. Double-check to make sure you've terminated all resources you created in this project.

Hands-On Projects Continued ────────────────────────────────

Project 8-4: Research Database Concepts

Estimated time: 30 minutes
Objective 3.5: Given a scenario, perform cloud migrations.
Resources:

- Internet access

Context:
Databases play a huge role in managing and using data in applications and websites. Think about how many times each day or each week you interact with databases: when you sign into your email account, when you post updates to social media, when you withdraw money from your bank account, when you pay for purchases at a store, and many, many more examples.

   You might never be responsible for managing a database—DBAs (database administrators) require a great deal of training. However, as a cloud professional, you will likely need to support and secure database storage, or you might need to migrate databases between the cloud and an on-prem data center or between cloud services. To do this, it's important to understand the terminology involved. To learn more about database concepts, search online for answers to the following questions:

1. What are the main differences between a database and a spreadsheet?
2. What is SQL? Give at least three points of description.
3. What is the primary difference between an RDBMS (Relational Database Management System) and a NoSQL, or nonrelational, database?
   a. What are advantages and disadvantages of each database type?
   b. Give an example of a database service in AWS, Azure, and GCP that supports relational databases.

   Be sure to answer the questions in your own words. The rubric in Table 8-2 shows how your responses for this project will be evaluated. Note that your instructor might choose to adjust the point distribution in this rubric.

Table 8-2   Grading rubric for Project 8-4

Task	Novice	Competent	Proficient	Earned
Database and spreadsheet differences	Generalized statements describing the differences **5 points**	Specific statements describing differences **10 points**	Detailed and thoughtful description of the differences **15 points**	
SQL description	Three generalized descriptive points **5 points**	Three specific descriptive points **10 points**	Three thoughtful descriptive points with supporting details **15 points**	
RDBMS and NoSQL comparison	Generalized statements describing the differences, advantages and disadvantages, and examples, with little cohesiveness **30 points**	Specific statements describing differences, advantages and disadvantages, and examples, with logical organization of ideas from beginning to end **45 points**	Detailed and thoughtful description of the differences, advantages and disadvantages, and examples, with clear organization of ideas, showing logical connections between thoughts **60 points**	
Mechanics	Several grammar and spelling errors **4 points**	Occasional grammar and spelling errors **7 points**	Appropriate grammar and spelling throughout **10 points**	
			Total	

Capstone Project 8: Host a Static Website

Note 17

Websites, applications, public cloud platforms, and related account options change often. While the instructions given in these projects were accurate at the time of writing, you might need to adjust the steps or options according to later changes.

Note to Instructors and Students: A rubric is provided for evaluating student performance on these projects. Please see Appendix D.

Estimated time: 45 minutes

Objective 3.2: Given a scenario, provision storage in cloud environments.

Resources:

- Public cloud account (such as AWS, Azure, or GCP)
- Internet access

Context:

In the Hands-on Projects for this module, you practiced creating storage buckets, adding objects to the buckets, and configuring access permissions for those objects. In this project, you will apply those skills to host a static website in a public cloud storage service.

Imagine you are building a small website for a local charity. You've decided that one way to keep costs down for maintaining the website is to design a static website that can be hosted in a public cloud storage bucket. This means there can be no server-side processing, such as accessing information from a database or managing login tasks. As you research the possibilities for static websites, you find there are some beautiful templates you can use to design an impressive website that will easily make a good impression on visitors to the site. But first, you need to make sure you have the infrastructure set up correctly in your public cloud account. You'll start with a very basic index file for your site as you experiment with access permissions.

Complete the following steps:

1. Create an **index.html** file to serve as the initial home page for your website. To do this, create a text document in Notepad or a similar simple text editor. Include the following text, and do not use any text formatting in your file; replace the bold, italicized text with your own text that is personalized and will identify you as the author:

```
<!DOCTYPE html>
<html lang="en">
<head>
    <meta charset="utf-8">
    <title>My Website</title>
    <style>
    body {
       font-family: Arial, Helvetica, sans-serif;
    }
    </style>
</head>
<body>
    <h1>My Static Webpage</h1>
    <p>This webpage is hosted in my S3 bucket.</p>
</body>
</html>
```

(continues)

Hands-On Projects Continued

Note 18

When you save your file, make sure to name the file **index.html**. To do this, you might need to save the file first as a .txt file, and then do a Save As function and type the .html file extension in place of the .txt file extension.

2. Do some research for your public cloud platform to find instructions for hosting a static website in that cloud. Some platforms require special settings for hosting a static website. For example, you might need to use a particular name for your bucket or container, or you might need to eliminate pieces of the HTML code (such as the header). As you do your research, keep in mind that for this project, you do not need to set up resources required to support a custom domain. For example, GCP requires a load balancer to use a custom domain, and this configuration is not required for this project. For this project, you also do not need to create an error file, also called a 404.html file.
3. In your selected public cloud platform, create a storage bucket or container and enable public access to this bucket or container. What is the name of your storage bucket or container?
4. Upload your index.html file to your bucket or container. If needed, enable public access to this object or blob. What steps did you need to take to enable public access to the file?
5. Visit the website's public URL in an incognito window to ensure anyone can access your website. If you receive any error messages here, troubleshoot and fix the problem. **Take a screenshot** of your website showing the public URL in the browser's address bar and the personalized text on the webpage; submit this visual with your answers to this project's questions.
6. Delete all resources you created for this project, including any resource groups, storage accounts, buckets, containers, objects, or blobs. Check through your account to ensure you permanently deleted or terminated any resources created in this project.

Note 19

Depending on the status of your account and the selections you made during this project, the resources you created can deplete your credits or accrue charges. Double-check to make sure you've terminated all resources you created in this project.

Solutions to Self-Check Questions

Section 8-1: Storage Types

1. Which file system is specific to Linux?

   Answer: b. BTRFS

   Explanation: BTRFS (B-Tree File System, pronounced "butter f-s") is a relatively new Linux file system.

2. What type of storage is the hard drive in a laptop?

   Answer: c. DAS

   Explanation: DAS (direct attached storage), the most familiar storage type to the typical user, is directly connected to the computer or server that uses it, such as the hard drive in a laptop.

3. Which protocol supports object storage communications?

   Answer: c. HTTPS

   Explanation: Object storage uses REST APIs and HTTP or the more secure version, HTTPS (Hypertext Transfer Protocol Secure).

Section 8-2: Storage Optimization Techniques

4. Which data optimization technique eliminates unnecessary copies of data?

   Answer: b. Deduplication

   Explanation: Deduplication eliminates multiple copies of the same data in a storage system.

5. Which of these storage tiers would be most appropriate for archived data?

   Answer: a. Glacier

   Explanation: AWS's Glacier storage tiers provide the coldest and cheapest storage for archived data that rarely needs to be accessed.

6. Which feature of CDN files helps ensure customers get current copies of cached data?

   Answer: c. TTL

   Explanation: The CDN (content delivery network) service manages the TTL (time to live) of files cached at edge locations to ensure updated files are requested from the origin point if the files have been sitting in the cache for too long.

Section 8-3: Cloud Storage Services

7. AWS file system policies are configured using _____.

   Answer: b. JSON

   Explanation: To change AWS file system policies, you must edit JSON (JavaScript Object Notation) code.

8. An object stored in Azure is called a _____.

   Answer: d. blob

   Explanation: In Azure, storage containers are analogous to AWS S3's buckets, and blobs are like S3 objects. You create a container, and then you upload objects, called blobs, to it.

9. GCP object-level permissions are set using _____.

   Answer: b. ACLs

   Explanation: Bucket-level permissions are set using GCP's IAM service, and object-level permissions are set using an ACL (access control list).

(continues)

Section 8-4: Creating and Storing Backups

10. What data characteristic ensures the data continues to exist?

    Answer: d. Durability

    Explanation: A CSP's guaranteed durability refers to the protection against losing a stored object.

11. What type of copy ensures the latest changes are always included in the backup?

    Answer: c. Synchronous replication

    Explanation: Synchronous replication writes data to the replica at the same time the data is written to primary storage. If a failure occurs with the primary data, the replica provides an exact, updated copy.

12. Which backup type creates the largest backup file?

    Answer: b. Full

    Explanation: A full backup creates the largest backup file because it copies all the original data, even old data that hasn't changed in a long time.

Section 8-5: Storage Security

13. Which of the following classification factors would be most secure?

    Answer: c. Classify by sensitivity

    Explanation: Data can be better secured when classified by similar sensitivity levels than by department, data type, or project.

14. Which of the following is the most effective form of data obfuscation?

    Answer: d. Tokenization

    Explanation: With tokenization, sensitive data is replaced by a token, which is random data unrelated to the original data and cannot be reversed to reveal the original data.

Module 9

Managing Cloud Performance

Module 9 Objectives

After reading this module, you will be able to:

1 Describe cloud monitoring tools and techniques.

2 Identify monitoring tools for logs and events.

3 Configure cloud monitoring resources.

4 Troubleshoot cloud performance issues.

Module 9 Outline

Study the module's outline to help you organize the content in your mind as you read.

Module 9 Scenario

"Hey, Sam, how's it going?" you ask as Nigel's 15-year-old son walks in the door. "Your dad will be back in a few minutes," you add. "He's fixing a problem with a printer."

"Hi," Sam mumbles as he shuffles over to Nigel's desk and flops into his office chair.

"What's wrong? You look mopey," you observe. Sam is a bright kid and normally very excited about one thing or another.

"Dad's going to be so mad at me," he groans. "I failed my English test today."

Just then, Kendra walks in and overhears Sam as he continues, "We've been reading short stories and talking about symbolism. Colors, weather, whatever. I don't know. Apparently, those authors always mean something more than what they say. It doesn't make sense, and then I flunk the test."

"Oh, I remember those discussions in high school English class," Kendra says as she smiles to herself. "I loved those stories! So much depth and meaning and significance. Math, however—I failed algebra...more than once," she confesses with a sheepish grin and an eye roll.

"But algebra is easy!" Sam argues. "You learn the rules and follow the steps. It's logical. Symbolism—how are you supposed to know what the author was thinking, when they say one thing but mean something else? It doesn't make sense."

"Ah, well, our minds all work differently, I guess," replies Kendra. "Algebra didn't make sense to me—how are you supposed to use letters that aren't really numbers when you're calculating things?"

"Will your dad really be mad?" you ask Sam. "He seems like a pretty laid-back guy to me."

"Well, he won't ground me or anything," Sam replies. "Dad says grades are indicators of what you need to work harder on. But I'd rather work on learning more about computers. That's a lot more interesting than old stories."

"Hmm, your dad's right," nods Kendra. "Grades show you what you're doing well and what needs more attention. But computers tell stories, too. And sometimes, you need to be able to look underneath the plain meaning of things to discover what's really going on with a computer system."

"Oh, like when you're monitoring the network," you add, as you think about the detective work it took to identify the printer problem Nigel's working on.

"Yes, and monitoring the cloud," adds Kendra. "Sometimes the problem you see isn't really the problem. You have to think about the bigger context, the clues you have, and even consider the information that you're missing, not just the information you have."

The next morning, as you, Kendra, and Nigel meet to go over your cloud migration plans, Nigel mentions to Kendra, "Thanks for chatting with Sam yesterday. He was really bummed about his English grade. But he was also a little bit excited to see how studying symbolism can help him work better with computers."

"My pleasure," says Kendra as she settles into her chair. "He's a good kid."

Before the conversation could turn to the meeting agenda, you wonder out loud, "Kendra, something you said yesterday has been stuck in my head. You said, 'Sometimes the problem you see isn't really the problem.' With our on-prem network, we can go look at devices and cabling and everything to find out what the real problem is. How do we do that in the cloud?"

"Ah, good question," replies Kendra. "In the cloud, we have to rely on monitoring tools to help us see what's going on. It's an awful lot of data, so we also have to rely on tools to help analyze the information and even respond automatically to some of the problems."

"Okay, just give us the research questions already," jokes Nigel.

"Ha—right," grins Kendra. "Let's look up information on these questions," she adds as she scribbles on a page in her notebook.

- How are cloud resources monitored?
- How are cloud expenses kept within budget?
- How are problems addressed?
- How are cloud resources recovered after a crisis?

Section 9-1: Monitoring Resources

Certification

1.2 Explain the factors that contribute to capacity planning.

1.4 Given a scenario, analyze the solution design in support of the business requirements.

2.2 Given a scenario, secure a network in a cloud environment.

2.5 Given a scenario, implement measures to meet security requirements.

4.1 Given a scenario, configure logging, monitoring, and alerting to maintain operational status.

4.2 Given a scenario, maintain efficient operation of a cloud environment.

4.4 Given a scenario, apply proper automation and orchestration techniques.

4.5 Given a scenario, perform appropriate backup and restore operations.

Throughout this course, you've learned about different types of clouds, various services you can run in the cloud, and how to create resources in the cloud. You've learned how to organize those resources in virtual networks and subnets, and how to connect resources in the cloud and back to your on-prem data center. All of this is great until something goes wrong. How can you monitor your cloud for problems? How can you make sure that your users have an optimal experience interacting with your cloud resources? And how can you ensure this all stays within your budget?

In this module, you learn about how to manage your cloud's transparency, or observability, to monitor resources and respond to problems. You also learn how to manage your cloud's capacity to support services and resources and how to optimize both performance and cost efficiency. In the next module, you learn more about how to automate maintenance processes to minimize the demand on IT staff's time and further optimize cloud performance and security. To begin, you first need to explore what resources can be targeted by your monitoring tools as well as what information can be collected.

Targets to Monitor

Many variables contribute to the fluctuation of cloud performance and costs. For example, a VM server will perform best if its CPU utilization remains below 80 percent. However, if CPU utilization falls below 10 percent for an extended period, this might indicate the VM instance is no longer needed and should be deallocated. As you can see, managing the capacity of your cloud resources can help you optimize both cloud performance and expenses.

Many of the cloud resources you've been working with—such as VM instances, storage buckets and volumes, databases, gateways, and load balancers—generate API messages that report various metrics for those resources. Monitoring tools, whether native to the CSP's platform or installed from a third-party monitoring service, capture information from these APIs and organize the data to report on the health, activities, and expenses of the monitored resources. Specific metrics, or KPIs (key performance indicators), are covered by these APIs.

For example, consider a running VM instance in the cloud. A KPI for the VM might be CPU utilization so you can increase the number of vCPUs for that VM when needed (called vertical scaling) or, instead, spin up additional VMs in the server cluster (called horizontal scaling) if existing VMs show signs of strain. Other metrics typically include data in or data out and disk read or write operations. All these metrics help indicate the VM's health, performance, and cost.

Note **1**

This concept of continuously monitoring a server's hardware (or virtual hardware) to track its overall health is borrowed from the on-prem data center. For example, an on-prem server monitoring solution might use IPMI (Intelligent Platform Management Interface) standards to watch and configure a server's hardware status, including power consumption, temperature, and fan speeds.

Figure 9-1 shows some metrics monitored by default in AWS for three running VM instances in EC2. Notice the different color lines for each instance and the various KPIs being monitored, such as CPU utilization, disk reads and writes, and network traffic. This figure also shows that three alarms are helping to monitor cloud resources. If one of the alarms is triggered, a cloud admin would need to dig into the alarm's information to determine what went wrong and whether the related resources need additional attention.

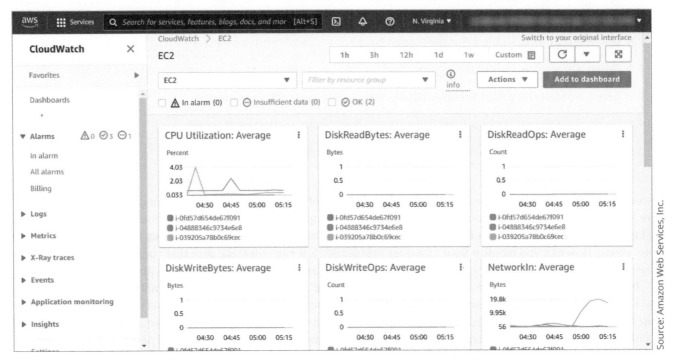

Figure 9-1   Some EC2 KPIs: CPU utilization, disk read and write operations, and network activity

Data collected on these metrics can be monitored on a service's or resource's own page, such as the page for a specific VM instance, or data from many services can be collected in a central location to give a bigger picture of a cloud deployment's overall health. For example, AWS provides the CloudWatch service, which allows cloud technicians to monitor metrics across AWS services and collate this data in one or more dashboards, track events, or generate alerts. Figure 9-2 shows the cross service dashboard in CloudWatch. Azure Monitor and GCP's Cloud Monitoring perform similar functions in their respective platforms.

Common metrics to track include the following:

- **Overall utilization**—How much storage space is used? How much memory or CPU capacity is being used consistently, and are those numbers pushing the boundaries of available resources or budget? Are resources bursting beyond normal thresholds? Is throughput peaking near available limits? These KPIs will indicate whether system load is increasing and so your cloud needs increased capacity, or perhaps even whether you should decrease its available capacity.

- **Elasticity usage**—You already know that scalability refers to a cloud resource's ability to scale up or down to adjust to variable demand. Elasticity refers to a cloud resource's ability to scale up or down automatically without requiring intervention from a cloud admin. For example, if more storage space is needed, does the storage service adjust automatically and dynamically to this demand, or does scaling require input from an admin? Elastic services might be appropriate in some scenarios but counterproductive in others, depending on how often the resource's needs fluctuate, how much money is saved by minimizing resource allocation at any given time, and whether the resource can handle a fluctuating environment or if it requires a more stable allocation.

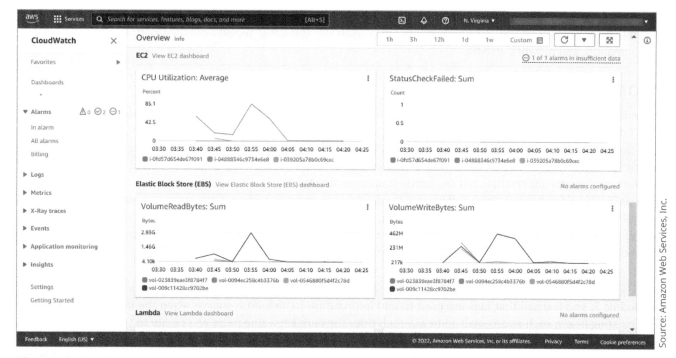

Figure 9-2   The cross service dashboard includes data on EC2 and EBS

- *Performance*—Cloud performance is determined by latency measurements and relative health of cloud resources while minimizing disruptive incidents. By reporting based on metrics detailed in any relevant SLAs you're responsible for meeting, you can track whether you're achieving expected performance standards.

- *System or service availability*—An individual system's or service's availability is measured by uptime versus downtime, connectivity to other services, and the health and performance of its various components. This is similar in concept to the on-prem KPIs of MTBF (mean time between failure), MTTF (mean time to failure), and MTTR (mean time to repair) that are reported for hardware such as disk drives and routers. Problems in any of these areas can indicate the need for further investigation to identify the cause of the problem and try to fix it. Many times, an SLA also requires a certain minimum uptime.

- *Cost*—Budget limitations, business needs, and company policies require that costs of cloud resources be adequately tracked. Cloud cost monitoring and optimization provide an opportunity to granularly monitor cloud consumption per user, customer, team, project, or department and make adjustments where needed. These costs might not necessarily be charged to the IT Department's budget, however. Consider the following arrangements:
  - *Chargeback model*—Many companies use a chargeback model where expenses for specific resources or resource groups are instead charged back to a specific department in the organization according to who is using those resources. For example, if an accounting application is running in the cloud, the charges for that application's resources could be tracked separately and charged to the Accounting Department.
  - *Showback model*—In contrast, a showback model tracks usage of cloud resources without attributing specific costs to that usage. This serves the purpose of increasing cost awareness without introducing the complexity of separately tracking funding for cloud services.

All this information can be collected by monitoring tools that observe cloud services from the cloud platform's perspective. In other words, these tools don't function within the individual resources but watch from the outside, like security cameras watching the outside of a building.

Alternatively, you can also install a local agent inside, say, an instance's OS to collect metrics from an insider's perspective. This would be similar to installing security cameras throughout the interior of a building. For example, AWS's CloudWatch Agent can be installed on an EC2 server instance running either Linux or Windows, or it can be installed in on-prem servers for hybrid cloud monitoring. The agent collects and reports metrics associated with counters in Windows Performance Monitor for a Windows server, which includes performance information on the OS and its applications, services, and drivers. On Linux systems, the agent reports detailed performance data on CPU, disk, memory, and network activity.

Monitoring Tools

Some monitoring processes, such as logs, offer retroactive analysis of past events, and other monitoring processes provide intermittent insights into a resource's state or performance. In contrast, some monitoring tools support ConMon (continuous monitoring), which means the tool can provide near-immediate feedback on performance or security metrics in a continuous, unbroken manner. For example, a line graph showing data on inbound network traffic could provide continuous information, not intermittent measurements.

Alerts and alarms can inform staff when a threshold is breached or when a concerning event occurs. In contrast, you might need to disable alerting when performing maintenance, which is sometimes called maintenance mode. When implementing monitoring tools, verify continuous monitoring is in use where it's needed and consider the differences in timeliness for each monitoring strategy as you read about them in this module.

Identifying Cloud Resources

In Module 7, you learned that tags are used to add information to a cloud resource when the information doesn't fit into existing fields, such as an email address or job title. Tags are key-value pairs you create to track resources within whatever organization you need. For example, you might use tagging to categorize resources by project or department. You can use tags to track cloud expenses and correlate those expenses to departmental budgets within your company. In a cloud environment where you might have difficulty taking inventory of all cloud resources and tracking those resources throughout their various lifecycle phases, tagging can help identify and monitor this expansive, abstract infrastructure.

To use tags effectively, it helps to create a comprehensive tagging policy early in the cloud deployment process. Designed well, tags can increase the business value of cloud resources as well as make the IT staff's work easier. Two layers of tag design include the following:

- *Explicit tagging*—Use key-value pairs to create useful fields for identifying and tracking resources. For example, you might create a key named "Department," and a possible value for this field could be "Accounting."
- *Implicit tagging*—Use naming conventions to increase consistency across resources and to increase saturation of information while requiring fewer fields. For example, you might begin the names of all EC2 instances used by Human Resources with the letters "HR" followed by other needed information (such as project, purpose, location, etc.).

Many tags can be designed around naming conventions already in place for an on-prem network. Also consider which costs need to be tracked by tags and how those costs are allocated to various budgets by department, project, or initiative. You might also use tags to identify access policies for resources and services. For example, identify sensitive resources as "internal" or "classified," and tag less secure resources as "public" or "open."

Capturing Network Traffic

Monitoring a network involves more than watching each individual resource. You also need to capture traffic between these resources and analyze this traffic for signs of problems, such as network congestion or a security issue.

If you've taken a networking class, you've probably learned about many of the methods used to collect network traffic on-prem. For example, the Wireshark application can capture network traffic crossing a specific interface. The captured traffic can be analyzed in-depth to determine what information is being transmitted, which protocols are in use, and what security gaps need to be addressed. You can even install a device called a network TAP (test access point), or packet sniffer, in line with network traffic to capture traffic flowing between various devices. Figure 9-3 shows a basic TAP. A packet broker near the TAP can sort this traffic, decrypt TLS traffic, mask sensitive data, and send different types of traffic to devices designed to further monitor and analyze traffic. Common targets include a WAF (web application firewall), a SIEM (security information and event management) tool, or an IDS/IPS (intrusion detection system/intrusion prevention system). Many network attacks can be detected with these tools.

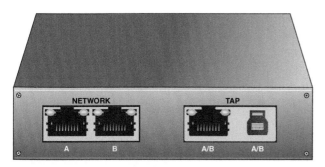

Figure 9-3   Network TAP

What about cloud networks? You can't exactly insert a TAP device on the cable between two switches when you don't manage switches in the cloud. Some vendors have created solutions to help bridge the gap between traditional packet brokers and cloud infrastructure. These solutions can capture cloud-based traffic and direct that traffic to an on-prem or cloud-hosted packet broker for monitoring and analysis. These tools are designed to distinguish between your cloud's traffic versus someone else's cloud traffic, even though both networks might use the same underlying physical infrastructure. Other, newer packet brokers are designed for hybrid or cloud deployments and can work across the entire infrastructure, whether physical, virtual, or cloud.

Monitoring User Experience

All monitoring is designed, in the end, to provide a satisfactory user experience, whether from ensuring security, performance, or availability of network resources. For example, as user density increases, capacity of resources (such as virtual desktops) needed by those users should increase to meet fluctuating demand. Still, some tools are designed specifically to collect information on the user's experience of IT services. ITSM (IT service management) tools help IT teams monitor several customer-facing processes to better meet user needs and expectations. Some of these core practices include the following:

- *Service request management*—Requests for permissions, updates, or enhancements
- *Knowledge management*—Organization of accumulated knowledge specific to the organization
- *IT asset management*—Oversight of asset life cycles and configurations
- *Incident management*—Responses to unplanned disruptions to restore services
- *Problem management*—Discovery and mitigation of underlying problems that lead to incidents
- *Change management*—Oversight of changes to any IT system while minimizing disruptions

All these service management tools can benefit from incorporating and integrating a company's cloud systems and automation capabilities. Newer ITSM tools revolve around the core concepts of DevOps that offer cross-department cooperation and collaboration.

Dashboards

Dashboards play a crucial role in monitoring cloud resources. A well-structured dashboard can give a cloud technician a quick overview of critical services and draw attention to issues that might indicate problems. Too much information in a dashboard causes confusion and overwhelm. Too little information decreases relevance. Poorly organized information takes too much time for a human admin to digest and decreases efficiency. Consider the following tips to designing an effective dashboard:

- *Five-second rule*—When you're looking for an answer to a frequently asked question, you should be able to identify the information you need on the dashboard within about five seconds. If it takes longer to find what you're looking for, clean up the clutter and organize the information more logically.
- *First things first*—News stories typically start with an eye-catching headline, followed by just enough information to hook you into the story. The next paragraph or two in a news article gives the most newsworthy information. This is followed by additional details that might not be relevant or interesting to all readers. This organization of content is sometimes described as an inverted triangle (see Figure 9-4). Similarly, your dashboard tells a constantly changing story of what's happening in your cloud. You want to see the most critical indicators first, which alert you to key metrics and changes. This should be followed by data showing trends over time, so that you can see the big picture of where these key metrics fit. Finally, a good dashboard includes more in-depth details at the bottom where you can follow the data trail and answer more specific questions, if needed.

- *Birds of a feather*—Group related pieces of information near each other. In some cases, you might be able to label the groups, which makes it easier to understand how they're related to each other. Similarly, make sure that any labels you use make sense and are easy to interpret. Don't use such short or cryptic abbreviations that it's difficult to understand what they mean. Be consistent in your naming conventions.

- *Less is more*—Have you ever wondered why phone numbers in the United States consist of seven digits (not counting area code)? Human minds can consume and remember only about seven distinct pieces of information at one time. Similarly, most people can only absorb about five to nine KPIs on a dashboard at a time. Even with all the available layers of information, you'll want fewer than 10 visualizations, or widgets, on the entire dashboard.

- *A picture is worth a thousand words*—Choose your visualizations carefully. For example, consider whether a line chart, stacked chart, pie chart, or dial will better reveal the meaning behind the data. You can use colors to quickly track and analyze trends for one resource in comparison to another, and you can use timeframes (the range of time covered by the visualization, such as 1 hour, 12 hours, or 2 days) and time increments (the time between each data point on the visualization, such as 1 minute, 15 minutes, or 1 hour) to better target the indicators you're looking for.

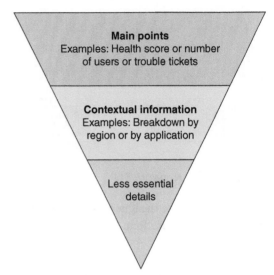

Figure 9-4   The information with the most impact comes first, followed by more detailed information

- *It's what you don't see*—Dashboards are made up of more than graphs, text, and boxes. Space between these visualizations is also important to assist the human eye in breaking down the information to absorb it. Leave sufficient and consistent white space between visualizations for easy comprehension of the information that is there.

How do you choose which data should be included on your dashboard? In the past, IT professionals have been primarily concerned with technical KPIs and thresholds that indicate how well the technology is performing in comparison to what it might be capable of. In today's cloud-run businesses, you've got to learn to think about the bigger picture. How do your cloud services fit into the business strategy of your organization? More specifically, how are users experiencing the services provided by your cloud resources? As many experts are now saying, "Slow is the new down." Outages might not be common in this five or six 9s world, but these days, slow services will lose business almost as quickly as outages will.

Dashboards provide a passive reporting of performance data that requires active monitoring from humans to catch and respond to problems. Much of this process can be automated, however. The options for doing this vary depending on your cloud platform. You learn more about automation techniques in the next module.

Note ②

While it's important to limit the amount of data presented on a single dashboard, you'll also want to limit the number of dashboards you need to monitor. Not only does this reduce the number of screens you need to check regularly; it's also less expensive. CSPs often charge for running additional dashboards.

Remember This

- Monitoring tools capture information from cloud resource APIs and organize the data to report on the health, activities, and expenses of monitored resources.
- Various monitoring processes offer retroactive analysis of past events, provide intermittent insights into a resource's state or performance, or provide near-immediate feedback on metrics in a continuous, unbroken manner.
- A well-structured dashboard can give a cloud technician a quick overview of critical services and draw attention to issues that might indicate problems.

Self-Check

1. _____ refers to a resource's ability to scale automatically.

   a. Utilization

   b. Availability

   c. Performance

   d. Elasticity

2. Which resource indicates a breached threshold?

   a. Alarm

   b. Tag

   c. Packet broker

   d. Metric

3. True or false: It's important to pack as much information as possible into a dashboard.

   a. True, because running extra dashboards costs money.

   b. False, because humans can only absorb so much information at a time.

   c. True, because extra space in a dashboard can be distracting.

   d. False, because the most detailed information should be positioned at the top of the dashboard.

○ Check your answers at the end of this module.

Section 9-2: Events and Logs

> **Certification**
>
> 1.2 Explain the factors that contribute to capacity planning.
> --
> 2.2 Given a scenario, secure a network in a cloud environment.
> --
> 2.3 Given a scenario, apply the appropriate OS and application security controls.
> --
> 4.1 Given a scenario, configure logging, monitoring, and alerting to maintain operational status.

You've already learned that metrics track information, such as performance and resource utilization. These metrics can be monitored using tools that capture live data, which is reported on dashboards. Two other common data sources for monitoring cloud services are events and logs.

Events

An **event** is a detectable change in a cloud service or resource that you're monitoring. For example, when a VM instance changes from a running state to a down state, that change registers as an event. Event collection occurs automatically behind the scenes and, in most cases, causes no additional actions to be taken. Occasionally, however, an event needs more attention. What happens next depends partly on the cloud platform you're using and partly on how you've configured the monitoring services within that platform.

An important aspect of event collection is **event correlation**. Events are generated from many resources throughout your cloud, and often these events are related. By identifying relationships between events through event correlation, monitoring tools can identify event patterns or anomalies that indicate performance or security problems. For example, IDP (intrusion detection and prevention) systems rely on event correlation processes to identify activities of concern. An IDP system might detect an account that hasn't been used in months suddenly has dozens of failed sign-in attempts. Perhaps the IDP system also detects a successful sign-in attempt to that account, followed by commands being executed from it. The IDP might also associate this activity with an earlier port scan that came from the same IP address now being used to interact with the user account. Out of thousands or even millions of logged events, event correlation connects these dots to reveal an attack in progress.

As you can see, the more events available to a monitoring system, the more likely the system can identify symptoms of a problem. On the other hand, collecting too many events slows down scanning processes and increases the likelihood of **false positives**, or false indicators of problems. Event collection policies need to be designed so they can determine which events are tracked and how they're responded to.

Logs

Whereas metrics and events generate data in near real time, **logs** collect streams of data over time to show historical insights and reveal usage patterns and anomalies. Logs typically include data collected from events or metrics and then make that data available for retroactive queries and analysis. Three common types of logs include the following:

- *Access/authentication*—A network server logs authentication attempts, both failed and successful, and might also log other access information.
- *System*—An OS keeps logs containing information about its drivers, system processes, and errors. Network systems can log traffic flows; database systems can log changes to data content or design; automated systems can log configuration changes; and security systems can log security events.
- *Application*—Application logs can collect a variety of event types, depending on how the software developer designed the application. These logs might include periodic information on the state of the application, its performance, or changes to data.

As you can imagine, logs generate a massive amount of data in a very short time. One of the biggest expenses related to logs is long-time storage of all this data. Keeping log data for a period allows cloud admins to investigate problems during troubleshooting, conduct forensic analysis during or after a security breach, and generate required reports to prove compliance with standards and regulations. In some cases, companies are required to keep log data for a period of years to meet compliance standards.

Another significant expense related to logging is the indexing process for these logs. Indexing organizes and labels data in the log for easy searching and analysis. This process is performed by an indexing engine and requires a lot of compute resources. Sometimes the expense of log management can be reduced by making trade-offs in what types and levels of indexing are performed.

> **Note 3**
>
> An important part of the logging process is removing sensitive data from the logs before storing captured traffic. This step is called **log scrubbing**.

In the end, logs need to be analyzed by some service. In AWS, the CloudWatch Logs Insights service provides built-in log analytics for AWS logs. Similarly, Azure Monitor Logs offers log analytics services as does GCP's Log Analytics service. You can also pull in services from other vendors, such as Splunk (splunk.com) or Rapid7 (rapid7.com), both of whom offer cloud SIEM products in addition to other cloud monitoring and log analysis solutions.

Syslog

On-prem networks rely on data-gathering technologies such as syslog and SNMP (Simple Network Management Protocol) to collect health, performance, security, and availability information on network resources. This data is sent to and analyzed by a log management tool. In some cases, a SIEM (Security Information and Event Management) solution provides log analysis, especially in the context of security.

Similarly, in the cloud, event logs and additional information are routinely recorded by many types of devices. These logs can be centrally collected via the syslog utility. **Syslog** is a standard for generating, storing, and processing messages about events on many networked systems, whether on-prem or in the cloud. It describes methods for detecting and reporting events and specifies the format and contents of messages. The syslog standard addresses three primary components, as illustrated in Figure 9-5 and described next.

Event message format

Event message transmission

Event message handling

Figure 9-5 Three components of the syslog standard

- *Event message format*—Event messages must be organized and formatted in a specific manner with certain types of information included, although flexibility to this format is built in to allow syslog's use in a wide variety of environments and scenarios.
- *Event message transmission*—Event messages are transported across the network on port 514. Syslog messages secured by TLS are transported instead over port 6514.
- *Event message handling*—The syslog utility on all monitored devices and on the syslog server follow protocols for creating, handling, analyzing, and storing event messages.

The syslog standard also defines two roles for devices participating in logging events:

- *Generator*—This is a device that is monitored by a syslog-compatible application and issues event information.
- *Collector*—This server gathers event messages from generators.

Level	State indicated
0	Emergency! System unusable
1	Alert–Immediate action needed
2	Critical–Critical condition
3	Error–Error condition
4	Warning–Warning condition
5	Notification–Normal but significant condition
6	Informational–Informational message only
7	Debugging–Helpful for debugging

Figure 9-6 Syslog security levels

You likely don't want to collect every possible event message, as that would generate massive amounts of data to be stored and analyzed. Unless this level of documentation is necessary for compliance purposes, you'll probably want to limit the types of messages generated, transmitted, and stored. For this purpose, syslog assigns a severity level, also called a logging level or priority value, to each event. For example, "0" indicates an emergency situation, whereas "7" points to specific information that might help in debugging a problem, as shown in Figure 9-6. You configure a filter on the device so that it sends all events from a specific level and above to the syslog server. Furthermore, you can filter syslog messages by the facility, or machine process, that created the event, such as the kernel (facility "0"), users (facility "1"), or security and authorization (facility "4").

The filters and other syslog configurations you implement on each device must be carefully considered in situations where you need to conform to regulatory compliance requirements. In some cases, you must be able to track every movement of every user. By referring to information stored in your logs, you should be able to answer the question, "Who did what activity when and in what way?" When tracking this level of information, the collective data is called an audit log, or audit trail. The data in these logs is consistent and thorough enough to retroactively prove compliance and also to defensibly prove user actions (that is, your logs document user action in a way that is presentable in a court of law). This data is often used in forensics investigations to determine how a particular problem occurred, especially if criminal investigations are involved. Make sure you know exactly what types of actions and other events you must log on your network to meet relevant compliance standards.

Bear in mind that the syslog utility doesn't alert you to any problems, but it does keep a history of messages issued by the system. It's up to you to monitor the system log for issues, review the logs regularly for missed problems, or filter log data to monitor packet flow when troubleshooting a problem or checking for patterns that might indicate developing problems. Most UNIX and Linux desktop operating systems provide a GUI application for easily reviewing and filtering the information in system logs. Other applications are available for sifting through syslog data and generating alerts.

Using the information collected in event logs and system logs for security and fault management requires thoughtful data filtering and sorting. After all, you can't assume that all the information in these logs points to a problem, even if it is marked with a warning. For example, you might have typed your password incorrectly while trying to log on to your computer, thus generating a log entry. Still, sometimes seemingly innocuous information turns out to be exactly the data you need to diagnose a problem.

SNMP Communications

In contrast to syslog, which collects log information on a central syslog server, organizations often use enterprise-wide network management systems to perform real-time monitoring functions across an entire network. Hundreds of such tools exist. All rely on a similar architecture (see Figure 9-7), in which the following entities work together:

- *NMS (network management system) server*—At least one network management console, which may be a server or workstation, depending on the size of the network, collects data from multiple managed devices at regular intervals in a process called polling.

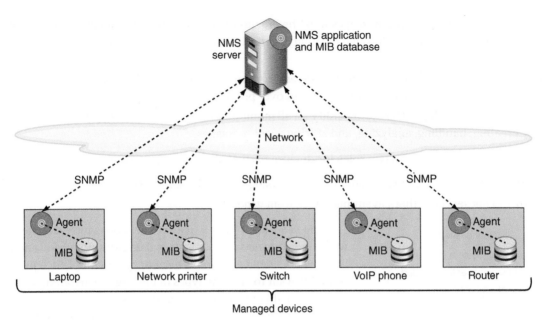

Figure 9-7   Network management architecture

- *Managed device*—Any network node monitored by the NMS is a managed device. Each managed device may contain several managed objects. This can be any characteristic of the device that is monitored, including components such as a processor, memory, hard disk, or NIC, or intangibles such as performance or utilization. Each managed object is assigned an OID (object identifier), which is standardized across all NMSs.

- *Network management agent*—Each managed device runs a network management agent, which is a software routine that collects information about the device's operation and provides it to the NMS. For example, on a server, an agent can measure how many users are connected to the server or what percentage of the processor's resources are used at any given time. So as not to affect the performance of a device while collecting information, agents demand minimal processing resources.

- *MIB (Management Information Base)*—The list of objects managed by the NMS, as well as the descriptions of these objects, are kept in the MIB (Management Information Base). The MIB also contains data about an object's performance in a database format that can be mined and analyzed. The MIB is designed in a top-down, hierarchical tree structure that supports faster and more efficient analysis.

Agents communicate information about managed devices via any one of several application-layer protocols. On modern networks, most agents use **SNMP (Simple Network Management Protocol)**, which is part of the TCP/IP suite of protocols and typically runs over UDP ports 161 and 162 (though it can be configured to run over TCP ports 10161 and 10162). Port 161 is used to send information from the manager to the installed agents, while port 162 is used for agents to send messages to the manager. One characteristic that sets SNMP apart from syslog is that SNMP can be used to reconfigure managed devices. Additionally, SNMP is used more for real-time network monitoring rather than retroactive analysis.

There are a few, key SNMP messages used to communicate between the NMS and managed devices. As you can see in the following list, most of these conversations are initiated by the NMS:

- *Get Request*—The NMS sends a request for data to the agent on a managed device. See the left side of Figure 9-8.

- *Get Response*—The agent sends a response with the requested information.

- *Get Next*—The NMS might then request the next row of data in the MIB database.

- *Walk*—With this one command, the NMS can issue the equivalent of a sequence of SNMP Get Next messages to walk through sequential rows in the MIB database on a monitored device.

- *Trap*—An agent can be programmed to detect certain abnormal conditions that prompt the generation of Trap messages, where the agent sends the NMS unsolicited data once the specified conditions on the managed device are met (see the right side of Figure 9-8). For example, on a Cisco server, you could use the command

snmp trap link-status to instruct the agent to send an alert if or when an interface fails. The trap can later be disabled with the command **no snmp trap link-status**. Trap messages can alert network administrators of unresponsive services or devices, power supply issues, high temperatures, and tripped circuit breakers, which allows technicians to identify and address problems quickly—hopefully before users start to notice the problem. A report of a tripped circuit breaker eliminates the need for further investigation into why a specific device isn't responsive. Or an unresponsive service, such as DHCP, could be restarted remotely.

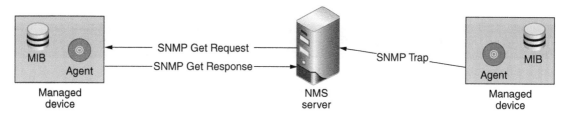

Figure 9-8   SNMP message types

Most, but not all, network management applications support multiple versions of SNMP. SNMPv3 is the most secure version of the protocol. However, some administrators have hesitated to upgrade to SNMPv3 because it requires more complex configuration. Therefore, SNMPv2 is still widely used, despite the many SNMP vulnerabilities listed in the CVE (Common Vulnerabilities and Exposures), one of which is displayed in Figure 9-9. When using older versions of SNMP, it's important to incorporate additional security measures, such as the following:

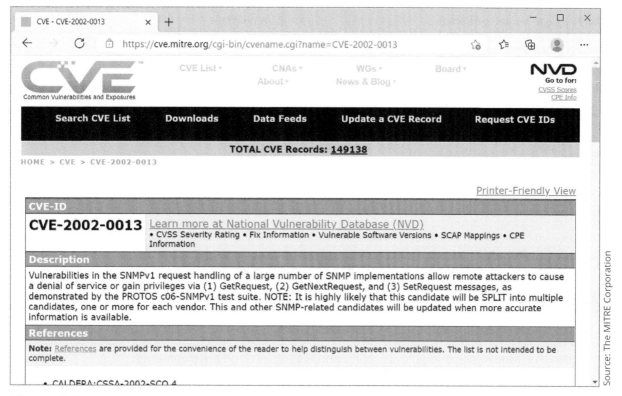

Figure 9-9   One of many SNMP vulnerabilities listed in the CVE

- Disable SNMP on devices where it's not needed.
- Limit approved sources of SNMP messages.
- Require read-only mode so devices can't be reconfigured using SNMP messages.
- Configure strong passwords, called community strings, on SNMP-managed devices.

- Use different community strings on different types of devices so, for example, a compromised UPS (which incorporates less secure protections) doesn't result in a compromised router using the same community string.

Although you can configure syslog on VM instances in the cloud or send SNMP messages from on-prem to the cloud, cloud-native monitoring solutions are more efficient, effective, and elegant. The next section discusses various monitoring tools built into AWS, Azure, and GCP.

Remember This

- An event is a detectable change in a cloud service that you're monitoring.
- Logs collect streams of data over time to show historical insights and reveal usage patterns and anomalies.
- Syslog is a standard for generating, storing, and processing messages about events on many networked systems.
- Agents communicate information about managed devices via any one of several application-layer protocols, most commonly SNMP (Simple Network Management Protocol).

Self-Check

4. Which of the following is an example of an event?
   - **a.** A VM's CPU utilization increases.
   - **b.** A storage bucket is deleted.
   - **c.** A VPC receives incoming traffic.
   - **d.** A ping fails.

5. Which process protects private information?
   - **a.** Event correlation
   - **b.** Trend analysis
   - **c.** Severity categorization
   - **d.** Log scrubbing

6. Which of the following is used to analyze logs?
   - **a.** SIEM
   - **b.** SNMP
   - **c.** Syslog
   - **d.** CVE

○ Check your answers at the end of this module.

Section 9-3: Analysis and Response

Certification

1.2 Explain the factors that contribute to capacity planning.

1.3 Explain the importance of high availability and scaling in cloud environments.

2.5 Given a scenario, implement measures to meet security requirements.

3.1 Given a scenario, integrate components into a cloud solution.

4.1 Given a scenario, configure logging, monitoring, and alerting to maintain operational status.

4.3 Given a scenario, optimize cloud environments.

4.4 Given a scenario, apply proper automation and orchestration techniques.

Now that you've seen where performance data is collected from—including metrics, events, and logs—consider what happens next to the data. Figure 9-10 shows the way data flows through a typical cloud monitoring system. There are, of course, variations for each platform. This diagram shows a general overview to help you understand where the data can come from and then what can be done with it.

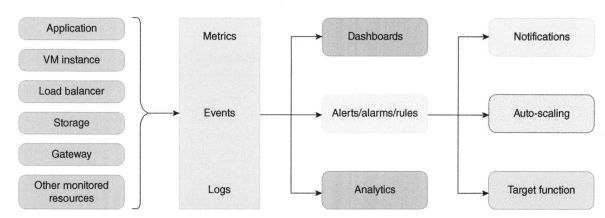

Figure 9-10   Cloud monitoring data collection and response

Dashboards provide a passive viewpoint for cloud admins to monitor cloud resources. This information might prompt further research or immediate human intervention. Alerts, alarms, and rules, however, can help automate responses and thereby relieve technicians of some of the time commitment required for cloud monitoring. In this section, you learn more about alerts, alarms, and rules in the AWS, Azure, and GCP environments.

Monitoring in AWS

AWS relies primarily on the CloudWatch service to provide monitoring capabilities. Many of the available features are free and included by default. Metrics about every AWS service you use can be tracked through CloudWatch dashboards. However, you can also configure alarms that send notifications directly to cloud admins via text and email, or notifications can automatically trigger changes on your behalf.

An AWS alarm monitors a single metric over a specified period. If the metric exceeds a threshold during that time, the alarm is activated and performs whatever response you programmed into it, such as sending a notification to SNS (Simple Notification Service) or enacting an auto-scaling policy. You can also show alarm states on your dashboards, as shown in Figure 9-11.

For example, suppose you collect information on an instance's CPU utilization every minute. If that utilization level exceeds a certain threshold for more than, say, five minutes, then the alarm might be configured to send a notification to SNS, which then sends an email to the cloud admin. If the CPU utilization spikes above the threshold for only one or two minutes, however, the alarm is not triggered. It's helpful to first understand the purpose and role of SNS notifications, and then alarm configuration options will make more sense.

SNS Notifications

An SNS notification can send text or email messages to human users. It can also support what is called event-driven computing. Recall that microservices and serverless architectures increase efficiency of applications and encourage evolution of individual components by decoupling, or isolating, services. In this environment, publish/subscribe messaging (pub/sub messaging for short) allows the service components to talk to each other about events that happen within each service while the services themselves continue to function independently of one another.

Pub/sub messaging refers to asynchronous communication between event producers (such as monitored resources) and event consumers (such as a monitoring service). The event producer publishes messages, and the event consumer subscribes to message channels. Monitoring is a common use of this technique, but it's not the only one. The decoupling of monolithic applications into microservices also relies on pub/sub messaging.

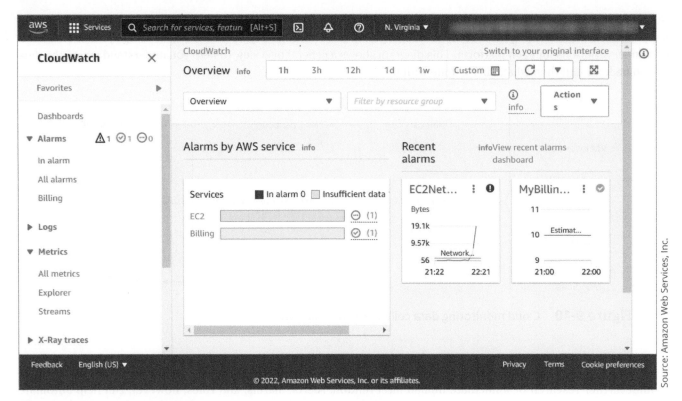

Figure 9-11 This dashboard shows one alarm in the ALARM state

For example, suppose the building blocks of a large and complex (called monolithic) application are separated into various, independently run services. Maybe you have a database, a web-based user interface, an authentication service, perhaps a payment platform, and a variety of other microservices that, collectively, make the app work. Each of these components runs in a separate environment, and each can be evolved and maintained separately due to their reliance on API-based communication, as you've already learned. Each microservice might be an event producer that broadcasts, or publishes, a message when an event occurs, such as a customer purchasing an item. Another microservice might subscribe to the first service's messaging channel. When the event consumer receives a message meeting certain requirements, it responds with its own action, such as generating a ticket to pull the purchased item from warehouse shelves.

As events occur within each component, communication must be triggered that keeps all related components in sync. The component experiencing the event publishes a message to all subscribers of that particular topic. Subscribers might include human users but can also include other components of the application or related resources. Each event serves as part of a larger process that emanates throughout the decoupled application. This arrangement is called **event-driven architecture** where an event in one service triggers an event in another service, thus enabling communication throughout the entire architecture. As you can see, SNS is much more than a notification service for humans.

CloudWatch Alarm Configuration

CloudWatch relies on the same SNS system to handle messages in response to alarms. Figure 9-12 shows some of the configuration options for an alarm threshold.

Notice that you can select a logical argument such as the following:

- >= (greater than or equal to)
- <= (less than or equal to)
- > (greater than)
- < (less than)

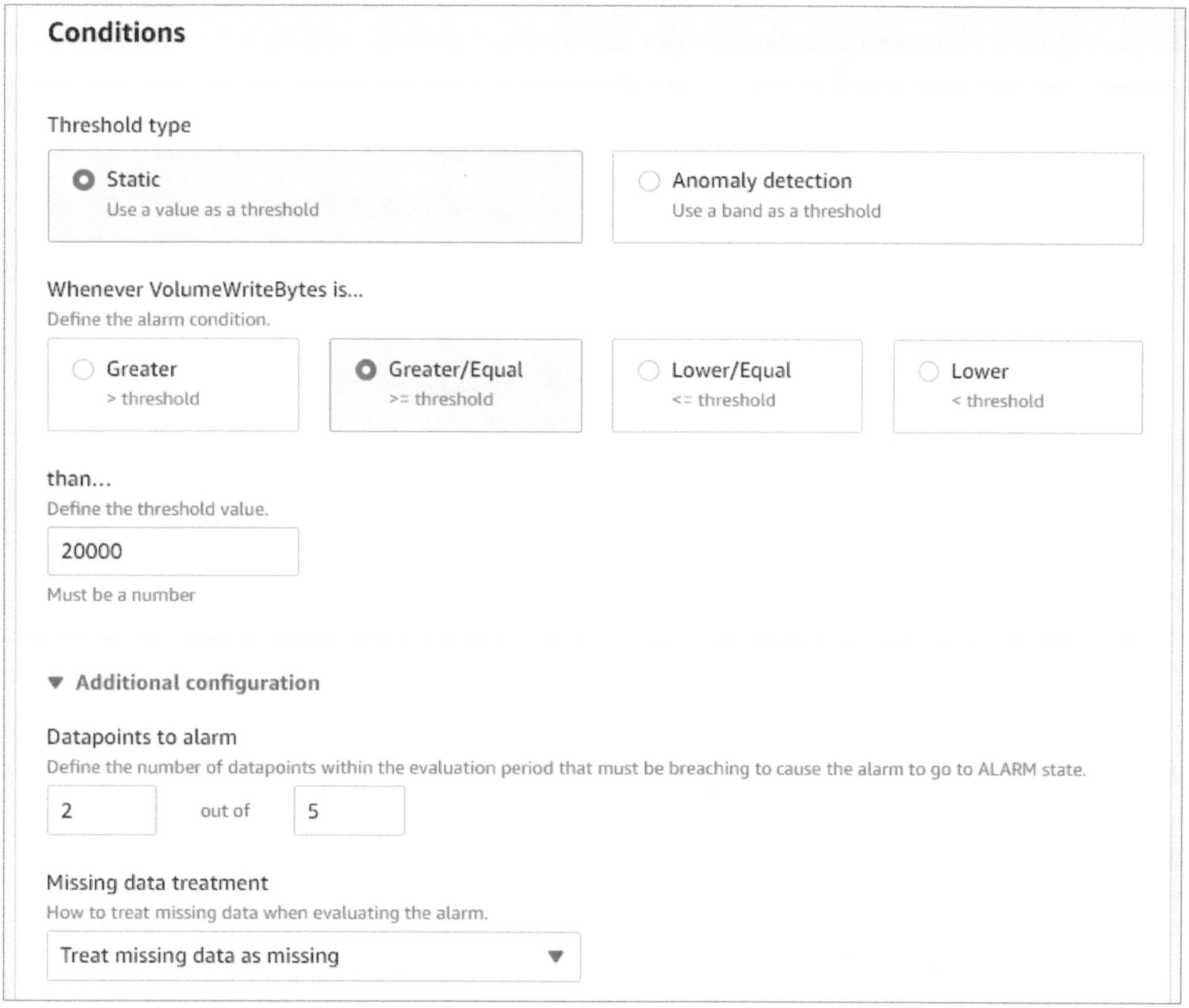

Conditions

Threshold type

○ **Static**
Use a value as a threshold

○ **Anomaly detection**
Use a band as a threshold

Whenever VolumeWriteBytes is...
Define the alarm condition.

○ **Greater**
\> threshold

● **Greater/Equal**
\>= threshold

○ **Lower/Equal**
<= threshold

○ **Lower**
< threshold

than...
Define the threshold value.

20000

Must be a number

▼ **Additional configuration**

Datapoints to alarm
Define the number of datapoints within the evaluation period that must be breaching to cause the alarm to go to ALARM state.

2   out of   5

Missing data treatment
How to treat missing data when evaluating the alarm.

Treat missing data as missing ▼

Figure 9-12   Configure a threshold and an action for the alarm to take

Figure 9-13 shows where the displayed threshold configuration falls on the metric's existing data. The red line indicates the alarm's threshold.

You can further restrict the alarm to a number of occurrences within a specified range of data points. For example, perhaps you only want the alarm to trigger if three of five data points exceed the threshold, but not when just one or two data points rise above the threshold.

Notice that you can also set various types of actions. A notification action might send an email or text to the cloud admin. An auto-scaling action, on the other hand, could stop, terminate, reboot, or recover an instance, which is a type of cloud bursting. For example, suppose you have an alarm configured to detect CPU utilization below 10 percent for more than one day. This alarm is designed to detect instances that are not currently being used. The alarm could trigger a stop instance action, which shuts down the instance until it's needed again.

How do you know where to configure alarm thresholds? This is really an art form rather than a science. With more experience, you'll get a better feel for what settings and thresholds miss important metric changes (called false negatives, where relevant indicators are missed) or, conversely, overwhelm your team with too many false positives. You'll understand the nuances of your cloud and integral systems, learning where problems are most likely to occur and what kinds of indicators give you an early warning that can help you avoid problems in the first

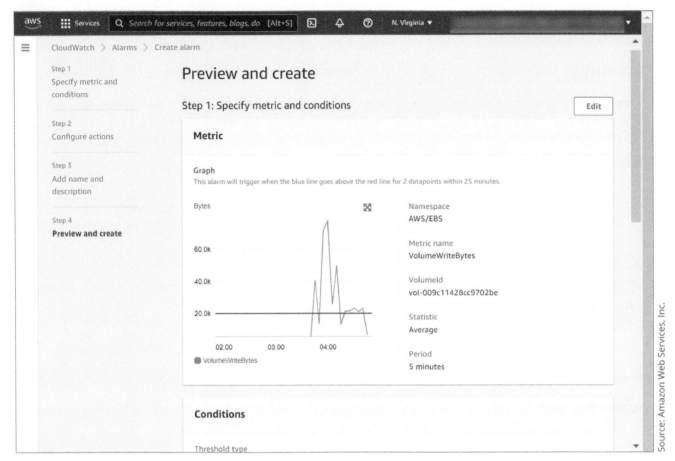

Figure 9-13   Greater than or equal to will trigger an alarm when the metric rises above the red line

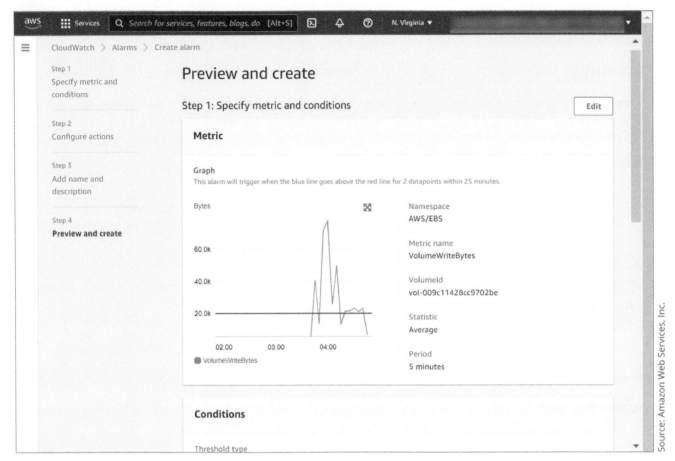

Figure 9-14   True or false positives and negatives

place. Figure 9-14 can help you understand the relationship between true or false positives and negatives.

As you begin configuring alarms, first gather information on target object baselines. What's normal for that object's metrics? At what point does deviation from those baselines indicate a true problem? How long should that deviation be in play before you want to receive a notification or make an automated change? Consider the following tips for alarm configuration:

• **Fine-tune your alarm thresholds**—If your acceptable band of values is too narrow, you'll have loads of false positives. If the acceptable band is too wide, you'll likely miss important indicators of problems creeping in. Watch the visualizations and metrics closely when setting thresholds to determine if you're satisfied with the resulting level of reporting. Also adjust your thresholds as needed for existing conditions. For example, if you're updating a server, you can expect increased traffic across connected network interfaces. You don't want this planned traffic to unnecessarily trigger alarms.

• **Configure granular or escalated notifications**—For example, more sensitive alarms that are more likely to result in false positives or low-priority alarms that require attention but little troubleshooting can be assigned to first- or second-tier IT staff. Alarms that indicate more complex problems or that are monitoring more critical services can send notifications directly to more experienced staff and admins. The people handling alarms will also need policies that clearly define how issues should be communicated to other staff, if needed, such as when a first-tier employee needs to escalate the alarm to someone more qualified to handle a difficult problem.

- *Choose notification types that resonate with staff*—For example, if you're consistently overwhelmed by emails but your phone never leaves your side, you might prefer text messages. If you tend to forget a text message moments after you read it, emails might work better. That said, never set up an email filter for the notifications coming to your inbox. "Out of sight, out of mind" presents a significant threat to follow-through on alarm notifications.

- *Include backup monitoring for critical services*—Just like with other parts of the infrastructure, avoid relying on a single point of failure for monitoring systems. A single monitoring solution can fail, leaving crucial red flags unnoticed until a pending failure starts costing users productivity time.

- *Explore monitoring tools and resources from third-party vendors*—Cloud monitoring is a crowded market with several excellent tools available to adaptively monitor resources, cut costs, and optimize services. For example, Datadog (datadoghq.com) collates data from servers, containers, databases, and third-party services into a single pane of glass with sophisticated monitoring algorithms. ParkMyCloud (parkmycloud. com), on the other hand, monitors and helps reduce cloud costs by identifying ways to optimize a cloud budget.

- *Configure monitoring tools throughout the cloud stack*—For example, APM (application performance management) tools monitor and can, in some cases, help manage applications for maximum performance and reliability. While AWS's CloudWatch provides some APM features, many third-party tools provide more in-depth functionality for monitoring applications. Examples include Stackify (stackify.com), Raygun APM (raygun.com), and New Relic APM (newrelic.com).

- *Consider that alarms can't monitor every possible indicator of a problem*—Sometimes problems that crop up are unpredictable and not indicated by the thresholds you are currently monitoring. If you regularly skim through your logs, reports, and dashboards, you might notice a problem that is not triggering an alarm but should (i.e., a false negative). When a problem does occur, you can do some forensic research to determine what early indicators you missed and how you might configure alarms to detect those red flags sooner. Also, these performance anomalies can sometimes be captured by third-party tools designed specifically for this purpose, such as Watchdog by Datadog. These tools rely on ML (machine learning) technologies to detect problems you might not think to look for.

Note 4

These alarm configuration tips apply to other cloud platforms as well, although the features might be called something else, such as alerts, rules, or policies.

Grow with Cengage Unlimited!

If you'd like more information about machine learning, use your Cengage Unlimited subscription to go to *Data Communication and Computer Networks: A Business User's Approach*, 9th edition, Chapter 7, and read the section titled "Data Analytics." If you don't have a Cengage Unlimited subscription, you can find more information at cengage.com/unlimited.

CloudWatch Events and Rules

Whereas alarms respond to continual metric changes, such as the rising and falling of CPU utilization, event rules respond to events, such as when an EC2 instance shuts down or an object in a storage bucket is deleted. When the specified event occurs, a rule is triggered that can initiate a corresponding action in a different service. This could be a simple response, such as pushing an SNS notification. Or it could be something much more complex, such as creating a new VM from a snapshot. Event rules are often configured to trigger Lambda functions. Lambda is a serverless computing service in AWS that can perform various compute functions without requiring the configuration or maintenance of underlying VM instances.

> **You're Ready**
>
> You're now ready to complete Project 9-1: Monitor Your AWS Cloud. You can complete the project now or wait until you've finished all the readings for this module.

Monitoring in Azure

The Azure Monitor service collects two kinds of data on the resources it monitors: metrics and logs. Metrics consist of lightweight, numerical data collected in real time and reported live in visualizations. Logs are more complex data, including both numerical and text data types, describing system events or activities and collected over time for retroactive analysis. Data from metrics and logs is retained at no charge for a few weeks, depending on the type of data and the current pricing scheme. If you need to keep data longer than that, you can send it to a storage account for paid storage.

Alerts can trigger when specific thresholds are breached or when certain events occur. An alert activates an action group that can notify cloud technicians or perform an automated response, such as creating a new web server. Each action group's reach should be limited to its resource group.

Figure 9-15 shows the configuration blade for creating a new action group and the sub-configuration for an Email/SMS/Push/Voice action type. Figure 9-16 shows available event levels that a new alert rule can monitor, which is conceptually comparable to syslog severity levels.

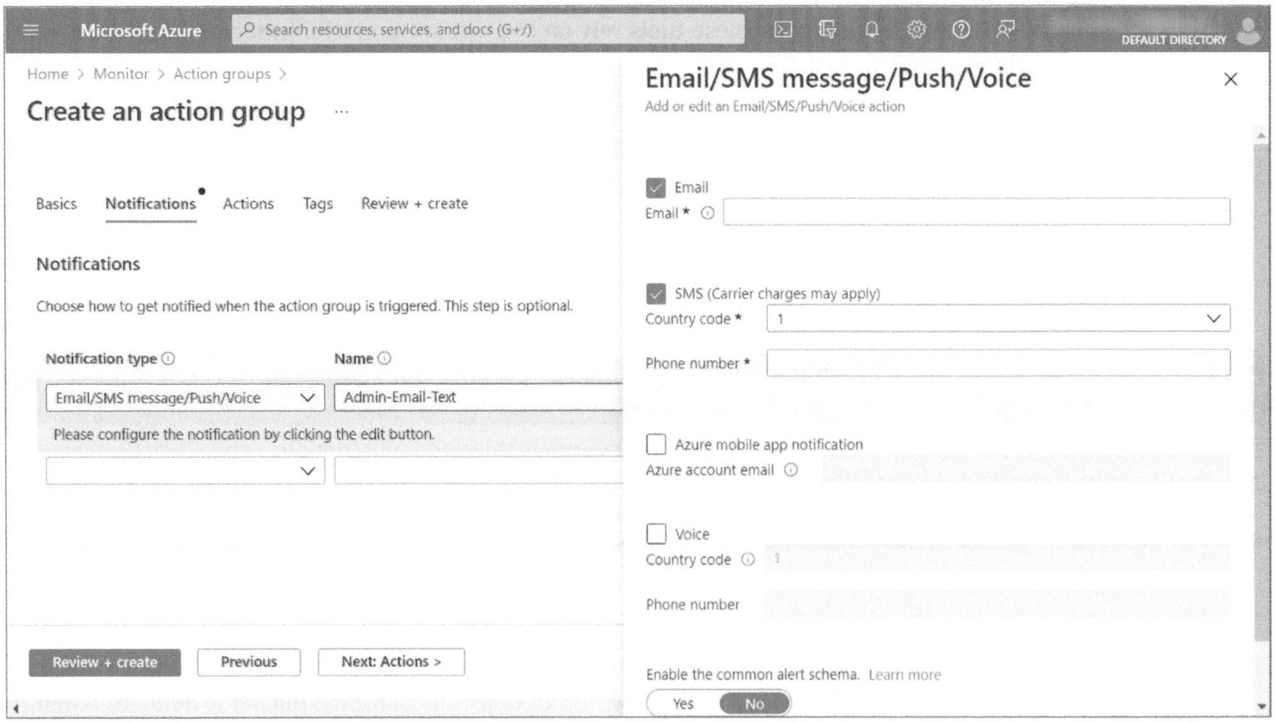

Figure 9-15 Configure a notification via email, text message, Azure app, or voice message

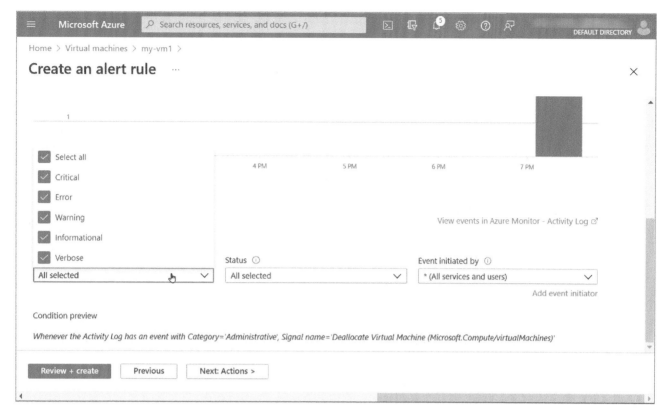

Figure 9-16   Choose a resource to monitor and a condition that triggers a specific action

You're Ready

You're now ready to complete Project 9-2: Monitor Your Azure Cloud. You can complete the project now or wait until you've finished all the readings for this module.

Monitoring in GCP

GCP offers monitoring services through Cloud Monitoring, which is part of the Operations Suite and can also be used to monitor resources in hybrid and multi-cloud environments. Some basic system metrics are monitored by default. Other metrics can be monitored as well by installing an agent on the monitored resource, defining custom metrics, or analyzing logs collected by Cloud Logging.

As shown in Figure 9-17, you can create an alerting policy on any number of available metrics and, when violated (see Figure 9-18), it will send a notification. Notification channels, such as email messages or texts via SMS (short message service), transmit information about triggered alerts.

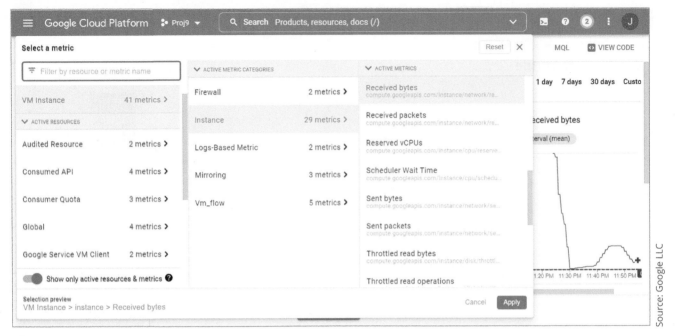

Figure 9-17   VM instance metrics for monitoring

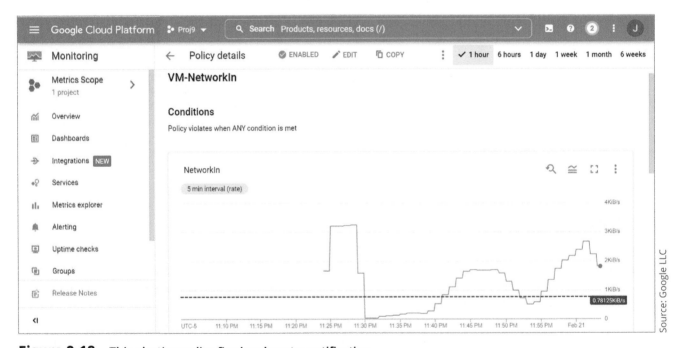

Figure 9-18   This alerting policy fired and sent a notification

Other notification types are available through integrated third-party services, such as Slack (slack.com), and are configured through the Alerting page in the Monitoring service, as shown in Figure 9-19.

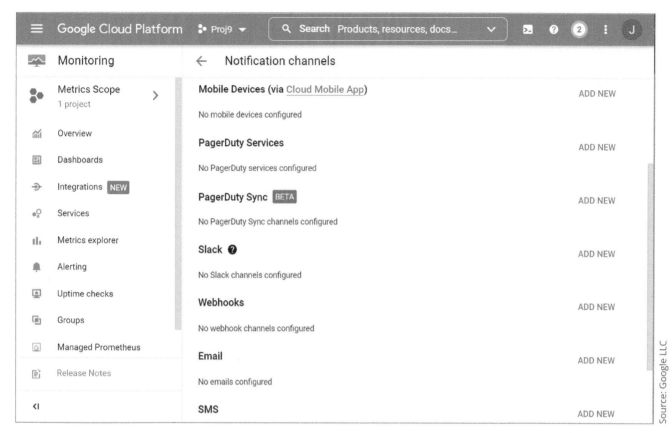

Figure 9-19   Add a notification channel

You're Ready

You're now ready to complete Project 9-3: Monitor Your GCP Cloud. You can complete the project now or wait until you've finished all the readings for this module.

Remember This

- AWS relies primarily on the CloudWatch service to provide monitoring capabilities.
- As events occur within each component, communication is triggered that keeps all related components in sync; this is called event-driven architecture.
- The Azure Monitor service collects two kinds of data on the resources it monitors: metrics and logs.
- GCP offers monitoring services through Cloud Monitoring, which is part of the Operations Suite and can also be used to monitor resources in hybrid and multi-cloud environments.

Self-Check

7. An event producer _____ messages.
   - **a.** subscribes to
   - **b.** analyzes
   - **c.** responds to
   - **d.** publishes

8. What kind of application relies on event-driven architecture?
   - **a.** Monolithic
   - **b.** Decoupled
   - **c.** Complex
   - **d.** Independent

9. What does the symbol >= stand for?
   - **a.** Less than
   - **b.** Greater than
   - **c.** Less than or equal to
   - **d.** Greater than or equal to

○ Check your answers at the end of this module.

Section 9-4: Troubleshooting Performance

Certification

4.3 Given a scenario, optimize cloud environments.

4.5 Given a scenario, perform appropriate backup and restore operations.

4.6 Given a scenario, perform disaster recovery tasks.

5.3 Given a scenario, troubleshoot deployment issues.

5.5 Given a scenario, troubleshoot common performance issues.

Despite all preparations, problems still occur. Monitoring helps identify symptoms of problems. How can you use this information to find the source of a problem? And how do you respond to the problems that surface?

Utilization Issues

A significant portion of the monitoring you will do in the cloud relates to how resource utilization supports performance. The information you collect will inform your work troubleshooting performance degradation issues. The following list explores some tips for improving performance on various factors:

- *CPU*—CPU resources are monitored by a CPU utilization measurement, as shown in Figure 9-20. Very low CPU utilization could indicate you have too many instances running, and you might want to configure the cluster to automatically reduce the number of servers in the cluster. Very high CPU utilization (typically over 85 or 90 percent) indicates the need for scaling out the cluster by adding more instances. Recall that this technique is called right-sizing—resources are increased or decreased according to need.

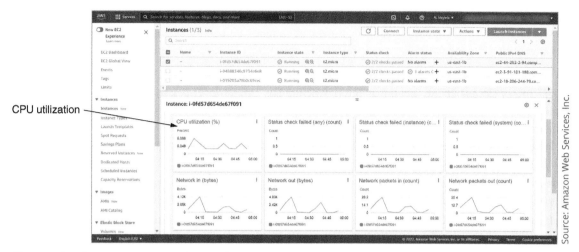

Figure 9-20   CPU utilization monitored in EC2

- **GPU**—When using a GPU, the GPU utilization metric can be monitored in much the same way as CPU utilization. This metric might trigger an autoscaling action, or it might trigger an alert to a cloud admin. You can also monitor metrics for a GPU's memory utilization, temperature, or power usage.

- **Memory**—Memory utilization is another critical metric to monitor clusters for too little or too much demand on the existing instances. Unlike other metrics, typical cloud monitoring services (such as CloudWatch) don't offer memory monitoring for VM instances because they don't have the necessary visibility into processes the instance is running within its own OS. To monitor memory utilization, the instances themselves must push RAM utilization information to the monitoring service. Some cloud providers, such as AWS, offer prebuilt scripts you can run on each instance where this configuration is needed. In contrast, memory utilization can be monitored for clusters in services such as AWS's ECS (Elastic Cluster Service), depending on the cloud service being used and the alarm configuration.

- **Storage**—Commonly monitored storage metrics include the following metrics:

  - IOPS (input/output operations per second), which indicates speed or throughput. IOPS might be calculated from DiskReadOps (disk read operations) or DiskWriteOps (disk write operations).
  - DiskReadBytes or DiskWriteBytes, which indicate data volume. Data volume information is especially relevant to determining storage costs and checking remaining capacity in cases where storage space is reserved (such as with block storage).

Scaling Issues

Problems from overwhelmed virtual resources aren't the only issues faced with a cloud deployment's performance. For example, you might run into limitations of the physical hardware underneath the virtual layer. Many cloud providers, especially for the public cloud, use oversubscription, or overprovisioning, to increase their customer base faster than their physical infrastructure can support. This strategy is common even within a company's own data center where, for example, you might deploy more storage space than you have available on your physical storage devices. You then increase the physical storage only as your need for storage space nears your hardware's current capacity. You read about this technique in Module 2 when you learned about the overcommitment ratio of vCPUs to available threads.

Additionally, oversubscription can cause problems for you as a public cloud customer if many customers draw on the CSP's physical infrastructure at the same time beyond typical bandwidth levels. In this case, you might not receive actual performance levels consistent with your realistic expectations. One way to avoid this problem is to ensure you choose a reputable public cloud provider who is known for maintaining sufficient physical infrastructure to meet fluctuating customer demand. Another option is to replicate some of your resources across the cloud provider's physical data centers so that, if one AZ is overwhelmed, your services can run on duplicate resources in another AZ.

One of the most common methods of balancing resource costs with performance is to configure automatic scaling, or auto-scaling. Auto-scaling configurations, however, can cause problems if scaling doesn't happen responsively to changing demands. The following list describes some common problems you might face with auto-scaling clusters of EC2 instances:

- *Conflicting policies*—If auto-scaling is not performing as expected, check to confirm you don't have multiple policies being triggered at the same time. For example, if one policy says to scale out but another policy says to scale in on the same trigger, you might get results you didn't want and, therefore, degrade performance. In this case, you can check the related alarm's history or the auto-scaling group's history to see if two auto-scaling policies are being triggered simultaneously.
- *Inadequate policy*—If an auto-scaling group's minimum or maximum capacity has already been reached, additional scaling in or out, respectively, won't work. These thresholds might need to be adjusted.
- *Stuck instance*—Even if an instance was automatically marked for creation or termination, occasionally an instance will get stuck in a Pending:Wait or Terminating:Wait state. This can distort auto-scaling group metrics. The instance should eventually time out, but you can push the process from the CLI (command line interface), if needed.

Similar to auto-scaling, automatic replication is designed to increase performance or increase availability and redundancy. Also similar to auto-scaling, replication processes can snag or fail. The following list examines some common replication issues:

- *Incorrect role*—To create replicated resources, the service performing the replication must have appropriate permissions through an assigned role. If the service is attempting to replicate while assigned the wrong role, the replication will fail.
- *Insufficient access*—If the replica is supposed to be created in a different account and the service does not have permission to create or upload resources into that account, replication will fail.
- *Missing or incorrect tags*—Resources intended to be replicated must be appropriately tagged at the time of creation. If the creation process does not assign tags during creation or is using the wrong tags, replication will fail.

Restoration from Backup

When things do go wrong, you'll need processes for restoring data and functions from your backups. Most of the time, backups rely on redundant resources of some kind, whether that's a redundant web server or redundant copies of data. An in-place backup is a redundancy that can take over immediately, meaning the backup is already in place and only requires a simple configuration change. These backups should be kept in an alternate location so issues affecting the primary resource won't also affect the backup. You might instead need to recover files or configurations from backup before activating these backups. For example, you can use versioning in a storage bucket to restore files if the active versions were damaged or accidentally deleted. You can also use a recovery point to restore a backed-up resource such as a VM instance or even a database.

Many cloud platforms offer built-in backup services. For example, AWS Backup provides managed backup protection throughout your AWS environment. Backups can be automated, monitored, and encrypted. Azure Backup similarly offers backup management throughout many Azure services. Although GCP does not offer a comprehensive managed backup service, it does include backup features within specific services, such as Backup for GKE (Google Kubernetes Engine) and Persistent Disk snapshots.

You're Ready

You're now ready to complete Project 9-4: Research Python Concepts. You can complete the project now or wait until you've finished the other projects for this module.

Remember This

- A significant portion of cloud monitoring relates to how resource utilization supports performance.
- Auto-scaling configurations can cause problems if scaling doesn't happen responsively to changing demands.
- An in-place backup is a redundancy that can take over immediately, meaning the backup is already in place and only requires a simple configuration change.

Self-Check

10. Which technique adjusts resources to match demand?
    - **a.** Cloud bursting
    - **b.** Right sizing
    - **c.** Oversubscription
    - **d.** Replication

11. Which of the following problems could result in an orphaned resource whose expenses are not properly tracked?
    - **a.** Incorrect role
    - **b.** Conflicting policies
    - **c.** Missing or incorrect tags
    - **d.** Stuck instance

○ Check your answers at the end of this module.

Module Summary

Section 9-1: Monitoring Resources

- Monitoring tools capture information from cloud resource APIs and organize the data to report on the health, activities, and expenses of monitored resources.
- Various monitoring processes offer retroactive analysis of past events, provide intermittent insights into a resource's state or performance, or provide near-immediate feedback on metrics in a continuous, unbroken manner.
- A well-structured dashboard can give a cloud technician a quick overview of critical services and draw attention to issues that might indicate problems.

Section 9-2: Events and Logs

- An event is a detectable change in a cloud service that you're monitoring.
- Logs collect streams of data over time to show historical insights and reveal usage patterns and anomalies.
- Syslog is a standard for generating, storing, and processing messages about events on many networked systems.
- Agents communicate information about managed devices via any one of several application-layer protocols, most commonly SNMP (Simple Network Management Protocol).

Section 9-3: Analysis and Response

- AWS relies primarily on the CloudWatch service to provide monitoring capabilities.
- As events occur within each component, communication is triggered that keeps all related components in sync; this is called event-driven architecture.

- The Azure Monitor service collects two kinds of data on the resources it monitors: metrics and logs.
- GCP offers monitoring services through Cloud Monitoring, which is part of the Operations Suite and can also be used to monitor resources in hybrid and multi-cloud environments.

Section 9-4: Troubleshooting Performance

- A significant portion of cloud monitoring relates to how resource utilization supports performance.
- Auto-scaling configurations can cause problems if scaling doesn't happen responsively to changing demands.
- An in-place backup is a redundancy that can take over immediately, meaning the backup is already in place and only requires a simple configuration change.

Key Terms

For definitions of key terms, see the Glossary.

audit log	ITSM (IT service management)	severity level
ConMon (continuous monitoring)	log	SNMP (Simple Network
event	log scrubbing	Management Protocol)
event correlation	ML (machine learning)	syslog
event-driven architecture	packet broker	tag
false positive	pub/sub messaging	TAP (test access point)

Acronyms Checklist

The acronyms in Table 9-1 are listed in the Cloud+ objectives and could appear on the Cloud+ exam. This means that exam questions might use any of these acronyms in context so that you must know the meaning of the acronym to answer the question correctly. Make sure you're familiar with what each acronym stands for and the general concept of the term itself. All these acronyms are used in context in this module.

Table 9-1   Module 9 acronyms

Acronym	Spelled out
IPMI	Intelligent Platform Management Interface
MTBF	mean time between failure
MTTF	mean time to failure
MTTR	mean time to repair or mean time to recovery
SNMP	Simple Network Management Protocol

Review Questions

1. Which CPU utilization measurement most likely does NOT indicate a problem?

   a. 100 percent
   b. 95 percent
   c. 50 percent
   d. 5 percent

2. Which strategy tracks cloud usage but not cloud costs?

   a. Log monitoring
   b. Chargeback model
   c. Showback model
   d. Event monitoring

3. When you create a tag called Project on all your EC2 instances, what kind of tagging are you using?

   a. Implicit
   b. Inherent
   c. Native
   d. Explicit

4. Which visualization would be the best fit for a KPI whose status fluctuates significantly and quickly?

   a. Dial
   b. Line chart
   c. Stacked chart
   d. Pie chart

5. Which of the following is NOT defined by syslog?

   a. Message transmission
   b. Message format
   c. Message security
   d. Message handling

6. How can you get deeper insight into your VM server's OS metrics?

   a. Configure logging.
   b. Install an agent.
   c. Customize your dashboard.
   d. Add more notifications.

7. Which of the following problems is caused by CSP-side configurations?

   a. Oversubscription
   b. Auto-scaling configuration
   c. Incorrect tags
   d. Incorrect role

8. Which tool can monitor cloud traffic across all resources hosted in a VPC?

   a. Wireshark
   b. Explicit tagging
   c. Packet broker
   d. Syslog

9. Which syslog severity level would be appropriate for an event that reports the catastrophic failure of a critical web server?

   a. 1
   b. 3
   c. 5
   d. 7

10. What information can help you determine where to set an alarm's threshold?

   a. Alert severity level
   b. Resource baselines
   c. Number of subscriptions
   d. Automated responses

Scenario-Based Questions

Question 9-1

Heidi is investigating a connectivity problem involving AWS EC2 instances running in a particular region. The problem began about three weeks ago and has resulted in repeatedly rebooting or recovering the server instances in this cluster. The servers appear to be caught in a cycle where the system's automated attempts at solving the problem seem to trigger the problem all over again. Heidi wants to go back to the first few error messages collected to see if she can determine what started the problem in the first place. What sort of data does Heidi need to access to examine this information?

   a. Metric reports
   b. Event logs
   c. EC2 metrics
   d. EC2 analytics

Question 9-2

Rex is managing a cluster of four web servers with a load balancer on the front end. His company's website has recently started receiving a significant increase in traffic due to a successful advertising campaign, and so he's ready to increase the budget available for running this cluster of web servers. However, Rex needs to decide whether to scale up or scale out. Currently, he has three reserved instances running in the cluster and one on-demand instance. He needs to improve performance capacity overall by about 25 percent. What approach should Rex take to reach his new capacity goal while minimizing the impact on his budget?

   a. Add another reserved instance to the cluster.

   b. Allocate more resources to all four existing servers.

   c. Add two more on-demand instances.

   d. Allocate more resources to the one existing, on-demand server.

Question 9-3

Kylie works for a retail chain that hosts its own e-commerce site. The site relies on three databases: one that holds the product catalog, one that stores historical order data, and a third that processes payments as purchases are made. To minimize DR costs while increasing her company's preparedness, Kylie has decided to invest in a failover service for one database to reduce RTO and RPO for that data to seconds. Which database should she choose?

   a. The historical orders database

   b. The product catalog database

   c. The customer loyalty database

   d. The payment processing database

Hands-On Projects

Note 5

Websites, applications, public cloud platforms, and related account options change often. While the instructions given in these projects were accurate at the time of writing, you might need to adjust the steps or options according to later changes.

Note to Instructors and Students: A rubric is provided for evaluating student performance on these projects. Please see Appendix D.

Project 9-1: Monitor Your AWS Cloud

Estimated time: 45 minutes

Objective 4.1: Given a scenario, configure logging, monitoring, and alerting to maintain operational status.

Resources:

- AWS account
- Access to an active email account
- Internet access

Context:

Generating notifications in response to an alarm is a great way to familiarize yourself with some of the basic monitoring services and options in AWS. In this project, you'll configure an alarm for a Windows VM and then trigger the alarm.

Note 6

At the time of this writing, all the services used in this project offered sufficient free tier limits to complete the project with no fees so long as you follow the instructions as written. To see a current list of free units included with AWS CloudWatch, search online for an Amazon CloudWatch pricing list, and check the "Free tier" portion of the pricing scheme. At the time of this writing, this information could be found at aws.amazon.com/cloudwatch/pricing.

Complete the following steps:

1. In your AWS Management Console, create a **Microsoft Windows Server** VM using the **t2.micro** type. In the Network settings section, add a security group rule that allows **All ICMP - IPv4** traffic from **Anywhere**. You can associate a key pair with the VM or not—you will not need to remote into it.
2. Before leaving the EC2 service, make note of the VM's instance ID. You will need this information later in this project.

Before you create an alert, you need an SNS topic, which will define where information about the alert will go. To create an SNS topic, complete the following steps:

3. Go to the **Simple Notification Service**, which is grouped in the Application Integration category. In the navigation pane on the left, click **Topics**. Click **Create topic**.
4. Select the **Standard** topic type. Give the topic a name, such as AdminAttn. The topic name could describe the resource the topic will be attached to (such as EC2), the application it's connected to, or the people or services that will be subscribed to it. Optionally, add a display name, such as your name, the name of your cloud network or resource, or the name of your organization. Click **Create topic**.

You now need to subscribe to this topic. Complete the following steps:

5. On the topic's page, scroll down and click **Create subscription**. For Protocol, choose **Email**. In the Endpoint field, enter your email address. You will need access to this email account to confirm the subscription. Click **Create subscription**.
6. When you receive the confirmation email, open it and click **Confirm subscription**.
7. To test your topic and subscription, return to the Topics page, click the topic to select it, and click **Publish message**. Give the message a subject line, such as Test message. Enter text for the message body. Click **Publish message**. Check your email to confirm the message came through. Did it work? If not, troubleshoot the problem.

Now you're ready to create your CloudWatch alarm. Complete the following steps:

8. Go to the **CloudWatch** service, which is grouped in the Management & Governance category. In the navigation pane's Metrics group, click **All metrics**. Because you created the VM at the beginning of this project, the EC2 tile should be listed in the Metrics pane under the Browse tab. If it's not, check your EC2 service to confirm your instance is fully initialized.
9. On the Metrics pane, click the **EC2** tile. Click **Per-Instance Metrics**. Click the check box to select the **NetworkIn** metric for the EC2 instance you created at the beginning of this project—confirm you're choosing the correct Instance ID from Step 2.
10. Click the **Graphed metrics** tab. In the Actions column, click the **Create alarm** icon (see Figure 9-21).

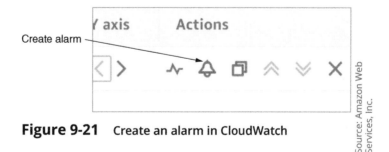

Figure 9-21 Create an alarm in CloudWatch

11. Change the Period field to **1 minute**. In the Conditions section, select **Greater/Equal** and define the threshold at **1500**. Click **Additional configuration** and notice that the Datapoints to alarm option is set at 1 out of 1. Click **Next**.

(continues)

Hands-On Projects Continued

12. Click in the *Send a notification to* field and select the topic you configured in Step 4. In addition to sending a notification, what other actions are available for this alarm? Click **Next**.
13. Give the alarm a name, such as EC2NetworkIn, and click **Next**. Click **Create alarm**.
14. On the All alarms page, what state is the alarm in?
15. Every 30 seconds or so, refresh the list of alarms until the alarm state changes. What state does the alarm change to?

Now that you have an alarm and you know your email subscription works, you're ready to trigger the alarm. Complete the following steps:

16. Click to select your alarm, and then click **View in metrics**. At the top of the screen, click **1h**.
17. In your browser, open a second tab and go to the EC2 service. Copy the VM's public IP address.
18. On your local computer, open a PowerShell or Command Prompt window. Enter the following command, using your VM's public IP address:

```
ping <ip-address> -t -l 1500
```

The -t switch runs the ping indefinitely until you tell it to stop. The -l switch increases the size of the ping packets. Note that the ping might not complete successfully; however, all you need to do is generate the incoming traffic so you can collect metrics on it.

19. While your ping is running in your PowerShell or Command Prompt window, repeatedly refresh the graphed metric in CloudWatch until the metric shows increased traffic and the alarm is triggered. What happens next? Note that it might take a minute or two for the alarm's action to take place. **Take a screenshot** showing the outcome of the alarm's action; submit this visual with your answers to this project's questions.
20. Return to the **EC2** service and check the Monitoring tab for your VM. If needed, click the **Refresh** icon. What other metrics show increased utilization?
21. Stop the ping (press **Ctrl+C** in the PowerShell or Command Prompt window) and wait a few minutes until the traffic level returns to normal. What happens to the alarm?
22. Delete all the resources you created in this project, including the VM, topic, subscription, and alarm. Check through your account to confirm that all related resources have been deleted.

Note 7

Depending on the status of your account and the selections you made during this project, the resources you created can deplete your credits or accrue charges. Double-check to make sure you've terminated all resources you created in this project.

Project 9-2: Monitor Your Azure Cloud

Estimated time: 45 minutes
Objective 4.1: Given a scenario, configure logging, monitoring, and alerting to maintain operational status.
Resources:

- Azure account
- Access to an active email account
- Internet access

Context:
Generating notifications in response to an alert is a great way to familiarize yourself with some of the basic monitoring services and options in Azure. In this project, you'll configure an alert rule for a Windows VM and then trigger the alert.

> **Note** 8
>
> At the time of this writing, all the services used in this project offered sufficient free limits to complete this project with no fees so long as you follow the instructions as written. To see a current list of free units included with Azure Monitor, search online for an Azure Monitor pricing list, and check the "Free Units Included" portion of the pricing schemes. At the time of this writing, this information could be found at azure.microsoft.com/en-us/pricing/details/monitor.

Complete the following steps:

1. In your Azure portal, create a new VM in a new resource group. Use the **Windows Server** image and the **B1s** VM size.

2. While the VM is being created, go to the Monitor service. In Monitor's navigation menu, click **Alerts**. Before you can configure an alert, you need an action group. Action groups are similar in concept to AWS's topics and determine where alert notifications are sent. At the top of the Alerts page, click **Create** and choose **Action group**.

3. Choose the resource group you created in Step 1. Give the action group a name, such as AdminAttn, and click **Next: Notifications**.

4. Select the **Email/SMS message/Push/Voice** action type. The Email/SMS message/Push/Voice blade opens. Select the **Email** check box and enter your email address in the field. Scroll down and click **OK**. Give the notification a name, such as MyEmail, and click **Review + create**.

5. Test the action group using the **Metric alert – Static threshold** sample type. Did it work? If not, troubleshoot the problem. When you're finished with the test, complete the creation of the action group.

6. By this time, your VM should be deployed. Return to the **Virtual machines** service and click your new VM. On the Overview page, click the **Monitoring** tab to see the various metrics running by default for your VM. What visualizations are listed?

7. In the VM's navigation menu, scroll down and click **Alerts**. Click **Create** and select **Alert rule**. In the list of signals, what signal types are included?

8. Search for **deallocate**, and then click **Deallocate Virtual Machine (Microsoft.Compute/virtualMachines)** from the **Administrative** monitor service. Leave the default Alert logic settings and click **Next: Actions**.

9. Click **Add action groups**, select the action group you created earlier in this project, and then click **Select**. Click **Next: Details**.

10. Make sure your resource group that you created in Step 1 is selected, and give the alert rule a name, such as VMStop. Click **Review + create**, and then click **Create**.

11. Click **Alert rules**. What severity is listed for your alert rule?

12. Return to the VM's Overview page, click **Stop**, and then click **OK**. Return to the Monitor service and examine the Alerts blade. What happens next? Note that you might need to wait a few minutes for the alarm's response to take place. **Take a screenshot** showing the outcome of the alert's action; submit this visual with your answers to this project's questions.

13. Delete all the resources created in this project by deleting the resource group from Step 1. Check through your account to confirm that all related resources have been deleted.

> **Note** 9
>
> Depending on the status of your account and the selections you made during this project, the resources you created can deplete your credits or accrue charges. Double-check to make sure you've terminated all resources you created in this project.

(continues)

Hands-On Projects Continued

Project 9-3: Monitor Your GCP Cloud

Estimated time: 45 minutes

Objective 4.1: Given a scenario, configure logging, monitoring, and alerting to maintain operational status.

Resources:

- GCP account
- Access to an active email account
- Internet access

Context:

Generating notifications in response to an alert is a great way to familiarize yourself with some of the basic monitoring services and options in GCP. In this project, you'll configure an alert policy for an Ubuntu VM and then trigger the alert.

> **Note 10**
>
> At the time of this writing, all the services used in this project offered sufficient free limits to complete the project with no fees so long as you follow the instructions as written. To see a current list of free allotments included with GCP Monitoring service, search online for a GCP Monitor pricing list, and check the "Free allotment per month" portion of the pricing schemes. At the time of this writing, this information could be found at cloud.google.com/stackdriver/pricing.

Complete the following steps:

1. In your GCP console, create a new project. Switch to the new project and create a VM instance using the **e2-micro** machine type and an **Ubuntu** boot disk. If you need to avoid accruing charges, be sure to select one of the free regions. (Search online for a current list of regions that support free instances in GCP.)

2. After the VM is deployed, select it in the list and, if necessary, click **SHOW INFO PANEL**, then click the **MONITORING** tab. Refresh the metrics every few minutes until the initial data appears. Which metrics are monitored here?

3. In the navigation menu, scroll down under OPERATIONS, point to **Monitoring**, and click **Overview**. (Note that you can hold down the Ctrl key on your keyboard to open the Monitoring overview in a different tab in your browser. You will need to view both Monitoring and Compute Engine services multiple times in this project.) Notice you have the option to create a dashboard, which would help you organize and monitor your alerts and other resources. In the left pane, click **Alerting**, and then click **CREATE POLICY**. Under step 1, click **ADD CONDITION**.

4. Give the condition a name, such as NetworkIn. Click the empty field in the Target section, and then select **VM Instance**. In the list of metrics that appears, scroll down and click **Received bytes**. In the Configuration section, configure the following settings:

   - Condition triggers if: **Any time series violates**
   - Condition: **is above**
   - Threshold: **800**
   - For: **1 minute**

   Click **ADD**, and then click **NEXT**.

5. In step 2, click the Notification Channels dropdown list, and click **MANAGE NOTIFICATION CHANNELS**. This opens a new tab in your browser where you can add an email channel. Scroll down and add your email address. Then close the notification channels tab in your browser and return to the **Create alerting policy** tab. Refresh the list of notification channels and select your email channel. Click **NEXT**.

6. Give the alert a name, such as VM-NetworkIn. Click **SAVE**.

7. Return to Compute Engine, go to your VM's page, and copy its external IP address.

8. On your local computer, open a PowerShell or Command Prompt window. Enter the following command, using the VM's public IP address:

$$\texttt{ping <ip-address> -t -l 1500}$$

The -t switch runs the ping indefinitely until you tell it to stop. The -l switch increases the size of the ping packets. Note that the ping might not complete successfully; however, all you need to do is generate the incoming traffic so you can collect metrics on it.

9. While your ping is running, return to the alerting policy's page in Monitoring, and watch it until the metric shows increased traffic and the alert is triggered. It could take several minutes for the alert to register. What happens next? **Take a screenshot** showing the outcome of the alert's action; submit this visual with your answers to this project's questions.

10. Return to your instance's page, and click the **OBSERVABILITY** tab. What metrics show increased utilization?

11. Stop the ping (press **Ctrl+C** in the PowerShell or Command Prompt window).

12. Delete the project you created in Step 1. Check through your account to confirm that all related resources have been deleted.

Note 11

Depending on the status of your account and the selections you made during this project, the resources you created can deplete your credits or accrue charges. Double-check to make sure you've terminated all resources you created in this project.

Project 9-4: Research Python Concepts

Estimated time: 30 minutes
Objective 4.4: Given a scenario, apply proper automation and orchestration techniques.
Group work: This project includes enhancements when assigned as a group project.
Resources:

- Internet access

Context:
In Module 8, you practiced editing bucket policies using JSON (JavaScript Object Notation). Whereas JSON is a set of rules defining how to format and present data, Python is a programming language that can be used to define and direct processes. It is often used in the cloud for a wide variety of tasks, including serverless applications, script automation, and cloud monitoring. You learn more about automation techniques in the next module. In the meantime, this project gives you a basic introduction to the concepts involved in using Python.

Exam Tip ✔

The CompTIA Cloud+ exam does not currently require that you know how to use Python. However, Python and many other coding languages are integral to using the cloud. If you plan to pursue a career in cloud, make sure you take at least one or two coding courses, if not more. You can also use online resources to start teaching yourself Python. At the time of this writing, a couple of good sites include learnpython.org and online-python.com.

Research online to answer the following questions:

1. In your own words, describe the difference between an interpreted coding language and a compiled coding language.
2. In your own words, explain what an IDE (integrated development environment) is and list three popular IDEs.

(continues)

Hands-On Projects Continued

3. Go to **python.org**. Within the documentation, find the Beginners Guide Overview. At the time of this writing, the document is located at **wiki.python.org/moin/BeginnersGuide/Overview**. Use this information to answer the following questions:

   a. What other languages are comparable to Python?
   b. Which OSs can run Python?
   c. What website can be used to check Python code?

4. A common test command that programmers practice when first learning how to code is to output the text line "Hello world." What code is needed to perform this task in Python?

5. What is Boto3, and what are some basic tasks you can use it for?

6. **For group assignments:** Each group member should choose a different coding language, such as Perl, Ruby, Scheme, or Java. Research what code is needed to print the text "Hello world" in that coding language, and then share your findings with the rest of the group. Answer the following questions:

   a. Which coding language did you research?
   b. What is the file extension for a file containing this language's code?
   c. What code in that language outputs the line "Hello world"?
   d. What patterns or differences do you notice as you compare the code from each language?

Capstone Project 9: Design an Alarm or Alert

Note 12

Websites, applications, public cloud platforms, and related account options change often. While the instructions given in these projects were accurate at the time of writing, you might need to adjust the steps or options according to later changes.

Note to Instructors and Students: A rubric is provided for evaluating student performance on these projects. Please see Appendix D.

Estimated time: 1.5 hours

Objective 5.5: Given a scenario, troubleshoot common performance issues.

Resources:

- Public cloud account (such as AWS, Azure, or GCP)
- Internet access

Context

In the Hands-On Projects for this module, you practiced creating an alarm or alert on an VM instance, and then triggering that alarm or alert by pushing the VM instance beyond the defined threshold. In this project, you will apply these skills to design your own alarm or alert (depending on the cloud platform you choose) using a different cloud service, and then trigger that alarm or alert.

Complete the following steps:

1. Choose a public cloud platform, such as AWS, Azure, or GCP. Choose a service, resource type, and resource metric within that platform to monitor. For example, you might choose to create an alarm for an EBS volume's read or write activity, or you might create an alert for an instance's CPU usage. A simple option for this project would be to create an alert on a storage volume attached to a VM instance, and then trigger the alert when the storage volume remains idle for more than one minute. However, you don't have to use this suggestion—you can come up with your own idea. Additionally, choose the service based on your ability to create a resource within that service. For example, you've had practice with some basic networking, security, and storage services. You might also be able to figure out another simple service that provides good documentation, such as AWS Lambda, AWS Lightsail, Azure Functions, or Google Kubernetes Engine. What platform and service did you choose?

Note 13

If you're having trouble coming up with ideas for an alarm or alert in this project, additional guidance is provided for creating an alarm in AWS on an EBS volume's idle time. You don't have to use these suggestions. However, the information is provided if you need the additional support in completing this project.

2. Create a simple resource within your chosen service that you will monitor. The resource does not need any complex configuration or expensive features. Many of the most popular cloud services offer detailed tutorials for creating practice resources.

   Tip: A simple option for this step would be to create an EC2 instance with an EBS root volume. You practiced this process in Hands-On Project 2-2. You can use the default settings for creating the root volume.

3. Create a topic subscription or notification channel, depending on what is appropriate for your chosen cloud platform, so you can receive emails when an alarm or alert will be triggered.

   Tip: Refer to the steps provided in this module's Hands-On Projects for more detailed guidance. For example, in AWS, you would create an SNS topic, and then create a subscription to that topic.

4. Create an alarm or alert that will trigger when you make a change to your resource or otherwise challenge your resource. For example, you might create an alarm that triggers when function code is invoked, or run. Or you might create an alarm that triggers when a storage volume sits idle for more than a minute. As you create the alarm or alert, examine the available metrics for monitoring your resource to help you decide which metric to choose. Make sure you choose a metric that you can easily control, and make sure you set the threshold at a point that you can easily exceed.

   What metric and threshold did you choose?

   Tip: If you're using the EBS volume suggestions in AWS, create a CloudWatch alarm on the EBS service. On the Metrics pane, click EBS, and then click Per-Volume Metrics. Find your EC2 instance's root volume in the list, and then choose the VolumeIdleTime metric for that volume. Change the Statistic to Maximum, and then change the Period to 1 minute. Define the threshold value at 1. On the next screen, choose your SNS topic, and then finish creating the alarm.

5. Do something to your resource to trigger the alarm or alert. **Take a screenshot** showing the alarm or alert in its triggered state or showing the email notification you received; include this visual with your responses to this project's questions.

   Tip: If you're using the EBS volume's idle time suggestions, you shouldn't need to do anything to trigger the alarm—it will automatically trigger within a couple of minutes while the EC2 instance sits idle.

6. Delete all resources you created for this project, including any resource groups, projects, notifications, alerts, or alarms. Check through your account to ensure you permanently deleted or terminated any resources created in this project.

Note 14

Depending on the status of your account and the selections you made during this project, the resources you created can deplete your credits or accrue charges. Double-check to make sure you've terminated all resources you created in this project.

Solutions to Self-Check Questions

Section 9-1: Monitoring Resources

1. _____ refers to a resource's ability to scale automatically.

   Answer: d. Elasticity

   Explanation: Elasticity refers to a cloud resource's ability to scale up or down automatically without requiring intervention from a cloud admin.

2. Which resource indicates a breached threshold?

   Answer: a. Alarm

   Explanation: Alerts and alarms can inform staff when a threshold is breached or when a concerning event occurs.

3. True or false: It's important to pack as much information as possible into a dashboard.

   Answer: b. False, because humans can only absorb so much information at a time.

   Explanation: Human minds can consume and remember only about seven distinct pieces of information at one time. Similarly, most people can only absorb about five to nine KPIs on a dashboard at a time.

Section 9-2: Events and Logs

4. Which of the following is an example of an event?

   Answer: b. A storage bucket is deleted.

   Explanation: An event is a detectable change in a cloud service or resource, such as the deletion of that resource.

5. Which process protects private information?

   Answer: d. Log scrubbing

   Explanation: Log scrubbing removes sensitive data from logs before storing captured traffic.

6. Which of the following is used to analyze logs?

   Answer: a. SIEM

   Explanation: Collected data is sent to and analyzed by a log management tool. In some cases, a SIEM (Security Information and Event Management) solution provides log analysis, especially in the context of security.

Section 9-3: Analysis and Response

7. An event producer _____ messages.

   Answer: d. publishes

   Explanation: An event producer publishes messages when events occur.

8. What kind of application relies on event-driven architecture?

   Answer: b. Decoupled

   Explanation: Each event in an event-driven architecture serves as part of a larger process that emanates throughout a decoupled application.

9. What does the symbol >= stand for?

   Answer: d. Greater than or equal to

   Explanation: The symbol >= combines the logical argument > (greater than) with the logical argument = (equal to), and it collectively means "greater than or equal to."

Section 9-4: Troubleshooting Performance

10. Which technique adjusts resources to match demand?

    Answer: b. Right sizing

    Explanation: Right sizing means resources are increased or decreased according to need.

11. Which of the following problems could result in an orphaned resource whose expenses are not properly tracked?

    Answer: c. Missing or incorrect tags

    Explanation: Resources must be appropriately tagged to allow for proper tracking of expenses. An untagged or improperly tagged resource could be left running without being properly identified and tracked.

Module 10

Cloud Automation

Module 10 Objectives

After reading this module, you will be able to:

1   Explain the purpose and common tools of cloud automation.

2   Describe common cloud maintenance processes.

3   Configure common cloud automation services.

4   Troubleshoot automation issues.

Module 10 Outline

Study the module's outline to help you organize the content in your mind as you read.

Module 10 Scenario

"I passed!" you announce as you walk in the door and throw a thumbs-up and a cheesy grin at the security camera.

"What's going on?" Kendra asks as she peeks cautiously out of her office door.

"All that research we've been doing for the cloud …" you begin. "I thought I might put my knowledge to the test, literally, and take the Cloud+ exam. So I did. And I passed!"

"Wow, that's awesome!" Kendra exclaims.

"Way to go!" Nigel agrees as he offers a double high-five.

"Seriously, that shows a lot of initiative," Kendra adds. "Goes to show how much we've all learned over these past few months."

"Now if only our cloud would show that much initiative," you jokingly suggest, "and build itself."

"Ha! That would be a smart cloud," Nigel laughs.

"Actually, it might not be so far-fetched," suggests Kendra. "I've been reading up on some pretty amazing tools for automating cloud deployment."

"That still takes a lot of work up front," you say as the wheels in your head start turning. "But if we design our cloud with the intention of building in a lot of automation, it wouldn't take nearly so much work to keep it running smoothly later."

"All hail our resident cloud expert," Nigel jokes. "You actually sounded like you knew what you were talking about just then."

"Well, I had to study up on automation for the exam. I've only touched the surface, though," you add. "Automation is a whole field of expertise all on its own."

"This is true," Kendra agrees.

"Which part?" asks Nigel as he realizes she's been staring into space and not really listening.

"Oh! Building in automation, I mean," Kendra says as she starts thinking aloud. "You know, that's really the piece I've been missing with our cloud migration plans, that part about how to keep the cloud running smoothly without needing so much micromanaging from us."

"Right—we can set it up to almost run on its own," you add. "You can't totally ignore it, of course, but you don't have to get bogged down in so much of the tedious, nitpicky stuff … if you set it up right."

"You know," Nigel muses, "I think this is kind of like your management style, Kendra."

"How's that?" Kendra asks with a quizzical look.

"The way you set us up to do our own research, to come up with our own ideas, to keep learning," explains Nigel. "You don't tell us what we have to know. You ask questions, we go find our own answers, and then come back and share what we learned."

"This is true," you add. "I really appreciate how you share your curiosity instead of dictating what we must do and how. It makes me want to know even more and gives me confidence to find my blind spots so I can keep learning."

"Aw, now I'm blushing," grins Kendra. "Okay, well, enough of that," she says as she recovers her composure. "How can we incorporate some of these automation tools into our cloud?"

"Can I ask the questions this time?" Nigel pleads excitedly.

"Go for it," Kendra says.

Nigel pauses for a moment to think and then starts scribbling on the whiteboard in Kendra's office:

- How does automation work in the cloud?
- What tasks can automation tools perform?
- What automation tools do cloud platforms offer?
- What can go wrong with automation?

Section 10-1: Automation Workflow

Certification

1.1 Compare and contrast the different types of cloud models.

1.4 Given a scenario, analyze the solution design in support of the business requirements.

2.3 Given a scenario, apply the appropriate OS and application security controls.

3.1 Given a scenario, integrate components into a cloud solution.

4.1 Given a scenario, configure logging, monitoring, and alerting to maintain operational status.

4.2 Given a scenario, maintain efficient operation of a cloud environment.

4.4 Given a scenario, apply proper automation and orchestration techniques.

5.3 Given a scenario, troubleshoot deployment issues.

Have you ever seen a movie or cartoon where a genius inventor is woken up in the morning by an alarm clock, a robot lifts him out of bed, and robot arms reach in and start combing his hair and brushing his teeth; meanwhile, the coffee pot starts dripping automatically, and the can of dog food is cut open and dumped in the dog's bowl? Audiences have long been fascinated with the idea of automation, and moviemakers play on this interest with often humorous results. The opening scene to the classic movie *Back to the Future* illustrates a perfect example of one inventor's shenanigans gone hilariously wrong. Also, search online for images of Rube Goldberg machines (https://www.rubegoldberg.org/), which make simple tasks complicated in the interest of automation.

Thankfully, cloud automation is more productive, more streamlined, and generally less traumatic. Automation refers to the use of software-based solutions to perform a process or procedure with minimal human intervention. In the physical world, this might look like cars that can park themselves, digital assistants like Siri or Alexa that can start your coffee pot in the morning, or drones that can deliver packages (see Figure 10-1). In the cloud, this might look like an automated process for creating, cloning, or shutting down a VM instance or a server cluster, configuring a virtual network, or deploying an extensive and complex cloud environment. The idea with cloud automation is to reduce the demand on human staff's time while increasing accuracy and repeatability of common tasks.

Source: iStock.com

Figure 10-1   Companies like Amazon (amazon.com) and UPS (ups. com) are experimenting with automated drone delivery of packages

Think about the steps you take to create a new VM. You choose the boot source, size (sometimes called shape), network connections, security configurations, and storage allocations. The first time you do this, you must think through the options and implications of your decisions. However, the next time you need a VM with the same configuration, you don't have to invest so much thought. If this is a configuration you use often, you eventually reach a point where creating the new VM consists of a series of mind-numbing clicks where you implement the same decisions you made the first time. The more boring or repetitive the task, the more likely you'll make a mistake. The thing is, humans tend to be particularly bad at doing the same thing exactly the same way over and over. Computers, however, are very good at doing exactly what you tell them to do and doing it exactly the same way every time. When you find yourself doing the same thing repeatedly, this is often an ideal candidate for automation.

Why Automate?

Automation in the cloud accomplishes several important goals, such as the following:

- *Faster deployment, adjustments, and corrections*—As you learned in Module 9, monitoring tools can be programmed to respond automatically to problems. Automated tools can also deploy or resize resources quickly and only when needed.
- *Better control*—Standardized processes are easier to define, monitor, and replicate. When you know a task is performed the same way every single time, you can better predict the effects of those changes and fine-tune the process as needed.
- *Lower costs*—With fewer errors and less demand on staff's time, your team can focus on higher-level, strategic activities that add value to your organization while paying less for cloud management and resources.
- *More secure*—It might seem counterintuitive to think of security increasing when admins hand off some control to the computer. However, a well-orchestrated system is much less likely to suffer from vulnerabilities due to misconfigurations and other human error.

Modern automation tools designed for the cloud offer flexible, robust features that can help your organization take full advantage of the cost-saving and performance benefits the cloud has to offer. Some of the maintenance and security tasks that these tools can perform include the following:

- Create snapshots and backups.
- Clone, resize, or remove resources.
- Apply patches and updates.
- Generate internal API communications.
- Restart or shut down VM instances.
- Enable or disable alerts.
- Detect signs of an attack.
- Quarantine compromised resources.
- Manage security rules.
- Migrate traffic to redundant resources.

Infrastructure as Code (IaC)

How does all this work? How can you set up a cloud system to make good decisions and perform complex tasks reliably without human intervention?

To understand the basic principles of automation, it helps to first understand the concept of a runbook. A **runbook** is a collection of physical or digital documents that outline the precise steps to complete procedures or operations in a specific IT environment. For example, an admin might document the steps to provision a new server, update a running VM instance, or recover from a database backup. Considering what you've learned in this course, you could write your own runbook for how to create a virtual network with an Internet-accessible subnet in AWS, Azure, or GCP. A good runbook provides sufficient detail so other people could follow the steps and obtain the exact same results each time.

Good runbook management keeps the documentation current and well organized, as well as accessible by the right people. This documentation might be stored in some kind of CMS (content management system) or knowledge base.

A runbook is typically designed to be read and followed by humans. However, consider what you could do with a runbook that is written in a computer-readable language, such as a programming language or scripting language. With sufficient detail, you could create runbooks that could spin up a VM, create or replicate a database, or configure a virtual network with multiple servers. This application of the runbook concept in an automated environment is called IaC (infrastructure as code), where the steps needed to configure or change a cloud environment are written in code and are deployed all at one time rather than requiring the human admin to complete one step of the deployment at a time in a GUI.

Now imagine that you've created several runbooks, all designed to work together to create multiple nodes and all the related security, networking, and OS configurations. In cooperation, these runbooks could create a large and complex testing environment complete with network services, security groups, VMs running various OSs, and predictable access keys and passwords as desired. Collections of automated processes like this in a carefully choreographed manner is the essence of orchestration. Where automation performs a single task (such as create a VM), orchestration designs a series of tasks in a workflow (such as creating an entire testing environment). GCP's Deployment Manager service, for example, allows you to design a separate template for each resource (such as a VM) that you want to create automatically, and then you collect multiple templates in a configuration file to deploy many resources in parallel.

IaC allows the execution of multiple tasks, phases, or deployments from a playbook, which is the collection of tasks orchestrated in a specific sequence. Orchestration sequencing is a key part of designing effective IaC templates. For example, you might have a playbook that deploys all the resources needed for a specific solution that relies on multiple cloud services, such as a database, containers, storage buckets, or VM instances. Contained within the overall solution template would be steps to deploy certain resources in certain ways and in a certain order.

Documenting and designing infrastructure as code presents many benefits. For example, IaC and the related automation and orchestration tools enable a more consistent environment throughout the process of developing, testing, deploying, and patching an application or service. During an app's development phase—or later, as changes are made—developers need an environment that is as nearly identical to the app's final production environment as possible. Typical environment phases such as the following could all be deployed from essentially the same IaC script:

- **Development**—This is a controlled environment where an app can be developed or changed to implement new features and improvements or to eliminate bugs.
- **Staging**—Usually a different team deploys the app in a staging environment for QA (quality assurance) testing, where testers try to identify bugs or security loopholes and run performance tests.
- **Production**—This is the live environment where users interact with the active version of the app.
- **Duplicate production**—It's not uncommon for an organization to run a duplicate production environment, at least temporarily, for an application or other services. One environment is active while the other environment receives updates, allows for further testing, or serves as a backup. This is called a blue-green deployment (see Figure 10-2), where one environment is active while the other is passive, waiting on standby or receiving updates. A router, load balancer, or other networking configuration (such as DNS) sends traffic only to the currently active environment and then changes traffic to the other environment after updates or other changes are successfully applied.

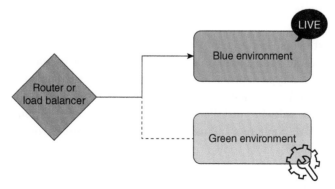

Figure 10-2 The blue environment is live while the green environment receives updates

> **Note 1**
>
> A blue-green deployment is also used for DR (disaster recovery) where the active environment handles the load while the passive environment remains in standby, ready to take over in case of an emergency.

IaC can ensure that all these environments are properly synced and updated. Think about how quickly applications are changed and updated in a DevOps-based organization. New releases might occur every day, even multiple times a day. By maintaining consistency between the various environments representing stages of an app's development, IaC helps minimize problems as the app is transitioned from one environment to the next.

IaC also assists in troubleshooting efforts or security investigations. What was the state of a cloud environment when a particular network connection went down or when a problematic intrusion occurred? In a large, active organization—or even in a small company—it could be nearly impossible to remember who made what changes if everything is done manually, where a staff person gives direct reconfiguration commands to the cloud deployment.

In contrast, by first defining a cloud environment in a text file, changes to that environment can be tracked by examining historical versions of the file. Each time a change is executed in an environment, the previous state of the environment is still documented in the earlier version of the file. This is especially useful when you experience a problem with the new configuration and must roll back to a previous configuration. This reversion can be accomplished by deploying the previous environment's configuration file.

Because IaC provides documentation of each automated environmental configuration along the way, troubleshooting or security teams can investigate historical changes made in the cloud environment to determine when a problem occurred and why. In essence, IaC provides a "paper trail" (digital, of course). This same IaC documentation also helps in meeting regulatory standards to prove historical compliance, which is essential during audits or court-ordered investigations. And IaC processes increase consistency across an organization's staff members, especially when the organization experiences staff turnover.

Automation Tools

Automation tools might be built into the cloud platform or provided by third-party vendor applications that interact with resources through APIs. Many of these tools are primarily managed through a CLI and rely on a variety of programming languages, such as Python, and file formats, such as JSON (JavaScript Object Notation; pronounced "j-son") and YAML (YAML Ain't Markup Language; rhymes with "camel"). Some of these tools offer a web GUI or cloud portal, especially if you're using the paid version of the application. Most of these tools work from templates of some kind for managing deployments. However, by understanding the underlying file format and programming languages, you can also write scripts or custom programming to design automated processes unique to your environment.

No single tool can meet all your automation needs. Some automation tasks address infrastructure provisioning or server configurations while other automation workflows target management of applications or IAM accounts. A tool that attempts to address all these areas typically doesn't handle any of them well. As a result, you need to know about the wide range of tools available to wisely choose which combination of tools will best serve your situation.

To begin, it's important to distinguish between two major categories of automation tools: provisioning and configuration management. You learned about some common automated tasks in the previous module where you read about auto-scaling features. Auto-scaling is a type of provisioning task. However, creating the resource is only the beginning. Automated processes might also need to configure, update, and reconfigure these resources over time to ensure they meet a certain standard of settings, software installations, and security configurations or to adapt to changing factors. This latter process is part of CM (configuration management). While many automation tools can do some of both these processes (provisioning and CM), most tools are specialized for one or the other. Whereas provisioning tools deploy new cloud resources, CM tools configure existing resources to match a particular configuration template. Both categories of automation tools are discussed in this section.

Popular Automation Tools

Let's start with provisioning tools. Following is a list of the most popular cloud automation tools for performing infrastructure provisioning tasks:

- *AWS's CloudFormation*—AWS's built-in solution for managing IaC, CloudFormation allows you to create a template of many AWS resources (collectively called a stack) that can all be deployed or deleted together. For example, you might want to duplicate an existing infrastructure in one region over to other regions for increased resistance to outages. Templates are configured using YAML or JSON, both of which are machine readable while also being human-reader friendly.

- *Azure's Resource Manager*—All resource deployment and management in Azure happens through the Resource Manager. Whether you manage resources through the portal, PowerShell, Azure CLI, or REST API clients, this activity passes through the Resource Manager. From an existing deployment of one or more resources, or just before deploying a newly configured resource, you can generate a template of that resource's configuration to be reused for automation. The template is a JSON file. Figure 10-3 shows a template for a VM in Azure. From this screen, you could download the template for further editing, add it to your Azure library for later use, or deploy the included resources.

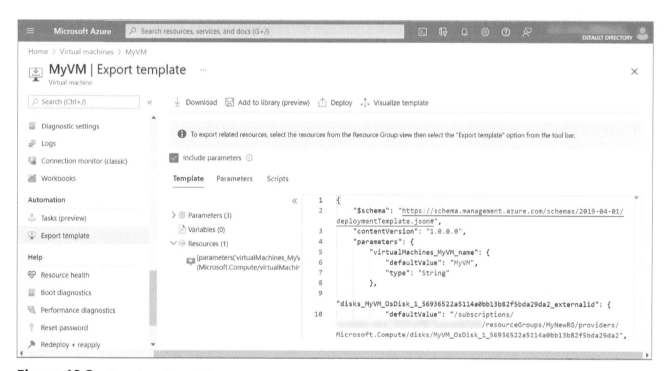

Figure 10-3 Template for a VM

- *GCP's Deployment Manager*—In Deployment Manager, you can create configuration files using YAML to repeatedly deploy many resources in parallel. You can track individual resources for deployment in templates, which serve as building blocks for the configuration deployment and can be reused in multiple configurations.

- *Terraform*—Terraform was developed by HashiCorp (hashicorp.com) and provides cloud-agnostic infrastructure provisioning. The open-source version is free to the public while the enterprise version offers additional features, such as GUI, collaboration, and governance capabilities that work well in an enterprise environment where many teams rely on the same tools. To use Terraform, you first create a plan using Terraform language, which is declarative in nature, meaning you describe the outcome rather than the steps to get there. Next, you apply the plan to deploy the configuration to your cloud or multi-cloud. Terraform works with AWS, Azure, GCP, and more than 150 other service providers.

Now consider CM tools. The following is a list of popular tools used primarily for CM:

- *Ansible*—Another open-source (but not free) automation tool, Ansible (ansible.com) is sponsored by Red Hat and relies on YAML. Ansible requires no agent installation on managed nodes and, instead, connects to these nodes via SSH by default. For this reason, Ansible is generally considered easier to set up than other third-party options. To automate changes, you create a text inventory file that contains definitions of variables for managed machines. You can create playbooks to orchestrate automation of multiple nodes at one time.

- *Chef*—Chef (chef.io) is an open-source CM tool that can be used to configure and manage large numbers of nodes such as servers and network devices both on-prem and in the cloud. Built on Ruby, a programming language that is easy for beginners to learn, configurations are stored in recipes that are grouped in cookbooks.

- *Puppet*—Puppet (puppet.com) is another CM tool similar to Chef but has been around longer. The Puppet DSL (Domain-Specific Language) is based on Ruby. Open-source Puppet is free to use while the enterprise version is free only for up to 10 nodes. Puppet and Chef both rely on an agent installed on each managed node, which then reports to the master server for CM.

- *SaltStack Config*—SaltStack Config, previously known as SaltStack and currently owned by VMware, is a CM component of the VMware vRealize Automation suite (vmware.com/products/vrealize-automation.html). SaltStack Config provides event-driven automation to detect problems and enforce the desired state of managed resources. SaltStack Config requires the installation of an agent, called a minion, on managed devices, and communication between the minions and the salt master server is bidirectional. A pillar file stores configuration details in YAML, JSON, or other formats. The original SaltStack was built on the open-source Salt, which is still free to the public at saltproject.io. The latest SaltStack Config is only available through VMware's vRealize Automation platform.

- *AWS's Systems Manager*—Systems Manager (formerly known as SSM) is AWS's built-in tool for configuring and managing EC2 instances, on-prem servers and VMs, and some other AWS resources through automated processes. Systems Manager's capabilities include several automation and maintenance tools for native interactions with AWS resources at scale.

- *Azure's Automation*—Azure Automation can be used for CM, update management, and process automation. With the CM feature, you can enforce a desired state for your VMs and other monitored resources, including on-prem, physical machines. Process automation offers the ability to create runbooks in three ways: graphically, in PowerShell, or by using Python to automate cloud management tasks.

- *GCP's Config Controller*—Powered by Kubernetes, Config Controller can provision and orchestrate GCP resources. Declarative configurations can be tracked through the Git repository for versioning, and configuration drift is repaired automatically.

Differentiating Factors

For now, these lists might look like a hodgepodge of tools providing no clear sense of direction on how to choose one tool over another. Let's explore some of the ways to differentiate each of these tools from the others. Differentiating factors include the following:

- *Push model versus pull model*—In a **push model**, the server pushes out configuration changes to managed resources, as shown in Figure 10-4. In a **pull model**, managed resources check in with the server to retrieve configuration details. The push model works well when the managed resources are easily identified and located, and they're consistently reachable through established network connections. For more transient resources, such as auto-scaled VMs, the pull model is typically more effective. Puppet and Chef use the pull model, whereas SaltStack Config and Ansible use more of a push configuration (although SaltStack Config actually uses some of both models).

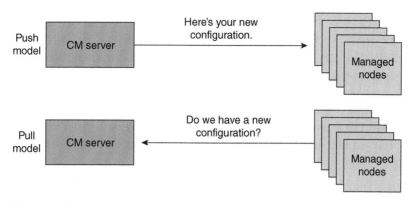

Figure 10-4   Push model versus pull model

- ***Immutable versus idempotent***—Immutable environments or resources aren't changed after they're deployed. They're deployed in the state they're intended to be used. If you need to make changes, you destroy the old resources and replace them with new resources that meet your desired configurations. Idempotent, however, means that you can run the configuration and it will make needed changes to the environment without destroying existing resources. Ansible and Chef rely on idempotent techniques whereas Terraform, CloudFormation, and AWS's auto-scaling groups take an immutable approach to resources.

- ***Imperative versus declarative***—Imperative tools require that you give them the exact steps you want taken to complete a task. Declarative tools, however, require less hand-holding. You tell the tool the outcome you want, and the tool figures out how to accomplish that goal. Chef and Ansible take an imperative approach whereas Terraform, SaltStack Config, Puppet, and CloudFormation all offer a declarative style.

Advanced Cloud Services

Cloud computing enables a host of new technologies that were unfeasible or impossible before cloud. Some of these technologies are not only enabled by cloud but are also used to improve cloud security and automation processes. This section explores some of these more advanced services.

Data Analytics

One of the most impactful modern influences of the Internet and cloud-based technologies on businesses is data analytics. An industry in its own right, data analytics is the study of raw data to detect patterns, anomalies, and insights that can inform research, business processes, regulatory measures, and many other efforts. Cloud computing uniquely enables data analytics due to the simple fact cloud makes available nearly unlimited processing power, storage space, and network bandwidth.

For example, extremely large data sets can be accessed through cloud platforms. These data sets inform the analysis work of many businesses and industries. Businesses themselves collect large volumes of data during daily business activities, including transactions, research, customer interactions, and personal information. These massive data sets are collectively referred to as big data. This data might be collected by companies, governments, or entire industries, and the data might be structured or unstructured. One example is global climate data made available by the National Oceanic and Atmospheric Administration at ncdc.noaa.gov/cdo-web/.

The three most common types of big data are as follows:

- Social data, such as that collected from social media platforms
- Machine data collected from sensors (such as traffic cams or medical devices), logs, and other automated sources
- Transactional data, such as purchases, payments, and invoices

Machine Learning (ML) and Artificial Intelligence (AI)

The cloud and big data make possible other cutting-edge technologies as well, such as AI (artificial intelligence) and ML (machine learning). **AI (artificial intelligence)** refers to a computer's ability to adapt its behavior according to ongoing input. This kind of computer processing starts to resemble human thought processes where responses to input aren't necessarily predictable. For example, have you attempted to carry on a conversation with a personal assistant such as Alexa or Siri? Sometimes, these assistants' responses can be surprising, even in humorous ways. Furthermore, AI enables a computer to continue to learn and adapt. **ML (machine learning)** is a process where computers learn from data analysis rather than from explicit programming. There are many approaches to the logic of ML. Three of the most common are the following:

- *Supervised learning*—The computer is given labeled data, such as videos of vehicles that are each identified by make and model. The computer studies the data to learn how to identify the same items later in unlabeled videos.

- *Unsupervised learning*—The computer is given unlabeled data and expected to identify patterns that might not be known to human programmers. For example, a computer might be given medical data and asked to determine what factors might indicate the likelihood of someone developing heart disease or cancer.

- *Reinforcement learning*—The computer engages in trial-and-error learning where helpful responses are rewarded and poor responses are not. For example, AWS's DeepRacer service uses reinforcement learning to teach a virtual vehicle how to drive along a simulated road course (see Figure 10-5). Turns that keep the vehicle on the road are preferred while turns that lead the vehicle off the road force-stop the simulation. In DeepRacer competitions, students develop algorithms to try to train their AI models faster and with fewer errors.

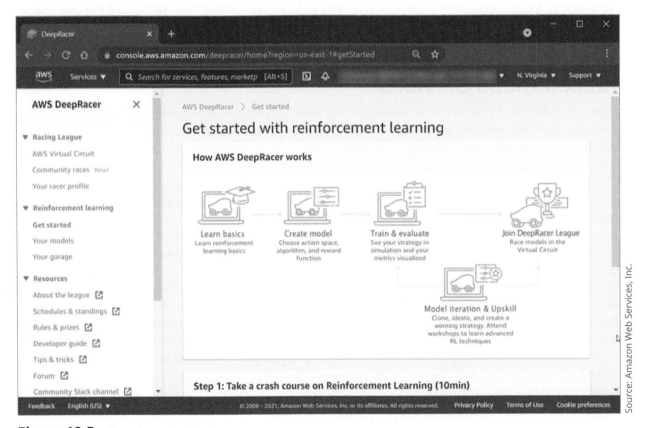

Figure 10-5 DeepRacer in AWS

AI and ML in Automation

Many of the automation tools you've learned about in this module are used to deploy AI and ML infrastructure. Similarly, AI and ML are used to support many automated tasks, such as application testing, resource scaling, network routing, and security adaptations. For example, AI and ML processes are increasingly used to ensure quality assurance during application development and testing. ML systems can challenge an application's API functionalities in ways humans can't effectively do, while tracking results and learning from the experience.

Through the rest of this module, you learn about many of the tasks commonly automated in the cloud, the cloud services available for helping with these processes, and the kinds of problems you might face.

You're Ready

You're now ready to complete Project 10-1: Research Automation Tools. You can complete the project now or wait until you've finished all the readings for this module.

Remember This

- Automation refers to the use of software-based solutions to perform a process or procedure with minimal human intervention.
- Some of the maintenance and security tasks that can be performed by automation tools include performing routine operations, applying updates, generating internal API communications, restarting or shutting down resources, and migrating traffic to redundant resources.
- Orchestration sequencing is a key component of designing effective IaC (infrastructure as code) templates.
- Automation tools might be built into the cloud platform or provided by third-party vendor applications that interact with resources through APIs.
- AI (artificial intelligence) refers to a computer's ability to adapt its behavior according to ongoing input, and ML (machine learning) is a process where computers learn from data analysis rather than from explicit programming.

Self-Check

1. Automation increases _____.
   - **a.** costs
   - **b.** response time
   - **c.** security
   - **d.** errors

2. Which CM tool does not require installation of an agent?
   - **a.** Chef
   - **b.** Ansible
   - **c.** Puppet
   - **d.** Terraform

3. Which process is most directly responsible for Siri's ability to answer a spoken question?
   - **a.** IaC
   - **b.** CM
   - **c.** ML
   - **d.** AI

○ Check your answers at the end of this module.

Section 10-2: Cloud Maintenance Processes

Certification

2.2 Given a scenario, secure a network in a cloud environment.

2.3 Given a scenario, apply the appropriate OS and application security controls.

2.4 Given a scenario, apply data security and compliance controls in cloud environments.

2.5 Given a scenario, implement measures to meet security requirements.

3.1 Given a scenario, integrate components into a cloud solution.

4.1 Given a scenario, configure logging, monitoring, and alerting to maintain operational status.

4.2 Given a scenario, maintain efficient operation of a cloud environment.

4.4 Given a scenario, apply proper automation and orchestration techniques.

4.6 Given a scenario, perform disaster recovery tasks.

Let's say you've migrated to the cloud, built out your cloud networks and server instances, and established your storage spaces and databases. Does this mean you're finished? Actually, no, it does not. Even if your workloads required predictable, unvarying resources that never need changes, your cloud still requires regular attention and maintenance to function smoothly. Common cloud maintenance tasks include the following:

- Resource monitoring
- Patch and update management
- Storage and backup management
- Log management
- Security monitoring and management
- Troubleshooting

For example, you might need to regularly check logs for signs of issues that have not been noticed yet. Good log management also includes archiving older log data and deleting log data that has expired. You might also need to monitor cloud resource settings, such as time zones or IP addresses, to ensure that nothing has been changed. Cloud-based servers require patches and updates just like on-prem virtual and physical servers do, and this requires regular checks to ensure no critical updates have been missed or failed. Any existing alert system will need to be monitored and fine-tuned to minimize false positives, catch missed red flags, and respond quickly to indicators of problems.

Because maintenance activities can impact the performance of affected resources, much of this work must be completed within a maintenance window to minimize disruption to cloud services. Timeliness is also critical when responding to issues related to security or disaster recovery. This reality creates a demand on IT staff that can be time-consuming or even impossible to handle manually.

Standard cloud maintenance tasks and maintenance schedules receive much of the focus of automation capabilities. Almost any action that is repeated in basically the same way every time can be automated. In many cases, you can also include orchestration when appropriate. Maintenance automation and orchestration tasks could include any of the following activities:

- Clearing or archiving logs
- Compressing drives or storage
- Removing orphaned resources
- Reclaiming resources as needed
- Removing stale DNS entries

- Removing outdated rules from a firewall or security group
- Removing inactive accounts
- Maintaining ACLs for target objects

A comprehensive tool for automated and orchestrated cloud maintenance is a CMP (cloud management platform). According to Gartner (gartner.com), a CMP must, at minimum, include the following features: incorporate self-service interfaces, provision system images, enable metering and billing, and provide workload optimization. Examples of CMP tools include RightScale CMP from Flexera (flexera.com), Cisco's CloudCenter (cisco.com), and VMware's vRealize Suite (vmware.com).

The responsibility for maintenance tasks will vary by cloud service model, just as the responsibility for security varies. Recall the division of security responsibility illustrated earlier in Figure 6-2. Figure 10-6 illustrates a similar division of labor when it comes to maintenance responsibilities, which shifts according to SaaS, PaaS, or IaaS service models.

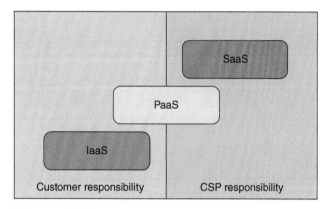

Figure 10-6   The distribution of maintenance responsibility varies by cloud service model

Many cloud platforms or services also come with a predefined level of customer support from the vendor to help cloud customers better manage their cloud resources. Customer support agreements will outline the extent to which you can rely on this vendor support. Another option, especially when managing a hybrid cloud, is to outsource some of these management tasks to an MSP (managed service provider). For example, an MSP might oversee your disaster recovery or backup processes, a database migration, CM, or even helpdesk support. The MSP itself might outsource some of the services it provides, partnering with a NOC (network operations center; pronounced "knock") that does the actual monitoring.

Regardless of who is responsible for which processes, automating these tasks means that problems are addressed sooner, patches are applied more consistently across the server fleet, IT staff are freed to focus on more complex tasks directly beneficial to business endeavors, and productivity increases for everyone relying on these cloud services.

Lifecycle Management

Many changes made to a resource, system, or environment are planned and expected. For example, updates and patches are typical changes expected to happen frequently throughout the life cycle of a resource. The following list describes some of the concepts used in managing resource life cycles:

- *Roadmaps*—A roadmap defines significant phases of a resource's life cycle. For example, a new product might initially be deployed to a small test market with the intent of trying new but unpolished features. Later phases in the roadmap might include a series of large-scale releases or incremental improvements to the solution's scope or target market.

- *Version control*—Version control is a process for tracking changes over time. The code in a template used to deploy resources can be kept for historical analysis as changes are made to the deployment and for post-deployment validation. Older versions of the deployment's configurations can be reviewed as needed, changes to current configurations are thoroughly documented, and future changes can be evaluated and tested before deployment. Version control is a foundational concept in managing a development pipeline where changes are proposed, tested, and released in a continual cycle and often in an automated fashion. When one or more proposed changes are incorporated into the production environment, a new version of that deployment is created, documented, and stored. A popular VCS (version control system) is Git. Figure 10-7 shows a sample pipeline where new versions are released after changes are developed and tested.

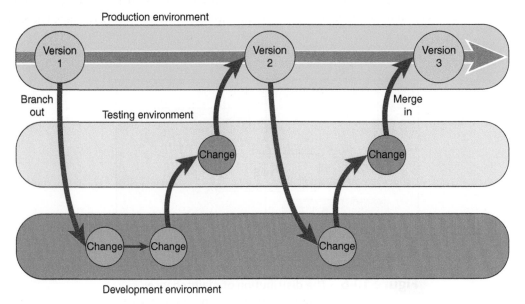

Figure 10-7   Versions in a sample development pipeline

- *Updates and upgrades*—Regular updates address bugs and close security gaps, and upgrades add new features.
- *Migrations*—As a system grows, it might need to be migrated to a different platform or environment. Planning from the beginning for possible migration targets can make this process easier and more effective.
- *Deprecations*—No system is designed to last forever. Using a modular design can help with anticipating the need to deprecate features or portions of a system. Designers should also consider what portions of a system might need to be preserved or migrated to a new system when the current system reaches its end of life.

Types of Updates

One of the more complex maintenance processes is applying updates to cloud resources. This is because the update process can disrupt normal business operations as resources are changed, power cycled, or replaced with new deployments. Cloud elements that might require updates in a public or private cloud include the following:

- Virtual machines and server clusters
- Networking components and virtual appliances (such as firewalls or load balancers)
- Storage components
- Applications
- Hypervisors and agents installed on VMs

Not all updates are created equal. Some updates apply small fixes to minor bugs while other, more critical updates patch security loopholes and vulnerabilities to protect resources against known threats. The terms used to describe various types of updates are not standardized in the industry and can be used in any number of ways for different purposes. For example, Microsoft releases regular and small updates that might be grouped together over time in a larger update called a build. Updates that address specific security issues are called security updates; updates that address other high-priority issues are called critical updates. Yet, Microsoft updates of all kinds are sometimes referred to as hotfixes. Figure 10-8 shows output from the `Get-Hotfix` cmdlet (pronounced "command-let," which is a command run in Windows PowerShell). The figure shows a history of applied updates and security updates in Windows. It's important to familiarize yourself with the update terminology used by your organization's vendors so you know which updates are the most critical.

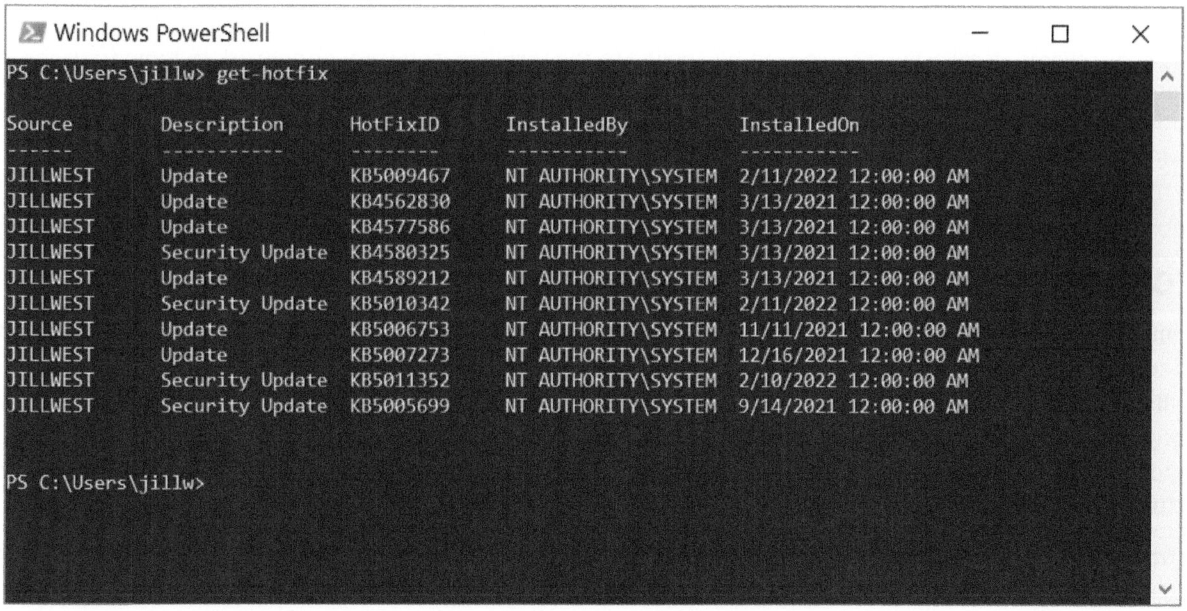

Figure 10-8   In Windows, a hotfix might refer to almost any kind of update, depending on the context

Keeping in mind that these terms have variable meanings when used by different vendors, the following list gives a general description of each concept:

- *Hotfix*—For many vendors, a hotfix is typically a smaller-scale update that addresses a specific issue, receives less testing, might not require restarting the system, or might be intended only for temporary use. It might not even be released to the public if it's addressing an issue for one or a handful of customers experiencing a unique issue in a given environment. For example, a driver required for a specialized piece of hardware might interfere with normal functioning of an application. A hotfix—either to the driver or to the application—could restore most or all functionality until the next scheduled update, which should include a permanent correction of the problem. One challenge with hotfixes is ensuring that all servers in a cluster receive the same hotfixes. This is especially important in a failover cluster, where a backup server must be able to take over a failed server's workload at any time, and so both servers must be identically configured.
- *Patch*—Patch and update often refer to the same thing, or a patch might be a smaller update, more like a hotfix. A patch is released to the public to fix bugs or security loopholes and add new features or enhancements.
- *Version update*—This is a larger-scale update that justifies a new version number. Sometimes the number increases to a new integer, such as going from version 3 to version 4, and sometimes the vendor only adds a decimal place, such as going to version 3.1.
- *Rollback*—The opposite of an update is a rollback. When an update causes a problem, a rollback will revert the system to its state from before the update was applied. Rollbacks are sometimes applied automatically when the system detects an error and, other times, the rollback is initiated by the user.

Note **2**

While this isn't as relevant in the cloud, know that firmware also sometimes needs patching to fix bugs, add features, or close security loopholes. You'll find firmware on all kinds of physical devices, including switches, routers, firewalls, printers, security cameras, and smart devices. Many of these devices might be managed through cloud services. For example, smart home devices occasionally need firmware updates that are applied through a cloud-based app.

Exam Tip ✔

Security professionals have taken the concept of a patch and applied it to vulnerability mitigation. When a new vulnerability is discovered, a collection of rules can be applied to the resource, software, or network to temporarily provide protection from related threats. This is called a **virtual patch**. Virtual patching is often performed by or through a WAF (web application firewall) or an IPS (intrusion prevention system). It's also called external patching or just-in-time patching. The virtual patch can provide protection until the vendor's security patch can be obtained and applied.

Patching and Update Methodologies

Different patching methodologies are required for different kinds of resources. This might be obvious at first, but also consider that even different OSs on VMs must be updated from different sources with different settings and steps. You might also need to apply different patch rules and restrictions to servers hosting a particular application or service. This kind of granular control should be built into your update management or patch management solution.

Patch or update management across cloud platforms that offer this feature consists of some standard operating procedures, including the following:

- *Installing agents*—Many patch management solutions require that you install a small app called an agent that can monitor and control managed resources. In major cloud platforms, such as AWS and others, this agent is often preinstalled on a VM, depending on which image you used to create the VM.

- *Scanning*—Resources (such as servers, applications, or storage systems) must be scanned for missing patches or other known vulnerabilities. This is especially important for open-source software where patches aren't automatically pushed to existing installations. Scans should be conducted at all layers of the stack for which you're responsible: network, operating system, and application.

- *Testing*—You'll want to test any new patches to ensure they won't create new problems in your particular environment. Consider resource dependencies for each element to be patched and how those dependencies will be affected by the update. You'll also need to consider patch dependencies, which means that some patches might need to be installed before other patches. These dependencies sometimes necessitate a specific order of operations.

- *Choosing update targets*—You can patch resources in groups to better control which resources get which updates and when. AWS calls these patch groups. For example, a web server cluster might be able to handle current updates with no problem, while current updates might "break" a server hosting a legacy application. The tags feature you learned about in a previous module works well for this purpose. You might tag VMs according to their environment (such as testing, staging, or production) or desired patch window (such as "Sunday night").

- *Considering backups ... and more backups*—You might schedule a backup of data to occur just before updates are applied, which is recommended by most OS and software makers. To back up services, you might stagger maintenance windows for different groups of servers so one group can be updated while another group handles the active workload. This way, only a few servers at a time are exposed to the inherent unpredictability of applying updates. Consider the following three techniques:

  - *Blue-green deployment*—You read earlier about blue-green deployments. With this technique, one environment enters a passive state and receives updates and follow-up testing while another environment identical in size and configuration handles the active workload. When the updates are complete, all traffic is switched to the updated environment.

○ *Canary deployment*—In this scenario, a small number of servers are updated, and a small amount of user traffic, perhaps one or two percent, is directed to those updated servers as a test run. If all goes well, the updates are then deployed to the rest of the fleet.

○ *Rolling deployment*—Also called a rolling update, in this scenario, traffic is directed away from a few servers at a time so they can be updated. As each server is updated, it begins to handle traffic again so the next wave of servers can be updated. Eventually, the entire fleet has received the update.

- *Scheduling maintenance windows*—Applying patches can interfere with performance; therefore, maintenance windows must be carefully selected. Other factors affecting maintenance window schedules include the following:

  ○ When planning a maintenance window, you might want to spread scheduled updates across multiple maintenance windows. For example, you could update inactive, failover servers first as a test run before updating active servers.

  ○ Often, you can also choose what percentage of servers should be running update processes at any given time and at what point before the maintenance window closes no more update processes should be initiated.

  ○ Determine how many errors may occur before the update process should be halted and an admin notified.

  ○ You'll also need to consider how critical pending updates might be—patching a critical security vulnerability will need to be completed sooner and more quickly, even if that means taking a harder hit on performance.

- *Monitoring compliance and completion rates*—The patch management solution provides a dashboard or some other reporting feature to show which patches were successfully applied and which machines are still out of compliance.

Automation and Security

Many patches directly address security issues. These patches are considered critical or even urgent and, in most cases, should be applied as soon as reasonably possible. Another type of security update applies specifically to anti-malware solutions. Many of these tools use signatures to identify patterns of code that are known to indicate specific vulnerabilities, exploits, or other undesirable traffic. As this knowledge base expands, anti-malware solutions require updates to their database of signatures. Many vendors release these signature updates daily or even multiple times a day.

Considering that patches are intended to fix bugs and close security loopholes, it's easy to think that every patch should be applied right after its release. However, the patching process itself presents some risk to a company's network and systems. For this reason, more risk-averse companies will often delay the application of a patch until it has been thoroughly tested by their own technicians or publicly tested in the open market. While signature updates should be applied at least daily, other types of updates might not happen as often. In some cases, these updates might accumulate over a week or a month, and then all the updates are applied together at one time, which is called a rollup. The monthly Windows update is an example of the rollup model. Urgent security patches might be released between monthly updates. Otherwise, most updates are held for the scheduled release each month.

In defining a company's patching policy, a common method is to identify the current, stable release as N. A company that lags behind the current release by one iteration, then, is using an N-1 patching policy. The patch that is two releases older than the current release is identified as N-2.

Knowing that patches are designed to fix problems, these policies are often debated among various IT professionals on which is the best approach. And even if a company typically waits to apply each release, there are times when a new patch addresses critical issues and must be applied sooner rather than later.

Automating Security

Applying updates isn't the only security-related process that can be automated. Consider the following possibilities:

- *Firewalls*—You can set default security groups to ensure that new instances are automatically protected. You can also bridge services for additional features, such as creating an automated Lambda function that makes needed changes to security groups or detects configurations that need attention, such as conflicting rules or port vulnerabilities. Furthermore, CLI and API access to platform-native firewall services can be leveraged to create custom scripts or integration with third-party tools. For example, tools like Puppet and Chef lend themselves well to automatic configuration and validation of firewall rules.

- ***IDS and IPS***—Cloud-native IDS (intrusion detection system) and IPS solutions are core security automation tools, designed specifically for perimeter-fluid cloud environments. These tools generate alerts and even mitigate attacks automatically to help protect your cloud resources. For example, AWS's GuardDuty relies on ML, anomaly detection, and threat intelligence to identify threats and trigger CloudWatch events or Lambda functions. Similarly, Microsoft Defender for Identity relies on learning-based analytics to better monitor activities, identify threats, and prioritize alerts for follow-up by security staff. In the interest of layered security, HIDS (host-based IDS) and HIPS (host-based IPS) solutions installed on VM instances can also trigger alerts or automated functions.

- ***FIM***—Another tool in the fight against malware is FIM (file integrity monitoring). Some files, such as program, application, or system files, should almost never change except when receiving a patch or upgrade. Malware, however, will attempt to change these files to embed itself and conduct other destructive processes. FIM tools will detect these changes and generate an alert. FIM works by establishing a baseline of protected files and then systematically comparing the files over time to that baseline. Any time a discrepancy is discovered, an alert is triggered.

- ***Log analytics***—Logs such as VPC flow logs can capture security-related events, which are scanned for signs of abnormal activity that, in turn, trigger alerts. Although cloud resources generate massive volumes of log data, you can take advantage of built-in log analytics services to comb through that data and identify problem indicators. In some cases, you can automate response workflows such as quarantining a VM or virtual network, collecting additional information from the compromised resource, and rolling back that resource to a known good state. In essence, log analytics that trigger automated responses can be a form of automated forensics.

- ***IAM scripting***—Using scripting that interacts with APIs or orchestrated functions in services such as AWS Lambda, you can automate user account management tasks. These tasks might include user account creation, removal, or disablement. Through automation, you can also standardize account configurations such as roles, permissions, resource access, initial password, and tags.

Securing Automation

You've already learned about several security techniques that can be automated to increase the security of your cloud resources and overall network. Similarly, automation itself needs to be secured. The following list explores best practices for creating secure scripts used in automation processes or in any other processes (such as programming scripts or client-side and server-side scripts for websites):

- ***Accounts***—Each resource can be assigned its own role that provides needed permissions. For example, a resource (such as a Lambda function) that needs to create a VM instance can be assigned a VM creation role that includes no other permissions. Similarly, users should be given separate accounts for different job roles. For example, a cloud admin might need a more privileged user account for some tasks that must be performed infrequently. However, this same user might be given a less privileged account for daily tasks.

- ***Passwords***—Do not include passwords to services or resources within a script, which is called a hard-coded password. Instead, assign roles to resources that provide the least permissions needed for each resource to do its job, and manage secrets (such as authentication keys) through a secrets management service or password vault.

- ***Authentication***—Cloud-based authentication processes generally support key-based authentication instead of being restricted to less secure password authentication. Recall that key-based authentication, also called cryptographic authentication, uses public and private key pairs to confirm a user's or resource's identity and permissions and, when needed, to establish secure communications between the client and the server. Keys can be stored in a KMS (key management service), such as AWS's KMS, so you don't have to transport keys to the cloud. KMS also logs all access or changes to keys for auditing later. Figure 10-9 shows some of the options for configuring a key in AWS's KMS.

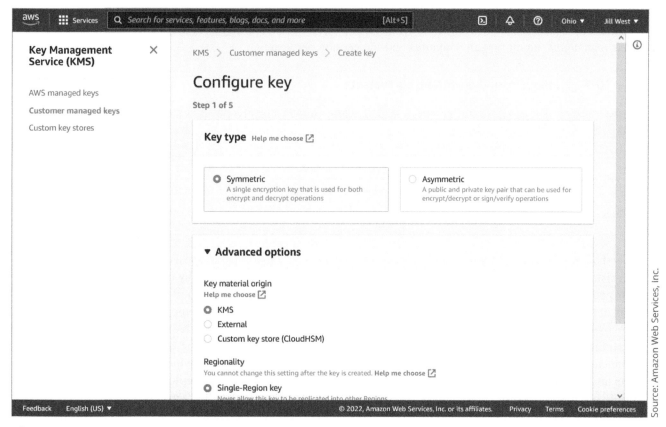

Figure 10-9   Create a key in AWS KMS

Automated Disaster Recovery

When it comes to security, disaster recovery plays an important role. Keeping resources functioning during a crisis and restoring full functionality afterward help ensure that vulnerabilities and threats don't complicate an already stressful situation.

In Module 8, you learned about durability for data stored in the cloud. For example, AWS S3 offers 11 nines durability, which is a 99.999999999 percent guarantee that an object stored in S3 will not be lost. This number of nines is also used in calculating HA (high availability) of cloud resources. In the world of networking, the term *availability* refers to how consistently and reliably a connection, system, or other network resource can be accessed by authorized personnel. It's often expressed as a percentage, such as 98 percent or 99.5 percent. For example, a server that allows staff to log on and use its programs and data 99.999 percent of the time is considered highly available, whereas one that is functional only 99.9 percent of the time is significantly less available.

In fact, the number of 9s in a system's availability rating is sometimes referred to colloquially as "four 9s" (99.99 percent) or "three 9s" (99.9 percent) availability. You might hear a network manager use the term in a statement such as, "We're a four 9s shop." This could be an impressive track record for a small ISP or a school's LMS (learning management system). For a hospital network, however, where lives are at stake, four nines likely wouldn't be enough. Four nines availability means that, each year on average, there could be as much as 52.6 minutes when you can't get to your resources.

> **Note 3**
>
> Similar terms include *reliability*, which refers to how well a resource functions without errors, and *resiliency*, which refers to a resource's ability to recover from errors even if it becomes unavailable during the outage.

One way to consider availability is by measuring a system or network's uptime, which is the duration or percentage of time it functions normally between failures. As shown in Table 10-1, a system that experiences 99.999 percent uptime is *unavailable* no more than 5 minutes and 15 seconds per year.

Table 10-1   Availability and downtime equivalents

Availability	Downtime per day	Downtime per month	Downtime per year
99%	14 minutes, 23 seconds	7 hours, 18 minutes, 17 seconds	87 hours, 39 minutes, 29 seconds
99.9%	1 minute, 26 seconds	43 minutes, 49 seconds	8 hours, 45 minutes, 56 seconds
99.99%	8 seconds	4 minutes, 22 seconds	52 minutes, 35 seconds
99.999%	0.4 seconds	26 seconds	5 minutes, 15 seconds

Now that you understand the significance of uptime, how can automation increase a cloud deployment's availability, or resistance to downtime, especially in the face of provider outages experienced by cloud customers? Many third-party providers offer automated disaster recovery solutions. Similarly, most major cloud providers include automated DR tools in their platforms. For example, AWS's CloudEndure offers automated resiliency that can potentially reduce RPO (recovery point objective) to less than a second and RTO (recovery time objective) to a few minutes.

CloudEndure and similar services work by performing automatic failover when an outage occurs. Designed well, redundancies can compensate even for widespread, regional outages by a cloud provider and many related services (such as Internet connectivity or DNS). Health checks can be used to perform post-deployment validation or escalate a return to normal status through a primary, secondary, and even tertiary failover infrastructure. For example, a static website can give users information temporarily when the outage first occurs. Then the failover web server takes over until the primary web server returns to functionality.

Remember This

- Because maintenance activities can impact the performance of affected resources, much of this work must be completed within a maintenance window to minimize disruption to cloud services.
- A roadmap defines significant phases of a resource's life cycle, and version control is a process for tracking changes over time.
- Some updates apply small fixes to minor bugs, whereas other, more critical updates patch security loopholes and vulnerabilities to protect resources against known threats.
- You might stagger maintenance windows for different groups of servers so one group can be updated while another group handles the active workload, such as when using a blue-green deployment, a canary deployment, or a rolling deployment.
- In defining a company's patching policy, a common method is to identify the current, stable release as N; a company that lags behind the current release by one iteration is using an N-1 patching policy.
- Automated disaster recovery services work by performing automatic failover when an outage occurs.

Self-Check

4. What factor primarily determines the division of responsibility for maintenance tasks?
   a. Logging configuration
   b. Service model
   c. Subscription service
   d. Lifecycle phase

5. What is the opposite of an update?

   a. Virtual patch   **c.** Failover
   b. Hotfix   **d.** Rollback

6. What lifecycle feature would enable you to deploy an earlier state of a web server's configuration?

   a. Migration   **c.** Roadmap
   b. Versioning   **d.** Signature

○ Check your answers at the end of this module.

Section 10-3: Cloud Automation Services

Certification

2.3 Given a scenario, apply the appropriate OS and application security controls.

2.5 Given a scenario, implement measures to meet security requirements.

4.2 Given a scenario, maintain efficient operation of a cloud environment.

4.4 Given a scenario, apply proper automation and orchestration techniques.

IaC relies on code-based interactions with cloud platforms. When you're first learning how to use and troubleshoot resources in the cloud, you typically start out using GUI consoles and dashboards. As you become more comfortable with the cloud features and options, you might find yourself drawn to the ease and convenience of working from the CLI where you can also use code to control your cloud resources. AWS, Azure, and GCP, as well as many other CSPs, offer one or more CLI tools. Using a CLI is one way you can create scripts for deploying cloud resources, which gives you the option to automate this and many other tasks. Let's take a quick tour of some of these CLI tools.

AWS CLI

The AWS CLI is a tool you install on your computer so you can use your local computer's CLI to interact with AWS services. From your computer's command line, such as Windows PowerShell, you can perform similar tasks to those you would do in the AWS Management Console through your browser. The commands interact with AWS's public APIs and account credentials stored on your computer. The AWS CLI can be installed on Windows, Linux, macOS, and Unix computers. It relies on TCP port 443, so if you have problems with it, check to make sure this port is enabled on your firewalls.

To install the AWS CLI, you download an installation package, which includes all the dependencies needed to install and run the AWS CLI on your computer. Make sure to source the package directly from AWS using their instructions for your OS. And ensure that you choose the most recent, stable AWS CLI version. If you have formerly installed an older version of AWS CLI, you will likely need to uninstall that version first.

After installation, you configure the AWS CLI with security credentials, default output format, and default AWS region. This can be accomplished easily using the `configure` command.

The AWS CLI's command syntax consists of a base call to the AWS program (written as `aws`), a command that identifies the AWS service, a subcommand that identifies the operation, and any options or parameters, as shown here:

```
aws <command> <subcommand> [options and parameters]
```

For example, a commonly used command is `ec2`, which interacts with the EC2 service in AWS. If you want to get help on this command, enter `aws ec2 help`. If you want to list your existing instances, enter `aws ec2 describe-instances`. You could also add parameters to this command in the form of filters. The following example shows a filter that limits output to instances with the instance type t2.micro:

```
aws ec2 describe-instances --filters "Name=instance-type, Values=t2.micro"
```

Table 10-2 shows some common commands used in the AWS CLI.

Table 10-2   Common AWS CLI commands

Command	Description
`aws --version`	Gives the installed version of AWS CLI, which is a good way to confirm the installation was successful
`aws help`	Gives information about AWS CLI options and top-level commands
`aws ec2 help`	Gives information about EC2 commands
`aws ec2 describe-instances help`	Gives verbose information about the describe-instances operation
`aws ec2 describe-instances`	Lists all EC2 instances

`aws ec2 run-instances`
`--image-id ami-xxxxxxxx`
`--count 1`
`--instance-type t2.micro`
`--key-name MyKeyPair`
`--security-group-ids sg-xxxxxxxx`
`--subnet-id subnet-xxxxxxxx`
	Creates a t2.micro instance using a specific AMI, key pair, security group, and subnet

`aws ec2 terminate-instances` `--instance-ids i-xxxxxxxx`	Terminates an instance identified by its Instance ID

AWS also offers a similar tool within the console called CloudShell, as shown in Figure 10-10. The CloudShell service opens a CLI pane in your browser where you can use the same AWS CLI commands without having to install any software on your local computer. In a project at the end of this module, you practice using AWS CloudShell to create, modify, and terminate an EC2 instance.

Source: Amazon Web Services, Inc.

Figure 10-10   Use the AWS CloudShell in your browser

Azure CLI

The Azure CLI can run in the Azure Cloud Shell in your browser, or you can download and install the Azure CLI for use through your computer's CLI, such as PowerShell in Windows. Launch Cloud Shell from the portal as shown in Figure 10-11, and then choose a subscription to associate the session with. To install Azure CLI, download the installation package for your OS and complete the installation. This is a much more straightforward process in Windows for Command Prompt or PowerShell than in other OSs. If you're using a Linux system, macOS system, or the WSL (Windows Subsystem for Linux), you'll need to check the Azure site for specific instructions. After installing Azure CLI, you then open your computer's shell, open an Azure session with the `az login` command, and sign in using your Azure credentials.

Figure 10-11   Use the Azure Cloud Shell directly in your browser

Similar to the AWS CLI, you start all Azure CLI commands with the base call `az`. Check the installed version with the `az --version` command. Table 10-3 shows a few additional, common Azure commands.

Table 10-3   Common Azure CLI commands

Command	Description
`az --version`	Gives the installed version of Azure CLI, which is a good way to confirm the installation was successful
`az --help`	Gives information about Azure CLI options and top-level commands
`az interactive`	Enables interactive mode, which displays help information as you work, provides auto-completion, and gives examples
`az find vm`	Uses AI to find popular commands containing the search term *vm*
`az vm --help`	Gives information about the `vm` command
`az vm list`	Lists details of all VMs associated with the current subscription
`az vm create -n NewVM -g MyRG --image UbuntuLTS`	Creates a VM using a specific name, group, and image
`az vm delete -g MyRG -n NewVM --yes`	Deletes a specific VM without prompting for confirmation

Note 4

An older version of the Azure CLI, now called the classic CLI, used the base call `azure`.

GCP CLI

The Google Cloud CLI includes several command-line tools, depending on the tasks you're performing. The following list describes some of the most important tools:

- *gcloud*—Among many other capabilities, gcloud is used to create, start, and manage VM instances, networks, firewall rules, disk storage, and more.
- *gsutil*—This tool is designed specifically to manage Google Cloud Storage.
- *bq*—This CLI tool is used for managing Google BigQuery, which is a data analytics service that operates in conjunction with Google Storage.
- *kubectl*—The kubectl tool is used to manage Kubernetes container clusters.

To use any of these CLI tools, you install the free Google Cloud CLI installer from cloud.google.com/sdk/. Alternatively, you can access the Google Cloud Shell in the GCP console (see Figure 10-12). The Google Cloud Shell is a Debian-based VM with preinstalled utilities such as gcloud and is accessed directly through your browser.

Figure 10-12 Use the Google Cloud Shell directly in your browser

Table 10-4 shows a few simple commands you can use in gcloud.

Table 10-4 Common gcloud commands

Command	Description
`gcloud -h`	Gives information about the gcloud commands and shows the major groupings of commands and their syntax
`gcloud compute -h`	Gives information about the compute group of gcloud commands and shows the major subgroupings of these commands and their syntax
`gcloud compute --help`	Gives verbose information about the compute group commands
`gcloud compute instances list`	Lists all compute instances
`gcloud compute instances create my-instance --zone=us-east4-b`	Creates the VM instance named "my-instance" in one of the N. Virginia zones
`gcloud compute instances start my-instance`	Starts the VM instance named "my-instance"
`gcloud compute instances delete my-instance`	Deletes the VM instance named "my-instance"

Patching in AWS

Earlier in this module, you learned about AWS's Systems Manager. One of the components of Systems Manager is Patch Manager, which can be used to automatically scan managed instances for patch compliance and, if desired, apply updates to these instances. You can use patch baselines to manage approved or rejected patches. Figure 10-13 shows some of the configurations for the default Windows patch baseline. You can create maintenance windows to automate patching processes. Patch Manager is integrated with AWS IAM and CloudWatch for increased automation and notification capabilities as well as auditing abilities.

To function, Systems Manager relies on the SSM Agent installed on managed instances. The agent is preinstalled on many of the more popular AMIs (Amazon Machine Images), such as Windows Server, Amazon Linux, and Ubuntu Server. When scheduling automated update tasks, know that the SSM Agent itself needs to be regularly updated as well. This task can also be automated.

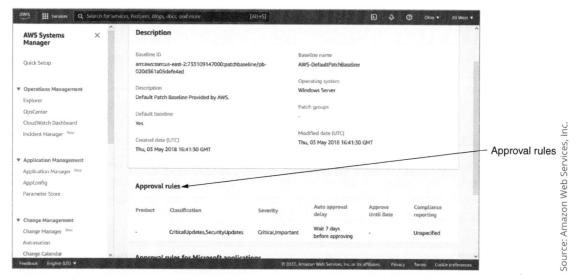

Figure 10-13   This default patch baseline allows all critical or security updates on managed Windows instances

Automated patching tasks occur within restrictions defined by a maintenance window. Figure 10-14 shows some of the available settings for a maintenance window in AWS. You can schedule frequent windows, such as every 30 minutes, or schedule windows further apart, such as every Sunday. You can also decide at what point within the maintenance window new tasks will no longer be initiated. This is helpful to prevent time-consuming updates or other tasks from beginning moments before the window closes.

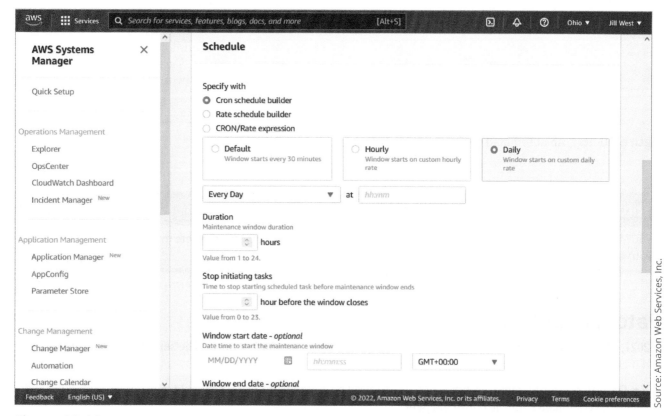

Figure 10-14   Configure maintenance window start frequency and duration

Patching in Azure

Update management in Azure is provided through the Azure Automation service. To access Azure Automation, you need an automation account. This is similar in concept to the storage account you used in an earlier module.

Figure 10-15 shows a VM that is noncompliant due to a missing security update. Figure 10-16 shows the update deployment dashboard as updates are being applied to the VM.

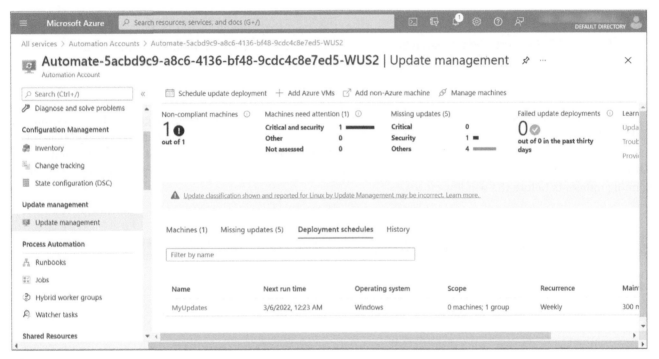

Figure 10-15   An automated update is scheduled

Patching in GCP

In 2021, GCP released a new suite of tools designed to manage updates for VM fleets. The service is called VM Manager, and it consists of three components, as follows:

- *OS patch management*—Applies patches to VM OSs on demand or by schedule and reports activities and patch compliance for the entire VM fleet.
- *OS inventory management*—Presents information on installed OSs.
- *OS configuration management*—Installs, removes, or updates software.

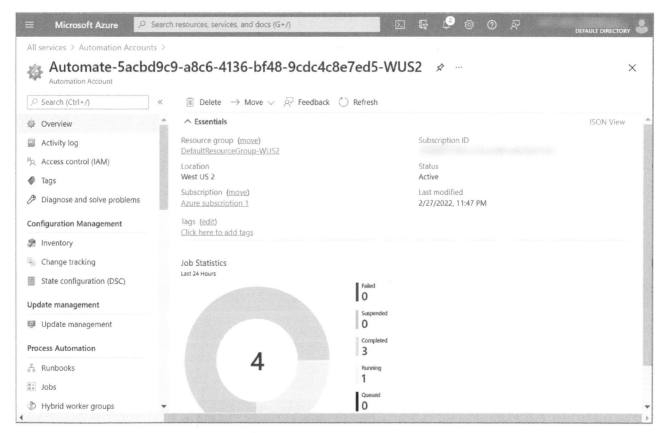

Figure 10-16   Three completed updates and one in progress

When creating a project, you can decide if VM Manager should be activated by default on all VMs or manually on selected VMs. Most VM images in Compute Engine already contain the OS Config agent, and this agent must be activated on each VM to enable communications with VM Manager. You can install the agent on other images as well. The agent uses built-in OS utilities to retrieve files for an update, apply the update, adjust the VM's state, or collect logs on the VM.

Figure 10-17 shows the OS patch management dashboard with three VMs needing updates, and two of these VMs need important or security updates.

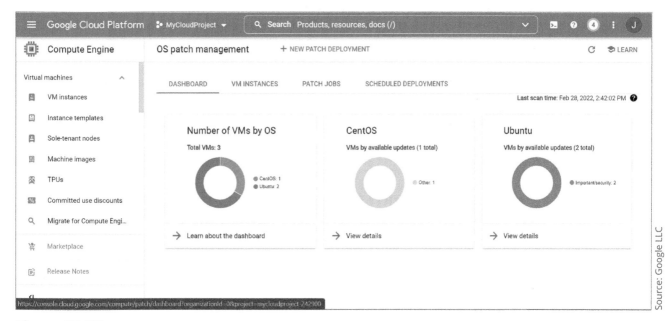

Figure 10-17   OS patch management in VM Manager

Figure 10-18 shows options for scheduling the patch deployment.

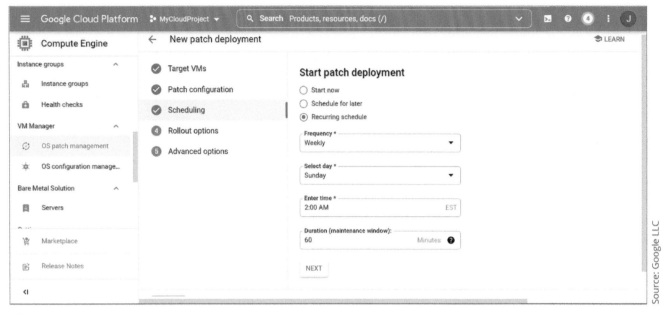

Figure 10-18 Schedule patch deployment

You're Ready

You're now ready to complete Project 10-4: Automated Patching in GCP. You can complete the project now or wait until you've finished all the readings for this module.

Remember This

- The AWS CLI is a tool you install on your computer so you can use your local computer's CLI to interact with AWS services.
- The Azure CLI can run in the Azure Cloud Shell in your browser, or you can download and install the Azure CLI for use through your computer's CLI, such as PowerShell in Windows.
- The Google Cloud CLI includes several command-line tools, depending on the tasks you're performing.
- Automated patching tasks in AWS Systems Manager occur within restrictions defined by a maintenance window.
- To access Azure Automation, you need an automation account.
- GCP's VM Manager agent uses built-in OS utilities to retrieve files for an update, apply the update, adjust the VM's state, or collect logs on the VM.

Self-Check

7. What software provides a bridge of communication between an OS and an update automation tool?
   a. Agent
   b. CLI
   c. Patch
   d. AMI

8. What text initiates communication with an installed CLI application?
   a. Parameter
   b. Base call
   c. Subcommand
   d. Filter

○ Check your answers at the end of this module.

Section 10-4: Troubleshooting Automation Issues

● **Certification**

5.3 Given a scenario, troubleshoot deployment issues.

5.6 Given a scenario, troubleshoot automation or orchestration issues.

When deploying resources through IaC, troubleshooting problems becomes more efficient, and the problems themselves are more easily traced. For example, consider how to troubleshoot a server configuration issue. If the server worked correctly previously, you can examine the IaC script to determine what change to the server's configuration caused the problems. If it has never worked correctly, examining the script responsible for deploying the server might reveal a misconfiguration or a poorly defined environmental variable. Fixing the script can result in repeatable deployments free of that particular problem.

Common Automation Issues

Other problems you might encounter with automation processes include the following:

- *Deprecated features*—As newer technologies emerge, older features are deprecated. Vendors regularly publish notifications on pending changes to features or deprecation of older features.
- *API version incompatibility*—To pressure customers to upgrade their systems, vendors sometimes remove compatibility of their REST APIs with older client systems. As the customer, again, you can rely on published information to anticipate coming changes and adjust IaC scripts and templates.
- *Patching failure*—When applying updates to adapt to feature and API changes, sometimes the patch itself fails. For example, the resource receiving the patch might not have enough available storage space or conflicting patch processes might be running at the same time. Typically, systems are designed to revert to a previous configuration if an automated patch process fails and to also send an alert to admins.
- *Change management failure*—The purpose of change management is to incorporate accountability for changes made to a system. When automation plays a role in changes made, sometimes the automated changes fall outside the purview of change management oversight, and sometimes change management approval doesn't reach far enough to anticipate automatic adjustments. Solving this problem requires a big-picture approach to the implementation of cloud automation so that proper accountability continues to apply while allowing automation tools to do the job they're designed to do.

Breakdowns in Workflow

Unfortunately, automation is not a failproof system. Things can still go wrong, especially during the initial setup phase. Automated systems rely on predictable configurations to find resources for monitoring or actions to trigger. Successful workflows also rely on well-planned processes and user training. Consider the following obstacles to the establishment of successful automation workflows:

- Don't rely on users' fascination with new technologies to ensure that users follow the correct steps to initiate automated processes. Adequate training and follow-through are essential. For example, a sophisticated trouble ticketing system isn't much help if employees continue to email or text IT staff when there's a problem instead of filing a trouble ticket through the system. In cases such as this, gentle and consistent reminders, along with assistance in learning to use the system and the eventual rejection of all manual requests, can help users get used to a new system. Additionally, ensuring the new system works well with quick responses from IT staff can demonstrate to users how the new system will help enhance productivity.
- Incomplete automated workflows apply automation for part of the process but not all of it. For example, an automated approval process for purchase orders that relies on manual transfer to your financial software is not true automation. You'll experience bottlenecks in the workflow and continuing issues with errors. Design workflows to complete a process from start to finish.

- Automating a workflow that is already not working well will only make it worse. Fix the broken process first, then consider how to automate it.
- No workflow will stay the same forever. Things change, and the workflow must be adapted for new variables. Review your automations, workflows, and system output regularly for signs of problems. Sources of these problems might include any of the following:
  - ○ Account mismatch issues, such as updated credentials
  - ○ Server name, IP address, or location changes, which might be caused by a change management failure
  - ○ Version or feature mismatch
  - ○ Job validation issues, where the automation system is unable to validate the workflow
  - ○ Batch job scheduling issues, where a task dependency is not scheduled to occur at the right point in the process
  - ○ Automation tool incompatibility, where tools are unable to adequately communicate with each other

A well-tuned automation system will save you time and save your company money by increasing efficiency and reducing risk and loss from human error. Training yourself on how to better automate and orchestrate your cloud processes will also help ensure your employability as cloud computing becomes the new status quo.

Exam Tip ✔

Studying for and earning your CompTIA Cloud+ certification is an entry point into your career as a cloud professional. You've laid a solid foundation in your ability to learn and work with the cloud. Yet there is still much more to learn, with the related technologies changing and maturing every day. No one is an expert in all areas of the cloud, so don't let what you don't know intimidate you. Keep asking good questions, researching new developments, and challenging yourself to explore and experiment with cloud services and platforms.

Remember This

- When deploying resources through IaC, troubleshooting problems becomes more efficient, and the problems themselves are more easily traced.
- Common problems with automated processes include deprecated features, API version incompatibility, patching failures, and change management failure.
- Whereas automated systems rely on predictable configurations to find resources for monitoring or actions to trigger, successful workflows rely on well-planned processes and user training.

Self-Check

9. An improperly documented server name change is a type of _____.
   - **a.** patch failure
   - **b.** deprecated feature
   - **c.** API version incompatibility
   - **d.** change management failure

10. What is caused by manual portions of a workflow?
    - **a.** Account mismatch
    - **b.** Bottleneck
    - **c.** Job validation
    - **d.** Task dependency

○ Check your answers at the end of this module.

Module Summary

Section 10-1: Automation Workflow

- Automation refers to the use of software-based solutions to perform a process or procedure with minimal human intervention.
- Some of the maintenance and security tasks that can be performed by automation tools include performing routine operations, applying updates, generating internal API communications, restarting or shutting down resources, and migrating traffic to redundant resources.
- Orchestration sequencing is a key component of designing effective IaC (infrastructure as code) templates.
- Automation tools might be built into the cloud platform or provided by third-party vendor applications that interact with resources through APIs.
- AI (artificial intelligence) refers to a computer's ability to adapt its behavior according to ongoing input, and ML (machine learning) is a process where computers learn from data analysis rather than from explicit programming.

Section 10-2: Cloud Maintenance Processes

- Because maintenance activities can impact the performance of affected resources, much of this work must be completed within a maintenance window to minimize disruption to cloud services.
- A roadmap defines significant phases of a resource's life cycle, and version control is a process for tracking changes over time.
- Some updates apply small fixes to minor bugs, whereas other, more critical updates patch security loopholes and vulnerabilities to protect resources against known threats.
- You might stagger maintenance windows for different groups of servers so one group can be updated while another group handles the active workload, such as when using a blue-green deployment, a canary deployment, or a rolling deployment.
- In defining a company's patching policy, a common method is to identify the current, stable release as N; a company that lags behind the current release by one iteration is using an N-1 patching policy.
- Automated disaster recovery services work by performing automatic failover when an outage occurs.

Section 10-3: Cloud Automation Services

- The AWS CLI is a tool you install on your computer so you can use your local computer's CLI to interact with AWS services.
- The Azure CLI can run in the Azure Cloud Shell in your browser, or you can download and install the Azure CLI for use through your computer's CLI, such as PowerShell in Windows.
- The Google Cloud CLI includes several command-line tools, depending on the tasks you're performing.
- Automated patching tasks in AWS Systems Manager occur within restrictions defined by a maintenance window.
- To access Azure Automation, you need an automation account.
- GCP's VM Manager agent uses built-in OS utilities to retrieve files for an update, apply the update, adjust the VM's state, or collect logs on the VM.

Section 10-4: Troubleshooting Automation Issues

- When deploying resources through IaC, troubleshooting problems becomes more efficient, and the problems themselves are more easily traced.
- Common problems with automated processes include deprecated features, API version incompatibility, patching failures, and change management failure.
- Whereas automated systems rely on predictable configurations to find resources for monitoring or actions to trigger, successful workflows rely on well-planned processes and user training.

Key Terms

For definitions of key terms, see the Glossary.

AI (artificial intelligence)	N-1	rollup
data analytics	playbook	runbook
failover cluster	pull model	signature
FIM (file integrity monitoring)	push model	version control
IaC (infrastructure as code)	roadmap	virtual patch

Acronyms Checklist

The acronyms in Table 10-5 are listed in the Cloud+ objectives and could appear on the Cloud+ exam. This means that exam questions might use any of these acronyms in context so that you must know the meaning of the acronym to answer the question correctly. Make sure you're familiar with what each acronym stands for and the general concept of the term itself. All these acronyms are used in context in this module.

Table 10-5 Module 10 acronyms

Acronym	Spelled out
CMS	content management system
FIM	file integrity monitoring
MSP	managed service provider
NOC	network operations center
QA	quality assurance

Review Questions

1. Which of these tools can be installed on your computer? Choose TWO.

   a. AWS CLI
   b. AWS CloudShell
   c. Azure CLI
   d. Azure Cloud Shell

2. Which kind of tool relies most on disposable resources?

   a. Declarative
   b. Imperative
   c. Idempotent
   d. Immutable

3. When testing a new automation script, the deployment of a web server repeatedly fails. What characteristic of the script is most likely responsible for the problem?

   a. Hardcoded passwords
   b. Container environment
   c. Patching
   d. Sequencing

4. Which technique pulls away a small number of servers at a time for updates throughout the entire deployment process?

   a. Canary
   b. Rolling
   c. Virtual
   d. Blue-green

5. Which term refers to a resource's track record of functioning error-free?

   a. Availability
   b. Durability
   c. Resiliency
   d. Reliability

6. Which technology requires computers to uncover hidden patterns?

   a. Supervised learning
   b. Artificial learning
   c. Unsupervised learning
   d. Reinforcement learning

7. Which of the following tools requires detailed instructions on how you want a group of resources deployed?

   a. Chef
   b. Terraform
   c. CloudFormation
   d. SaltStack Config

8. Which environment is primarily focused on ensuring consistent quality throughout an application's design?

   a. Production
   b. Development
   c. Duplicate production
   d. Staging

9. Which type of machine learning will most likely result in serendipitous discoveries not anticipated by human designers?

   a. Supervised learning
   b. Reinforcement learning
   c. Unsupervised learning
   d. Artificial learning

10. What technique will protect root system files?

   a. QA
   b. CMS
   c. FIM
   d. NOC

Scenario-Based Questions

Question 10-1

Terry is preparing a lab activity for his students where they'll be practicing patching techniques on a variety of operating system configurations. Terry needs to deploy several VMs in the lab, and he'll need to be able to make multiple changes to the VM configurations during the course of the activity. Which of the following tools would be most useful for automated deployment in this situation?

   a. Ansible
   b. CloudFormation
   c. Python
   d. Terraform

Question 10-2

Mateo is troubleshooting a recurring issue with one of his applications running on a private cloud in his company's on-prem network. It seems the OS patches are not being applied properly, with frequent errors showing the VM is not in compliance with his patch management policies. Mateo is looking for indications of other patches that need to be applied to fix this problem. Which of the following components most likely needs to be updated?

   a. The underlying hypervisor
   b. The local database
   c. The running application
   d. The local agent on the VM

Question 10-3

Dominique and her team are ready to deploy updates to a core business application running in their organization's cloud. They've spun up a second, identical environment to their production environment, applied the updates, and completed testing. Because of the nature of the updates, however, the team has decided there's a moderate risk of problems during the deployment even after all the prep work they've done. Dominique has asked for suggestions on how to minimize the impact of these anticipated issues should they occur. Which of the following strategies would best ensure the deployment goes smoothly with minimal impact on users while giving Dominique's team the time and opportunity they need to resolve issues that might arise?

   a. Create a third environment for additional testing.
   b. Update a few servers in the original environment that is handling live traffic.

c. Transfer a small percentage of live traffic to the updated environment.

d. Create a third environment that is given only the portion of updates least likely to cause problems.

Hands-On Projects

Note 5

Websites, applications, public cloud platforms, and related account options change often. While the instructions given in these projects were accurate at the time of writing, you might need to adjust the steps or options according to later changes.

Note to Instructors and Students: A rubric is provided for evaluating student performance on these projects. Please see Appendix D.

Project 10-1: Research Automation Tools

Estimated time: 45 minutes

Objective 4.4: Given a scenario, apply proper automation and orchestration techniques.

Resources:

- Internet access

Context:

While the installation and configuration of most of the automation tools in this module exceed the scope of this course, it's simply easier to understand what the tools offer if you've seen one or more of them in action. In this project, you'll research an automation tool covered in this module and watch a video of it being used in a cloud platform of your choice. First, decide on which tool you'd like to research. Choose from the following list:

- Terraform
- Ansible
- Chef
- Puppet
- SaltStack Config

Next, find a video online showing your selected tool being used in the cloud platform of your choice, such as AWS, Azure, or GCP. After watching the video, answer the following questions:

1. What tool and cloud platform did you choose? What is the link to the video you watched?
2. What activities were performed in the video using this tool in this cloud platform? Give a detailed description of the processes covered in the video.
3. What cloud platform services interacted with this tool?
4. How would you explain the purpose of this tool to an executive in your company?

Be sure to answer the questions in your own words. The grading rubric in Table 10-6 shows how your responses for this project will be evaluated. Note that your instructor might choose to adjust the point distribution in this rubric.

Hands-On Projects Continued

Table 10-6   Grading rubric for Project 10-1

Task	Novice	Competent	Proficient	Earned
Identify tool, platform, and video	One item is given **5 points**	Two items are given **10 points**	All three items are given **15 points**	
Activities description	Vague, general description **5 points**	Specific description giving multiple steps **15 points**	Thoughtful, detailed description giving multiple steps and examples **25 points**	
Cloud platform services listed	One or two items listed with no supporting details **5 points**	Multiple items listed with supporting details and description **15 points**	Multiple items listed with supporting details and explanation of how these services fit into the overall activity **25 points**	
Explanation of tool's purpose	Generalized statements describing the tool with little cohesiveness **5 points**	Specific statements describing the tool with logical organization of ideas from beginning to end **15 points**	Detailed and thoughtful statements describing the tool with clear organization of ideas, showing logical connections between thoughts **25 points**	
Mechanics	Several grammar and spelling errors **4 points**	Occasional grammar and spelling errors **7 points**	Appropriate grammar and spelling throughout **10 points**	
Total				

Project 10-2: Automated Patching in AWS

Estimated time: 45 minutes
Objective 4.2: Given a scenario, maintain efficient operation of a cloud environment.
Resources:

- AWS account
- Internet access

Context:

CloudShell is an AWS service that allows you to use a CLI from within the AWS management console to interact with resources and services. Practicing with CloudShell will give you some idea of how IaC scripting works. In this project, you'll enable CloudShell and practice some commands, including creating an EC2 instance. You'll then use the console to configure automated patching on your instance using Systems Manager. Automating patching processes is a good way to reduce the workload on staff and increase timeliness of patches.

If you're using an AWS Academy account, skip to Step 3. If you're using a standard AWS account, create an IAM role before proceeding by completing the following steps:

1. Go to the IAM dashboard and click **Roles** in the navigation pane. Click **Create role**. Select **AWS service**, and then select **EC2**. Click **Next**.
2. Select **AmazonEC2RoleforSSM** and click **Next**. Give the role a name, such as MyEC2Role. Click **Create role**. Keep the role name handy, as you will need it again shortly.

For all users, you're now ready to enable and practice using the CloudShell environment in your AWS console. Complete the following steps:

3. In the search box at the top of your console, enter **CloudShell**. Read the information in the pop-up box, and then click **Close**. AWS will initialize the CloudShell environment for your account. Notice the CloudShell icon is now available at the top of your screen for future access.

(continues)

4. Enter **aws help**. What command gives a list of available help topics? Press the **Spacebar** to continue through the help output, and type **q** when you're ready to return to the shell prompt.

5. Refer to Table 10-2 earlier in the module for some common AWS commands. Request information on the EC2 service. What command did you enter?

Now you're ready to create an EC2 instance using CloudShell. Complete the following steps:

6. Use CloudShell to deploy an EC2 instance. You'll need the following information to create your command:

   • Start with the command text:

     ```
     aws ec2 run-instances --image-id ami-xxxxxxxx --count 1 --instance-type
     t2.micro --key-name MyKeyPair
     ```

   • Replace the AMI text in the sample command with the AMI ID for a Windows Server system. Where did you find this information?
   • Replace the key name with the name of a key pair in your account.
   • What command did you run that successfully deployed an EC2 instance?

Note 6

It might feel inconvenient to find the required information and type a long command the first time you run a command like this, such as finding a key pair name and an AMI ID. However, once you collect this information, you can repeat this command many times much faster than working through the console over and over. Once your command is created, you can repeat this activity as many times as needed, knowing that every resource will receive exactly the same configuration information.

7. Type **q** to quit from the output about your new instance. Enter the command **aws ec2 describe-instances** to confirm your instance is listed. What is your instance's image ID?

Now that you have created an instance, you're ready to practice making a change to the instance's configuration using CloudShell. So that you can enable automatic patching later in this project, you will associate an instance profile to the instance. AWS Academy users will attach the instance profile called "Lab Role." Standard account users will attach the instance profile from the role created in Step 2; the instance profile uses the same name as the role you created. Complete the following steps:

8. Enter the following command, replacing <your-instance-id> with your instance's ID and using the correct instance profile name:

   ```
   aws ec2 associate-iam-instance-profile --instance-id <your-instance-id>
   --iam-instance-profile Name="Lab Role"
   ```

Now you're ready to create a maintenance window that will carry out the patch automation tasks. Complete the following steps:

9. Go to the **Systems Manager** console. Systems Manager is listed in the Management & Governance category. In the navigation pane, click **Maintenance Windows**, and then click **Create Maintenance Window**.

10. Give the maintenance window a name, such as MyMW. In the Schedule section, make sure **Cron schedule builder** is selected, and select **Daily**. Configure the window to start every **Sunday** at **02:00**. Set the duration for **5** hours and stop initiating tasks **1** hour before the window closes. Click **Create maintenance window**.

You're now ready to configure patching for your instance. Complete the following steps:

11. In the navigation pane, click **Patch Manager**, and then click **Configure patching**. In the Instances to patch section, click **Select instances manually**. Select your Windows instance in the list that appears. (If you don't see your instance in the list, it might not be fully validated yet. If you need to troubleshoot, return to the EC2

Hands-On Projects Continued

service and confirm the EC2 instance has completed all its status checks. Sometimes it takes several minutes before the instance will show up in Patch Manager. Also confirm the instance profile was properly applied.) In the Patching schedule section, select the maintenance window you created in Step 10. What are the two options in the Patching operation section? Leave the default selection and click **Configure patching**.

12. Patch Manager shows a list of patch baselines. Each OS has a default patch baseline, and some OSs have other available patch baselines as well. Based on this information, which patch baseline did you just use?

13. Click that patch baseline's Baseline ID. Which updates are automatically approved? How long does Systems Manager wait before automatically approving the updates?

14. In the navigation pane, click **Maintenance Windows**, and then click the maintenance window you created in Step 10. Notice you can edit the maintenance window or perform other actions. On the **Tasks** tab, how many tasks are listed for this maintenance window? If you were to leave the maintenance window running for a few weeks, you would start to see entries on the History tab as well.

Now you're ready to delete the resources created in this project. Terminate the EC2 instance using CloudShell, and then use the console to ensure all other resources are deleted. Complete the following steps:

15. In CloudShell, enter the following command:

```
aws ec2 terminate-instances --instance-id <your-instance-id>
```

16. Use CloudShell to show that your instance is being shut down. **Take a screenshot** of the command you used and the portion of the output showing a shutdown is in progress; submit this visual with your answers to this project's questions.

17. Delete all the remaining resources you created for this project, including the IAM role, maintenance window, and any remaining EC2 instances. Check through your account to confirm that all related resources have been deleted.

Note 7

Depending on the status of your account and the selections you made during this project, the resources you created can deplete your credits or accrue charges. Double-check to make sure you've terminated all resources you created in this project.

Project 10-3: Automated Patching in Azure

Estimated time: 1 hour
Objective 4.2: Given a scenario, maintain efficient operation of a cloud environment.
Resources:

- Azure account
- Internet access

Context:

Cloud Shell is an Azure service that allows you to use a CLI from within the Azure portal to interact with resources and services. Practicing with Cloud Shell will give you some idea of how IaC scripting works. In this project, you'll enable Cloud Shell and practice some commands, including creating a VM. You'll then enable automated updates on the VM using Update management. Automating updates is a good way to reduce the workload on staff and increase timeliness of updates.

Complete the following steps:

1. In your Azure portal, click the **Cloud Shell** icon at the top of the screen, and select the **Bash** shell. Bash is a Linux-native CLI environment. To function, Azure Cloud Shell needs a storage account. Choose your subscription, and then click **Create storage**. Note that an Azure for Students Starter subscription cannot be used to create a storage account.

2. When the terminal connects, enter the command **az --version**. What version of Azure CLI is your Cloud Shell using? Notice that Azure also gives version information for its components, such as SSH and Python.

You're now ready to practice using your Azure Cloud Shell. Complete the following steps:

3. Enter **az --help**. Near the top of the list, what command allows you to manage your Azure subscription information?
4. Refer to Table 10-3 earlier in the module for some common Azure commands. Request some commonly used commands containing the text *vm*. What command did you enter?

Before creating other resources, you need to create a new resource group. It's important to place this resource group in a region that supports the type of automation used in this project. For simplicity's sake, you'll use West US 2. Complete the following step:

5. Use Cloud Shell to create a resource group. Enter the following command, using your own name for your resource group:

```
az group create -l westus2 -n MyNewRG
```

Now you're ready to create a VM using the Cloud Shell. Complete the following steps:

6. Use Cloud Shell to create a VM instance. You'll need the following information to create your command:

   - Start with the command text:

   ```
   az vm create -n NewVM -g MyNewRG --image Win2019Datacenter --size
   Standard_B1s --public-ip-sku Standard --admin-username thisisme --admin-
   password MyP@ssword123
   ```

   - Replace the resource group name with your resource group you created in Step 5.
   - If desired, you can replace the provided text with other text, such as the VM's name or the admin password.
   - What command did you run that successfully deployed a VM instance?

Note 8

It might feel inconvenient to find the required information and type a long command the first time you run a command like this, such as finding an image name or instance size. However, once you collect this information, you can repeat this command many times much faster than working through the console over and over. Once your command is created, you can repeat this activity as many times as needed, knowing that every resource will receive exactly the same configuration information.

When your deployment is complete, you're ready to enable update management on this VM using the portal. Complete the following steps:

7. Close the Cloud Shell pane and go to the **Virtual machines** blade. Click the new VM in the list. If you see a message saying the VM's agent status is not ready, wait until it is. (Navigate away from this screen and back to it every few minutes to get update information, as the Refresh button does not affect the message.) In the VM's navigation pane, click **Guest + host updates**, and then click **Go to Update management**. Leave all default selections, which will create a new default Log Analytics workspace and a new default Automation account. Click **Enable**.
8. Wait until the solution is enabled. Note that you might get an error message; however, there is a good chance the process succeeded. On the **All services** blade, in the **Analytics** category, click **Log Analytics workspaces**. Click the workspace listed, and then click **Virtual machines** in the workspace's navigation pane. If your VM is listed here, update management is likely enabled.

Hands-On Projects Continued

Now you're ready to schedule ongoing, automatic updates. Complete the following steps:

9. On the **All services** blade, in the **Management and governance** category, click **Automation Accounts**. Click the Automation account listed, click **Update management** in the account's navigation pane, and then click **Schedule update deployment**.

10. Give the update deployment a name, such as MyUpdates. Click under Groups to update, select your subscription, select the resource group you created in Step 5, click **Add**, and click **OK**.

11. Click the dropdown list to show available update classifications. What classifications are listed? Deselect all update classifications except **Critical updates** and **Security updates**.

12. Click under Schedule settings and leave the default start time. Under Recurrence, click **Recurring**. Set the update deployment to occur every **1** week on **Sunday**, and then click **OK**.

13. You won't use Pre-scripts or Post-scripts in this project. However, these features can be used to accomplish certain tasks immediately before or after the update deployment. For example, you might want to shut down a VM before applying an update. Set the Maintenance window to **300** minutes, and then click **Create**.

The update information will take several minutes to register. In the meantime, let's explore what resources you've created so far. Complete the following steps:

14. Go to the list of resource groups. You created one resource group in Step 1 so you could use Cloud Shell. Which resource group contains this storage account?

15. You created another resource group in Step 5. What is the name of that resource group?

16. Looking at the other resource groups listed, which one was created by default in Step 7?

17. What resources are listed in this default resource group that are not typically included in a resource group when you simply create a new VM?

18. By now, your updates should have registered with the Automation account. Return to your Automation account's Update management blade. If your VM is not yet listed, wait a few more minutes. What updates is your machine missing? Note that you might need to wait a few more minutes after the VM appears in the list until needed update information is reported. If you were to leave these resources running, where would the completed deployments be listed?

Now you're ready to delete the resources created in this project using both Cloud Shell and the portal. Complete the following steps:

19. In Cloud Shell, enter the following command, replacing the appropriate text with your resource group name and your VM's name:

```
az vm delete -g MyNewRG -n NewVM --yes
```

20. Use Cloud Shell to show that your VM has been deleted. **Take a screenshot** of the command you used and the output showing your VM no longer exists; submit this visual with your answers to this project's questions.

21. Use Cloud Shell to delete the resource group you created in Step 5. What command did you use?

22. Delete the remaining resources you created in this project by deleting the default resource group you created in Step 7. You might want to leave the Cloud Shell storage resource group for future use. Check through your account to confirm that all other resources have been deleted.

Note 9

Depending on the status of your account and the selections you made during this project, the resources you created can deplete your credits or accrue charges. Double-check to make sure you've terminated all resources you created in this project.

Project 10-4: Automated Patching in GCP

Estimated time: 1 hour
Objective 4.2: Given a scenario, maintain efficient operation of a cloud environment.
Resources:

- GCP account
- Internet access

Context:

The Google Cloud Shell is a GCP service that allows you to use a CLI from within the GCP console to interact with resources and services. Practicing with Cloud Shell will give you some idea of how IaC scripting works. In this project, you'll enable Cloud Shell and practice some commands, including creating a Compute Engine instance. You'll then use the console to configure automated patching on your instance.

Complete the following steps:

1. In your GCP console, create a new project, and switch to the new project.
2. At the top of your GCP console, click **Activate Cloud Shell**. When the Cloud Shell pane opens, if necessary, close the information box by clicking **Got it!**
3. Enter the command `gcloud --version`. Notice you're given version numbers for several components. What is your version of Google Cloud SDK? What is your version of gsutil?

You're now ready to start using gcloud. Complete the following steps:

4. Enter the command `help`. Enter the command `gcloud help`. Press the **Spacebar** to keep moving forward. When you're ready, type **q** to quit.
5. Refer to Table 10-4 earlier in the module for some common gcloud commands. Request information on any running instances. What command did you enter? Authorize use of your credentials or enable APIs, if needed.

Now you're ready to create a new VM instance using Cloud Shell. Complete the following steps:

6. Use the Cloud Shell to deploy a Compute Engine instance. You'll need the following information to create your command:

    - Start with the command text:

      ```
      gcloud compute instances create my-instance --zone=us-east1-b
      --image-family=ubuntu-2004-lts --image-project=ubuntu-os-cloud
      --machine-type=e2-micro
      ```
    - If desired, you can replace the instance name with a different name.
    - What command did you run that successfully deployed a VM instance?

> ## Note 10
>
> It might feel inconvenient to find the required information and type a long command the first time you run a command like this, such as finding an image name or instance size. However, once you collect this information, you can repeat this command many times much faster than working through the console over and over. Once your command is created, you can repeat this activity as many times as needed, knowing that every resource will receive exactly the same configuration information.

When your deployment is complete, you're ready to enable VM Manager in your project. Complete the following steps:

7. Close the Cloud Shell pane and go to the list of **VM instances** in Compute Engine. VM Manager can be enabled automatically by visiting any VM Manager page. In the navigation pane, under VM Manager, click **OS patch management**. On the OS patch management page, scroll down, if necessary, and click **ENABLE VM MANAGER**.

Hands-On Projects Continued

8. After VM Manager is enabled, click the **VM INSTANCES** tab. Notice that no VM instances are listed yet. This is because there is one more step that must be completed manually before management can begin. In your Cloud Shell, enter the following command to enable the OS Config service API:

```
gcloud services enable osconfig.googleapis.com
```

You might need to wait several minutes (even up to an hour) for the VM to show up in your OS patch management list. Once it does, you're ready to schedule a patch deployment. Complete the following steps:

9. Click **NEW PATCH DEPLOYMENT**. Select VM instances manually and choose your VM. Click **NEXT**. Give the deployment a name, and then click **NEXT**.
10. Schedule a recurring patch deployment for **Sundays** at **2:00 AM** with a **60** minute maintenance window. Click **NEXT**.
11. Leave all other default settings and complete the deployment.
12. If you were to leave these resources in place, your completed patch deployment would show on the PATCH JOBS tab. On which tab would you be able to edit this deployment or run it now?

Now you're ready to delete the resources created in this project using the Cloud Shell. Complete the following steps:

13. In Cloud Shell, enter the following command, replacing the appropriate text with your VM's name and zone:

```
gcloud compute instances delete my-instance --zone=us-east1-b
```

14. Use Cloud Shell to show that your VM has been deleted. **Take a screenshot** of the command you used and the output showing your VM no longer exists; submit this visual with your answers to this project's questions.
15. Use Cloud Shell to delete the project you created in Step 1. What command did you use?
16. Check through your account to confirm that the project is deleted and no related resources were created outside of that project.

Note 11

Depending on the status of your account and the selections you made during this project, the resources you created can deplete your credits or accrue charges. Double-check to make sure you've terminated all resources you created in this project.

Capstone Project 10: Create a Cloud Deployment

Note 12

Websites, applications, public cloud platforms, and related account options change often. While the instructions given in these projects were accurate at the time of writing, you might need to adjust the steps or options according to later changes.

Note to Instructors and Students: A rubric is provided for evaluating student performance on these projects. Please see Appendix D.

Estimated time: 90 minutes

Objective 3.1: Given a scenario, integrate components into a cloud solution.

Group work: This project includes enhancements when assigned as a group project.

Resources:

- Public cloud account (such as AWS, Azure, or GCP)
- Drawing app, such as Visio or app.diagrams.net
- Internet access

(continues)

Context:

Throughout this course, you've learned to deploy compute, networking, security, and storage resources. In this final Capstone Project, you will combine your skills from previous modules to create a complete cloud deployment. Complete the following steps:

1. Choose a public cloud platform. Ensure you have MFA enabled on your root account. **Take a screenshot** showing where MFA is required; submit this visual with your responses to this project's questions.

2. Create a storage container or bucket that contains a static website. Use the sample website text from Capstone Project 8 as a starting point. However, make significant changes to the code to ensure your website is unique and reflects some of the information you have learned in this course. For example, you should change the name of the webpage and insert text identifying yourself. You might also include a statement or two about what you have learned, what more you would like to learn, or how this webpage fits into your cloud deployment for this Capstone Project. Open the webpage in a separate tab and **take a screenshot** of your webpage; submit this visual with your responses to this project's questions.

3. Create a VPC, VNet, or subnet with Internet access. Refer to Module 4 for guidance on how to give resources within a VPC, VNet, or subnet access to the Internet. For example, in AWS, you need an Internet gateway and a related route. Create a second VPC, VNet, or subnet that does NOT have access to the Internet. Make sure the IP address spaces for these two networks do not overlap. Create a peering connection between them. Refer to Capstone Project 5 for guidance on creating a peering connection. **Take a screenshot** showing the peering connection; submit this visual with your responses to this project's questions.

4. Deploy a VM in each VPC, VNet, or subnet so that one has access to the Internet and the other one does not. Refer to Module 2 for a review of how to deploy VM instances. Make sure one instance is deployed in your public VPC, VNet, or subnet; place the other instance in your private VPC, VNet, or subnet. Use a drawing app, such as Visio or app.diagrams.net, to **draw a network diagram** showing the VPCs/VNets/subnets and their resources, with logical connections, CIDR ranges, gateways, firewall rules, and relative position of each resource. This diagram does not need to be complex but should give another person an accurate understanding of the relationships between your deployed resources.

5. Make sure both VMs can send and receive pings. Recall this means you will need to allow ICMP into each VPC, VNet, or subnet. Refer to the projects in Module 6 to review how to make these changes. For each VM, ping a location on the Internet (such as Google's DNS server at 8.8.8.8) to prove one VM has access to the Internet and the other one does not. **Take screenshots** showing the ping output for each VM; submit these visuals with your responses to this project's questions.

6. Apply an alert or alarm, or enable automatic updates for one of the VMs. Refer to projects in Module 9 for guidance on how to do this. **Take a screenshot** showing this configuration; submit this visual with your responses to this project's questions.

7. Use your cloud platform's pricing tools to calculate the cost of your deployment for one year. Refer to Module 3 for reminders on how to use each cloud platform's pricing calculators. **Take a screenshot** of your results; submit this visual with your responses to this project's questions.

8. Fully document your entire deployment. If you used all free tier resources, or if you are using an AWS Academy account, your instructor might want you to preserve your deployment for now. You can also document your deployment so that you could display your work in a portfolio or during a job interview. You might use screenshots along with your network diagram. You might also export configuration files, snapshots, or image files for one or more of your resources for later use. This portion of the project is not graded so you can think through how best to collect and organize this information for your purposes. The information will be relevant for you in your job applications and in your future cloud work. One of the best ways to impress employers during a job interview is to show evidence like this of your practical skills.

9. **For group assignments**: Practice presenting your full cloud deployment to one or more group members as you would during a job interview. Assume your audience knows nothing of your deployment, and give a sufficient overview using diagrams and demonstrations so your audience can understand the resources and how they are related. Highlight the skills you acquired to design this deployment. Be prepared to

Hands-On Projects Continued

answer questions. When you are part of the audience for another group member's presentation, ask at least one question to clarify anything you don't understand about their deployment. What questions were you asked during your presentation, and how did you answer these questions? What questions do you think you should prepare for if you were to present this deployment during a job interview?

10. When you're finished with the deployment, delete all resources. Check through your account to confirm no resources are continuing to drain credits or accrue charges.

> **Note 13**
>
> Depending on the status of your account and the selections you made during this project, the resources you created can deplete your credits or accrue charges. Double-check to make sure you've terminated all resources you created in this project.

Solutions to Self-Check Questions

Section 10-1: Automation Workflow

1. Automation increases _____.

   Answer: c. security

   Explanation: A well-orchestrated system is much less likely to suffer from vulnerabilities due to misconfigurations and other human error, thus increasing security.

2. Which CM tool does not require installation of an agent?

   Answer: b. Ansible

   Explanation: Ansible requires no agent installation on managed nodes and, instead, connects to these nodes via SSH by default.

3. Which process is most directly responsible for Siri's ability to answer a spoken question?

   Answer: d. AI

   Explanation: AI (artificial intelligence) refers to a computer's ability to adapt its behavior according to ongoing input, such as a spoken question.

Section 10-2: Cloud Maintenance Processes

4. What factor primarily determines the division of responsibility for maintenance tasks?

   Answer: b. Service model

   Explanation: The responsibility for maintenance tasks will vary by cloud service model, just as the responsibility for security varies.

5. What is the opposite of an update?

   Answer: d. Rollback

   Explanation: The opposite of an update is a rollback. When an update causes a problem, a rollback will revert the system to its state from before the update was applied.

6. What lifecycle feature would enable you to deploy an earlier state of a web server's configuration?

   Answer: b. Versioning

   Explanation: Versioning tracks changes along the way so historical changes can be referenced.

Section 10-3: Cloud Automation Services

7. What software provides a bridge of communication between an OS and an update automation tool?

   Answer: a. Agent

   Explanation: An agent uses built-in OS utilities to retrieve files for an update, apply the update, adjust the VM's state, or collect logs on the VM. It handles communications with the update automation or CM (configuration management) tool.

8. What text initiates communication with an installed CLI application?

   Answer: b. Base call

   Explanation: Most of the common cloud CLIs' command syntax begin with a base call to the cloud program, such as aws for the AWS CLI and az for the Azure CLI.

Section 10-4: Troubleshooting Automation Issues

9. An improperly documented server name change is a type of _____.

   Answer: d. change management failure

   Explanation: Improperly documented server name, IP address, or location changes might be caused by a change management failure.

10. What is caused by manual portions of a workflow?

    Answer: b. Bottleneck

    Explanation: Incomplete automated workflows apply automation for part of the process but not all of it; this causes bottlenecks in the workflow and continuing issues with errors.

Appendix A

CompTIA Cloud+ Exam Objectives Mapped to Modules

These tables provide a complete list of the latest CompTIA Cloud+ CVO-003 certification exam objectives. The official list of objectives is available at CompTIA's website, *comptia.org*. For your reference, the following tables list each exam objective and the module and section that explains the objective, plus the amount of the exam that will cover each certification domain.

Domain 1.0 Cloud Architecture and Design—13% of Examination

1.1   Compare and contrast the different types of cloud models.

Objective	Module	Section
• Deployment models	1	Section 1-2: Cloud Deployment Models
– Public	1	Section 1-2: Cloud Deployment Models
– Private	1	Section 1-2: Cloud Deployment Models
– Hybrid	1	Section 1-2: Cloud Deployment Models
	5	Section 5-1: Hybrid Cloud and Multi-Cloud Networking
– Community	1	Section 1-2: Cloud Deployment Models
– Cloud within a cloud	1	Section 1-2: Cloud Deployment Models
– Multicloud	1	Section 1-2: Cloud Deployment Models
	5	Section 5-1: Hybrid Cloud and Multi-Cloud Networking
– Multitenancy	1	Section 1-2: Cloud Deployment Models
• Service models	1	Section 1-3: Cloud Service Models
– Infrastructure as a Service (IaaS)	1	Section 1-3: Cloud Service Models
– Platform as a Service (PaaS)	1	Section 1-3: Cloud Service Models
– Software as a Service (SaaS)	1	Section 1-3: Cloud Service Models
• Advanced cloud services	10	Section 10-1: Automation Workflow
– Internet of Things (IoT)	1	Section 1-4: Cloud Service Providers

(continues)

1.1   Compare and contrast the different types of cloud models. *(Continued)*

Objective	Module	Section
– Serverless	2	Section 2-4: VM Alternatives
– Machine learning/Artificial intelligence (AI)	10	Section 10-1: Automation Workflow
• Shared responsibility model	6	Section 6-1: Cloud Security Configurations

1.2   Explain the factors that contribute to capacity planning.

Objective	Module	Section
• Requirements	2	Section 2-1: Virtualization Technologies
– Hardware	2	Section 2-1: Virtualization Technologies Section 2-3: VMs in the Cloud
– Software	2	Section 2-1: Virtualization Technologies Section 2-3: VMs in the Cloud
	3	Section 3-1: Migration Planning
– Budgetary	9	Section 9-1: Monitoring Resources
– Business need analysis	9	Section 9-1: Monitoring Resources
• Standard templates	2	Section 2-3: VMs in the Cloud
• Licensing	2	Section 2-2: Virtualized Processing and Memory
– Per-user	2	Section 2-2: Virtualized Processing and Memory
– Socket-based	2	Section 2-2: Virtualized Processing and Memory
– Volume-based	2	Section 2-2: Virtualized Processing and Memory
– Core-based	2	Section 2-2: Virtualized Processing and Memory
– Subscription	3	Section 3-3: Deployment Testing and Validation
• User density	9	Section 9-1: Monitoring Resources
• System load	9	Section 9-1: Monitoring Resources
• Trend analysis	9	Section 9-1: Monitoring Resources
– Baselines	9	Section 9-3: Analysis and Response
– Patterns	9	Section 9-2: Events and Logs
– Anomalies	9	Section 9-2: Events and Logs
• Performance capacity planning	3	Section 3-5: Planning for Problems

1.3   Explain the importance of high availability and scaling in cloud environments.

Objective	Module	Section
• Hypervisors	2	Section 2-1: Virtualization Technologies
– Affinity	2	Section 2-3: VMs in the Cloud
– Anti-affinity	2	Section 2-3: VMs in the Cloud
• Oversubscription	2	Section 2-2: Virtualized Processing and Memory
– Compute	2	Section 2-2: Virtualized Processing and Memory
– Network	5	Section 5-1: Hybrid Cloud and Multi-Cloud Networking
– Storage	8	Section 8-2: Storage Optimization Techniques

Objective	Module	Section
• Regions and zones	8	Section 8-3: Cloud Storage Services
		Section 8-5: Storage Security
• Applications	2	Section 2-4: VM Alternatives
• Containers	2	Section 2-4: VM Alternatives
• Clusters	5	Section 5-2: Extending Network Services
• High availability of network functions	4	Section 4-1: Networking Concepts in the Cloud
	5	Section 5-2: Extending Network Services
– Switches	4	Section 4-1: Networking Concepts in the Cloud
– Routers	4	Section 4-1: Networking Concepts in the Cloud
– Load balancers	5	Section 5-2: Extending Network Services
– Firewalls	6	Section 6-2: Virtual Network Security
• Avoid single points of failure	8	Section 8-4: Creating and Storing Backups
• Scalability	1	Section 1-2: Cloud Deployment Models
	3	Section 3-3: Deployment Testing and Validation
– Auto-scaling	3	Section 3-3: Deployment Testing and Validation
		Section 3-5: Planning for Problems
– Horizontal scaling	3	Section 3-5: Planning for Problems
– Vertical scaling	3	Section 3-5: Planning for Problems
– Cloud bursting	9	Section 9-3: Analysis and Response

1.4   Given a scenario, analyze the solution design in support of the business requirements.

Objective	Module	Section
• Requirement analysis	3	Section 3-1: Migration Planning
– Software	3	Section 3-1: Migration Planning
– Hardware	3	Section 3-1: Migration Planning
– Integration	3	Section 3-1: Migration Planning
– Budgetary	3	Section 3-1: Migration Planning
– Compliance	1	Section 1-2: Cloud Deployment Models
	8	Section 8-2: Storage Optimization Techniques
		Section 8-5: Storage Security
– Service-level agreement (SLA)	3	Section 3-3: Deployment Testing and Validation
– User and business needs	1	Section 1-1: Characteristics of Cloud Computing
– Security	1	Section 1-3: Cloud Service Models
	6	Section 6-1: Cloud Security Configurations
– Network requirements	4	Section 4-2: IP Address Spaces
▪ Sizing	4	Section 4-2: IP Address Spaces
▪ Subnetting	4	Section 4-2: IP Address Spaces
▪ Routing	5	Section 5-2: Extending Network Services

(continues)

1.4   Given a scenario, analyze the solution design in support of the business requirements. *(Continued)*

Objective	Module	Section
• Environments	3	Section 3-5: Planning for Problems
	10	Section 10-1: Automation Workflow
– Development	10	Section 10-1: Automation Workflow
– Quality assurance (QA)	10	Section 10-1: Automation Workflow
– Staging	10	Section 10-1: Automation Workflow
– Blue-green	10	Section 10-1: Automation Workflow
– Production	10	Section 10-1: Automation Workflow
– Disaster recovery (DR)	3	Section 3-5: Planning for Problems
• Testing techniques	3	Section 3-3: Deployment Testing and Validation
– Vulnerability testing	3	Section 3-3: Deployment Testing and Validation
– Penetration testing	3	Section 3-3: Deployment Testing and Validation
– Performance testing	3	Section 3-3: Deployment Testing and Validation
– Regression testing	3	Section 3-3: Deployment Testing and Validation
– Functional testing	3	Section 3-3: Deployment Testing and Validation
– Usability testing	3	Section 3-3: Deployment Testing and Validation

Domain 2.0 Security—20% of Examination

2.1   Given a scenario, configure identity and access management.

Objective	Module	Section
• Identification and authorization	7	Section 7-1: Cloud Accounts
		Section 7-3: Authorization to Cloud Objects
– Privileged access management	7	Section 7-1: Cloud Accounts
– Logical access management	7	Section 7-1: Cloud Accounts
– Account life-cycle management	6	Section 6-1: Cloud Security Configurations
	7	Section 7-1: Cloud Accounts
▪ Provision and deprovision accounts	7	Section 7-1: Cloud Accounts
– Access controls	7	Section 7-3: Authorization to Cloud Objects
▪ Role-based	7	Section 7-3: Authorization to Cloud Objects
▪ Discretionary	7	Section 7-3: Authorization to Cloud Objects
▪ Non-discretionary	7	Section 7-3: Authorization to Cloud Objects
▪ Mandatory	7	Section 7-3: Authorization to Cloud Objects
• Directory services	7	Section 7-2: Authentication
		Section 7-4: IAM for Hybrid Clouds
– Lightweight directory access protocol (LDAP)	7	Section 7-2: Authentication
• Federation	7	Section 7-2: Authentication
		Section 7-4: IAM for Hybrid Clouds
• Certificate management	7	Section 7-2: Authentication

Objective	Module	Section
• Multifactor authentication (MFA)	7	Section 7-2: Authentication
• Single sign-on (SSO)	7	Section 7-2: Authentication
– Security assertion markup language (SAML)	7	Section 7-2: Authentication
• Public key infrastructure (PKI)	7	Section 7-2: Authentication
• Secret management	7	Section 7-2: Authentication
• Key management	6	Section 6-5: Troubleshooting Cloud Security
	7	Section 7-2: Authentication

2.2   Given a scenario, secure a network in a cloud environment.

Objective	Module	Section
• Network segmentation	4	Section 4-3: Networking in AWS
– Virtual LAN (VLAN)/Virtual extensible LAN (VXLAN)/Generic network virtualization encapsulation (GENEVE)	5	Section 5-1: Hybrid Cloud and Multi-Cloud Networking
– Micro-segmentation	6	Section 6-1: Cloud Security Configurations
– Tiering	4	Section 4-3: Networking in AWS
• Protocols	5	Section 5-1: Hybrid Cloud and Multi-Cloud Networking
		Section 5-2: Extending Network Services
	6	Section 6-4: Data Security
– Domain name service (DNS)	5	Section 5-2: Extending Network Services
	6	Section 6-4: Data Security
▪ DNS over HTTPS (DoH)/DNS over TLS (DoT)	6	Section 6-4: Data Security
▪ DNS security (DNSSEC)	6	Section 6-4: Data Security
– Network time protocol (NTP)	6	Section 6-4: Data Security
▪ Network time security (NTS)	6	Section 6-4: Data Security
– Encryption	5	Section 5-1: Hybrid Cloud and Multi-Cloud Networking
	6	Section 6-4: Data Security
▪ IPSec	5	Section 5-1: Hybrid Cloud and Multi-Cloud Networking
▪ Transport layer security (TLS)	6	Section 6-4: Data Security
▪ Hypertext transfer protocol secure (HTTPS)	6	Section 6-4: Data Security
– Tunneling	5	Section 5-3: Troubleshooting Cloud Connectivity
▪ Secure Shell (SSH)	5	Section 5-1: Hybrid Cloud and Multi-Cloud Networking
		Section 5-3: Troubleshooting Cloud Connectivity
▪ Layer 2 tunneling protocol (L2TP)/Point-to-point tunneling protocol (PPTP)	5	Section 5-1: Hybrid Cloud and Multi-Cloud Networking
▪ Generic routing encapsulation (GRE)	5	Section 5-1: Hybrid Cloud and Multi-Cloud Networking
• Network services	6	Section 6-2: Virtual Network Security
– Firewalls	6	Section 6-2: Virtual Network Security

(continues)

2.2   Given a scenario, secure a network in a cloud environment. *(Continued)*

Objective	Module	Section
▪ Stateful	6	Section 6-2: Virtual Network Security
▪ Stateless	6	Section 6-2: Virtual Network Security
– Web application firewall (WAF)	6	Section 6-3: Compute Security
– Application delivery controller (ADC)	6	Section 6-3: Compute Security
– Intrusion protection system (IPS)/Intrusion detection system (IDS)	6 10	Section 6-2: Virtual Network Security Section 10-2: Cloud Maintenance Processes
– Date loss prevention (DLP)	6	Section 6-4: Data Security
– Network access control (NAC)	6	Section 6-2: Virtual Network Security
– Packet brokers	9	Section 9-1: Monitoring Resources
• Log and event monitoring	9	Section 9-2: Events and Logs
• Network flows	6	Section 6-2: Virtual Network Security
• Hardening and configuration changes	5 6	Section 5-3: Troubleshooting Cloud Connectivity Section 6-3: Compute Security
– Disabling unnecessary ports and services	6	Section 6-3: Compute Security Section 6-4: Data Security
– Disabling weak protocols and ciphers	6	Section 6-4: Data Security
– Firmware upgrades	6	Section 6-3: Compute Security
– Control ingress and egress traffic	5 6	Section 5-3: Troubleshooting Cloud Connectivity Section 6-2: Virtual Network Security
▪ Allow list (previously known as whitelisting) or blocklist (previously known as blacklisting)	6	Section 6-2: Virtual Network Security
▪ Proxy servers	5	Section 5-3: Troubleshooting Cloud Connectivity
– Distributed denial of service (DDoS) protection	6	Section 6-2: Virtual Network Security Section 6-3: Compute Security

2.3   Given a scenario, apply the appropriate OS and application security controls.

Objective	Module	Section
• Policies	6	Section 6-1: Cloud Security Configurations
– Password complexity	7	Section 7-2: Authentication
– Account lockout	7	Section 7-2: Authentication
– Application approved list (previously known as whitelisting)	6	Section 6-1: Cloud Security Configurations
– Software feature	6	Section 6-1: Cloud Security Configurations
– User/group	7 8	Section 7-3: Authorization to Cloud Objects Section 8-2: Storage Optimization Techniques Section 8-5: Storage Security
• User permissions	7 10	Section 7-1: Cloud Accounts Section 7-3: Authorization to Cloud Objects Section 10-2: Cloud Maintenance Processes

Objective	Module	Section
• Antivirus/anti-malware/endpoint detection and response (EDR)	6	Section 6-3: Compute Security
• Host-based IDS (HIDS)/Host-based IPS (HIPS)	6	Section 6-3: Compute Security
	10	Section 10-2: Cloud Maintenance Processes
• Hardened baselines	6	Section 6-3: Compute Security
– Single function	6	Section 6-3: Compute Security
• File integrity	7	Section 7-2: Authentication
	10	Section 10-2: Cloud Maintenance Processes
• Log and event monitoring	9	Section 9-2: Events and Logs
• Configuration management	10	Section 10-1: Automation Workflow
		Section 10-3: Cloud Automation Services
• Builds	3	Section 3-4: Cloud Agility
– Stable	3	Section 3-4: Cloud Agility
– Long-term support (LTS)	3	Section 3-4: Cloud Agility
– Beta	3	Section 3-4: Cloud Agility
– Canary	3	Section 3-4: Cloud Agility
• Operating system (OS) upgrades	6	Section 6-3: Compute Security
• Encryption	6	Section 6-4: Data Security
– Application programming interface (API) endpoint	6	Section 6-4: Data Security
– Application	6	Section 6-4: Data Security
– OS	6	Section 6-4: Data Security
– Storage	6	Section 6-4: Data Security
– Filesystem	8	Section 8-3: Cloud Storage Services
		Section 8-4: Creating and Storing Backups
• Mandatory access control	7	Section 7-3: Authorization to Cloud Objects
• Software firewall	6	Section 6-3: Compute Security

2.4   Given a scenario, apply data security and compliance controls in cloud environments.

Objective	Module	Section
• Encryption	6	Section 6-4: Data Security
• Integrity	6	Section 6-4: Data Security
	10	Section 10-2: Cloud Maintenance Processes
– Hashing algorithms	6	Section 6-4: Data Security
– Digital signatures	7	Section 7-2: Authentication
– File integrity monitoring (FIM)	10	Section 10-2: Cloud Maintenance Processes
• Classification	7	Section 7-3: Authorization to Cloud Objects

(continues)

2.4   Given a scenario, apply data security and compliance controls in cloud environments. *(Continued)*

Objective	Module	Section
• Segmentation	4	Section 4-3: Networking in AWS
		Section 4-4: Networking in Azure
		Section 4-5: Networking in GCP
	6	Section 6-1: Cloud Security Configurations
• Access control	7	Section 7-3: Authorization to Cloud Objects
• Impact of laws and regulations	1	Section 1-2: Cloud Deployment Models
– Legal hold	8	Section 8-2: Storage Optimization Techniques
• Records management	8	Section 8-1: Storage Types
		Section 8-2: Storage Optimization Techniques
– Versioning	8	Section 8-2: Storage Optimization Techniques
– Retention	8	Section 8-2: Storage Optimization Techniques
– Destruction	8	Section 8-2: Storage Optimization Techniques
– Write once read many	8	Section 8-1: Storage Types
• Data loss prevention (DLP)	6	Section 6-4: Data Security
• Cloud access security broker (CASB)	6	Section 6-2: Virtual Network Security

2.5   Given a scenario, implement measures to meet security requirements.

Objective	Module	Section
• Tools	6	Section 6-1: Cloud Security Configurations
– Vulnerability scanners	6	Section 6-1: Cloud Security Configurations
– Port scanners	6	Section 6-1: Cloud Security Configurations
• Vulnerability assessment	3	Section 3-3: Deployment Testing and Validation
	6	Section 6-1: Cloud Security Configurations
– Default and common credential scans	6	Section 6-1: Cloud Security Configurations
– Credentialed scans	6	Section 6-1: Cloud Security Configurations
– Network-based scans	6	Section 6-1: Cloud Security Configurations
– Agent-based scans	6	Section 6-1: Cloud Security Configurations
	9	Section 9-1: Monitoring Resources
		Section 9-3: Analysis and Response
– Service availabilities	6	Section 6-1: Cloud Security Configurations
• Security patches	10	Section 10-2: Cloud Maintenance Processes
– Hot fixes	10	Section 10-2: Cloud Maintenance Processes
– Scheduled updates	10	Section 10-2: Cloud Maintenance Processes
		Section 10-3: Cloud Automation Services
– Virtual patches	10	Section 10-2: Cloud Maintenance Processes
– Signature updates	10	Section 10-2: Cloud Maintenance Processes
– Rollups	10	Section 10-2: Cloud Maintenance Processes
• Risk register	6	Section 6-1: Cloud Security Configurations

Objective	Module	Section
• Prioritization of patch application	10	Section 10-2: Cloud Maintenance Processes
• Deactivate default accounts	6	Section 6-3: Compute Security
	7	Section 7-1: Cloud Accounts
• Impacts of security tools on systems and services	6	Section 6-5: Troubleshooting Cloud Security
• Effects of cloud service models on security implementation	1	Section 1-3: Cloud Service Models

2.6   Explain the importance of incident response procedures.

Objective	Module	Section
• Preparation	3	Section 3-5: Planning for Problems
– Documentation	3	Section 3-5: Planning for Problems
– Call trees	3	Section 3-5: Planning for Problems
– Training	3	Section 3-5: Planning for Problems
– Tabletops	3	Section 3-5: Planning for Problems
– Documented incident types/categories	3	Section 3-5: Planning for Problems
– Roles and responsibilities	3	Section 3-5: Planning for Problems
• Incident response procedures	3	Section 3-5: Planning for Problems
– Identification	3	Section 3-5: Planning for Problems
▪ Scope	3	Section 3-5: Planning for Problems
– Investigation	3	Section 3-5: Planning for Problems
– Containment, eradication, and recovery	3	Section 3-5: Planning for Problems
▪ Isolation	3	Section 3-5: Planning for Problems
▪ Evidence acquisition	3	Section 3-5: Planning for Problems
▪ Chain of custody	3	Section 3-5: Planning for Problems
– Post-incident and lessons learned	3	Section 3-5: Planning for Problems
▪ Root cause analysis	3	Section 3-5: Planning for Problems

Domain 3.0 Deployment—23% of Examination

3.1   Given a scenario, integrate components into a cloud solution.

Objective	Module	Section
• Subscription services	3	Section 3-3: Deployment Testing and Validation
– File subscriptions	3	Section 3-3: Deployment Testing and Validation
– Communications	3	Section 3-3: Deployment Testing and Validation
	9	Section 9-3: Analysis and Response
▪ Email	3	Section 3-3: Deployment Testing and Validation
	9	Section 9-3: Analysis and Response
▪ Voice over IP (VoIP)	3	Section 3-3: Deployment Testing and Validation

3.1   Given a scenario, integrate components into a cloud solution. *(Continued)*

Objective	Module	Section
▪ Messaging	3	Section 3-3: Deployment Testing and Validation
	9	Section 9-3: Analysis and Response
– Collaboration	3	Section 3-3: Deployment Testing and Validation
– Virtual desktop infrastructure (VDI)	2	Section 2-1: Virtualization Technologies
– Directory and identity services	7	Section 7-2: Authentication
– Cloud resources	10	Section 10-2: Cloud Maintenance Processes
▪ IaaS	10	Section 10-2: Cloud Maintenance Processes
▪ PaaS	10	Section 10-2: Cloud Maintenance Processes
▪ SaaS	10	Section 10-2: Cloud Maintenance Processes
● Provisioning resources	2	Section 2-3: VMs in the Cloud
	3	Section 3-1: Migration Planning
– Compute	2	Section 2-3: VMs in the Cloud
	3	Section 3-1: Migration Planning
– Storage	3	Section 3-1: Migration Planning
	8	Section 8-2: Storage Optimization Techniques
		Section 8-3: Cloud Storage Services
– Network	4	Section 4-2: IP Address Spaces
		Section 4-3: Networking in AWS
		Section 4-4: Networking in Azure
		Section 4-5: Networking in GCP
● Application	2	Section 2-4: VM Alternatives
	3	Section 3-4: Cloud Agility
– Serverless	2	Section 2-4: VM Alternatives
● Deploying virtual machines (VMs) and custom images	2	Section 2-3: VMs in the Cloud
● Templates	2	Section 2-3: VMs in the Cloud
	10	Section 10-1: Automation Workflow
– OS templates	2	Section 2-3: VMs in the Cloud
– Solution templates	10	Section 10-1: Automation Workflow
● Identity management	7	Section 7-3: Authorization to Cloud Objects
		Section 7-4: IAM for Hybrid Clouds
● Containers	2	Section 2-4: VM Alternatives
– Configure variables	2	Section 2-4: VM Alternatives
– Configure secrets	2	Section 2-4: VM Alternatives
– Persistent storage	2	Section 2-4: VM Alternatives
● Auto-scaling	3	Section 3-3: Deployment Testing and Validation
		Section 3-5: Planning for Problems
● Post-deployment validation	10	Section 10-2: Cloud Maintenance Processes

3.2   Given a scenario, provision storage in cloud environments.

Objective	Module	Section
• Types	8	Section 8-1: Storage Types
– Block	8	Section 8-1: Storage Types
		Section 8-3: Cloud Storage Services
▪ Storage area network (SAN)	8	Section 8-1: Storage Types
○ Zoning	8	Section 8-1: Storage Types
– File	8	Section 8-1: Storage Types
		Section 8-3: Cloud Storage Services
▪ Network attached storage (NAS)	8	Section 8-1: Storage Types
– Object	8	Section 8-1: Storage Types
		Section 8-3: Cloud Storage Services
▪ Tenants	8	Section 8-2: Storage Optimization Techniques
▪ Buckets	8	Section 8-3: Cloud Storage Services
• Tiers	8	Section 8-2: Storage Optimization Techniques
		Section 8-3: Cloud Storage Services
– Flash	8	Section 8-2: Storage Optimization Techniques
– Hybrid	8	Section 8-2: Storage Optimization Techniques
– Spinning disks	8	Section 8-4: Creating and Storing Backups
– Long-term	8	Section 8-2: Storage Optimization Techniques
• Input/output operations per second (IOPS) and read/write	8	Section 8-2: Storage Optimization Techniques
• Protocols	8	Section 8-1: Storage Types
– Network file system (NFS)	8	Section 8-1: Storage Types
– Common internet file system (CIFS)	8	Section 8-1: Storage Types
– Internet small computer system interface (iSCSI)	8	Section 8-1: Storage Types
– Fibre Channel (FC)	8	Section 8-1: Storage Types
– Non-volatile memory express over fabrics (NVMe-oF)	8	Section 8-1: Storage Types
• Redundant array of inexpensive disks (RAID)	8	Section 8-1: Storage Types
– 0	8	Section 8-1: Storage Types
– 1	8	Section 8-1: Storage Types
– 5	8	Section 8-1: Storage Types
– 6	8	Section 8-1: Storage Types
– 10	8	Section 8-1: Storage Types
• Storage system features	8	Section 8-2: Storage Optimization Techniques
– Compression	8	Section 8-2: Storage Optimization Techniques
– Deduplication	8	Section 8-2: Storage Optimization Techniques
– Thin provisioning	8	Section 8-2: Storage Optimization Techniques
– Thick provisioning	8	Section 8-2: Storage Optimization Techniques
– Replication	8	Section 8-4: Creating and Storing Backups

(continues)

3.2   Given a scenario, provision storage in cloud environments. *(Continued)*

Objective	Module	Section
• User quotas	8	Section 8-4: Creating and Storing Backups
• Hyperconverged	8	Section 8-1: Storage Types
• Software-defined storage (SDS)	8	Section 8-1: Storage Types

3.3   Given a scenario, deploy cloud networking solutions.

Objective	Module	Section
• Services	5	Section 5-2: Extending Network Services
– Dynamic host configuration protocol (DHCP)	5	Section 5-2: Extending Network Services
– NTP	6	Section 6-4: Data Security
– DNS	5	Section 5-2: Extending Network Services
– Content delivery network (CDN)	8	Section 8-2: Storage Optimization Techniques
– IP address management (IPAM)	4	Section 4-3: Networking in AWS
	5	Section 5-2: Extending Network Services
• Virtual private networks (VPNs)	5	Section 5-1: Hybrid Cloud and Multi-Cloud Networking
– Site-to-site	5	Section 5-1: Hybrid Cloud and Multi-Cloud Networking
– Point-to-point	5	Section 5-1: Hybrid Cloud and Multi-Cloud Networking
– Point-to-site	5	Section 5-1: Hybrid Cloud and Multi-Cloud Networking
– IPSec	5	Section 5-1: Hybrid Cloud and Multi-Cloud Networking
– Multiprotocol label switching (MPLS)	5	Section 5-1: Hybrid Cloud and Multi-Cloud Networking
• Virtual routing	2	Section 2-1: Virtualization Technologies
	4	Section 4-3: Networking in AWS
		Section 4-4: Networking in Azure
		Section 4-5: Networking in GCP
	5	Section 5-2: Extending Network Services
– Dynamic and static routing	5	Section 5-2: Extending Network Services
– Virtual network interface controller (vNIC)	2	Section 2-1: Virtualization Technologies
– Subnetting	4	Section 4-3: Networking in AWS
		Section 4-4: Networking in Azure
		Section 4-5: Networking in GCP
• Network appliances	5	Section 5-2: Extending Network Services
– Load balancers	5	Section 5-2: Extending Network Services
– Firewalls	6	Section 6-2: Virtual Network Security
• Virtual private cloud (VPC)	4	Section 4-3: Networking in AWS
	5	Section 5-1: Hybrid Cloud and Multi-Cloud Networking
– Hub and spoke	5	Section 5-1: Hybrid Cloud and Multi-Cloud Networking
– Peering	5	Section 5-1: Hybrid Cloud and Multi-Cloud Networking
• VLAN/VXLAN/GENEVE	5	Section 5-1: Hybrid Cloud and Multi-Cloud Networking
• Single root input/output virtualization (SR-IOV)	4	Section 4-2: IP Address Spaces
• Software-defined network (SDN)	4	Section 4-1: Networking Concepts in the Cloud

3.4   Given a scenario, configure the appropriate compute sizing for a deployment.

Objective	Module	Section
• Virtualization	2	Section 2-1: Virtualization Technologies
– Hypervisors	2	Section 2-1: Virtualization Technologies
▪ Type 1	2	Section 2-1: Virtualization Technologies
▪ Type 2	2	Section 2-1: Virtualization Technologies
– Simultaneous multi-threading (SMT)	2	Section 2-2: Virtualized Processing and Memory
– Dynamic allocations	2	Section 2-1: Virtualization Technologies
– Oversubscription	2	Section 2-2: Virtualized Processing and Memory
• Central processing unit (CPU)/virtual CPU (vCPU)	2	Section 2-1: Virtualization Technologies Section 2-2: Virtualized Processing and Memory
• Graphics processing unit (GPU)	2	Section 2-1: Virtualization Technologies
– Virtual	2	Section 2-1: Virtualization Technologies
▪ Shared	2	Section 2-1: Virtualization Technologies
– Pass-through	2	Section 2-1: Virtualization Technologies
• Clock speed/Instructions per cycle (IPC)	2	Section 2-2: Virtualized Processing and Memory
• Hyperconverged	8	Section 8-1: Storage Types
• Memory	2	Section 2-2: Virtualized Processing and Memory
– Dynamic allocation	2	Section 2-2: Virtualized Processing and Memory
– Ballooning	2	Section 2-2: Virtualized Processing and Memory

3.5   Given a scenario, perform cloud migrations.

Objective	Module	Section
• Physical to virtual (P2V)	3	Section 3-2: Migration Execution
• Virtual to virtual (V2V)	3	Section 3-2: Migration Execution
• Cloud-to-cloud migrations	3	Section 3-2: Migration Execution
– Vendor lock-in	3	Section 3-2: Migration Execution
– PaaS or SaaS migrations	3	Section 3-2: Migration Execution
▪ Access control lists (ACLs)	3	Section 3-2: Migration Execution
▪ Firewalls	3	Section 3-2: Migration Execution
• Storage migrations	8	Section 8-1: Storage Types
– Block	8	Section 8-1: Storage Types
– File	8	Section 8-1: Storage Types
– Object	8	Section 8-1: Storage Types
• Database migrations	3	Section 3-2: Migration Execution
– Cross-service migrations	3	Section 3-2: Migration Execution
– Relational	8	Section 8-1: Storage Types
– Non-relational	8	Section 8-1: Storage Types

Domain 4.0 Operations and Support—22% of Examination

4.1 Given a scenario, configure logging, monitoring, and alerting to maintain operational status.

Objective	Module	Section
• Logging	9	Section 9-2: Events and Logs
– Collectors	9	Section 9-2: Events and Logs
▪ Simple network management protocol (SNMP)	9	Section 9-2: Events and Logs
▪ Syslog	9	Section 9-2: Events and Logs
– Analysis	9	Section 9-2: Events and Logs
– Severity categorization	9	Section 9-2: Events and Logs
– Audits	9	Section 9-2: Events and Logs
– Types	9	Section 9-2: Events and Logs
▪ Access/authentication	9	Section 9-2: Events and Logs
▪ System	9	Section 9-2: Events and Logs
▪ Application	9	Section 9-2: Events and Logs
– Automation	10	Section 10-2: Cloud Maintenance Processes
– Trending	9	Section 9-1: Monitoring Resources
• Monitoring	9	Section 9-1: Monitoring Resources
– Baselines	9	Section 9-3: Analysis and Response
– Thresholds	9	Section 9-1: Monitoring Resources
– Tagging	9	Section 9-1: Monitoring Resources
– Log scrubbing	9	Section 9-2: Events and Logs
– Performance monitoring	9	Section 9-1: Monitoring Resources
▪ Application	9	Section 9-2: Events and Logs Section 9-3: Analysis and Response
▪ Infrastructure components	9	Section 9-1: Monitoring Resources
– Resource utilization	9	Section 9-1: Monitoring Resources
– Availability	9	Section 9-1: Monitoring Resources
▪ SLA-defined uptime requirements	9	Section 9-1: Monitoring Resources
– Verification of continuous monitoring activities	9	Section 9-1: Monitoring Resources
– Service management tool integration	9	Section 9-1: Monitoring Resources
• Alerting	9	Section 9-1: Monitoring Resources
– Common messaging methods	9	Section 9-3: Analysis and Response
– Enable/disable alerts	9 10	Section 9-1: Monitoring Resources Section 10-1: Automation Workflow Section 10-2: Cloud Maintenance Processes
▪ Maintenance mode	9	Section 9-1: Monitoring Resources
– Appropriate responses	9	Section 9-3: Analysis and Response
– Policies for categorizing and communicating alerts	9	Section 9-3: Analysis and Response

4.2 Given a scenario, maintain efficient operation of a cloud environment.

Objective	Module	Section
• Confirm completion of backups	8	Section 8-4: Creating and Storing Backups
• Life-cycle management	8	Section 8-2: Storage Optimization Techniques
	10	Section 10-2: Cloud Maintenance Processes
– Roadmaps	10	Section 10-2: Cloud Maintenance Processes
– Old/current/new versions	10	Section 10-2: Cloud Maintenance Processes
– Upgrading and migrating systems	10	Section 10-2: Cloud Maintenance Processes
		Section 10-3: Cloud Automation Services
– Deprecations or end of life	10	Section 10-2: Cloud Maintenance Processes
• Change management	3	Section 3-2: Migration Execution
• Asset management	3	Section 3-2: Migration Execution
– Configuration management database (CMDB)	3	Section 3-2: Migration Execution
• Patching	10	Section 10-2: Cloud Maintenance Processes
– Features or enhancements	10	Section 10-2: Cloud Maintenance Processes
– Fixes for broken or critical infrastructure or applications	10	Section 10-2: Cloud Maintenance Processes
– Scope of cloud elements to be patched	10	Section 10-2: Cloud Maintenance Processes
▪ Hypervisors	10	Section 10-2: Cloud Maintenance Processes
▪ VMs	10	Section 10-2: Cloud Maintenance Processes
		Section 10-3: Cloud Automation Services
▪ Virtual appliances	10	Section 10-2: Cloud Maintenance Processes
▪ Networking components	10	Section 10-2: Cloud Maintenance Processes
▪ Applications	10	Section 10-2: Cloud Maintenance Processes
▪ Storage components	10	Section 10-2: Cloud Maintenance Processes
▪ Firmware	10	Section 10-2: Cloud Maintenance Processes
▪ Software	10	Section 10-2: Cloud Maintenance Processes
▪ OS	10	Section 10-2: Cloud Maintenance Processes
		Section 10-3: Cloud Automation Services
– Policies	10	Section 10-2: Cloud Maintenance Processes
▪ n-1	10	Section 10-2: Cloud Maintenance Processes
– Rollbacks	10	Section 10-2: Cloud Maintenance Processes
• Impacts of process improvements on systems	10	Section 10-2: Cloud Maintenance Processes
• Upgrade methods	10	Section 10-1: Automation Workflow
		Section 10-2: Cloud Maintenance Processes
– Rolling upgrades	10	Section 10-2: Cloud Maintenance Processes
– Blue-green	10	Section 10-2: Cloud Maintenance Processes
– Canary	10	Section 10-2: Cloud Maintenance Processes
– Active-passive	10	Section 10-1: Automation Workflow
– Development/QA/production/DR	10	Section 10-1: Automation Workflow

(continues)

4.2 Given a scenario, maintain efficient operation of a cloud environment. *(Continued)*

Objective	Module	Section
• Dashboard and reporting	9	Section 9-1: Monitoring Resources
– Tagging	9	Section 9-1: Monitoring Resources
– Costs	9	Section 9-1: Monitoring Resources
▪ Chargebacks	9	Section 9-1: Monitoring Resources
▪ Showbacks	9	Section 9-1: Monitoring Resources
– Elasticity usage	9	Section 9-1: Monitoring Resources
– Connectivity	9	Section 9-1: Monitoring Resources
– Latency	9	Section 9-1: Monitoring Resources
– Capacity	9	Section 9-1: Monitoring Resources
– Incidents	9	Section 9-1: Monitoring Resources
– Health	9	Section 9-1: Monitoring Resources
– Overall utilization	9	Section 9-1: Monitoring Resources
– Availability	9	Section 9-1: Monitoring Resources

4.3 Given a scenario, optimize cloud environments.

Objective	Module	Section
• Right-sizing	3	Section 3-3: Deployment Testing and Validation
	9	Section 3-5: Planning for Problems
		Section 9-4: Troubleshooting Performance
– Auto-scaling	3	Section 3-5: Planning for Problems
– Horizontal scaling	3	Section 3-5: Planning for Problems
– Vertical scaling	3	Section 3-5: Planning for Problems
– Cloud bursting	9	Section 9-3: Analysis and Response
• Compute	2	Section 2-1: Virtualization Technologies
	9	Section 9-4: Troubleshooting Performance
– CPUs	2	Section 2-1: Virtualization Technologies
		Section 2-2: Virtualized Processing and Memory
– GPUs	2	Section 2-1: Virtualization Technologies
– Memory	2	Section 2-1: Virtualization Technologies
		Section 2-2: Virtualized Processing and Memory
– Containers	2	Section 2-4: VM Alternatives
• Storage	8	Section 8-2: Storage Optimization Techniques
	9	Section 9-4: Troubleshooting Performance
– Tiers	8	Section 8-2: Storage Optimization Techniques
▪ Adaptive optimization	8	Section 8-2: Storage Optimization Techniques
– IOPS	8	Section 8-2: Storage Optimization Techniques
– Capacity	8	Section 8-2: Storage Optimization Techniques
– Deduplication	8	Section 8-2: Storage Optimization Techniques
– Compression	8	Section 8-2: Storage Optimization Techniques

Objective	Module	Section
• Network	5	Section 5-1: Hybrid Cloud and Multi-Cloud Networking
– Bandwidth	5	Section 5-1: Hybrid Cloud and Multi-Cloud Networking
– Network interface controllers (NICs)	2	Section 2-1: Virtualization Technologies
– Latency	5	Section 5-1: Hybrid Cloud and Multi-Cloud Networking
– SDN	4	Section 4-1: Networking Concepts in the Cloud
– Edge computing	8	Section 8-2: Storage Optimization Techniques
▪ CDN	8	Section 8-2: Storage Optimization Techniques
• Placement	2	Section 2-3: VMs in the Cloud
– Geographical	4	Section 4-3: Networking in AWS Section 4-4: Networking in Azure Section 4-5: Networking in GCP
– Cluster placement	2	Section 2-3: VMs in the Cloud
– Redundancy	8	Section 8-4: Creating and Storing Backups
– Colocation	5	Section 5-1: Hybrid Cloud and Multi-Cloud Networking
• Device drivers and firmware	2	Section 2-1: Virtualization Technologies
– Generic	2	Section 2-1: Virtualization Technologies
– Vendor	2	Section 2-1: Virtualization Technologies
– Open source	2	Section 2-1: Virtualization Technologies

4.4 Given a scenario, apply proper automation and orchestration techniques.

Objective	Module	Section
• Infrastructure as code	10	Section 10-1: Automation Workflow
– Infrastructure components and their integration	10	Section 10-1: Automation Workflow
• Continuous integration/continuous deployments (CI/CD)	3	Section 3-4: Cloud Agility
• Version control	10	Section 10-2: Cloud Maintenance Processes
• Configuration management	10	Section 10-1: Automation Workflow
– Playbook	10	Section 10-1: Automation Workflow
• Containers	10	Section 10-1: Automation Workflow
• Automation activities	9 10	Section 9-1: Monitoring Resources Section 10-1: Automation Workflow
– Routine operations	10	Section 10-1: Automation Workflow
– Updates	10	Section 10-1: Automation Workflow Section 10-3: Cloud Automation Services
– Scaling	9	Section 9-1: Monitoring Resources Section 9-3: Analysis and Response
– Shutdowns	10	Section 10-1: Automation Workflow
– Restarts	10	Section 10-1: Automation Workflow
– Create internal APIs	10	Section 10-1: Automation Workflow

(continues)

Objective	Module	Section
• Restoration methods	3	Section 3-5: Planning for Problems
	8	Section 8-4: Creating and Storing Backups
	9	Section 9-4: Troubleshooting Performance
– In place	9	Section 9-4: Troubleshooting Performance
– Alternate location	3	Section 3-5: Planning for Problems
	9	Section 9-4: Troubleshooting Performance
– Restore files	8	Section 8-4: Creating and Storing Backups
	9	Section 9-4: Troubleshooting Performance
– Snapshot	8	Section 8-4: Creating and Storing Backups

4.6 Given a scenario, perform disaster recovery tasks.

Objective	Module	Section
• Failovers	3	Section 3-5: Planning for Problems
	10	Section 10-2: Cloud Maintenance Processes
• Failback	3	Section 3-5: Planning for Problems
• Restore backups	3	Section 3-5: Planning for Problems
	8	Section 8-4: Creating and Storing Backups
	9	Section 9-4: Troubleshooting Performance
• Replication	8	Section 8-4: Creating and Storing Backups
• Network configurations	8	Section 8-4: Creating and Storing Backups
• On-premises and cloud sites	2	Section 2-3: VMs in the Cloud
	3	Section 3-5: Planning for Problems
– Hot	3	Section 3-5: Planning for Problems
– Warm	3	Section 3-5: Planning for Problems
– Cold	3	Section 3-5: Planning for Problems
• Requirements	3	Section 3-5: Planning for Problems
– RPO	3	Section 3-5: Planning for Problems
– RTO	3	Section 3-5: Planning for Problems
– SLA	3	Section 3-5: Planning for Problems
– Corporate guidelines	3	Section 3-5: Planning for Problems
• Documentation	3	Section 3-5: Planning for Problems
– DR kit	3	Section 3-5: Planning for Problems
– Playbook	3	Section 3-5: Planning for Problems
– Network diagram	4	Section 4-3: Networking in AWS
		Section 4-4: Networking in Azure
		Section 4-5: Networking in GCP
• Geographical datacenter requirements	4	Section 4-3: Networking in AWS
		Section 4-4: Networking in Azure
		Section 4-5: Networking in GCP

Domain 5.0 Troubleshooting—22% of Examination

5.1 Given a scenario, use the troubleshooting methodology to resolve cloud-related issues.

Objective	Module	Section
• Always consider corporate policies, procedures, and impacts before implementing changes.	1	Section 1-5: Troubleshooting Methodology
1. Identify the problem	1	Section 1-5: Troubleshooting Methodology
■ Question the user and identify user changes to the computer and perform backups before making changes.	1	Section 1-5: Troubleshooting Methodology
■ Inquire regarding environmental or infrastructure changes	1	Section 1-5: Troubleshooting Methodology
2. Establish a theory of probable cause (question the obvious)	1	Section 1-5: Troubleshooting Methodology
■ If necessary, conduct external or internal research based on symptoms	1	Section 1-5: Troubleshooting Methodology
3. Test the theory to determine cause	1	Section 1-5: Troubleshooting Methodology
■ Once the theory is confirmed, determine the next steps to resolve the problem	1	Section 1-5: Troubleshooting Methodology
■ If the theory is not confirmed, re-establish a new theory or escalate	1	Section 1-5: Troubleshooting Methodology
4. Establish a plan of action to resolve the problem and implement the solution	1	Section 1-5: Troubleshooting Methodology
5. Verify full system functionality and, if applicable, implement preventive measures	1	Section 1-5: Troubleshooting Methodology
6. Document the findings, actions, and outcomes throughout the process.	1	Section 1-5: Troubleshooting Methodology

5.2 Given a scenario, troubleshoot security issues.

Objective	Module	Section
• Privilege	7	Section 7-5: Troubleshooting Cloud IAM
– Missing	7	Section 7-5: Troubleshooting Cloud IAM
– Incomplete	7	Section 7-5: Troubleshooting Cloud IAM
– Escalation	7	Section 7-5: Troubleshooting Cloud IAM
– Keys	6	Section 6-5: Troubleshooting Cloud Security
• Authentication	7	Section 7-5: Troubleshooting Cloud IAM
• Authorization	7	Section 7-5: Troubleshooting Cloud IAM
• Security groups	6	Section 6-2: Virtual Network Security Section 6-5: Troubleshooting Cloud Security
– Network security groups	6	Section 6-2: Virtual Network Security Section 6-5: Troubleshooting Cloud Security
– Directory security groups	7	Section 7-5: Troubleshooting Cloud IAM

Objective	Module	Section
• Keys and certificates	7	Section 7-2: Authentication
		Section 7-5: Troubleshooting Cloud IAM
– Expired	7	Section 7-5: Troubleshooting Cloud IAM
– Revoked	7	Section 7-2: Authentication
– Trust	7	Section 7-5: Troubleshooting Cloud IAM
– Compromised	7	Section 7-2: Authentication
– Misconfigured	7	Section 7-5: Troubleshooting Cloud IAM
• Misconfigured or misapplied policies	6	Section 6-5: Troubleshooting Cloud Security
• Data security issues	6	Section 6-1: Cloud Security Configurations
		Section 6-4: Data Security
		Section 6-5: Troubleshooting Cloud Security
– Unencrypted data	6	Section 6-1: Cloud Security Configurations
		Section 6-5: Troubleshooting Cloud Security
– Data breaches	6	Section 6-1: Cloud Security Configurations
		Section 6-5: Troubleshooting Cloud Security
– Misclassification	6	Section 6-5: Troubleshooting Cloud Security
– Lack of encryption in protocols	6	Section 6-4: Data Security
– Insecure ciphers	6	Section 6-4: Data Security
• Exposed endpoints	7	Section 7-2: Authentication
• Misconfigured or failed security appliances	6	Section 6-5: Troubleshooting Cloud Security
– IPS	6	Section 6-5: Troubleshooting Cloud Security
– IDS	6	Section 6-5: Troubleshooting Cloud Security
– NAC	6	Section 6-5: Troubleshooting Cloud Security
– WAF	6	Section 6-5: Troubleshooting Cloud Security
• Unsupported protocols	6	Section 6-4: Data Security
• External/internal attacks	6	Section 6-1: Cloud Security Configurations

5.3 Given a scenario, troubleshoot deployment issues.

Objective	Module	Section
• Connectivity issues	3	Section 3-3: Deployment Testing and Validation
	5	Section 5-3: Troubleshooting Cloud Connectivity
– Cloud service provider (CSP) or Internet service provider (ISP) outages	3	Section 3-3: Deployment Testing and Validation
• Performance degradation	5	Section 5-3: Troubleshooting Cloud Connectivity
	9	Section 9-4: Troubleshooting Performance
– Latency	5	Section 5-3: Troubleshooting Cloud Connectivity
• Configurations	10	Section 10-1: Automation Workflow
– Scripts	10	Section 10-1: Automation Workflow
		Section 10-4: Troubleshooting Automation Issues

(continues)

5.3 Given a scenario, troubleshoot deployment issues. *(Continued)*

Objective	Module	Section
• Applications in containers	2	Section 2-4: VM Alternatives
• Misconfigured templates	2	Section 2-3: VMs in the Cloud
• Missing or incorrect tags	9	Section 9-4: Troubleshooting Performance
• Insufficient capacity	3	Section 3-5: Planning for Problems
– Scaling configurations	3	Section 3-5: Planning for Problems
– Compute	3	Section 3-5: Planning for Problems
– Storage	3	Section 3-5: Planning for Problems
– Bandwidth issues	3	Section 3-5: Planning for Problems
– Oversubscription	9	Section 9-4: Troubleshooting Performance
• Licensing issues	3	Section 3-3: Deployment Testing and Validation
• Vendor-related issues	3	Section 3-2: Migration Execution
– Migrations of vendors or platforms	3	Section 3-2: Migration Execution
– Integration of vendors or platforms	3	Section 3-2: Migration Execution
– API request limits	3	Section 3-5: Planning for Problems
– Cost or billing issues	3	Section 3-2: Migration Execution

5.4 Given a scenario, troubleshoot connectivity issues.

Objective	Module	Section
• Network security group misconfigurations	5	Section 5-3: Troubleshooting Cloud Connectivity
– ACL	5	Section 5-3: Troubleshooting Cloud Connectivity
	6	Section 6-5: Troubleshooting Cloud Security
– Inheritance	7	Section 7-5: Troubleshooting Cloud IAM
• Common networking configuration issues	5	Section 5-1: Hybrid Cloud and Multi-Cloud Networking
		Section 5-2: Extending Network Services
		Section 5-3: Troubleshooting Cloud Connectivity
– Peering	5	Section 5-3: Troubleshooting Cloud Connectivity
– Incorrect subnet	5	Section 5-3: Troubleshooting Cloud Connectivity
– Incorrect IP address	5	Section 5-3: Troubleshooting Cloud Connectivity
– Incorrect IP space	5	Section 5-3: Troubleshooting Cloud Connectivity
– Routes	5	Section 5-2: Extending Network Services
▪ Default	5	Section 5-3: Troubleshooting Cloud Connectivity
▪ Static	5	Section 5-2: Extending Network Services
		Section 5-3: Troubleshooting Cloud Connectivity
▪ Dynamic	5	Section 5-2: Extending Network Services
– Firewall	5	Section 5-3: Troubleshooting Cloud Connectivity
	6	Section 6-5: Troubleshooting Cloud Security
▪ Incorrectly administered micro-segmentation	6	Section 6-5: Troubleshooting Cloud Security

Objective	Module	Section
– Network address translation (NAT)	5	Section 5-3: Troubleshooting Cloud Connectivity
▪ VPN	5	Section 5-1: Hybrid Cloud and Multi-Cloud Networking
▪ Source	5	Section 5-3: Troubleshooting Cloud Connectivity
▪ Destination	5	Section 5-3: Troubleshooting Cloud Connectivity
– Load balancers	5	Section 5-3: Troubleshooting Cloud Connectivity
▪ Methods	5	Section 5-3: Troubleshooting Cloud Connectivity
▪ Headers	5	Section 5-3: Troubleshooting Cloud Connectivity
▪ Protocols	5	Section 5-3: Troubleshooting Cloud Connectivity
▪ Encryption	5	Section 5-3: Troubleshooting Cloud Connectivity
▪ Back ends	5	Section 5-3: Troubleshooting Cloud Connectivity
▪ Front ends	5	Section 5-3: Troubleshooting Cloud Connectivity
– DNS records	5	Section 5-3: Troubleshooting Cloud Connectivity
– VLAN/VXLAN/GENEVE	5	Section 5-1: Hybrid Cloud and Multi-Cloud Networking
– Proxy	5	Section 5-3: Troubleshooting Cloud Connectivity
– Maximum transmission unit (MTU)	5	Section 5-1: Hybrid Cloud and Multi-Cloud Networking
– Quality of service (QoS)	5	Section 5-3: Troubleshooting Cloud Connectivity
– Time synchronization issues	3	Section 3-3: Deployment Testing and Validation
• Network troubleshooting tools	5	Section 5-3: Troubleshooting Cloud Connectivity
– ping	5	Section 5-3: Troubleshooting Cloud Connectivity
– tracert/traceroute	5	Section 5-3: Troubleshooting Cloud Connectivity
– flushdns	5	Section 5-3: Troubleshooting Cloud Connectivity
– ipconfig/ifconfig/ip	5	Section 5-3: Troubleshooting Cloud Connectivity
– nslookup/dig	5	Section 5-3: Troubleshooting Cloud Connectivity
– netstat/ss	5	Section 5-3: Troubleshooting Cloud Connectivity
– route	5	Section 5-3: Troubleshooting Cloud Connectivity
– arp	5	Section 5-3: Troubleshooting Cloud Connectivity
– curl	5	Section 5-3: Troubleshooting Cloud Connectivity
– Packet capture	5	Section 5-3: Troubleshooting Cloud Connectivity
	6	Section 6-2: Virtual Network Security
– Packet analyzer	5	Section 5-3: Troubleshooting Cloud Connectivity
	6	Section 6-2: Virtual Network Security
– OpenSSL client	5	Section 5-1: Hybrid Cloud and Multi-Cloud Networking
	6	Section 6-4: Data Security

5.5   Given a scenario, troubleshoot common performance issues.

Objective	Module	Section
• Resource utilization	9	Section 9-4: Troubleshooting Performance
– CPU	9	Section 9-4: Troubleshooting Performance
– GPU	9	Section 9-4: Troubleshooting Performance
– Memory	9	Section 9-4: Troubleshooting Performance
– Storage	9	Section 9-4: Troubleshooting Performance
▪ I/O	9	Section 9-4: Troubleshooting Performance
▪ Capacity	9	Section 9-4: Troubleshooting Performance
– Network bandwidth	5	Section 5-3: Troubleshooting Cloud Connectivity
– Network latency	5	Section 5-3: Troubleshooting Cloud Connectivity
– Replication	9	Section 9-4: Troubleshooting Performance
– Scaling	9	Section 9-4: Troubleshooting Performance
• Application	2	Section 2-4: VM Alternatives
– Memory management	2	Section 2-4: VM Alternatives
– Service overload	2	Section 2-4: VM Alternatives
• Incorrectly configured or failed load balancing	5	Section 5-3: Troubleshooting Cloud Connectivity

5.6   Given a scenario, troubleshoot automation or orchestration issues.

Objective	Module	Section
• Account mismatches	10	Section 10-4: Troubleshooting Automation Issues
• Change management failures	10	Section 10-4: Troubleshooting Automation Issues
• Server name changes	10	Section 10-4: Troubleshooting Automation Issues
• IP address changes	10	Section 10-4: Troubleshooting Automation Issues
• Location changes	10	Section 10-4: Troubleshooting Automation Issues
• Version/feature mismatch	10	Section 10-4: Troubleshooting Automation Issues
• Automation tool incompatibility	10	Section 10-4: Troubleshooting Automation Issues
– Deprecated features	10	Section 10-4: Troubleshooting Automation Issues
– API version incompatibility	10	Section 10-4: Troubleshooting Automation Issues
• Job validation issue	10	Section 10-4: Troubleshooting Automation Issues
• Patching failure	10	Section 10-4: Troubleshooting Automation Issues

Appendix B

Modules Mapped to CompTIA Cloud+ Exam Objectives

These tables provide a complete list of the latest CompTIA Cloud+ CV0-003 certification exam objectives mapped to each section within each module. The official list of objectives is available at CompTIA's website, comptia. org. For your reference, the following tables list each line item from the objectives covered in each module and section.

Module 1: Introduction to Cloud Computing

Sections and headings	Objectives
Section 1-1: Characteristics of Cloud Computing • CompTIA Cloud+ Certification • Other Cloud Certifications • What Is Cloud Computing? • What Do I Need to Know?	**Obj. 1.4: Given a scenario, analyze the solution design in support of the business requirements.** • User and business needs

Section 1-2: Cloud Deployment Models
 	
• Public Cloud
• Private Cloud
• Hybrid Cloud
• Multi-Cloud
• Community Cloud
• Cloud Within a Cloud
	Obj. 1.1: Compare and contrast the different types of cloud models.
	
	• Deployment models
	  – Public
	  – Private
	  – Hybrid
	  – Community
	  – Cloud within a cloud
	  – Multicloud
	  – Multitenancy
	
	Obj. 1.3: Explain the importance of high availability and scaling in cloud environments.
	
	• Scalability

(continues)

Module 1: Introduction to Cloud Computing *(Continued)*

Sections and headings	Objectives
	Obj. 1.4: Given a scenario, analyze the solution design in support of the business requirements. • Requirement analysis – Compliance **Obj. 2.4: Given a scenario, apply data security and compliance controls in cloud environments.** • Impacts of laws and regulations

Section 1-3: Cloud Service Models
 	
• Common Cloud Service Models
• Service Model Security Concerns
	Obj. 1.1: Compare and contrast the different types of cloud models.
	
	• Service models
	  – Infrastructure as a Service (IaaS)
	  – Platform as a Service (PaaS)
	  – Software as a Service (SaaS)
	
	Obj. 1.4: Given a scenario, analyze the solution design in support of the business requirements.
	
	• Requirement analysis
	  – Security
	
	Obj. 2.5: Given a scenario, implement measures to meet security requirements.
	
	• Effects of cloud service models on security implementation

Section 1-4: Cloud Service Providers • PaaS and IaaS Providers • Common Cloud Services • Internet of Things (IoT)	**Obj. 1.1: Compare and contrast the different types of cloud models.** • Advanced cloud services – Internet of Things (IoT)

Section 1-5: Troubleshooting Methodology
 	
• Common Cloud Computing Problems
• Troubleshooting Steps
• Preventive Measures
	Obj. 5.1: Given a scenario, use the troubleshooting methodology to resolve cloud-related issues.
	
	• Always consider corporate policies, procedures, and impacts before implementing changes.
	  1. Identify the problem.
	     – Question the user and identify user changes to the computer and perform backups before making changes.
	     – Inquire regarding environmental or infrastructure changes.
	  2. Establish a theory of probable cause (question the obvious).
	     – If necessary, conduct external or internal research based on symptoms.
	  3. Test the theory to determine cause.
	     – Once the theory is confirmed, determine the next steps to resolve the problem.
	     – If the theory is not confirmed, re-establish a new theory or escalate.
	  4. Establish a plan of action to resolve the problem and implement the solution.
	  5. Verify full system functionality and, if applicable, implement preventive measures.
	  6. Document the findings, actions, and outcomes throughout the process.

Module 2: Virtual Hardware

Sections and headings	Objectives

Section 2-1: Virtualization Technologies
 	
• Virtual Machines (VMs)
• Hypervisors
• Network Connection Types
• VM Configuration
	Obj. 1.2: Explain the factors that contribute to capacity planning.
	
	• Requirements
	 – Hardware
	 – Software
	
	Obj. 1.3: Explain the importance of high availability and scaling in cloud environments.
	
	• Hypervisors
	• Oversubscription
	 – Storage
	
	Obj. 3.1: Given a scenario, integrate components into a cloud solution.
	
	• Subscription services
	 – Virtual desktop infrastructure (VDI)
	
	Obj. 3.3: Given a scenario, deploy cloud networking solutions.
	
	• Virtual routing
	 – Virtual network interface controller (vNIC)
	
	Obj. 3.4: Given a scenario, configure the appropriate compute sizing for a deployment.
	
	• Virtualization
	 – Hypervisors
	  ▪ Type 1
	  ▪ Type 2
	 – Dynamic allocations
	• Central processing unit (CPU)/virtual CPU (vCPU)
	• Graphics processing unit (GPU)
	 – Virtual
	  ▪ Shared
	 – Pass-through
	
	Obj. 4.3: Given a scenario, optimize cloud environments.
	
	• Compute
	 – CPUs
	 – GPUs
	 – Memory
	• Network
	 – Network interface controllers (NICs)
	• Device drivers and firmware
	 – Generic
	 – Vendor
	 – Open source

(continues)

Module 2: Virtual Hardware *(Continued)*

Sections and headings	Objectives
Section 2-2: Virtualized Processing and Memory • CPU Management • Memory Management	**Obj. 1.2: Explain the factors that contribute to capacity planning.** • Licensing – Per-user – Socket-based – Volume-based – Core-based **Obj. 1.3: Explain the importance of high availability and scaling in cloud environments.** • Oversubscription – Compute **Obj. 3.1: Given a scenario, integrate components into a cloud solution.** • Provisioning resources – Compute **Obj. 3.4: Given a scenario, configure the appropriate compute sizing for a deployment.** • Virtualization – Simultaneous multi-threading (SMT) – Oversubscription • Central processing unit (CPU)/virtual CPU (vCPU) • Cloud speed/Instructions per cycle (IPC) • Memory – Dynamic allocation – Ballooning **Obj. 4.3: Given a scenario, optimize cloud environments.** • Compute – CPUs – Memory
Section 2-3: VMs in the Cloud • VM Instance Types • Instance Templates • Affinity • Allocation Factors	**Obj. 1.2: Explain the factors that contribute to capacity planning.** • Requirements – Hardware – Software • Standard templates **Obj. 1.3: Explain the importance of high availability and scaling in cloud environments.** • Hypervisors – Affinity – Anti-affinity **Obj. 3.1: Given a scenario, integrate components into a cloud solution.** • Deploying virtual machines (VMs) and custom images • Templates – OS templates **Obj. 4.3: Given a scenario, optimize cloud environments.** • Placement – Cluster placement

Sections and headings	Objectives
	Obj. 4.6: Given a scenario, perform disaster recovery tasks. • On-premises and cloud sites **Obj. 5.3: Given a scenario, troubleshoot deployment issues.** • Misconfigured templates

Section 2-4: VM Alternatives
• Serverless Computing
• Containers
• Supporting Containers
• Troubleshooting Applications in Containers
	Obj. 1.1: Compare and contrast the different types of cloud models.
	• Advanced cloud services
	  – Serverless
	
	Obj. 1.3: Explain the importance of high availability and scaling in cloud environments.
	• Applications
	• Containers
	
	Obj. 3.1: Given a scenario, integrate components into a cloud solution.
	• Application
	  – Serverless
	• Containers
	  – Configure variables
	  – Configure secrets
	  – Persistent storage
	
	Obj. 4.3: Given a scenario, optimize cloud environments.
	• Compute
	  – Containers
	
	Obj. 5.3: Given a scenario, troubleshoot deployment issues.
	• Applications in containers
	
	Obj. 5.5: Given a scenario, troubleshoot common performance issues.
	• Application
	  – Memory management
	  – Service overload

Module 3: Migration to the Cloud

Sections and headings	Objectives
Section 3-1: Migration Planning • Cloud Migration Phases • Transition Assessment • Migration Plan • Migration Strategies • Timing	**Obj. 1.2: Explain the factors that contribute to capacity planning.** • Requirements – Software

(continues)

Module 3: Migration to the Cloud *(Continued)*

Sections and headings	Objectives

	Obj. 1.4: Given a scenario, analyze the solution design in support of the business requirements.
	
	• Requirement analysis
	  – Software
	  – Hardware
	  – Integration
	  – Budgetary

Section 3-2: Migration Execution
 	
• Change Management
• Deployment Automation
• Data Transfer
• VM Migrations
• Storage Migration
• Cloud-to-Cloud Migrations
	Obj. 3.1: Given a scenario, integrate components into a cloud solution.
	• Provisioning resources
	  – Compute
	  – Storage
	
	Obj. 3.5: Given a scenario, perform cloud migrations.
	• Physical to virtual (P2V)
	• Virtual to virtual (V2V)
	• Cloud-to-cloud migrations
	  – Vendor lock-in
	  – PaaS or SaaS migrations
	    ▪ Access control lists (ACLs)
	    ▪ Firewalls
	• Database migrations
	  – Cross-service migrations
	
	Obj. 4.2: Given a scenario, maintain efficient operation of a cloud environment.
	• Change management
	• Asset management
	  – Configuration management database (CMDB)
	
	Obj. 5.3: Given a scenario, troubleshoot deployment issues.
	• Vendor-related issues
	  – Migrations of vendors or platforms
	  – Integration of vendors or platforms
	  – Cost or billing issues

Section 3-3: Deployment Testing and Validation
 	
• Testing Types
• Testing Considerations
• Test Analysis
• Common Deployment Issues
	Obj. 1.2: Explain the factors that contribute to capacity planning.
	• Licensing
	  – Subscription
	
	Obj. 1.3: Explain the importance of high availability and scaling in cloud environments.
	• Scalability
	  – Auto-scaling

Sections and headings	Objectives

	Obj. 1.4: Given a scenario, analyze the solution design in support of the business requirements.
	
	• Requirement analysis
	   – Service-level agreement (SLA)
	• Testing techniques
	   – Vulnerability testing
	   – Penetration testing
	   – Performance testing
	   – Regression testing
	   – Functional testing
	   – Usability testing
	
	Obj. 2.4: Given a scenario, apply data security and compliance controls in cloud environments.
	
	• Integrity
	
	Obj. 2.5: Given a scenario, implement measures to meet security requirements.
	
	• Vulnerability assessment
	
	Obj. 3.1: Given a scenario, integrate components into a cloud solution.
	
	• Subscription services
	   – File subscription
	   – Communications
	      ■ Email
	      ■ Voice over IP (VoIP)
	      ■ Messaging
	   – Collaboration
	• Auto-scaling
	
	Obj. 4.3: Given a scenario, optimize cloud environments.
	
	• Right-sizing
	
	Obj. 5.3: Given a scenario, troubleshoot deployment issues.
	
	• Connectivity issues
	   – Cloud service provider (CSP) or Internet service provider (ISP) outages
	• Licensing issues
	
	Obj. 5.4: Given a scenario, troubleshoot connectivity issues.
	
	• Common networking configuration issues
	   – Time synchronization issues

Section 3-4: Cloud Agility
 	
• Project Management
• Application Life Cycle
• Builds
	Obj. 2.3: Given a scenario, apply the appropriate OS and application security controls.
	
	• Builds
	   – Stable
	   – Long-term support (LTS)
	   – Beta
	   – Canary

(continues)

Module 3: Migration to the Cloud *(Continued)*

Sections and headings	Objectives
	Obj. 3.1: Given a scenario, integrate components into a cloud solution. • Application **Obj. 4.4: Given a scenario, apply proper automation and orchestration techniques.** • Continuous integration/continuous deployment (CI/CD)

Section 3-5: Planning for Problems
• Capacity Limitations
• Capacity Planning
• Business Continuity Planning
• Disaster Recovery
	Obj. 1.2: Explain the factors that contribute to capacity planning.
	• Performance capacity planning
	Obj. 1.3: Explain the importance of high availability and scaling in cloud environments.
	• Scalability
	  – Auto-scaling
	  – Horizontal scaling
	  – Vertical scaling
	Obj. 1.4: Given a scenario, analyze the solution design in support of the business requirements.
	• Environments
	  – Disaster recovery (DR)
	Obj. 2.6: Explain the importance of incident response procedures.
	• Preparation
	  – Documentation
	  – Call trees
	  – Training
	  – Tabletops
	  – Documented incident types/categories
	  – Roles and responsibilities
	• Incident response procedures
	  – Identification
	    ▪ Scope
	  – Investigation
	  – Containment, eradication, and recovery
	    ▪ Isolation
	    ▪ Evidence acquisition
	    ▪ Chain of custody
	  – Post-incident and lessons learned
	    ▪ Root cause analysis
	Obj. 3.1: Given a scenario, integrate components into a cloud solution.
	• Auto-scaling
	Obj. 4.3: Given a scenario, optimize cloud environments.
	• Right-sizing
	  – Auto-scaling
	  – Horizontal scaling
	  – Vertical scaling
	Obj. 4.5: Given a scenario, perform appropriate backup and restore operations.
	• Backup and restore policies
	  – Recovery time objective (RTO)
	  – Recovery point objective (RPO)

Sections and headings	Objectives

	Obj. 4.6: Given a scenario, perform disaster recovery tasks.
	• Failovers
	• Failback
	• Restore backups
	• On-premises and cloud sites
	   – Hot
	   – Warm
	   – Cold
	• Requirements
	   – RPO
	   – RTO
	   – SLA
	   – Corporate guidelines
	• Documentation
	   – DR kit
	   – Playbook
	
	Obj. 5.3: Given a scenario, troubleshoot deployment issues.
	• Insufficient capacity
	   – Scaling configurations
	   – Compute
	   – Storage
	   – Bandwidth issues
	• Vendor-related issues
	   – API request limits

Module 4: Cloud Networking

Sections and headings	Objectives

Section 4-1: Networking Concepts in the Cloud
 	
• Networking Concepts
• From OSI Model to Cloud Stack
• Software-Defined Networking in the Cloud
	Obj. 1.3: Explain the importance of high availability and scaling in cloud environments.
	• High availability of network functions
	   – Switches
	   – Routers
	
	Obj. 3.3: Given a scenario, deploy cloud networking solutions.
	• Software-defined network (SDN)
	
	Obj. 4.3: Given a scenario, optimize cloud environments.
	• Network
	   – SDN

(continues)

Module 4: Cloud Networking *(Continued)*

Sections and headings	Objectives

Section 4-2: IP Address Spaces
 	
• IP Addressing
• Subnetting
• Cloud Network Interfaces
	Obj. 1.4: Given a scenario, analyze the solution design in support of the business requirements.
	• Requirement analysis
	  – Network requirements
	    ▪ Sizing
	    ▪ Subnetting
	
	Obj. 3.1: Given a scenario, integrate components into a cloud solution.
	• Provisioning resources
	• Network
	
	Obj. 3.3: Given a scenario, deploy cloud networking solutions.
	• Single root input/output virtualization (SR-IOV)

Section 4-3: Networking in AWS
 	
• Regions in AWS
• Availability Zones in AWS
• VPCs in AWS
• Subnets in AWS
• Gateways and Route Tables in AWS
	Obj. 2.2: Given a scenario, secure a network in a cloud environment.
	• Network segmentation
	  – Tiering
	
	Obj. 2.4: Given a scenario, apply data security and compliance controls in cloud environments.
	• Segmentation
	
	Obj. 3.1: Given a scenario, integrate components into a cloud solution.
	• Provisioning resources
	  – Network
	
	Obj. 3.3: Given a scenario, deploy cloud networking solutions.
	• Services
	  – IP address management (IPAM)
	• Virtual routing
	  – Subnetting
	• Virtual private cloud (VPC)
	
	Obj. 4.3: Given a scenario, optimize cloud environments.
	• Placement
	• Geographical
	
	Obj. 4.6: Given a scenario, perform disaster recovery tasks.
	• Documentation
	  – Network diagram
	• Geographical datacenter requirements

Section 4-4: Networking in Azure
 	
• Regions and Availability Zones in Azure
• VNets and Subnets in Azure
• Route Tables in Azure
	Obj. 2.4: Given a scenario, apply data security and compliance controls in cloud environments.
	• Segmentation
	
	Obj. 3.1: Given a scenario, integrate components into a cloud solution.
	• Provisioning resources
	  – Network
	
	Obj. 3.3: Given a scenario, deploy cloud networking solutions.
	• Virtual routing
	  – Subnetting

Sections and headings	Objectives

	Obj. 4.3: Given a scenario, optimize cloud environments.
	• Placement
	  – Geographical
	
	Obj. 4.6: Given a scenario, perform disaster recovery tasks.
	• Documentation
	  – Network diagram
	• Geographical datacenter requirements

Section 4-5: Networking in GCP
 	
• Regions and Zones in GCP
• VPCs and Subnets in GCP
• Routes in GCP
	Obj. 2.4: Given a scenario, apply data security and compliance controls in cloud environments.
	• Segmentation
	
	Obj. 3.1: Given a scenario, integrate components into a cloud solution.
	• Provisioning resources
	  – Network
	
	Obj. 3.3: Given a scenario, deploy cloud networking solutions.
	• Virtual routing
	  – Subnetting
	
	Obj. 4.3: Given a scenario, optimize cloud environments.
	• Placement
	  – Geographical
	
	Obj. 4.6: Given a scenario, perform disaster recovery tasks.
	• Documentation
	  – Network diagram
	• Geographical datacenter requirements

Module 5: Cloud Connectivity and Troubleshooting

Sections and headings	Objectives

Section 5-1: Hybrid Cloud and Multi-Cloud Networking
 	
• Connecting Networks
• Virtual LAN (VLAN)
• Virtual Extensible LAN (VXLAN)
• Generic Network Virtualization Encapsulation (GENEVE)
	Obj. 1.1: Compare and contrast the different types of cloud models.
	• Deployment models
	  – Hybrid
	  – Multicloud
	
	Obj. 1.3: Explain the importance of high availability and scaling in cloud environments.
	• Protocols
	  – Encryption
	    ▪ IPSec
	  – Tunneling
	    ▪ Layer 2 tunneling protocol (L2TP)/Point-to-point tunneling protocol (PPTP)
	    ▪ Generic routing encapsulation (GRE)

(continues)

Module 5: Cloud Connectivity and Troubleshooting *(Continued)*

Sections and headings	Objectives
	Obj. 2.2: Given a scenario, secure a network in a cloud environment. • Network segmentation – Virtual LAN (VLAN)/Virtual extensible LAN (VXLAN)/Generic network virtualization encapsulation (GENEVE)

	Obj. 3.3: Given a scenario, deploy cloud networking solutions.
	• Virtual private networks (VPNs)
	  – Site-to-site
	  – Point-to-point
	  – Point-to-site
	  – IPSec
	  – Multiprotocol label switching (MPLS)
	• Virtual private cloud (VPC)
	  – Hub and spoke
	  – Peering
	• VLAN/VXLAN/GENEVE

	Obj. 4.3: Given a scenario, optimize cloud environments.
	• Network
	  – Bandwidth
	  – Latency
	• Placement
	  – Colocation

	Obj. 5.4: Given a scenario, troubleshoot connectivity issues.
	• Common networking configuration issues
	  – Network address translation (NAT)
	    ▪ VPN
	  – VLAN/VXLAN/GENEVE
	  – Maximum transmission unit (MTU)
	• Network troubleshooting tools
	  – OpenSSL client

Section 5-2: Extending Network Services
• DHCP Services
• DNS Services
• Routing
• Load Balancing
	Obj. 1.3: Explain the importance of high availability and scaling in cloud environments.
	• Clusters
	• High availability of network functions
	  – Load balancers
	
	Obj. 1.4: Given a scenario, analyze the solution design in support of the business requirements.
	• Requirement analysis
	  – Network requirements
	    ▪ Routing
	
	Obj. 2.2: Given a scenario, secure a network in a cloud environment.
	• Protocols
	  – Domain name service (DNS)

Sections and headings	Objectives

	Obj. 3.3: Given a scenario, deploy cloud networking solutions.
	• Services
	  – Dynamic host configuration protocol (DHCP)
	  – DNS
	  – IP address management (IPAM)
	• Virtual routing
	  – Dynamic and static routing
	
	Obj. 5.4: Given a scenario, troubleshoot connectivity issues.
	• Common networking configuration issues
	  – Routes
	    ▪ Static
	    ▪ Dynamic

Section 5-3: Troubleshooting Cloud Connectivity
 	
• Common Troubleshooting Commands
• Common Connectivity Problems
	Obj. 2.2: Given a scenario, secure a network in a cloud environment.
	• Protocols
	  – Tunneling
	    ▪ Secure Shell (SSH)
	• Hardening and configuration changes
	  – Control ingress and egress traffic
	    ▪ Proxy servers
	
	Obj. 5.3: Given a scenario, troubleshoot deployment issues.
	• Connectivity issues
	• Performance degradation
	  – Latency
	
	Obj. 5.4: Given a scenario, troubleshoot connectivity issues.
	• Network security group misconfigurations
	  – ACL
	• Common networking configuration issues
	  – Peering
	  – Incorrect subnet
	  – Incorrect IP address
	  – Incorrect IP space
	  – Routes
	    ▪ Default
	    ▪ vStatic
	  – Firewalls
	  – Network address translation (NAT)
	    ▪ Source
	    ▪ Destination
	  – Load balancers
	    ▪ Methods
	    ▪ Headers
	    ▪ Protocols
	    ▪ Encryption
	    ▪ Back ends
	    ▪ Front ends
	  – DNS records
	  – Proxy
	  – Quality of service (QoS)

(continues)

Module 5: Cloud Connectivity and Troubleshooting *(Continued)*

Sections and headings	Objectives

	Network troubleshooting tools
	
	 – ping
	 – tracert/traceroute
	 – flushdns
	 – ipconfig/ifconfig/ip
	 – nslookup/dig
	 – netstat/ss
	 – route
	 – arp
	 – curl
	 – Packet capture
	 – Packet analyzer
	
	 Obj. 5.5: Given a scenario, troubleshoot common performance issues.
	
	 • Resource utilization
	    – Network bandwidth
	    – Network latency
	 • Incorrectly configured or failed load balancing

Module 6: Securing Cloud Resources

Sections and headings	Objectives

Section 6-1: Cloud Security Configurations
 	
 • Threats to Cloud Security
 • Scanning Tools
 • Cloud-Based Approaches to Security
 • Supporting Shadow IT
	Obj. 1.1: Compare and contrast the different types of cloud models.
	
	 • Shared responsibility model
	
	 Obj. 1.4: Given a scenario, analyze the solution design in support of the business requirements.
	
	 • Requirement analysis
	    – Security
	
	 Obj. 2.1: Given a scenario, configure identity and access management.
	
	 • Identification and authorization
	    – Account life-cycle management
	
	 Obj. 2.2: Given a scenario, secure a network in a cloud environment.
	
	 • Network segmentation
	    – Micro-segmentation
	
	 Obj. 2.3: Given a scenario, apply the appropriate OS and application security controls.
	
	 • Policies
	    – Application approved list (previously known as whitelisting)
	    – Software feature
	
	 Obj. 2.4: Given a scenario, apply data security and compliance controls in cloud environments.
	
	 • Segmentation

Module 6: Securing Cloud Resources *(Continued)*

Sections and headings	Objectives

	Obj. 2.5: Given a scenario, implement measures to meet security requirements.
	• Tools
	  – Vulnerability scanners
	  – Port scanners
	• Vulnerability assessment
	  – Default and common credential scans
	  – Credentialed scans
	  – Network-based scans
	  – Agent-based scans
	  – Service availabilities
	• Risk register
	
	Obj. 5.2: Given a scenario, troubleshoot security issues.
	• Data security issues
	  – Unencrypted data
	  – Data breaches
	• External/internal attacks

Section 6-2: Virtual Network Security
• Allow and Deny Rules
• AWS VPCs and Subnets
• Azure Virtual Networks
• GCP VPCs
• Securing Hybrid and Multi-Clouds
	Obj. 1.3: Explain the importance of high availability and scaling in cloud environments.
	• High availability of network functions
	  – Firewalls
	
	Obj. 2.2: Given a scenario, secure a network in a cloud environment.
	• Network services
	  – Firewalls
	    ▪ Stateful
	    ▪ Stateless
	  – Intrusion protection system (IPS)/Intrusion detection system (IDS)
	  – Network access control (NAC)
	• Network flows
	• Hardening and configuration changes
	  – Control ingress and egress traffic
	    ▪ Allow list (previously known as whitelisting) and blocklist (previously known as blacklisting)
	  – Distributed denial of service (DDoS) protection
	
	Obj. 2.4: Given a scenario, apply data security and compliance controls in cloud environments.
	• Cloud access security broker (CASB)
	
	Obj. 3.3: Given a scenario, deploy cloud networking solutions.
	• Network appliances
	  – Firewalls
	
	Obj. 5.2: Given a scenario, troubleshoot security issues.
	• Security groups
	  – Network security groups

(continues)

Module 6: Securing Cloud Resources *(Continued)*

Sections and headings	Objectives

	Obj. 5.4: Given a scenario, troubleshoot connectivity issues.
	• Network troubleshooting tools
	  – Packet capture
	  – Packet analyzer

Section 6-3: Compute Security
• Device Hardening
• Application Security
	Obj. 2.2: Given a scenario, secure a network in a cloud environment.
	• Network services
	  – Web application firewall (WAF)
	  – Application delivery controller (ADC)
	• Hardening and configuration changes
	  – Disabling unnecessary ports and services
	  – Firmware upgrades
	  – Distributed denial of service (DDoS) protection
	
	Obj. 2.3: Given a scenario, apply the appropriate OS and application security controls.
	• Antivirus/anti-malware/endpoint detection and response (EDR)
	• Host-based IDS (HIDS)/Host-based IPS (HIPS)
	• Hardened baselines
	  – Single function
	• Operating system upgrades
	• Software firewall
	
	Obj. 2.5: Given a scenario, implement measures to meet security requirements.
	• Deactivate default accounts

Section 6-4: Data Security
• Encrypting Data
• Securing Protocols
	Obj. 2.2: Given a scenario, secure a network in a cloud environment.
	• Protocols
	  – Domain name service (DNS)
	    ▪ DNS over HTTPS (DoH)/DNS over TLS (DoT)
	    ▪ DNS security (DNSSEC)
	  – Network time protocol (NTP)
	    ▪ Network time security (NTS)
	  – Encryption
	    ▪ Transport layer security (TLS)
	    ▪ Hypertext transfer protocol secure (HTTPS)
	• Network services
	  – Data loss prevention (DLP)
	• Hardening and configuration changes
	  – Disabling weak protocols and ciphers
	
	Obj. 2.3: Given a scenario, apply the appropriate OS and application security controls.
	• Encryption
	  – Application programming interface (API) endpoint
	  – Application
	  – OS
	  – Storage

Sections and headings	Objectives
	Obj. 2.4: Given a scenario, apply data security and compliance controls in cloud environments. • Encryption • Integrity – Hashing algorithms • Data loss prevention (DLP)
	Obj. 3.3: Given a scenario, deploy cloud networking solutions. • Services – NTP **Obj. 5.2: Given a scenario, troubleshoot security issues.** • Data security issues – Lack of encryption in protocols – Insecure ciphers • Unsupported protocols **Obj. 5.4: Given a scenario, troubleshoot connectivity issues.** • Network troubleshooting tools – OpenSSL client
Section 6-5: Troubleshooting Cloud Security • Security Misconfigurations • Data Misclassification • Key Management	**Obj. 2.1: Given a scenario, configure identity and access management.** • Key management **Obj. 2.5: Given a scenario, implement measures to meet security requirements.** • Impacts of security tools on systems and services **Obj. 5.2: Given a scenario, troubleshoot security issues.** • Privilege – Keys • Security groups – Network security groups • Misconfigured or misapplied policies • Data security issues – Unencrypted data – Data breaches – Misclassification • Misconfigured or failed security appliances – IPS – IDS – NAC – WAF **Obj. 5.4: Given a scenario, troubleshoot connectivity issues.** • Network security group misconfigurations – ACL • Common networking configuration issues – Firewalls ▪ Incorrectly administered micro-segmentation

Module 7: Identity and Access Management

Sections and headings	Objectives

Section 7-1: Cloud Accounts
 	
• Identity
• Account Management
• Privileged Access Management (PAM)
	Obj. 2.1: Given a scenario, configure identity and access management.
	• Identification and authentication
	  – Privileged access management
	  – Logical access management
	  – Account life-cycle management
	    ▪ Provision and deprovision accounts
	
	Obj. 2.3: Given a scenario, apply the appropriate OS and application security controls.
	• User permissions
	
	Obj. 2.5: Given a scenario, implement measures to meet security requirements.
	• Deactivate default accounts

Section 7-2: Authentication
 	
• Authentication Processes
• Password Policies
• Multifactor Authentication (MFA)
• Certificate-Based Authentication
• Single Sign-On
• Digital Signatures
• Securing Secrets
	Obj. 2.1: Given a scenario, configure identity and access management.
	• Directory services
	  – Lightweight directory access protocol (LDAP)
	• Federation
	• Certificate management
	• Multifactor authentication (MFA)
	• Single sign-on (SSO)
	  – Security assertion markup language (SAML)
	• Public key infrastructure (PKI)
	• Secret management
	• Key management
	
	Obj. 2.3: Given a scenario, apply the appropriate OS and application security controls.
	• Policies
	  – Password complexity
	  – Account lockout
	• File integrity
	
	Obj. 2.4: Given a scenario, apply data security and compliance controls in cloud environments.
	• Integrity
	  – Digital signatures
	
	Obj. 3.1: Given a scenario, integrate components into a cloud solution.
	• Subscription services
	  – Directory and identity services
	
	Obj. 4.4: Given a scenario, apply proper automation and orchestration techniques.
	• Secure scripting
	  – Password vaults

Sections and headings	Objectives

	Obj. 5.2: Given a scenario, troubleshoot security issues.
	
	• Keys and certificates
	  – Revoked
	  – Compromised
	• Exposed endpoints

Section 7-3: Authorization to Cloud Objects
 	
• AWS Identity and Access Management (IAM)
• Azure Identity and Access Management (IAM)
• GCP Identity and Access Management (IAM)
	Obj. 2.1: Given a scenario, configure identity and access management.
	
	• Identification and authorization
	  – Access controls
	    ▪ Role-based
	    ▪ Discretionary
	    ▪ Non-discretionary
	    ▪ Mandatory
	
	Obj. 2.3: Given a scenario, apply the appropriate OS and application security controls.
	
	• Policies
	  – User/group
	• User permissions
	• Mandatory access control
	
	Obj. 2.4: Given a scenario, apply data security and compliance controls in cloud environments.
	
	• Classification
	• Access control
	
	Obj. 3.1: Given a scenario, integrate components into a cloud solution.
	
	• Identity management

Section 7-4: IAM for Hybrid Clouds • AWS IAM in a Hybrid or Multi-Cloud • Azure IAM in a Hybrid Cloud • GCP IAM in a Hybrid Cloud	**Obj. 2.1: Given a scenario, configure identity and access management.** • Directory services • Federation **Obj. 3.1: Given a scenario, integrate components into a cloud solution.** • Identity management

Section 7-5: Troubleshooting Cloud IAM
 	
• Common IAM Issues
• Troubleshooting Privilege Issues
	Obj. 5.2: Given a scenario, troubleshoot security issues.
	
	• Privilege
	  – Missing
	  – Incomplete
	  – Escalation
	• Authentication
	• Authorization
	• Security groups
	  – Directory security groups
	• Keys and certificates
	  – Expired
	  – Trust
	  – Misconfigured
	
	Obj. 5.4: Given a scenario, troubleshoot connectivity issues.
	
	• Network security group misconfigurations
	  – Inheritance

Module 8: Cloud Storage

Sections and headings	Objectives

Section 8-1: Storage Types
• On-Prem Storage Technologies
• Cloud Storage Technologies
• Storage Migrations
	Obj. 2.3: Given a scenario, apply the appropriate OS and application security controls.
	• Policies
	  – Filesystem
	
	Obj. 2.4: Given a scenario, apply data security and compliance controls in cloud environments.
	• Records management
	  – Write once read many
	
	Obj. 3.2: Given a scenario, provision storage in cloud environments.
	• Types
	  – Block
	    ▪ Storage area network (SAN)
	    ▪ Zoning
	  – File
	    ▪ Network attached storage (NAS)
	  – Object
	• Protocols
	  – Network file system (NFS)
	  – Common Internet file system (CIFS)
	  – Internet small computer system interface (iSCSI)
	  – Fibre Channel (FC)
	  – Non-volatile memory express over fabrics (NVMe-oF)
	• Redundant array of inexpensive disks (RAID)
	  – 0
	  – 1
	  – 5
	  – 6
	  – 10
	• Hyperconverged
	• Software-defined storage (SDS)
	
	Obj. 3.4: Given a scenario, configure the appropriate compute sizing for a deployment.
	• Hyperconverged
	
	Obj. 3.5: Given a scenario, perform cloud migrations.
	• Storage migrations
	  – Block
	  – File
	  – Object
	• Database migrations
	  – Relational
	  – Non-relational

Sections and headings	Objectives
Section 8-2: Storage Optimization Techniques • Storage Capacity • Data Optimization • Data Lifecycle • Edge Computing	**Obj. 1.3: Explain the importance of high availability and scaling in cloud environments.** • Oversubscription – Storage **Obj. 1.4: Given a scenario, analyze the solution design in support of the business requirements.** • Requirement analysis – Compliance **Obj. 2.3: Given a scenario, apply the appropriate OS and application security controls.** • Policies – User/group **Obj. 2.4: Given a scenario, apply data security and compliance controls in cloud environments.** • Impacts of laws and regulations – Legal hold • Records management – Versioning – Retention – Destruction **Obj. 3.1: Given a scenario, integrate components into a cloud solution.** • Provisioning resources – Storage **Obj. 3.2: Given a scenario, provision storage in cloud environments.** • Types – Object ▪ Tenants • Tiers – Flash – Hybrid – Long-term • Input/output operations per second (IOPS) and read/write • Storage system features – Compression – Deduplication – Thin provisioning – Thick provisioning **Obj. 3.3: Given a scenario, deploy cloud networking solutions.** • Services – Content delivery network (CDN)

(continues)

Module 8: Cloud Storage *(Continued)*

Sections and headings	Objectives

	Obj. 4.2: Given a scenario, maintain efficient operation of a cloud environment.
	
	• Life-cycle management
	
	Obj. 4.3: Given a scenario, optimize cloud environments.
	
	• Storage
	  – Tiers
	    ▪ Adaptive optimization
	  – IOPS
	  – Capacity
	  – Deduplication
	  – Compression
	• Network
	  – Edge computing
	    ▪ CDN

Section 8-3: Cloud Storage Services
 	
• AWS Storage Services
• Azure Storage Services
• GCP Storage Services
	Obj. 1.3: Explain the importance of high availability and scaling in cloud environments.
	
	• Regions and zones
	
	Obj. 2.3: Given a scenario, apply the appropriate OS and application security controls.
	
	• Encryption
	  – Filesystem
	
	Obj. 3.1: Given a scenario, integrate components into a cloud solution.
	
	• Provisioning resources
	  – Storage
	
	Obj. 3.2: Given a scenario, provision storage in cloud environments.
	
	• Types
	  – Block
	  – File
	  – Object
	    ▪ Buckets
	• Tiers

Section 8-4: Creating and Storing Backups
 	
• Protection Capabilities
• Backup Types
• Redundancy Levels
• Backup Considerations
	Obj. 1.3: Explain the importance of high availability and scaling in cloud environments.
	
	• Regions and zones
	• Avoid single point of failure
	
	Obj. 2.3: Given a scenario, apply the appropriate OS and application security controls.
	
	• Encryption
	  – Filesystem
	
	Obj. 3.2: Given a scenario, provision storage in cloud environments.
	
	• Tiers
	  – Spinning disks
	  – Long-term

Sections and headings	Objectives
	Storage system features
	– Replication
	• User quotas
	Obj. 4.2: Given a scenario, maintain efficient operation of a cloud environment.
	• Confirm completion of backups
	Obj. 4.3: Given a scenario, optimize cloud environments.
	• Placement
	– Redundancy
	Obj. 4.5: Given a scenario, perform appropriate backup and restore operations.
	• Backup types
	– Incremental
	– Differential
	– Full
	– Synthetic full
	– Snapshot
	• Backup objects
	– Application-level backup
	– Filesystem backup
	– Database dumps
	– Configure files
	• Backup targets
	– Tape
	– Disk
	– Object
	• Backup and restore policies
	– Retention
	– Schedules
	– Location
	– SLAs
	– 3-2-1 rule
	■ Three copies of data
	■ Two different media
	■ One copy off site
	• Restoration methods
	– Restore files
	– Snapshot
	Obj. 4.6: Given a scenario, perform disaster recovery tasks.
	• Restore backups
	• Replication
	• Network configurations

(continues)

Module 8: Cloud Storage *(Continued)*

Sections and headings	Objectives

Section 8-5: Storage Security
• Data Classification
• Data Obfuscation
	Obj. 1.3: Explain the importance of high availability and scaling in cloud environments.
	• Regions and zones
	
	Obj. 1.4: Given a scenario, analyze the solution design in support of the business requirements.
	• Requirement analysis
	  – Compliance
	
	Obj. 2.3: Given a scenario, apply the appropriate OS and application security controls.
	• Policies
	  – User/group

Module 9: Managing Cloud Performance

Sections and headings	Objectives

Section 9-1: Monitoring Resources
• Targets to Monitor
• Monitoring Tools
• Dashboards
	Obj. 1.2: Explain the factors that contribute to capacity planning.
	• Requirements
	  – Budgetary
	  – Business need analysis
	• User density
	• System load
	• Trend analysis
	
	Obj. 1.4: Given a scenario, analyze the solution design in support of the business requirements.
	• Environments
	
	Obj. 2.2: Given a scenario, secure a network in a cloud environment.
	• Network services
	  – Packet brokers
	
	Obj. 2.5: Given a scenario, implement measures to meet security requirements.
	• Vulnerability assessment
	  – Agent-based scans

Sections and headings	Objectives

	Obj. 4.1: Given a scenario, configure logging, monitoring, and alerting to maintain operational status.
	• Logging
	  – Trending
	• Monitoring
	  – Thresholds
	  – Tagging
	  – Performance monitoring
	    ■ Infrastructure components
	  – Resource utilization
	  – Availability
	    ■ SLA-defined uptime requirements
	  – Verification of continuous monitoring activities
	  – Service management tool integration
	• Alerting
	  – Enable/disable alerts
	    ■ Maintenance mode
	
	Obj. 4.2: Given a scenario, maintain efficient operation of a cloud environment.
	• Dashboard and reporting
	  – Tagging
	  – Costs
	    ■ Chargebacks
	    ■ Showbacks
	  – Elasticity usage
	  – Connectivity
	  – Latency
	  – Capacity
	  – Incidents
	  – Health
	  – Overall utilization
	  – Availability
	
	Obj. 4.4: Given a scenario, apply proper automation and orchestration techniques.
	• Automation activities
	  – Scaling
	
	Obj. 4.5: Given a scenario, perform appropriate backup and restore operations.
	• Backup and restore policies
	  – Mean time to recovery (MTTR)

(continues)

Module 9: Managing Cloud Performance *(Continued)*

Sections and headings	Objectives

Section 9-2: Events and Logs
 	
• Events
• Logs
• Syslog
• SNMP Communications
	Obj. 1.2: Explain the factors that contribute to capacity planning.
	
	• Trend analysis
	  – Patterns
	  – Anomalies
	
	Obj. 2.2: Given a scenario, secure a network in a cloud environment.
	
	• Log and event monitoring
	
	Obj. 2.3: Given a scenario, apply the appropriate OS and application security controls.
	
	• Log and event monitoring
	
	Obj. 4.1: Given a scenario, configure logging, monitoring, and alerting to maintain operational status.
	
	• Logging
	  – Collectors
	    ▪ Simple network management protocol (SNMP)
	    ▪ Syslog
	  – Analysis
	  – Severity categorization
	  – Audits
	  – Types
	    ▪ Access/authentication
	    ▪ System
	    ▪ Application
	• Monitoring
	  – Log scrubbing
	  – Performance monitoring
	    ▪ Application

Section 9-3: Analysis and Response
 	
• Monitoring in AWS
• Monitoring in Azure
• Monitoring in GCP
	Obj. 1.2: Explain the factors that contribute to capacity planning.
	
	• Trend analysis
	  – Baselines
	  – Anomalies
	
	Obj. 1.3: Explain the importance of high availability and scaling in cloud environments.
	
	• Scalability
	  – Cloud bursting
	
	Obj. 2.5: Given a scenario, implement measures to meet security requirements.
	
	• Vulnerability assessment
	  – Agent-based scans
	
	Obj. 3.1: Given a scenario, integrate components into a cloud solution.
	
	• Subscription services
	  – Communications
	    ▪ Email
	    ▪ Messaging

Sections and headings	Objectives

	Obj. 4.1: Given a scenario, configure logging, monitoring, and alerting to maintain operational status.
	
	• Monitoring
	  – Baselines
	  – Performance monitoring
	    ▪ Application
	• Alerting
	  – Common messaging methods
	  – Appropriate responses
	  – Policies for categorizing and communicating alerts
	
	Obj. 4.3: Given a scenario, optimize cloud environments.
	
	• Right-sizing
	  – Cloud bursting
	
	Obj. 4.4: Given a scenario, apply proper automation and orchestration techniques.
	
	• Automation activities
	  – Scaling

Section 9-4: Troubleshooting Performance
 	
• Utilization Issues
• Scaling Issues
• Restoration from Backup
	Obj. 4.3: Given a scenario, optimize cloud environments.
	
	• Right-sizing
	• Compute
	• Storage
	
	Obj. 4.5: Given a scenario, perform appropriate backup and restore operations.
	
	• Restoration methods
	  – In place
	  – Alternate location
	  – Restore files
	
	Obj. 4.6: Given a scenario, perform disaster recovery tasks.
	
	• Restore backups
	
	Obj. 5.3: Given a scenario, troubleshoot deployment issues.
	
	• Performance degradation
	• Missing or incorrect tags
	• Insufficient capacity
	  – Oversubscription
	
	Obj. 5.5: Given a scenario, troubleshoot common performance issues.
	
	• Resource utilization
	  – CPU
	  – GPU
	  – Memory
	  – Storage
	    ▪ I/O
	    ▪ Capacity
	  – Replication
	  – Scaling

Module 10: Cloud Automation

Sections and headings	Objectives

Section 10-1: Automation Workflow
 	
• Why Automate?
• Infrastructure as Code (IaC)
• Automation Tools
• Advanced Cloud Services
	Obj. 1.1: Compare and contrast the different types of cloud models.
	
	• Advanced cloud services
	  – Machine learning/Artificial intelligence (AI)
	
	Obj. 1.4: Given a scenario, analyze the solution design in support of the business requirements.
	
	• Environments
	  – Development
	  – Quality assurance (QA)
	  – Staging
	  – Blue-green
	  – Production
	
	Obj. 2.3: Given a scenario, apply the appropriate OS and application security controls.
	
	• Configuration management
	
	Obj. 3.1: Given a scenario, integrate components into a cloud solution.
	
	• Templates
	  – Solution templates
	
	Obj. 4.1: Given a scenario, configure logging, monitoring, and alerting to maintain operational status.
	
	• Alerting
	  – Enable/disable alerts
	
	Obj. 4.2: Given a scenario, maintain efficient operation of a cloud environment.
	
	• Upgrade methods
	  – Active-passive
	  – Development/QA/production/DR
	
	Obj. 4.4: Given a scenario, apply proper automation and orchestration techniques.
	
	• Infrastructure as code
	  – Infrastructure components and their integration
	• Configuration management
	  – Playbook
	• Containers
	• Automation activities
	  – Routine operations
	  – Updates
	  – Shutdowns
	  – Restarts
	  – Create internal APIs
	• Orchestration sequencing
	
	Obj. 5.3: Given a scenario, troubleshoot deployment issues.
	
	• Configurations
	  – Scripts

Sections and headings	Objectives

Section 10-2: Cloud Maintenance Processes
 	
• Lifecycle Management
• Types of Updates
• Patching and Update Methodologies
• Automation and Security
• Automated Disaster Recovery
	Obj. 2.2: Given a scenario, secure a network in a cloud environment.
	• Network services
	  – Intrusion protection system (IPS)/Intrusion detection system (IDS)
	
	Obj. 2.3: Given a scenario, apply the appropriate OS and application security controls.
	• User permissions
	• Host-based IDS (HIDS)/Host-based IPS (HIPS)
	• File integrity
	
	Obj. 2.4: Given a scenario, apply data security and compliance controls in cloud environments.
	• Integrity
	  – File integrity monitoring (FIM)
	
	Obj. 2.5: Given a scenario, implement measures to meet security requirements.
	• Security patches
	  – Hot fixes
	  – Scheduled updates
	  – Virtual patches
	  – Signature updates
	  – Rollups
	• Prioritization of patch application
	
	Obj. 3.1: Given a scenario, integrate components into a cloud solution.
	• Subscription services
	  – Cloud resources
	    ▪ IaaS
	    ▪ PaaS
	    ▪ SaaS
	• Post-deployment validation
	
	Obj. 4.1: Given a scenario, configure logging, monitoring, and alerting to maintain operational status.
	• Logging
	  – Automation
	• Alerting
	  – Enable/disable alerts
	
	Obj. 4.2: Given a scenario, maintain efficient operation of a cloud environment.
	• Life-cycle management
	  – Roadmaps
	  – Old/current/new versions
	  – Upgrading and migrating systems
	  – Deprecations or end of life

(continues)

Module 10: Cloud Automation *(Continued)*

Sections and headings	Objectives
	• Patching
	– Features or enhancements
	– Fixes for broken or critical infrastructure or applications
	– Scope of cloud elements to be patched
	▪ Hypervisors
	▪ VMs
	▪ Virtual appliances
	▪ Networking components
	▪ Applications
	▪ Storage components
	▪ Firmware
	▪ Software
	▪ OS
	– Policies
	▪ n-1
	– Rollbacks
	• Impacts of process improvements on systems
	• Upgrade methods
	– Rolling upgrades
	– Blue-green
	– Canary
	– Active-passive
	Obj. 4.4: Given a scenario, apply proper automation and orchestration techniques.
	• Version control
	• Secure scripting
	– No hardcoded passwords
	– Use of individual service accounts
	– Password vaults
	– Key-based authentication
	Obj. 4.6: Given a scenario, perform disaster recovery tasks.
	• Failovers

Section 10-3: Cloud Automation Services
 	
• AWS CLI
• Azure CLI
• GCP CLI
• Patching in AWS
• Patching in Azure
• Patching in GCP
	Obj. 2.3: Given a scenario, apply the appropriate OS and application security controls.
	
	• Configuration management
	
	Obj. 2.5: Given a scenario, implement measures to meet security requirements.
	
	• Security patches
	  – Scheduled updates
	
	Obj. 4.2: Given a scenario, maintain efficient operation of a cloud environment.
	
	• Life-cycle management
	  – Upgrading and migrating systems

Sections and headings	Objectives

	• Patching
	  – Scope of cloud elements to be patched
	    ▪ VMs
	    ▪ OS
	
	Obj. 4.4: Given a scenario, apply proper automation and orchestration techniques.
	• Automation activities
	  – Updates

Section 10-4: Troubleshooting Automation Issues
 	
• Common Automation Issues
• Breakdowns in Workflow
	Obj. 5.3: Given a scenario, troubleshoot deployment issues.
	• Configurations
	  – Scripts
	
	Obj. 5.6: Given a scenario, troubleshoot automation or orchestration issues.
	• Account mismatches
	• Change management failures
	• Server name changes
	• IP address changes
	• Location changes
	• Version/feature mismatch
	• Automation tool incompatibility
	  – Deprecated features
	  – API version incompatibility
	• Job validation issue
	• Patching failure

Appendix C

CompTIA Cloud+ Acronyms

Table C-1 provides a complete list of acronyms listed in the latest CompTIA Cloud+ CV0-003 certification exam objectives. The official list of objectives is available at CompTIA's website, comptia.org.

Table C-1 CompTIA Cloud+ Acronyms

Acronym	Spellout
AAA	Authentication, Authorization, and Accounting
ACL	Access Control List
ADC	Application Delivery Controller
AES	Advanced Encryption Standard
AI	Artificial Intelligence
API	Application Programming Interface
ARP	Address Resolution Protocol
BCP	Business Continuity Plan
BGP	Border Gateway Protocol
BIA	Business Impact Analysis
CAB	Change Advisory Board
CAS	Content Addressed Storage
CASB	Cloud Access Security Broker
CD	Continuous Deployment
CDN	Content Delivery Network
CI	Continuous Integration
CIFS	Common Internet File System
CIIS	Client Integration Implementation Service
CMDB	Configuration Management Database
CMS	Content Management System
CNA	Converged Network Adapter
COL	Co-Location

Acronym	Spellout
COOP	Continuity of Operations Plan
CPU	Central Processing Unit
CRL	Certificate Revocation List
CRM	Customer Relationship Management
CSP	Content Service Provider
DAC	Discretionary Access Control
DAS	Direct Attached Storage
DBaaS	Database as a Service
DBMS	Database Management Server
DDoS	Distributed Denial of Service
DFS	Distributed File System
DHCP	Dynamic Host Configuration Protocol
DLP	Data Loss Prevention
DMZ	Demilitarized Zone
DNS	Domain Name Service
DNSSEC	DNS Security
DoH	DNS over HTTPS
DoT	DNS over TLS
DR	Disaster Recovery
DRP	Disaster Recovery Plan
DSA	Distributed Services Architecture
EDR	Endpoint Detection and Response
FC	Fibre Channel
FCoE	Fibre Channel over Ethernet
FIM	File Integrity Monitoring
FTP	File Transfer Protocol
FTPS	FTP over SSL
GENEVE	Generic Network Virtualization Encapsulation
GPT	GUID Partition Table
GPU	Graphics Processing Unit
GRE	Generic Routing Encapsulation
GUI	Graphical User Interface
HA	High Availability
HBA	Host Bus Adapter
HIDS	Host-Based IDS
HIPS	Host-Based IPS
HTTPS	Hypertext Transfer Protocol Secure
IaaS	Infrastructure as a Service
ICMP	Internet Control Management Protocol

Acronym	Spellout
IDS	Intrusion Detection System
IFCP	Internet Fibre Channel Protocol
IGRP	Interior Gateway Routing Protocol
I/O	Input/Output
IOPS	Input/Output Operations Per Second
IoT	Internet of Things
IPAM	IP Address Management
IPC	Instructions Per Cycle
IPMI	Intelligent Platform Management Interface
IPS	Intrusion Prevention System
IPSec	IP Security
IQN	Initiator Qualified Name
iSCSI	Internet Small Computer System Interface
ISNS	Internet Storage Name Service
ISP	Internet Service Provider
JBOD	Just a Bunch of Disks
KVM	Kernel Virtual Machine, Keyboard Video Mouse
L2TP	Layer 2 Tunneling Protocol
LAN	Local Area Network
LDAP	Lightweight Directory Access Protocol
LTS	Long-Term Support
LUN	Logical Unit Number
MAC	Mandatory Access Control
MBR	Master Boot Record
MDF	Main Distribution Facility
MFA	Multi-Factor Authentication
ML	Machine Learning
MPIO	MultiPath I/O
MPLS	Multiprotocol Label Switching
MSP	Managed Service Provider
MTBF	Mean Time Between Failure
MTTF	Mean Time To Failure
MTTR	Mean Time To Repair
MTU	Maximum Transmission Unit
NAC	Network Access Control
NAS	Network Attached Storage
NAT	Network Address Translation
NFS	Network File System
NIC	Network Interface Controller

Acronym	Spellout
NOC	Network Operations Center
NPIV	N_Port ID Virtualization
NTFS	New Technology File System
NTP	Network Time Protocol
NTS	Network Time Security
NVMe	Nonvolatile Memory Express
NVMe-oF	NVMe over Fabrics
ODBC	Open Database Connectivity
OLA	Operational Level Agreement
OS	Operating System
OSPF	Open Shortest Path First
P2P	Physical to Physical
P2V	Physical to Virtual
PaaS	Platform as a Service
PAT	Port Address Translation
PBX	Private (or Public) Branch Exchange
PIT	Point-in-Time (backup or snapshot)
PKI	Public Key Infrastructure
PPTP	Point-to-Point Tunneling Protocol
QA	Quality Assurance
QoS	Quality of Service
RAID	Redundant Array of Inexpensive Disks
RDP	Remote Desktop Protocol
ReFS	Resilient File System
RPO	Recovery Point Objective
RTO	Recovery Time Objectives
SaaS	Software as a Service
SAML	Security Assertion Markup Language
SAN	Storage Area Network
SAS	Serial Attached SCSI
SATA	Serial Advanced Technology Attachment
SCP	Session Control Protocol
SCSI	Small Computer System Interface
SDLC	Software Development Life Cycle
SDN	Software-Defined Network
SDS	Software-Defined Storage
SFTP	Secure FTP
SHA	Secure Hash Algorithm
SIP	Session Initiation Protocol

Acronym	Spellout
SLA	Service-Level Agreement
SMB	Server Message Block
SMT	Simultaneous Multi-Threading
SNMP	Simple Network Management Protocol
SR-IOV	Single-Root Input/Output Virtualization
SSD	Solid State Disk
SSH	Secure Shell
SSL	Secure Sockets Layer
SSO	Single Sign-On
TCO	Total Cost of Operations
TCP	Transmission Control Protocol
TKIP	Temporal Key Integrity Protocol
TLS	Transport Layer Security
TPM	Trusted Platform Module
TTL	Time to Live
UAT	User Acceptance Testing
UDP	Universal Datagram Protocol
UPS	Universal Power Supply
V2P	Virtual to Physical
V2V	Virtual to Virtual
VAT	Virtual Allocation Table
vCPU	Virtual CPU
VDI	Virtual Desktop Infrastructure
vGPU	Virtual Graphics Processing Unit
VHD	Virtual Hard Disk
VLAN	Virtual LAN
VM	Virtual Machine
VMFS	Virtual Machine File System
VNC	Virtual Network Computing
vNIC	Virtual NIC
VoIP	Voice over IP
VPC	Virtual Private Cloud
VPN	Virtual Private Network
vRAM	Virtual RAM
vSAN	Virtual SAN
vSwitch	Virtual Switch
VTL	Virtual Tape Library
VXLAN	Virtual Extensible LAN
WAF	Web Application Firewall

Acronym	Spellout
WAN	Wide Area Network
WMI	Windows Management Implementation
WWNN	World Wide Node Name
WWPN	World Wide Port Name
XaaS	Anything as a Service
ZFS	Z File System

Appendix D

Rubric for Hands-On Projects and Capstone Projects

Criteria	Beginning	Developing	Proficient	Exemplary	Score
Responses to questions	All missing or incorrect **[0 points]**	Most missing or incorrect **[15 points]**	Little missing or incorrect **[20 points]**	All complete **[25 points]**	
Other deliverables	Missing **[0 points]**	Present but missing most or all the required information **[15 points]**	Present but missing some of the required information **[20 points]**	Present and contains all the required information **[25 points]**	
Critical thinking and engagement	Student shows little to no evidence of attempting to meet the performance requirements of the assignment **[0 points]**	Student retains their existing understanding while attempting to meet the performance requirements of the assignment **[15 points]**	Student challenges their existing understanding and shows evidence of new learning **[20 points]**	Student challenges their existing understanding and displays creative and original insights **[25 points]**	
Mechanics	Grammar, spelling, punctuation, and formatting make student's message difficult to understand **[0 points]**	Grammar, spelling, punctuation, and formatting detract from student's message **[15 points]**	Grammar, spelling, punctuation, and formatting support student's message **[20 points]**	Grammar, spelling, punctuation, and formatting enhance student's message **[25 points]**	
				Total	

Rubric for Discussion Assignments

Task	Developing	Proficient	Exemplary	Score
Initial post	Generalized statements **[30 points]**	Some specific statements with supporting evidence **[40 points]**	Self-reflective discussion with specific and thoughtful statements and supporting evidence **[50 points]**	
Initial post: Mechanics	• Length < 100 words • Several grammar and spelling errors **[5 points]**	• Length = 100 words • Occasional grammar and spelling errors **[7 points]**	• Length > 100 words • Appropriate grammar and spelling **[10 points]**	
Response 1	Brief response showing little engagement or critical thinking **[5 points]**	Detailed response with specific contributions to the discussion **[10 points]**	Thoughtful response with specific examples or details and open-ended questions that invite deeper discussion of the topic **[15 points]**	
Response 2	Brief response showing little engagement or critical thinking **[5 points]**	Detailed response with specific contributions to the discussion **[10 points]**	Thoughtful response with specific examples or details and open-ended questions that invite deeper discussion of the topic **[15 points]**	
Both responses: Mechanics	• Length < 50 words each • Several grammar and spelling errors **[5 points]**	• Length = 50 words each • Occasional grammar and spelling errors **[7 points]**	• Length > 50 words each • Appropriate grammar and spelling **[10 points]**	
			Total	

Glossary

A

AD (Active Directory)   A collection of services on Windows Server that manages access to resources on a network. *Mod. 7*

ADC (application delivery controller)   A device or software that increases application responsiveness over the Internet by load balancing and filtering traffic, handling encryption processes, and incorporating traffic shaping and monitoring techniques. *Mod. 6*

affinity   The requirement that guest VMs reside on the same physical host. *Mod. 2*

agent-based scan   Software that relies on small applications called agents installed on various devices to gain deeper visibility into a network and its resource configurations. *Mod. 6*

agility   The ability to adapt quickly to market demands according to increased or decreased feature use within a system or application. *Mod. 3*

AI (artificial intelligence)   The ability of computers to adapt to changing circumstances. *Mod. 10*

Alibaba Cloud   The China-based cloud computing platform offered by Alibaba Group. *Mod. 1*

allow list   A list of rules defining which traffic is allowed to pass. Previously called *whitelisting*. *Mod. 6*

ALM (application lifecycle management)   The oversight of an application through its development, maintenance, and retirement. *Mod. 3*

AMD-V (AMD virtualization)   The HAV (hardware-assisted virtualization) technology available on AMD CPUs that enables a CPU to support virtualization processes. *Mod. 2*

anti-affinity   The requirement that guest VMs reside on different physical hosts. *Mod. 2*

API (application programming interface)   A request made in a specific format to a program. *Mod. 1*

application-level backup   Backup strategies for components of an application that ensure none of the infrastructure resources (such as VMs or code resources) rely on a single point of failure and that all resource configurations are saved for future reference. *Mod. 8*

AS (autonomous system)   A group of networks, often on the same domain, that are operated by the same organization. *Mod. 5*

asset management   The oversight of components that provide value to a business throughout their life cycles. *Mod. 3*

audit log   A collection of data in logs that is consistent and thorough enough to retroactively prove compliance and also to defensibly prove user actions. *Mod. 9*

authentication   A process usually managed by a server that proves the identity of a client and determines whether that client is allowed to access a secured system. *Mod. 7*

automation   The use of technology to perform a task with minimal human intervention. *Mod. 1*

auto-scaling   The ability of a virtual resource to automatically increase or decrease in capacity as demand on the resource changes. *Mod. 3*

AWS (Amazon Web Services)   A subsidiary of Amazon that is headquartered in Seattle, Washington, and provides extensive cloud computing services to businesses and individuals. *Mod. 1*

AZ (availability zone)   An isolated data center in a geographic region that provides independent power, cooling, and network infrastructure to cloud consumers. *Mod. 4*

Azure   Microsoft's cloud computing platform that is designed for optimal compatibility with existing Microsoft products. *Mod. 1*

B

ballooning   A memory management technique that allows a host system to reclaim some memory that is currently allocated to a guest VM. *Mod. 2*

baseline   A record of how a system operates under normal conditions. *Mod. 3*

BC (business continuity)   A company's ability to weather a failure, crisis, or disaster while maintaining continuity of operations, especially for critical services to customers and income-generating activities. *Mod. 3*

beta   A system build that benefits from user testing on earlier builds and is generally updated less often than earlier releases, such as every six weeks. *Mod. 3*

BGP (Border Gateway Protocol)   Dubbed the "protocol of the Internet," this routing protocol is the only current EGP and is capable of considering many factors in its routing metrics. *Mod. 5*

big data   Data that consists of high levels of variety in high volumes and arriving in high velocity (the three Vs). *Mod. 8*

blast radius   The extent of system vulnerability to a destructive event such as a security breach or device failure. *Mod. 7*

block list   A list of rules defining which traffic is prevented from passing. Also called *deny list*; previously called *blacklisting*. *Mod. 6*

block zoning   A block storage initiative that increases efficiency of block storage space and decreases latency by dividing the overall space into zones for specific types of data. *Mod. 8*

broad network access   The ability to connect to cloud-hosted resources from anywhere on the Internet using a variety of device types. *Mod. 1*

build   The deployment of a working application, website, or other system from source code files. *Mod. 3*

C

CAB (change advisory board) A team that reviews complex, expensive, or high-risk change requests to make a final determination of whether to proceed with the change. *Mod. 3*

call tree A formal structure that defines who should be contacted, in what order, and how to contact them. Automated call tree systems can perform these calls, texts, or emails automatically. *Mod. 3*

canary build A system build that incorporates all new changes but tends to be very unstable. *Mod. 3*

CapEx (capital expenditures) Costs whose benefits are experienced over a long period of time after the investment is made. *Mod. 3*

CASB (cloud access security broker) A security appliance, either physical or virtual and hosted on-prem or in the cloud, that is designed to detect applications and other resources running within a domain and monitor those resources according to policies set by the organization. *Mod. 6*

CCPA (California Consumer Privacy Act) A California law that applies only to medium and large businesses and enforces some data privacy standards that exceed those set by the GDPR in Europe. *Mod. 1*

CDN (content delivery network) A distributed storage structure that allows customers to store files in locations closer to where their users are located. *Mod. 8*

chain of custody Documentation that describes evidence, including when it was collected, who collected it, its condition, and how it was secured and transferred from one responsible party to the next. *Mod. 3*

change management Carefully defined processes to evaluate the need for a change, the cost of the change, a plan for making the change with minimal disruption, and a backup plan if the change doesn't work as expected. *Mod. 3*

channel System iterations of the same build type. *Mod. 3*

CIA (confidentiality, integrity, and availability) triad A three-tenet, standard security model describing the primary ways that encryption protects data. Confidentiality ensures that data can only be viewed by its intended recipient or at its intended destination. Integrity ensures that data was not modified after the sender transmitted it and before the receiver picked it up. Availability ensures that data is available to and accessible by the intended recipient when needed. *Mod. 6*

CIDR (classless interdomain routing) notation A shorthand method for identifying network and host bits in an IP address. *Mod. 4*

cipher A mathematical code used to scramble data into a format that can only be read by reversing the cipher. *Mod. 6*

cloud within a cloud A layer of virtualization running on top of a virtualized cloud environment. *Mod. 1*

cluster A group of devices or resources that appear as a single device or resource to the rest of the network. *Mod. 2*

CMDB (configuration management database) A relational database used to track information, such as configuration and maintenance, on hardware and software assets, which are referred to as CI (configuration items). *Mod. 3*

colocation facility A data center facility where ISPs, CSPs, and other organizations can rent hardware or rack space for their own hardware. *Mod. 3*

community cloud A cloud deployment model in which flexible data storage, applications, or services are managed centrally by an organization or service provider on hardware dedicated to a specific group of organizations. *Mod. 1*

compression A process that reduces the number of bits needed to store data by recoding the data in a more efficient manner. *Mod. 8*

ConMon (continuous monitoring) A characteristic of a monitoring tool that provides near immediate feedback on performance or security measures. *Mod. 9*

container A lightweight, self-contained environment that provides the services needed to run an application in nearly any OS environment. *Mod. 2*

continuous delivery A DevOps practice where changes are deployed in small increments on a short schedule, such as every 24 hours, rather than being delayed for larger, less frequent updates. *Mod. 3*

continuous deployment A DevOps practice that deploys new code as soon as it passes testing, rather than waiting for a scheduled release. *Mod. 3*

continuous integration A DevOps practice of continuously merging all code changes from all developers working on a project. *Mod. 3*

core The processor component in a CPU. *Mod. 2*

credentialed scan A scan in which the scanning tool is provided with default or common credentials, such as "admin" for the username, or actual credentials for sensitive accounts. *Mod. 6*

CRM (customer relationship management) A product that assists a business with managing data from interactions with customers, potential customers, vendors, and associates. *Mod. 1*

cross-service migration The migration of a resource from one service type in a cloud platform to a different service type in the same platform. *Mod. 3*

CSP (cloud service provider) A business that offers one or more cloud services to other businesses or individuals. *Mod. 1*

D

DAC (discretionary access control) A method of access control where users decide for themselves who has access to their resources. *Mod. 7*

DAS (direct attached storage) Storage that is directly attached to the computer or server that uses it. *Mod. 8*

data analytics The study of raw data to detect patterns, anomalies, and insights that can inform research, business processes, regulatory measures, and many other efforts. *Mod. 10*

database dump A file created using the database software's export facility that contains the database's metadata, the database's content, or both. *Mod. 8*

DDoS (distributed denial of service) attack   An attack in which multiple computers simultaneously flood a target with traffic, rendering the target unable to function. Most often, this type of attack is performed by a botnet made up of numerous malware-infected machines without the owners' knowledge. *Mod. 6*

deduplication   A process that eliminates multiple copies of data in a storage system. *Mod. 8*

deny list   A list of rules defining which traffic is prevented from passing. Also called *block list*; previously called *blacklisting*. *Mod. 6*

dev (developer) build   A system build that is released often, such as weekly, as bugs in the canary version are addressed. *Mod. 3*

DevOps (development and operations)   A cultural shift toward continuous collaboration between development teams and operations teams that brings highly responsive application updates. *Mod.3*

DHCP (Dynamic Host Configuration Protocol)   A protocol that manages the dynamic distribution of IP addresses on a network. *Mod. 2*

digital certificate   A small file containing verified identification information and the public key of the entity whose identity is being authenticated. *Mod. 7*

digital signature   A security procedure that uses public key cryptography to assign a code to a document, and only the identified user possesses the private key needed to prove their identity as the signer. *Mod. 7*

DLP (data loss prevention)   A security technique that uses software to monitor confidential data, track data access and ownership, and prevent it from being copied or transmitted off the network. *Mod. 6*

DNS (Domain Name System or Domain Name Service)   A hierarchical approach to tracking domain names and their addresses, devised in the mid-1980s. *Mod. 5*

DNSSEC (DNS Security Extension)   Extensions to the DNS protocol that requires verification of DNS records using public key cryptography. *Mod. 6*

DoH (DNS over HTTPS)   A secured version of DNS where encrypted DNS messages are sent using HTTPS instead of UDP. *Mod. 6*

DoS (denial of service) attack   An attack in which a legitimate user is unable to access normal network resources because of an attacker's intervention. Most often, this type of attack is achieved by flooding a system with so many requests for services that it can't respond to any of them. *Mod. 6*

DoT (DNS over TLS)   A secured version of DNS where TLS (Transport Layer Security) encrypts traditional, UDP (User Datagram Protocol) traffic used for DNS. *Mod. 6*

DR (disaster recovery)   Strategies and tools designed to facilitate an organization's recovery from an adverse incident. *Mod. 2*

DR kit (disaster recovery kit)   A collection of items that will be needed during a crisis and is already organized and accessible before the emergency occurs. *Mod. 3*

driver   Firmware an OS uses to know how to interact with a device. *Mod. 2*

durability   The resistance of data to errors due to corruption or loss. *Mod. 8*

E

edge computing   The placement of computing devices, data, or connections at or near the location of their use. *Mod. 8*

EDR (endpoint detection and response)   A service that detects and monitors endpoints in a network or cloud deployment. *Mod. 6*

egress traffic   Traffic exiting a network or system. *Mod. 2*

elasticity   A cloud resource's ability to scale up or down automatically without requiring human intervention. *Mod. 2*

encryption   The use of an algorithm to scramble data into a format that can be read only by reversing the algorithm—that is, by decrypting the data—to keep the information private. *Mod. 6*

Eucalyptus (Elastic Utility Computing Architecture for Linking Your Programs To Useful Systems)   A partially open-source private cloud platform designed for optimal compatibility with Amazon's cloud services to create hybrid cloud deployments. *Mod. 1*

event   A detectable change in a cloud resource's state. *Mod. 9*

event correlation   The process of identifying relationships between events to identify event patterns. *Mod. 9*

event-driven architecture   A design strategy that uses events to trigger communications between microservices. *Mod. 9*

F

FaaS (Function as a Service)   The management of individual processes or functions in the cloud rather than managing an entire OS environment. *Mod. 2*

failback   The process of restoring services to their primary location after a failover. *Mod. 3*

failover   The process of transferring services to backup systems in response to a failure or during maintenance. *Mod. 3*

failover cluster   A group of servers supporting a high-availability (HA) service by providing failover protection from the loss of one or more active servers in the cluster to one or more inactive servers. *Mod. 10*

false positive   An indication of a problem that isn't actually a problem. *Mod. 9*

federation   The process of managing user identities across organizations in a trust-based relationship. *Mod. 7*

FIM (file integrity monitoring)   A security technique that alerts the system of any changes made to files that shouldn't change, such as operating system files. *Mod. 10*

FTS (follow the sun)   A time management model used in customer support or software development where staff in one time zone hands off work at the end of the day to staff in a time zone several hours west to maximize work hours throughout a 24-hour day. *Mod. 3*

functional testing   A testing strategy that confirms a system works as expected and meets predefined requirements. *Mod. 3*

G

GCP (Google Cloud Platform)   Google's collection of public cloud computing services, designed to take advantage of Google's own extensive physical infrastructure around the globe. *Mod. 1*

GDPR (General Data Protection Regulation)   A European Union law establishing broad-reaching data protection standards for any information that could be tied to a single individual. *Mod. 1*

GENEVE (Generic Network Virtualization Encapsulation)   A European Union law establishing broad-reaching data protection standards for any information that could be tied to a single individual. *Mod. 1*

GPU (graphics processing unit)   Processing cores onboard a graphics card. *Mod. 2*

guest   A VM running in a hypervisor on a physical computer. *Mod. 2*

H

HA (high availability)   The percentage of time during which a system, resource, or network functions reliably. *Mod. 2*

hardened baseline   Documentation of all configuration changes needed to secure a system and its OS. *Mod. 6*

hashing   The transformation of data through an algorithm that is mathematically irreversible and generally reduces the amount of space needed for the data. Hashing is mostly used to ensure data integrity—that is, to verify the data has not been altered. *Mod. 6*

HCI (hyperconverged infrastructure)   An implementation of software-defined compute, networking, and storage services all in one solution, typically provided by a single vendor and managed through a single interface that, like public cloud, relies on API calls. *Mod. 8*

HIPAA (Health Insurance Portability and Accountability Act)   A United States law that, among other things, establishes data protection standards for medical information. *Mod. 1*

horizontal scaling   The process of increasing the number of resources. *Mod. 3*

host   A physical computer running a hypervisor to support guest VMs. *Mod. 2*

HT (hyperthreading)   The ability of an Intel CPU to schedule two series of tasks at one time so that a single physical core appears to have two logical cores. *Mod. 2*

hub-and-spoke   A VPC peering architecture where a central device, such as AWS's Transit Gateway, or a central network, such as Azure's hub virtual network, connect many VPCs to each other. *Mod. 5*

hybrid cloud   A cloud deployment model in which both private and public clouds or both cloud-based and on-prem services are used simultaneously. *Mod. 1*

hybrid cloud storage   The distribution of stored data across cloud-based services and personal devices or on-prem storage. Mod. 8

hypervisor   The element of virtualization software that manages multiple guest machines and their connections to the host (and, by association, to a physical network). Also called a *VMM (virtual machine manager). Mod. 2*

I

IaaS (Infrastructure as a Service)   A cloud service that allows consumers to deploy a cloud-based network with services such as operating systems, network configurations, storage, and virtual devices. *Mod. 1*

IaC (infrastructure as code)   The provisioning and management of IT infrastructure through computer-readable configuration files that can be automated rather than interactive tools that require manual configuration. *Mod. 10*

IAM (identity and access management)   A framework of techniques and tools for managing the identities of people and applications that allow for access to cloud resources. *Mod. 7*

IBM Cloud   The cloud computing services suite offered by IBM, parts of which were formerly known as SoftLayer or Bluemix. *Mod. 1*

identity   A digital entity that can be given access to resources through roles and permissions. *Mod. 7*

IG or IGW (Internet gateway)   A virtual gateway device that provides a connection between internal, private resources and the public Internet. *Mod. 4*

ingress traffic   Traffic entering a network or system. *Mod. 2*

instance   A specific resource, such as a VM, hosted in a cloud platform. *Mod. 2*

IoT (Internet of Things)   Devices connected to the Internet that normally wouldn't be expected to do so. *Mod. 1*

IPAM (IP address management)   A product, service, or application that provides a way to plan, deploy, and monitor a network's IP address space. *Mod. 4*

IPsec (Internet Protocol security)   A network layer protocol that defines encryption, authentication, and key management for TCP/IP transmissions. IPsec is an enhancement to IPv4 and is native to IPv6. *Mod. 5*

ISO/IEC 27001   An information security certification showing that an organization conforms to the best practices defined by the certification's standards. *Mod. 1*

ITIL (IT Infrastructure Library)   A collection of publications that define best practices in IT. *Mod. 3*

ITSM (IT service management)   A collection of tools and strategies used to help IT teams manage several customer-facing processes to better meet user needs. *Mod. 9*

IX or IXP (Internet exchange point)   A physical location where Internet traffic crosses from one provider's infrastructure to another. *Mod. 3*

K

key   A series of characters that is combined with a block of data during the data's encryption. *Mod. 6*

key-value database   A database that contains any number of key-value pairs for each record. *Mod. 8*

knowledge base   A collection of information, configurations, troubleshooting scenarios, and helpful tips relevant to a specific network or service. *Mod. 1*

KPI (key performance indicator)   A specific performance factor measured to indicate the efficiency and functioning of a system. *Mod. 3*

Kubernetes   An open-source container management service developed by Google. *Mod. 2*

L

latency   The delay between the transmission of a signal and its receipt. *Mod. 1*

legal hold   A court-ordered notification preventing the deletion of identified data. *Mod. 8*

lifecycle rule   Storage configurations that enforce the automatic transition of data from one storage tier to another based on various factors, such as age or time since last access. *Mod. 8*

load balancing   The distribution of traffic over multiple components or links to optimize performance and fault tolerance. *Mod. 5*

load testing   A testing strategy that pushes a system beyond its normal workload conditions to determine how well it adapts to higher demands. *Mod. 3*

log   A collection of streams of data over time that show historical insights and reveal usage patterns or anomalies. *Mod. 9*

log scrubbing   An important part of the logging process that removes sensitive data from the logs before storing captured traffic. *Mod. 9*

logical access control   The management of access to logical resources, such as a network or workstations. *Mod. 7*

LTS (long-term support)   An especially stable system build that is intended to remain mostly unchanged for two years or longer. *Mod. 3*

M

MAC (mandatory access control)   A method of access control where resources are organized into hierarchical classifications, such as "confidential" or "top secret," and grouped into categories, such as by department. Users, then,

are also classified and categorized. If a user's classification and category match those of a resource, then the user is given access. *Mod. 7*

measured service   The ability to charge for cloud resource usage according to an incremented schedule based on the type of service being used. *Mod. 1*

memory bursting   The ability of a VM to temporarily increase its consumption of physical memory to a maximum limit defined by the hypervisor. *Mod. 2*

MFA (multifactor authentication)   An authentication process that requires information from two or more categories of authentication factors. *Mod. 7*

micro-segmentation   A security technique that allows for granular control of traffic and workflows within a cloud-based network. *Mod. 6*

microservice   A component of an application that can be run in a separate cloud resource than other application components. *Mod. 2*

ML (machine learning)   The ability of computers to learn from data analysis rather than from explicit programming. *Mod. 9*

multi-cloud   A cloud deployment model in which a customer incorporates cloud services from multiple vendors at one time. *Mod. 1*

multitenancy   The support of multiple customers' processes on the same hardware. *Mod. 1*

N

N-1   The patch release one iteration before the current, stable release. *Mod. 10*

NAC (network access control)   One or more security techniques for managing users' or resources' access to a network and its resources. *Mod. 6*

NAS (network attached storage)   A specialized storage device or group of storage devices that provides centralized, fault-tolerant file system storage and relies on network infrastructure to provide file access. *Mod. 8*

NAT (network address translation)   A technique in which interfaces on a private network are temporarily assigned a public IP address by a gateway when accessing a public network. *Mod. 4*

NAT-T (NAT-Traversal)   A protocol that is used to communicate IP addresses and port numbers through a VPN that would otherwise be encrypted in the VPN tunnel. *Mod. 5*

NDA (nondisclosure agreement)   A legal agreement designed to restrict sharing of proprietary information by employees, partners, vendors, or customers. *Mod. 1*

network-based scan   Software designed to scan devices connected to the network to check configurations and identify network security gaps. *Mod. 6*

NFV (network functions virtualization)   A network architecture that merges physical and virtual network devices. *Mod. 4*

NGW (NAT gateway) A virtual gateway device that provides resources in a subnet with egress-only access to the Internet. *Mod. 4*

NIST (National Institute of Standards and Technology) A nonregulatory agency that is part of the U.S. Department of Commerce and promotes measurements, standards, and technology in support of innovation and industrial competition. *Mod. 1*

NTS (Network Time Security) A secured version of NTP (Network Time Protocol) using the TLS authentication mechanism. *Mod. 6*

NVMe-oF (nonvolatile memory express over fabric) A SAN (storage area network) connection technology that applies the NVMe technology to connections between servers and the SAN. *Mod. 8*

O

on-demand self-service The ability to add, adjust, or remove cloud services at any time by the service subscriber or other users. *Mod. 1*

online migration The migration of a system while it is still running to prevent or minimize downtime. Also called *live migration*. *Mod. 3*

OpenSSL A command-line tool available for Linux and Windows systems that is used to test secure connections, gather information on security configurations, and manage certificates. *Mod. 6*

OpenStack An open-source private cloud platform that enables organizations to create and host their own compute, storage, and networking cloud services. *Mod. 1*

OpEx (operational expenditures) Costs whose benefits are experienced in about the same period as when the expenses are paid for those benefits. *Mod. 3*

Oracle Cloud The cloud computing platform offered by Oracle as a rebranding of their existing On Demand services. *Mod. 1*

orchestration The design, development, and optimization of automation processes. *Mod. 1*

overcommitment ratio The ratio of the number of vCPUs allocated to VMs on a host compared to the number of CPU threads (logical cores) available on the physical host. Also called oversubscription. *Mod. 2*

P

P2P (physical to physical) The process of migrating an OS and its dependencies (configurations, applications, and data) from one physical environment to another. *Mod. 3*

P2V (physical to virtual) The process of migrating an OS and its dependencies (configurations, applications, and data) from a physical machine to a virtual machine. *Mod. 3*

PaaS (Platform as a Service) An intermediate level of cloud capability that allows consumers to deploy applications on various platforms without having to manage lower-layer infrastructure. *Mod. 1*

packet broker A physical or virtual device that can sort captured traffic, decrypt TLS traffic, mask sensitive data, and send different types of traffic to devices designed to monitor and analyze network traffic. *Mod. 9*

PAM (privileged access management) A subnet of IAM (identity and access management) that applies stricter rules and safety precautions specifically to users who are given elevated permissions to do their jobs. *Mod. 7*

password vault Secure storage for passwords. *Mod. 7*

PCI DSS (Payment Card Industry Data Security Standard) A data protection standard applying to any company that accesses, stores, processes, or transmits credit card information. *Mod. 1*

peering connection The joining of VPCs in such a way that traffic is routed via private IP addresses and not over the Internet. *Mod. 4*

pen (penetration) testing A testing strategy that scans a network for vulnerabilities and takes advantage of those gaps to investigate potential security flaws. *Mod. 3*

performance testing A testing strategy that challenges a system to determine its responsiveness and stability under various conditions. *Mod. 3*

persistent storage A virtual storage device that continues to exist even when an instance or container is terminated. *Mod. 2*

PKI (public key infrastructure) The use of certificate authorities to associate public keys with certain users. *Mod. 7*

placement group In AWS, a logical group of instances all hosted in the same AZ that are used to determine the affinity of these instances. *Mod. 2*

playbook (1) A document that provides succinct, organized information that is easy to access and follow during the stress of an emergency. (2) A collection of automated tasks orchestrated in a specific sequence. *Mod. 3, Mod. 10*

POP (point of presence) A data center facility at which a provider rents out space to allow for dedicated connection services. *Mod. 3*

port scanner Software that searches a server, switch, router, or other device for open ports that might be vulnerable to attack. *Mod. 6*

principle of least privilege A security measure that ensures users are only given enough access and privileges to do their jobs, and these privileges are terminated as soon as the person no longer needs them. *Mod. 7*

private cloud A cloud deployment model in which flexible data storage, applications, or services are managed centrally by an organization or service provider on hardware dedicated to that one organization. *Mod. 1*

private IP address An IP address that can be used on a private network but not on the Internet. IEEE recommends the following IP address ranges for private use: 10.0.0.0/8, 172.16.0.0/12, and 192.168.0.0/16. *Mod. 4*

private subnet A cloud-based subnet in which hosted resources are protected from Internet traffic. *Mod. 4*

privilege escalation attack   The use of existing privileges to gain information about a system or to further escalate access privileges. *Mod. 7*

project   An effort that has a clearly defined beginning and ending. *Mod. 3*

project management   The application of specific skills, tools, and techniques to manage processes in such a way that the desired outcome is achieved. *Mod. 3*

pub/sub messaging   Asynchronous communication between event producers and event consumers. *Mod. 9*

public cloud   A cloud deployment model in which shared and flexible data storage, applications, or services are managed centrally by service providers. *Mod. 1*

public IP address   An IP address that is valid for use on public networks, such as the Internet. *Mod. 4*

public subnet   A cloud-based subnet in which hosted resources are provided a direct route to the Internet. *Mod. 4*

pull model   A client-server model where the client checks in with the server every so often to determine if the client should make configuration changes. *Mod. 10*

push mode   A client-server model where configuration changes are pushed out from the server at the time the changes should be made by the clients. *Mod. 10l*

Q

QoS (Quality of Service)   A group of techniques for adjusting the priority a network assigns to various types of transmissions. *Mod. 5*

R

RAID (Redundant Array of Independent Disks or Redundant Array of Inexpensive Disks)   A distribution of data copies stored on multiple disk drives; provides a level of data security, performance improvement, or both. *Mod. 8*

rapid elasticity   The ability to increase or decrease the number or size of cloud resources according to demand. *Mod. 1*

RBAC (role-based access control)   A method of access control where a network administrator assigns only the privileges and permissions necessary for users to perform the role required by their position in an organization. Also called *nondiscretionary access control. Mod. 7*

record   An item whose content provides evidence of communications, decisions, and actions during business activities. *Mod. 8*

records management   The process of identifying and protecting items that qualify as records and is an important component of storage services. *Mod 8*

region   A geographic location of a CSP's physical data center. *Mod. 4*

regression testing   A testing strategy that tests preexisting functionality after a change to confirm that changes haven't negatively impacted other systems. *Mod. 3*

resiliency   The ability of a system to withstand and compensate for failures or outages while continuing to function. *Mod. 2*

resource pooling   The availability of physical and virtual cloud resources to multiple subscribers according to consumer demand without regard to geographic location. *Mod. 1*

RFC (Request for Comments) 1918   An IETF publication specifying best practices for address allocation on private networks. *Mod. 4*

RFP (request for proposals)   A document that lays out the terms by which a job should be completed and invites vendors to propose their ideas on how to meet those terms. *Mod. 3*

right sizing   The process of balancing performance and capacity needs with budgetary needs. *Mod. 3*

risk register   A project management tool that can be used to document cybersecurity risks, background information on these risks, mitigation strategies specific to each risk, plans for responding should a vulnerability be attacked, and team members with responsibilities related to each risk. *Mod. 6*

roadmap   A plan that defines significant phases of a resource's life cycle. *Mod. 10*

rollup   A collection of updates or patches accumulated over a period of time and applied together. *Mod. 10*

root   The master user in a cloud account or compute system that retains complete access and action permissions, no matter what permissions are also given to other users. *Mod. 7*

root-cause analysis   A formal procedure that identifies all the contributing factors that allowed the incident to happen. *Mod. 3*

route table   A list of routes used to manage traffic to and from a cloud-based resource. *Mod. 4*

runbook   A collection of physical or digital documents that outline the precise steps to complete procedures or operations in a specific IT environment. *Mod. 10*

S

SaaS (Software as a Service)   The provision of application services through the cloud where those applications can be accessed from many different types of devices without having to manage any of the underlying infrastructure. *Mod. 1*

SAN (storage area network)   A distinct network of storage devices and the infrastructure that supports them in providing centralized, fault-tolerant block storage. *Mod. 8*

screened subnet   An area on the perimeter of a network that is less protected than the internal network and provides internal resources with a transitive connection to external resources. Previously called *DMZ (demilitarized zone). Mod. 6*

SDDC (software-defined data center)   A data center where the infrastructure is provided as virtualized services. *Mod. 4*

SDLC (software development life cycle)   The phases of planning, creating, testing, and deploying an application. *Mod. 3*

SDN (software-defined networking) A centralized approach to networking that removes most of the decision-making power from network devices and instead handles that responsibility at a software level. *Mod. 4*

SDS (software-defined storage) A storage technology that virtualizes the storage infrastructure to provide highly scalable, manageable storage space on top of generic (as opposed to proprietary) and diverse hardware. *Mod. 8*

secret Information required to authenticate to a service, such as a password or an API key. *Mod. 2*

secrets management A system that handles the secure storage and distribution of keys, passwords, authorization tokens, and other files used to secure access to resources. *Mod. 7*

serverless computing A cloud-native, streamlined technology for hosting cloud-based applications where a customer accesses a CSP-managed server for short bursts only when needed by an application or service. *Mod. 2*

severity level A number assigned by syslog to indicate the criticality of an event. Also called *logging level* or *priority value*. *Mod. 9*

shadow IT IT resources or systems in an organization that were not submitted to formal approval processes and likely exist outside the knowledge or oversight of the IT department. *Mod. 3*

shared responsibility model The division of labor between a cloud service provider and a cloud customer for the management, configuration, and security of a cloud service. *Mod. 6*

signature Identifiable patterns of code that are known to indicate specific vulnerabilities, exploits, or other undesirable traffic. *Mod. 10*

SLA (service-level agreement) A contract defining service standards from a company to its customer and options for recourse should those service levels not be met. *Mod. 1*

SMT (simultaneous multithreading) The brand-agnostic term for the ability of a CPU to schedule two series of tasks at one time so that a single physical core appears to have two logical cores. *Mod. 2*

snapshot A record of the state of a VM or data storage at a particular point in time. *Mod. 8*

SNMP (Simple Network Management Protocol) An application layer protocol in the TCP/IP suite used to monitor and manage devices on a network. *Mod. 9*

SOC (Service Organization Control) report A report produced by an audit performed according to the standards defined by SSAE 18. *Mod. 1*

SOP (standard operating procedure) The steps defined for a specific process within an organization to maintain consistency and avoid errors. *Mod. 3*

SR-IOV (single root input/output virtualization) A virtualization technology that alters the way the physical host distributes use of its physical NICs so network traffic passes directly to the physical NIC rather than processing traffic through the hypervisor's internal, virtual switch. *Mod. 4*

SSAE (Statement on Standards for Attestation Engagements No. 18) A standard used to determine an organization's compliance with appropriate audit regulations, guidelines, and requirements. *Mod. 1*

SSL (Secure Sockets Layer) A method of encrypting TCP/IP transmissions—including webpages and data entered into web forms—en route between the client and server using public key encryption technology. *Mod. 6*

SSO (single sign-on) A form of authentication in which a client signs in one time to access multiple systems or resources. *Mod. 7*

stable release A system build that incorporates features that have been fully tested and should be free of bugs or security gaps. The stable build is appropriate for use in a production environment. *Mod. 3*

storage migration The process of moving blocks or volumes of data from one storage medium to another. *Mod. 3*

storage tier A pricing schema that places data in various storage technologies where storage costs decrease as access costs increase. *Mod. 8*

stratum A number that indicates an NTP (Network Time Protocol) server's location within the NTP hierarchy relative to a stratum-1 server. *Mod. 6*

subnetting The segmentation of networks into smaller networks called subnets, and the process of calculating address spaces for these subnets within the larger network. *Mod. 4*

subscription A license that requires the customer to pay a monthly or annual fee per user or per device for as long as they use the license. *Mod. 3*

synthetic full backup A backup created from the most recent full backup and any applicable incremental or differential backups. *Mod. 8*

syslog A standard for generating, storing, and processing messages about events on many networked systems, whether on-prem or in the cloud. *Mod. 9*

T

tag A key-value pair used to track resources, especially in a cloud platform. *Mod. 9*

TAP (test access point) A device connected between two devices on a network that can capture all traffic traversing the connection, for example, between a switch and a router. *Mod. 9*

template A configuration file that determines particular parameters for deployment of identical resources. *Mod. 2*

tenant A cloud customer whose cloud services are running on specific hardware. *Mod. 1*

thread The ability of a CPU's core to perform one series of tasks. *Mod. 2*

tiering A segmentation technique that, in some implementations, divides a customer's cloud space into three logical areas with varying degrees of isolation from the Internet. *Mod. 4*

TLS (Transport Layer Security) A version of SSL standardized by the IETF (Internet Engineering Task Force). TLS uses slightly different encryption algorithms than SSL but otherwise is very similar to the most recent version of SSL. *Mod. 6*

tokenization A data obfuscation technique that replaces sensitive data with random data called a token. *Mod. 8*

type 1 hypervisor A hypervisor that installs as a minimal OS on the firmware of the physical host with no other underlying OS. *Mod. 2*

type 2 hypervisor A hypervisor that installs in a host OS as an application. *Mod. 2*

U

usability testing A testing strategy that asks users to test the system while developers observe the users and the system. *Mod. 3*

user quota A limitation on how much storage space any individual user can consume. *Mod. 8*

V

V2P (virtual to physical) The process of migrating an OS and its dependencies (configurations, applications, and data) from a virtual machine to a physical machine. *Mod. 3*

V2V (virtual to virtual) The process of migrating an OS and its dependencies (configurations, applications, and data) from one virtual environment to another. *Mod. 3*

vCPU (virtual CPU) One logical thread of processing power allotted to a VM. *Mod. 2*

VDI (virtual desktop infrastructure) A remote desktop implementation that offers VM instances for remote access clients. *Mod. 2*

vendor lock-in The ominous expense of changing vendors that often prevents customers from considering competitors' products. *Mod. 3*

version control A process for tracking changes over time. *Mod. 10*

versioning The technique of keeping older versions of the data as a backup or to document changes in the data, such as for compliance or regulatory purposes. *Mod. 8*

vertical scaling The process of increasing the capacity of an existing resource. *Mod. 3*

virtual memory Space on a storage drive temporarily used for storing memory files called pages when a system's memory resources are overtaxed. *Mod. 2*

virtual patch A collection of rules designed to close a security gap from a recently discovered vulnerability. *Mod. 10*

virtualization The emulation of part or all of a computer or network. *Mod. 1*

VLAN (virtual LAN) A network within a network that is logically defined by grouping ports on a switch so that some of the local traffic on the switch is forced to go through a router, thereby limiting the traffic to a smaller broadcast domain. *Mod. 5*

VM (virtual machine) A logical computer running an operating system that borrows hardware resources from its physical host computer and otherwise functions as a completely independent system. *Mod. 2*

VMware A subsidiary of Dell Technologies providing virtualization and cloud products and services. *Mod. 1*

VNet A software-defined portion of a larger, cloud-based network. *Mod. 4*

vNIC (virtual NIC) A logically defined network interface associated with a VM. *Mod. 2*

volume-based licensing Software licensing designed to allow many users under one license. *Mod. 2*

VPC (virtual private cloud) A software-defined portion of a larger, cloud-based network. *Mod. 4*

VPN (virtual private network) A virtual connection between two geographically distant locations that provides access to network resources between a client and a remote network, two remote networks, or two remote hosts over the Internet. *Mod. 1*

vRAM (virtual RAM) The amount of the host's physical memory reserved for a VM's use. *Mod. 2*

VT (Virtualization Technology) The HAV (hardware-assisted virtualization) technology available on Intel CPUs that enables a CPU to support virtualization processes. *Mod. 2*

vulnerability scanner Software that evaluates network resources for security weaknesses. *Mod. 6*

vulnerability testing A testing strategy that identifies a system's security weaknesses, with or without malicious intent. *Mod. 3*

VXLAN (virtual extensible LAN) A transport layer segmentation technology that inserts the MAC address next to the UDP header, essentially creating a layer 2 network overlay above layer 3. *Mod. 5*

W

WAF (web application firewall) A firewall service that can be installed either on-prem or in the cloud and protects web apps by inspecting, monitoring, and filtering traffic coming into the web app. *Mod. 6*

waterfall method A linear path of software development with a clearly defined beginning and ending and a distinct progression of phases in between. *Mod. 3*

workflow The steps of a process, typically an automated process. *Mod. 3*

Z

zero-trust security model A security approach that assumes nothing in the network is trustworthy until proven otherwise. *Mod. 6*

Index

A

access control list (ACL), 324
account hijacking, 217
account management, 217, 264–265
Active Directory (AD), 267, 277
advanced persistent threats (APTs), 217
affinity, 57–58
agent-based scans, 219
agility, defined, 103
AI. *See* artificial intelligence (AI)
alarm/alert design, 384–385
Alibaba Cloud, 19
allocation factors, 59
allow list, 224
ALM. *See* application lifecycle management (ALM)
Amazon Machine Image (AMI) ID, 56
Amazon Web Services (AWS), 4, 19
    account with, 31–32
    availability zones in, 140
    CLI, 409–410
    CloudFormation, 395
    cloud monitoring, 378–380
    cloud peering in, 210–211
    configure security in, 253–254
    configure VPC and subnets in, 162–163
    deploy a VM in, 70–72
    Directory Service, 281–282
    Elastic Block Store, 321
    Elastic Container Repository service, 63
    Elastic Container Service, 63, 64
    Elastic Kubernetes Service, 64
    explore VPN options in, 204–206
    gateways and route tables in, 144–148
    IAM, 275–276, 281–282
    manage storage in, 339–341
    manage users and permissions in, 292–294
    monitoring in, 363–368
    patching in, 412–414, 423–425
    pricing calculator, 118–119
    regions in, 139
    security group, 127
    serverless services, 61, 63
    storage services, 319–321
    subnets in, 135, 143, 225–229
    Systems Manager, 396
    VM instance types for, 55
    VPCs in, 140–142, 225–229
AMD virtualization (AMD-V), 44
Ansible tool, 396
anti-affinity rule, 57
antivirus, 230
application delivery controller (ADC), 236
application-level backup, 327
application lifecycle management (ALM), 102–103
application programming interface (API), 10, 217
application security, 236
application security group (ASG), 231
artificial intelligence (AI), 398–399
asset management, 88
audit log, 359
authentication, 266
    backups, 332
    certificate-based, 270
    defined, 267
    digital signatures, 272

issues, 285
    multifactor authentication, 269
    password policies, 267–269
    process, 267
    securing secrets, 272–274
    single sign-on, 270–271
authentication, authorization, and accounting (AAA), 266
authorization issues, 285
authorization, to cloud objects
    AWS IAM, 275–276
    Azure IAM, 277–279
    GCP IAM, 279–280
automation, 7. See also automation workflow
    tools research, 422–423
automation workflow, 391–392
    artificial intelligence, 398–399
    data analytics, 397
    differentiating factors, 396–397
    infrastructure as code, 392–394
    machine learning, 398–399
    popular automation tools, 395–396
    tools, 394
    troubleshooting automation issues, 417–418
autonomous system (AS), 188
autonomous system number (ASN), 188
auto-scaling, 97
availability zones (AZs), 57, 140
    in AWS, 140
    in Azure, 150
AWS. *See* Amazon Web Services (AWS)
AZs. *See* availability zones (AZs)
Azure, 4, 19
    account with, 33–34
    Automation, 396
    CLI, 410–411
    cloud monitoring, 380–381
    cloud peering in, 210–211
    configure a VNet and subnets in, 164–165
    configure security in, 254–256
    deploy a VM in, 72–74
    explore VPN options in, 207–208
    IAM, 277–279, 282–283
    manage storage in, 341–342
    monitoring in, 368–369
    patching in, 414, 425–427
    pricing calculator, 119–120
    regions and availability zones in, 150
    Resource Manager, 395
    route tables in, 152
    serverless services, 61
    storage services, 322–323
    subnets in, 150–151
    virtual networks, 229–231
    VM instance types for, 55
    VNet in, 139, 150–151
Azure Active Directory (Azure AD), 277, 294–295
Azure Blob storage, 322

B

backup restoration, 332–333
backup rotation, 332
backups, creating and storing, 326–327
    considerations, 332–333
    protection capabilities, 327–329

    redundancy levels, 331–332
    types, 329–330
ballooning, 53
bare-metal hypervisor, 42
baselines, 82
BCP. *See* business continuity plan (BCP)
beta release, 104
big data, 306
binary large objects (BLOBs), 322, 323
blast radius, 265
block list, 224
block storage, 311–312
block zoning, 311
Border Gateway Protocol (BGP), 188
bridged mode, 45
broad network access, 5
build, 104
business continuity (BC), 82, 108
business continuity plan (BCP), 108–109

C

California Consumer Privacy Act (CCPA), 10
call tree, 109
canary build, 104
capital expenditures (CapEx), 84
CASB. *See* cloud access security broker (CASB)
central processing unit (CPU), 41, 46, 50–51, 372
certificate authority (CA), 273–274
certificate-based authentication, 270, 273–274
Certified Cloud Security Professional (CCSP) certification, 3
Certified Information Systems Security Professional (CISSP) certification, 3
chain of custody, 112
change advisory board (CAB), 88
change management, 87–88
channel, 104
chargeback model, 353
Chef tool, 396
CIDR (classless interdomain routing) notation, 134, 136
cipher, 240
classless interdomain routing (CIDR) notation, 134, 136
CLI. *See* command-line interface (CLI)
client access license (CAL), 52
cloning, 328
cloud access security broker (CASB), 233–234
cloud accounts, 263
    account management, 264–265
    identity, 263–264
    privileged access management, 265
cloud agility
    application lifecycle management, 102–103
    build, 104
    project management, 101–102
cloud architecture, 83
cloud-based approaches to security, 220
    DevSecOps, 220–221
    micro-segmentation, 221–222
cloud-based database services, 327
cloud-based file systems, 327
cloud computing
    certifications, 30–31
    characteristics of, 2–7
    description of, 4–6